ABC Dictionary of Chinese Proverbs

ABC CHINESE DICTIONARY SERIES

Victor H. Mair, General Editor

The ABC Chinese Dictionary Series aims to provide a complete set of convenient and reliable reference tools for all those who need to deal with Chinese words and characters. A unique feature of the series is the adoption of a strict alphabetical order, the fastest and most user-friendly way to look up words in a Chinese dictionary. Most volumes contain graphically oriented indices to assist in finding characters whose pronunciation is not known. The ABC dictionaries and compilations rely on the best expertise available in China and North America and are based on the application of radically new strategies for the study of Sinitic languages and the Chinese writing system, including the first clear distinction between the etymology of words, on the one hand, and the evolution of shapes, sounds, and meanings of characters, on the other. While aiming for conciseness and accuracy, series volumes also strive to apply the highest standards of lexicography in all respects, including compatibility with computer technology for information processing.

Other titles in the series:

ABC Chinese-English Dictionary, Desk Reference Edition
Edited by John DeFrancis

ABC Chinese-English Dictionary, Pocket Edition
Edited by John DeFrancis

ABC Dictionary of Chinese Proverbs
Edited by John S. Rohsenow

ABC Dictionary of Sino-Japanese Readings
A Select List of Japanese Readings of Chinese Characters
According to Pinyin Alphabetical Order
Edited by Victor H. Mair

ABC Dictionary
of
Chinese Proverbs
汉英谚语词典

by

John S. Rohsenow

University of Hawai'i Press

Honolulu

Library of Congress Cataloging-in-Publication data

Rohsenow, John Snowden.
  ABC dictionary of Chinese proverbs / John S. Rohsenow.
    p. cm. — (ABC dictionary of Chinese proverbs)
  Includes bibliographical references and index.
  ISBN 0-8248-2221-8 (alk. paper)
    1. Proverbs, Chinese—Dictionaries. 2. Chinese language—Dictionaries—English. I.
Title: Dictionary of Chinese proverbs. II. Title. III. Series.

PL1273 .R64 2002
398.9'951'03—dc21   2001033588
ISBN-13: 978-0-8248-2770-0 (pbk)
ISBN-10: 0-8248-2770-8 (pbk)

University of Hawai'i Press books are printed on acid-free paper and
meet the guidelines for permanence and durability of the
Council on Library Resources.

Text prepared by Thomas E. Bishop of Wenlin Institute, Inc.

Printed by Versa Press, Inc.

www.uhpress.hawaii.edu

Contents

Foreword

This dictionary of Chinese proverbs, edited by John S. Rohsenow, is a welcome addition to the ABC series of Chinese dictionaries published by the University of Hawai'i Press. All other Chinese-English dictionaries of comparable quality are either badly out of date or long out of print. The need for an up-to-date work of this nature is particularly pressing because of the vital role proverbial language has traditionally played and still plays in Chinese speech and literature. There is probably no other major linguistic community on earth that is so fond of proverbs as that of the Chinese. So we are indeed fortunate to have this excellent new tool for the study of Chinese proverbs.

Yet this book is more than just a handy listing of Chinese maxims and aphorisms from the past and the present with reliable English translations. The author also provides cogent explanations of the figurative meanings of these often earthy and culturally specific sayings, and gives citations to actual usages in literature. In addition, he has provided an extremely insightful introduction in which the reasons for the persistence of proverbial language into the twenty-first century are spelled out persuasively.

Last, but certainly not least, this dictionary is very easy to use, being arranged in the single-sort alphabetical order and with scrupulous attention to the official romanized orthography (*Hànyǔ Pīnyīn Zhèngcífǎ*) of the People's Republic of China. It may be noted that Professor Rohsenow is the translator of the "Basic Rules for Hanyu Pinyin Orthography" established by the State Language Commission of the PRC and published as Appendix I of the *ABC Chinese-English Dictionary* edited by John DeFrancis. Professor Rohsenow's translation of the official orthographical rules for Pinyin have also been accepted by the International Standards Organization. For all of these reasons, I fully expect that the *ABC Dictionary of Chinese Proverbs (Yànyǔ)* will become a standard reference work for students and specialists of Chinese language, literature, society, and history.

Victor H. Mair
Swarthmore, Pennsylvania

Acknowledgments

The data for the present study were first collected in China while I was a National Endowment for the Humanities fellow at the Institute of Linguistics at the Chinese Academy of Social Sciences in Beijing. My research in China was also partially supported by a grant from the Campus Research Board of the University of Illinois at Chicago (UIC).

I am grateful to the Institute for the Humanities at UIC for providing me with a fellowship for the year 1992-1993 to initiate this dictionary project, and especially to Mary Beth Rose, Gene Ruoff, and Linda Vavara. In 1994-1995, the project was also supported by a grant (RT-21567-94) from the National Endowment for the Humanities (Research Tools Division), and had additional support from UIC's Campus Research Board throughout the project. Final editing of the manuscript was again supported by a grant from the UIC Institute for the Humanities. The initial manuscript of this dictionary was the recipient of a First Annual Tuttle Language Grant for Asian Language Publication Research in 1995.

A work of this nature and magnitude is inevitably the result of collaboration. I especially wish to thank Professor Guo Jianzhong of Hangzhou University and Professor Pan Da'an of California State Polytechnic University, without whom this work would not have been possible. Guo Lu Ping provided invaluable assistance in the initial proofreading and in checking Chinese literary sources. Ann K. Ning undertook the onerous job of the final proofreading of the Chinese characters. I also wish to thank the librarians at the East Asian Collection of the library of the University of Illinois at Champaign-Urbana, and also the Center for East Asian Studies at the University of Chicago for providing me access to the East Asian Collection of the University of Chicago's Regenstein Library.

The computerscript for this dictionary was typed by Mathew Calo, Joel Felix, and Lysa Lei. The character insertion was done by Robert Zhe Zhang, using Wenlin software with the advice and assistance of its designer, Tom Bishop of Wenlin Institute, Inc. (www.wenlin.com), whose technical help has also been invaluable in actually producing this book. In the initial stages of this work, able technical assistance was provided by the staff of the UIC Computer Center, most especially Edward Zawacki. Professor Yin Binyong of the Chinese State Language Commission checked the Hanyu pinyin. Ms. Lisa Zhao of the UIC Library formatted the Bibliography. Cynthia Lowe did the proofreading.

All of that having been said, I am of course solely responsible for any deficiencies or errors which remain.

For assistance and encouragement, I specifically wish to thank the late Wolfram Eberhard, Hui-ch'ing Chang, Marcia Farr, Hill Gates, Guo Luyi, Paul Hockings, Bronislawa Kordas, Ellen Laing, Michael Leiber, Y. C. Li, J. Macevichius, Donald Marshall, M. C. Paris, David Rolston, Allen Scott Bookseller, Arthur Wolf, and Dale Woolley. I also wish to express my gratitude to Patricia Crosby and Ann Ludeman at the University of Hawai'i Press, as well as to John DeFrancis and Victor Mair, the general editors of the ABC series. The general editors and I also wish to express our gratitude to the Freeman Foundation for their support of the ABC dictionary series.

My heartfelt love and gratitude go to my wife, Betty Jacobsen, without whose love, encouragement and assistance this work could not have been completed. My love and thanks also go to my parents and siblings for their love and support over the years.

Chicago
June 4, 2001

Introduction

"To understand a proverb, and the interpretation;
the words of the wise, and their dark sayings." –*Proverbs 1,6*

"From childhood I read many, many poems and verses, and listened to
many, many proverbs. And everywhere I went, I picked up proverbs."
–*Jiang Zemin, CCP General Party Secretary*, Newsweek, *March 12, 1990*

In 1956 when the president of Beijing University, the demographer Ma Yanchu warned against the dangers of China's rapid post-liberation surge in population growth, Chinese Communist Party Chairman Mao Zedong is said to have replied characteristically by citing a proverb: *Zhòngrén shíchái huǒyàn gāo*, "The more people (there are to) collect firewood, the higher the flames will grow." Describing the supposed popular reaction against "rightist" political elements that same year, Mao cited the proverb: *Lǎoshǔ guò jiē, rénren hàn dǎ*, "When a rat crosses the street, everyone cries out and beats it." Expressing his opposition to the requirement that scientists, educators, and administrators be more "Red" than "expert," Mao's pragmatic successor Deng Xiaoping quoted a proverb from his native Sichuan: *Bùguǎn hēi māo, bái māo, zhǐ zhuā dào lǎoshǔ jiùshì hǎo māo*, "It doesn't matter if a cat is black or white, as long as it can catch mice." In an interview with the American magazine *Newsweek* cited above, Chinese Communist Party General Secretary Jiang Zemin legitimized his Party's anti-corruption campaign by quoting the proverb: *Shàngliáng bù zhèng, xiàliáng wāi*, "When the main beam is not upright, the entire structure will be crooked." Clearly these traditional proverbs (*yànyǔ*) continue to play a central role in the thinking and rhetoric of China's leaders to the present day.

Unlike the much studied and translated four-character traditional fused literary idioms or set phrases known as *chéngyǔ* (成语), these *yànyǔ* (谚语), or "proverbs," are ultimately the heritage of thousands of years of China's primarily illiterate, oral, peasant-based culture, in terms of which the present communist leaders of the Peoples Republic for ideological reasons continue to characterize her tortured transformation into a modern industrialized nation-state. Let us here examine the nature, definition, history and function which such proverbs have played in traditional society, as well as the reasons for their continuing currency in the Peoples Republic and other Chinese communities today.

Anyone living and interacting within Chinese society, whether it be on the mainland of China, Hong Kong, Taiwan, Singapore or elsewhere becomes aware of the all-pervading nature of proverbs and proverbial sayings in Chinese life, both in daily speech, as well as in Chinese writings and other media. Some of these are in fact maxims or quotations or paraphrases of quotations from the so-called Chinese "Classics," cited for so many hundreds of years that they have become proverbial, regardless of whether their written version or source is known to the speakers who use them. Thus *qiān lǐ zhī xíng, shǐ yú zú xià*, (literally) "A thousand league journey begins with [what is] under [one's] foot," is attributed to the old Taoist Master known as Lǎozǐ, and transcribed in the third century B.C.E. work known as the *Dào Dé Jīng*, "The Classic of the Way and Integrity," although some believe it to be in fact an even older proverb with an even longer oral history quoted by the Old Master. From the Analects of Master Kong (*Kǒng Fūzǐ* or "Confucius"), which was promulgated and memorized as state orthodoxy for most of the last two thousand years, come dozens of similar maxims, made proverbial by long familiarity: *Zǐ yuē: Sìhǎi zhī nèi, jiē xiōngdì yě*, now usually translated: "The Master said: Within the four seas, all [men] are brothers." Or again from the Confucian Analects: *Sān rén tóngxíng, bì yǒu wǒ shī*, "If three [of us] are walking together, there must be [at least one who can be] my teacher"; that is, no matter how educated one is, one can always learn something from others. Even today, despite China's massive problems with overpopulation, a familiar dictum of Mèngzǐ or "Mencius" is still often quoted: *Wú xiào yǒu sān, wú hòu wéi dà*; "There are three [ways of being] unfilial [to one's parents, and] the greatest [of these] is to have no posterity."

But against hundreds of such often-quoted maxims which have over the years become "proverbial," there are a far greater number of anonymous colloquial proverbs in common use. The first one I can remember hearing, from a cook from Shandong, is *not* in the Confucian Analects; to sum up her view on the all-pervasiveness of nepotism in human affairs, she tartly observed: *Gǒu bù chī shǐ, rén bù piānxīn*, "When dogs stop eating excrement, people will stop practicing favoritism," or something like "People will stop playing favorites, when Hell freezes over."

In their writing and speaking, educated Chinese continue to use the older, more "literary" proverbs, and can sometimes give sources for some of them if asked, but they of course also use many of the more common colloquial proverbs and proverbial expressions as well. On the other hand, uneducated, often illiterate Chinese people also use quite a few of the more common, older "classical" proverbs, giving their speech the authority of antiquity, while at the same time they employ an even larger number of those earthy, witty, pomposity-piercing proverbs for which peasants are famous all over the world. Recently, a worker at a university in China where I have spent a good deal of time over the last twenty years delighted me by rendering her verdict on an extramarital affair between two married faculty members by using a proverb I had never heard before: *Mǔ gǒu bù chū pìgǔ, gōng gǒu nán shàng*, "If female dogs don't present their posteriors, it is hard for male dogs to mount them."

According to Francis Bacon's Essay (1517), ". . . the genius, wit, and spirit of a nation are discovered in its proverbs." But what is a proverb? The term has been widely used, yet it is difficult to define. The English statesman Lord John Russell is credited with the characterization of proverbs which has come down to us "proverbially" as "the wisdom of many and the wit of one."[1] *The American College Dictionary* (1957) defines a proverb as a "short pithy saying . . . popularly known and repeated, usually expressing simply and concretely, though often metaphorically, a truth based on common sense or the practical experience of mankind."[2] Neal Norrick, a contemporary paremiologist, after reviewing numerous studies of, and writing on the subject, noted that "proverbs are consistently described as self-contained, pithy, traditional expressions with didactic content and fixed poetic form." (1985:31) Norrick then presents two of his own more technical definitions: an "ethnographic" definition of the proverb in English as "a traditional, conversational didactic genre with a general meaning, a potential free conversational turn, preferably with figurative meaning," along with his more general "supra-cultural" definition of proverbs in general as "a typically spoken, conversational form with didactic function and not associated with any particular source."(1985:78–79) Proverbs, then, can be differentiated on the basis of both formal as well as semantic criteria from other rhetorical forms such as colloquial phrases ("to face the music"); aphorisms or maxims ("Brevity is the soul of wit," or "The truth shall make you free"); clichés ("so much for the facts"; "white as snow"); Wellerisms ("I see, said the blind carpenter as he picked up his hammer and saw"); and other related rhetorical figures. (Cf. Norrick 1985:32, 65–74).

Similar problems exist in Chinese, where the terminology in this area is also not consistently defined or applied, and is still a matter for discussion.[3] The Chinese term I take to be equivalent to the English word "proverb" in the sense just given is *yànyǔ* (谚语). There have been varying uses of this term *yànyǔ* in Chinese, both historically and in contemporary Chinese discussions of the subject. We may take as representative of the better treatments Sun Zhiping's (1982) definition, which addresses the structure, meaning, and usage of *yànyǔ* in Chinese: "*Yànyǔ* are complete sentences, expressing a judgment or an inference, [which] may be used to validate [or to] represent [one's] own [individual] views, [whereas] *chéngyǔ, xiēhòuyǔ*, and *súyǔ* generally can only serve as parts of a sentence, [and are] used to give a concrete description or expression of the quality, state, degree, etc. of some objective material phenomenon." [(1984:3)—my translation] Discussion and analyses in Chinese similar to those in English summarized by Norrick above allow us to differentiate this term *yànyŭ* (proverb) from other related Chinese rhetorical terms such as *shúyŭ* (熟语, familiar sayings), *súyŭ* (俗语, colloquial expressions), *géyán* (格言, maxims), *chéngyŭ* (成语, fused phrase literary expressions), *xiēhòuyŭ* (歇后语, enigmatic folk similes or truncated witticisms), as well as from the modern term *guànyòngyŭ* (惯用语, idiom, in the technical linguistic sense of a group of words used invariantly whose meaning cannot be determined from the sum of its parts).

As we have noted, proverbs are fundamentally an oral form consisting of complete sentences, which reduce the observations, experiences, and wisdom of ordinary people into short, pithy, colloquial statements and judgments, employing familiar images and tropes phrased in easily memorizable forms. Thus, for example, the *yànyŭ: qiăo fù nán wéi wú mǐ zhī chuī*, ("[Even] the cleverest housewife cannot cook [a meal] without rice") is comparable in its meaning and usage to the English proverb "One cannot make bricks without straw." *Súyŭ* or colloquial expressions, on the other hand, are equally familiar colloquial set phrases, images or tropes, but which consist only of sentence fragments used for description, such as *jǐng lǐ lāo qǐ; yòu diào jìn chí lǐ*, literally: "to scoop something from inside the well, only to drop it into the pond," that is, to get out of one calamity, only to get into another, comparable to the English colloquial expression, "out of the frying pan, into the fire." Note that both the Chinese example just cited and "out of the frying pan, . . ." etc. are sentence fragments, and that neither one expresses an observation or judgment, but rather merely describes a situation. On the other hand, the English proverb "Out of sight, out of mind," while grammatically parallel to the "frying pan" example, *does* express an observation of cause and effect, i.e., that [when one is] not seen [for some time], [one tends to be] forgotten [by others]. Similarly, the classical four character proverb *chún wáng chǐ hán*, "[When] the lips are gone, the teeth are cold," is a complete (if elliptical) sentence consisting of two subject + verb clauses, and also expresses cause and effect metaphor, and thus qualifies as a proverb, despite its use of literary Chinese phrasing and its four-character, *chéngyŭ*-like appearance.

As Obelkevitch (1987:44) rightly notes, however, "what [really] defines the proverb . . . is not its internal organization, but its external *function*, [which is] . . . usually moral and didactic: people *use* proverbs to tell others what to do in a given situation or what attitude to take towards it. Proverbs, then, are 'strategies for situations,' but they are strategies with authority, formulating some part of a society's common sense, its values and ways of doing things." Proverbs employ familiar images and tropes to capture the experience and values shared by successive generations; they are repeatedly quoted and appealed to for persuasion, in argumentation, and as guides for daily living. In the mouths of ordinary peasant farmers, craftspersons and tradespeople, they are "mini-texts" of a commonly shared "oral literature" which possess authority by virtue of their constant repetition and use. [My italics –JSR][4]

Géyán or maxims are usually also complete statements, likewise expressing judgments or observations, but differing in that they are quotations, that is, guides for behavior taken from the writings attributed to some famous author or work in the past. Thus they usually have a decidedly written flavor in lexical choice, grammar, and style, even if they have over the years become "proverbial" in use and their original written sources or authors forgotten or unknown by their users. Thus, numerous quotations from the Confucian Analects (*Lùnyŭ*) such as the "Within the four seas, all men are brothers" example cited above have become "proverbial" even beyond China's borders, although their source is often forgotten. Similarly, the famous line from the *Dào Dé Jīng* also cited above: *qiān lǐ zhī xíng, shǐ yú zú xià*, now usually paraphrased in English as "The longest journey begins with (but) a single step," may in fact be an even older popular proverb with an even longer oral history which was simply quoted by or attributed to the old Taoist master *Lăozǐ* in that third century B.C.E. work.

Another basically written form is the ubiquitous *chéngyŭ*, set phrases or fused phrase idioms. *Chéngyŭ* are also fixed literary expressions or idioms, usually consisting of four characters, employing the vocabulary and structures of literary Chinese (*wényán*), which are often taken from or contain allusions (*diǎngù*) to classical written works. Thus China's "Chicken

Little," the man of the ancient kingdom of Qi who also worried that the sky might fall, has become immortalized in the *chéngyǔ: Qǐ rén yōu tiān*, literally, "the man of Qi worries about the sky," used to this day by educated writers and speakers to mean "(entertaining) groundless or unnecessary fears." Unlike most *chéngyǔ*, this particular example can be read as a complete subject-plus-verb sentence, but it does not express an observation or judgment, and thus does *not* qualify as a proverb. Four syllable colloquial sentences such as *Hǎoshì duō mó*, "The road to happiness is strewn with setbacks," often equated with Shakespeare's "The course of true love never did run smooth," and the more literary *Néngzhě duō láo*, "Able persons [should] do more work," do fulfill the criteria for proverbs and should not be misclassified as *chéngyǔ* descriptive expressions. *Chéngyǔ* are included along with the other terms discussed here under the general heading of *shúyǔ*, or familiar sayings, because so many have passed into common use and are widely used, even in contemporary vernacular (*báihuà*) writing, as well as in the speech of educated speakers.

Finally, certainly in modern speech and writing and even in some older written works one encounters another primarily spoken form, *xiēhòuyǔ*, enigmatic folk similes or truncated witticisms. A true *xiēhòuyǔ* is a two-part allegorical saying consisting first of a descriptive phrase, always stated and often preceded by a verb of explicit comparison (e.g., *hǎo bǐ* . . . , "it's just like . . ."; thus the term simile). This first metaphorical image is then followed by a pause, then followed by a second phrase, often left unspoken, which either directly or indirectly resolves and explains the relevance of the simile to which the first part of the *xiēhòuyǔ* has been applied metaphorically. For example, recalling the old days when upper class Chinese girls and women's feet were every day tightly wrapped with long cotton strips of cloth in order to deform them into erotically attractive (to men) "golden lily" feet, a certain person's lecture might therefore be described as "(just like) an old [Chinese] woman's foot-binding bandages—[i.e.,] both long and stinky!" Often the resolution of the metaphor involves a double-entendre or pun on the superficial meaning of the second part of the *xiēhòuyǔ*, as when Mao Zedong described himself to the visiting American journalist Edgar Snow as (being like) "a [bald-shaven Buddhist] monk under an umbrella" (*héshang dǎsǎn*). As Mao did not complete the *xiēhòuyǔ* and as Snow did not know the hidden meaning of the second part of this enigmatic folk simile: *wú fǎ, wú tiān*, literally: "having neither hair nor Heaven [above him]," he could only take Mao's image literally. But the literal meaning of the resolution of the simile is not the true meaning; *wú fǎ, wú tiān* is in fact homophonous with Mao's truly intended meaning, a four character fused phrase idiom meaning "[bound by] neither [earthly] law [*fǎ* = hair/law], nor by Heaven [above]."[5]

Some of the earliest recorded types of proverbs are the so-called "agricultural proverbs" (*nóngyàn* 农谚) and "weather proverbs" (*qìxiàng yànyǔ* 气象谚语) which encapsulate traditional observations and advice concerning the weather and various agricultural practices in different areas of China over the centuries. We have examples of collections of these types of proverbs dating as far back as the Eastern Han dynasty, eighteen hundred years ago, when Cuī Shí (崔寔) first collected proverbs as part of his *Sì Mín Yuè Lìng* (四民月令, Farmers' Monthly Guide). Similar collections in succeeding times containing proverbs on various aspects of agriculture, animal husbandry, aquaculture, and other farming side production are Wú Lùjī's (吴陆玑) *Máo Shī Cǎo Mù Niǎo Shòu Chóng Yú Shū* (毛诗草木鸟兽虫鱼疏, Mao's Annotations on Plant, Tree, Bird, Animal, Insect and Fish Metaphors) in the Three Kingdoms period; Jiǎ Sìxié's (贾思勰) *Qí Mín Yào Shù* (齐民要术, Important Skills for Commoners) in the Northern Wei dynasty; Chén Fū's (陈敷) *Nóng Shū* (农书, Book of Agriculture) in the Song dynasty; Lóu Yuánlǐ's (娄元礼) *Tiánjiā Wǔ Háng* (田家五行, The Farmer's Five Skills) in the Yuan dynasty; and Xú Guāngqǐ's (徐光启) *Nóng Zhèng Quán Shū* (农政全书, Complete Book of Agricultural Management) in the Ming.

Not until the Song dynasty were there works purely devoted to the collection of proverbs *per se*. The first two such collections produced in the Song were Gong Yízhèng's (龚颐正) *Shì Cháng Tán* (释常谈, Explanations of Common Sayings) and Zhōu Shǒuzhòng's (周守忠) *Gǔ-Jīn Yàn* (古今谚, Ancient and Contemporary Proverbs). Other outstanding such works in succeeding centuries are Yáng Shēng'ān's (杨升庵) similarly titled *Gǔ-Jīn Yàn* in the Ming dynasty, followed by Dù Wénlán's (杜文澜) *Gǔ Yáoyàn* (古谣谚) and Zēng Tíngméi's (曾廷枚) *Gǔ Yàn Tán* (古谚谈, Casual Comments on Ancient Proverbs) in the Qing. The tradition of collection and compilation of Chinese proverbs in modern times was continued in such works as Lǐ Jiàntáng's (李鉴堂) *Súyǔ Kǎo Yuán* (俗语考原, Origins of Common Sayings); Shǐ Xiāngzāi's (史襄哉) *Zhōnghuá Yàn Hǎi* (中华谚海, China's Sea of Proverbs); and Zhū Yǔzūn's (朱雨尊) *Mínjiān Yànyǔ Quánjí* (民间谚语全集, Complete Collection of Popular Proverbs). In addition to these specialized works, agricultural, weather, and general proverbs peculiar to a particular locality were often included in local gazetteers (*dìfāngzhì* 地方志) over the years.[6]

In his comprehensive evaluation of literary theory and criticism up until his own time entitled *Wén Xīn Diào Lóng* (文心调龙, The Literary Mind and the Carving of Dragons), the sixth century Liang dynasty scholar Liú Xié (刘勰) in his chapter on Epistolary Writing (*Shū Jì* 书记) noted that "Proverbs [*yàn* 谚] are direct statements . . . Duke Mu of [the kingdom of] Zou said: 'A leaky bag can still hold things' . . . The *Tài Shì* [(太誓, Great Vow) section in the Lǐ Jì (礼记, Record of Rites)] says: 'The Ancients had a saying: A hen should not crow at dawn.' And in the *Dà Yǎ* [(大雅, Great Elegantiae) section of the *Shī Jīng* (诗经, Poetry Classic)] it is said: 'Through grief one grows old.' Both of these are proverbs from antiquity which are quoted in the Classics . . ." After quoting additonal examples of "proverbs employed in literary writings" found in such ancient works, Liu concluded: "In literature there is nothing more vulgar than proverbs, but they were used by the sages in [these] classic works, so how can one ignore them?"[7]

For additional examples of proverbs in ancient writings, we can cite proverbs in many classic works from pre-Qin times. In the third century B.C.E. Discourses of the Domains (*Guó Yǔ* 国语) we find *Cóng shàn rú dèng; cóng è rú bèng*; "To follow goodness is to rise, [but] to follow evil is to fall." In the Intrigues of the Warring States (*Zhàn Guó Cè* 战国策) we find *Nìng wéi jī kǒu; wú wéi niú hòu*; "Better to be the head of a chicken than the tail of an ox," and in the *Hán Fēi Zǐ* (韩菲子), *Yuán shuǐ nán jiù jìn huǒ; yuán qīn bùrú jìn lín*; "[Just as] distant water cannot extinguish nearby fires, [so] distant relatives are not as good as nearby neighbors," which are all pairs of balanced rhymed couplets. In the classic Historical Records (*Shǐ Jì* 史记) written by Sīmǎ Qiān (司马迁) in the former (Western) Han dynasty (206 B.C.E. to 24 C.E.) we find proverbs which are still in current use today, such as *Zhōngyán nì'ěr lìyú xíng*; "Honest advice, [though] unpleasant to the ear, benefits [one's] conduct," and also the proverb: *Chǐ yǒu suǒ duǎn; cùn yǒu suǒ cháng*, literally "Some[times a] foot [may be too] long, [or an] inch, too short," meaning that everyone has both strong and weak points.

Strictly speaking a Chinese proverb is a grammatically complete sentence expressing an observation or judgment based on experience. Agricultural proverbs (*nóngyán*) and weather proverbs (*qìxiàng yànyǔ*) usually refer to local conditions and do not gain national currency, with the exception of a few general ones such as *zhāoxiá zhǔ yǔ; wǎnxiá zhǔ qíng*, equivalent to the English proverb "Red sky at night, sailor's/shepherd's delight; red sky in the morning, sailor/shepherd take warning." For this reason, as in most Chinese collections of Chinese proverbs, there are very few such proverbs included in this dictionary.

In terms of formal structure, Chinese proverbs usually consist of one or two lines of four or more syllables each, using either colloquial or literary (*wényán*) style. The grammar of Chinese proverbs is largely determined by the basic topic-comment structure of Chinese sentences, which—unlike in poetry—can outweigh formal considerations of parallelism. Thus in *qiān lǐ sòng émáo; lǐ qīng, rényì zhòng*, "[When] a goose feather is sent a thousand miles, [although] the gift [itself] is light, the [accompanying] sentiment is weighty," or "It's the thought that counts," the two lines each of five syllables together form one sentence, but lack the strict grammatical parallelism and rhyme required by classical Chinese poetry. This is true even when the two lines do end-rhyme, as proverbs often do for ease of memorization, as in the extremely colloquial doggerel proverb *Hǎo jiè, hǎo huán; zài jiè bù nán*, "Well borrowed and well returned; borrowing again will not be spurned." Formal grammatical parallelism usually occurs when the same structure is repeated for contrast or comparison, as in the now prover-bial quotation from the Discourses of the Domains (*Guó Yǔ*) cited above: *Cóng shàn rú dèng; cóng è rú bēng,* "To follow goodness is to rise; to follow evil is to fall."

Like proverbs all over the world, some may be taken literally, and some are to be under-stood metaphorically. Thus *Jūnzi dòng kǒu, bù dòng shǒu,* "Gentlemen move [their] mouths, not [their] hands," is a fairly straightforward injunction to resolve disagreements through peaceful speech rather than through physical conflict, whereas *Zhēn jīn bù pà huǒ,* "True gold fears not the fire," is to be understood metaphorically to mean that a person of in-tegrity can stand severe moral testing. The more literary *Qiǎo fù nán wéi wú mǐ zhī chuī,* "[Even] the cleverest housewife cannot cook a meal without rice," is understood metaphor-ically as equivalent to the English "One cannot make bricks without straw." Often explicit metaphors or implicit similes are combined with literal advice or judgments in parallel lines, as in the proverb *Kuàimǎ yī biān; kuài rén yī yán,* "[Just as a] fast horse [needs only] one [touch of the] whip, [so a] straightforward person needs only a word [in order to under-stand]," or an expansion of the proverb from the Han dynasty *Shǐ Jì* cited above, *Liángyào kǔkǒu lìyú bìng; zhōngyán nì'ěr lìyú xíng,* "[Just as] good medicine [which is] bitter in the mouth [is] good for [one's] illness, [so] sincere advice [which] offends the ear [is] beneficial to [one's] conduct." Often only the first of the two lines of such familiar proverbs is cited, the other being implied by suggestion, thus making them appear similar to enigmatic folk simi-les (*xiēhòuyǔ*), discussed above. For example, the first, metaphorical part of some two-part proverbs can take on the meaning of the unsaid second part, as in *Bào sǐ liú pí,* "[When a] leopard dies, [it] leaves [its] skin," which is often used alone with the meaning of the unspo-ken second part, . . . *rén sǐ liú míng,* "[(so) when a] person dies, [(s)he] leaves his (or her) reputation."[8]

Proverbs often follow fixed formulae, such as the comparative A *bùrú* B single line pattern, as in *Bǎi wén bùrú yī jiàn,* "Hearing [(about) something] a hundred times is not as good as see-ing [it] once," or the two line *nìng (kě)* A . . . , *bù* B . . . comparative pattern, e.g., *nìngkě wéi yùsuì, bù kě wǎ quán,* "[It is] better to be a shattered jade [vessel] than an unbroken [piece of] porcelain," meaning that it is better to die in glory than to live in dishonor. A much more popular formula may be seen in *Tiān bù pà, dì bù pà; zhǐpà Guǎngdōng rén shuō Pǔtōnghuà,* "Fear nothing in Heaven or on Earth; the only thing to be feared is Cantonese speaking Man-darin," where the set doggerel formula *Tiān bù pà, dì bù pà; zhǐpà* . . . may be completed with anything a contemporary speaker wishes to make fun of, as long as it contains the requisite number of syllables and can be made to end-rhyme with *pà.*

Single line proverbs in Chinese generally tend to have between five and eight syllables, although—as we have noted above—there are proverbs consisting of four syllables, both lit-erary and colloquial in their wording, which—being complete grammatical sentences con-taining a moral, judgment or observation—are in fact proverbs, *not* to be confused with the more descriptive four syllable literary fixed phrase idioms known as *chéngyǔ.* Given the topic-comment structure of Chinese sentences and the fact that proverbs in Chinese almost always consist of monosyllabic and disyllabic words (*cí*), proverbs with lines of seven or eight sylla-bles generally fall into a four plus three syllable or four plus four syllable pattern, respectively, for each line, with the topic introduced in the first four syllables, and the comment in the remaining syllables. An example of a seven syllable proverb is *Chē dào shān qián, bì yǒu lù,* "[When the] cart gets to the mountain, there must be a way [through]," meaning that things always work themselves out, while the now proverbial quotation attributed to Confucius cited above, *Sān rén tóng xíng, bì yǒu wǒ shī,* "[When] three [of us] persons are walking together, [one of the other two] must be my teacher," i.e., that one can always learn something from others, illustrates the four plus four syllable pattern. Proverbs of nine syllables are few (e.g., *Hào jiào de māo dǎi bùzhù lǎoshǔ,* "Cats who like to mew can't catch mice," meaning that people who brag a lot probably are "all talk and little action") and proverbs of ten or more syllables are rare, usually consisting of couplets of paired five, six, seven or eight syllable lines, often rhymed.[9]

While it is true that proverbs and proverbial wisdom have long played and continue to play a large part within most of the world's non-literate, orally-based peasant cultures, the Chinese perhaps more than any other people are world-renowned for their proverbs, and proverbs have long played and continue to play an important role in both their oral and written traditions up to the present day.

The history of Chinese proverbs in both speech and writing is best examined in terms of the interaction in Chinese society between the so-called "great tradition" of the educated literati versus the so-called "little tradition" of the common people, primarily the peasantry. This distinction was proposed by Robert Redfield (1956:50–51) in an essay encouraging anthropologists to begin to study the farmers or peasants of settled agricultural state societies, rather than confining themselves to the study of simpler hunting and gathering societies. More than five thousand years ago, the land in east Asia which we now think of as China developed settled agricultural communities along the Yellow River, and eventually evolved hierarchical societies based on peasant labor and the agricultural surplus which such a social organization can produce. Along with this more stratified society, there also occurred the development of writing, first as a tool for divination and later for recording grain distribution, taxes, and the numerous other affairs necessary for the management of this more complex social organization.

The earliest written records we have consist of divination inscriptions incised on "oracle bones" and turtle shells (jiǎgǔwén) and cast bronze inscriptions dealing mostly with divination, wars, and affairs of state. But writing later also began to be used to record some of the classics of the pre-literate oral tradition. From the fifth through third centuries B.C.E. we have recorded traditional peasant poetry in the *Shī Jīng* or Poetry Classic, rituals of divination in the *Yìjīng* (易经) or Book of Changes, and later the written records of the sayings of the Taoist Master Lǎozǐ, of Confucius, of Mencius and others. These early written "Classics," which became the canon of the great tradition of the Chinese literati, like other written texts such as the Iliad and the Odyssey, the Ramayana, the Bible, the Koran, Beowulf, the *Chanson de Roland* and the *Kalevala*, to name but a few, are artifacts of a much older primary *oral* tradition which have been fixed and codified thanks to the technological invention of writing.

It must be remembered, however, that the preservers and transmitters of the great written tradition were that very small percentage of society who were literate, the so-called "literati" or scholar-gentry who effectively ruled China's peasantry for most of the last two thousand years after the institution of the civil service in the Han dynasty (202 B.C.E. to 220 C.E.). Even after the invention of printing in China in the eighth century, that technology was still used primarily to record and disseminate the ideology and affairs of the great tradition: official histories, dictionaries, moral philosophy, poetry, essays, semi-popular almanacs, religious texts and other classic works. Writing and printing were not used to record and disseminate the sayings of the vast majority of the illiterate peasant population which supported the great tradition of the literati, even though that peasantry comprised well over ninety percent of the population for most of China's long history. Still today, over eighty percent of China's 1.4 billion people are peasant farmers, and despite the substantial efforts of the government of the People's Republic since 1949 to promote literacy, only about half of them are meaningfully literate, leaving the other more than half a billion either illiterate or only minimally literate and still immersed in the tradition of orality.

As the Qing dynasty scholar Dù Wénlán (杜文澜) noted in the Introduction to his *Gǔ Yáoyàn* (古谣谚: 凡例), "The rise of ballads and proverbs began with spoken language, not inscribed in writing."[10] It is true, however, that *some* of the *súhuà*, the "vulgar sayings" (the usual Chinese term for proverbs and proverbial expressions) of the common people have been transmitted to us through written texts. This may be because the non-literate peasantry, who produced the surplus which supported the imperial system and the scholar-gentry class who ruled them, have always at least in theory occupied a place of honor in the hierarchy of traditional Chinese society, just below the emperor and the literati, and above the merchants, who were officially denigrated as exploitative middlemen often strictly regulated by sumptuary laws. In fact, the yearly imperial examinations—prerequisite to entry into the educated civil service which ruled the empire in the emperor's name—were (at least in theory) open to any peasant family who could afford to raise and educate a son (*sic*) through the years of memorizing the Confucian classics upon which those examinations were based. As the proverb tells us: *Guān chū yú mín, mín chū yú tǔ*, "Officials come from the people, [just as] the people come from the soil."

Perhaps because of this ideology, in later times some of the proverbs and other "vulgar" sayings of the peasants were occasionally recorded and passed down to us in local gazetteers, sometimes in poetry, and—in more recent centuries—in the popular *xiǎoshuō* ("little talk" or fiction) which has had a semi-subterranean history among the literate scholar-gentry for generations, for example, such famous Ming and Qing dynasty works as *Rúlín Wàishǐ* (The Scholars), *Hónglóu Mèng* (Dream of the Red Chamber), the erotic *Jīn Píng Méi* (Golden Lotus) and the ever popular and slightly subversive *Shuǐhú Zhuàn* (Water Margin).

Other proverbs come down through such picaresque works such as the semi-historical *Sānguó Yǎnyì* (The Romance of the Three Kingdoms), and the *Xīyóu Jì*, (Journey to the West, or Monkey), both of which are written codifications of traditional popular oral legends handed down over countless generations by storytellers who roamed county fairs and city markets, as well as through the ever popular local Chinese "operas," such as Peking opera, *kūnqǔ* opera, etc.[11] These traditions survive in Chinese speaking communities today, in Hong Kong and Taiwan as well as on the *shūchǎng* or "storytelling stages" which one still occasionally finds in refurbished temples converted into neighborhood parks and recreation centers in mainland China. They also survive in the modern media, where they continue to provide material for radio, television, and cinema, just as the episodes of the Hindu Ramayana epic provide similar fare for the television and movie industry in India to this day.

The mandarinate of scholar-officials as ruling civil servants was first established in the Han dynasty. Nearly a millennium later written civil service exams to test candidates' literary abilities and knowledge of the Confucian classics was institutionalized in the Sui dynasty. The succeeding Tang dynasty established state-supported schools and authorized editions of those classics to help train potential scholar-officials. Thus, literacy and education became the official criteria for entry into the ruling class of scholar-gentry. As this "great tradition" became firmly established, it is safe to say that the peasantry—as participants, however marginal, in a society run by literates—also acquired at least some oral familiarity with certain proverbialized maxims of the canonized Great Tradition by which they were ruled, which they in turn employed in their own argumentation, declamation, storytelling, and oral performances, and which to some extent influenced their own oral style. To use Goody's (1987) term, this "feedback" thus "closed the loop" between the origin of proverbs in the orality-based little traditions of the common people and the incorporation of sayings and maxims from the literate great tradition into popular oral culture, so that the two thereafter continued to interact in an ongoing dialectical relationship.

This picture of the society which produced the Chinese proverbs, both "high" and "low," in this dictionary is exactly that "composite cultural structure comprised of great and little traditions which have interacted in the past and which are still interacting today" which Redfield described. "The historian and the humanist . . . both can conceive of the civilization which they study as a persisting and characteristic, but also always changing, interaction between little and great traditions . . .; the learning of the great tradition is an outgrowth of the little tradition, and [in turn becomes] . . . an exemplar for the people who carry the little tradition. Great and little traditions are dimensions of one another . . ."[12]

We see then that China's proverbs, originally exemplars and bearers of the "little traditions" of the peasantry, are at base oral forms, with a long history certainly dating back long before, later running parallel with and standing in a dialectical relationship to, the "great tradition" of the literate minority. In discussing the "orality of language," Walter Ong (1982) first reminds us of the linguist's basic creed that ". . . language is so overwhelmingly *oral* that of all the many thousands of languages—possibly tens of thousands—spoken in the course of human history, only around 106 have ever been committed to writing to a degree sufficient to have produced literature, and most have never been written at all. Of the some 3000 languages spoken that exist today, only some 78 have a literature.[13] There is no way to calculate how many languages have disappeared or been transmuted into other languages before writing came along. Even now, hundreds of languages in active use are never written at all: no one has worked out an effective way to write them." Thus, Ong concludes, "The basic orality of language is permanent." [1982:7]

This is to say that for most of humankind's existence on this planet, most human beings have lived in small, face-to-face traditional orality-based societies, societies virtually untouched by the technology of writing. Ong also proposes that formulaic expressions such as proverbs, fixed sayings, clichés, etc. play an important function in such traditional orality-based societies for the storage, processing, and transmission of knowledge and community values.

While Ong admits that totally orality-based cultures in the strict sense now hardly exist, "since [almost] every culture knows of writing and has some experience of its effects," nevertheless he contends that ". . . to varying degrees, many cultures and subcultures, even in a high-technology ambiance, preserve much of the mind-set" of such traditional orality-based societies. [1982:11][14] I suggest that over their long history, the vast majority of China's people, both before and even after the invention of writing, have lived (and many still do live) in such a primarily orality-based culture. Of such societies, Ong observes: "Many modern cultures that have known writing for centuries but have never interiorized it . . . rely heavily on formulaic thought and expression still," emphasizing oral traditions over written ones. [Ong 1982:26]

Proverbs are one important formulaic way of storing and processing knowledge in such traditional orality-based cultures. As Ong notes, "formulas help implement rhythmic discourse and also act as mnemonic aids in their own right, as set expressions circulating through the mouths and ears of all." [1982:36] Thus, for example, the balanced, rhymed English proverb "Red sky in the morning, sailor (/shepherd) take warning; red sky at night, sailor's (/shepherd's) delight" is neatly paralleled in both structure and content by the Chinese qìxiàng yànyǔ or weather proverb cited above: zhāoxiá chū yǔ; wǎnxiá chū qíng, "a rosy dawn means rain; a rosy dusk means clear," making both equally easy to memorize and remember. "Fixed, often rhythmically balanced expressions of this sort . . . can be found occasionally in print, indeed can be 'looked up' in books of sayings, but in oral cultures they are not occasional. They are incessant . . . Heavy patterning and communal fixed forms [of the type commonly found in proverbs –JSR] in oral[ity-based] cultures serve some of the purposes of writing in chirographic [i.e., writing] cultures . . ." [1982:36; my additions –JSR]

We can see then that—as in other parts of the world—proverbs were an integral part of China's primarily peasant, traditional orality-based culture, assisting in the storage, processing, and transmission of knowledge and traditional cultural values, and continuing to influence the rhetoric of the majority of the population even after the invention of writing and the creation of the literate great tradition.

Understanding Chinese proverbs as an integral part of such a primarily orality-based culture suggests an explanation for the continuing existence and functioning of proverbs in traditional Chinese society, both among the overwhelming majority of illiterate Chinese peasants as well as for their persistence among the minority of literate scholar-gentry. However, given the great strides in literacy made by the government of the People's Republic of China since 1949, and the spread of modern communications media since that time, how can we account for their continuing currency in educated and uneducated speech and their continuing popularity in written materials in China throughout the twentieth century? To answer this question, we must examine three factors: the reasons for the decline of proverbs in Western Europe, the linguistic and literary revolutions which took place in China in the twentieth century, and the socio-political history of the establishment of the People's Republic under the leadership of the Chinese Communist Party.

For purposes of comparison, let us first briefly examine the fate of proverbs in Europe and especially in English. As Obelkevitch notes in "Proverbs and Social History":

. . . in pre-industrial Europe it was the peasants, the majority of the population, who used proverbs most; with their oral culture and face-to-face social relations they have continued to do so down to the present day. Although proverbs are learned as well as popular in their origins, their content largely reflected peasant needs and realities; . . . there seems to have been a saying, or several, for every contingency in agriculture, and in life . . . In the nineteenth century, the English equivalents of a peasantry, the small farmers, cottagers and farm laborers, also tended to be heavy users; Russia, the land with the most peasants [in Europe] apparently had the most proverbs of all. [1987:45–46]

Looking just at written sources, Obelkevitch notes that there were seven thousand proverbs in Sebastian Frank's 1541 German collection, almost twelve thousand in Tilley's modern (1950) dictionary of English 16th and 17th century proverbs and proverbial phrases and more than twenty thousand each in two German collections of 17th century proverbs. "Since then the curve has turned downward, the losses outnumbering the gains. Of the English proverbs current in the 17th century, the majority have fallen out of common use and are not familiar; today the total in active service probably does not exceed a thousand." [1987:52]

In a fascinating and detailed analysis, Obelkevitch traces this decline in the use and appreciation of proverbs from Elizabethan England—"soaked with proverbs"—down to their present greatly reduced number and status. Let us examine Obelkevitch's summary explanation for the reasons for this decline, which may also provide us with a basis for understanding the reasons for the continuing existence of proverbs in China today.

Perhaps there is now something unacceptable in the very notion of collective wisdom; more to the modern individualist taste is Wilde's quip that "a truth ceases to be a truth when more than one person believes it"; . . . educated people have many reasons not to use proverbs: . . . that the purpose of life is to fulfil an inner potential, that happiness can be achieved and ought to be pursued, that in the process one becomes a unique individual—all of this clashes with one or another assumption implicit in proverbs. Proverbs put the collective before the individual, the recurrent and stereotyped before the unique, external rules before self-determination, common sense before the individual vision, survival before happiness . . . To use proverbs would deny the individuality of both speaker and listener. In this view, those who use proverbs are either linguistically lazy or lacking in originality, their poverty of language reflecting poverty of experience and poverty of imagination. Proverbs are seen as part of a restricted code that encapsulates experience and imprisons it; they are conversation-stoppers. [1987:65]

In contrast to the decline in the use of proverbs and collective "proverbial wisdom" in Europe and North America, let us now examine both the linguistic and literary revolutions which occurred in China in the twentieth century, and their implications for the continuing positive valuation of proverbs up to the present.

Despite almost one hundred years of Western aggression, the ancient imperial system of emperor at the top, a literate civil service chosen by written examinations based on the Confucian classics, and a population consisting overwhelmingly of illiterate peasant farmers making up the bulk of the population managed to stagger into the twentieth century. The civil service examinations were abolished in 1905, and after the revolutionary uprising of 1911 the Qing dynasty formally collapsed when the last emperor was forced to abdicate in 1912. Until that time, as we have seen, for most of the previous two thousand years literacy was effectively monopolized by the small class of literati, the scholar-gentry who ruled China in the emperor's name. By "monopolized" I mean that full literacy consisted of the ability to read and write "classical" or "literary" Chinese, a written language not based on any living spoken language, but rather on the grammar, vocabulary, and style of pre-Han written classical Chinese, drawn from the classical Confucian canon of works written in the 5th to 3rd centuries B.C.E. This is something akin to speakers of modern English only being able to write in Old English or Latin, but in a non-alphabetic script! While this did provide a common written *lingua franca* for the literate minority of educated speakers of China's many diverse "dialects" throughout the empire, it also ensured that literacy, and hence education, and hence political power, remained in the hands of that very small percentage of the population capable of supporting their sons through the many years of study necessary to pass the imperial civil service examinations and join the extremely small ruling class of scholar-gentry.

This was the linguistic situation with regard to written literacy throughout almost all of the last two thousand years of China's history. It helps to explain the continuing persistence of the tradition of orality not only among the majority of the non-literati population, but also even among the minority of literates. Because all of the texts that they read, as well as those they were required to write, did not reflect any contemporary spoken language, much of their education consisted of oral repetition and rote memorization of classical texts, many of which, although written, were originally structured for oral memorization by people who still lived in an overwhelmingly oral culture.

Soon after the fall of the Qing dynasty and the founding of the Nationalist Republic of China in 1911 came the modernization movement eventually identified with the "May 4th Movement," which focused on linguistic and literary reform. (The "May 4th Movement" was named after the student demonstrations on May 4th, 1919, held in opposition to China's un-just treatment at the Treaty of Versailles at the end of World War I.) In order to facilitate the promotion of widespread literacy and democratize China's "feudal" culture, those Chi-nese intellectuals who had been trained abroad in America, Europe, and Japan, or in the new Western-influenced missionary universities in China, broke with tradition, abandoned the centuries-old Chinese literary tradition, and deliberately proposed a new "national (spo-ken) language" (*Guóyǔ* 国语, now called Mandarin Chinese) based on the spoken dialect of Beijing, the capital. They also created a new style of writing which still employs the non-alphabetic Chinese character writing system, but which is in its grammar and vocabulary much closer to the contemporary spoken language, and thus more accessible to those able to speak it. Under the banner of the New Literature Movement, democratic writers such as Hu Shi and Lu Xun worked to encourage writing in this new "unadorned" *báihuàwén* (白话文) style in-stead of in the traditional "literary Chinese" *wényánwén* (文言文) style, the standard style of writing based on centuries-old classical Chinese which had persisted through the end of the Qing dynasty. Progressive writers such as Hu Shi, Lu Xun, Pa Jin, Cao Yu, Mao Dun, and Lao She struggled to create a modern literary style appropriate to the new China they hoped to build. In their attempts to capture the ideas, concerns and actual language of ordinary peo-ple in this new medium, they naturally included such colloquial forms as proverbs and other types of familiar *shúyǔ* expressions of the common people in their essays, articles, short sto-ries, novels and plays. Hu Shi's pioneering and influential article, "Tentative Suggestions for Literary Reform" (1917), specifically concluded with the admonition, "Do not avoid popular expressions."

In 1932 Chen Wangdao (陈望道), the pioneering rhetorician of this new vernacular *báihuàwén* writing style, in his influential *Xiūcíxué Fāfán* (修辞学发凡, Introduction to Rhetoric), included in his chapter on quotations not only famous proverbs from the classics, but also anonymous popular proverbs, as well as a section on the history and structure of the lowly enigmatic folk simile (*xiēhòuyǔ*) discussed above.

The dominant struggle in China in the second quarter of the twentieth century was between the urban-based Nationalist ("KMT") Party led by Sun Yat-sen's successor, General Chiang Kai-shek, and the Soviet-supported Chinese Communist Party, founded in Shanghai in 1921. After the failure of the Communist-led uprising among the urban workers in Shanghai in 1927,[15] the communists fled to the country and thereafter concentrated on organizing the peasant farmers, following the revolutionary theories and tactics of their new leader, himself a self-educated peasant named Mao Zedong.

After the Chinese communists' "Long March" of 1934–36, in which they retreated to the mountain caves of Yan'an in the remote northwest reaches of China for the duration of the War of Resistance against Japan, they continued to devote themselves to Mao Zedong's new strategy of mobilizing China's peasantry. From then until the Japanese surrender in 1945, Mao concentrated on the recruitment and indoctrination of a cadre of peasant leaders, to whom he often personally lectured on politics, economics, and ideology. While basic literacy classes were of course part of their instruction, Mao did not wait or rely on literacy as a core component of his educational program. Rather he spoke directly, and trained others to speak directly, to the peasant masses whom he intended to mobilize. (The official "Collected Works" of Mao Zedong consist in large part of literacized versions of these talks, and their oral flavor still comes through, despite heavy retroactive editing by official Communist Party historians for public consumption.) The style employed by Mao in his lectures and writings, which were deliberately phrased in terms of a rhetoric calculated to communicate with China's illiterate peasantry, included many proverbs and proverbial sayings and allusions, and formed the basis for much of the style of later communist writing and public speaking in "post-Liberation" China after 1949.

Mao, like Stalin, Khruschev, and other Soviet leaders, was famous for his application of traditional proverbs, particularly "earthy" ones, to the complex issues of modernizing a traditional peasant-based agricultural society, as well as for his own oracular, proverb-like utterances. In the famous "little red book" of his say-ings, we see that Mao chose as his metaphor for China's unrelenting struggle to modernize and create a new communal society the traditional *chéngyǔ* phrase *Yúgōng Yí Shān* (愚公移山). This is an allusion to the proverbial folk story of the "Foolish Old Man [Who] Moved the Mountain," relentlessly shoveling away at it, confident that his descendants would continue his work, generation after generation, until the obstacle was removed. Mao deflated U.S. "imperialism" by comparing it to the proverbial image of a traditional paper [maché] tiger['s head] carried in dragon dance parades: fierce-looking on the outside, but easily poked through with a touch of a finger. Later during the Cultural Revolution, he criticized arrogant Party bureaucrats using the proverbial image of a "tiger's backside—(thinking themselves to be) untouchable." And when Mao's "closest comrade in arms" and heir apparent Lin Biao found his plot to usurp Mao's power exposed and attempted to flee to the Soviet Union in his son's air force plane, Mao was widely quoted as having reacted by using the fatalistic Ningbo proverb as the first part of a *xiēhòuyǔ* folk simile: *Tiān yào xiàyǔ, niáng yào jiàrén—Méi bànfǎ!* "The heavens will rain [and] widows will remarry; it can't be helped!"

The roots of the propagandistic fiction, poetry, and drama which dominated the People's Republic of China for at least the third quarter of the twentieth century can of course be traced back to the Marxist influence of the Soviet Union which launched the "proletarian literature" of the 1920s. In order to explain the currency of proverbs and other such popular colloquial expressions in the oral and written culture of the People's Republic, however, we must pay particular attention to Mao's famous Talks on Literature and Art given in Yan'an in 1942. He explicitly stressed to writers and artists the importance of the mass audience and of employing a populist language and style accessible to the majority of that audience, including the use of proverbs, folk idioms and other such familiar expressions as he himself so often did. To quote Edward Gunn's *Rewriting Chinese: Style and Innovation in Twentieth Century Chinese Prose* (1991:134), "The period of the War of Resistance to Japan (1937–1945) and the subsequent decades of Maoist leadership are remembered in [China's] literary history for the rise and predominance of works executing the prescriptions of Socialist Realism and [of] Mao Zedong's Yan'an Talks (1942)."

Out of this conscious redirection of art and literature developed the so-called "Potato School" (*shānyaodàn pài*) of "native soil" literature, which was characterized by a deliberate emphasis on folk (i.e., peasant) and regional features, perhaps best seen in Zhao Shuli's 1943 work *Lǐ Yǒucái Bǎnhuà* (李有才板话, The Rhymes of Li Youcai). In such works the proverbs, proverbial expressions, and also those fused phrase *chéngyǔ* idioms which had already passed into popular usage in northern (Mandarin) Chinese became required elements of this new style. As Gunn notes, ". . . *yanyu* proverbs and *chengyu* patterned idioms were given a high value as essential elements of a work." (1991:138) In this way, many originally regional familiar sayings and proverbs gained wider currency and passed into the emerging standard of the new national language and written style. By "the 1940s and early 1950s, the wave of writing that sought authenticity through the use of regional speech and idioms was followed by a wave of glossaries, dictionaries, and studies of these features." (1991:79) This conscious political decision to promote proverbs and folk idioms in the creation of a new literary style as part of the formation of a new society to be founded on the communal values and orally based rhetoric of the traditional peasantry explains the widespread inclusion of proverbs in modern Chinese literature within the People's Republic after 1949.

These basic directions, stemming from the linguistic and literary reform associated with the May 4th movement, from Mao Zedong's pronouncements in his Yan'an Talks, and from the resultant "Potato School" of literature all combined to promote the currency of proverbs and other colloquial expressions within the emerging standard of the new "Mandarin" national language, as well as in Chinese fiction, drama, and other writings past the end of the Maoist era and into the last quarter of the twentieth century. It should be stressed that these expressions should not be viewed as simply a kind of superficial "window dressing," calculated to give an air of peasant legitimacy to a revolutionary movement. The question remains: *why* is it that the *proverb*, that specific rhetorical device, was chosen and has served as an important part of the rhetorical arsenal of the Chinese revolutionary movement and continues to have such currency in China today?

To answer this question, I suggest that we should go back to Obelkevitch's explanation of why proverbs did not survive in Europe, especially among the educated upper and middle classes. The heart of Obelkevitch's explanation is this: "Proverbs put the *collective* before the *individual*, the *recurrent* and *stereotyped* before the *unique*, *external* rules before *self*-determination, *common* sense before the *individual* vision, *survival* before *happiness*." [1987:65, my italics –JSR]

Individuality, uniqueness, self-determination, individual vision, (individual) happiness, these are the positive values of modern European and North American society, especially among the educated middle and upper classes, which Obelkevitch tells us led to the decline of the popularity of proverbs in the West. But these values of the "collective over the individual," the "recurrent before the unique," "external rules over self-determination," accepting the traditional "common[ly shared] sense" (i.e., traditional Chinese peasant values) over any individual's personal vision, and the assurance of basic "survival" for all before the luxury of "happiness" for a privileged few are not just the ideals theoretically espoused by Mao Zedong and the Chinese Communist Party; they are in fact the ideals and values of traditional Chinese peasant society. It is exactly the Chinese Communist Party's endorsement of those basic Chinese values which may be said to account for the Chinese peasantry's support for the communist movement and the many undeniable successes of communism in China since 1949. And these are still the traditional values which many of China's older leaders (rightly or wrongly) wish to preserve.

I have tried to document that the common thread running though the persistence of proverbs in Chinese society is their function as both a rhetorical mainstay and an integral bearer of traditional knowledge and values in China's millennia-old tradition of orality. I have further tried to demonstrate that the history of proverbs in China throughout the twentieth century in both speaking and writing was intimately related to deliberate attempts to preserve traditional Chinese communal values and to incorporate the orally-based rhetoric of the peasantry into the emerging linguistic style of the "New China." Assuming that China is able to achieve its other goals of widespread literacy, education, industrialization, and modernization in the new global context, it remains to be seen whether those traditional values and that orally-based tradition can or will survive.

Notes:

1. Taylor, A. in Mieder, W. and Dundes, A. 1981:3, 61.

2. *American College Dictionary*, 1957; quoted in Mieder and Dundes 1981:141,159.

3. Cf. Qū Pǔ 1992:17–32; Sūn Zhìpíng et al.,1984:2–3; Sūn Wéizhāng 1989:292–344; Táng Qǐyùn 1981:55–87; Wáng Yì 1961:44–58; Wáng Qín 1980:1–8; Wēn Duānzhèng 1985:1–18; Wǔ Zhànkūn & Mǎ Guófàn 1980:1–22; Zhōngguó Mínjiān Wénxué Jíchéng 1990:1–8.

4. Advising missionaries and visitors to China in 1874, Alfred Lister noted, "The usefulness of [proverbs] . . . dealing with . . . the Chinese cannot be exaggerated. It is the peculiar advantage attaching to the citation of a proverb that it is something beyond dispute, accepted and settled as true, a first principle, like the axioms of science, or the multiplication table [for a Westerner]. The silencing effect of an apt and telling proverb, let off, as it were, right in the faces of a possibly angry, and certainly gesticulating and blatant Chinese crowd must be seen to be observed. If it happen to be a proverb from the classics, so much the better." [Lister, 1981:248]

5. *Life* magazine 70:4:46–48, April 1971; Rohsenow 1991:ix.

6. *Zhōngguó Mínjiān Wénxué Jíchéng—Níngxià Juàn* 1990:5

7. Zhào Zhòngyì, 1982:233–238; the English translation is from Shih, V. 1983:294–295.

8. A note on translation: The generic word *rén* in Chinese is easily translated as "person." More difficult are the non-gender-marked (spoken) third-person singular pronoun *tā* and places where English demands a singular pronoun. Where convenient, I have tried to avoid overly sexist translations, without committing solecisms, by using "(s)he," "they," etc. Where the original proverb is sexist, I have rendered it so.

9. For a detailed analysis of the structure of Chinese proverbs, see Táng Qǐyùn 1981:64–73.

10. Jì Chéngjiā et al., 1981:1.

11. For a more detailed treatment of the history of intertextuality between the Chinese oral tradition and proverbs in Chinese literature, see Rohsenow, J. S., 2001.

12. Redfield, R. 1956:50–51,58.

13. Edmonson, 1971: 323;332, quoted in Ong 1982:7.

14. I do not endorse Ong's concept of "primary oral cultures," which has been criticized by Street (1987), Tannen (1982), and others.

15. The abortive 1927 Shanghai uprising was dramatized by André Malraux in his novel *La Condition Humaine* (Man's Fate).

How to Use This Dictionary

Following the principles of this ABC series, the entries are arranged alphabetically, in a strict "letter-by-letter" order, ignoring word spaces and punctuation. Tones also do not affect the order (since all the proverbs are alphabetically distinct). Thus, the proverb beginning with the word *guāngzhe* comes before the one beginning with the words *guān jǐng*; and, the proverb beginning *chǐ yǐn* precedes the one beginning *chǐ yǐ qiàn*. The romanization is standard *Hànyǔ Pīnyīn*, following the *Hànyǔ Pīnyīn Cíhuì* and the word (*cí* 词) division rules set forth in the *Hànyǔ Pīnyīn Zhèngcífǎ* as jointly promulgated in 1988 by the PRC State Language Commission and State Education Commission.[1]

The romanization is followed by the simplified characters (*jiǎntǐzì* 简体字) which have been standard in China since the 1950s. The characters are punctuated according to contemporary Chinese convention, but for the convenience of English readers, the romanization is punctuated according to English conventions.

    *   An asterisk after the romanization marks the most commonly occurring proverbs.

    ( )   Parentheses surround optional portions of the proverbs and explanations.

    [ ]   Square brackets enclose English words within the translation which must be understood but which do not correspond directly to any of the Chinese words in the proverb.

    /   Slashes separate variants.

    " "   Double quotation marks are used for equivalent or related English proverbs or proverbial sayings.

    (lit) (fig) — Unless the translation is self-explanatory, there is first a literal (lit) translation followed by a figurative (fig) translation, which explains the meaning.

    (1) (2) (3) — Alternative meanings are numbered sequentially.

    "Cf." refers to works in which examples of the proverb in question may be found; since many *yànyǔ* appear in the popular traditional vernacular novels listed on the following page, the abbreviations for those novels (DRC, etc.) are used in the citations. "See also," "vs.," and "q.v." are cross-references to the first several words of other entries in this dictionary. Sometimes there is a "note" referring to other related expressions or facts. A proverb may contain or refer to a *chéngyǔ* 成语, fixed literary idiom or set phrase, or to a *súyǔ* 俗语, a traditional proverbial expression.[2]

    A *bibliography* of works of and about *yànyǔ* and related topics is followed by an *index* of names, places and topics contained within the entries.

Notes:

    1. For my English translation of the *Hànyǔ Pīnyīn Zhèngcífǎ Jīběn Guīzé* or "Basic Rules for Hanyu Pinyin Orthography," see the appendix to DeFrancis, (ed.), *ABC Chinese-English Dictionary*, University of Hawai'i Press, 1996, pp. 835–845.

    2. Many of the four-character proverbs cited herein which might first appear to be *chéngyǔ* are here word-divided according to their own internal grammar, and not according to the arbitrary AB-CD, one-formula-fits-all compromise convention for real *chéngyǔ* dictated by the *Hànyǔ Pīnyīn Zhèngcífǎ*. But when such a proverb is sometimes also used as (or has been misanalyzed as) a *chéngyǔ*, that form is also noted within the entry, and listed in the index.

Abbreviations for Popular Novels

DRC   *Dream of the Red Chamber*

           or *A Dream of Red Mansions*

           or *Story of the Stone* —— *Hónglóu Mèng* 红楼梦

JPM   *Golden Lotus* or *The Plum in the Golden Vase* —— *Jīn Píng Méi* 金瓶梅

JW   *Journey to the West* or *Monkey* —— *Xīyóu Jì* 西游记

R3K   *Romance of the Three Kingdoms* —— *Sān Guó Yǎnyì* 三国演义

WM   *Water Margin* or *Outlaws of the Marsh* —— *Shuǐhǔ Zhuàn* 水浒传

           also translated by Pearl Buck as *All Men Are Brothers*

A

1 **Ài fàn yǒu fàn; xī yī yǒu yī.** 爱饭有饭，惜衣有衣。[Those who] treasure [their] food [will always] have food [and those who] take care of [their] clothing [will always] have clothes [to wear]. [An admonition to thrift; see also *bùyī nuǎn* below.]

2 **Ái gǒu yǎo de rén bù dōu shì zéi.** 挨狗咬的人不都是贼。(lit) Not all who are bitten by dogs are thieves. (fig) One should not make judgments based on superficial appearances. Things are not always as they (first) appear.

3 **Áiguo shé yǎo, jiàn shàn pǎo.** 挨过蛇咬，见鳝跑。(lit) [One who has been] bitten by a snake [at the] sight [of an] eel [will] run away. (fig) "Once bitten, twice shy." [See also *yīzhāo bèi shé yǎo* below.]

4 **Ài huā, lián pén ài; ài nǚ, téng nǚxu.** 爱花连盆爱，爱女疼女婿。(lit) [If one] loves a flower, [one will] love [its] pot; [if one really] loves [one's] daughter, [one will also] love [one's] son-in-law. (fig) "Love me, love my dog." [Note the *chengyu*: *àiwū-jíwū*, "love for a person extends even to the crows on his roof."]

5 **Ài huā, lián pén ài; yuàn jī, lián wō yuàn.** 爱花连盆爱，怨鸡连窝怨。(lit) [If one] loves a flower, [one will] love [its] pot; [if one] hates a chicken, [one will] hate [its] coop [as well]. (fig) If one has strong feelings about some person(s), one will also be for or against everything associated with them.

6 **Ài jiào de máquè bù zhǎng ròu.** 爱叫的麻雀不长肉。(lit) Sparrows who love to chirp won't put on weight. (fig) People who like to talk a lot won't make any substantial achievements. [See also *huì jiào de gǒu* below.]

7 **Ài jiào de mǔjī bù xiàdàn.** 爱叫的母鸡不下蛋。(lit) Cackling hens do not lay eggs. (fig) Boastful people are good at nothing. [See also *duō míng zhī māo* and *huì zhuō lǎoshǔ* below.]

8 **Ài jīn sì jīn; ái yù sì yù.** 挨金似金，挨玉似玉。(lit) [One who is] close to gold [is] like gold [and one who is] close to jade [is] like jade. (fig) A good environment produces good people. People are influenced by the company they keep. [Cf. *Érnǚ Yīngxióng Zhuàn*, chap. 37; see also *jìn zhū zhě chì* below.]

9 **Āi mò dàyú xīn sǐ.** 哀莫大于心死。(lit) [Of] grief, there is none greater than a dead mind/heart. (fig) There is nothing more grievous than a mind/heart which has stopped thinking/feeling. [Cf. *Zhuāngzǐ: Tián Zǐfāng*; now more popularly *āi mò guòyú xīn sǐ*.]

10 **Ài pán, bù jī shǔ.** 爱盘不击鼠。(lit) [If one] loves the plate, one doesn't strike the mouse [on it]. (fig) One won't go all out to solve a problem if it involves someone with whom one has some connection. People can't avoid being partial. [See also *gǒu bù chī shǐ* below.]

11 **Ài qīn zuòqīn.** 爱亲做亲。(lit) Loving families make [good] in-laws. (fig) Loving families make for happy marriages. [Cf. *Rúlín Wàishǐ*, chap. 21; note: *zuòqīn* "become relatives by marriage"; *qìngjia*, "in-laws"; see also *ér-nǚ qīn* below.]

12 **Ǎirén duō qiǎojì.** 矮人多巧计。Short people are always good at schemes. [See also *ǎizi dù lǐ* below.]

13 **Ái yī quán, dé yī zhāo; ái shí quán, biàn Zhūgé.** 挨一拳，得一招，挨十拳，变诸葛。(lit) Receive one blow, [and one] learns a lesson; receive ten blows, [and one] becomes a huge Zhuge [Liang, the mastermind]. (fig) One can learn much from failure or "hard knocks." [Note: Zhuge Liang was the master strategist in *R3K*.]

14 **Ài zài xīnli, hěn zài miànpí.** 爱在心里，狠在面皮。Love [your] children in [your] heart, [but] be stern [with them] in [your] manner. [Rhyme.]

15 **Āizhe tiějiang huì dǎ dīng; āizhe mùjiang huì lājù.** 挨着铁匠会打钉，挨着木匠会拉锯。(lit) [If one stays] close to a blacksmith, [one will] learn to hammer out nails; [if one stays] close to a carpenter, [one will] learn how to use a saw. (fig) One can always learn something from those one associates with. [See also *cuō yào sān nián* and *gēnzhe wǎjiang* and *rù háng sān rì* and *sān tiān zhù zài* and *shú dú Tángshī* below.]

16 **Ài zhī yù qí fù; qīn zhī yù qí guì.** 爱之欲其富，亲之欲其贵。(lit) [To] love them [is to] desire their enrichment; [to be] dear [to] them [is to] desire their honor. (fig) One hopes that those dear to one will win riches and honor. [Cf. *Shǐ Jì: Sān Wáng Shì Jiā.*]

17 **Ǎizi dù lǐ gēda duō.** * 矮子肚里疙瘩多。(lit) In the bellies of short people there are many schemes. (fig) Short people are notorious for hatching schemes. [Note: *gēda*, (lit) "lumps" or "bumps," here refers to schemes in a derogatory sense; see also *ǎirén duō qiǎojì* above.]

18 **Ǎizi miànqián, mò shuō duǎn huà.** * 矮子面前，莫说短话。(lit) In front of short people, don't talk about shortness. (fig) One should not discuss others' shortcomings in their presence (in order to avoid hurting their feelings). [See also *dāngzhe ǎirén* below.]

19 **Àn dǎ húli, míng dǎ láng.** 暗打狐狸，明打狼。(lit) Hunt foxes stealthily, [and] hunt wolves openly [just as they themselves do]. (fig) Different opponents require different appropriate strategies. [See also *bīng wú cháng shì* and *guānmén dǎ gǒu* and *qīng ná níqiu* below.]

20 **Àndào de mǔjī bù xiàdàn.** 按倒的母鸡不下蛋。(lit) A hen [which is] forced [to nest] won't lay eggs. (fig) One cannot force people to do things they do not want to do. [See also the following entry.]

B

21 **Àn niú tóu, chībude cǎo.** 按牛头, 吃不得草。 (lit) [Although] the ox's head is pressed down, [it] won't eat grass. (fig) Tactics which rely purely on force will not succeed. "You can lead a horse to water, but you can't make it drink." [See also *niú bù hē shuǐ* below and the preceding entry.]

22 **Ào bùkě zhǎng; yù bùkě zòng.** 傲不可长, 欲不可纵。 (lit) Pride [should] not be permitted to grow, [and] desire [should] not be permitted to run amok. (fig) Pride and desire should be controlled. [Cf. *Lǐjì: Qū Lǐ Shàng.*]

23 **Àoqì sǔn cái.** 傲气损才。 Arrogance (or stubbornness) [can] cost [one a] fortune. [Cf. the modern *shuōshū*-based *Wǔ Sōng*; chap. 3 and chap. 6.]

B

1 **Bǎduò de bù huāng, chéngchuán de wěndang.** 把舵的不慌, 乘船的稳当。 (lit) [If the] helmsman is not nervous, the passengers [will feel] secure. (fig) If the leader appears confident, his or her followers will gain confidence also. [See also *tóumǎ bù huāng* and *zhǎngduò de (xīn)* below.]

2 **Báibù diào zài diàn gāng lǐ, qiān dàn héshuǐ xǐ bù qīng.** 白布掉在靛缸里, 千担河水洗不清。 (lit) [If a piece of] white cloth falls into an indigo dyeing vat, a thousand tons of river water can't wash [it] clean. (fig) Once one has been implicated, it is difficult to regain people's good opinion. [One *dàn* is equal to fifty kilograms.]

3 **Bǎi bù wéi duō; yī bù wéi shǎo.** 百不为多, 一不为少。 (lit) A hundred is not too many, [and] one is not too few. (fig) Things are valued for their quality, not merely for their quantity. One can never have too much of a good thing.

4 **Bǎi chǐ gāntóu, gèng jìnyībù.** 百尺杆头, 更进一步。 (lit) [Even a] one-hundred foot [tall] bamboo [can] progress even one [more] step. (fig) After having achieved a fair degree of success, one should try to do still better. [Originally a message of Buddhist self-cultivation; also said *bǎi chǐ gāntóu, jìn qǔ yī bù.*]

5 **Bǎidù, bǎi dào jiāngbiān; zào tǎ, zào dào tǎ jiān.** 摆渡摆到江边, 造塔造到塔尖。 (lit) [If you] ferry [people], ferry [them] to the [opposite] river bank; [if you] build a pagoda, build [it up] to the top. (fig) If you do anything (for others), do it thoroughly. [Rhyme; see also *bāng rén, bāng dàodǐ* and *sòng fó, sòng dào Xī* below.]

6 **Báijiǔ hóng rén miàn; huángjīn hēi shì xīn.** 白酒红人面, 黄金黑世心。 [Just as] white liquor makes people's faces turn red, [so] yellow gold makes people's hearts turn black [i.e., evil]. [Cf. *Chū Kè Pāi'àn Jīngqí*, chap. 14.]

7 **Bàijūn zhī jiàng, bùzú yán yǒng.** 败军之将, 不足言勇。 The general of a defeated army is not entitled to claim bravery. [Cf. *JW*, chap. 31.]

8 **Bǎi liàn cái chéng gāng.** 百炼才成钢。 (lit) Only after much tempering is steel produced. (fig) True character must be tested in hardship. [Derived from the *chengyu*: *bǎiliàn-chénggāng.*]

9 **Bǎi lǐ bù fàn qiáo; qiān lǐ bù fàn dí.** 百里不贩樵, 千里不贩籴。 (lit) Do not [travel] a hundred *li* to sell firewood [or a] thousand *li* to buy grain. (fig) Don't waste your time in unprofitable undertakings. [A pre-1949 *yanyu*; cf. *Shǐ Jì: Huòzhí Lièzhuàn.*]

10 **Bǎi lǐ, bùtóng fēng; qiān lǐ, bùtóng sú.** 百里不同风, 千里不同俗。 (lit) [Travel one] hundred *li* [and] the customs are not the same; [travel one] thousand *li* [and] the practices are different. (fig) Customs differ from place to place, even though they may be only a short distance apart. [Cf. *Érnǚ Yīngxióng Zhuàn*, chap. 17; note: traditionally, one *li* equaled approximately one-half of a kilometer; see also *chūmén sān li* and *gé dào bù xiàyǔ* below.]

11 **Bái māo, hēi māo, néng dǎi hàozi jiùshi hǎo māo.** 白猫, 黑猫, 能逮耗子就是好猫。 (lit) • [It doesn't matter if a] cat [is] black or white, [as long as it] can catch mice, it's a good cat. (fig) One's ideological persuasion is not important, as long as one can get the job done. [Attributed to Deng Xiaoping as an example of his pragmatic policies, for which he was criticized during the Cultural Revolution; see also *bùguǎn hēi māo* below.]

12 **Bǎi mì wèimiǎn yī shū.** 百密未免一疏。 (lit) One hundred careful plannings cannot avoid one slip. (fig) There are bound to be oversights even in the most well conceived plan. [Note: *zhōumì*, "careful, thorough"; *shūlòu*, "oversight," also said *bǎi mì zòng yǒu yī shū.*]

13 **Bǎinián chéngshì bùzú; yīdàn huài zhī yǒuyú.** 百年成事不足; 一旦坏之有余。 A hundred years are not enough to accomplish anything great, [but] one day is more than enough to ruin it. [Rhyme; see also *chái wū yī dài yān* below.]

14 **Bài qí yǒu shèng zhāo.** 败棋有胜招。 (lit) [In a] losing chess [game], there is [still a chance for a] winning move. (fig) Although when one is involved in a difficult situation it may appear hopeless, nevertheless there is still a chance to win, so remain calm and try your best.

15 **Bǎi rén bǎi xìng; gèrén gèxìng.** 百人百姓, 个人个性。 (lit) [Just as] each person [has] a different surname, [so] each individual [has] a different character. (fig) Different people think and behave differently. [Note: the one-word term (*lǎo*)*bǎixìng*, (lit) "(old) hundred surnames," refers to the common people.]

B

16 **Bǎi rén chī bǎi wèi.** 百人吃百味。(lit) A hundred people have a hundred different tastes. (fig) (1) "Each to his own taste." (2) It is impossible to please everyone.

17 **Bǎi rì chuáng qián wú xiàozǐ.** 百日床前无孝子。(lit) [After] one hundred days before [an ailing parent's] bed, there are no filial sons. (fig) Even a dutiful child will lose patience if his parent is confined to bed for too long. [More commonly said jiǔ bìngchuáng qián below.]

18 **Bǎi rì kǎnchái, yī rì shāo.** 百日砍柴，一日烧。(lit) The firewood cut over a hundred days [will be] burnt in one day. (fig) One should make long-term preparations against a time of emergency. [See also yǎngbīng qiān rì below.]

19 **Bǎi shèng nán lǜ dí; sān zhē nǎi liángyī.** 百胜难虑敌，三折乃良医。(lit) [Even a general who has won a] hundred victories [may be] hard put to see through the enemy['s stratagems, but one who has] broken [his] arm three [times will] be a good doctor. (fig) One cannot always depend on past successes to guarantee future success, but one can always learn from lessons drawn from failure. [A rhymed line from a poem by the Tang dynasty poet Liu Yuxi; see also sān zhé gōng zhī below.]

20 **Bǎi shìyí zǎo, bùyí chí.*** 百事宜早，不易迟。[In] all things better [to make preparations] early [rather] than later.

21 **Bǎisuì guāngyīn rú guòkè.** 百岁光阴如过客。(lit) [Even a] hundred-year-old [person] is [but a] traveler passing by. (fig) Human life is short.

22 **Báitiān bù zuò kuīxīnshì, yèbàn qiāomén bù chījīng.** 白天不做亏心事，夜半敲门不吃惊。(lit) [If one does] not do bad things in the daytime, one need not be alarmed at knocks on the door in the middle of the night. (fig) "A quiet conscience sleeps in thunder." [See also bù zuò kuīxīnshì and méi zuò kuīxīnshì and rìjiān bù zuò below.]

23 **Báitóu rú xīn; qīng gài rúgù.** 白头如新，倾盖如故。(lit) White heads as [though] new[ly met]; two canopi[ed chariots] tipping [toward each other] as [though] old friends. (fig) With some people one maintains a long acquaintanceship without any real understanding for years; with others one becomes intimate friends upon first meeting. [Cf. This is termed a yanyu in Shǐ Jì: Lú Zhòng Lián Zhōu Yáng Lièzhuàn; note: qīng gài, (lit) "inclined [carriage] canopies [touching]"; (fig) "Two passing canopied carriages draw near to talk."]

24 **Bǎiwàn mǎi zhái; qiānwàn mǎi lín.** 百万买宅，千万买邻。(lit) [It may cost a] million to buy a house, [but] ten million to find [good] neighbors. (fig) Good neighbors are hard to find. Good neighbors are even more important than the quality of one's house. [A line from a Song dynasty poem by Xīng Qíjí; see also fángzi hǎo zhù and qiānjīn mǎi chǎn below.]

25 **Bǎiwén bùrú yījiàn.** 百闻不如一见。(lit) A hundred words of hearsay are not as good as one look [at the reality]. (fig) One look is worth a thousand words. "Seeing is believing." [Cf. Hàn Shū: Zhào Chōng Guó Zhuàn; in Jīngshì Tōngyán, chap. 5: qiān wén bùrú yī jiàn; see also tīng qiān biàn below.]

26 **Bǎi wú yī yòng shì shūshēng.** 百无一用是书生。(lit) Not a useful one in a hundred, that's scholars. (fig) Scholars are basically impractical. "Those who can, do; those who can't, teach." [In traditional times, Chinese scholars could not do any practical work; from a Qing dynasty poem by Huáng Jǐngrén; see also xiùcai zàofǎn below.]

27 **Bǎi yàng mǐ yǎng bǎi yàng rén.** 百样米养百样人。(lit) A hundred kinds of rice nourish a hundred kinds of people. (fig) People differ greatly in their minds and character. [See also yī yàng mǐ below.]

28 **Bǎi zhàng zhīhòu, háojié tǐng shēng.** 百仗之后，豪杰挺生。[Only] after a hundred battles are [true] heroes produced.

29 **Bàizǐ huítóu biàn zuò jiā.** 败子回头便作家。A prodigal son [who] returns will revitalize [his] family['s affairs]. [Cf. Èr Kè Pāi'àn Jīngqí, chap. 22; Xǐngshì Héngyán, chap. 17; see also the following entry; note: bàijiāzǐ, "spendthrift; wastrel; prodigal."]

30 **Bàizǐ huítóu, jīnbùhuàn.** 败子回头金不换。(lit) A prodigal son [who] returns [can]not be exchanged for gold. (fig) Nothing is more valued than a reformed prodigal. [Cf. Érnǚ Yīngxióng Zhuàn, chap. 15; see also làngzǐ-huítóu and the preceding and the following entries.]

31 **Bàizǐ ruò shōuxīn, yóu rú guǐ biàn rén.** 败子若收心，由如鬼变人。If prodigal son repents, it is like a ghost changing into a human being. [Cf. Chū Kè Pāi'àn Jīngqí, chap. 15.]

32 **Bǎi zú zhī chóng, sǐ ér bù jiāng.** 百足之虫，死而不僵。(lit) A centipede dies but never stiffens. (fig) A powerful person or family still has some influence or political power even after decline or ruin. [Cf. DRC, chap. 2; see also dà chuán lànle below.]

33 **Bále máo de fènghuáng bùrú jī.*** 拔了毛的凤凰不如鸡。(lit) A plucked phoenix is not as [good as a] chicken. (fig) One who is out of office or favor becomes a nobody. A defective thing is of no value, no matter how superior it used to be. [See also dézhì māor and fènghuáng luò jià and sǐ zhīfū below.]

34 **Bān bu dǎo húlu, sǎ bu liǎo yóu.** 搬不倒葫芦，洒不了油。(lit) [If we] don't tip [the] bottle gourd, [we] can't spill [out] the oil. (fig) If one does not employ certain means, one can't achieve one's goal. "You can't make an omelet without breaking some eggs." [Cf. Yuè Fēi Zhuàn, chap. 82.]

35 **Bàn bù Lúnyǔ zhì tiānxià.** 半部论语治天下。(lit) [Using only] half of the Analects of Confucius, [one can] rule the country. (fig) (1) One can bring peace and order to the country using only half of

B

the Confucian Analects. (2) One need not be a complete Confucian in order to be a ruler.

36　**Bāng lǐ, bù bāng qīn.** 帮里，不帮亲。(lit) Support [those who have] right [on their side], not [just those who are your] relatives. (fig) Act according to correct principles in doing everything regardless of your relationship to those you are dealing with. [See also *duàn lǐ, bù duàn qīn* below.]

37　**Bāng rén, bāng dàodǐ; sòng fó, sòng dào Xī.** 帮人帮到底，送佛送到西。(lit) [When you] help others, help [them] completely, [just as when you see someone off,] see [him] off [all the way] to the West[ern] Heaven. [A rhyme; *Xī* "West" here refers to *Xītiān*, the Western Heaven of Buddhism; see also *bǎidù, bǎi dào* above and *jiù rén, jiù dàodǐ* and *sòng fó, sòng dào Xī* below.]

38　**Bàngtóu chū xiàozǐ; zhùtóu chū wǔnì.** 棒头出孝子，箸头出忤逆。(lit) A club produces filial sons; chopsticks produce disobedient [ones]. (fig) Strict discipline produces dutiful children whereas indulgence produces disobedient ones. "Spare the rod and spoil the child." [Cf. *Chū Kè Pāi'àn Jīngqí*, chap. 13.]

39　**Bàn jiǔ róngyì, qǐngkè nán; qǐngkè róngyì, kuǎnkè nán.** 办酒容易，请客难；请客容易，款客难。It's easier to make a feast than to get the guests to come, [and] it's easier to get guests to come than to entertain them properly.

40　**Bānjiū xián shù, bānjiū qǐ.** 斑鸠嫌树斑鸠起。(lit) [When a] turtledove dislikes a tree, [the] turtledove leaves. (fig) If someone is tired of a place, (s)he will leave immediately.

41　**Bàn jūn rú bàn hǔ.** 伴君如伴虎。Attending upon a king is [as dangerous as] keeping company with a tiger. [Cf. *Yuè Fēi Zhuàn*, chap. 8.]

42　**Bàn rén de zhuāngzi bùzài gāo.** 绊人的桩子不在高。A stake [in the ground which] causes people to stumble [does] not [have to be] high. (fig) People fail because they overlook seemingly insignificant obstacles.

43　**Bǎo dài gānliang; nuǎn dài yī.** 饱带干粮，暖带衣。(lit) Carry [extra] food when full and [extra] clothes when warm. (fig) Always be "prepared for a rainy day."

44　**Bǎo de yī rén; bǎobude yī mén.** 保得一人，保不得一门。[One] can protect one person, [but one] cannot protect a whole family. [Cf. *Wǔ Sòng*, chap. 2.]

45　**Bǎo hàn bù zhǐ è hàn jī.*** 饱汉不知饿汉饥。(lit) A full person [can]not [truly] understand a starving person's hunger. (fig) One can't sympathize with the starving on a full stomach. [Cf. *Guānchǎng Xiànxíng Jì*, chap. 45; also said *bào rén bù zhī è rén jī*; see also *mǎ shàng bù zhī* and *qí lǘ bù zhī* and *sānshí wǎnshang* below.]

46　**Bǎojiàn bì fù lièshì; qí fāng bìxū liángyī.** 宝剑必付烈士，奇方必须良医。(lit) [A] valuable sword should be granted [to a] person of high endeavor, [and an] uncommon prescription should be handled [by a] good doctor. (fig) Resources should be given to those who can make full use of them. [See also the following entry.]

47　**Bǎojiàn mài yǔ lièshì; hóngfěn zèngyǔ jiārén.** 宝剑卖与烈士，红粉赠与佳人。[A] valuable sword [should be] sold to a person of high endeavor [and high quality] rouge [should be] granted to a beauty. (fig) Resources should be given to those who can make the best use of them. [See also the preceding entry.]

48　**Bǎonuǎn shēng xiánshì; jīhán fā dào xīn.** 饱暖生闲事，饥寒发盗心。[Those who are] amply fed [and] clothed [are inclined to] get into trouble, [whereas] hunger [and] cold breed [the temptation to] steal. [Cf. *JPM*, chap. 25; also said *bǎonuǎn sì yínyù; jīhán qǐ dào xīn*, "Those who are well fed and warm are inclined to be lustful, etc." in *Èr Kè Pāi'àn Jīngqí*, chap. 21; compare *yīshí zú érhòu* below; see also the following entry.]

49　**Bǎonuǎn sī yínyù.*** 饱暖思淫欲。[When one is] full [and] warm [i.e., when one has enough to eat and to wear, one's] thoughts turn to carnal desires. [Usually said of wealthy people in traditional China; *Èr Kè Pāi'àn Jīngqí*, chap. 28; *Píng Yāo Zhuàn*, chap. 35; see also the preceding entry.]

50　**Bào sǐ, liú pí; rén sǐ, liúmíng.** 豹死留皮，人死留名。[Just as when a] leopard dies, [it] leaves [its] skin, [so when a] person dies, [(s)he] leaves his (or her) reputation.

51　**Bǎobiǎn shì mǎizhǔ; (hècǎi shì xiánrén).** 褒贬是买主，(喝彩是闲人)。[One who] criticizes [the goods] is a [potential] buyer, [but one who simply] praises [the goods] is only an idler (passing time by window shopping). [See also *xián huò zhèngshì* below.]

52　**Bāozi yǒu ròu, bùzài zhě shàng.** 包子有肉，不在褶上。(lit) [Whether or not a] dumpling [is decently filled] with meat [can]not [be judged] from [how well the decorative] folds [are made on the outside]. (fig) Whether someone is good, (talented, wealthy, etc.) cannot be judged by superficial appearance. "Don't judge a book by its cover."

53　**Bāshí suì de mā méi ràng láng gǎnshàng.** 八十岁的妈没让狼赶上。(lit) [Even the] eighty-year-old mother didn't let the wolf catch up [with her]. (fig) Everyone can find hidden reserves of strength when necessary.

54　**Bāxiān guò hǎi, gè xiǎn shéntōng / qí néng.** 八仙过海，各显神通/其能。(lit) [When the] Eight Taoist Immortals cross the ocean, [each] one displays [his or her own] (special) ability. (fig) Each individual in a group has his or her own special talent or way of dealing with things. [Based on a famous folktale in which each of the Immortals used his or her own special skill in crossing the sea; also used as a *xiēhòuyǔ*.]

55　**"Bā" zì yámen cháo nán kāi, yǒulǐ wú qián mò jìnlái.** "八"字衙门朝南开，有理无钱莫近来。(lit) The yamen [gate] faces south, open wide [like the Chinese character for] "eight"; [if you're] right but poor, don't go inside. (fig) Without money for bribes, don't expect any justice from a magistrate [in traditional China]. [Rhyme;

the *yámen* was a county magistrate's office in traditional imperial China; see also *yámen bā zì* below.]

56 **Bèi rén jìdu bǐ bèi rén liánmǐn hǎo.** 被人忌妒比被人怜悯好。[It is] better to be envied by others than to be pitied by others. [This is a rephrasing of *yǔqí shòu rén* . . . below.]

57 **Bēishāng yōuchóu bùrú wòjǐn quántou.** 悲伤忧愁不如握紧拳头。(lit) Better than to feel sad and worry is to clench [one's] fist. (fig) It is better to fight against one's enemy than to lapse into despair and distress.

58 **Bèitóu lǐ zuòshì zhōng xiǎodé.** 被头里做事终晓得。[Although done] beneath a [bed] quilt, [secrets will] be known sooner or later. "Truth will out." [See also *chái duī lǐ cáng* and *zhǐ bāo bu zhù huǒ* below.]

59 **Bèiwō lǐ bù jiànle zhēn, bù shì pópo, jiùshì sūn.** 被窝里不见了针,不是婆婆就是孙。(lit) [If] a needle is missing in the bedding, if it's not granny [who took it], then it's a grandchild. (fig) The source of a problem must lie within. [Cf. Ding Ling's modern novel: *Tàiyáng Zhào Zài Sānggān Hé Shàng*, chap. 31.]

60 **Bèi yǔ lín guò de rén bù pà lùshui.** 被雨淋过的人不怕露水。(lit) One who has been drenched by the rain is not afraid of dew drops. (fig) One who has gone through hardships is not afraid of (minor) setbacks.

61 **Běndì jiāng bù là.** 本地姜不辣。(lit) The local ginger is not [considered] spicy. (fig) Local products or talent are never valued by local people. [See also *yuǎn lái de héshang* below.]

62 **Bèn niǎo xiān fēi*, (zǎo rù lín).** 笨鸟先飞(早入林)。(lit) A clumsy bird [has to] fly first [ahead of its peers] (in order to enter the forest earlier). (fig) The slow need to start early and work harder. [Usually said modestly of oneself to explain one's making preparations earlier than others; *not* "The early bird gets the worm"; cf. *DRC*, chap. 67. *Bèn niǎo xiān fēi* has become a common colloquial expression; see also *númǎ qiān lǐ* below and the following entry.]

63 **Bèn rén xiān qǐshēn; bèn niǎo zǎo chū lín.** 笨人先起身,笨鸟早出林。(lit) A slow-witted person [has to] get up earlier, [just as a] clumsy bird [has to] fly out of the woods earlier. (fig) People of little competence have to start working earlier than others. [Usually said self-deprecatingly to explain why one needs to start early; see the more common *bèn niǎo xiān fēi* just above.]

64 **Běn xiǎo lì wēi; běn dà lì kuān.** 本小利微,本大利宽。Small [brings] small profits, [and] big capital [brings] big profits. [Cf. *Jǐngshì Tōngyán*, chap. 31.]

65 **Biàn cháng bǎi guǒ néng chéng xiān.** 遍尝百果能成仙。(lit) Eat every [kind of one] hundred [kinds of] fruit [and you] can become a god. (fig) Eating fruit makes one healthy.

66 **Biǎndan méi zā, liǎngtóu dǎ tā.** 扁担没扎,两头打塌。(lit) [When the] carrying pole has not been secured [at both ends], [the loads at] both ends slip off. (fig) If one tries to get two things at once one may end up getting neither. [This play on words is also used as a *xiēhòuyǔ*.]

67 **Biǎndan shì tiáo lóng; yīshēng chī bù qióng.** 扁担是条龙,一生吃不穷。A shoulder [carrying] pole is [like a] dragon; [one can depend on it for] a living all one's life. [A rhyme; said before 1949 by porters, meaning that one must rely on one's own efforts to make a living.]

68 **Biān kuāng, biān lǒu, quán zài shōukǒu; miáo lóng, miáo fèng, nán zài diǎn jīng.** 编筐,编篓全在收口,描龙描凤,难在点睛。(lit) [In] weaving [rush] baskets, [the most difficult part lies] in tying off [their] openings; [in] drawing dragons or phoenixes, [the most] difficult [part lies] in drawing in [their] eyes. (fig) One should attach great importance to the finishing touches of a job. [Cf. the *chengyu*: *huàlóng-diǎnjīng*, "to add the finishing touch."]

69 **Biān zhǐ shāng ròu; èyǔ rùgǔ.** 鞭只伤肉,恶语入骨。(lit) Whipping only wounds the flesh, [but] evil words cut to the bone. (fig) Harsh words can do more damage to a person than physical punishment. [See also *gùnzi shāng ròu* and *lì dāo shāng tǐ* below.]

70 **Biǎo zhuàng bùrú lǐ zhuàng.** 表壮不如里壮。(lit) [Better to be] strong inside than [to be] strong outside. (fig) (1) [Originally:] [An] able [husband] outside [working to support a family is] not as good as [an] able [wife] inside [working and saving to take care of the family]. (2) Inner strength is more important than outward appearance. [Of individuals, families, etc.; *WM*, chap. 24.]

71 **Biérén de ròu tiē bù dào zìjǐ shēnshang.** 别人的肉贴不到自己身上。(lit) Other people's flesh can't be pasted on [one's] own body. (fig) Other people's children cannot be as close as one's own. [See also *shǒubèi yě shì ròu* below.]

72 **Biérén pì chòu; zìjiā xiāng.** 别人屁臭,自家香。(lit) Other people's flatulence stinks, [but] one's own is fragrant. (fig) Some people criticize as defects in others what they (seem to) treasure in themselves.

73 **Biérén qiú wǒ sānchūn yǔ; wǒ qù qiúrén liùyuè shuāng.** 别人求我三春雨,我去求人六月霜。(lit) [When] people come to ask one for help, [they are as warm as] spring rain; [when] one goes to ask others for help, [they are as cold as] frost in June. (fig) It's easier to give help than to get it. Human feelings are shallow. [Cf. *Jǐngshì Tōngyán*, chap. 25.]

74 **Bié shí róngyì; jiàn shí nán.** 别时容易,见时难。(lit) Parting is easy [but] meeting is difficult. (fig) After parting, one does not know when one will meet again. [A line from a Southern Tang *cí* poem by Li Yu: "Làng Tǎo Shā: Huái Jìn."]

75 **Bìkǒu shēn cáng shé; ānshēn chùchù láo.** 闭口深藏舌,安身处处牢。(lit) Close [your] mouth [and] hide [your] tongue, [and you'll be able to] settle down securely wherever [you go].

B

(fig) Prudence in speech will keep one safe. [Cf. *Xīngshì Héngyán*, chap. 35; see also *bìng cóng kǒu rù* below.]

76 **Bìmén jiā zhōng zuò, huò cóng tiānshàng lái.** 闭门家中坐，祸从天上来。[Even though one] sits at home behind closed doors, [unexpected] disaster [may] befall [him]. [Cf. *Xīngshì Héngyán*, chap. 16; *Chū Kè Pāi'àn Jīngqí*, chap. 15.]

77 **Bīng bài rú shān dǎo.** 兵败如山倒。(lit) Troops defeated are like a landslide. (fig) A rout is like a landslide. [Cf. *Yuè Fēi Zhuàn*, chap. 24.]

78 **Bīng bù yàn zhà.** 兵不厌诈。(lit) Soldiers [can]not reject deceit. (fig) In war, nothing can be considered deceitful. All's fair in war.

79 **Bìng cóng kǒu rù; huò cóng kǒu chū.** 病从口入，祸从口出。(lit) Illness enters via the mouth, [and] ills come out of it. (fig) Loose talk can cause trouble. [Rhyme; see also *kǒu shé cónglái* and *rénshēng sàng jiā* and *sān cùn shé* below and the following entry.]

80 **Bìng cóng kǒu rù; yán duō bì shī.** 病从口入，言多必失。(lit) Illness enters via the mouth; [if one's] words are too many, [one] must [suffer a] loss. (fig) Careless talk leads to trouble. "The less said the better." [Rhyme; see also the preceding entry.]

81 **Bīngdòng sān chǐ, fēi yī rì zhī hán.** 冰冻三尺，非一日之寒。(lit) (Ice) frozen three feet [thick does] not [form from] one day's coldness. (fig) The present situation must be the result of a long-term process [e.g., (1) Such high accomplishments must be the result of long-term efforts, or (2) such situations don't develop overnight]. This trouble has been brewing for quite some time. [Cf. *Lùn Héng: Zhuàng Liú* by Wang Cong in the Eastern Han dynasty; vs. *dī dòng sān chǐ* below.]

82 **Bìngfū duō chángshòu.*** 病夫多长寿。(lit) Sick people generally live longer. (fig) Things weak in appearance may have a strong life force.

83 **Bīng guì yú yǒng, bù zàiyú duō.** 兵贵于勇，不在于多。[The value of] troops lies in [their] valor, not in [their] large number. [See also *bīng zài jīng* below.]

84 **Bīng hútu yī gè; jiàng hútu yī duī.** 兵糊涂一个，将糊涂一堆。(lit) A muddle-headed soldier [only affects himself] alone; a muddle-headed general [will harm] the whole bunch. (fig) Leaders bear a heavy responsibility for those they lead. [See also *bīng sǒng, sǒng yī gè* and *jiàngshuài wúnéng* below.]

85 **Bìng jiā yú xiǎo yù.** 病加于小愈。(lit) Illness [may] increase at [the time of a] small improvement. (fig) One's illness may take a turn for the worse when one starts to feel a little better, (because one becomes careless). [Said as a caution.]

86 **Bìngjí luàn tóuyī.** 病急乱投医。(lit) [When one's] sickness is serious, [one will] in desperation turn to [any] doctor. (fig) When one is in dire straits, one will clutch desperately at any solution. "Any port in a storm." [Cf. *DRC*, chap. 57.]

87 **Bīng lái jiàng dǎng; shuǐ lái tǔ yǎn.** 兵来将挡，水来土掩。[When enemy] soldiers come, [send a] general to stop [them; when flood] waters come, [use] earth to block [them]. (fig) Use different, appropriate tactics to cope with different situations. [Cf. *JPM*, chap. 48; *R3K*, chap. 73.]

88 **Bìng lái rú bēn mǎ; bìng qù rú bùxíng.** 病来如奔马，病去如步行。(lit) Sicknesses come as [if on a] charging horse, [but] they go away as [if] on foot. (fig) Illnesses beset one suddenly, but take a longer time to recover from. [See also the following entry.]

89 **Bìng lái rú shān dǎo; bìng qù rú chōusī.** 病来如山倒，病去如抽丝。Sickness comes [on as fast] as an avalanche, [but] it departs [as slowly] as pulling silk [off of a cocoon]. [Cf. *DRC*, chap. 52; see also the preceding entry.]

90 **Bīngmǎ bù lí zhèn; láng hǔ bù lí shān.** 兵马不离阵，狼虎不离山。(lit) Soldiers [and] horses [can]not leave [their] battle formations, nor [can] wolves [and] tigers leave the mountains. (fig) One can do nothing if one gives up one's advantages.

91 **Bīngmǎ wèi dòng, liángcǎo xiānxíng.** 兵马未动，粮草先行。(lit) Before the soldiers [and] horses [have started to] move, [their] provisions and fodder [must be] taken care of first. (fig) One should make ample preparations before taking any action in order to ensure success. [Cf. *Yuè Fēi Zhuàn*, chap. 5; see also *wú liáng, bù dòngbīng* below.]

92 **Bìngrén bù jìzuǐ, pǎo duàn dàifu tuǐ.** 病人不忌嘴，跑断大夫腿。(lit) [If one] doesn't restrict [one's] diet [when one is ill, the] doctor [will] run [his] legs off [to no avail]. (fig) Patients must cooperate with their doctors. [In traditional Chinese medicine, it is believed that one should avoid certain kinds of food when one takes certain medicines.]

93 **Bìngrén duō cháng mìng.** 病人多长命。People [who easily succumb to] illness mostly live longer.

94 **Bìng rù gāohuāng, bù kě jiù yào.*** 病入膏肓，不可救药。(lit) [One who is] sick to the core can't be cured [by any] medicine. (fig) When things come to a certain stage, there's nothing anyone can do to save the situation (literally, or sometimes referring to corruption). [Cf. *Zuǒ Zhuàn: Chén Gōng 10 Nián*; note: *gāo* refers to the tip of the heart; *huāng* is the diaphragm; *bìng rú gāohuāng*, "sick to the core," is used alone as a *chengyu* meaning "beyond cure."]

95 **Bīng shǎng bù yú rì.** 兵响不踰日。Soldiers' pay [should] not be a day late. [See also *jūn shǎng bù yú yuè* below.]

96 **Bīng sǒng, sǒng yī gè; jiàng sǒng, sǒng yī wō.** 兵悚悚一个，将悚悚一窝。(lit) A weak soldier [is a weak soldier] alone; [but a] weak general [will make] all the soldiers [weak]. [More commonly *bīng xióng, xióng yī gè*, etc. (q.v.); see also *bīng hútu yī gè* above and *yī jiàng wú móu* below.]

97 **Bīng suí jiànglìng, cǎo suí fēng.** 兵随将令，草随风。(lit) Soldiers follow [their] commander's orders [like] grass follows the wind. (fig) Lower levels must take directions from higher levels.

98 **Bīng tàn bù tóng lú.** 冰炭不同炉。(lit) Ice [and red hot] charcoal [can]not co-exist [in one] container. (fig) People of contrasting characters cannot co-exist or cooperate. [Cf. *Wǔ Sōng*, chap. 1; *Sān Xiá Wǔ Yì*, chap. 34; this is a paraphrase of *Hán Fēizǐ: Xiǎn Xué*: "*bīng tàn bù tóng qì*"; see also the following entry.]

99 **Bīng tàn bù tóng lú; shàn è bù tóng tú.** 冰炭不同炉，善恶不同途。(lit) [Just as] ice [and] coal [can]not [remain] together in a stove, [so] goodness [and] evil [can]not walk [on the] same road. (fig) Good and evil cannot coexist. [Rhyme; cf. Han Feizi's *Xiǎn Xué*: "*bìng tàn bù tóng qì*"; see also the preceding entry.]

100 **Bīng wú cháng shì; shuǐ wú cháng xíng.** 兵无常势，水无常形。(lit) Troops have no fixed [battlefield] strategy [just as] water has no constant shape [but adapts itself to whatever container it is in]. (fig) One should seek to find whatever strategy or method is best suited to resolving each individual problem. [Cf. Sūnzǐ's *Bīngfǎ (The Art of War)*: *Xū Shí Piān*.]

101 **Bīng wú jiàng ér bù dòng; shé wú tóu ér bù xíng.** 兵无将而不动，蛇无头而不行。(lit) An army without a general won't move, [just as] a snake without a head won't move. (fig) Forces without a leader cannot accomplish anything. [See also *shé wú tóu* below.]

102 **Bīng xióng, xióng yī gè; jiàng xióng, xióng yī wō.** 兵熊熊一个，将熊熊一窝。(lit) A soldier of no ability [is a matter which affects] himself only, [but] a general of no ability [will] disable the whole lot. (fig) Any group must have competent leaders. [See also *bīng sóng, sóng yī gè* above and *jiàngshuài wúnéng* below.]

103 **Bīng zài jīng, (ér bù zài duō).** 兵在精(而不在多)。[The value of] troops lies in [their] quality, (not [just] in [their] quantity). [Also said *bīng guì yú jīng*; see also *bīng guì yú yǒng* above and *jiàng zài móu* below and the following entry.]

104 **Bīng zài jīng ér bù zài duō; jiàng zài móu ér bù zài yǒng.*** 兵在精而不在多，将在谋而不在勇。[Just as] troops [are valued for their] quality and not [just] for numbers, [so] generals [are valued] for their tactics, not [just] for [their] bravery. [Cf. the Ming dynasty biography *Yīng Lièzhuàn*; the two parts may be reversed.]

105 **Bīng zhì sǐdì érhòu shēng.** 兵置死地而后生。(lit) Soldiers put [in a do or] die position [will] come out alive. (fig) Soldiers fight best when in desperation. [Cf. Sūnzǐ's *Bīngfǎ (The Art of War)*: *Jiǔ Dì Piān*.]

106 **Bì qí ruìqì, jī qí duò guī.** 避其锐气，击其惰归。(lit) Avoid [your enemy]'s fighting spirit [and] attack [when] his [morale is] declining. (fig) Avoid the enemy when his morale is high, and strike him when his morale is flagging. [Cf. Sūnzǐ's *Bīngfǎ (The Art of War)*: *Jūn Zhēng*.]

107 **Bì xué fūrén.** 婢学夫人。(lit) [The] maid imitates [her] mistress. (fig) Inferiors imitate their superiors. "Like master, like man."

108 **Bìzhe de zuǐ fēi bù jìn cāngying.** 闭着的嘴飞不进苍蝇。(lit) A closed mouth does not [permit] flies to enter. (fig) Prudence in speech invites no trouble.

109 **Bí zhī suǒ xǐ bùkě rèn; kǒu zhī suǒ shì bùkě suí.** 鼻之所喜不可任，口之所嗜不可随。(lit) [One] should not take too much that pleases [one's] nose, nor should one eat too much that pleases [one's] mouth. (fig) One should not give way to one's desires.

110 **Bù bǐ bù zhīdao; yī bǐ, xià yī tiào.** 不比不知道，一比，吓一跳。[If one does] not make comparisons, [one will] not know [the truth]; once [one] compares, [one will be] greatly surprised. [A rhyme said, e.g., of the necessity of *shuō kǔ*, "recounting the bitterness" of life in pre-1949 China.]

111 **Bù chī làjiāo, bù fāshāo.** 不吃辣椒，不发烧。(lit) [If one does] not eat red peppers, [one will] not feel hot. (fig) One will not feel qualms of fear, guilt or pangs of conscience if one hasn't done anything wrong. [Rhyme.]

112 **Bù chī bái bù chī.** 不吃白不吃。(lit) [If one does] not eat, [one is] wasting [one's share of] food. (fig) When something is free, one might as well take some as not. [See also *dàjiā mǎ('ér)*, *dàjiā qí* below.]

113 **Bù chī yú, kǒu bù xīng.** 不吃鱼，口不腥。(lit) [If one does] not eat fish, [one's] mouth [will] not smell fishy. (fig) If one doesn't exploit petty advantages, one will not get into trouble.

114 **Bù dǎ, bù (chéng) xiāngshí.** 不打，不(成)相识。(lit) No fighting, no[t develop] acquaintance. (fig) From an exchange of blows, friendship grows. Sometimes friendship can grow out of confrontation. [An allusion to the fellowship of the heroes of the novel *Shuǐhǔ Zhuàn*; cf. WM, chap. 38; *Érnǚ Yīngxióng Zhuàn*, chap. 10; also said *bù dǎ, bù chéngjiāo*; see also *hǎohàn bù dǎ* below.]

115 **Bù dāng héshang, bù zhī tóu lěng.** 不当和尚，不知头冷。(lit) [One who has] not been a monk [does] not know [the feeling of a] cold head. (fig) One cannot know the true meaning of hardship until one has experienced it oneself. [Note: Buddhist monks traditionally have their heads shaved; see also *bù tiāo dànzi* and the following entry.]

116 **Bù dāng héshang, bù zhī zhāijiè kǔ.** 不当和尚，不知斋戒苦。[One who has] not been a monk [does not] know the suffering of [being on a] vegetarian diet. [See also the preceding entry.]

117 **Bù dāngjiā, bù zhī cháimǐ guì.** 不当家，不知柴米贵。(lit) [If one is] not the household head, [one can]not know how expensive rice and firewood are. (fig) Only the one who takes responsibility knows how difficult it is to get anything done. [See also the following entry.]

118 **Bù dāngjiā, bù zhī cháimǐ guì; bù yǎng ér, bù zhī fùmǔ ēn.** 不当家不知柴米贵，不养儿不知父母恩。[Just as if one has] not been the head of a household, [one does not] know the cost of fuel [and] rice, [so one who has] not raised children, does not appreciate his parent's kindness.

B

[See also *yǎng ér fāng zhī* below and the preceding entry.]

119 **Bù dào chuán fān, bù tiào hé.** 不到船翻, 不跳河。 (lit) [One will] not jump into the river until the boat overturns. (fig) People won't take risks or make sacrifices until they have to.

120 **Bù dào huǒhou, bù jiē guō.** 不到火候, 不揭锅。 (lit) Don't take the lid off the pot until the food is ripe. (fig) Don't take action until the time is ripe. [See also *bù jiàn tùzi* below and the following two entries.]

121 **Bù dào jiāngbiān, bù tuō xié.** 不到江边, 不脱鞋。 (lit) Don't take off [your] shoes until [you] come to the river bank. (fig) Take action when the right time comes. [See also the two preceding entries.]

122 **Bù dào Sū-Háng, sǐ de yuānwang.** 不到苏杭, 死的冤枉。 [One who has] not visited [Suzhou and] Hang[zhou in life will] die not [having lived a] worthwhile [life]. [Both spots are famous for their scenic beauty; rhyme; see also *shàng yǒu tiāntáng* and *Sū-Háng bù dào* below and the following entry.]

123 **Bù dào Sū-Háng, wǎng wéirén.** 不到苏航往为人。 [If one has] never been to Su[zhou and] Hang[zhou], [one's] life has not been worthwhile. [Both spots are famous for their scenic beauty; also said as *Sū-Háng bù dào*, etc.; see also *shàng yǒu tiāntáng* below and the preceding entry.]

124 **Bù dào Xītiān, bù zhī fó dàxiǎo.** 不到西天, 不知佛大小。 (lit) [If one has] not visited the Western Heaven, [one can]not know the [relative] sizes [i.e., ranks] of the Buddhas. (fig) If one has not had personal experience, one cannot understand things (completely). [Note: *Xītiān* refers to the "Western Heaven" of Buddhism, sometimes identified with India; see also *bù dāng héshang* above.]

125 **Bù dǒng zhuāng dǒng, yǒngshì fàntǒng.** 不懂装懂, 永世饭桶。 [If one] pretends to know [what one really does] not know, [one will remain] good-for-nothing all [one's] life. [Rhyme.]

126 **Bùgān-bùjìng; chīle méi bìng.** 不干不净, 吃了没病。 [Even if the food is] not clean, [if one] eats it, one won't get sick. [A rhyme popularly said by common people to excuse unsanitary conditions or as a charm to ward off disease, something like "A little dirt is good for your system" or "Everyone must eat a pound of dirt before they die"; cf. Lao She's play: *Lóng Xū Gōu*, ("Dragon Beard Ditch"), Act 1; see also *chī de lāta* and *yǎn bùjiàn wéi jìng* below.]

127 **Bù gān jǐ shì, bù zhāngkǒu; yī wèn yáotóu sānbùzhī.** 不干己事不张口, 一问摇头三不知。 (lit) [About] matters [that] don't concern [you], do not open [your] mouth, [and] when questioned, always shake [your] head "no" [in answer]. (fig) It is best to remain reticent about other people's affairs and to refuse to make any comment on matters that don't concern you. [Cf. *DRC*, chap. 55; see also *sān gè bù kāikǒu* and *yī wèn sān bù zhī* below.]

128 **Bù guài zìjiā máshéng duǎn, zhǐ guài tā jiā gǔ jǐng shēn.** 不怪自家麻绳短, 只怪他家古井深。 (lit) [Some people do] not blame the shortness of their own rope, [but] rather blame the deepness of the old well. (fig) Some people overlook their own shortcomings and try to put the blame on their circumstances. [Also said as *bù hèn shéng duǎn, zhǐ yuàn jǐng shēn*.]

129 **Bùguǎn hēi māo, bái māo; néng zhuōzhe lǎoshǔ de jiùshì hǎo māo.** 不管黑猫白猫, 能捉着老鼠的就是好猫。 (lit) It doesn't matter [if a] cat [is] black [or] white; [as long as it] can catch mice, it's a good cat. [Attributed to Deng Xiaoping as an example of his pragmatic policies, for which he was criticized during the Cultural Revolution; see also *bái māo, hēi māo* above.]

130 **Bù guǎnxiánshì, zhōng wú shì.** 不管闲事终无事。 Don't meddle in other people's business [and you will] not have any trouble. [Cf. *Fēngshén Yǎnyì*, chap. 25.]

131 **Bù guì chǐ zhī bì, ér zhòng cùn zhī yīn.** 不贵尺之璧, 而重寸之阴。 (lit) Treasure not a foot long [piece of] jade, [rather] treasure an inch of time. (fig) Time is the most important thing. [Cf. *Huái Nán Zǐ: Yuán Dào Xùn*; see also *chǐ bì fēi bǎo* and *yī cùn guāngyīn* below.]

132 **Bù huì chēngchuán, lài hé wān.** 不会撑船, 赖河湾。 (lit) [One who] cannot steer the boat blames the bends in the river. (fig) One who is incompetent always tries to shift the blame elsewhere; "a poor workman blames his tools." [See also *bù shàn shǐ chuán* and *bù shì chēng chuánshǒu* below.]

133 **Bù huì dǎzhàng, bù chīliáng; bù huì chànggē, bù mài táng.** 不会打仗不吃粮, 不会唱歌不卖糖。 (lit) [If one] can't fight, one cannot eat [army] rations; [if one] can't sing, one cannot sell sweet [pear] syrup. (fig) If one is not competent, one should not be in the trade. [Rhyme; this kind of rhymed doggerel couplet is known as *shùnkǒuliū(r)*; note: street vendors in traditional China sang to tout their medicines in a kind of "medicine show"; note: *lígāo táng*, sweet pear cough medicine.]

134 **Bù huì zuòguān, kàn qián yàng.** 不会做官, 看前样。 (lit) [If you] don't know how to perform [your duties] as a [newly appointed] official, [just] follow the example [of those who came] before [you]. (fig) If you don't know how to do your job, just copy those around you.

135 **Bù jiāng xīnkǔ yì, nán dé shìrén cái.** 不将辛苦意, 难得世人财。 (lit) Without making hard efforts, it is difficult to get worldly wealth. (fig) One can't make money without a lot of effort. [Cf. *JPM*, chap. 59; also said . . . *nán jìn shì jiàn cài*.]

136 **Bù jiàn kě yù, shǐ xīn bù luàn.** 不见可欲, 使心不乱。 (lit) Never having seen [what one] might desire leaves one's heart undisturbed. (fig) One doesn't miss what one has never seen or experienced. [Rhyme; cf. *Lǎozǐ (Dào Dé Jīng)*, chap. 3; *Xǐngshì Héngyán*, chap. 30.]

B

137 **Bù jiàn tùzi, bù sā yīng.** 不见兔子不撒鹰。 (lit) [Until you] see the hare, don't loose the falcon. (fig) Do not take any action before the time is right. [See also *bù dào huǒhou* above and *jiàn tù fàngyīng* below.]

138 **Bù jiàn zhēn fó, bù niàn zhēn jīng.** 不见真佛, 不念真经。 (lit) [Until you] see a true Buddha, don't chant true [Buddhist] scriptures. (fig) Don't speak frankly or waste your breath until you encounter someone who can truly understand or help the situation. [See also the following entry.]

139 **Bù jiàn zhēn fó, bù shāoxiāng.*** 不见真佛, 不烧香。 (lit) Don't burn real joss sticks until you see a true Buddha. (fig) Don't bother to ask for help until you encounter someone who can truly understand or help the situation. [Cf. *DRC*, chap. 6; see also the preceding entry.]

140 **Bù jīng chúzi shǒu, nándé wǔxiāng wèi.** 不经厨子手, 难得五香味。 (lit) [If it has] not passed through the hands of a [professional] cook, it is difficult to get [the food to] taste good. (fig) Only specialists can make fine products. [Note: *wǔxiāng* refers to the five standard seasoning spices used in Chinese cooking.]

141 **Bù jīng dōng hán, bù zhī chūn nuǎn.** 不经冬寒, 不知春暖。 (lit) Without having experienced the cold of winter, one cannot appreciate the warmth of spring. (fig) One cannot truly appreciate happiness without having gone through hardship.

142 **Bù jīng yī shì, bù zhǎng yī zhì.** 不经一事, 不长一智。 (lit) Without experiencing a thing, one can't grow in knowledge. (fig) Wisdom comes from experience. [Rhyme; cf. *DRC*, chap. 60; see also *chī yī qiàn, zhǎng yī zhì* and *jīng yī shì* below.]

143 **Bù jìn shānmén, bù shòujiè.** 不进山门, 不受戒。 (lit) [Those who have] not "entered the Mountain Gates" [i.e., become a Buddhist monk or nun], don't [have to] follow [Buddhist] scriptures. (fig) Those who are not members of a particular group need not observe its rules and regulations. [I.e., Why should *I* care?]

144 **Bù juǎn kùjiǎo, bù guòhé; bù mō dǐxì, bù kāi-qiāng.** 不卷裤脚不过河, 不摸底细不开腔。 Before you roll up [the bottoms of your] trouser legs, don't cross the river; before [you] really know the true state of things, don't open your mouth.

145 **Bù kàn chī de, kàn chuān de.** 不看吃的看穿的。 Don't look at what (s)he eats [but] what (s)he wears [and you'll know whether (s)he's rich or poor.]

146 **Bù kàn jiā zhōng bǎo; dān kàn mén qián cǎo.** 不看家中宝, 单看门前草。 (lit) [The wealth of a farm family may be] seen not by the [amount of] treasure within the house, [but] by simply looking at the piles of [rice] straw in front of [their] door. [A rhyme said to be common among peasants before 1949.]

147 **Bù kě bù pèng, gǔtou bù yìng.** 不磕不碰, 骨头不硬。 (lit) Without being knocked around a bit, [one's] bones won't be[come] hard. (fig) One can't become strong without first being tempered by "hard knocks."

148 **Bù kě quán xìn, yě bù kě bù xìn.** 不可全信, 也不可不信。 Do not either believe totally nor totally disbelieve [people, news, reports, etc., but rather make up your own mind].

149 **Bù liàn gùxiāng shēng chù hǎo; shòu ēn shēnchù biàn wéi jiā.** 不恋故乡生处好, 受恩深处便为家。 Don't feel that [your] native place [where you were] born and brought up is superior; better to make [your] home where [you have been] shown great kindness. [Cf. *Xǐngshì Héngyán*, chap. 10; note: *ēnhuì* "favor, kindness, honesty."]

150 **Bǔ lòu chèn tiān qíng; wèi kě xiān jué jǐng.** 补漏趁天晴, 未渴先掘井。 (lit) Mend the roof while the weather is fine, [and when you are] not yet thirsty, dig the well beforehand. (fig) Always be prepared in advance.

151 **Bù mián zhī yè cháng; jiǔ jiāo zhī rénxīn.** 不眠之夜长; 久交知人心。 (lit) [Only when one can] not sleep, [does one] learn how long the night is; [only by] long acquaintance [does one] learn a person['s true] character.

152 **Bù néng yǎo rén, jiù bié zīyá.** 不能咬人, 就别龇牙。 (lit) [If you] can't bite people, don't bare [your] teeth. (fig) Don't show your anger if you can't do anything about the situation.

153 **Bù pà bù shíhuò, jiù pà huò bǐ huò.** 不怕不识货, 就怕货比货。 It doesn't matter if one is not familiar with [the quality of] goods; what really matters is comparing goods with each other. [Often said by salesmen touting their wares; cf. *Wǔ Sōng*, chap. 8.]

154 **Bù pà èsǐ, shéi kěn fànfǎ?** 不怕饿死, 谁肯犯法? (lit) If one did not fear starving to death, who would dare to violate the law? (fig) One must be truly hard-pressed to (be forced to) commit crimes. [Said sympathetically.]

155 **Bùpà fēnglàng dà, jiù pà jiǎng bù qí.** 不怕风浪大, 就怕桨不齐。 (lit) Do not fear strong winds [and] high waves; what [one should] worry about is not rowing in unison. (fig) However difficult the task, the key to success lies in making collective efforts. [See also *sān rén yītiáoxīn* and *xiélì shān chéng yù* and *zhǐyào jiǎng huā qí* and *zhòngrén yìxīn* below.]

156 **Bùpà gāi zhài de jīng qióng, jiù pà tǎozhài de yīngxióng.** 不怕该债的精穷, 就怕讨债的英雄。 (lit) It's not how poverty-stricken the debtor is; it's the aggressiveness of the bill-collector that matters. (fig) Even the poorest debtor has to pay something when he meets a harsh bill collector. [Rhyme; cf. *Rúlín Wàishǐ*, chap. 52.]

157 **Bùpà guān, zhǐpà guǎn.** 不怕官, 只怕管。 (lit) Don't worry about officials, only worry about officiating! (fig) Don't be concerned about high officials; only the one who officiates directly over you! [Cf. *Xǐngshì Héngyán*, chap. 26.]

B

158 **Bùpà hóngliǎn Guān Yé, jiù pà mǐnzuǐ púsà.** 不怕红脸官爷，就怕抿嘴菩萨。 (lit) Never mind the [straightforward] red-faced "Guan Gong," it's the closed-mouth "Smiling Buddha" one has to be on guard against. (fig) It's easy to deal with straightforward people, but hard to deal with those who always appear to be superficially friendly (as one never knows what they're really thinking). [Note: *mǐn zuǐ yǐ xiào*, "to smile with one's mouth closed"; Guan Ye is another name for Guan Gong, the easily angered but straightforward hero of *R3K*; see also *míng qiāng yǐ duǒ* and *zhǐ rènde zhengyǎn* below the following entry.]

159 **Bùpà hǔ láng dāngmiàn zuò; zhǐpà rén qián liǎngmiàn dāo.** 不怕虎狼当面坐，只怕人前两面刀。 (lit) Do not fear tigers [and] wolves [i.e., bandits] sitting [openly] in front of you; what [one should] guard against are two-faced "double-dealers." (fig) Open enemies are not to be feared as much as sly double-dealers. [See *liǎngmiàn pài* "double-dealer"; *liǎngmiàn sāndāo* "double-dealing"; see also *bùpà míngchù* and the following entries.]

160 **Bùpà liàn bù chéng; jiù pà xīn bù héng.*** 不怕练不成；就怕心不恒。 (lit) Do not worry about not being able to master [a skill]; what [one has to] be concerned about is lack of perseverance. (fig) One's skills cannot be perfected without perseverance in practice. [Rhyme; cf. *héngxīn*, "perseverance"; see also *bùpà qiān zhāo* and *yī rì liàn* below.]

161 **Bùpà lù yuǎn, zhǐpà zhì duǎn.** 不怕路远，只怕志短。 (lit) Fear not a long road; fear only short ambition. (fig) However difficult the goal is, one can achieve it as long as one is determined to do so. [See also *bùpà rén qióng* and *yǒuzhìzhě* below.]

162 **Bùpà màn, jiù pà zhàn.** 不怕慢，就怕站。 (lit) Don't worry about being slow; only worry about standing still. (fig) A slow progress holds some promise, but to stand still promises failure. [Rhyme; also said *bùpà màn; quán pà zhàn*; see also *màn zǒu qiáng rú xiē* below.]

163 **Bùpà míngchù qiāng hé gùn; zhǐpà yīnyáng liǎngmiàn dāo.** 不怕明处枪和棍，只怕阴阳两面刀。 It's easy to dodge a spear or a club out in the open, but hard to guard against a hidden double-edged sword. [Note: *yīnyáng-guàiqì*, "mystifying, enigmatic, deliberately ambiguous"; see also *bùpà hóngliǎn* above and *míng qiāng yǐ duǒ* below.]

164 **Bùpà qiān zhāo huì, zhǐpà yī zhāo shú.** 不怕千招会，只怕一招熟。 (lit) Do not worry about mastering a thousand skills; [one] only needs one perfected skill. (fig) Many an imperfect skill is nothing; one perfect skill is everything. [See also *bùpà liàn bù chéng* above and *shí shì bàn tōng* below.]

165 **Bùpà qiān zhāo qiǎo; jiù pà yī zhāo cuò.** 不怕千招巧；就怕一招错。 (lit) Do not worry about making a thousand clever moves; what [one has to] fear is one bad move. (fig) Even if you have made many clever moves before, one wrong move will ruin the whole game. [Note: here *zhāo* refers to "moves" in Chinese chess; see also *yī zhāo bùshèn* below.]

166 **Bùpà rén bùjìng, jiù pà jǐ bù zhèng.** 不怕人不敬，就怕己不正。 Don't worry [that] people won't respect [you]; what [you should] worry about [is your own behavior being] incorrect. (fig) One will always get respect if one behaves properly.

167 **Bùpà rén bù qǐng; zhǐpà yì bù jīng.** 不怕人不请，只怕艺不精。 (lit) Don't worry [that] no one will employ [you], what [you should] worry about [is whether your] skill is perfected or not. (fig) People will always come to you if you have perfected your abilities. [Rhyme.]

168 **Bùpà rén lǎo, zhǐpà xīn lǎo.** 不怕人老，只怕心老。 (lit) Do not be concerned about being old; be concerned about a mind which is old. (fig) One is not as old as one looks, only as old as one thinks one is. [Cf. the colloquial *suyu* expression: *rén lǎo, xīn bu lǎo*; "old in body, but not in spirit."]

169 **Bùpà rén qióng, zhǐpà zhì duǎn.** 不怕人穷，只怕志短。 (lit) It is not poverty that is to be feared; it is low ambition. (fig) It is not poverty, but lack of lofty aspiration that is to be regretted. [See also *bùpà lù yuǎn* above.]

170 **Bùpà shào shí kǔ; nándé lǎolái fú.** 不怕少时苦，难得老来福。 Don't worry about having a hard time when young; [what's] difficult is [ensuring a] happy life in old age. [Rhyme.]

171 **Bùpà yīwàn, zhǐpà wànyī.*** 不怕一万，只怕万一。 (lit) Do not be concerned about one thousand; only be concerned about a thousand [to] one. (fig) It is not predictable things which one has to worry about, it's rare unforeseen happenings which one should be on guard against; it's always wise to play (it) safe.

172 **Bù qì, bù chóu; huó dào báitóu.** 不气不愁，活到白头。 Don't get angry or worried [and you will] live [long] till [all your] hair [becomes] white. [Rhyme.]

173 **Bù qí mǎ, bù shuāijiāo; bù dǎshuǐ, bù diào shāo.** 不骑马，不摔跤，不打水，不掉梢。 (lit) [If you] don't ride a horse, [you] won't fall off; [if you] don't draw water, [you] won't drop the bucket. (fig) If one does nothing, one commits no errors. [Rhyme; see also *duō zuò, duō cuò* below.]

174 **Bù rù hǔxué, yān dé hǔzǐ?** 不入虎穴，焉得虎子？ (lit) [If one does] not [dare to] enter the tiger's lair, how [can one] obtain tiger cubs? (fig) "Nothing ventured, nothing gained." [Cf. the Han dynasty *Dōng Guān Hàn Jì: Bān Chāo Zhuàn*; *Sān Guó Zhì: Lǚ Méng Zhuàn*; *Hòu Hàn Shū: Bān Chāo Zhuàn*; JW, chap. 83; *Èr Kè Pāi'àn Jīngqí*, chap. 40; now more commonly said· "... *bù dé hǔzǐ*; ... one cannot obtain tiger cubs."]

175 **Bù rúyì shì cháng bā-jiǔ; kě yǔ rén yán wú èr-sān.** 不如意事常八九，可与人言无二三。 [There are] always eight [or] nine [out of ten things in one's life which are] unsatisfactory, [and] fewer than two [or] three [secret thoughts which] can be shared with others. [Cf. *Xǐngshì Héngyán*, chap. 32.]

B

176 **Bù sā dà wǎng, bù dé dà yú.*** 不撒大网, 不得大鱼。(lit) [If one does] not cast a big net, [one can]not get big fish. (fig) One cannot make great accomplishments without making great efforts or taking great pains.

177 **Bù shàn shǐ chuán, xián gǎng qū; bùshàn xiězì, xián bǐ tū.** 不善驶船嫌港曲, 不善写字嫌笔秃。(lit) A bad boatman complains of the bends in the port; a bad calligrapher complains of the baldness of his writing brush. (fig) An incompetent person always tries to shift the blame elsewhere; "a poor workman blames his tools." [The first part is a later version of *bù shàn cāo zhōu ér wù hé zhī qū*; see also *bù huì chēngchuán* above and *bù shì chēng chuánshǒu* below.]

178 **Bù shì chēng chuánshǒu, xiū lái nòng zhúgān.** 不是撑船手, 休来弄竹竿。(lit) [If one is] not a boatman, [one] should not take hold of the barge-pole. (fig) One should not take upon oneself work that one doesn't know how to do. [Usually said as a criticism; e.g., you don't know what you're doing; see also *bù huì chēngchuán* above and *bù shàn shǐ chuán* above.]

179 **Bù shì dōngfēng yādǎo xīfēng, jiùshì xīfēng yàdǎo dōngfēng.** 不是东风压倒西风, 就是西风压倒东风。(lit) If the east wind doesn't prevail over the west wind, then the west wind is [bound] to prevail over the east wind. (fig) One of two forces must prevail over the other. [In this form often used by Mao Zedong, e.g., in his *Zài Gé Guó Gōngchǎndǎng Hé Gōngréndǎng Mòsīkē Huìyì Shàng de Jiǎnghuà*; originally from *DRC*, chap. 82.]

180 **Bù shì jīng ròu, bù bā gǔ; bù shì féiròu bù bā pí.** 不是精肉不巴骨, 不是肥肉不巴皮。(lit) [What] is not lean meat does not adhere to the bone, [and what] is not fat does not adhere to the skin. (fig) Like bonds to like; "birds of a feather flock together."

181 **Bù shì yīfān hán chègǔ, zěn dé méihuā pūbí xiāng.** 不是一番寒彻骨, 怎得梅花扑鼻香。(lit) Were it not for periods of bone-chilling winter cold, how could the nose-piercing fragrance of [winter] plum blossoms be obtained? (fig) One cannot enjoy the pleasures of life without enduring some hardships. [Cf. *Hé Diǎn*, chap. 10; *Xǐngshì Héngyán*, chap. 22.]

182 **Bù shì yījiā rén, bù jìn yījiā mén.** 不是一家人, 不进一家门。(lit) If they were not [like members of] a family, [they would] not enter the same gate. (fig) Those who fit together seem to get together; "birds of a feather flock together."

183 **Bù shì yuānjia, bù jù tóu.** 不是冤家, 不聚头。(lit) [If we/they/you were] not rivals/enemies, there would be no encounter. (fig) Enemies and lovers are pre-destined to meet; opponents always meet. [Cf. *DRC*, chap. 29; note: *yuānjia*, (lit. "enemy" or "rival" or "opponent") is also a term of endearment commonly used by women to refer to their husbands or sometimes children; see also *yuānjia lù zhǎi* below.]

184 **Bù shòu kǔ zhōng kǔ, nán wéi rén shàng rén.** 不受苦中苦, 难为人上人。Without the most terrible sufferings, one cannot be a superior person. [Also said *chī de kǔ zhong kǔ, fāng wèi rén shàng rén*; see also the following entry.]

185 **Bù shòu móliàn, bù chéng fó.** 不受磨练不成佛。(lit) Without tempering oneself, [one] can't become a Buddha. (fig) One cannot be a superior person without undergoing hardships and trials. [See also the preceding entry.]

186 **Bù shuō, bù xiào, bù chéng shìdào.** 不说, 不笑, 不成世道。(lit) Without talk [and] laughter, it's not a good life. (fig) A good life is full of talk and laughter. [Rhyme.]

187 **Bù tān piányi, bù shàngdàng.** 不贪便宜, 不上当。[If you do] not try to get things cheaply all the time, [you will] not be taken in. [Also said *bù tú piányi . . .*]

188 **Bù tiāo dànzi, bù zhī zhòng; bù zǒu cháng lù, bù zhī yuǎn.** 不挑担子不知重, 不走长路不知远。(lit) [If one does] not carry a load [oneself, one will] not know how heavy [it is]; [if one does] not walk a long distance, [one will] not [truly] know how long [it is]. (fig) One cannot truly understand things without having personally experienced them. [See also *bù dāng héshang* above.]

189 **Bù tīng lǎorén yán, bìdìng shòu jīhán.** 不听老人言, 必定受饥寒。[If one does] not listen to the words of [one's] elders, [one will] surely go hungry [and] cold. [See also the following two entries.]

190 **Bù tīng lǎorén yán, chīkǔ zài yǎnqián.** 不听老人言, 吃苦在眼前。[If one does] not listen to the words of one's elders, one will suffer immediately. [Rhyme; see also *jiǎ yǒu yī lǎo* below.]

191 **Bù tīng lǎorén yán, yīshì kǔ huánglián.** 不听老人言, 一世苦黄连。[If one does] not listen to the advice of old people, [one will] live in poverty all one's life. [Rhyme; note: *chīkǔ huánglián*, (lit) "eat bitter Chinese goldthread (medicine)," is a metaphor for leading a bitter existence; see also the preceding two entries.]

192 **Bù tú guōbā chī, bù zài guō biān zhuàn.** 不图锅巴吃, 不在锅边转。(lit) [If one were] not planning to eat rice crust, [one would] not be circling around the cooking pan. (fig) People do not hang around without a purpose. [Note: *guōbā* refers to crispy rice cooked hard on the bottom of a *wok* or Chinese round-bottomed frying pan.]

193 **Bù tú jīnnián zhú, dàn tú láinián sǔn.** 不图今年竹, 但图来年笋。(lit) Don't [just] think of this year's bamboo, but [rather] think of next year's bamboo shoots [which are eaten in winter and spring]. (fig) Think about long-term benefits rather than immediate gains. [This colloquial *suyu* expression is often used with the understood force of a proverb.]

194 **Bù tú lì, bù qǐzǎo.** 不图利, 不起早。[If one] sees no profit [in it], no [one will] get up early. (fig) No one gets up early (to work) unless it is in their best interest to do so. [See also *rén wú lì jǐ* below.]

B

195 **Bù wéi liángxiàng, dāng wèi liángyī.** 不为良相，当为良医。(lit) [If one can]not be a good [prime] minister, [then] be a good doctor. (fig) If one has ability, even if one can't be president, one can still do something beneficial for others.

196 **Bù xià dàhǎi, nán dé míngzhū.** 不下大海，难得明珠。(lit) Without going out into the sea, it is difficult to get pearls. (fig) "Nothing ventured, nothing gained"; "No pain, no gain."

197 **Bù xiàng, bù shì xì; tài xiàng, bù shì yì.** 不像不是戏，太像不是艺。[Going] too far [from life] is not drama; being too true [to life] is not art.

198 **Bù xiào yǒu sān; wú hòu wéi dà.** * 不孝有三，无后为大。(lit) [As to] unfiliality, there are three [types, and the] greatest [of these] is to have no descendants. (fig) There are three major offenses against filial piety of which not producing an heir is the worst. [The others are: (1) not supporting one's parents when they are alive and (2) not giving them a decent burial when they pass away; cf. Mencius, *Mèngzǐ: Lí Lóu, Xià*.]

199 **Bù xíng chūnfēng, nán dé qiūyǔ.** 不行春风，难得秋雨。(lit) [If the] spring winds do not blow, there will be no autumn rains. (fig) There is always a cause for every result. [Originally a *nóngyàn* or farming proverb.]

200 **Bù xìn hǎorén yán, bì yǒu xī huáng shì.** 不信好人言，必有恓惶事。(lit) If one does not take good advice, one is bound to have troubles. [Cf. *Xǐngshì Héngyán*, chap. 6; see also *bù tīng lǎorén yán* above.]

201 **Bù yǐ chéng-bài lùn yīngxióng.** 不以成败论英雄。Not [merely by their] successes [or] failures [are] heroes [to be] judged, [but by their] courage].

202 **Bù yī guīju, bù chéng fāngyuán.** 不依规矩，不成方圆。(lit) Without a compass and square, [one can]not form [squares and] circles. (fig) One can't do a job well without following the rules and regulations. [Cf. *Zàishēng Yuán*, chap. 79; this is a paraphrase of Mencius (*Mèngzǐ: Lí Lóu, Shàng*); *guīju*, (lit) "compass and square," now means "rules; regulations."]

203 **Bù yīn, bù lóng, bù chéng gū gōng.** 不瘖不聋，不成姑公。(lit) [Unless one pretends to be] stupid and deaf, it is difficult to be a mother-in-law or father-in-law. (fig) If one wishes to be a good parent (in-law), one had best pretend to be ignorant and deaf toward one's married children's business. [Rhyme; advice to parents-in-law; cf. *Jìnghuā Yuán*, chap. 93.]

204 **Bùyī nuǎn; cài gēn tián.** 布衣暖，菜根甜。(lit) [Simple] clothing is warm, [and] vegetable roots are sweet. (fig) Live a simple and thrifty life; never be luxurious and lavish. [An admonition to thrift; note: *bùyī*, (lit) "cloth clothing," is also used to refer to the common people; see also *ài fàn yǒu fàn* above.]

205 **Bù yīn yúfū yǐn, zěn dé jiàn bōtāo?** 不因渔夫引，怎得见波涛？(lit) Without a fisherman as a guide, how can one see the waves? (fig) Without the guidance of one who knows, how can one experience inspiring or surprising things? [Cf. *Xīyáng Jì*, chap. 57.]

206 **Bù yòng pīlì shǒuduàn, xiǎn bù chū púsà xīncháng.** 不用霹雳手段，显不出菩萨心肠。(lit) [If one does] not adopt severe measures, [one can]not manifest [one's] Buddha-like kindness. (fig) You can't really help people unless you're willing to criticize their mistakes frankly. [Advice to a potential critic; note: *púsà xīncháng*, (lit) "Bhoddhisatva's heart," has a figurative meaning of "kindhearted and merciful."]

207 **Bù yǒu qiáofū tà pò yún, shìjiān nǎ dé zhī qí chù.** 不有樵夫踏破云，世间哪得知其处。(lit) Without woodcutters climbing [high on the mountains] through the clouds, the world would never know [about and enjoy] their [scenic] spots. (fig) One won't be able to enter new realms of learning without some pioneers taking great pains. [From the Song dynasty author Liu Jin's poem "Yán Kōng Yán."]

208 **Bù zháo jiā rén, nòngbude jiā guǐ.** 不着家人，弄不得家鬼。[If there were] no one [in the] family conspiring [with others outside the family], [there would be] no trouble within the family. [Cf. *JPM*, chaps. 47; 90.]

209 **Bù zhī qí rén, guān qí yǒu.** 不知其人，观其友。(lit) [If you do] not know this person, look at his friends. (fig) "A man is known by the company he keeps." [Also said *bù guān qí rén, dàn guān qí yǒu*, "One does not need to see the person himself; it's enough just to see his friends"; see also *yù shí qí rén* below.]

210 **Bù zhī shuǐ shēnqiǎn, qièmò jí xià hé.** 不知水深浅，切莫急下河。(lit) Without knowing the depth of the water, never go hastily into the river. (fig) Never plunge into hasty action without first investigating the situation. [See also *yào zhī hé shēnqiǎn* below.]

211 **Bù zhī zhě bù zuò zuì.** 不知者不作罪。(lit) One who does not know [should] not get convicted. (fig) It is not a crime to make an error if one does not know how things stand; ignorance can be forgiven. [Cf. *JW*, chap. 33; *DRC*, chap. 28; also said *bù zhī zhě bù guài*.]

212 **Bù zuò kuīxīnshì, bù pà guǐ jiàomén.** 不做亏心事，不怕鬼叫门。(lit) If one has not done anything to trouble one's conscience, one need not be afraid of any devils who call at the door. (fig) "A quiet conscience sleeps in thunder." [See also *báitiān bù zuò* above and *méi zuò kuīxīnshì* and *rìjiān bù zuò* below.]

213 **Bù zuò zhōngrén, bù zuò bǎo; yīshì bù fánnǎo.** 不做中人，不做保，一世不烦恼。[If one does] not stand as a middle man [or] witness nor as a guarantor [for anybody], [one will be] at ease all [one's] life. [Rhyme.]

C

1 **Cái bù lòubái.** 财不露白。 (lit) Never show off [your] money or property [to others] to no purpose. (fig) Don't flash your money around, (as people become jealous easily). [See also *jīn-yín bù lòubái* and *qiáncái bù lòu* below.]

2 **Càidāo bù néng xiāo zìjǐ de bǐng.** 菜刀不能削自己的柄。 (lit) A kitchen knife cannot cut its own handle. (fig) (1) Never harm your own people. (2) However able one is, there's always something beyond one's ability. (3) One always needs help from others. [See also *kuàidāo bù xiāo* below.]

3 **Cǎi dòng héhuā, qiāndòng ǒu.** 采动荷花，牵动藕。 (lit) [If one] plucks the lotus flower, [one will] also affect [its] roots. (fig) When one attacks one problem, other persons or things connected with it will also be affected.

4 **Cái dòng rénxīn.** 财动人心。 (lit) Wealth moves people's hearts. (fig) Money and wealth tempt people. "Money makes the mare go." [See also *qián kě tōng shén* below.]

5 **Cǎi huā fēng kǔ mì fāng tián.** 采花蜂苦蜜方甜。 (lit) Only because of the hardships of the bees who harvest the flowers [is there] sweet honey. (fig) "No pain, no gain."

6 **Cài méi yán, wúwèi; huà méi lǐ, wúlì.** 菜没盐无味，话没理无力。 [Just as] dishes without salt are tasteless, [so] words without reason are powerless.

7 **Cái qù, shēn ānlè.** 财去，身安乐。 [If one] loses property, [at least one] gains personal security. [Said as a (self-)consolation, as in the *chengyu*-like phrases: *cái qù rén ān* and *pòcái xiāo zāi*, "If one loses property, at least one will avoid calamity"; see also *pòcái shì dǎng zāi* and *huānxǐ pòcái* below.]

8 **Cái yā núbì; yì yā dāng háng.** 财压奴婢，艺压当行。 [Just as] wealth [can] bring servants to their knees, [so superior] craftsmanship [can allow one to] achieve superiority [over one's] colleagues in the same trade. [Cf. *Érnǚ Yīngxióng Zhuàn*, chap. 21; note: *dāng háng* is equivalent to *nèiháng*, "insiders in the trade."]

9 **Cáizhì néng zuò dǎi; cōngming bù wéi fēi.** 才智能作歹，聪明不为非。 (lit) Intelligence can [be used to] do evil, [but a truly] wise [person will] not [use his or her intelligence to] do evil. (fig) Truly intelligent people never use their intelligence to do evil things. [Note the phrases *cōngmíng cáizhì*, "intelligent and clever," and *wéifēi-zuòdǎi*, "to do evil things."]

10 **Cáizhu shuō qióng huà; guānggùn shuō xióng huà.** 财主说穷话，光棍说熊话。 A rich person talks [like a] poor [one]; a clever guy pretends to be foolish. (fig) Truly clever people never display their riches or talent. [See also *gāoguān qí shòu mǎ* below.]

11 **Cánhuā méi rén dài; zì jiāo méi rén ài.** 残花没人戴，自骄没人爱。 A withered flower won't be worn by anyone, [and] a conceited person won't be liked by anyone. [Rhyme.]

12 **Cāngtiān yǒu yǎn.** 苍天有眼。 (lit) Heaven has eyes. (fig) Heaven sees all. Heaven will protect the good and punish the wicked. [Note: *cāngtiān*, (lit) "blue sky," here refers to Heaven; also said *Lǎotiān yǒu yǎn*, "Heaven has eyes."]

13 **Cāngying bù bào méi fèngr de jīdàn.** 苍蝇不抱没缝儿的鸡蛋。 (lit) No fly will go for uncracked eggs. (fig) No one can take advantage of someone unless (s)he has some sort of problem in the first place. [Cf. *DRC*, chap. 61; also said *cāngyíng dīng pò dàn*, "Flies go for cracked eggs."]

14 **Cǎo bù mí yīng yǎn; shuǐ bù mí yú yǎn.** 草不迷鹰眼，水不迷鱼眼。 (lit) Grass cannot mislead an eagle's eye, nor water a fishes' eye. (fig) A clever person won't be perplexed by superficial phenomena. [See *míngyǎnrén*, "a person with a discerning eye"; see also *zhìzhě kàn huǒ* below.]

15 **Cǎo lǐ shī zhēn, cǎo lǐ xún.** 草里失针，草里寻。 (lit) [If you] lose a needle in the grass, look for [it] in the grass. (fig) Wherever you take a loss, that's the place you should try to make it up. [See also *nǎr diēdǎo, nǎr pá qǐ* below.]

16 **Cáo nèi wú shí, zhū gǒng zhū.** 槽内无食，猪拱猪。 (lit) [When] there's no fodder in the trough, pigs jostle each other. (fig) Shortage of supplies will lead to internal conflicts. [Note: *gǒngzhū*, (lit) "push the pig," is also the name of a popular card game.]

17 **Cǎo pà yánshuāng, shuāng pà rì; èrén zì yǒu èrén mó.** (草怕严霜，霜怕日，)恶人自有恶人磨。 [Just as] grass fears severe frost [which in turn] fears sun, [so one] evil person [will be] tormented by another evil person. [The second part (q.v.) is most commonly used alone.]

18 **Cǎo rù niú kǒu, qí mìng bù jiǔ.** 草入牛口，其命不久。 (lit) [When] grass enters a cow's mouth, it won't last long. (fig) When one is in a dangerous situation, one's chances of survival are not great. [Cf. *Gǔ-Jīn Xiǎoshuō*, chap. 36; note: *cǎokòu*, "rural bandits."]

19 **Cáotóu mǎi mǎ, kàn mǔzi.** 槽头买马，看母子。 (lit) [If you're in the] stable [when buying a young] horse, [first] look at [its] mother. (fig) One can judge a person by his or her mother. [Cf. *Xǐngshì Yīnyuán Zhuàn*, chap. 52.]

20 **Cǎo yǎn zhī fēngxiàng.** 草偃知风向。 (lit) [By the way the] grass bends, [one can] know the direction of the wind. (fig) Specific events are signs or harbingers of larger social or political trends. [See also *yī yè shì fēngxiàng* below.]

C

21 **Cǎoyào yī wèi, qìsǐ míngyī.*** 草药一味，气死名医。 (lit) One species of a medicinal herb [can] shame a famous doctor. (fig) Sometimes medicinal herbs can cure diseases which even a good doctor can't cure. [See also *piānfāng zhì dà bìng* below.]

22 **Cǎozì chūle gé, shénxiān rènbude.** 草字出了格，神仙认不得。 (lit) [Free style cursive] "grass" characters written outside the lines, [even a] god cannot make out. (fig) It's almost impossible to read sloppy handwriting. [Cf. *Wǔ Sōng*, chap. 2.]

23 **Céng jīng cānghǎi, nán wéi shuǐ.** 曾经沧海，难为水。 (lit) Having experienced the great ocean, it is difficult to appreciate [ordinary] waters. (fig) For one who has had great experiences, ordinary experiences pale by comparison. [This is a line paraphrasing Mencius (*Mèngzǐ: Jìn Xīn Shàng*) from a poem entitled "Lí Sī" by the Tang dynasty poet Yuán Zhěn in which he compares the vastness of his love for his wife to the experience of a great ocean which dwarfs all other waters by comparison. Note: *céngjīng-cānghǎi* can be used as a *chengyu* expression meaning "having sailed the seven seas"; "having seen much of the world." See also *guān yú hǎi zhě* below.]

24 **Céng zháo mài táng jūnzǐ hǒng, dào jīn bù xìn kǒu tián rén.** 曾着卖糖君子哄，到今不信口甜人。 (lit) Once taken in by a candy seller, the gentleman will never believe anyone who mouths sweet [words]. (fig) "Once burned, twice shy." [Cf. *JW*, chap. 72; *Èr Kè Pāi'àn Jīngqí*, chap. 26.]

25 **Cè yǐn zhī xīn, rén jiē yǒu zhī.** 侧隐之心，人皆有之。 (lit) A sense of pity, all people have it. (fig) All people have a sense of compassion. [Cf. Mencius, *Mèngzǐ: Gào Zǐ Shàng*; *Húdié Mèng*, chap. 2; *Jǐngshì Tōngyán*, chap. 22.]

26 **Chái duī lǐ cáng bu zhù huǒ; shāizi lǐ chéng bu zhù shuǐ.** 柴堆里藏不住火，筛子里盛不住水。 Fire can't be hidden in a pile of firewood, nor can water be kept in a sieve. (fig) Truth cannot be suppressed. The truth will (come) out in the end. [See also *bèitóu lǐ zuòshì* above and *mán de guò rén* and *shuǐ luò shítou* and *zhǐ bǎo bu zhù huǒ* below.]

27 **Chái wú sān gēn, huǒ bù zháo.** 柴无三根，火不着。 (lit) Without [at least] three sticks of wood, [one] cannot light a fire. (fig) One cannot accomplish anything alone. "In unity lies strength." [See also *dān zé yì zhé* below.]

28 **Chāi wū yī dài yān, qǐ wū sān dàn mǐ.** 拆屋一袋烟，起屋三担米。 (lit) [It needs only the time it takes to smoke] one packet of tobacco to level a house [to the ground, but it takes] three hundred catties of rice [to feed the workers to] build one. (fig) It is easy to destroy things but difficult to create them. [Note: one *dàn* is a unit of measure equal to one hundred *jīn*, "catties," or fifty kilograms; see also *bǎinián chéngshì* above.]

29 **Chá jiàn yuān yú zhě bùxiáng; zhì liào yǐnnì zhě yǒu yāng.** 察见渊鱼者不祥；智料隐匿者有殃。 (lit) [To be able to] see fish swimming in

a deep pond is inauspicious, [and to be] clever [enough to] spot hidden people or things [is to] invite trouble. (fig) One who is too perceptive or too wise will invite trouble. "There's such a thing as being too clever." [Rhyme; cf. *Lièzǐ: Shuō Fù* and *Hán Fēizǐ: Shuō Lín Shàng*.]

30 **Cháng'ān suī hǎo, bù shì jiǔ liàn zhī jiā.** 长安虽好，不是久恋之家。 (lit) Although Chang'an [the capital of the Tang dynasty] is good, it's not a place to become attached to for long [since it's not your hometown]. (fig) However good a strange place is, one should not stay there long, but rather return home as one ought to. [Cf. *JW*, chap. 96; vs. *bù liàn gùxiāng* above; see also *chùchù yǒu lù* and *Liáng yuán suī hǎo* below.]

31 **Cháng biānzi bù dǎ zhuǎnwān niú.** 长鞭子不打转弯牛。 Don't [use a] long whip on an ox [that is] making a turn while plowing. [Note: It is natural that an ox pulling a plow will go slower while making a turn.] (fig) When a person realizes his or her mistakes and starts to do something to correct them, (s)he should not be pressed too hard, but should be given time to correct the mistakes.

32 **Cháng dī yào fáng lǎoshǔ dòng; dà shù yào fáng zhùxīnchóng.** 长堤要防老鼠洞，大树要防蛀心虫。 (lit) [In] long dikes [one] should guard against rat holes [and in the centers of] big trees against wood boring worms. (fig) One should always pay attention to petty but potentially harmful troubles (hidden) within one's own group. [Rhyme.]

33 **Cháng huà bùrú duǎn shuō.** 长话不如短说。 (lit) Long speech is not as good as short talk. (fig) Better come to the point directly than to take the long way around [in one's speech].

34 **Cháng Jiāng hòu làng cuī qián làng; (yī tì xīnrén huàn jiù rén).** 长江后浪催前浪，(一替新人换旧人)。 (lit) [Just as in] the Yangtse River, the waves behind push on those ahead, ([so] newcomers replace the old-[timers]). (fig) Inevitably each generation is replaced by (and often surpassed by) the next. [Cf. *Wǔ Sōng*, chap. 1; now said ". . . tuī qián làng; yī dài xīn rén huàn jiù rén"; the second half is often omitted.]

35 **Cháng jiāng yǒu rì, sī wú rì; mò dài wú shí, xiǎng yǒu shí.** 常将有日思无日，莫待无时想有时。 (1) [If in] times of plenty [you] always recall [your] times of want, [you'll] have no need in times of want to yearn for [your] times of plenty. (2) [Even] if [you] have [money], remember when [you] didn't [and be frugal], [and] if [you] don't have any, don't think about when you had [money], [but rather just work hard and be frugal].

36 **Cháng lǐ chūlai, cháng lǐ rè.** 肠里出来，肠里热。 [Toward those who have] come out from one's guts, [one's] guts are warm. (fig) One is most attached to one's own children. [See also *gè yǎng de* below.]

37 **Cháng mà bù jīng; cháng dǎ bù pà.** * 常骂不惊, 常打不怕。 (lit) Repeated scolding and beating won't frighten [a child]. (fig) Repeated punishments on a person will have increasingly less effect.

38 **Cháng pān gāoshān, tuǐ bù ruǎn; cháng guò xiāntán, bù pà jiāo.** 常攀高山腿不软, 常过险滩不怕礁。 (lit) [If one] often climbs high mountains, [one's] legs will not be weak; [if one] often passes over dangerous shoals, one won't be afraid of reefs. (fig) One who has gone through hardships has developed fortitude and won't easily yield to difficulties.

39 **Cháng tiān dēngcǎo, mǎn tiān yóu.** 长添灯草, 满添油。 (lit) Replenish [the supply of lamplighting] rushes [when the original one is still] long, [and] replenish the oil supply [(even) when the lamp is] full. (fig) It is best to make one's preparations early.

40 **Cháng tòng bùrú duǎn tòng.** 长痛不如短痛。 (lit) Rather [suffer greater] pains for a short time than [lesser] pains for a long time. (fig) It's better to get painful things over with quickly.

41 **Cháng xiàn fàng yuǎn yào.** 长线放远鹞。 (lit) The longer the string, the higher the kite will fly. (fig) If one makes a long-term plan, the more successful one will be. [Cf. *Dàng Kòu Zhì*, chap. 73.]

42 **Chàngxì de bù mán dǎ luó de.** 唱戏的不瞒打锣的。 (lit) [A Chinese] opera singer [does] not hide anything from [the accompanist who] strikes the gong. (fig) Partners should not hide anything from one another.

43 **Chàngxì de sān tiān bù chàng, zuǐ shēng; dǎ tiě de sān tiān bù dǎ, shǒu shēng.** 唱戏的三天不唱嘴生, 打铁的三天不打手生。 (lit) [An] opera singer who does not sing for three days [will get] rusty, [and a] blacksmith [who does] not strike for three days [will] also. (fig) One has to keep practicing to keep one's skill up. [See also *quán bù lǐ shǒu* below.]

44 **Cháng xiù shàn wǔ; duō qián shàn gǔ.** 长袖善舞, 多钱善贾。 [Just as] long sleeves [enhance a] good dancer, [so] great wealth [makes it] easier to do business or get ahead. [Rhyme; *Hán Fēizǐ: Wǔ Dù*.]

45 **Chàngxì yào sǎngzi; lā gōng yào bǎngzi.** 唱戏要嗓子, 拉弓要膀子。 (lit) Opera singers depend on [their] voices, [and] bow-pullers on [their] (upper) arms. (fig) Skill or expertise is needed in doing everything. [Rhyme; note: "bow-pullers" can be either archers or fiddle players.]

46 **Cháng yè rú xiǎonián.** 长夜如小年。 A long night [can be as long] as a short year. [Said, e.g., of sleepless or long winter nights; note: *xiǎonián* refers to a short lunar year in which the last month has only 29 days.]

47 **Cháng zài hébiān zhuàn, bù pà shuǐ shī jiǎo.** * 常在河边转, 不怕水湿脚。 (lit) [Those who] often take a turn along the river bank won't be afraid to wet their feet. (fig) Being in proximity to badness, one is prepared to deal with it; one comes to understand the criminal mind. [See also the following entry.]

48 **Cháng zài hébiān zǒu, nánmiǎn tàshī xié.** 长在河边走, 难免踏湿鞋。 [If one] often walks by the riverside, [it's] difficult to avoid getting [one's] shoes wet. (fig) People often become tainted or give in to temptation [e.g., when handling money]. "It comes with the territory."

49 **Chángzi zhù zài ǎi yán xià, bùdé bù dītóu.** 长子住在矮檐下, 不得不低头。 (lit) [When] a tall person stays under low eaves, he has no choice but to lower his head. (fig) One has no choice but to submit to circumstances. [Also said (jì) zài ǎi yán xià and rén zài wūyán xià (see below).]

50 **Chányán sān zhì, címǔ bù qīn.** 谗言三至, 慈母不亲。 (lit) [If] slanderous talk [about her offspring] comes [to her] three times, [even a] loving mother will not love [them anymore]. (fig) Rumors or lies repeated often enough will be taken to be true. [Cf. *Zhànguó Cè: Qín Cè 2*.] [See also sān rén chéng hǔ below.]

51 **Chǎo dòu, dàhuǒ chī; zhà guō, yī rén dān.** 炒豆大伙吃, 炸锅一人担。 (lit) Roasted beans, everyone eats, [but when the] pot [gets] burned, [only] one is responsible. (fig) Everyone enjoys the benefits, but when something goes wrong only one person is held responsible. [Note: zhàguō is also a colloquial expression meaning "to wrangle loudly."]

52 **Cháo jū zhī fēng; xué chù zhī yǔ.** 巢居知风, 穴处知雨。 (lit) [Those] living [in] nests [can] predict the wind, [and those] living [in] caves [can] predict the rain [from the moisture]. (fig) Those with experience can tell what's going to happen in a familiar or sensitive environment. [See also chūn jiāngshuǐ nuǎn below.]

53 **Cháo lǐ wú rén, mò zuò guān.** 朝里无人, 莫作官。 [If] at [the imperial court [you] have no friends, it is difficult to be an official. [Also said cháo lǐ yǒu rén, hǎo zuò guān, "If one has friends at court one can be an official."]

54 **Cháo pà èrshí; rén pà sìshí.** 潮怕二十, 人怕四十。 (lit) The tide ebbs [after the] 20[th of the lunar month]; people turn [old after the age of] 40. (fig) Treasure time and work hard while you're young.

55 **Cháoshān de bù shì quán wèile jìng shén.** 朝山的不是全为了敬神。 (lit) Not all pilgrims [come] to worship gods. (fig) The same group of people may not all have the same motives or purposes; one must expect variation. [Note: cháoshān de, (lit) "mountain climbers," here refers to those pilgrims who visit Buddhist temples in remote places; the expression cháoshān jìnxiāng, "Pilgrim(s) presenting incense," is often printed on pilgrims' bags or clothes.]

56 **Cháotíng bù chāi è bīng.** 朝廷不差饿兵。 (lit) The imperial court does not send hungry soldiers [into battle]. (fig) One cannot ask others to work for nothing. [Cf. *Guānchǎng Xiànxíng Jì*, chap. 31 and *Dàng Kòu Zhì*, chap. 87; see also sān rì wú liáng below.]

C

57 **Cháotíng bùkě yī rì wú jūn.** 朝廷不可一日无君。(lit) The imperial court cannot [afford even] one day without [its] ruler. (fig) A country cannot afford to be without a leader. [Cf. *JW*, chap. 40; see also *guó bùkě yī rì wú jūn* below.]

58 **Cháotíng hái yǒu sān ménzi qióng qīn.** 朝廷还有三门子穷亲。(lit) Even the emperor has branches of the family [with] poor relations. (fig) Everyone has some poor relatives. [Cf. *DRC*, chap. 6; note: *sān ménzi* refers to branches of an extended family; see also *huángdì yě yǒu* below.]

59 **Chā zhī háolí, miù yǐ qiān lǐ.** 差之毫厘，谬以千里。(lit) An error [the breadth] of a single hair ✿ [can] lead [one] astray one thousand leagues. (fig) The smallest mistake can have far-reaching consequences. [Also "... *shī zhī qiān lǐ*" in JW, chap. 36; originally "*chā ruò háolí*, etc." in the Confucian *Book of Rites* (Lǐjì: *Jīng Jiě*); see also *shī zhī háolí* below; one *lǐ* equals one-half of a kilometer.]

60 **Chē bàn liú bàn, qí huò lì xiàn.** 拆半留半，其祸立见。[If one] destroys half [but] leaves [the other] half, its disaster[ous results will soon be] seen. (fig) In dealing with a situation, one should do a thorough job, leaving no potential problems undealt with. [Note: the last character (见) is here pronounced (*xiàn*).]

61 **Chē dào méi è lù.** 车到没恶路。(lit) [Wherever] a cart goes, there's no bad road. (fig) Things will sort themselves out in the end. There's always a way out. [Cf. *Xǐngshì Yīnyuán Zhuàn*, chap. 83; see also the following entry.]

62 **Chē dào shān qián bì yǒu lù.** 车到山前必有路。(lit) [When the cart] gets to the mountains, there will have to be a way [through]. (fig) Things always work out in the end (so don't worry about them). "Cross that bridge when you come to it." [See also *chuán dào qiáotóu* below and the preceding entry.]

63 **Chē duō, ài zhé; chuán duō, cā biān.** 车多碍辙；船多，擦边。(lit) Too much car(t) traffic will cause a jam; too many boats will rub against each other. (fig) "Too many cooks spoil the broth."

64 **Chéng dàshì bù jì xiǎo chóu.** 成大事不记小仇。[One who has aspirations to] do great things won't begrudge trifling insults or slights. [See also *dàrén bù jì* and *jūnzǐ bù jiàn* below.]

65 **Chéng dàshì zhě bù xī xiǎofèi.** 成大事者不惜小费。One who accomplishes great things does not begrudge petty expenditures or losses. [Cf. *JPM*, chap. 1; *Xīyáng Jì*, chap. 19.]

66 **Chènggǎn xīngxīng liáng rénxīn.** 秤秆星星量人心。The steelyard's [calibration] marks measure the honesty of the person [who uses it (i.e., the seller), vs. dishonest peddlers who alter the scales or manipulate them]. [Note: before 1949 steelyard scales were marked with sixteen star symbols, one for each ounce of weight.]

67 **Chénggōng bù huǐ.** 成功不毁。(lit) Accomplishments [should] not be destroyed. (fig) Once something has been accomplished, it should not be wantonly destroyed.

68 **Chéngjiàn bùkě yǒu; dìngjiàn bùkě wú.** 成见不可有；定见不可无。(lit) Preconceived views [one] should not have; definite opinions [one] shouldn't be without. (fig) One should not harbor any preconceptions but should have one's own ideas about everything.

69 **Chéngjiā yóurú jiān tiāo tǔ, bài jiā yóurú làng chōng shā.** 成家犹如肩挑土，败家犹如浪冲沙。To establish [and maintain] a family is as [hard as] carrying earth on [one's] shoulders; to ruin a family is as [easy as] waves washing away the sand. [See also *chénglǐ zhī nán* below.]

70 **Chéng jiā zhī zǐ, xī fèn rú jīn; (bài jiā zhī zǐ, huī jīn rú fèn /tǔ).** 成家之子惜粪如金，(败家之子挥金如粪／土)。(lit) The children who succeed in establishing themselves [well in life are those who are so frugal as to] value [anything as insignificant as] dung as [being like] gold; ([while those] children who ruin [their] families [are those who] throw gold around like dung). (fig) Frugality is the key to success in life, (while excessive spending will lead to ruination). [The second part is often omitted; note: *huī jīn rú tú*, "to throw money around like dirt."]

71 **Chénglǐ zhī nán rú dēng tiān; fùbài zhī yì rú liǎo máo.** 成立之难如登天，覆败之易如燎毛。Getting established [in life] is as difficult as ascending to heaven, [but] ruination [of one's family and career] is as easy as burning up a hair. [See also *chéngjiā yóurú* above and *zǎnqián hǎobǐ* below.]

72 **Chéngmén shīhuǒ, yāngjí chí yú.** 城门失火，殃及池鱼。(lit) [When the] city gate is on fire, [it] endangers even the fish [in the] moat [when the water is pumped out to extinguish the fire]. (fig) Innocent bystanders are often injured. Things often have un-thought-of far-reaching consequences.

73 **Chéngmíng měi zài qióngkǔ rì; bàishì duō yú dézhì shí.** 成名每在穷苦日，败事多于得志时。Success is always [won] when [one is] in poverty, failure usually [comes] when [one is] successful (so be careful!).

74 **Chéngqián-bìhòu, (zhìbìng-jiùrén).** 惩前毖后，(治病救人)。(lit) [One must] learn from former [mistakes in order to] avoid [similar ones] later, ([and] cure the illness to save the [sick] person.) (fig) One must learn from past mistakes in order to avoid future ones (and take all actions, however unpleasant, which are necessary to correct the situation). [The first part is a Ming dynasty *chengyu* derived from the *Shījīng: Zhōu Sòng: Xiǎo Bì*. The second part was added by Mao Zedong to produce a slogan, often quoted by Communist leaders as justification for criticism and their drastic actions; see also *yán zhě wúzuì* and *zhī wú bù yán* below.]

75 **Chéngrén bù zìzài; zìzài bù chéngrén.** 成人不自在，自在不成人。A person of [great] accomplishments [can]not be carefree, [and a] carefree [person can]not be a person of [great] accomplishments. [Cf. *Xǐngshì Héngyán*, chap. 17.]

76 **Chéng rén chē, zài rén huàn.** 乘 人 车，载 人 患。 (lit) [If one] rides in [someone's] cart, [one should] share [his] sorrows. (fig) One should share the difficulties of those to whom one is indebted. [Cf. Sima Qian's *Shǐ Jì*: *Huái Yīn Hóu Lièzhuàn*; see also *chī nǎ jiā jiǔ* below.]

77 **(Chéngshì bù shuō;) jìwǎng bù jiù.** (成事不说,) 既往不咎。 (lit) (What's [already] done [does] not [need to be] spoken [about];) what's past [need] not [be] blamed. (fig) One should "let bygones be bygones." [The two parts are used separately as idiomatic phrases, each equivalent to "let bygones be bygones"; the second part is more commonly said alone; cf. *Jìnghuā Yuán*; chap. 6.]

78 **Chéngsǐ dǎndà de; èsǐ dǎnxiǎo de.** 撑死胆大的，饿死胆小的。 (lit) [Those who] die of overeating [are the] bold, [while those who] die of hunger [are the] timid. (fig) The bold get rich, while the timid usually suffer from poverty.

79 **Chéngtiān dǎ hú; bù rèn xī.** 成天打壶，不认锡。 (lit) [Although one] makes tea kettles [from it] all day long, [one may still] not [be able to] tell tin [from other metals]. (fig) A person may not fully understand what is (going on) around him or her all the time.

80 **Chèngtuó suī xiǎo, yā qiānjīn.** 秤砣虽小，压千斤。 (lit) The sliding weight [of a steelyard scale], although small, can balance a thousand catties. (fig) An unimpressive person may have hidden talents or ambitions. [Cf. *JW*, chap. 31; note: literally, one *jīn* or "catty" is equal to one-half kilogram, but *qiānjīn* is figuratively taken to mean "a ton; a great weight."]

81 **Chéng yóu qínjiǎn; pò yóu shē.** 成由勤俭，破由奢。 Success [comes] from diligence [and] thrift, [while] bankruptcy [results] from extravagance. [Originally a line from a Tang dynasty poem by Li Shangyin.]

82 **Chéng zé wéi wáng; bài zé wéi zéi.** 成则为王，败则为贼。 (lit) Succeed and [you] are a king; be defeated and [you] are [considered] a bandit. (fig) Legitimacy goes to the victor; losers are always in the wrong. [Cf. *DRC*, chap. 2; traditionally the losers in Chinese civil wars are always described as bandits.]

83 **Chèn huǒ rè, bǔ lòu guō.** 趁火热，补漏锅。 (lit) Mend the leaking pot while it's already hot. (fig) Grasp the opportunity to make up for the loss. Turn losses into opportunities. [This is *not* equivalent to "Strike while the iron is hot"; compare *chèn rè (hǎo) dǎtiě* below.]

84 **Chēn quán bù dǎ xiào miàn.** 嗔拳不打笑面。 (lit) [An] angry fist [will] not strike a smiling face. (fig) If you put on a smiling face, even your enemies won't strike you; a smile is the best defense. [Cf. *JPM*, chap. 96; also said *shén shǒu bù dǎ xiào liǎn rén*.]

85 **Chèn rè (hǎo) dǎtiě.** 趁热(好)打铁。 (lit) While [it's] hot, (it's easier to) beat iron [into shape]. (fig) It's easier to) strike while the iron is hot. [Compare *chèn huǒ rè* and *dǎnglìng guǒzi* below; *chènrè-dǎtiě* is used as a *chengyu*; see also the following entry.]

86 **(Chèn shuǐ huò ní;) chèn rè dǎ tiě.** (趁水和泥,) 趁热打铁。 (lit) (While the water [lasts], mix the plaster); while [it is] hot, strike the iron. (fig) Seize the opportunity when it arises. "Strike while the iron is hot." "Make hay while the sun shines." [See also the preceding entry.]

87 **Chèn wǒ shí nián yùn; yǒu bìng zǎo lái yī.** 趁我十年运，有病早来医。 [While] I [am having] ten years [of] good luck, [if you] are sick, come [see the] doctor [i.e., me] as soon as possible. (fig) If you need any favors done, come and see me while I am still in a position to help others out. [See also the contemporary saying: *yǒuquán bù yòng, guòqī zuòfèi* below.]

88 **Chē xíng bàn pō, tíngbùdé.** 车行半坡，停不得。 (lit) [When pulling a] cart, never stop half way up the slope. (fig) Never stop half-way in doing anything; don't lose your momentum.

89 **Chē zǒu chēdào; mǎ zǒu mǎdào.** 车走车道，马走马道。 (lit) [Let] the cart travel the main road [and] the horse travel the bridle path. (fig) One should not interfere with another's business. [Rhyme; see also *chuán duō bù ài gǎng* and *dàlù tōngtiān* below.]

90 **Chībǎo de māo bù zhuō hàozi.** 吃饱的猫不捉耗子。 (lit) A cat that is full doesn't catch mice. (fig) When one has achieved enough to satisfy one's needs, one won't continue to make further efforts.

91 **Chǐ bì fēi bǎo; cùn yīn shì jìng.** 尺璧非宝，寸阴是竞。 (lit) A round piece of jade a foot [in diameter is] not [to be reckoned] treasure, [but an] inch of time [on a sundial] is [worth] striving for. (fig) Time is priceless. [From the "Thousand Character Classic" *Qiān Zì Wén*. Now often said . . . *cùn yīn shì jīn*, "an inch of time is [worth] gold" to create structural parallelism; note: *bì* refers to a round flat piece of jade with a hole in the center used for ceremonial burial purposes in ancient China; *cùnyīn* is now used as one word to mean "a very short time"; see also *yī cùn guāngyīn* below.]

92 **Chī bu liǎo, dōuzhe zǒu.** 吃不了，兜着走。 (lit) [What you] can't eat, [you'll have to] take with [you]. (fig) One has to bear the consequences of one's actions. [Now sometimes also used jokingly to refer to taking leftovers home from restaurants; cf. *DRC*, chap. 23; *JPM*, chap. 13.]

93 **Chī bù qióng, chuān bù qióng; bù huì jīngjì, yīshì qióng.** 吃不穷穿不穷，不会经济一世穷。 (lit) Eating [will] not impoverish [one] nor will clothing, [but] not being able to plan [a budget] [will make one] poor for a lifetime. (fig) The ordinary necessities of life will not impoverish one; what will make one poor all one's life is to live beyond one's means. [Rhyme; also said . . . *bù huì jìsuàn*, ". . . cannot budget," etc.; see also *chīfàn, chuān yī* and *chuān bù qióng* below.]

94 **Chī cōng, chī suàn, bù chī jiāng [/jiàng].** 吃葱，吃蒜，不吃姜[/将]。 (lit) [One may] eat onions, [or] eat garlic, [but one should] not eat ginger. (pun/fig) Whatever one may do, one should not let oneself be goaded into action by others. [Note:

jiāng, "ginger" is a pun on jiàng, "general" as in the Chinese chess ploy called jíjiàngfǎ, "goading another into action."]

95 **Chī de hǎo; shuō de hǎo.** 吃的好，说的好。 [When you] eat well [of someone's food, then] speak well of them. [Cf. *Wǔ Sōng*, chap. 3; often said about providing banquets to visiting authorities so they will make a good report; see also *chī rénjiā de* and *dé rén qiáncái* below.]

96 **Chī de kuī, zuò yī duī.*** 吃得亏，坐一堆。 [One who is] able to take small losses [can] live [in harmony] with others. [Rhyme; see also *chīkuī de shì guāi* and *chī yī fēn kuī* below.]

97 **Chī de kǔ zhōng kǔ, fāng wéi rén shàng rén.** 吃得苦中苦，方为人上人。 Only those who have tasted the bitterest of the bitter can become people [who] stand out among others. [Cf. *Guānchǎng Xiànxíng Jì*, chap. 1.]

98 **Chī de kǔ zhōng kǔ, fāng zhī tián zhōng tián.** 吃得苦中苦，方知甜中甜。 Only one who has tasted the bitterest of the bitter can appreciate the sweetest of the sweet. [See also *chīguò kǔtou* above.]

99 **Chī de lāta; zuò dé Púsà.** 吃的邋遢，做得菩萨。 (lit) [One who] eats carelessly [will] become a Buddha. (fig) One need not pay too much attention to cleanliness or sanitation when eating. [Said as an excuse or as a preventative charm by careless eaters; see also *bùgān-bùjìng* above.]

100 **Chī dú shū shū, qiān lǐ miànmù.** 尺读书疏，千里面目。 [To read someone's] letters [and] official reports [is to see his] face [though he is a] thousand miles [away]. [Rhyme; cf. *Yán Shì Jiā Xùn: Zá Yì*.]

101 **Chīfàn, chuān yī liàng jiādàng.*** 吃饭穿衣量家当。 (lit) [In spending money on] eating [and] clothing, [one should] measure [one's] capital. (fig) One should calculate one's expenditures based on one's resources and live within one's means. [See also *chī bù qióng* above and *kàn cài chīfàn* below.]

102 **Chīfàn fáng yē; xíng lù fáng diē.** 吃饭防噎，行路防跌。 (lit) Guard against choking [when you] eat, [and] against stumbling [when] walking. (fig) Be careful in everything you do in life. [Rhyme; cf. WM, chap. 10; chap. 33.]

103 **Chīguò kǔtou, fāng zhī tiántou.** 吃过苦头，方知甜头。 (lit) Only [one who has] tasted bitterness can know sweetness. (fig) Only those who have suffered can really appreciate sweetness. [Rhyme; see also *chī de kǔ zhōng kǔ* below.]

104 **Chī hàn bùkěn ráorén; ráorén bù shì chī hàn.** 痴汉不肯饶人，饶人不是痴汉。 (lit) A foolish person isn't willing to pardon others; to forgive others is not [to be a] fool. (fig) One who forgives others is wise. [See also *rànglù bù shì* and *ráorén bù shì* below.]

105 **Chī huā màn fā, dàqì-wǎnchéng.** 迟花慢发，大器晚成。 [Just as] late flowers mature slowly, [so] great men succeed late [in life]. [Cf. *Rúlín Wàishǐ*, chap. 49; note: *dàqì-wǎnchéng*, from *Lǎozǐ*, is used as a *chengyu*; see also *chī kāi de huā* and *hǎo fàn bùpà wǎn* below.]

106 **Chī jìn wèidao, yán hǎo; zǒubiàn tiānxià, niáng hǎo.** 吃尽味道盐好，走遍天下娘好。 [Just as] of all the flavors [one] eats, salt [tastes the] best, [so] wherever [one] goes in the world, [one's] mother is dearest.

107 **Chī jiǔ bù yán gōngwù shì.*** 吃酒不言公务事。 [While] drinking never talk public business. [See also *jiǔ bù yán gōng* below.]

108 **Chī jiǔ tú zuì; fàngzhài tú lì.** 吃酒图醉，放债图利。 (lit) [One] drinks liquor to get drunk, [and] one] lends money to get interest. (fig) There is always some motive for every action. [Note: here *tú* is a verb meaning "to seek."]

109 **Chí kāi de huā wèibì bù xiāngyàn.** 迟开的花未必不香艳。 (lit) Late-blooming flowers are not [necessarily] unfragrant. (fig) Men who become famous late in life do not necessarily have few achievements. [See also *chí huā màn fā* above.]

110 **Chīkuī de shì guāi; zhàn piányi de shì dāi.** 吃亏的是乖，占便宜的是呆。 [One who] suffers petty losses is wise; [one who] takes petty advantages is foolish. [Rhyme; see also *chī de kuī* above and the following entry.]

111 **Chīkuī rén cháng zài.** 吃亏人常在。 [One who] takes losses will live [a] long [life because (s)he] will always have a clear conscience. [See also the preceding entry.]

112 **Chīkuī wǎngwǎng jiùshì zhàn piányi.** 吃亏往往就是占便宜。 Suffering [a loss] is [really] a gain [in the long run because of the knowledge and/or goodwill gained thereby]. [See also *chī yī fēn kuī* below.]

113 **chīkuī xuéguāi dàijià gāo, bèn hàn fēi cǐ xué bù dào.** 吃亏学乖代价高，笨汉非此学不到。 To suffer and learn a lesson, [one] pays a high price, [but] a fool can't learn any other way. [Rhymed couplet]

114 **Chīle hétún, bǎi yàng wúwèi.** 吃了河豚，百样无味。 (lit) [After] having eaten globefish [the rarest delicacy], [one feels] nothing else to be tasty. (fig) One who has had the best regards everything else as inferior.

115 **Chīle sān tiān sù, jiù xiǎng shàng Xītiān.*** 吃了三天素，就想上西天。 (lit) After practicing vegetarianism for only three days, [one should not] aspire to ascend to the Western Heaven [i.e., to become a Buddha]. (fig) It's impossible to become successful or famous without first "paying your dues" through hard efforts.

116 **Chīlì bù zhuànqián; zhuànqián bù chīlì.** 吃力不赚钱，赚钱不吃力。 [Those who] work hard do not make [big] money, [and those who] make [good] money do not [have to] work hard. [Said of business people before 1949 and in the 1990s.]

117 **Chí lǐ wú yú, xiā wéi dà.** 池里无鱼，虾为大。 (lit) [When] there are no fish in the pond, the shrimp becomes the biggest. (fig) When people of real talent or authority are absent, lesser people take over. [See also *shān zhōng wú lǎohǔ* below.]

118 **Chī lì yào bōpí; qiānniú yào qiān bí.** 吃栗要剥皮，牵牛要牵鼻。[To] eat a chestnut, [one] has to remove the shell; [to] lead an ox, [one] has to lead [it by its] nose. (fig) In solving any problem, one has to grasp the essential point. [Rhyme; see also *qiānniú, yào qiān* below.]

119 **Chī nǎ jiā jiǔ, shuō nǎ jiā huà.** 吃哪家酒, 说哪家话。(lit) [If one] consumes someone's liquor, [one must] speak their language. (fig) One has to speak for the person from whom one receives favors or bribes. [See also *chéng rén chē* and *chī rénjiā de* below.]

120 **Chí qiǎn bù néng yǎng dà yú.*** 池浅不能养大鱼。(lit) Big fish can't be raised in a shallow pond. (fig) With no scope to bring their talents into full play, talented people will probably leave for greener pastures. [See also *shuǐ qiǎn, yǎng bu zhù* below.]

121 **Chī rén de shīzi bù lù chǐ.** 吃人的狮子不露齿。(lit) A man-eating lion never shows its fangs. (fig) The most dangerous people are those who hide their true colors. [See also *ègǒu yǎo rén* and *yǎo rén gǒu* below.]

122 **Chī rénjiā de, zuǐ ruǎn; ná rénjiā de, shǒu duǎn.*** 吃人家的，嘴软，拿人家的，手短。(lit) [After] eating another's [food], [one's] mouth is softened; [after] taking someone's [present] [one's] reach is shortened [because then they can expose you for bribery]. (fig) Once someone in power has taken favors or bribes from you, they no longer have power over you because you can always expose their corruption. [Now often used of Communist party cadres or officials who have accepted bribes or favors; see also *chī de hǎo* above.]

123 **Chī rénjiā wǎn bàn; bèi rénjia shǐhuan.** 吃人家碗半，被人家使唤。[After you have] eaten [even] half a bowl [of someone else's food, you are] at [that] person's beck and call. [Rhyme; cf. *JPM*, chap. 58; also said *chī tā yī wǎn, píng shǐ huàn* in *Hé Diǎn*, chap. 6; see also *shòu rén yī fàn* above.]

124 **Chī rén miànqián bùdé shuō mèng.** 痴人面前不得说梦。(lit) To an idiot, [one] ought not tell fantastic tales [or (s)he will believe them]. (fig) Don't talk to the ill-informed about things beyond their ken. Don't waste your time talking to fools. [Note: *chī rén shuō mèng*, "idiotic nonsense."]

125 **Chī rén yīkǒu, bào rén yī dǒu.** 吃人一口，报人一斗。Eat one mouthful of [someone's] rice, [and one day you will have to] return one bushel to them. (fig) If one takes petty advantages of others, one will suffer great losses some day. [Rhyme; note a *dǒu* is a unit of measure for grain equal to ten liters.]

126 **Chī rén zìyǒu chī fú.** 痴人自有痴福。(lit) Foolish people have fool's luck. (fig) "Fortune favors fools."

127 **Chī shā mántou, dāngbude fàn.** 吃杀馒头，当不得饭。(lit) [No matter] how much you eat, steamed bread can't equal rice [for a meal]. (fig) A substitute can never compare with the original. [Said by southern Chinese, who principally eat rice, as opposed to northerners, who eat wheat-based foods such as noodles and steamed bread.] [Cf. *Chū Kè Pāi'àn Jīngqí*, chap. 26.]

128 **Chī shāobing háiyào péi tuòmo.** 吃烧饼还要赔唾沫。(lit) [Even] when eating pancakes, [one] must add saliva. (fig) In doing anything, one must invest (or lose) something in order to gain something (or to make a profit). [Cf. *Xǐngshì Yīnyuán Zhuàn*, chap. 80.]

129 **Chīshuǐ bù wàng jué jǐng rén.** 吃水不忘掘井人。(lit) When drinking water, don't forget those who dug the well. (fig) Don't be ungrateful to those who have helped you in the past. [See also *guò hé mò wàng* below.]

130 **Chī xiǎo kuī, zhàn dà piányi.** 吃小亏，占大便宜。(lit) Take small losses [for the sake of] earning big gains [later on]. (fig) "Lose a penny [in order to] gain a pound." [Note: during the Cultural Revolution Liu Shaoqi was criticized for recommending *chī xiǎo kuī, zhàn dà piányi* ("suffer a little to gain a lot") as a strategy for the Chinese Communist party; see also *chī yī fēn kuī* and *zhàn xiǎopiányi* below.]

131 **Chī yào bù mán lángzhōng.*** 吃药不瞒郎中。(lit) [One who has] taken medicine [should] not hide [from one's] doctor [what kind of medicine one has taken]. (fig) Be frank with those who are trying to help you [or they won't be able to help you]. [Cf. *Dàng Kòu Zhì*, chap. 99; note: *lángzhōng* refers to a physician trained in herbal medicine.]

132 **Chī yào bù tóu fāng, nǎpà yòng chuán zhuāng.** 吃药不投方，哪怕用船装。(lit) [If one] takes medicine without the correct prescription, [one won't be cured] even if [one takes a] shipload full. (fig) In doing anything one should adopt methods appropriate to the particular situation, or it will be of no use. [Rhyme.]

133 **Chī yào sān nián huì xíngyī.*** 吃药三年会行医。(lit) [One who] takes medicine [for] three years can become a doctor. (fig) One who has long connections with a trade will become experienced. [See also *jiǔ bìng chéng liángyī* and *sān zhé gōng zhī* below.]

134 **Chī yī fēn kuī, wúliàng fú; shī piányi chù shì piányi.** 吃一分亏无量福，失便宜处是便宜。(lit) To suffer a small loss [is] a boundless blessing; the place [where one] loses is a gain. (fig) If you make a small concession (so as to let others gain a little), in the long run you'll gain; the small loss you suffer is a benefit. Don't always try to get the best of others every time; be willing to lose a little for a long-term gain in good will. [Cf. *Jīngshì Tōngyán*, chap. 3; see also *chīkuī wǎngwǎng* and *chī xiǎo kuī* above.]

135 **Chī yī huí kuī, xué yī huí guāi.** 吃一回亏，学一回乖。Suffer a loss [and] learn a lesson. [See also *chī yī qiàn* below.]

136 **Chǐ yǐn chuān dī, néng piāo yī yì.** 尺蚓穿堤能漂一邑。(lit) A one foot long earthworm, [if it] pierces a dike, can submerge [an entire] city. (fig) If one does not guard against little defects

C

or problems, great disasters will eventually occur. [See also *xiǎo dòng bù bǔ* below.]

137 **Chī yī qiàn, zhǎng yī zhì.*** 吃一堑，长一智。 (lit) Fall in a ditch [and] grow in wisdom. (fig) "A fall in a pit, a gain in wit"; one learns valuable lessons from setbacks. [Cited in Mao Zedong's *On Practice*; see also *chī yī huí kuī* and *bù jīng yī shì* above and *shàng huí dàng* below.]

138 **Chī yǒu suǒ duǎn; cùn yǒu suǒ cháng.** 尺有所短，寸有所长。 (lit) A [linear] foot [can be too] short [and] an inch [can be too] long. (fig) Just as a foot may be too short in one case while an inch may be too long in another, so every person has his weak points as well as his strong points. [Cf. *Shǐ Jì: Bái Qǐ Wáng Jiàn Lièzhuàn*; note: one Chinese "foot" or *chǐ* (equals one-third of a meter) contains ten Chinese "inches" or *cùn*.]

139 **Chī zài Guǎngdōng; chuān zài Shànghǎi.** 吃在广东；穿在上海。 (lit) Eat in Guangdong (province), [and get your] clothing in Shanghai. (fig) The best food (in China) is in Guangdong and the best clothes are made in Shanghai. [A popular saying in twentieth century China; see also *shēng Dōng Wú* below.]

140 **Chīzhāi bùrú xíngshàn.** 吃斋不如行善。 (lit) [It is] better to do good works than to be a vegetarian. (fig) Better to do good to others than to engage in self-cultivation. [Note: both vegetarianism and doing good deeds are religious practices of Buddhism.]

141 **Chīzhāi néng chéng fó, niúmǎ shàng Xītiān.** 吃斋能成佛，牛马上西天。 (lit) [If anyone who] lives on a vegetarian diet can [ascend to the Western Heaven and] become a Buddha, [then] oxen [and] horses, [who eat only grass,] can [get there too]. (fig) (1) One should do everything in a down-to-earth manner, without any illusions. (2) One cannot accomplish things only by wishful thinking. [See also *chīzhāi bùrú* above.]

142 **Chǒng gǒu shàng zào; chǒng zǐ bùxiào.** 宠狗上灶，宠子不孝。 [Just as] a spoiled dog [will] climb onto the kitchen stove [to eat, so] a spoiled child is not filial. [Rhyme.]

143 **Chóngsūn yǒu lǐ gào tàigōng.** 重孙有里告太公。 (lit) [Even] a great-grandson [may] bring a lawsuit against his great-grandfather [if he] has reason [on his side]. (fig) All persons stand equal before reason. [Cf. *Wǔ Sōng*, chap. 6; in traditional Chinese society, normally no family member would ever take legal action against another, especially someone senior in generation.]

144 **Chōu dāo duàn shuǐ, shuǐ gèng liú; jiè jiǔ xiāochóu, chóu gèng chóu.** 抽刀断水水更流，借酒消愁愁更愁。 [If one] draws [one's] sword to stop the water, the water [will] flow even more [when the sword is removed]; [similarly,] drowning [one's] sorrows in drink [only] makes them worse. [The order of the two halves may be reversed; see also *jiè jiǔ xiāochóu* and *yào bù néng zhǐ* below.]

145 **Chōu dāo nán rù qiào.** 抽刀难入鞘。 A sword drawn is difficult [to put back] into [its] sheath. (fig) Things once started are hard to stop, even though one may wish to.

146 **Chǒu póniáng hào cháfěn.** 丑婆娘好搽粉。 (lit) An ugly woman likes to make herself up. (fig) People try hard to cover their shortcomings.

147 **Chǒu rén bù shí chǒu.** 丑人不识丑。 (lit) An ugly person does not realize his or her ugliness. (fig) One who has shortcomings is unwilling to admit them (even though others criticize or point them out).

148 **Chǒu rén duō zuòguài.** 丑人多作怪。 Ugly people are inclined to behave strangely [in order to draw attention to themselves]. [Usually said of women; note the *chengyu*: *niúnie-zuòtài*, "behaving coyly; affectedly bashful."]

149 **Chóurén xiāngjiàn, fènwài yǎnhóng.** 仇人相见，分外眼红。 [When] enemies encounter one another, [their] eyes [become] especially red with fury. [See also *ēnrén xiāngjiàn* below.]

150 **Chóurén xiāngjiàn, fènwài yǎn míng.** 仇人相见，分外眼明。 [When] two foes meet, [they] recognize [each other] immediately. [Cf. *JPM*, chap. 87; *Shuǐhǔ Quán Zhuàn*, chap. 3; *Jīngshì Tōngyán*, chap. 40; see also *ēnrén xiāngjiàn* below.]

151 **Chǒu shì jiā zhōng bǎo; (kě miǎn rě fánnǎo).** 丑是家中宝，(可免惹烦恼)。 Ugliness [in a wife] is a blessing for a family, ([which] can avoid arousing trouble). [Rhyme; cf. *JPM*, chap. 91; the second part is often omitted.]

152 **Chǒu xífù pà jiàn gōngpó.** 丑媳妇怕见公婆。 (lit) An ugly bride is afraid to meet her parents-in-law. (fig) One who has done evil things is afraid to face people. [Cf. *JPM*, chap. 72; see also the following entry.]

153 **Chǒu xífù zǒng (děi yào) jiàn gōngpó.** 丑媳妇总(得要)见公婆。 An ugly bride will eventually (have to) meet her parents-in-law. (fig) Truth will come to light sooner or later. [Cf. *Liáo Zhāi Zhì Yì* (Strange Stories from a Chinese Studio): *Lián Chéng*.]

154 **Chòu yú bù jiàn rén jiàomài.** 臭鱼不见人叫卖。 (lit) [One] never sees people crying "stinking fish for sale." (fig) A "skeleton in one's closet" should not be shown to outsiders. "Don't wash your dirty linen in public." [See also *jiāchǒu bùkě* below.]

155 **Chuán bù lí duò; kè bù lí huò.** 船不离舵，客不离货。 (lit) [Just as a] ship [can]not be separated from [its] rudder, [so a] trader [can]not be separated from [his] goods. (fig) A merchant without merchandise is not a merchant. [Rhyme; note: *kèshāng*, "traveling trader"; see also *guān bù lí yìn* below.]

156 **Chuān bù qióng; chī bù qióng; suànpán bù dào, yīshì qióng.** 穿不穷，吃不穷，算盘不到，一世穷。 (lit) [Buying] clothing and food won't reduce [one] to poverty, [but if] an abacus is not present [to budget your money, you'll be] poor all [your] life. [Cf. *Wǔ Sōng*, chap. 6; see also *chī bù qióng* and *chīfàn, chuān yī* above.]

157 **Chuán dào jiāngxīn, bǔ lòu chí.** 船到江心, 补漏迟。 (lit) [When the] boat reaches midstream, [it will be] too late to mend the leaks. (fig) One should take action before trouble occurs.

158 **Chuán dào qiáotóu zì huì zhí, (chē dào shān qián bì yǒu lù).** 船到桥头自会直, (车到山前必有路)。 (lit) [When the] boat comes to the bridge [underpass], [it] will go through straight by itself; ([when the] cart gets to the mountains, there must be a way to get over them). (fig) Things always work out by themselves. "Cross that bridge when you come to it." [These two lines may be used separately as two separate yanyu; see chē dào shān qián above.]

159 **Chuán duō bù ài gǎng; chē duō bù ài lù.** 船多不碍港, 车多不碍路。 (lit) Boats, [however] many, won't block the harbor, [and] vehicles, [however] many, won't block the road. (fig) Each should go his own way and not interfere with each other('s business). [Cf. JPM, chap. 7, 16, and 74; see also chē zǒu chēdào above and gèrén chuán below.]

160 **Chuángtóu yǒu luó gǔ, wù pà wú rén kū.** 床头有箩谷, 勿怕无人哭。 (lit) [If one] has baskets of grain [at] the head of [one's] bed, there is no need to fear [that] no one [will] cry [over one's death]. (fig) If one has sufficient property, one's heirs will remain filial. [Also said chuáng tóu yǒu gǔ, rén zhèng kū; see also jiǔ bìngchuáng qián below.]

161 **Chuān guǎng, yú dà.** 川广鱼大。 (lit) Great rivers [breed] big fish. (fig) (1) If the ruler is kind and benevolent, people will gather around him. (2) If the conditions are favorable, outstanding people will appear. [Cf. Wén Zhǐ: Shàng Dé; see also shuǐ kuǎn, yú dà below.]

162 **Chuān hēi yī, bào hēi zhù.** 穿黑衣, 抱黑柱。 (lit) [Those who] wear black embrace the black pillar. (fig) People protect others of their own kind. [Cf. JPM, chap. 72.]

163 **Chuánjiā háizi huì fúshuǐ.** 船家孩子会浮水。 (lit) A boatman's child knows how to float. (fig) One who comes from the family of a certain trade is certain to know something of it. [See also gēnzhe wǎjiang below.]

164 **Chuán kào duò; fān kào fēng; lì jiàn háiyào kào qiáng gōng.** 船靠舵, 帆靠风, 利箭还要靠强弓。 (lit) Steering a ship depends on the helm, sailing a ship depends on the wind, [and] a sharp arrow depends on a strong bow. (fig) External conditions are important in accomplishing anything. [See also chuán wú shuǐ nán below.]

165 **Chuántóu bù yù, zhuǎn duò xiāngféng.** 船头不遇, 转舵相逢。 [If] boats' bows do not meet [bow to bow], [they will] meet [after a] change in course. (fig) If we do not meet here, we will meet somewhere else. People are bound to run into each other somewhere or other. [See also dàhǎi fúpíng and shuāngrì bù zháo below.]

166 **Chuān wà bù zhī jiǎoxià nuǎn; tuō wà cái zhī jiǎoxià hán.** 穿袜不知脚下暖, 脱袜才知脚下寒。 (lit) While wearing stockings, [one does]

not feel [one's] feet are warm until one is barefooted [and one's] feet are cold. (fig) One doesn't realize the true value of what one has until one loses it. [Rhyme; see also jǐng gān cái zhī and yǒu mǎo, bù zhī below.]

167 **Chuán wú shuǐ nán xíng; niǎo wú yì nán fēi.** 船无水难行, 鸟无翼难飞。 (lit) Boats can't move without water [and] birds can't fly without wings. (fig) Without certain necessary conditions, nothing can be accomplished. [See also chuán kào duò above.]

168 **Chuányán guò huà, zì tǎo áimà.** 传言过话, 自讨挨骂。 To pass on rumors and slanders [is to] invite curses upon oneself. [Rhyme.]

169 **Chuān yī dài mào, gèrén suǒ hào.** 穿衣戴帽, 个人所好。 (lit) [As to what kind of] clothes [or] hats [one] wears, each person has that which [(s)he] likes. (fig) Everyone has his or her own preferences (in clothing). [Rhyme.]

170 **Chuán zài wàn jīn, zhǎngduò yī rén.** 船载万斤, 掌舵一人。 (lit) A ship carrying thousands of pounds [of cargo, depends] solely on the helmsman. (fig) Leaders bear a heavy responsibility.

171 **Chuānzhēn yào gè yǐn xiàn rén.** 穿针要个引线人。 (lit) To thread a needle one needs a "thread carrier." (fig) A "go-between" is necessary to accomplish anything. [Cf. Érnǚ Yīngxióng Zhuàn, chap. 24; see also wú zhēn bù yǐn xiàn below.]

172 **Chuánzhǔ bù shǐ chuán kè lāqiàn.** 船主不使船客拉纤。 (lit) A boatman should never ask his passengers to tow the boat. (fig) One should not impose on one's guests.

173 **Chūbīng bù yóu jiàng.** 出兵不由将。 (lit) Soldiers [who are fighting] on the battlefields [can]not be directed by generals [as each soldier has to fight on his own]. (fig) People "in the trenches" have to make decisions on the spot according to the immediate circumstances. [Cf. Xīyáng Jì, chap. 23; see also jiàng zàiwài below.]

174 **Chūchù bùrú jù chù.** 出处不如聚处。 (lit) [The price at the] place of production is not as [cheap as at the] wholesale buyers. (fig) Because of competition, sometimes local products are even cheaper at the wholesalers than in the place where they are produced. [Cf. jù chù refers to a jísàndì, "collection and distribution center."]

175 **Chùchù yǒu lù tōng Cháng'ān.** 处处有路通长安。 (lit) All roads lead to Chang'an. (fig) "All roads lead to Rome." [Chang'an was the capital of the Western Han, Sui, and Tang dynasties; see also Cháng'ān suī hǎo above.]

176 **Chū de mén duō, shòu de zuì duō.** 出的门多, 受的罪多。 One who travels a lot suffers a lot. [See also chūwài yī lǐ below.]

177 **Chuī huǒ tǒng, liǎngtóu tōng.** 吹火筒, 两头通。 (lit) [A] fire-blowing tube [is] open at both ends. (fig) (1) A tactful person [can] mediate between two parties in conflict. (2) Some people (can) show a different face to everyone.

C

178 **Chuī shénme fēng, xià shénme yǔ.** 吹什么风，下什么雨。 (lit) Different types of wind [foretell] different types of rain. (fig) There's always a sign before things happen. [Also said *guā shénme fēng,* etc.]

179 **Chū jià cóng qīn; zàijià yóu shēn.** 初嫁从亲，再嫁由身。 [The] first [time a woman marries she] follows [her] parents' [wishes], [but when she] marries again, [it is] according to [her] own [wishes]. [From traditional China; cf. *WM,* chap. 25.]

180 **Chūjià de guīnǚ kū shì xiào; luòdì de jǔzǐ xiào shì kū.** 出嫁的闺女哭是笑，落地的举了笑是哭。 (lit) The weeping of a daughter who is going to be married is [really] laughter; the laughter of a scholar who fails in the imperial exam is [really] weeping. (fig) In life, crying is not necessarily an expression of sadness, nor laughter an expression of happiness. [Note: *jǔzǐ* or *jǔrén* was a successful candidate in the imperial examinations in the Ming and Qing dynasties, who was then entitled to take the highest level of imperial examinations.]

181 **Chūjiāo píng yīguān; jiǔ jiāo píng xuéshí.** 初交凭衣冠，久交凭学识。 [On] first contact, [one's impression of a person] depends on clothing; [after] long acquaintance, [one's assessment is] based on knowledge.

182 **Chūjiā róngyì; guī jiā nán.** 出家容易，归家难。 (lit) It's easier to become a monk than to stop being one. (fig) It's easier to get into things than out of them. [Note: *chūjiā,* (lit) "leaving home," refers to the practice of becoming a Buddhist monk or nun; also said *chūjiā róngyì; huàn sú nán.*]

183 **Chūjiā sān tiān, fó zài miànqián; chūjiā sān nián, fó zài Xītiān; chūjiā rú chū chéng fó yǒuyú.** 出家三天佛在面前，出家三年佛在西天，出家如出成佛有余。 (lit) [After] being a monk for three days, one feels as if the Buddha was just in front of one; [after] being a monk for three years, one feels as if the Buddha was [far away] in the Western Heaven; [after many years when one gets the] original feeling back, one feels as if one has become a Buddha oneself and more [as the Buddha has truly entered one's heart]. (fig) One has to go through a certain period of time to come to understand the world or to grasp the true essence of knowledge or learning. [Note: *chūjiā* means to become a Buddhist monk or nun.]

184 **Chūkǒu xū chéngshí; kǒushé shì huò jī.** 出口须诚实，口舌是祸机。 [What] comes out of [one's] mouth should be honest; the mouth [and] tongue [are the] causes of disaster. [Cf. *Xǐngshì Héngyán,* chap. 33; see also *bìng cóng kǒu rù* above and *kǒu shì huò zhī mén* below.]

185 **Chúle Líng Shān bié yǒu fó.** 除了灵山别有佛。 (lit) In addition to [this] Spirit Mountain, there are other Buddhas [elsewhere]. (fig) If one cannot find what one needs in one place, one can always go and seek someplace else. [Also said "... hái yǒu fó"; note: *líng shān* or *líng zhòu shān* refers to the place where Buddhas live; see also the following entry.]

186 **Chúle Líng Shān yě yǒu sì.** 出了灵山也有寺。 (lit) [When one has] left Mount Ling, there are other temples. (fig) One can always find a way of (making a) living somewhere else. [Note: *Líng Shān,* ("Spirit Mountain"), also the name of the highest peak in the Western Hills outside of Beijing, here simply stands for any mountain where spirits live; see also the preceding entry.]

187 **Chúle sǐ fǎ, háiyǒu huó fǎ.** 除了死法，还有活法。 (lit) In addition to rigid ways, there are [always] flexible ways [to do things]. (fig) "There is more than one way to skin a cat." [Cf. *Hé Diǎn,* chap. 1; see also *cǐ lù bù tōng* below.]

188 **Chū lín sǔnzi xiān dǎduàn.** 出林笋子先打断。 (lit) The bamboo shoots which grow outside [the edge of a bamboo] grove [will be the] first to be broken off. (fig) One who "sticks one's neck out" will be the first to be attacked. [See also *chū shuǐ chuán'ér* and *chūtóu chuánzi* and *qiāng dǎ chūtóu* below.]

189 **Chūmén bù lòubái.*** 出门不露白。 When you are out of doors, never show [your] silver [money]. [See also *cái bù lòubái* above.]

190 **Chūmén bù rèn huò.** 出门不认货。 (lit) [Once] the goods are carried out [of the store, the boss] refuses to acknowledge them [i.e., have them returned]. (fig) After you buy it, it's your problem; *caveat emptor.* [Originally *chūmén fú rèn huò* in *Hé Diǎn,* chap. 10.]

191 **Chūmén guān tiānsè; jìn mén kàn liǎnsè.** 出门观天色，进门看脸色。 (lit) [When you] go outdoors, look at the color of the sky; [when you] go indoors, look at the expressions on people's faces. (fig) Just as one should watch for changes in the weather, so one should pay attention to changes in mood of one's elders. [This rhyme was advice given to newly married daughters-in-law as a code of conduct in their husbands' families; see also *pīchái, kàn chái* and *rùmén xiū wèn* and *shàng shān kàn shānshì* below.]

192 **Chūmén sān bù yuǎn, yòushì yī céng tiān.** 出门三步远，又是一层天。 (lit) Three steps away from home, is another [level of the] world. (fig) Every place is different; every situation is different. [In traditional Chinese mythology, the universe is divided into nine "levels" or worlds: *jiǔ chóng tiān*; see also *gé chóng lóubǎn* below and the following entry.]

193 **Chūmén sān lǐ dì, zǒng suàn wàiláirén.** 出门三里地，总算外来人。 (lit) [One who has] gone three miles away from home is always [regarded as] a stranger. (fig) Customs differ from place to place (even though they may not be far away from each other). [See also *bǎi lǐ, bùtóng* above and *gé dào bù xiàyǔ* below and the preceding entry.]

194 **Chūn bù zhòng, qiū bù shōu.** 春不种，秋不收。 (lit) Without spring sowing, [there will be] no autumn harvest. (fig) One must exert some effort in order to accomplish anything.

195 **Chūn dòng gǔtou; qiū dòng ròu.** 春冻骨头，秋冻肉。 (lit) Spring freezes the bones, [while] autumn [only] freezes the flesh. (fig) Spring cold is more severe than autumn cold.

196 **Chūn jiāngshuǐ nuǎn, yā xiān zhī.** 春江水暖鸭先知。 (lit) [In the] spring [when the] river waters [get] warm, the ducks are the first to know. (fig) (1) [Usually used literally to describe] the coming of spring. (2) People with experience on the inside are the first to know of coming changes. [See also *cháo jǔ zhī fēng* above.]

197 **Chǔnrén jiáoshé; zhìzhě dòng nǎo.** 蠢人嚼舌，智者动脑。 Foolish people wag their tongues, [while] wise people use their brains.

198 **Chūntiān hái'ér liǎn, yī tiān biàn sān biàn.** 春天孩儿脸，一天变三变。 Spring [weather is] like a child's face, changing three times a day. [Rhyme; see also *xiǎo háizi de liǎn* below.]

199 **Chún wáng, chǐ hán.** 唇亡齿寒。 (lit) [If the] lips are gone, the teeth are cold. (fig) If one (of two interdependent things) falls, the other is in danger. [Cf. *Mòzǐ: Fēi Gōng*; *R3K*, chap. 119; used, e.g., to describe the relationship between Korea and China at the time of the *Kàng Měi Yuán Cháo Zhànzhēng*, "War to Resist U.S. Aggression and Aid Korea" (1950–1953); this is often used as a chengyu, as in *chúnwáng-chǐhán guānxi*, describing two things as being in an interdependent relationship.]

200 **Chūn wǔ, qiū dòng; (lǎolái wú bìng).*** 春捂秋冻,(老来无病)。 Muffle [yourself] up in spring [and stay] cold [in] autumn, ([so that even when you] get old [you'll] be healthy). (fig) In spring, continue to keep on warm garments (in order to avoid catching cold), and in the autumn, delay putting on thick garments (so as to build up your resistance to the cold gradually), (in order to strengthen your resistance in your later years). [See also *dōng bù jǐ wēn* and *dòng jiǔ, wǔ sì* and *duō yī, duō hán* below.]

201 **Chūnxiāo yīkè zhí qiānjīn.** 春宵一刻值千金。 A quarter of an hour of a spring night is worth a thousand [ounces of] gold. [Cf. *Hé Diǎn*, chap. 4; a line from a Song dynasty poem "Chūn Yè" by Su Shi, often used as a metaphor for the first night of marriage.]

202 **Chūnyǔ guì rú yóu.** 春雨贵如油。 Spring rain is as precious as oil. [Cf. *Xǐngshì Yīnyuán Zhuàn*, chap. 8.]

203 **Chúqù yī sǐ wú dànàn; rén dào yàofàn wú zài qióng.** 除去一死无大难；人到要饭无再穷。 (lit) There's no greater disaster than one's death [and] no greater poverty than begging. (fig) The worst things that can happen are death or starvation, so why worry?

204 **Chǔ shān bùpà pō dǒu.** 处山不怕坡陡。 (lit) [One who] lives in the mountains is not afraid [to climb] slopes [which are] steep. (fig) Living in poor conditions one becomes accustomed to inconveniences or hardships in life.

205 **Chūshēng niúdú bù pà hǔ.** 初生牛犊不怕虎。 See the following entry.

206 **Chūshēngzhīdú bù jù/wèi hǔ.** 初生之犊不惧/畏虎。 (lit) A newborn calf fears not the tiger. (fig) The innocent or naive don't know enough to be afraid. "Fools rush in where angels fear to tread." [Rhyme; cf. *R3K*, chap. 74; *chūshēngzhīdú* is now taken as a set noun phrase; this is now more commonly said *chūshēng niúdú bù pà hǔ*.]

207 **Chúshī pà tái zào; cáiféng pà pí'ǎo.*** 厨师怕抬灶，裁缝怕皮袄。 (lit) Cooks are reluctant to carry stoves [and] tailors to make fur coats. (fig) There are difficult parts to every job. [Rhyme.]

208 **Chǔshì yí dài chūnfēng.** 处事宜带春风。 (lit) [In] dealing [with one's] affairs, [it is] appropriate to be as [warm as a] spring breeze. (fig) Always deal with others with a smile. [A line from a poem entitled "Yòu Mèng Yǐng" by the Qing dynasty poet Zhang Chao.]

209 **Chūshǒu jiàn gāodī.** 出手见高低。 [Whether one is] skilled or not [will soon be] seen [once one] sets to work.

210 **Chū shuǐ cái kàn liǎng tuǐ ní.** 出水才看两腿泥。 (lit) Only after [one] comes out of the water can [one] see [from] the mud on [one's] two legs [how deep the mud was]. (fig) One never knows the final consequences until things are all finished.

211 **Chū shuǐ chuán'ér xiān làn dǐ.** 出水船儿先烂底。 The ship out of water [is the one which will have its] bottom rotten first. (fig) The one who "sticks one's neck out" will be attacked first. [See also *chū lín sǔnzi* above and *chūtóu chuánzi* and *qiāng dǎ chūtóuniǎo* below.]

212 **Chú sǐ wú dà zāi.** 除死无大灾。 (lit) Excepting death, there are no big disasters. (fig) Always keep things in perspective.

213 **Chūtóu chuánzi xiān xiùlàn.** 出头椽子先朽烂。 (lit) Rafter ends [that] jut out [from under the roof will] rot first. (fig) People in the limelight bear the brunt of attack. [Cf. *JPM*, chap. 86; see also *chū lín sǔnzi* above and *chū shuǐ chuán'ér* and *qiāng dǎ chūtóuniǎo* below.]

214 **Chūwài yī lǐ bùrú jiā lǐ.** 出外一里不如家里。 (lit) It's better to stay at home than to go abroad [even] a half kilometer. (fig) "There's no place like home." "East or west, home is best." [Rhyme; cf. *WM*, chap. 61; one *lǐ* equals one-half kilometer; see also *zàijiā qiān rì hǎo* below.]

215 **Chú yī è, zhǎng shí shàn.** 锄一恶，长十善。 Eliminating one evil increases [one's] good deeds by ten.

216 **Chú zhōng yǒu shèngfàn; lùshang yǒu jī rén.** 厨中有剩饭，路上有饥人。 (lit) In the kitchen, there is surplus rice, [while] on the streets there are starving people. (fig) Rich people always have a surplus, while poor people are starving. "The rich get richer and the poor get poorer." [Cf. *JW*, chap. 57.]

217 **Cíbēi tài guò, dāng zuò'è.** 慈悲太过，当作恶。 [To show] too much mercy [toward evildoers] is to do evil [oneself].

C

218 **Cǐchù bù liú rén, zì yǒu liú rén chù.** 此处不留人，自有留人处。 [If I'm] not welcome to stay here, [I] can always go where [I am] welcome. [Cf. *Gǔ-Jīn Xiǎoshuō*, chap. 3; *Xǐngshì Héngyán*, chap. 24; *Xǐngshì Yīnyuán Zhuàn*, chap. 77.]

219 **Cǐdì wú yín sānbǎi liǎng.** 此地无银三百两。 (lit) [A fool named Third Brother Zhang posts a sign saying] "Three hundred ounces of silver are not buried here." (fig) Some people are so obvious as to be foolish. Some things are "a dead give-away." [The thief who then stole the silver also left a sign: *duì mén Wáng Èr bùcéng tōu*, "Second [Brother] Wang [who lives] next door hasn't stolen [anything]"; from a popular folk story.]

220 **Cǐdì wú zhūshā, hóngtǔ wéi guì.** 此地无朱砂，红土为贵。 (lit) [In] this place there is no [red] cinnabar, [so] red soil is taken as valuable. (fig) In the absence of really high quality, something of less quality will do; *faut de mieux*; "In the land of the blind, the one-eyed man is king."

221 **Cǐ lù bù tōng, nà lù tōng.** 此路不通，那路通。 (lit) [If] this road doesn't go through, that road will go through. (fig) There are more ways than one to achieve one's goal. "There's more than one way to skin a cat." [*Cǐlù-bùtōng* has become a set phrase meaning "dead end; blind alley"; see also *chúle sǐ fǎ* above.]

222 **Címǔ duō bài ér.** 慈母多败儿。 A mother [who lavishes too] much love [on her] children spoils [them]. [Cf. *Hán Fēizǐ: Xiǎn Xué*; see also *ér pà niáng jiāo* below.]

223 **Cǐ yīshí, bǐ yīshí.** 此一时，彼一时。 (lit) This [is] one time [and] that [was] one [other] time. (fig) Times change. Things are different now from what they were before.

224 **Cì zǐ qiānjīn bùrú cì zǐ yī yì.** 赐子千金不如赐子一艺。 Better than to give [one's] son [a] thousand [ounces of] gold [is] to teach him a skill. [See also *yì bù yà shēn* below.]

225 **Cónglái hǎoshì duō fēngxiǎn; zìgǔ guā'ér kǔ hòu tián.** 从来好事多风险，自古瓜儿苦后甜。 (lit) [It has] ever [been the case that the realization of] good things is usually [preceded by] difficulties, [just as it has] always [been that] melons [taste] bitter before [they taste] sweet. (fig) The road to happiness is never smooth. [Rhyme; the noun suffix *-ér* is pronounced as an independent syllable to preserve the meter (*jiézòu*).]

226 **Cōngming běn shì kǔ gōngfu.** 聪明本是苦工夫。 The root of cleverness is hard effort.

227 **Cōngming fǎn bèi cōngming wù.** 聪明反被聪明误。 (lit) Cleverness [may] be taken in by itself. (fig) Clever people may be victims of their own cleverness. "Cleverness may overreach itself." [Cf. *Zàishēng Yuán*, chap. 75; see also *guānggùn dǎ jiǔ jiǔ* and *hóuzi jīnglíng* below.]

228 **Cōngming yīshì, hútu yīshí.** 聪明一世，糊涂一时。 (lit) Clever one lifetime, muddled one time. (fig) A lifetime of cleverness can be interrupted by moments of stupidity. "Smart as a rule, but this time a fool." "Even Homer sometimes nods." [Cf. *Xǐngshì Héngyán*, chap. 37; see also *shèngrén yě yǒu* and *zhìzhě qiān lǜ* below and the following entry.]

229 **Cōngmíng yīshì, měngdǒng yīshí.** 聪明一世，懵懂一时。 [One can be] clever [for] a lifetime, [and still be] muddle-headed [at least] once [in one's life]. [Cf. *Érnǚ Yīngxióng Zhuàn*, chap. 18; *Xǐngshì Héngyán*, chap. 75; now more commonly: *cōngmíng yī shì; hútu yì shí*, as in Lao She's novel: *Luòtuo Xiángzi* (Rickshaw); see also preceding entry.]

230 **Cóngqián zuòguo shì, méi xīng yīqí lái.** 从前做过事，没兴一齐来。 [All] the [bad] things [one] has done in the past [will be recompensed with] ill luck all at once. [Cf. *Dōng Zhōu Lièguó Zhì*, chap. 33.]

231 **Cóng shàn rú dēng; cóng è rú bēng.** 从善如登，从恶如崩。 (lit) To follow goodness is to rise; to follow evil is to fall. (fig) It requires effort to follow examples of goodness, but it is easy to follow bad examples. [Rhyme; cf. *Guó Yǔ: Zhōu Yǔ, Xià*.]

232 **Cóng xiǎo'ér dìng bāshí.** 从小儿定八十。 (lit) From the child [one can] know [the adult of] eighty. (fig) "The child is father of the man."

233 **Cōng zhě tīng yú wúshēng; míng zhě jiàn yú wúxíng.** 聪者听于无声，明者见于无形。 (lit) A clever person hears what [others do] not hear; an intelligent person sees what [others do] not see. (fig) A clever person can foretell what will follow from present events. [Cf. *Shǐ Jì: Huái Nán Héng Shān Lièzhuàn*; see also *cháo jū zhī fēng* above.]

234 **Cùn tiě rù mù, jiǔ niú nán bá.** 寸铁入木，九牛难拔。 (lit) An inch of iron driven into wood can hardly be pulled out by nine oxen. (fig) It's easier to do things than to undo them once they're done.

235 **Cūn wú dà shù, pénghāo wéi lín.** 村无大树，蓬蒿为林。 (lit) [If a] village has no big trees, [short] bushes are [regarded as a] forest. (fig) If there are not any talented people in an area, then persons of lower ability are mistakenly regarded as prominent. [Said either critically by others, or modestly of oneself; note *péng*, "bitter fleabane" and *hāo*, "wormwood," here refer to bushes of short height; cf. the Qing dynasty author Zhái Hào's *Tōng Sú Biān: Cǎo Mù* and *Jìn Shū: Chén Yún Zhuàn*; see also *cǐdì wú zhūshā* above and *shān zhōng wú lǎohǔ* below.]

236 **Cuō yào sān nián huì xíngyī.** 撮药三年会行医。 (lit) [Having] filled prescriptions [in a drugstore for] three years, [one] can be a doctor. (fig) One is bound to pick something up just by associating with specialists. [See also *āizhe tiějiang* above and *rù háng sān rì* and *sān tiān zhù zài* and *shú dú Tángshī* below.]

D

1　**Dà bài xiǎo, wèi zhāngkǒu; xiǎo bài dà, wú kě nài.** 大拜小为张口，小拜大无可奈。 [When people in] higher [positions] pay respect to [people in] lower [positions, it] is because [they need] to ask [for their help]; [when people in] lower [positions] pay respect to [people in] higher [positions, it] is because [they] have no choice. [Cf. the *chengyu*: *wúkě-nàihé*, "to have no alternative."]

2　**Dà bìng cóng shā qǐ; dà zéi cóng guā qǐ.** 大病从痧起，大贼从瓜起。 (lit) [Just as a] serious illness [may] start from [an insignificant illness like] sunstroke, [so a] big thief [may] develop from [the theft of a] melon. (fig) One must pay attention to small errors and transgressions at the beginning, and "nip them in the bud." [See also *dà chuán hái pà* below.]

3　**Dǎ bù duàn de qīn; mà bù duàn de lín.** 打不断的亲，骂不断的邻。 (lit) Fighting or name-calling won't break off the relations between relatives or the friendship between neighbors. (fig) Relatives and neighbors are so close that fighting or name-calling won't affect their long-term relationship. [Cf. JW, chap. 94.]

4　**Dà bù zhèng, xiǎo bùjìng.** 大不正，小不敬。 [If the] older [generation's behavior is] not upright, the young [will] not respect [them]. [Cf. JPM, chap. 76.]

5　**Dǎchái wèn qiáofū; shǐ chuán wèn shāogōng.** 打柴问樵夫，驶船问艄公。 (lit) [To] cut firewood, [one must] ask a woodcutter; [to] sail a boat, one must ask a boatman. (fig) If one wants to do something, one should ask an expert for advice.

6　**Dàchóng bù chī fú ròu.** 大虫不吃伏肉。 (lit) A tiger never eats an animal who has submitted. (fig) The strong (should) never bully the weak who have already submitted. "Don't kick a man when he's down." [Cf. WM, chap. 2; note: *dàchóng* (lit) "big worm" is a colloquial term for "tiger."]

7　**Dàchóng chī xiǎo chóng.** 大虫吃小虫。 (lit) Big tigers eat smaller tigers. (fig) [Usually said of traditional officials:] the strong(er) (always) bully the weak(er). "Big fish eat little fish." [Note: *dàchóng* (lit) "big worm" is a colloquial term for "tiger"; see also *dà yú chī xiǎo yú* below.]

8　**Dàchóng è shā bù chī ér.** 大虫恶杀不吃儿。 (lit) [However] ferocious a tiger [is, it will] not eat [its own] cubs. (fig) Parents won't do any harm to their children. [Cf. Jīngshì Tōngyán, chap. 20; note: *dàchóng* (lit) "big worm" is a colloquial term for "tiger."]

9　**Dà chuán hái pà dīng yǎn lòu.** 大船还怕钉眼漏。 (lit) [Even a] big ship can't stand a hole as [small as] a nail. (fig) One may suffer great loses if one neglects trifles. [See also *dà bìng cóng shā qǐ* above and *xiǎo dòng bù bǔ* below.]

10　**Dà chuán lànle háiyǒu sānqiān gè dīng.** 大船烂了还有三千个钉。 (lit) After a big ship has rotted away, there still remain three thousand nails. (fig) Even if it has gone bankrupt, a wealthy family still has some property to fall back on. [See also *bǎi zú zhī chóng* above; *fùle pín*; *qióng suī qióng*; *shòu sǐ de luòtuo* and *tóng pén lànle* below.]

11　**Dàchù-zhuóyǎn; xiǎo chù zhuóshǒu.** 大处着眼，小处着手。 [Always] keep the whole picture in mind, [but] carry out the immediate tasks detail by detail. [Note: *dàchù-zhuóyǎn* has become a set phrase.]

12　**Dàdǎn tiānxià qù dé; xiǎoxīn cùnbù-nánxíng.** 大胆天下去得，小心寸步难行。 [Be] bold [and you] can go anywhere in the world; [be] overly prudent [and you] can hardly take one step forward. [Cf. Jǐngshì Tōngyán, chap. 21; note the *chengyu*: *cùnbù-nánxíng* meaning "unable to do anything." Vs. *xiǎoxīn tiānxià* below.]

13　**Dà dào yánjiē zǒu, wú zāng bù dìngzuì.** 大盗沿街走，无赃不定罪。 (lit) [A] great robber [may] walk along the streets [because without the] spoils, he cannot be proven] guilty. (fig) Without concrete proof, one cannot accuse someone. [See also *qiángdào yánjiē* below.]

14　**Dǎ de yāhuan; xià de xiǎojie.** 打的丫鬟，吓的小姐。 (lit) Smack the maid [and] frighten [her] mistress. (fig) Punish one as an example to others. [Cf. Wǔ Sōng, chap. 3; see also *dǎle luózi* and *dǎle yātou* below and the colloquial *suyu* expression: *shā jī gěi hóuzi kàn*, "(to) kill a chicken in order to frighten the monkeys."]

15　**Dǎ de yī quán qù; miǎnde bǎi quán lái.** 打的一拳去，免得百拳来。 Strike one blow first [and you'll] avoid being struck a hundred blows. [Cf. Wǔ Sōng, chap. 2; see also *dǎ rén bù guò* below.]

16　**Dàfēng chuī dǎo wútóng shù, zǒng yǒu pángrén shuō chángduǎn.** 大风吹倒梧桐树，总有旁人说长短。 (lit) [If a] strong wind blows over a Chinese parasol tree, there will always be onlookers [who will] gossip about the matter. (fig) Whenever something unusual happens, people will always gossip about the causes (so just ignore them). [Note: *shuō cháng dào duǎn*, "to gossip about others"; see also *fènghuáng fēishang* below.]

17　**Dà gǒu pá qiáng, xiǎo gǒu kàn yàng.** 大狗爬墙，小狗看样。 (lit) [If an] old dog climbs a wall, a young dog will follow suit. (fig) "Like father, like son." [Rhyme; derogatory.]

18　**Dǎ gǒu yào yòng qín hǔ lì.** 打狗要用擒虎力。 (lit) [If one wants] to strike a dog, [one] should use the same strength as [if one were] trying to catch a tiger. (fig) One should never underestimate one's enemy.

19 **Dǎ gǒu (zhīqián, yào) kàn zhǔrén (miàn).** 打狗
（之前，要）看主人（面）。(lit) (Before) [you]
beat a dog, [you'd] better think about [its] mas-
ter('s face). (fig) Before you attack someone, better first find out who else you are likely to offend.
[Rhyme; cf. *JPM*, chap. 79; this is a rhymed version of *dǎ gǒu kàn zhǔrén*; see also *dǎle yātou* and
yào dǎ, kàn niáng below.]

20 **Dàguān bùyào qián, bùrú zǎo guītián; xiǎo guān
bù suǒ qián, érnǚ wú yīnyuán.** 大官不要钱，
不如早归田；小官不索钱，儿女无姻缘。
(lit) A high official [who does] not take bribes
had better retire; a petty official [who does] not
extort money [will] not [be able to get his] sons
and daughters married. (fig) Corrupt officials get
rich while honest officials suffer from poverty.
[Rhyme; note: *guītián*, (lit) "go back to (one's)
fields," means "to retire from public life."]

21 **Dàhǎi bùjìn lòu zhī.** 大海不禁漏卮。(lit)
[Even] the ocean is not immune from [being
dried up by] seepage. (fig) No matter how much
one accumulates, if one spends foolishly, it will
be exhausted in the end. [*Lòu zhī* refers to a leaky
ancient wine vessel; cf. *Xǐngshì Yīnyuán Zhuàn*,
chap. 94.]

22 **Dàhǎi bù xián shuǐ duō; dà shān bù xián tǔ duō.**
大海不嫌水多；大山不嫌土多。(lit) The
oceans do not dislike [there being too] much
water [and] the mountains do not dislike [there
being too] much earth. (fig) A person of great
knowledge will not refuse to absorb more knowledge. The more learned one becomes, the more
one realizes how much more there is to learn.
[Rhyme; see also *jiàn cù suī lì* below.]

23 **Dàhǎi fúpíng yě yǒu xiāngféng zhī rì.** 大海浮萍
也有相逢之日。(lit) [Even] patches of float-
ing duckweed on the ocean may meet some day.
(fig) Who knows when one will meet (again) by
chance? It's a small world. [Cf. *Jǐngshì Tōngyán*,
chap. 11; see also *chuántóu bù yù* above and
shuāngrì bù zháo below.]

24 **Dà hé lǐ yǒu shuǐ, xiǎo hé mǎn.** 大河里有水，
小河满。(lit) If there's water in the big rivers,
the small rivers will be full. (fig) The individual
will get rich if the community prospers. [See also
guó lǐ yǒu and *xiǎo hé zhǎngshuǐ* below and the
following entry.]

25 **Dà hé wú shuǐ, xiǎo hé gān.** 大河无水，小河
干。(lit) [When the] big rivers have no water,
the small rivers run dry. (fig) The individual will
have nothing if the community has none [so we
should all work hard for the common good]. [See
also the preceding entry.]

26 **Dà hé yǒu yú; xiǎo hé yǒu xiā.** 大河有鱼，小
河有虾。(lit) Big rivers have fish [while] small
rivers have shrimp. (fig) Big or small, each place
has its own advantages.

27 **Dǎ hǔ hái děi qīnxiōngdì; shàngzhèn xū jiào fù-zǐ
bīng.** 打虎还得亲兄弟，上阵须叫父子兵。
(lit) [To] hunt tigers [one] must have a brother's
help, [and to go] into battle [one] needs [the help
of] an army of fathers and sons. (fig) Only very
close friends and relatives will risk their lives to

help you in times of danger. [Note: *qīnxiōngdì* literally refers to "blood brothers"; cf. *JW*, chap.
81.]

28 **Dǎ hǔ yào lì; zhuō hóu yào zhì.** 打虎要力，捉
猴要智。(lit) To fight a tiger requires strength,
[but] to catch a monkey requires intelligence.
(fig) Different problems must be dealt with in different ways.

29 **Dǎi gè què'r, hái děi diū bǎ mǐ.** 逮个雀儿，还得
丢把米。(lit) [Even to] catch a sparrow, [one]
has to spill a little rice. (fig) If one wants to accomplish anything, one has to put forth some effort or
investment.

30 **Dāizhě bù lái; láizhě bù dāi.** 呆者不来，来者不
呆。(lit) The stupid wouldn't come [and] those
who [do] come aren't stupid. (fig) People usually
have some (ulterior) motive for coming, so be
careful! [Rhyme; see also *láizhě bùshàn* below.]

31 **Dāizi bāngmáng; yuè bāng, yuè máng.*** 呆子帮
忙，越帮越忙。[When a] fool helps, the more
(s)he helps, the more difficult [the job becomes].

32 **Dàjiā guīnǚ, xiǎo jiā qī.** 大家闺女，小家妻。
(lit) [A] daughter [from a] rich family [should not]
marry into an ordinary family. (fig) People should
marry within their own social class. [Note: the
chengyu: méndāng-hùduì, "well-matched in social
and economic status for marriage."]

33 **Dàjiā mǎ('ér), dàjiā qí.** 大家马（儿），大家骑。
(lit) Everybody [has the right to] ride the communal horse. (fig) Everyone has a right to enjoy
a commonly shared benefit. [Cf. *Érnǚ Yīngxióng
Zhuàn*, chap. 38; see also *gōngzhòng mǎ* below.]

34 **Dà jiàng wú qì cái.** 大匠无弃材。(lit) A great
craftsman has no wasted materials. (fig) (1) A
great craftsman makes use of every bit of his materials. (2) A great leader can make the best use
of the abilities of each of his subordinates.

35 **Dà jiān sì zhōng; dà zhà shì xìn.** 大奸似忠，大
诈是信。The most treacherous look loyal [and]
the most deceitful look trustworthy.

36 **Dǎ jǐng fánghàn; jī gǔ fáng jī.** 打井防旱，积谷
防饥。(lit) Dig wells [to provide] against times
of drought; store grain [to provide] against times
of famine. (fig) One should always be prepared
against hard times ahead.

37 **Dǎ jìn tiānxià wú díshǒu, jǐnfáng Gāoyóu Jīn
Déjiē.** 打尽天下无敌手，谨防高邮晋
阶。(lit) [Even if you can] beat [everyone in] the
world [and] no one is [your] equal, still [you must]
guard against Jin Dejie, [the hero of] Gaoyou
[county in Jiangsu province]. (fig) There's always someone better and stronger to beware of.
[Based on a popular Qing dynasty story.]

38 **Dà jiǔ zuì rén; dàhuà nǎorén.** 大酒醉人，大
话恼人。(lit) [Just as] strong liquor gets people
drunk, [so] big talk [i.e., bragging] gets people an-
noyed.

39 **Dǎle héshang, mǎn sì xiū.** 打了和尚，满寺
羞。(lit) [When one] monk gets beaten, the
whole temple [is] shamed. (fig) If one member of
a group is attacked or insulted, the whole group
is injured.

40 **Dǎléi de yǔ xià bù cháng.*** 打雷的雨下不长。 (lit) Rain [accompanied by] thunder [will] not last long. (fig) Anything that comes fast, goes fast. [A modern paraphrase of *Lǎozǐ*, chap. 23.]

41 **Dǎle luózi, mǎ yě jīng.** 打了骡子，马也惊。 (lit) [If one] beats a mule the horse(s) will also be frightened. (fig) If one is punished the others will be frightened; punish one as an example to others. [See also *dǎ de yāhuan* above, and the colloquial *súyǔ* expression: *shā jī gěi hóu kàn*, "(to) kill a chicken in order to frighten the monkeys."]

42 **Dǎle yātou, chǒule xiǎojie.** 打了丫头，丑了小姐。 (lit) [If one] has beaten the servant girl, [one] has made [her] mistress lose face. (fig) Before you attack someone, you had better consider who his or her superior is. [See also *dǎ gǒu zhīqián* and *dǎ de yāhuan* above.]

43 **Dà lì shǐ fānchuán.** 大力驶翻船。 (lit) [Too] strong a force applied [will] overturn a boat. (fig) One should do everything in a manner appropriate to that particular situation.

44 **Dà lòu, lòu bù gān; xì lòu, lòu gān táng.** 大漏漏不干，细漏漏干塘。 (lit) A big leak [will soon be noticed and stopped up so that] everything will not leak out, [while] a small leak [may be overlooked and the] pond [will become] dry. (fig) Small problems or hidden dangers are often the most harmful in the long run.

45 **Dàlù shēng zài zuǐ biān.** 大路生在嘴边。 (lit) The highway comes out of [one's] mouth. (fig) (If you're lost, just) ask and you'll know which way to go. [Cf. *Dàng Kòu Zhì*, chap. 80; *Hé Diǎn*, chap. 6; see also *lù zài zuǐ biān* and *zuǐ dǐxià* below.]

46 **Dàlù tōngtiān, gè zǒu yī biān.** 大路通天，各走一边。 (lit) The highway leads to Heaven, [but] each goes his own way. (fig) Do not interfere with other people's business. [Rhyme; see also *chē zǒu chēdào* above.]

47 **Dàmén guān de jǐn, wāifēng chuī bù jìn.** 大门关得紧，歪风吹不进。 (lit) [If one's] gate is tightly closed, no ill wind can blow in. (fig) If one observes strict standards of conduct, one won't be influenced by evil practices. [Rhyme.]

48 **Dànàn bù sǐ, bì yǒu hòufú (/hòu lù).** 大难不死，必有后福(/后禄)。 [One who] survives a great disaster must [be destined] for good fortune [ever] after. [Also said . . . *bì yǒu hòu lù* in *Gǔ-Jīn Xiǎoshuō*, chap. 21.]

49 **Dān chí, bù dān cuò.** 担[/耽]迟不担[/耽]错。 [Better to] be slow than to be wrong. [Cf. *Wǔ Sōng*, chap. 2; see also *máng lǐ yào zhēnzhuó* and *zuòshì guò chí* below.]

50 **Dà néng yǎn xiǎo; hǎi nà bǎi chuān.** 大能掩小，海纳百川。 (lit) The great [can] cover [the transgressions of] the small, [just as] the sea [can] hold water from hundreds of rivers. (fig) One should always be large-minded; *noblesse oblige*. [Note: *yǎngài*, "to cover"; see also *dàrén bù jì* below.]

51 **Dāng bó niúméng; bù dāng pò jǐ shī.** 当搏牛虻，不当破虮虱。 (lit) [When one] ought to be catching horseflies [which can sting], [one] should not [waste one's time] picking nits [(lit) breaking lice eggs]. (fig) One should keep the general goal in sight instead of getting bogged down in petty details.

52 **Dāngchāi de guān miàn shàng kàn qì; xíngchuán de kàn fēngshi shǐ péng.** 当差的官面上看气，行船的看风势使篷。 A "gofer" [always] watches his superior's countenance, [just as] a boatman trims his sails according to the force of the wind. [Note *dāngchāi de* refers to "runners" or assistants employed by *yámen* county magistrates in traditional China; see also *guān qīng, yámen shòu* below.]

53 **Dǎng de zhù qiān rén shǒu; wǔ bu zhù bǎi rén kǒu.** 挡得住千人手，捂不住百人口。 [One] can hold out against a thousand people's fists, [but one] cannot cover up a thousand people's mouths. (fig) Public opinion cannot be suppressed. [Rhyme; see also *fáng mín zhī kǒu* below.]

54 **Dāng duàn bù duàn; fǎn shòu qí luàn.** 当断不断，反受其乱。 (lit) [If one does] not decide [when one] ought to decide, then [one will] suffer the [(lit) its] consequences [later on]. (fig) Indecision invariably leads to trouble. [Rhyme; cf. *Dōng Zhōu Lièguó Zhì*, chap. 4]

55 **Dāng guān de dòngdong zuǐ; dāngbīng de pǎo shé tuǐ.** 当官的动动嘴，当兵的跑折腿。 An officer [only] gives orders, [but his] soldiers [have to] run their legs off [doing all the work]. [Rhyme; note: *dòngzuǐ*, "to talk without doing."]

56 **Dāng háng yàn dāng háng.** 当行厌当行。 People of the same trade dislike each other. [Cf. *JPM*, chap. 3; see also *tónghang shì yuānjia* below.]

57 **Dāngjiā cái zhī cháimǐ jià; yǎng zǐ fāng xiǎo fù niáng ēn.** 当家才知柴米价，养子方晓父娘恩。 One has to have been responsible for a household's affairs before one knows the price of rice and firewood [just as] one has to have raised children before one [can] understand parental love. [Cf. *JW*, chap. 28; see also *bù dāng héshang* above.]

58 **Dāngjiā rén; è shuǐgāng.** 当家人，恶水缸。 The one [who is] in charge of a household's affairs [is disliked as much as a] slop bucket [by all other family members]. [Usually said of an extended family in traditional China; cf. *JPM*, chap. 51; *DRC*, chap. 68; see also the following two entries.]

59 **Dāngjiā rén jí lǎo; jìn huǒ de shāojiāo.** 当家人疾老，进火的烧焦。 (lit) The one who is responsible for a household's affairs gets old faster [just as] things close to a fire get burned first. (fig) The heavy responsibility of managing a large traditional extended family's affairs takes its toll. [Rhyme.]

60 **Dāngjiā sān nián, gǒu yě xián.** 当家三年，狗也嫌。 One who is responsible for managing the household's affairs for three years is hated even

by the [family] dog. [Cf. *JPM*, chap. 75; see also the preceding two entries.]

61 **Dāngjúzhě mí; pángguānzhě qīng.** 当局者迷，旁观者清。(lit) Those [involved] in affairs are confused [while the] onlookers [see more] clearly. (fig) Outsiders can (often) see things more clearly or objectively than those involved. [Cf. *JPM*, chap. 24; *DRC*, chap. 55; *Érnǚ Yīngxióng Zhuàn*, chap. 26.]

62 **Dāngle bīng, bù rèn qīn; chīle liáng, bù rèn niáng.** 当了兵不认亲，吃了粮不认娘。(lit) Having become a soldier, [one should] not recognize [one's friends and] relations; having gone into government service, [one should] not recognize [even one's own] mother. (fig) When one makes a commitment to government or military service, one should not act in the interests of one's friends, relatives, or family. [Rhyme; note: *chī gōngjiā de liáng*, (lit) "to eat the common grain"; (fig) "to be in government service"; see also *gōng ér wàng sī* below.]

63 **Dānglìng guǒzi chèn xiān mài.** 当令果子趁鲜卖。(lit) Sell fruit in season when it is fresh. (fig) Do things at the proper time; "strike while the iron is hot." [See also *chèn rè hǎo* above.]

64 **Dāngmiàn bù qǔ, guòhòu mò huǐ.** 当面不取，过后莫悔。[If you] fail to take [when you've] got the chance, don't regret it later. [Cf. *WM*, chap. 15; see also *dāngquán ruò bù* and *yǒuquán bù yòng* below.]

65 **Dāngmiàn jiào zǐ; bēihòu jiào qī.** 当面教子，背后教妻。[One may] admonish one's children in the presence of others, [but one's] wife only in private. [See also *jiào fù chūlái* below.]

66 **Dāngmiàn shǔ qián bù wéi xiǎo jiàn.** 当面数钱不为小见。[On completing a transaction,] counting money right in front of the other party is not [to be] regarded as pettiness (or disrespect). [Rhyme.]

67 **Dāngquán ruò bù xíng fāngbiàn rú rù bǎo shān kōngshǒu huí.** 当权若不行方便如入宝山空手回。(lit) To be in [a position of] power [but] not help others is like returning from a treasure-hill empty-handed. [Originally a Buddhist exhortation to benevolence; later understood to mean not taking advantage of one's position for the benefit of oneself or one's friends and relatives; see also *dāngmiàn bù qǔ* above and *gōng mén lǐ* below.]

68 **Dāngzhe ǎirén, bié shuō ǎi huà.** 当着矮人，别说矮话。(lit) In front of dwarves one should not talk about midgets. (fig) Don't talk about people's shortcomings or defects in front of them. "Don't speak of halters in the house of a hanged man." [Cf. *DRC*, chap. 46; see also *ǎizi miànqián* above and *mò fàn rén huì* below.]

69 **Dà niú hǎo qiān; xiǎo hào nán zhuā.** 大牛好牵，小耗难抓。(lit) Leading an ox is easy [but] catching a mouse is difficult. (fig) Honest people are easy to deal with, but sly people are not.

70 **Dàn jiǔ duō bēi huì zuì rén.** 淡酒多杯会醉人。(lit) [Too] many cups of [even] light wine can make a person drunk. (fig) Many small problems can give rise to a major problem.

71 **(Dān sī bù chéng xiàn,) dú mù bù chéng lín.** (单丝不成线,) 独木不成林。(lit) (A single [strand of] silk does not make a thread, [and] one] single tree does not make a forest. (fig) Only in unity is there strength. [Cf. *DRC*, chap. 56; *Fēngshén Yǎnyì*, chap. 72; *Wǔ Sōng*, chap. 2; the second half is often used alone (q.v.).]

72 **Dàn tiān yī dǒu; bù tiān yīkǒu.** 但添一斗，不添一口。[It's] better to add one [more] bushel of rice [one time than to] add one [more] mouth [to feed for a lifetime to one's family or group.] [Rhyme; cf. *Érnǚ Yīngxióng Zhuàn*, chap. 30; note: *dànyuàn* "rather"; note: a *dǒu* is a large measure of grain equal to one deciliter.]

73 **Dàn xíng hǎoshì, mò wèn qiánchéng.** 但行好事，末问前程。[If one] really cares to do good deeds, never ask [what benefit one will get from it in the] future. [Cf. *Gǔ-Jīn Xiǎoshuō*, chap. 30; *Jìnghuā Yuán*, chap. 71; see also *shī ēn mò wàng bào* below.]

74 **Dǎn yù dà ér xīn yù xiǎo; zhì yù yuán ér xíng yù fāng.** 胆欲大而心欲小；智欲圆而行欲方。[One] should be both bold and careful [as well as] flexible in thought and upright in behavior. [Cf. *Huái Nán Zǐ; Zhǔ Shù Xùn*.]

75 **Dān zé yì zhé; zhòng zé nán cuī.** 单则易折，众则难摧。(lit) A single [stick is] easy to break; a group [of sticks is] hard to break. (fig) In unity lies strength. [Based on a popular story about a dying father's advice to his family, using chopsticks as an example; see also *chái wú sān gēn* above and the following entry.]

76 **Dān zhú bù chéng pái.*** 单竹不成排。(lit) A single bamboo cannot make a raft. (fig) In unity lies strength. [See also the preceding entry.]

77 **Dào bùtóng, bù xiāng wéi móu.** 道不同，不相为谋。[People of] different doctrines (or beliefs) won't unite in a common cause. [Cf. *Shǐ Jì: Lǎozǐ Hán Fēi Lièzhuàn*.]

78 **Dào chéng cóng, bì yǒu bài; rén chéngqún, bì chū guài.** 稻成丛，必有稗；人成群，必出怪。[Just as in a] thicket of rice, there must be "barnyard grass" [a weed that looks like rice], [so in every] crowd of people, there must be bad [ones]. [Rhyme.]

79 **Dào dào wú shī, yǒu chì bù fēi.** 道道无师，有翅不飞。[If one] misappropriates Taoism without [learning from a] master, [even] with wings [one can] not fly [up to heaven]. (fig) If one tries to copy without proper guidance or understanding, one can never become a true adept.

80 **Dāo dùn, shí lái mó; rén chǔn, mònàihé.** 刀钝石来磨，人蠢没奈何。A blunt knife may be sharpened on stone, [but if] a person is stupid, there is no help for it.

81 Dào duō, dǎchū mǐ lái; rén duō, jiǎng chū lǐ lái. 稻多打出米来，人多讲出理来。(lit) [Just as] many rice plants produce rice, [so] many people['s] discussion produces reason. (fig) "Many heads are better than one." [Rhyme.]

82 Dào gāo yī chǐ; mó gāo yī zhàng.* 道高一尺，魔高一仗。(lit) If the Tao/Buddha rises one foot, the demon rises ten feet. (fig) [Originally:] The virtuous are outnumbered by evil doers. [Now:] One just force outnumbers an opposing force, or, no sooner does one solve one problem than another arises. [Cf. Chū Kè Pāi'àn Jīngqí, chap. 36; JW, chap. 50; Mao Dun's novel Zǐyè (Midnight). The change in meaning is discussed by Guang Lu in Shū Lín 1979; note: ten Chinese feet (chǐ) equal one zhàng.]

83 Dāo kuài bùpà bózi cū. 刀快不怕脖子粗。(lit) A sharp knife [chops the head off fast,] however thick the neck may be. (fig) One can surmount any difficulty and undertake any task as long as one has strong determination and courage.

84 Dàolù bùpíng, pángrén xǐ. 道路不平，旁人躥。(lit) [If the] road is uneven, people's [constant] walking [will make it even]. (fig) If there's injustice, people will speak out. [Cf. Xīngshì Yīnyuán Zhuàn, chap. 23; see also lù bùpíng, yǒu rén cǎi below, and the suyu expression: lù jiàn bùpíng, bá dāo xiāng zhù, "[a swordsman] seeing an injustice on the highway draws his sword to assist"; note that bùpíng means both "uneven" and "unjust."]

85 Dǎoméi, kēshuì duō. 倒霉瞌睡多。(lit) [People having] bad luck often doze off. (fig) Those who are having a run of bad luck are often depressed.

86 Dāoqiāng wú yǎn. 刀枪无眼。(lit) Swords [and] spears have no eyes. (fig) Once weapons are taken up, it is inevitable that someone will be hurt. [Note: dāoqiāng, (lit) "swords [and] spears," means "weapons"; cf. Yuè Fēi Zhuàn, chap. 18.]

87 Dào shénme shān shàng, chàng shénme gē.* 到什么山上，唱什么歌。(lit) Whatever mountain [one] visits, [one should] sing its songs. (fig) One should follow the local customs or act appropriately according to the immediate situation. "When in Rome, do as the Romans do." [Cf. Mao Zedong's essay "Fǎnduì Dǎng Bāgǔ"; see also rùjìng wèn jìn below.]

88 Dào suī xiǎorén, zhì guò jūnzǐ. 盗虽小人，智过君子。Although robbers and thieves [are] petty persons, [they] surpass gentlemen in intelligence. (fig) Do not ignore or underestimate potentially harmful petty people. [See also zéi shì xiǎorén below.]

89 Dào wú jiǎo, qiè bù zháo. 盗无脚，窃不着。[If] thieves and robbers [did] not have [someone with a] foot ["on the inside"], [they] could not succeed. [Rhyme; see also zéi wú lǐ dǐ below.]

90 Dāozi yào kuài, duō jiā gāng; zhīshi yào shēn, gōngfu cháng. 刀子要快多加钢，知识要深工夫长。[For a] knife [to be] sharp [requires] adding more steel; [for] knowledge to be profound [requires] long hard work. [Rhyme.]

91 Dǎ qiáng bǎnr, fān shàngxià; qiánrén shìjiè, hòurén shōu. 打墙板儿翻上下，前人世界后人收。(lit) [Just as when] building [up] a wall, the form boards [constantly change their relative positions] up and down [as the wall gets higher], [so] the world [i.e., conditions of the forebears is inherited by [their] descendants. (fig) Sometimes a person or generation is up, and sometimes they're down; the fate of human beings is changeable. [Note: the first half is in JPM, chap. 90; shìjiè is sometimes tiántǔ, "lands."]

92 Dǎ qiáng yě shì dòngtǔ. 打墙也是动土。(lit) Building a wall also [requires] moving earth. (fig) Building a wall requires almost as much work as building a house, so why not build a house? If one is going to undertake something, why stop at half measures? Why not "go the whole hog"/go "all the way"? [Cf. DRC, chap. 29; note: dòngtǔ (lit) "moving earth"; (fig) "to build a house or tomb."]

93 Dà qū bì yǒu dà shēn. 大屈必有大伸。(lit) [After] great bending there must be great expansion. (fig) One who suffers great humiliation will have great accomplishments later. [See also dàzhàngfu néng qū below.]

94 Dǎ rén bù guò xiān xiàshǒu. 打人不过先下手。In a fight, it's best to strike the first blow. [Cf. Fēngshén Yǎnyì, chap. 3; see also dǎ de yī quán qù above.]

95 Dàrén bù jì xiǎorén guò. 大人不计小人过。A great man does not remember a petty person's trespasses. [Cf. JPM, chap. 51; see also chéng dàshì and dà néng yǎn xiǎo above and jūnzǐ bù jìn below.]

96 Dǎ rén mò dǎ xī; dào rén mò dào shí. 打人莫打膝，道人莫道实。(lit) Never strike a person on the knee (cap) [i.e., a vital spot], [and] never criticize a person completely. (fig) Always leave a person some "face" or a "way out." [Cf. Song dynasty Yuan Cai's Xuán Shī Shǐ Fàn, chap. 2.]

97 Dǎ rén sān rì yōu; màrén sān rì xiū. 打人三日忧，骂人三日羞。[If you] hit someone, [you will] worry [for] three days, [and if you] curse at someone, [you will feel] ashamed [for] three days. [Rhyme.]

98 Dǎrén xiū dǎ liǎn; màrén xiū jiēduǎn. 打人休打脸，骂人休揭短。In a fight, never smack [someone's] face [and] in a quarrel never rake up [someone's] faults. [Cf. JPM, chap. 86.]

99 Dǎrén yì quán; fáng rén yī jiǎo. 打人一拳，防人一脚。(lit) [If you] strike somebody [with] a fist, be prepared for a kick [back]. (fig) If one attacks others, one has to be prepared for retaliation.

100 Dǎ sǎn bùrú yún zhē rì; shān shàn bùrú zìlái fēng. 打伞不如云遮日，扇扇不如自来风。(lit) [To] protect [one from] the sun, better than an umbrella is [to have] clouds; [to] cool oneself, better than a fan is [to have] a natural breeze. (fig) A good opportunity is better than expending a lot of effort.

D

101 **Dǎ shé bù sǐ, zì yí qí hài.*** 打蛇不死，自遗其害。(lit) [If a] snake is not beaten to death, [one] will suffer harm [from] it [later]. (fig) In dealing with an enemy or a problem, deal with it completely, or it may come back to haunt you later. [Cf. *Xǐngshì Héngyán*, chap. 22; also said *dǎ shé bù sǐ, zhuǎn bēi yǎo rén*, "If a snake is not beaten to death, it will turn around and bite you"; see also *dí bùkě zòng* above and *fánghǔ-guīshān* below.]

102 **Dǎ shé, dǎ qī cùn.*** 打蛇，打七寸。(lit) [When] striking a snake, hit [it on the first] seven inches [i.e., on its neck]. (fig) Strike your enemy in a vital place. [Cf. *Hé Diǎn*, chap. 1; *Rúlín Wàishǐ*, chap. 14.]

103 **Dǎ shé xiān dǎ tóu; qín zéi xiān qín wáng.*** 打蛇先打头，擒贼先擒王。(lit) [Just as when] striking a snake, first strike [it on the] head, [so] to catch robbers, first catch [their] chief. (fig) Catching the ringleaders is most important.

104 **Dàshì huà xiǎo; xiǎoshì huà liǎo.** 大事化小，小事化了。(lit) Reduce big troubles into small ones, [and] small ones into nothing. (fig) Keep trouble to the minimum. Just let things pass. [Rhyme; a piece of advice; cf. *DRC*, chap. 62; *Guānchǎng Xiànxíng Jì*, chap. 47.]

105 **Dàshì, mán bu liǎo zhuāng xiāng; xiǎoshì, mèi bu zhù línjū.** 大事，瞒不了庄乡；小事，昧不住邻居。(lit) One can't keep a big secret in a village or a small one from one's neighbors. (fig) One can't cover up the truth from one's neighbors. [See also *yǒushì, nán mán sìlín* below.]

106 **Dǎ shì téng; mà shì ài.** 打是疼，骂是爱。(lit) Smacking is fondness [and] scolding is love. (fig) Smacking or scolding [usually one's husband or children] are signs of love. [Cf. *Xǐngshì Yīnyuán Zhuàn*, chap. 3; *Érnǚ Yīngxióng Zhuàn*, chap. 37; note: *téng'ài*, "to love dearly."]

107 **Dà shítou bù lí xiǎo shítou diàn.** 大石头不离小石头垫。(lit) [In building a wall] big stones cannot be separated from the small stones [needed] to fill in [the cracks between]. (fig) A leader or able person needs support from others to accomplish anything great. [See also *yī gè líba* and *mǔdan suī hǎo* below.]

108 **Dà shù dǐxià hǎo chéngliáng.** 大树底下好乘凉。(lit) Great trees are good for shade. (fig) A person's livelihood or career is assured if one has an influential patron. [Cf. *Hé Diǎn*, chap. 10; see also *dà shù zhīxià* below.]

109 **Dà shù dǐxia zhǎng bù chū hǎo cǎo.** 大树底下长不出好草。(lit) No fine grass will grow under a big tree. (fig) Young people who depend too much on their parents or inferiors who stand in awe of their superiors cannot develop themselves well or bring their own potential into full play.

110 **Dà shú nián chéng gébì huāng.** 大熟年成隔壁荒。(lit) A year of bumper harvest [for you might] be [one of] starvation [for your] neighbor. (fig) Favorable conditions are available to everyone, but it depends on one's own efforts to make the most of them.

111 **Dà shù zhīxià, cǎo bù zhān shuāng.** 大树之下，草不沾霜。(lit) The grass under big trees doesn't suffer frost. (fig) One who is under the protection of the rich and powerful won't be bullied or hurt. [Cf. *Xǐngshì Yīnyuán Zhuàn*, chap. 48; see also *dà shù zhīxià* above.]

112 **Dǎsǐ mài quán de; yānsǐ huìshuǐ de.** 打死卖拳的，淹死会水的。(lit) [It is the] professional boxer [who gets] beaten to death [and it is the] good swimmer [who] drowns. (fig) An able person often fails because of carelessness or negligence. Even an expert can be taken in. [See also *shàn yóu zhě nì* below.]

113 **Dǎtiě bùxī tàn.** 打铁不惜炭。(lit) [While] forging iron, spare no charcoal. (fig) Spare no effort if you want to accomplish anything successfully.

114 **Dǎtiě, kàn huǒhou; shuōhuà, kàn yǎnsè.** 打铁，看火候，说话，看眼色。[Just as when] forging iron, [one must] watch the state of the fire, [so while] speaking, [one must] watch the expression [in the eyes of one's listener]. [See also *chūmén guān tiānsè* above.]

115 **Dǎ tù de bù xián tù duō; chī yú de bùpà yú xīng.** 打兔的不嫌兔多，吃鱼的，不怕鱼腥。(lit) ●● Those who hunt hares never complain that there are too many hares, [and] those who love fish do not care about the smell of fish. (fig) "One can never have too much of a good thing." "The more the better."

116 **Dǎ yī rì huāgǔ, yóu yī rì jiānghú.** 打一日花鼓，游一日江湖。(lit) [As long as one] passes one['s] days beating the flower drum [i.e., as a street performer], then one is merely passing one['s] days as an aimless vagabond. (fig) Some people just idly waste their time going through the superficial motions without taking any initiative in the work of their lives. [Note: *huāgǔ* "flower-drum opera" is popular in Hunan, Hubei, Jiangxi, and Anhui provinces; note: *liúluò jiānghú* means "to live a vagabond life."]

117 **Dà yǒu dà nán; xiǎo yǒu xiǎo nán.** 大有大难，小有小难。(lit) The big have big difficulties [and] the small have small ones. (fig) Large or small, every group has difficulties of its own. [Said of families, groups, but not individuals; rhyme; also said *dà yǒu dà de nánchu; (xiǎo yǒu xiǎo de nánchu)*, as in *DRC*, chap. 6.]

118 **Dǎyóu de qián bù mǎi cù.** 打油的钱不买醋。Money for [cooking] oil [should] not [be used to] buy vinegar. (fig) One should make an overall budget or plan and then stick to it.

119 **Dà yú chī xiǎo yú; xiǎo yú chī xiāmi.** 大鱼吃小鱼，小鱼吃虾米。(lit) Big fish eat small fish, [and] small fish eat shrimp eggs. (fig) The strong bully the weak. [See also *dàchóng chī xiǎo chóng* above.]

120 **Dǎyú de bù lí chuán biān; dǎchái de bù lí shān biān.** 打鱼的不离船边，打柴的不离山边。(lit) Fishermen won't leave their boats, nor [will] woodcutters leave the mountains. (fig) People are tied to their means of making a living. [Rhyme; see also *jìn shān shǐ mù* below.]

121 **Dā zài lán lǐ biànshì cài; (zhuō zài lán lǐ biànshì xiè).** 搭 在 篮 里 便 是 菜，（捉 在 篮 里 便 是 蟹）。(fig) [Anything] thrown into a basket [counts as] food stuff ([and anything] caught in a basket [counts as] crabs). (fig) Something is better than nothing. Don't be choosy. Just make do with whatever is at hand. [Cf. *Xīngshì Héngyán*, chap. 3.]

122 **Dàzhàngfu néng qū néng shēn.** 大丈夫能屈能伸。(lit) A great man can bend [and] can extend. (fig) A great man knows when to pull back and when to give full play to his ambition. [A paraphrase of *Kǒngzǐ Jiā Yǔ: Qū Jié Jiě*; cf. *Wǔ Sōng*, chap. 6; see also *dà qū bì yǒu* and *shíshíwùzhě* below and the following entry.]

123 **Dàzhàngfu xiàngshí'érdòng.** 大丈夫相时而动。A great man (*sic*) considers the times [and circumstances] before [he] acts. [A paraphrase of *Zuǒ Zhuàn: Yǐn Gōng 11 Nián*; cf. *DRC*, chap. 4; note: *xiàngshí'érdòng* is an idiomatic phrase meaning "to bide one's time"; see also the preceding entry.]

124 **Dà zhě bùfú xiǎo.** 大者不服小。Those [in] higher [positions] never submit to those [in] lower [positions]. [Cf. *Liáo Zhāi Zhì Yì: Shào 9 Niáng*.]

125 **Dà zǒu, duō diē; dà jiáo, duō yē.** 大走多跌，大嚼多噎。[If one] walks too fast, [there are] more [chances to] fall; [if one] eats too fast, [there are] more [chances to] choke. (fig) One should never go to extremes in one's speech or behavior. [Rhyme.]

126 **Dé dào, duō zhù; shī dào, guǎ zhù.** 得道多助，失道寡助。(lit) [A cause which has] attained righteousness, many [will] support, [but a cause which has] lost right, [only a] few [will] support. (fig) A just cause enjoys abundant support, while an unjust cause finds little support. [Note: *dé dào* also refers to the Taoist concept of following the Tao or Way of the Universe. This is a quotation from Mencius (*Mèngzǐ: Gōng Sūn Chǒu, Xià*), often used by Mao Zedong; the two halves are used independently as *chengyu*; see also *dé rénxīn zhě* below.]

127 **Dé huángjīn bǎi jīn bùrú dé Jì Bù yī nuò.** 得黄金百斤不如得季布一诺。(lit) Better than to get a hundred catties of gold is to have one promise from Ji Bu. (fig) A trustworthy promise is more precious than gold. [Cf. *Shǐ Jì: Jì Bù Rǎng Bù Lièzhuàn*; note: Jibu, a general under Xiang Yu in the Han dynasty, was known for his trustworthiness; note: *nuòyán*, "promise(s)."]

128 **Děi fàngshǒu shí, xū fàngshǒu; děi ráorén chù, qiě ráorén.** 得放手时须放手，得饶人处且饶人。(lit) When [you] should let go, [you] must let go; where [you] should forgive people, then do so. (fig) Be lenient whenever you can; forgive others wherever you can. [Cf. *DRC*, chap. 61; *Xīngshì Héngyán*, chap. 5.]

129 **Děi hǎo xiū, biàn hǎo xiū.** 得好休，便好休。(lit) [If a dispute should be] let go, then [just] let it go. (fig) In dealing with conflicts or disputes, if possible don't prolong them, which may simply

make matters worse. [This is from the operatic version of *Xīxiāng Jì*, Act 4, Scene 2, from the famous aria entitled *Kǎo Hóng*, "Interrogating the Maid Hong Niang."]

130 **Děi rěn, qiě rěn; děi nài, qiě nài; bù rěn, bù nài; xiǎoshì chéng dà.** 得忍且忍，得耐且耐，不忍不耐，小事成大。(lit) [What you] should bear, bear; [when you should] be patient, be patient; [if you are] not forbearing [and] patient, small matters [can] become big [ones]. (fig) Restrain yourself as much as possible, otherwise small problems will become big ones.

131 **Dé kuàihuo, qiě kuàihuo.** 得快活且快活。(lit) [If one] gets happiness, then be happy. (fig) One should enjoy oneself whenever one gets the opportunity. "Gather ye rosebuds while ye may."

132 **Dé lǐ, ràng sān fēn.** 得理让三分。(lit) [Even if one] is right, [one should be willing to] give in thirty-percent. (fig) One should always be accommodating to others.

133 **Dēng bù diǎn, bù liàng; (lǐ bù shuō, bùmíng).** 灯不点不亮，(理不说不明)。[Just as] a lamp won't be bright until it is lit, ([so people will] not understand unless reason has been explained). [The first part is commonly used alone, with the second part left unsaid, like a *xiehouyu*; see also the following entry.]

134 **Dēng bù liàng, yào rén tī; rén bùmíng, yào rén tí.** 灯不亮要人剔，人不明要人提。[If the oil] lamp won't be bright, [its rush wick] should be trimmed; if people don't understand, someone has to explain. [Rhyme; see also the preceding entry.]

135 **Děng rén yì lǎo; děng chuán nán dào.** 等人易老，等船难到。Waiting for someone [to return], the anticipation or anxiety makes it] easy [to feel that one is getting old [faster], [just as] waiting for a ship to arrive [makes one feel time goes more] slowly. [See also *mǎ chí xián biān qīng* below.]

136 **Dēngtái zhào rén, bù zhào jǐ.** 灯台照人不照己。(lit) A lamp sheds light on others, [but] not on itself. (fig) One sees the shortcomings of others easily, but not one's own. [See also *húli bù zhī* and *lǘ bù zhī zì chǒu* and *niú bù zhī jiǎo wān* and *rén guàn shì jǐ guò* below.]

137 **Dé piányi chù shī piányi.*** 得便宜处失便宜。Wherever [one tries to] gain petty advantages, [one will] suffer a loss. [Cf. *Xīngshì Héngyán*, chap. 16; *Chū Kè Pāi'àn Jīngqí*, chap. 24.]

138 **Dé rén dīshuǐ zhī ēn, xū dāng yǒng quán xiāng bào.*** 得人滴水之恩，须当涌泉相报。(lit) [If one] receives a water drop of kindness, [one should] repay [it with a] flowing spring. (fig) One should repay several fold kindness that one received in times of difficulty.

139 **Dé rén qiáncái, yǔ rén xiāo zāi.** 得人钱财，与人消灾。(lit) [If a monk or a Taoist priest] gets money [from someone, he should pray that the] person [who gave the money may] avoid disaster. (fig) If you take favors from someone, you owe them a service. [Cf. *Xīngshì Yīnyuán Zhuàn*, chap. 34; see also *chī de hǎo* above and *duàn rén wǎn* below.]

D

140 **Dé rénxīn zhě dé tiānxià; shī rénxīn zhě shī tiānxià.** 得人心者得天下, 失人心者失天下。 Those who gain the people's hearts [will] gain [power] over all the world; those who lose in the people's hearts [will] lose [power] everywhere. [See also dé dào, duō zhù above and the following entry.]

141 **Dé rén zhě chāng; shī rén zhě wáng.** 得人者昌, 失人者亡。 (lit) One who wins over the people [will] prosper; one who loses the people [will] fail. [Cf. R3K, chap. 29; see also dé dào, duō zhù above and the preceding entry.]

142 **Déyì bùkě wàngxíng.** 得意不可忘形。 [Once one has] attained [one's] goal, [one] should not get carried away [with success]. [Note the chengyu: déyì wàngxíng, "to become dizzy with success"; see also the following entry.]

143 **Déyì bùkě zài wǎng.** 得意不可再往。 (lit) [Where one has] achieved success, [one] cannot expect [to do so] again. (fig) Don't expect to make a second success in a place where you have made one already. Quit while you're ahead. Don't push your luck. [Cf. Guānchǎng Xiànxíng Jì, chap. 53; Sān Xiá Wǔ Yì, chap. 10; see also the preceding entry.]

144 **Dé yīn róngyì; dé yùn nán.** 得音容易, 得韵难。 (lit) [In learning to sing Chinese opera] getting the sounds right is easier than getting the flavor right. (fig) In learning (artistic expression), it's easier to get the form right than to get the spirit right. [This is a quotation from a famous Beijing opera singer, Tan Fuyin; note: yùnwèi, "pleasing quality"; "charm (of singing)."]

145 **Dé yì sài dēngkē.** 得意赛登科。 (lit) Satisfaction with oneself far surpasses succeeding in the imperial examinations. (fig) Self-satisfaction is the most satisfying feeling. [Note: Under the traditional system, dēngkē meant to succeed in the provincial level imperial examinations leading to the rank of jìnshì.]

146 **Dé yī, wàng shí; dé shí, wàng bǎi.** 得一望十, 得十望百。 [If a person] gets one, [(s)he will] want ten; [if (s)he] gets ten, [(s)he will] long for a hundred. [Cf. Xīngshì Héngyán, chap. 33; note the colloquial súyǔ expression: dé cùn, jìn chǐ, "Give an inch, and (s)he/they'll want a foot."]

147 **Dézhì māor, xióng sì hǔ; bài líng yīngwǔ bùrú jī.** 得志猫儿雄似虎, 败翎鹦鹉不如鸡。 (lit) [A] cat [that] achieves [its] goal [acts as] fierce as a tiger; [a] parrot [whose] feathers fall off is less valued than a chicken. (fig) A petty person who succeeds in something puts on great airs, while a great person who has fallen from power is looked down upon. [Cf. Suí Táng Yǎnyì, chap. 8; JW, chap. 61; see also bǎle máo de fènghuáng above.]

148 **Dé zhòng guǐshén qīn.** 德重鬼神钦。 [A person of] noble character [and] high prestige [even] ghosts [and] gods hold in esteem. [Note: the chengyu: dégāo-wàngzhòng, "enjoying high prestige and commanding universal respect."]

149 **Diànfáng yǒu gè zhǔrén; miào lǐ yǒu gè zhùchí.** 店房有个主人，庙里有个住持。 (lit) [An] inn has an [inn]keeper, [and a] temple has an abbot. (fig) Wherever one goes, there is someone in charge. [Cf. DRC, chap. 48.]

150 **Diǎn làzhú bù zhī yóu jià.** 点蜡烛不知油价。 (lit) [One who] burns candles doesn't know the price of oil. (fig) One doesn't know about or is not interested in things which one is not directly connected with.

151 **Diǎn tǎ qī céng bùrú àn hù yī dēng.** 点塔七层不如暗护一灯。 (lit) Lighting up a seven-storied pagoda is not as [good as] lighting a lamp in a dark place. (fig) Better to do good which brings practical benefits to people rather than just for show. [See also jiù rén yī mìng and ruòbù yǔ rén and zàijiā jìng fùmǔ below.]

152 **Diāo bùzú; gǒu wěi xù.** 貂不足，狗尾续。 [Since there are] insufficient marten tails, dog tails [are used to] complete [the job]. (fig) When there's not enough of (of the original) good material, one has to make do with second rate material to finish up. It's a wretched sequel to a fine work. [A rhyme sometimes used self-deprecatingly by authors of sequels. Note: marten tails were used to decorate the black gauze caps worn by high officials in ancient China; as a chengyu: gǒu wěi xù diāo.]

153 **Diāo xī pímáo; xiàng hù yá.** 貂惜皮毛，象护牙。 (lit) The marten treasures [its] fur [and] the elephant protects [its ivory] tusks. (fig) People value their integrity and reputation most.

154 **Diàoyú bù zài jí shuǐ tān.** 钓鱼不在急水滩。 (lit) [Good] fishing is not on the banks [where the] water flows rapidly. (fig) Only act when conditions are favorable to your enterprise.

155 **Diàoyú yào wěn; zhuō yú yào hěn.** 钓鱼要稳，捉鱼要狠。 (lit) Casting for fish requires patience; landing a fish requires resolution. (fig) Each problem must be dealt with in its own way.

156 **Dí bùkě zòng.** 敌不可纵。 Don't let the enemy get away. [Cf. Zuǒ Zhuàn: Xī Gōng 33 Nián; see also dǎ shé bù sǐ above and fánghǔ-guīshān below.]

157 **Dì dòng sān chǐ, zì kāi fèng.** 地冻三尺，自开缝。 (lit) When the earth is frozen three feet deep, naturally [there will] appear cracks. (fig) When things get to a certain point, changes are naturally bound to occur. [Vs. bīng dòng sān chǐ above.]

158 **Dié dà, wǎn xiǎo; kēzhe, pèngzhe.** 碟大碗小，磕着碰着。 [If the] plate [is] big [and the] bowl [is] small, knocking [and] banging [are inevitable]. (fig) It's inevitable that there will be arguments or quarrels within a family or group. [Cf. DRC, chap. 83.]

159 **Diē yǒu bùrú niáng yǒu; niáng yǒu bùrú lǎopo yǒu; lǎopo yǒu hái yào kāikai kǒu; fú rú zì yǒu.** 爹有不如娘有，娘有不如老婆有，老婆有还要开开口，弗如自有。 (lit) Father having is not as good as Mother having; Mother having is not as good as [one's] wife having; [even if one's] wife has [it, one] still has to open up

[one's] mouth [to ask for it, which is still] not as good as having [it] oneself. (fig) Having things of one's own is best. "God bless the child that's got his own."

160 **Dìng fǎ bù shì fǎ.** 定法不是法。(lit) Fixed methods are not methods. (fig) Don't follow a rigid routine. Don't always "go by the book." [Cf. *Érnǚ Yīngxióng Zhuàn*, chap. 16.]

161 **Dìngshù nán táo.** 定数难逃。[What is] destined by fate is hard to avoid. [Cf. *R3K*, chap. 62; *Fēngshén Yǎnyì*, chap. 24; note: *dìngshù*, (lit) "fixed number," or *qìshù* are colloquial expressions for matters destined by fate.]

162 **Dī qí yě yǒu shénxian zhāo.** 低棋也有神仙着。(lit) A poor chess [player can] also make a remarkable move. (fig) People of little ability can sometimes do something remarkable. [Note: *zhāo(shù)* refers to a move in Chinese chess; from a Qing dynasty essay on poetry by Wang Yinggui entitled "Liú Nán Suí Bǐ," vol. 1; see also *yú zhě qiān lǜ* below.]

163 **Dītóu bùjiàn, táitóu jiàn.** 低头不见, 抬头见。(lit) [If you do] not see [someone while] looking down, [you'll] see [him or her while] looking up. (fig) One is always running into one's neighbors, so it is important to remain on good terms with them.

164 **Dìtóu wénshū, tiěgū tǒng.** 地头文书, 铁箍桶。(lit) Local documents [recording the decision in a legal case are like an] iron-hooped barrel. (fig) A case settled in the local court can hardly be reversed. Local authorities are most difficult to deal with. [Cf. *Rúlín Wàishǐ*, chap. 45.]

165 **Diūle bàng'er, bèi gǒu qī.** 丢了棒儿, 被狗欺。(lit) [When one] loses [one's] stick, [one will be] attacked by dogs. (fig) (1) One should always maintain one's defensive ability; never let your guard down. (2) If one loses one's patron, one will be attacked by others.

166 **Diū qián shì mǎizhǔ; shuōhuà shì xiánrén.** 丢钱是买主, 说话是闲人。(lit) [In business deals one who] puts down cash is a [true] customer, [while one who just] talks is [just] a bystander. (fig) Actions speak louder than words. [Cf. *Wǔ Sōng*, chap. 2; also said dī 递 qián . . ., etc.; see also *bǎobiǎn shì mǎizhǔ* above.]

167 **Dì yǒu gāodī; rén yǒu guìjiàn.** 地有高低, 人有贵贱。[Just as] land can be high or low, [so] people can be high or low [in social position].

168 (**Dì zài rén zhòng;**) **shì zài rén wéi.** (地在人种,) 事在人为。(lit) ([Whether the] land [is productive] depends on people's farming; [similarly] whether] things [can be accomplished] depends on the human effort. (fig) Human effort is the decisive factor in success. [The second part is usually used alone.]

169 **Dìzhǔ de suànpán yī xiǎng, nóngmín de yǎnlèi zhí tǎng.** 地主的算盘一响, 农民的眼泪直淌。Once [they hear the] sound of the landlord's abacus, the peasants' tears start to flow. [A rhyme from two modern communist novels describing a landlord's exploitation in traditional pre-1949 China.]

170 **Dōng bù jiè yī; xià bù jiè shàn.** 冬不借衣, 夏不借扇。(lit) Don't borrow clothes in winter nor fans in summer. (fig) Don't borrow things which are essential for the owner's own well-being.

171 **Dōng bù jí wēn; xià bù jí liáng.** 冬不极温, 夏不极凉。(lit) In winter don't dress too warmly [and] don't dress too coolly in summer. (fig) Both excessive warmth or coolness will make one sick. [A common Chinese folk belief; see also *chūn wǔ, qiū dōng* above and *dōng jiǔ, wǔ sì* and *duō yī, duō hán* below.]

172 **Dōng bùkě fèi gě; xià bùkě fèi qiú.** 冬不可废葛; 夏不可废裘。(lit) In winter [one] should not throw away hemp cloth[ing], nor fur [clothing] in summer. (fig) One should always be farsighted in one's planning. [Cf. *gě*, (lit) hemp cloth, refers generally to summer garments; *qiú* refers to fur garments.]

173 **Dōngfāng bù liàng, xīfāng liàng; hēile nánfāng yǒu běifāng.*** 东方不亮, 西方亮, 黑了南方有北方。(lit) [When it is] dark in the east, [it is] light in the west; [when things are] dark in the south there is still [light in] the north. (fig) No matter how dark things look at one time or place, there are always brighter prospects around the corner. There's always a way. [A rhyme quoted by Mao Zedong in his *Zhōngguó Gémìng Zhànzheng de Zhànlüè Wèntí* ("Problems of Strategy in China's Revolutionary War").]

174 **Dōng hé lǐ méi shuǐ, xī hé lǐ zǒu.** 东河里没水, 西河里走。(lit) [If] there's no water in the eastern river, [we may] go to the western river. (fig) There's always a way. [See also *chē dào méi è lù* and *dōngfāng bù liàng* above.]

175 **Dōngjì jìn bǔ; kāichūn dǎ hǔ.*** 冬季进补, 开春打虎。(lit) Take tonics in winter [and you can] beat a tiger in the spring. (fig) One should always prepare against the future. [Note: Chinese believe in taking tonics generally and also that one's digestion is better in winter.]

176 **Dòng jiǔ, wǔ sì.** 冻九, 捂四。[Stay] cold [in the] ninth [lunar month (October), and continue to] muffle [yourself] up [in the] fourth [lunar month (May), and you'll stay healthy]. [See also *chūn wǔ, qiū dōng* above.]

177 **Dòngle Tàisuì tóushàng tǔ, wú zāi yě yǒu huò.** 动了太岁头上土, 无灾也有祸。(lit) [If you] move the earth above the head of Taisui [the earth god], [you will] surely invite calamity or disaster [upon yourself]. (fig) If you provoke someone far superior in power or strength, it is certain that you'll get into trouble sooner or later. [Taisui is the God of Earth, equivalent to Jupiter; *Tàisuì tóu shàng dòng tǔ* "to provoke someone far superior in power or strength" is a common colloquial expression.]

178 **Dòng lǐ de shé, bù zhī chángduǎn.** 洞里的蛇, 不知长短。(lit) [When a] snake [is] in [its] hole, [one does] not know how long [it is]. (fig) When problems haven't been fully revealed, it's hard to evaluate the situation accurately.

D

179 **Dōngmén shī tiáo biǎndan, xīmén shuōshì zào-fǎn.** 东门失条扁担，西门说是造反。(lit) [When] a carrying-pole is lost at the east [city] gate, [rumors spread to the] west [city] gate [that there] is a rebellion [on the east side]. (fig) Never believe rumors. [Rhyme; see also *huà jīng sān zhāng zuǐ* below.]

180 **Dōng shān lǎohǔ chī rén; xī shān lǎohǔ yě chī rén.*** 东山老虎吃人，西山老虎也吃人。 (lit) Tigers in the eastern hills kill people, [and] so do tigers in the western hills. (fig) Evil people are the same everywhere on earth. [See also *tiānxià wūyā* below.]

181 **Dòngsǐ bù kǎo dēng qián huǒ; èsǐ bù tiǎn māo shèng shí.** 冻死不烤灯前火，饿死不舔猫剩食。(lit) [Even if you're] freezing to death, never warm [yourself] by a lamp, [and even if you're] starving to death, never lick a cat's left-overs. (fig) Even if one is in difficult circumstances, one should not compromise one's moral integrity. [See also *dòngsǐ yíngfēng* below.]

182 **Dòngsǐ xiánrén; è sǐ chán rén.** 冻死闲人，饿死馋人。(lit) Idlers freeze to death [and] greedy ones starve to death. (fig) One should work hard and be moderate in one's living habits.

183 **Dòngsǐ yíngfēng zhàn; èsǐ bù zhéyāo.** 冻死迎风站，饿死不折腰。(lit) [Even when] freezing to death, stand and face the wind, [and even when you're] starving to death, don't bend (at the waist). (fig) One should maintain one's integrity at all costs. [See also *dòngsǐ bù kǎo* above.]

184 **Dōngxi bùkě luàn chī; xiánhuà bùkě luàn jiǎng.** 东西不可乱吃，闲话不可乱讲。Don't eat anything indiscriminately [and] don't talk about anything loosely [or you'll get into trouble]. [See also *bìng cóng kǒu rù* above.]

185 **Dōng yǒu yí hán; xià yǒu qí yǔ.** 冬有祁寒，夏有奇雨。(lit) In winter there is extreme cold [and] in summer extraordinary downpours. (fig) Always prepare for the worst eventuality. [Note: *yí hàn* refers to the extreme cold of winter.]

186 **Dòufu duōle yī bāo shuǐ; kōnghuà duōle wú rén xìn.** 豆腐多了一包水，空话多了无人信。[If there is] a lot of beancurd, [there will be] a lot of water [running out of it, and if one makes] too much empty talk, no one [will] believe [you].

187 **Dòufu hǎo chī, mò nán tuī.** 豆腐好吃，磨难推。(lit) Beancurd is tasty, [but] pushing the millstone [to grind it] is hard. (fig) Anything good comes as the result of hard effort.

188 **Duāngōng bù shuō guǐ, dài lǐ méiyǒu mǐ.** 端公不说鬼，袋里没有米。(lit) [If a] shaman does not talk [about] ghosts, there won't be any rice in [his (sic)] bag. (fig) In order to achieve their goals, cheaters must tell lies, (so beware!)

189 **Duàn lǐ, bù duàn qīn.** 断理不断亲。 [One should] make judgments [based on truth or] reason, not [on whether one is] related [to someone or not]. [See also *bāng lǐ, bù bāng qīn* above.]

190 **Duān rén wǎn, guī rén guǎn.** 端人碗，归人管。(lit) [If you] hold a bowl [supplied by] another, [then you're] under his or her control. (fig) One who works for others is under their control. [Rhyme; see also *dé rén qiáncái* above.]

191 **Duànsòng yīshēng wéiyǒu jiǔ.** 断送一生惟有酒。(lit) The ruination of one life [comes] solely from liquor. (fig) Liquor can ruin a person's life. [Cf. *JW*, chap. 71.]

192 **Dú bìng, dúyào yī.** 毒病，毒药医。(lit) A malignant disease [has to be] treated with toxic medication. (fig) (One must) fight poison with poison; "fight fire with fire." [Note the *chengyu*: *yǐdú-gōngdú*, "use poison to attack poison."]

193 **Dú bùjìn de shū; zǒu bù wán de lù.*** 读不尽的书，走不完的路。(lit) [One] can never read all the books [and] never travel all the roads [in the world]. (fig) There are no limits to knowledge; there is no end to learning. [Rhyme; see also *shū náng wú dǐ* and *xué dào lǎo* below.]

194 **Dú chái nán shāo; dúzǐ nán jiāo.** 独柴难烧，独子难教。(lit) [Just as] burning a single stick of firewood is difficult, [so] is educating an "only son." (fig) Single children tend to be spoiled. [Rhyme.]

195 **Dùhé zì yǒu rén chēng gāo.** 渡河自有人撑篙。[When one gets to a] ferry crossing, there must be boat polers. (fig) Don't worry too early; there will surely be a way. [See also *chē dào shān qián* above.]

196 **Duī jīn bùrú jī gǔ.** 堆金不如积谷。(lit) Accumulating gold is not as [good as] storing up grain. (fig) It is better to labor diligently than to take risks trying to get rich.

197 **Duì kè bù děi chēn gǒu.** 对客不得嗔狗。(lit) Never swear at the dog in front of guests. (fig) It is not good to criticize one's subordinates before outsiders and make them lose face in public. [See also *dāngmiàn jiào zǐ* above.]

198 **Duìniú-tánqín, yīqiào-bùtōng.** 对牛弹琴，一窍不通。(lit) [When] "playing a lute to a cow," [there's] "not one chance of getting through" [to it]. (fig) Don't waste your time trying to explain things to fools. Don't "cast pearls before swine." [Cf. *Wǔ Sōng*, chap. 1; note: this saying has been formed by combining two separate fused phrase literary idioms or *chengyu*.]

199 **Duìzhe xiānsheng jiù jiǎng shū; duìzhe túfū biàn jiǎng zhū.** 对着先生就讲书，对着屠夫便讲猪。(lit) Talk about books with a teacher [and] talk about pigs with a butcher. (fig) Choose an appropriate topic when you talk to different people. [Rhyme.]

200 **Dù jī mò yǔ bǎo rén yán.** 肚饥莫与饱人言。(lit) A hungry person has no language [in common] with a full one. (fig) The poor and the rich have no common understanding. [See also *bǎo hàn bù zhī* above.]

201 **Dǔ jìn dào; yín jìn shā.** 赌近盗，淫近杀。(lit) Gambling is close [to] theft [and] lewdness to murder. (fig) Gambling often leads to theft, and lewdness (adultery, etc.) often leads to murder.

[Cf. *Jǐngshì Tōngyán*, chap. 35; see also *dǔ yǔ dào wéi lín* below.]

202 **Dǔ lǐ wú jūnzǐ.*** 赌里无君子。Among gamblers there are no gentlemen. [See also *dǔqián chǎng shàng* below.]

203 **Dú mù bù chéng lín.** 独木不成林。(lit) A single tree does not make a forest. (fig) Cooperation is necessary for success. [This is an idiomatic phrase meaning "one alone cannot accomplish much"; see also *dān sī bù chéng xiàn* above.]

204 **Dú mù nán zhī (dàshà).** 独木难支 (大厦)。(lit) A single log cannot prop up (a building). (fig) One person alone cannot save a bad situation. One cannot sustain adversity all by oneself. [Note: *dúmù-nánzhī* is used alone as a *chengyu* with this meaning.]

205 **Duō bùrú shǎo; shǎo bùrú hǎo.** 多不如少, 少不如好。[In artistic creation], more is not as [good as] less, [and] less is not as [good as] good [quality]. [Rhyme.]

206 **Duō dé bùrú xiàn dé.** 多得不如现得。(lit) Having more [on credit] is not as good as [what one can] have [in hand]. (fig) Credit is not as good as the same amount in cash. "A bird in the hand is worth two in the bush." [See also *shē sān bùdí* and *shí shē bùrú* below.]

207 **Duǒ de liǎo chūyī; duǒ bu liǎo shíwǔ.*** 躲得了初一, 躲不了十五。(lit) [One may] get off [paying one's debts on] the first [of the month, but] not by the fifteenth. (fig) Sooner or later, one has to face up to things. [Note: *duǒzhài*, "to avoid one's creditors."]

208 **Duō gè péngyou, duō tiáo lù; duō gè yuānjia, duō dào qiáng.** 多个朋友多条路, 多个冤家多道墙。One more friend, one more road [of opportunity for you]; one more opponent, one more wall [blocking your way]. [Cf. *Wǔ Sōng Yǎnyì*, chap. 18; note the expression: *ménlù duō*, "to have many connections or routes of opportunity."]

209 **Duō gè xiānglú, duō gè guǐ.** 多个香炉, 多个鬼。(lit) The more incense burners, the more devils. (fig) The more people involved, the more trouble there will be.

210 **Duō lǐ lāomo.** 多里捞摸。(lit) [From] among many [it is easier to] take. (fig) The more, the better. [Cf. *JW*, chap. 2; said by the Monkey King Sun Wukong of his three hundred and sixty tricks.]

211 **Duō míng zhī māo bǔ shǔ bì shǎo.** 多鸣之猫捕鼠必少。(lit) Cats which mew a lot must [be those which] catch few rats. (fig) People who talk a lot are usually "all talk and no action"; "barking dogs do not bite." [Rhyme; see also *ài jiào de mǔjī* above and *huì zhuō lǎoshǔ* below.]

212 **Duōnián lǎoniang, cuò jiǎn qídài.** 多年老娘, 错剪脐带。(lit) [Even an] experienced midwife [can] make blunders [in] cutting umbilical cords. (fig) Even an experienced worker may sometimes make mistakes. [See also *cōngming yīshì* above.]

213 **Duōnián línjū biànchéng qīn.** 多年邻居变成亲。Long-standing neighbors [will] become [as close as] relatives. [See also *jiǔ zhù línjū* and *yuǎnqīn bùrú* below.]

214 **Duō suàn shèng shǎo suàn.** 多算胜少算。(lit) More planning [will] conquer less planning. (fig) More strategy wins the battle. [Cf. *Sūnzǐ's Jì Piàn*; *Hàn Shū: Zhào Chōng Guó Zhuàn*.]

215 **Duō xiǎng chū zhìhuì.** 多想出智慧。Diligent thinking produces wisdom.

216 **Duō yán, zhòng suǒ jì.** 多言众所忌。Loquacity is disliked by everyone. [See also *duōzuǐ tǎorénxián* below.]

217 **Duō yī, duō hán; shǎo yī, bó hán.** 多衣多寒, 少衣薄寒。(lit) [In winter,] the more clothes [you wear], the colder [you feel]; the less [you wear], the less cold [you feel]. (fig) If one wears too much clothing in winter, it will reduce one's resistance to the cold, whereas wearing less clothing will help build up one's resistance to cold. [A common Chinese belief; see also *chūn wǔ, qiū dòng* and *dōng bù jí wēn* above.]

218 **Duō yī shì bùrú shǎo yī shì.** 多一事不如少一事。Better to do less than more [in order to avoid trouble]. [Usually attributed to bureaucrats; see also *duō zuò, duō cuò* below.]

219 **Duō yòngbīng bùrú qiǎo yòng jì.** 多用兵不如巧用计。(lit) Using more troops is not as good as using a clever strategy. (fig) Cleverness is better than brute force.

220 **Duō zāihuā, shǎo zāi cì; liúzhe rénqíng hǎo bànshì.** 多栽花少栽刺, 留着人情好办事。(lit) Plant more flowers [and] fewer thorns; always take others' feelings into consideration [and it will be] easier to handle [your] affairs. (fig) One's dealings with others in life will be easier if one always takes others' feelings into consideration. "You'll catch more flies with honey than with vinegar." [See also *jīngāng-nùmù* below.]

221 **Duōzuǐ tǎorénxián.** 多嘴讨人嫌。[One who] talks too much is disliked by everyone. [See also *duō yán, zhòng suǒ jì* above.]

222 **Duō zuò, duō cuò; shǎo zuò, shǎo cuò; bù zuò, bùcuò!** 多做多错, 少做少错, 不做不错! The more [one] does, the more mistakes; the less [one] does, the fewer mistakes; [if one] does nothing, [there will be no mistakes at all, which is] not bad! [A play on words between the literal and idiomatic meanings of *bùcuò*, "no mistake/not bad"; a satirical rhyme said of or attributed to bureaucrats; see also *duō yī shì* above and *shěngshì, wú shì* below.]

223 **Dǔqián chǎng shàng wú fù-zǐ.** 赌钱场上无父子。(lit) At the gambling table, there are no fathers and sons. (fig) When gambling, the only important thing is money. In gambling, there is no friendship or kinship; it's every man for himself. [Cf. *WM*, chap. 38; see also *dǔ lǐ wú jūnzǐ* above.]

224 **Dú quán nán dǎ hǔ.** 独拳难打虎。(lit) Single-handed, [it's] difficult to fight a tiger. (fig) One person alone cannot accomplish anything great.

225 **Dúshé zǒngshì qū zǒu; pángxiè zǒngshì héngxíng.** 毒蛇总是曲走, 螃蟹总是横行。Poisonous snakes always move in a zigzag manner, [and] crabs always scuttle sideways. (fig) Bad people's basic evil nature can't be changed.

226 **Dúshé zuǐ lǐ méi hǎo yá.** 毒蛇嘴里没好牙。 (lit) In the mouth of poisonous snakes there are no good teeth. (fig) Never believe anything from the mouth of an evil person. [See also *gǒu zuǐ lǐ* below.]

227 **Dúshū bù zhī yì bùrú kěn shùpí.** 读书不知意不如啃树皮。 Reading without understanding🕐 is as [tasteless as] chewing tree bark. [Rhyme.]

228 **Dú xíng bù kuì xíng; dú qǐn bù kuì shí.** 独行不愧形，独寝不愧食。 (lit) Walking alone, [one is] unashamed of [one's] behavior; sleeping [i.e., living] alone, [one is] unashamed of [one's] lifestyle. (fig) A gentleman is always a gentleman regardless of whether others observe him or not. [Rhyme; cf. *Yànzǐ Chūnqiū: Wài Piān 8 Zhī 4*; note:

qǐnshí "sleeping and eating" and *qǐjū-yǐnshí*, (lit) "rising, sleeping, drinking, eating," (fig) "daily activities."]

229 **Dǔ yǔ dào wéi lín.** 赌与盗为邻。 (lit) Gambling and robbery are neighbors. (fig) Gamblers inevitably turn to theft or robbery when they have lost all their money. [See also *dǔ jìn dào* above.]

230 **Dù zhòng ér mù zhé; xì dà ér qiáng huài.** 蠹众而木折，隙大而墙坏。 (lit) Too many worms and the rafter [will] snap; [when a] crack [gets too] big, the wall [will] crumble. (fig) Many small problems can bring disaster.

231 **Dúzǐ dé xī.** 独子得惜。 "Only-children" are treasured [by their parents]. [Cf. *Jǐngshì Tōngyán*, chap. 31.]

E

1 **É bù shí yú, dà guò yā.** 鹅不食鱼，大过鸭。 (lit) Geese, [which] don't eat fish, [grow] bigger than ducks, [which do]. (fig) External conditions, favorable or not, are not the decisive factors in success.

2 **È chūlai de jiànshi; qióng chūlai de cōngming.** 饿出来的见识，穷出来的聪明。 Out of hunger comes wisdom; out of poverty comes cleverness.

3 **È dùzi děngbude zǎodào huáng.** 饿肚子等不得早稻黄。 (lit) [When one is] hungry [one] can't wait for the early rice to ripen. (fig) When one is in dire straits, promises of future aid are of no help. [See also *yuǎn shuǐ bù jiù* below.]

4 **Ègǒu bù pà mùgùn.** 饿狗不怕木棍。 (lit) A hungry dog is not afraid of a wooden club. (fig) A wicked person in a tight corner will take desperate action. [See also *tùzi jíle* and *zhí xiàng gǎn gǒu* below.]

5 **Ègǒu yǎo rén, àn xià kǒu.** 恶狗咬人，暗下口。 (lit) [When] vicious dogs bite people [they] do so without warning. (fig) The most dangerous people to be wary of are those who hide their evil intentions. [See also *chī rén de* above and the following entry.]

6 **Ègǒu yǎo rén bù lù yá.** 恶狗咬人不露牙。 (lit) Fierce dogs bite people without showing [their] teeth. (fig) The most dangerous people to be wary of are those who hide their evil intentions. [See also the preceding entry.]

7 **È hǔ nán dòu dù lǐ shé.** 恶虎难斗肚里蛇。 (lit) [Even a] ferocious tiger is hard [put to] struggle [against a] snake inside [its] belly. (fig) It is harder to deal with an enemy within one's own ranks. A fortress is more easily attacked from within.

8 **È jī bù pà dǎ; è rén bù jiǎng liǎn.** 饿鸡不怕打；饿人不讲脸。 (lit) [Just as a] hungry chicken is not afraid of being beaten, [so a] hungry person is not afraid of losing face.

9 **È le tián rú mì; bǎole mì bù tián.** 饿了甜如蜜，饱了蜜不甜。 (lit) [When one is] hungry, [everything is as] sweet as honey, [but when one is] full, [even] honey is not sweet. (fig) "Hunger is the best sauce."

10 **È lóng nán dòu dìtóushé.** 恶龙难斗地头蛇。 (lit) [Even a] fierce dragon is hard [put to] struggle against a local snake. (fig) It's hard to deal with local tyrants on their own ground. [See also *qiáng lóng bù yā* below.]

11 **È mǎ, èrén qí.** 恶马，恶人骑。 (lit) A vicious horse [is] ridden [by a] vicious person. (fig) In the end the wicked will fall afoul of their own ilk. [See also *èrén zì yǒu* below.]

12 **Ēn'ài fūqī bù dàotóu.** 恩爱夫妻不到头。 An affectionate couple [can]not [live together] to the end [of their lives]. [A peasant belief.]

13 **Ēn bù fàngzhài.** 恩不放债。 (lit) Helping [others] is not lending money at interest [to be repaid]. (fig) One should not expect to be repaid for helping others.

14 **Ēn duō chéng yuàn.** 恩多成怨。 Too many kindnesses [can] lead to resentment.

15 **Ēn jiāng ēn bào; chóu jiāng chóu bào.** 恩将恩报，仇将仇报。 Return good for good [and] evil for evil. [Cf. *Gǔ-Jīn Xiǎoshuō*, chap. 31.]

16 **Ēnrén xiāngjiàn, fènwài yǎn míng; chóurén xiāngjiàn, fènwài yǎn zhēng.** 恩人相见分外眼明，仇人相见分外眼狰。 [When one] sees [one's] benefactor, [one's] eyes particularly brighten; [when one] sees [one's] enemy, [one's] eyes particularly flash [with hatred]. [Cf. the popular classical opera *Pípá Jì*, chap. 17; see also *chóurén xiāngjiàn* above.]

17 **Ěr bù tīng, xīn bù fán.** 耳不听，心不烦。 Don't listen [to rumors and] you won't be upset. [See also the more common *yányǔ: yǎn bùjiàn, xīn bù fán* below.]

18 **Ér bù xián mǔ chǒu; quǎn bù yuàn zhǔ pín.** 儿 不嫌母丑，犬不怨主贫。 (lit) A son doesn't care [if his] mother is ugly [or not, just as a] dog doesn't complain [if his] master is poor. (fig) People who are related have deep feelings for each other. "Blood is thicker than water." [See also *gǒu bù xián jiā pín* below.]

19 **Ér dà bù yóu niáng.** 儿大不由娘。 [Once] children grow up, [they] won't follow [their] parent['s wishes]. [Cf. *Xǐngshì Yīnyuán Zhuàn*; chap. 89; here *ér* "son(s)" and *niáng* "mother(s)" are metaphors for children and parents.]

20 **Ér duō, mǔ kǔ; yán duō, cài kǔ.** 儿多母苦，盐多菜苦。 [When there are] too many children, a mother suffers, [just as when there is] too much salt, the food tastes bad. [Rhyme.]

21 **Èrén cáng chòu shí.** 恶人藏臭食。 (lit) Evil people store up rotten food. (fig) Some selfish people store up surplus food even till it rots, although others may be starving. Some people are selfish beyond belief.

22 **Èrén nán xíng shànshì.** 恶人难行善事。 Wicked people rarely do anything good.

23 **Èrén xiān gàozhuàng.** 恶人先告状。 (lit) Evil doers sue first [i.e., play the plaintiff]. (fig) Evil doers often defend themselves by attacking their critics (first). "The best defense is a good offense."

24 **Èrén zì yǒu èrén mó.*** 恶人自有恶人魔。 (lit) Evil people will naturally be tortured by other evil people. (fig) Eventually evil people are fated to be tormented by others of their same ilk. One bad deed deserves another. [See *Xǐngshì Héngyán*, chap. 34; *Píng Yāo Zhuàn*, chap. 10; see also *cǎo pà yánshuāng* and *è mǎ, èrén qí* above and *tóng pén zhuàngle* below.]

25 **Èr hǔ xiāng dòu, bì yǒu yī shāng.** 二虎相斗，必 有一伤。 (lit) When two tigers fight, one is sure to be wounded. (fig) When two (powerful) people fight, one is sure to get hurt. [See also *liǎng hǔ xiāng dòu* below.]

26 **Ér-nǚ qīn, bèi bèi qīn; dǎduàn gēbo liánzhe jīn.** 儿女亲辈辈亲，打断胳膊连着筋。 In-law relations [endure] many generations [and cannot be broken, just as a] broken arm is still connected by its sinews. [Rhyme; note: *ér-nǚ qīn* refers to relations between in-laws; see also *ài qīn zuòqīn* above.]

27 **Érnǚ-qíngcháng, yīngxióng qìduǎn.** 儿女情长， 英雄气短。 (lit) [When] young people are passionately in love, [even] great men lose [their] ambition. (fig) When (young) men are in love, their ambition is reduced. [Note the *chengyu*: *érnǚ-qíngcháng*, "passionate love between men and women."]

28 **Ér pà niáng jiāo; miáo pà chóng yǎo.** 儿怕娘 娇，苗怕虫咬。 [With] sons [what one needs to] worry about [is their being] spoiled [by their] mother [just as] seedlings [may be] bitten [by] worms. [Rhyme; see also *címǔ duō bài ér* above.]

29 **Èr rén tóngxīn, qí lì duàn jīn.** 二人同心，其 力断金。 (lit) [When] two persons [are] of one mind, their [combined] sharpness [is powerful enough] to cut gold. (fig) In unity there is strength. [Rhyme.]

30 **Érsūn zì yǒu érsūn fú; mò wèi érsūn zuò mǎ niú.** 儿孙自有儿孙福，莫为儿孙做马牛。 Children will naturally have their own blessings [when they grow up]; [their parents] don't have to work like draft animals [for their children's future]. [Rhyme; cf. *Jǐngshì Tōngyán*, chap. 2 and 40; Mao Dun's *Chūn Cán Jí* (Spring Silkworms).]

31 **Ěr tīng wéi xū, yǎn jiàn wéi shí.** 耳听为虚，眼
• 见为实。 (lit) [What the] ears hear [may be] false; [what the] eyes see is true. (fig) Seeing is believing. [Cf. *Yuè Fēi Zhuàn*, chap. 30; see also the following entry.]

32 **Ěrwén bùrú qīn jiàn.** 耳闻不如亲见。 Hearsay is not as good as seeing for oneself. [Rhyme; cf. *JW*, chap. 48; see also the preceding entry.]

33 **Ér xíng qiān lǐ mǔ dānyōu; mǔ xíng qiān lǐ ér bù chóu.** 儿行千里母担忧，母行千里儿不愁。 [When a] son is a thousand leagues away, [his] mother's heart is heavy with worry, [but] it's not the same if the situation is reversed. [Rhyme; cf. *Yuè Fēi Zhuàn*, chap. 94.]

34 **Èrzhě bùkě jiān dé.** 二者不可兼得。 (lit) [You] cannot have both [at the same time]. (fig) You cannot "have your cake and eat it too."

35 **Érzi bù yǎng niáng, bái téng tā yī chǎng.** 儿子 不养娘，白疼他一场。 [When] a son does not support his mother, [her] affection for him was in vain. [Rhyme.]

36 **Ér zuò de ér dāng; yé zuò de yé dāng.** 儿做的儿 当，爷做的爷当。 A son is responsible for his own actions, [just as] a father is also responsible for *his* own actions. (fig) Each person is responsible for his own actions. [See also *yī rén zuòshì* below.]

37 **Èshì chuán qiān lǐ; hǎoshì bùchūmén.** 恶事传 千里，好事不出门。 Ill news is transmitted a thousand leagues; good news never gets beyond one's [own] door. [Also said *huàishì* . . . etc.; the order of the two halves may be reversed; technically one *lǐ* equals one-half kilometer.]

38 **Èsǐ bù zuò zéi; qūsǐ bù gàozhuàng.** 饿死不做 贼，屈死不告状。 (lit) [Even if you're] starving, don't be a thief, [and even if you're] extremely wronged, don't go to court. (fig) Poor people (in traditional China) could hardly get any justice.

39 **Èsǐ, shì xiǎo; shījié, shì dà.** 饿死事小，失节 事大。 (lit) To starve to death [is a] small matter, [but to] lose one's integrity [is a] great matter. (fig) To die is a small thing compared to betraying one's integrity. [Cf. Lu Xun's *Zhōngguó Xiǎoshuō Shǐ Lüè*; note: *shījié* originally referred to a woman losing her chastity or a widow dishonoring herself by remarrying.]

40 **È wéi huò zhī běn.** 恶为祸之本。 (lit) Evil is the root of disaster. (fig) Sin is the root of sorrow.

41 **Ēyú rénrén xǐ; zhíyán gègè xián.** 阿谀人人喜， 直言个个嫌。 Flattery, everybody likes; straight talk, everybody hates. [Cf. *Jǐngshì Tōngyán*, chap. 17.]

42 **Ēyú yǒu fú; zhíyán gǔ huò.** 阿谀有福，直言 贾祸。 Flattery brings fortune; [while] honest speech buys trouble. [Cf. *Hòu Hàn Yǎnyì*, chap. 47; see also the preceding entry.]

E

F

1 **Fǎ bù chuán liù ěr.** 法不传六耳。 (lit) A (secret) method [or trick should] not be transmitted to six ears. (fig) A secret should not be shared by more than two people. [Cf. *JPM*, chap. 73; *Érnǚ Yīngxióng Zhuàn*, chap. 4.]

2 **Fǎ bù zé zhòng.** 法不责众。 The law cannot be enforced [when] everyone [is an offender]. [Also said *fǎ bù zhì zhòng*.]

3 **Fà duǎn ér xīn cháng.** 发短而心长。 (lit) [The] short[er the] hair, the greater the mind. (fig) Older people are wiser. [Cf. *Zuǒ Zhuàn: Zhāo Gōng 3 Nián*; see also *gānzhe lǎolái tián* below.]

4 **Fǎ hū qí shàng, jǐn dé qí zhōng; fǎ hū qí zhōng, zé dé qí xià.** 法乎其上仅得其中，法乎其中则得其下。 (lit) [If one] takes as a model [something] better, [one will] only get a mediocre [copy]; [if one] takes as a model mediocrity, [one will] get [something] inferior [to that]. (fig) A copy will always be inferior to the model, so try to take the best model you can. [See also *qǔ fǎ hū shàng* below.]

5 **Fà luàn, zhǎo shūzi; xīn luàn, zhǎo péngyou.** 发乱，找梳子，心乱，找朋友。 [When your] hair is in a tangle, look for a comb; [when your] heart is in a tangle, look for a friend.

6 **Fāngcùn dìshang xiǎngcǎo; sān yè diàn nèi yǒu xiánrén.** 方寸地上生香草，三夜店内有贤人。 (lit) [Just as a] square inch [i.e., a small plot] of land [can] produce sweet grass, [so if one stays for] three nights in a small inn [one will meet] a person of virtue. (fig) There are virtuous people everywhere.

7 **Fáng dǎo, yā bù shārén; shétou dǎo, yā shārén.** 房倒压不杀人，舌头倒压杀人。 (lit) A house falling down [will] not crush people to death; [but] a tongue [rising and] falling [can] kill people. (fig) Gossip can harm people. [Cf. *JPM*, chap. 78; see also *bìng cóng kǒu rù* above.]

8 **Fāng de bù gǔn; yuán de bù wěn.** 方的不滚，圆的不稳。 (lit) Square [objects will] not roll, [while] round ones [can]not [stand] steady. (fig) Honest people are not flexible; flexible people are unsteady. No one is perfect in every situation. [See also *fāng shí bù kě* below.]

9 **Fáng fēng xiān yào dǔ dòng.** 防风先要堵洞。 (lit) To guard against the wind, the first [thing one] should [do] is stop up the holes [in the wall]. (fig) To protect against being corrupted, one should first resist small temptations.

10 **Fáng huàn yú wèirán.** 防患于未然。 (lit) [One should] prevent trouble before it happens. (fig) "An ounce of prevention is worth a pound of cure." [As a chengyu: *fánghuàn-wèirán*; see also *jūnzǐ fáng huàn wèi rán* below.]

11 **Fànghǔ-guīshān, bì yǒu hòuhuàn.** 放虎归山，必有后患。 (lit) [If one] releases a tiger back to the mountains, it's sure to be a source of trouble later on. (fig) Don't let your enemies off easily or you'll regret it later. [Rhyme; as a chengyu: *fànghǔ-guīshān*, also *zònghǔguīshān*, "to cause calamity for the future"; see also *dǎ shé bù sǐ* and *dí bùkě zòng* above and *yī rì zòng dí* below and the following entry.]

12 **Fànghǔ-guīshān, qín hǔ nán.** 放虎归山，擒虎难。 (lit) [After] releasing a tiger back to the mountains, [it's] difficult to catch the tiger [again]. (fig) If one releases a captured enemy, it is all the harder to capture him again. [Cf. *Wǔ Sōng*, chap. 6; note also the expression *fàng lóng rù hǎi*; *zònghǔguīshān*, (lit) "to release a dragon into the sea, and let a tiger go back to the mountains"; (fig) "to let a dangerous enemy go." See also *qín hǔ yì* below and the preceding entry.]

13 **Fáng jūnzǐ, bù fáng xiǎorén.*** 防君子，不防小人。 [Certain (cosmetic or ineffective) security measures may] stop a gentleman [but] not a low person.

14 **Fáng mín zhī kǒu shènyú fáng chuān.** 防民之口甚于防川。 It's more difficult to stop the people's mouths than to block a river. (fig) Public opinion cannot be stopped. [Cf. *Guó Yǔ: Zhōu Yǔ, Shàng*; see also *dǎng de zhù qiān rén* above.]

15 **Fāng mùtou bù gǔn; yuán mùtou bù wěn.** 方木头不滚，圆木头不稳。 (lit) Square logs do not roll [and] round logs are unsteady. (fig) There's nothing perfect in this world. [See also *shì ruò qiúquán* below.]

16 **Fáng rén bùrú fáng jǐ.** 防人不如防己。 [Better to] guard against [one's] own [misbehavior] than to guard against [criticism from] others.

17 **Fāng shí bù kěyǐ wéi mò; zhí mù bù kěyǐ wéi lún.** 方石不可以为磨，直木不可以为轮。 (lit) Square stones can't be made into millstones, nor straight boards into wheels. (fig) Employ people or things to their best advantage. [See also *fāng de bù gǔn* above.]

18 **Fáng xiǎo, chuáng kào qiáng; fáng dà, chuáng zhōngyāng; bùkě duìzhe mén, gèng yào yuǎnlí chuāng.** 房小床靠墙，房大床中央，不可对着门，更要远离窗。 [If the] room is small, [put the] bed against the wall; [if the] room is big, [put the] bed in the middle; never put the bed facing the door, [and] even more [importantly] keep [it] away from the windows [lest you catch cold, or people see you]. [Rhyme.]

19 **Fáng zài qiántou, shǎo chī kǔtou.*** 防在前头，少吃苦头。 (lit) [If one is] prepared in advance, [one will] suffer fewer losses. (fig) Always be prepared for a rainy day. [Rhyme.]

20 **Fángzi hǎo zhù; jiěfang nán chǔ.** 房子好住，街坊难处。 [It's] easy to live in [a nice] house, [but] difficult to get along with [one's] neighbors. [Rhyme; see also *bǎiwàn mǎi zhái* above and *qiānjīn mǎi chǎn* below; note *xiāngchǔ*, "to get along with."]

21 **Fàn hòu bǎi bù zǒu; (měi cān shǎo yīkǒu; qǔ gè lǎopo chǒu;) huó dào jiǔshíjiǔ.** 饭后百步走，(每餐少一口，取个老婆丑，)活到九十九。 (lit) Walk one hundred paces after meals, (eat one mouthful less at every meal, marry an ugly wife,) [and you'll] live to be ninety-nine. [A popular folk rhyme; the second and third parts are usually omitted.]

22 **Fánnǎo bù xún rén; rén zì xún fánnǎo.** 烦恼不寻人，人自寻烦恼。 Trouble doesn't seek people; people seek trouble.

23 **Fánshì kāitóu nán.** 凡事开头难。 The most difficult part of any task is getting started. [See also *fánshì zǒng yǒu kāitóu*.]

24 **Fánshì liú rénqíng; hòulái hǎo xiāngjiàn.** 凡事留人情，后来好相见。 In all matters, you should always remain on good terms with others, [so that] you [will be able to] face them again later.

25 **Fánshì zhǐpà gè qǐtóu.** 凡事只怕个起头。 (lit) [In] all matters, the only [thing to] worry about is the beginning. (fig) Things once started can't be stopped. [Cf. *Xǐngshì Héngyán*, chap. 3.]

26 **Fánshì zǒng yǒu kāitóu.** 凡事总有开头。 (lit) Everything must have a beginning. (fig) The most difficult part of any job is getting started. [More commonly *fánshì kāitóu nán* above. (q.v.)]

27 **Fàn sòng jī rén; huà sòng zhī rén.** 饭送饥人，话送知人。 (lit) [Save your] food [to] give to the hungry [and] save your words for those [who will] understand [you, i.e., your intimate friends and confidants].

28 **Fǎ wú sān rì yán.** 法无三日严。 (lit) The law won't be strictly observed [for more than] three days [running]. (fig) It is usually the case that a law is more strictly observed when it is first enacted. [Cf. *Érnǚ Yīngxióng Zhuàn*, chap. 40; see also *guān wú sān rì jǐn*.]

29 **Fēi de bù gāo, diē de bù zhòng.** 飞的不高，跌的不重。 (lit) When the flight is not high, the fall is not heavy. (fig) If one doesn't have high aspirations, one won't court great disasters. [Cf. *Érnǚ Yīngxióng Zhuàn*, chap. 14.]

30 **Fēi de gāo de niǎo qī de dī.** 飞得高的鸟栖得低。 (lit) The bird that flies high makes [its] nest low. (fig) A learned person never shows off his or her knowledge.

31 **Fēi'é- tóuhuǒ, zìqǔ fén shēn.** 飞蛾投火，自取焚身。 (lit) [When a] moth darts into a flame it brings destruction upon itself. (fig) "One who plays with fire will get burned." [The first part is also a *chengyu* and the two halves are used like a *xiehouyu*; cf. *Érnǚ Yīngxióng Zhuàn*, chap. 8; *WM*, chap. 27.]

32 **Féi jī bù xiàdàn.*** 肥鸡不下蛋。 (lit) A fat hen doesn't lay eggs. (fig) There's such a thing as too much of a good thing. [See also *hǎoshì guòtóu* below.]

see L5

33 **Fēi lǐ zhī cái, mò qǔ; fēi lǐ zhī shì, mò wéi.** 非理之财莫取，非理之事莫为。 Never obtain property unreasonably, nor do anything that goes against reason.

34 **Fēi qīn, yǒu yì, yīng kějìng; shì yǒu, wú qíng, bùkě jiāo.** 非亲有意，应可敬；是友无情，不可交。 Strangers who are sincere should be respected; friends who are not sincere should be dropped.

35 **Féi shuǐ bù guò biérén tián.** 肥水不过别人田。 (lit) Water beneficial to crops [should] not pass [to] other people's fields. (fig) Benefits should not be allowed to go to others. "Charity begins at home." [See also *piányi bù guò* below.]

36 **Fēngbào líntóu, bù zé gǎng.** 风暴临头，不择港。 (lit) [When a] storm is impending, [a ship will] not be choosy about [which] harbor [to anchor in]. (fig) When disaster is impeding, any way to avoid it is acceptable. "Any port in a storm."

37 **Fēng bù chuī, cǎo bù yáo.** 风不吹，草不摇。 (lit) [If] the wind doesn't move [it], the grass doesn't stir. (fig) There must be a cause or reason for every phenomena. "There's no smoke without fire." [See also *fēng cóng nǎli qǐ* and *làng cóng fēng lái* below and the following entry.]

38 **Fēng bù lái, shù bù dòng; chuán bù yáo, shuǐ bù hún.** 风不来树不动，船不摇水不浑。 (lit) [If] the wind doesn't come, the trees won't move; [if] the boatman doesn't row, the water won't be muddied. (fig) There must be a cause behind everything. [Cf. *WM*, chap. 20; *JPM*, chap. 75; see also the preceding entry.]

39 **Fèng bù lí cháo; lóng bù lí wō.** 凤不离巢，龙不离窝。 (lit) A phoenix won't leave its nest, nor a dragon its den. (fig) One won't leave the place where one makes a living. [Originally *fèng bù lí kē*, etc., where *kē* 窠 technically rhymes with *wō*; vs. *lóng bù lí hǎi* below.]

40 **Fēngcháo guòle, shìjiè zài.** 风潮过了，世界在。 (lit) [After the] storm has blown over, the world still remains. (fig) "(These) things always blow over." "Life goes on." [Often said of political movements.]

41 **Fēng cóng nǎli qǐ, yǔ cóng nǎli luò.** 风从哪里起，雨从哪里落。 (lit) Wherever the wind starts from, that's where the rains fall from [as well]. (fig) "Where there's smoke, there's fire." [See also *fēng bù chuī* above.]

42 **Fēng cuī rén, yǔ liú rén; xiàxuě, bù zǒu, hútu rén.** 风催人雨留人，下雪不走，糊涂人。 (lit) [When the] wind [blows, it] urges one [to leave, because when the] rain [falls,] one [has to] stay; [when it] starts snowing, [one who does] not leave [is a] fool. (fig) A clever person is always attuned to changes in the situation and acts promptly. [See also *qíng gǎn bùkěn zǒu* below.]

43 **Fēng duō chū wáng; rén duō chū jiàng.** 蜂多出王，人多出将。 (lit) [Just as] a crowd of bees produces a queen [bee, so] a crowd of people will produce a general. (fig) Leaders appear naturally from among the people. [Rhyme.]

44 **Féng è, bù pà; féng shàn, bù qī.** 逢恶不怕，逢善不欺。 [When you] encounter the wicked, do not fear [them, and when you] encounter the kind, do not bully [them].

F

45 **Fènghuáng bù rù wūyā cháo.** 凤凰不入乌鸦巢。 (lit) A phoenix won't enter a crow's nest. (fig) A noble person won't set foot into a commoner's home.

46 **Fènghuáng fēishang wútóng shù, zìyǒu pángrén shuō duǎn-cháng.** 凤凰飞上梧桐树，自有旁人说短长。 (lit) If a phoenix perches at the top of a [common] Chinese parasol tree, naturally there will be people gossiping about it. (fig) People will always gossip about any unusual person, incident, or behavior. [See also *dàfēng chuī dǎo* above.]

47 **Fènghuáng luò jià bùrú jī.** 凤凰落架不如鸡。 (lit) A phoenix stripped of its glory is not as good as a chicken. (fig) A powerful person who has lost power will be less respected than an ordinary person. [See also *bǎle máo de fènghuáng* and *dézhì māor* above and *hǔ sǐ, bù luò jià* below.]

48 **Féng rén qiěshuō sānfēnhuà; wèikě quán pāo yī piàn xīn.** 逢人且说三分话，未可全抛一片心。 (lit) [When you] meet others, only say thirty percent [of what you think]; do not completely reveal [what is in] your mind. (fig) Always speak with reservation and never pour out your heart to anyone. [Cf. *Jīngshì Tōngyán*, chap. 32.]

49 **Fèng shēng fèng; lóng shēng lóng; lǎoshǔ shēng de huì dǎ dòng.** 凤生凤，龙生龙，老鼠生的会打洞。 (lit) Phoenixes beget phoenixes [and] dragons beget dragons, [so] what is born of rats is capable of digging holes. (fig) One's behavior and attitudes are determined by one's family's class background. [This rhyme was a well-known political slogan during the Cultural Revolution, summarizing the theory of *xuètǒnglùn*, or "theory of [class] blood lines"; note also the rhymed Cultural Revolution slogan: *lǎozi yīngxióng, ér hǎohàn; lǎozi fǎndòng, ér hùndàn*, "if one's father was a hero, the son will be a good man; if one's father was a counter-revolutionary, the son will be a bad egg"; also said *lóng shēng lóng* (q.v.) below]

50 **Fēng wú cháng shùn; bīng wú cháng shèng.*** 风无常顺，兵无常胜。 (lit) Winds are not always favorable, [and] soldiers are not always victorious. (fig) One is bound to encounter some difficulties or obstacles in life. "You can't win them all." [Cf. *Xīngshì Héngyán*, chap. 34.]

51 **Fēngxiǎn lǐ chū yīngxióng; hǎilàng lǐ jiàn hǎohàn.** 风险里出英雄，海浪里见好汉。 (lit) In the dangers of the storm, [there] appear heroes; in the [danger of] the waves [one] sees good men. (fig) Heroes are produced by difficult circumstances. [See also *luànshì chū yīngxióng* below.]

52 **Féngzhe hǎochù, biàn ānshēn.** 逢着好处便安身。 [If you happen to] come across a good place, then [stay there and] settle down. [Cf. *Hé Diǎn*, chap. 7; see also *zài yī fāng* below.]

53 **Fēn jiā sān nián, chéng línjū.** 分家三年，成邻居。 [Brothers whose families have] lived apart for three years [after the death of their parents] become [just like] neighbors. [In traditional

China, brothers often divided up the family property and lived separately after the death of their parents; see also *shù dà, fēn chà* below.]

54 **Fěnshuā de wūyā, bái bù jiǔ.** 粉刷的乌鸦，白不久。 (lit) A white-washed crow won't [stay] white for long. (fig) Sooner or later truth will come out. "Truth will out."

55 **Fó shāo yī zhù xiāng; rén zhēng yīkǒuqì.** 佛烧一炷香，人争一口气。 [Just as] Buddhas [need to have] a stick of incense burned, [so] people [need] to have [a little] self-respect. [Cf. *Bái Máo Nǚ* (The White-Haired Girl).]

56 **Fó yào jīn zhuāng; rén yào yī zhuāng.** 佛要金装，人要衣装。 (lit) [Just as] Buddha [image]s need to be covered with gold, [so] people need to be covered with [fine] clothes. (fig) "Fine clothes make the man." "Fine feathers make fine birds." [Originally *fó shī jīn zhuāng, rén shì yī zhuāng*; cf. *Xīngshì Héngyán*, chap. 1; see also *mǎ kào ān zhuāng* below.]

57 **Fó zài xīntóu zuò; jiǔ ròu chuān cháng guò.** 佛在心头坐，酒肉穿肠过。 (lit) [If one has] Buddha in [one's] heart, [it doesn't matter that] wine [and] meat will pass through [one's] intestines. (fig) As long as one's intentions are noble, one need not observe all the rules and regulations. [Rhyme; originally said . . . *jiǔ ròu fúcháng guò*; cf. *Xīngshì Héngyán*, chap. 26; said as an excuse by Buddhist monks like the Southern Song dynasty monk Ji Gong, who violated the Buddhist taboo on eating meat and drinking wine.]

58 **Fù bù xué shē ér shē; pín bù xué jiǎn ér jiǎn.** 富不学奢而奢，贫不学俭而俭。 [When people become] rich [they will naturally be] luxurious without any instruction; [when one becomes] poor, [one will automatically] be thrifty without having to be taught.

59 **Fù cháo zhīxià wú wán luǎn.** 覆巢之下无完卵。 (lit) Beneath [an] overturned nest there are not unbroken eggs. (fig) If the base is destroyed, things which depend on it cannot survive. If the group is harmed, the individual can hardly survive. [See also *pò cháo zhīxià* below.]

60 **Fùguì bù yā xiānglǐ.** 富贵不压乡里。 [When one gets] rich, [one should] not oppress [one's] fellow townspeople. [Cf. *Xīngshì Héngyán*, chap. 20; see also *guān dà, bù yā* below.]

61 **Fùguì, cǎo tóu lù.** 富贵草头露。 Wealth and honors [are as short-lived as] dewdrops [on the] tips of grass. [See also the following entry.]

62 **Fùguì rú fúyún.*** 富贵如浮云。 Wealth and honors [are as ephemeral as] floating clouds. [Cf. the Confucian Analects: *Lúnyǔ: Shù Ér*; see also the preceding entry.]

63 **Fùguì tārén hé; pínjiàn qīnqi lí.** 富贵他人合，贫贱亲戚离。 [When one is] rich, others [will come and] gather around; [when one is] poor, [even, one's] relatives will distance [themselves]. [See also *pín jū nàoshì* and *qián jù rúxiōng* below.]

64 **Fùguì wú gēn; pín jiàn wú miáo.** 富贵无根，贫贱无苗。 (lit) There is no root for wealth or honors [and] no seedling for poverty. (fig) Riches, rank or poverty are not predestined.

65 **Fù hǔ, xiū kuān.** 缚虎休宽。(lit) [When] trussing [up a] tiger, [one should] not tie [it] loosely. (fig) One should be very careful when trying to capture a person of ability. [Cf. *Suí Táng Yǎnyì*, chap. 12; see also *shàn zhǔ, è ná* below.]

66 **Fú hǔ yào zhī hǔ xìng.*** 伏虎要知虎性。(lit) To tame a tiger [one] has to know its nature. (fig) To deal with (bad) people, one must understand how they think.

67 **Fù jiā yī xí jiǔ; qióng hàn bànnián liáng.** 富家一席酒，穷汉半年粮。[The cost of a] rich family's feast [is as much as] half a year's grain [for a] poor man['s family]. [Cf. *Xǐngshì Héngyán*, chap. 29.]

68 **Fǔ kuài bùpà mùchái yìng.** 斧快不怕木柴硬。(lit) [If the] axe is sharp, it doesn't matter how hard the wood is. (fig) An able person is not afraid to take up a difficult task.

69 **Fùle pín, hái chuān sān nián líng.** 富了贫还穿三年绫。(lit) [Even when a] rich [family] declines, [they can] still wear silk [clothing for] three years. (fig) A rich family has some property left even when they are in decline. [Cf. *Xǐngshì Yīnyuán Zhuàn*, chap. 8; see also *dà chuán lànle* above and *qióng suī qióng* and *shòu sǐ de luòtuo* and *tóng pén lànle* below.]

70 **Fùmǔ zhī chóu, bùgòngdàitiān.** 父母之仇，不共戴天。[One] cannot live under the same sky with the murderer of one's parents. [Note: *bùgòngdàitiān* is an idiomatic expression.]

71 **Fùnǚ néng dǐng bànbiāntiān.** 妇女能顶半边天。(lit) Women can hold up half the sky. (fig) Women can do whatever men can do. [A communist slogan often used by Mao Zedong.]

72 **Fūqī wú gé xiǔ zhī chóu.** 夫妻无隔宿之仇。Enmity between husband and wife doesn't last overnight. [Cf. *Rúlín Wàishǐ*, chap. 29; also said . . . *géyè zhī chóu*; see also *tiānshàng xiàyǔ* below.]

73 **Fùrén, sìjì chuān yī; qióngrén, yī chuān sìjì.** 富人四季穿衣，穷人衣穿四季。The rich wear [different] clothes [in the] four seasons, [while the] poor [have one set of] clothes [which they] wear [in all] four seasons. [Rhyme.]

74 **Fùrén, xīn hēi; qióngrén, shǒu hēi.** 富人，心黑；穷人，手黑。Rich people [have] black hearts, [while] poor people [have] black hands.

75 **Fùshé zhě shǒu, zhuàngshì jiě wàn.** 蝮蛇蜇手，壮士解腕。(lit) [If a] poisonous snake bites [his] hand, a brave man [will] cut off [his] wrist. (fig) One must be resolute in dealing with affairs; if one is unwilling to make small sacrifices, one will suffer greater losses.

76 **Fǔtóu chī záozi; záozi chī mùtou.** 斧头吃凿子，凿子吃木头。(lit) [An] axe [can] dent a chisel, [and a] chisel [can] dent wood. (fig) There is always one thing which can conquer another. [See also *yī wù xiáng yī wù* below.]

77 **Fú wú chóng shòu rì; huò yǒu bìng lái shí.** 福无重受日，祸有并来时。(lit) Fortune does not have repeated days of receiving, [but with] misfortune there [can] be times [when it] comes in doubles. (fig) Good fortune does not repeat itself, but ill fortune can come repeatedly. [Cf. *fú wú shuāng zhì* below.]

78 **Fù wú sān dài xiǎng.** 富无三代享。[A rich family's] prosperity won't be enjoyed for three generations [because spoiled children and grandchildren will squander it all].

79 **Fú wú shuāng zhì; huòbùdānxíng.** 福无双至，祸不单行。(Blessings never come in pairs, [and]) misfortunes never come singly. [Cf. *JW*, chap. 15; *WM*, chap. 37; note: *huòbùdānxíng* has become a set phrase; see also *fú wú chóng shòu rì* above.]

80 **Fù xián qiān kǒu shǎo; pín hèn yīshēn duō.** 富嫌千口少，贫恨一身多。[The] rich consider a thousand mouths [to feed as but] a few, [while a] poor [person considers himself to be one] too many.

81 **Fùxiōng shījiào, zǐdì bù kān.** 父兄失教，子弟不堪。(lit) If father [or] eldest brother neglects disciplining [his children or younger brothers], the children will be unworthy. [Cf. *Érnǚ Yīngxióng Zhuàn*, chap. 32; see also *yǎng bù jiào* below.]

82 **Fùyù niàn qī-zǐ; pínqióng sī niáng qīn.** 富裕念妻子；贫穷思娘亲。[When] rich, [one] thinks [only] of [one's] wife [and] children, [but when] poor, [one] thinks of [one's] parents [for help and comfort].

83 **Fù yù xíngjié, zǐ bì shārén.** 父欲行劫，子必杀人。(lit) [If] a father seeks to do robbery, [his] children will surely commit murder. (fig) If a father does something bad, his son will inevitably do something even worse. [See also *lǎozi tōu guā* below.]

84 **Fù zhài, zǐ huán.** 父债子还。A father's debts, a [dutiful] son is [obliged] to pay. [Cf. *Wǔ Sōng*, chap. 2.]

85 **Fú zhōng fú huò; huò zhōng yù fú.** 福中伏祸，祸中寓福。In good fortune lurks misfortune, [and] in misfortune lies good fortune. [See also *huò yǔ fú wéi lín* and *huò xī fú suǒ yǐ* below.]

86 **Fú zì tiān lái.** 福自天来。Blessings come from Heaven.

87 **Fù-zǐ wú gé xiǔ zhī chóu.** 父子无隔宿之仇。(lit) [Between] father [and] son there is no enmity which outlasts the night. (fig) Nothing should come between father and son. [Cf. *JW*, chap. 31; see also *fūqī wú gé xiǔ* above.]

F

G

1 **Gài guān lùn dìng.** 盖棺论定。(lit) [Only after they have] shut the coffin [can one] pronounce certainly. (fig) Final judgment can be passed on a person only after he or she dies. [Note: *gàiguānlùndìng* has become a set literary expression.]

2 **Gănchē sān nián, zhī mă xìng.** 赶车三年，知马性。(lit) [A driver who] drives a horse-cart [for] three years knows horse's natures [well]. (fig) One learns from experience.

3 **Gàn dà zé zhī xié.** 干大则枝斜。(lit) Big trunks have slanted branches. (fig) Big families often have good-for-nothing sons or grandsons.

4 **Gāng zé yì zhé, róu zé cháng cún.** 刚则易折，柔则常存。(lit) [Anything which is] unyielding will break easily; [anything which is] soft will last long. (fig) Those who are unyielding invite trouble, while those who are flexible will survive. [Note: *gāngqiáng*, "firm; unyielding."]

5 **Gànhuó bù yóu dōng, lèisǐ yě wú gōng.** 干活不由东，累死也无功。(lit) [If one does] not do [one's] work according to [one's] employer['s wishes], even [if one] works hard, [one] will not be rewarded. [Rhyme; cf. *dōngjia*, "boss."]

6 **Gān jǐng bì xiān jié.** 甘井必先竭。(lit) The well with sweet water will be exhausted first. (fig) People of ability are overburdened (and "burn out" early). [Cf. *Zhuāngzǐ: Shān Mù*; see also *néng zhě duō láo* and the following entry.]

7 **Gānquán bì jié; zhí mù bì fá.** 甘泉必竭，直木必伐。(lit) Sweet springs will run dry, [and] straight trees will be cut. (fig) People of ability are overburdened (and "burn out" early). [See also the preceding entry.]

8 **Găn rén bù kě găn shàng.** 赶人不可赶上。(lit) [When] driving people, [one] should not drive [them too] hard. (fig) Never drive others too hard. [Cf. *WM*, chap. 2.]

9 **Gān shǐ mǒ bù dào rén shēnshàng.** 干屎抹不到人身上。(lit) Dried dung cannot stick onto one's body. (fig) Slander cannot harm an honest person. [See also *shùshēn zhǎng de zhèng* below.]

10 **Găn shíwǔ bùrú găn chūyī.** 赶十五不如秆初一。(lit) Doing [something on the] fifteenth [of the month] is not as good as doing [it on the] first [day of the month]. (fig) Don't put things off. "Better earlier than later."

11 **Gān tǔ dǎ bù chéng gāo qiáng; méi qián gài bù qǐ wǎfáng.** 干土打不成高墙，没钱盖不起瓦房。(lit) High walls cannot be built with dry earth, [and] tiled roof houses cannot be built without money. (fig) One can do nothing without money.

12 **Gān yú bù néng gěi māo zuò zhěntou.** 干鱼不能给猫作枕头。(lit) A dried fish cannot be used as a cat's pillow [for it would be soon eaten up]. (fig) Don't leave temptation lying around. [Cf. *JW*, chap. 55.]

13 **Gānzhe lǎolái tián; làjiāo lǎolái hóng.** 甘蔗老来甜，辣椒老来红。(lit) [As they] get older, sugar cane [becomes] sweeter [and] peppers grow redder. (fig) The older people get, the more experienced and popular they become. [Note: *lǎoláihóng* refers to people becoming successful in their more mature years; see also *fā duǎn ér xīn cháng* above.]

14 **Gānzhe méiyǒu liǎngtóu tián.*** 甘蔗没有两头甜。(lit) There is no sugar cane that is sweet at both ends. (fig) One can't "have it both ways" in life. It's impossible to have something perfect; there are always two sides to everything. [See also *shì ruò qiúquán* below.]

15 **Gāofēi zhī niǎo, sǐ yú měishí; shēn qián zhī yú, sǐ yú fāng ěr.** 高飞之鸟死于美食，深潜之鱼死于芳饵。(lit) A high-flying bird [may] die for tasty food; deep-water fish [may] die for tasty bait. (fig) If one wants to love or capture someone, one must first give him or her what he or she desires.

16 **Gāoguān qí shòu mǎ.** 高官骑瘦马。(lit) High officials ride thin horses. (fig) The rich do not show off their wealth. [See also *cáizhu shuō qióng huà* above.]

17 **Gào rén sǐzuì, dé sǐzuì.** 告人死罪，得死罪。[Anyone who] lodges a [false] accusation against somebody for a capital crime [should] receive the death penalty. [Rhyme; cf. *JW*, chap. 83.]

18 **Gāoshān yǎng zhǐ, jīngxíng xíng zhǐ.** 高山仰止，景行行止。(lit) The high mountains [one may] look up at; the royal road, [one may] travel. (fig) One should look up to role models of high moral character and conduct and try to follow their example. [Originally from the Poetry Classic: *Shījīng: Xiǎo Yǎ: Chē Xiá*, quoted by Sima Qian in *Shǐ Jì*; note: *jīngxíng*, "royal road or highway," is a metaphor for "(one) taking the high [moral] road"; both halves are used independently as *chengyu*.]

19 **Gāo zhě bù shuō; shuōzhě bù gāo.** 高者不说，说者不高。[An] able person doesn't boast [and] a boaster is not able.

20 **Gēbo nǐng bu guò dàtuǐ.** 胳膊拧不过大腿。(lit) The arm cannot overcome the thigh. (fig) The weaker cannot overcome the stronger. [Cf. the *píngshū: Yuè Fēi Zhuàn*, chap. 43.]

21 **Gēbo (/gēbei) shé le, wǎng xiù lǐ cáng.** 胳膊(/胳臂)折了，往袖里藏。(lit) [If one's] elbow is broken, [one should] hide [it] in one's sleeve. (fig) (1) If one has some shortcomings or if one has done something stupid or wrong, one cannot let it be known to others. (2) One tends to cover up or protect one's own people. [Cf. *DRC*, chap. 7 and 68; *Guānchǎng Xiànxíng Jì*, chap. 11 and 36; see also *jiāchǒu bùkě* and the following entry.]

22 **Gēbo zǒngshì cháo lǐ wān.** 胳膊总是朝里弯。 (lit) [One's] arms always bend inward. (fig) One usually favors and protects one's own people. [See also *quántou cháo wài* and *zhū zhuǎ zhū qiān gǔn* below and the preceding entry.]

23 **Gé chóng dùpí, gé chóng shān.** 隔重肚皮，隔重山。 [A stepchild of a] different womb is separated [from his] stepmother and her own children as if they were] separated by mountains. [Cf. *Chū Kè Pāi'àn Jīngqí*, chap. 38; see also *hòumǔ de quántou* and *pí lǐ shēng de* below.]

24 **Gé chóng lóubǎn, gé chóng tiān.** 隔重楼板，隔重天。 (lit) A different floor, a different world. (fig) Every household is different. [Note: *jiǔ chóng tiān*, "nine different levels of heaven"; see also *chūmén sān bù* above.]

25 **Gèchù gè xiāngsú; yī chù yī guīju.** 各处各乡俗，一处一规矩。 (lit) Each place [has] its own local customs; [in] one place [there is] one code of conduct. (fig) Different places or groups have different standards or rules of behavior. [Rhyme; see also *shí lǐ bùtóng sú* below and the following entry.]

26 **Gé dào bù xiàyǔ; bǎi lǐ bùtóng fēng.** 隔道不下雨，百里不同风。 (lit) [Just as] across the road, [it can be] not raining [i.e., different weather], [so a] hundred leagues [away] there are different customs. (fig) Different places have different customs. [Note: *fēngsú xíguàn* "local customs"; one *(huá)lǐ* equals approximately one-half kilometer; see also *bǎi lǐ, bùtóng fēng* and *chūmén sān lǐ* above and the preceding entry.]

27 **Gé guō fàn'er xiāng.** 隔锅饭儿香。 (lit) Food from a different cooking pan tastes better. (fig) "The grass is always greener on the other side of the fence."

28 **Géháng, bù gé lǐ.** 隔行不隔理。 (lit) [Although the] trades [may be] different, [there is] no difference in principles. (fig) Although the professions or specializations may be different, the same basic principles underlie them. [Vs. the following entry.]

29 **Géháng rú géshān.** 隔行如隔山。 (lit) Different professions [are as different] as different mountains. (fig) Difference in profession makes people feel worlds apart. [Note: *géháng rú géshān* is used metaphorically to refer to being compartmentalized; see also *tóngháng shì yuānjia* below; vs. the preceding entry.]

30 **Gé hé qiān lǐ yuǎn.** 隔河千里远。 (lit) [Although] separated only by a river, [it's as though they were a] thousand leagues apart. (fig) It's hard to know the situation in a different place, (even though it may not be that far away). [See also *géshān rú gé tiān* below.]

31 **Gè jiāmén, gè jiā hù.** 各家门，各家户。 (lit) [Behind] every door [is a] separate household. (fig) People should mind their own business. [Cf. *Xīngshì Yīnyuán Zhuàn*, chap. 3, and *DRC*, chap. 71; see also *gèrén zì sǎo* below.]

32 **Gèjìn-suǒnéng, ànláo-fēnpèi.** 各尽所能，按劳分配。 [From] each according to [his] ability; [to] each according to [his] work. [This Marxist slogan is referred to as the Socialist Principle of Distribution; see also the following entry.]

33 **Gèjìn-suǒnéng, ànxū-fēnpèi.** 各尽所能，按需分配。 [From] each according to [his] ability; [to] each according to [his] needs. [This Marxist slogan is referred to as the Communist Principle of Distribution; see also the preceding entry.]

34 **Gēn bù zhèng, miáo bì wāi.** 根不正，苗必歪。 (lit) [If the] root is not straight, the seedling will be crooked. (fig) One's character and behavior later in life depend on one's early upbringing. "As the twig is bent, so grows the tree." [See also the following entry.]

35 **Gēn bù zhèng, miáo bù shèng.** 根不正，苗不盛。 (lit) [If the] root is not straight, the seedlings [will] not flourish. (fig) There can be no successful future for children without a good upbringing. [See also the preceding entry.]

36 **Gēng lǐ bù zháo, fàn lǐ zháo.** 羹里不着，饭里着。 (lit) [If one does] not meet in the soup, [one will] meet in the rice. (fig) If one creates an enemy, one is bound to encounter him sooner or later; it can't be avoided. [Cf. *Chū Kè Pāi'àn Jīngqí*, chap. 31; see also *yuānjia lù zhǎi* below.]

37 **Gēn hǔ jìn shān; gēn yīng fēi tiān.** 跟虎进山，跟鹰飞天。 (lit) [If one] follows a tiger, [one will] go into the mountains; [if one] follows an eagle, [one will] fly in the sky. (fig) One learns from the company one keeps. [See also *gēnzhe hǎorén* below.]

38 **Gé nián de huánglì, kànbude.** 隔年的皇历，看不得。 (lit) Last year's calendar is not to be looked at. (fig) One should not be bound by old, out of date rules.

39 **Gēn shēn bù jiǎn; wěi dà nán yáo.** 根深不剪，尾大难摇。 (lit) Deep roots are difficult to cut, [and] big tails are difficult to wave. (fig) When one's subordinates get too strong, they're hard to control.

40 **Gēn shēn bùpà fēng yáodòng; shù zhèng hé chóu yuè yǐng yí.** 根深不怕风摇动，树正何愁月影移。 (lit) A deep-rooted tree fears not the wind, [and] an upright tree does not worry about the moving shadow of the moon [distorting its image]. (fig) A frank and righteous person need not be afraid of slander. [See also *hǎorén shuō bù huài* and *jiǎo zhèng bùpà* and *shùshēn zhǎng de zhèng* below.]

41 **Gēnzhe hǎorén, xué hǎorén; (gēnzhe lǎohǔ, xué yǎo rén).** 跟着好人学好人，(跟着老虎学咬人)。 (lit) [When one] keeps good company, [one] learns to be good; ([when one] keeps company with tigers, [one] learns to bite people). (fig) One learns from the company one keeps. [Rhyme; the first half is more commonly used alone; see also *gēn hǔ jìn shān* above and the following entry.]

G

42 **Gēnzhe hǎorén, xué hǎorén; gēnzhe wūpó, tiào jiǎ shén.** 跟着好人学好人，跟着巫婆跳假神。 (lit) Keep company with good people [and you will] learn from them; keep company with witches [and you will] learn to go into trances. (fig) One is influenced by the company one keeps. [Also said gēn hǎorén, xué hǎorén; see also gēnzhe wǎjiang below and the preceding entry.]

43 **Gēnzhe qín de méi lǎn de; kànzhe yìng de méi ruǎn de.** 跟着勤的没懒的，看着硬的没软的。 Keep company with diligent [people and you] won't be lazy; keep company with tough [people and you] won't be soft (i.e., cowardly).

44 **Gēnzhe wǎjiang shuì sān tiān; bù huì gài fáng, yě huì bān zhuān.** 跟着瓦匠睡三天，不会盖房，也会搬砖。 (lit) [If you] stay with brick-layers for three nights, [you] may not learn how to build houses, [but] at least [you'll] learn how to carry bricks. (fig) One is influenced by those one spends time with. [See also āizhe tiějiang and gēnzhe hǎorén above and rù háng sān rì and sān tiān zhù zài and shú dú Tángshī below.]

45 **Gé qiáng xū yǒu ěr; chuāng wài qǐ wú rén?** 隔墙须有耳，窗外岂无人？ (lit) On the other side of the wall there must be ears; outside the window, how can there not be someone [eavesdropping]? (fig) One must always assume that someone is listening. "The walls have ears." [Cf. WM, chap. 16; see also lùshang shuōhuà below and the following entry.]

46 **Gé qiáng yǒu ěr.** 隔墙有耳。 (lit) On the other side of the wall there must be ears. (fig) "The walls have ears." One must be careful of eavesdroppers. [See also méiyǒu bù tòufēng and qiáng yǒu fèng below and the preceding entry.]

47 **Gèrén chuán dǐxià yǒu shuǐ, gèrén zì xíng.** 个人船底下有水，个人自行。 (lit) [Since] there's water under each individual's boat, [so] each person goes his [or her] own way. (fig) Each looks after him or herself and no one interferes with anyone else. You take care of your business and I'll take care of mine. [Cf. Píng Yāo Zhuàn, chap. 22; see also chuán duō bù ài above.]

48 **Gèrén de mèng, gèrén yuán.** 各人的梦，各人圆。 (lit) Each person [tries to] interpret [his or her] own dream. (fig) One must deal with the consequences of one's own actions. "As you make your bed, so you must lie in it." [Note: guān mèng, "to interpret dreams."]

49 **Gèrén lěngnuǎn, gèrén zì zhī.** 个人冷暖，个人自知。 (lit) Each individual knows best whether (s)he feels warm or chilly. (fig) One knows one's own situation best.

50 **Gè rén tóushang, yī fāng tiān.** 各人头上一方天。 (lit) Each person [has] a patch of sky over [his or her] head. (fig) Each person leads his or her own life. Each person has his or her own "space" and should not be interfered with by others. [See also rénrén tóu shàng dǐng below.]

51 **Gèrén xǐ miàn, gèrén guāng.** 个人洗面，个人光。 (lit) Each person washes [his (or her) own] face and] each one shines. (fig) Each takes care of his or her own affairs and derives his or her own benefit. "As one sows, so shall one reap." [Cf. Érmǚ Yīngxióng Zhuàn, chap. 13; see also gōng xiū, gōng dé below.]

52 **Gèrén yǒu gèrén de yuánfǎ.** 个人有个人的缘法。 (lit) Each person has his [or her] own destiny. (fig) Each person has his or her own predestined lot which predetermines our relations with each other, for good or ill. [Cf. DRC, chap. 49; note: yuánfèn, a Buddhist term meaning the lot or luck by which people are brought together; see also jì zài fó huì xià and yǒuyuán qiān lǐ below.]

53 **Gèrén zì sǎo mén qián xuě; mò guǎn tā jiā wǎ shàng shuāng.** 个人自扫门前雪，莫管他家瓦上霜。 (lit) Each person sweeps the snow before his own door; never mind the frost on another family's roof. (fig) (It's advisable for) every individual to keep within his own province and refrain from encroaching upon others. [Cf. Jǐngshì Tōngyán, chap. 24; advice traditional before 1949, which was criticized during the Cultural Revolution.]

54 **Géshān rú gé tiān.** 隔山如隔天。 (lit) [Areas] separated by mountains [are like] separate worlds. (fig) Customs differ greatly from locality to locality. [Note: géshān is also used to refer to a foster relationship; see also gé chóng dùpí and gé hé qiān lǐ yuǎn above.]

55 **Gè shīfu, gè chuánshòu; (gè bǎxì, gè biàn shǒu).** 各师傅各传授，(各把戏各变手)。 (lit) Every master teacher [has] his own teaching method ([and] every trick [has] its own artifice). [Rhyme; cf. Lǎo Cán Yóujì, chap. 13; note: biàn xì, "to do conjuring tricks"; see also xìfǎ rénrén below.]

56 **Gé shuǐ wú xiāngyīn.** 隔水无乡音。 People who are separated by water don't have the same local accent (or dialect).

57 **Gè yǎng de, gè téng.** 各养的，各疼。 (lit) [The children that] each [one] has raised, each [one] loves. (fig) Each person loves his own children. [Cf. Rúlín Wàishǐ, chap. 5; see also cháng lǐ chūlai above.]

58 **Gōng bù wǎng rén; dì bù kuī rén.** 工不枉人，地不亏人。 (lit) [An investment of] hard effort is never in vain, [just as] the land does not cheat [these] people [who invest hard efforts in tilling it]. (fig) The greater one's investment in terms of effort, the greater one's return will be.

59 **Gōngdao, bù gōngdao, zì yǒu tiānzhīdao.** 公道，不公道，自有天知道。 Whether [something is] just or not, only Heaven knows. [Rhyme.]

60 **Gōngdao shìjiān wéi báifà.** 公道世间惟白发 ◉ (lit) The only equal treatment in the world [is] white hair [i.e., time]. (fig) Only time treats everyone equally. [A line from a Tang dynasty poem by Du Mu, entitled "Sòng Yínzi Yī Jué."]

61 **Gōng dào, zìrán chéng.** 功到自然成。 (lit) [After] mastery has been achieved, success will naturally follow. (fig) Constant effort yields sure success. [Cf. *JW*, chap. 36; note: *gōngdào zìránchéng* is used alone as an idiom meaning "constant effort yields sure success"; see also *tiědǎ fángliáng* and *zhǐyào gōngfu shēn* below.]

62 **Gōngdào zì zài rénxīn.** 公道自在人心。 (lit) Justice resides naturally in people's hearts. (fig) In their hearts, everyone knows what is right.

63 **Gōng duō chū qiǎo yì.** 功多出巧艺。 (lit) More effort produces refined art. (fig) "Practice makes perfect." [Also said *gōng duō, yì jiù shóu.*]

64 **Gōng ér wàng sī; (guó ér wàng jiā).** 公而忘私，(国而忘家)。 Public [business comes] before private [affairs], ([and] the country [comes] before one's family). [Note: *gōng'érwàngsī* has become a *chengyu* referring to selflessness in the charge of one's official duties: see also *dāngle bīng* above and *gōngshì gōng bàn* and *xiān gōng (ér) hòu sī* below.]

65 **Gōngjìng bùrú cóngmìng.** 恭敬不如从命。 (lit) [Showing outward] respect is not as good as following orders. (fig) Obedience is a better way of showing respect than outward reverence. [Usually said self-deprecatingly when accepting an invitation; cf. *Jīngshì Tōngyán*, chap. 3; *DRC*, chap. 62; and Lao She's *Zhèng Hóng Qí Xià*.]

66 **Gōng mén lǐ hǎo xiūxíng.** 官门里好修行。 It's easier [for those who serve] in the yamen [to] "do good for others." [Cf. *Rúlín Wàishǐ*, chap. 25; note: The *yámen* was a county magistrate's office in traditional China; *xiūxíng* is a term meaning to practice Buddhism or Taoism; see also *dāngquán ruò* above.]

67 **Gōngpíng chūyú zhòng yì.** 公平出于众议。 (lit) Fairness comes out of public opinion. (fig) It is public opinion that decides whether something is fair or not. [See also *gǔ duō, chóng chū mǐ* and *línjú yǎnjing* and *shìfēi zì yǒu* and *zhòngrén yǎnjing* below.]

68 **Gōngpíng suànzhàng, yǒuyì cháng.** 公平算帐，友谊长。 A clear and open reckoning of accounts makes for long friendships. [See also *qīnxiōngdì míng suànzhàng* below.]

69 **Gōng rén jiàn piào, shēngkou jiàn liào.** 工人见票，牲口见料。 Civil servants seeing [bank] notes [are as greedy as] draft animals seeing fodder. [See also the following entry.]

70 **Gōng rén jiàn qián rú yíngzi jiàn xuè.** 工人见钱如蝇子见血。 Civil servants [are] as greedy for money as flies seeing blood. [Cf. *WM*, chap. 21; see also the preceding entry.]

71 **Gōngshì bù sī yì.** 公事不私议。 Public business [should] not be conducted in private. [See also the following entry.]

72 **Gōngshì gōng bàn.*** 公事公办。 (lit) Official business [should be] done [according to] official [principles]. (fig) One should not let personal considerations interfere with one's execution of one's public duties. [Note: *gōngshì-gōngbàn* is also used as a *chengyu*; see also *dāngle bīng* and *gōng ér wàng sī* above and *xiān gōng (ér) hòu sī* below.]

73 **Gōng shì gōng, sī shì sī.** 公是公，私是私。 Official [business] is official [business]; private [affairs] are private [affairs]. (fig) Public and private business should be kept separate. [See also *rénqíng guī rénqíng* below.]

74 **Gōng tài mǎn zé zhé; yuè tài mǎn zé quē.** 弓太满则折，月太满则缺。 (lit) [When a] bow [is pulled] too far, [it] will break; [when the] moon [is at its] fullest, [it] will wane. (fig) Things that reach their extreme will decline. [Cf. Sima Qian's *Shǐ Jì: Cài Zé Zhuàn*; see also *luòcháo zǒng yǒu* below.]

75 **Gōng xiū, gōng dé; pó xiū, pó dé; (bù xiū, bù dé).** 公修公得，婆修婆得，(不修不得)。 (lit) [When the] father-in-law does good, the father-in-law gains; [when the] mother-in-law does good, the mother-in-law gains; ([if one does]n't do [anything good], [one does]n't get [anything at all]). (fig) "As one sows, so shall one reap." [Cf. *JW*, chap. 96; note: *xiū(xíng)* means to practice Buddhism or Taoism; see also *gōng mén lǐ hǎo xiūxíng* above.]

76 **Gōng yìng, xián cháng duàn; rén jiàng, huò bì suí.** 弓硬弦长断，人强祸必随。 (lit) [Just as a] rigid bow always breaks its string, [so a] stubborn man inevitably invites disaster. (fig) Trouble will follow an unbending person, so be flexible. [Note: *juéjiàng*, "stubborn; unbending."]

77 **Gōng yù shàn qí shì, bì xiān lì qí qì.*** 工欲善其事，必先利其器。 (lit) A workman to do his work well must first sharpen his tools. (fig) Good preparation is prerequisite to the successful execution of a job. [Cf. the Confucian Analects: *Lúnyǔ: Wèi Líng Gōng*.]

78 **Gōngzhòng mǎ, gōngzhòng qí.** 公众马，公众骑。 (lit) The communal horse, everybody can ride. (fig) Seeing as it's there for the taking, one might as well take one's share. [See also *bù chī bái bù chī* and *dàjiā mǎ('ér)* above.]

79 **Gǒu bù chī shǐ, rén bù piānxīn.** 狗不吃屎，人不偏心。 [When] dogs [no longer] eat excrement, [then] human beings will no [longer] practice favoritism. [See also *rén yǒu liángxīn* below.]

80 **Gǒu bù shàngqián, yòng shí wèi; mǎ bù shàngtào, jiā biān dǎ.** 狗不上前用食喂，马不上套驾鞭打。 (lit) [If a] dog won't advance [toward you], use food to feed [it]; [if a] horse won't get into harness, use a whip to beat [it]. (fig) One must deal with different people or situations with different tactics.

81 **Gǒu bù xián jiā pín; (rén bù xián dì báo).** 狗不嫌家贫，(人不嫌地薄)。 (lit) [Just as a] dog doesn't dislike [its] poor master, ([so] people don't complain [about their] poor land). (fig) People are attached to their home place. "Be it ever so humble there's no place like home." [The second part is usually omitted; see also *ér bù xián* above.]

82 **Gǒu bù yǎo bàinián de; guān bù dǎ sòng qián de.** 狗不咬拜年的，官不打送钱的。 [Just as] dogs don't bite those [who come to] pay [formal] New Year's calls, [so] government officials don't [sentence to be] beat[en] those [who] send

[gifts of] money. [Rhyme, usually said of traditional magistrates before 1949; see also *guānfǔ bù dǎ* below.]

83 **Gǒu cháo pì zǒu; rén cháo shì zǒu.** 狗朝屁走，人朝势走。 [Just as] dogs follow [the smell of] flatulence, [so] people follow the power[ful]. [See also *gǒu bù chī shǐ* above and *gǒu yǎo chuān làn* below.]

84 **Gǒu chī shǐ; láng chī rén.** 狗吃屎，狼吃人。 (lit) Dogs eat excrement [and] wolves eat people. (fig) People cannot change their basic natures. "A leopard cannot change its spots." [Cf. *Érnǚ Yīngxióng Zhuàn,* chap. 31; see also *gǒu gǎi bùliǎo* and *gǒu zǒu qiān lǐ* and *jiāngshān yì gǎi* and *shé zuān de kūdòng* and *yī rén, yī xiàng* below.]

85 **Gǒu dōu yǒu qiào wěiba de shíhou.** 狗都有翘尾巴的时候。 (lit) Every dog has [his] time to stick up [his] tail. (fig) "Every dog will have his day." [Note: *qiào wěiba,* "to be cocky."]

86 **Gǒu dù lǐ cáng bu zhù rè zhī yóu.** 狗肚里藏不住热脂油。 (lit) No fatty oil can be kept in a dog's belly. (fig) A shallow person can keep nothing secret.

87 **Gǒu duō, bù pà láng; rén duō, bù pà hǔ.** 狗多不怕狼，人多不怕虎。 (lit) [When] dogs are many, [they] do not fear wolves; [when] people are many, [they] do not fear tigers. (fig) There is strength in numbers. [See also *hǎo hǔ jià bu zhù* below.]

88 **Gǒu gǎi bùliǎo chī shǐ.** 狗改不了吃屎。 (lit) Dogs cannot change eating excrement. (fig) Bad people cannot change their bad natures. [See also *gǒu chī shǐ* above.]

89 **Gǒu jí tiào qiáng; rén jí xuánliáng.** 狗急跳墙，人急悬梁。 (lit) [Just as a] cornered dog [will] leap [over a] wall, [so a] desperate person [will] hang [himself from a] roof beam. (fig) Desperate people will resort to desperate measures. [Rhyme; the first half is sometimes used alone as a *chengyu* metaphorically; see also *zhí xiàng gǎn gǒu* below.]

90 **Gǒu pà jiā wěi; rén pà shūlǐ.** 狗怕夹尾，人怕输理。 [Just as what] dogs dislike [most is running away with their] tails between [their legs, so what] people dislike [most is being [(shown to be) in the] wrong.

91 **Gǒu ròu gǔn sān gǔn, shénxiān zhàn bù wěn.** 狗肉滚三滚，神仙站不稳。 (lit) [After] dog meat [has been] boiled three times, [even] gods cannot resist [it]. (fig) No one can resist the temptation of delicious food. [Note: Inviting people to dine is a common way of asking for and repaying favors in Chinese society; vs. the following entry. Especially around Canton and in Northeast China dog meat is considered a "hot" strengthening food to protect against cold weather.]

92 **Gǒu ròu shàngbude tái pán; xī nǐba hú bu shàng bì.** 狗肉上不得台盘，稀泥巴糊不上壁。 (lit) Dog meat cannot be served [to guests, just as] watery mud cannot be used to plaster walls. (fig) Some people are worthless or hapless beyond helping. [Also said *gǒu ròu bù shàng zhuō:*

(lit) Dog meat cannot be served at table; vs. the preceding entry.]

93 **Gǒu shòu, zhǔrén xiū.** 狗瘦，主人羞。 (lit) [When a] dog is thin, [its] master [feels] ashamed. (fig) A leader feels ashamed when his or her subordinates misbehave.

94 **Gǒu tóu shàng chābude jīn huā.** 狗头上插不得金花。 (lit) [On a] dog's head [one] cannot place golden flowers. (fig) Some people, things, or situations are so bad, that attempts to beautify them simply make the whole situation worse.

95 **Gǒu tóu shàng gē bu zhù ròu gǔtou.** 狗头上搁不住肉骨头。 (lit) On a dog's head meaty bones can't be kept for long. (fig) Certain people or situations are just hopeless.

96 **Gǒu wéi bǎi bù wáng, zhǐshì mén qián láng.** 狗为百步王，只是门前狼。 (lit) A dog is a king [within a radius of] one hundred paces, but is only a wolf in front of [his master's] door. (fig) Everyone feels that he or she is important within their own small sphere. "Every cock crows on its own dunghill." [Rhyme.]

97 **Gǒuwō lǐ yǎng bù chū jīnqiánbào.** 狗窝里养不出金钱豹。 (lit) Spotted leopards can't be born in a doghouse. (fig) No person of high ability can be produced from a low environment. [Vs. *hánmén chū cáizǐ* below.]

98 **Gǒuyǎn kàn rén dī.** 狗眼看人低。 (lit) [From the lowly perspective of a] dog's eyes, everyone looks short. (fig) A snobbish person looks down on those poorer or weaker than himself. [Note the colloquial *suyu* expression: *gǒuyǎn kàn rén,* "to look down on others; to be snobbish."]

99 **Gǒu yǎo chuān làn de; rén tiǎn chuān hǎo de.** 狗咬穿烂的，人舔穿好的。 Dogs bite the raggedly dressed, [while] people "lick up to" [i.e., flatter] the well-dressed. [See also *gǒu cháo pì zǒu* above.]

100 **Gǒu yǎo gǒu, liǎng zuǐ máo.** 狗咬狗，两嘴毛。 (lit) [When] dog bites dog, both [get a] mouthful of hair. (fig) When two (bad) parties engage in (an unjustifiable) dispute, they both end up losing or looking badly. "A curse upon both their houses." [Often used to describe two of the speaker's enemies fighting; *gǒu-yǎo-gǒu* refers to a "dog-eat-dog" conflict.]

101 **Gǒu yǎo rén, yǒu yào yī; rén yǎo rén, méi yào zhì.** 狗咬人有药医，人咬人没药治。 [When a] person is bit[ten by a] dog, there are medicines [which can] cure [him, but if] one is bit[ten by another] person, there is no medicine [which can] cure [him]. (fig) One who is falsely accused in a legal action is hard put to defend himself or herself. [See also *ruǎndāozi shārén* and *yù jiā zhī zuì* below.]

102 **Gǒu yě yǒu sān shēng kāng fēn.** 狗也有三升糠分。 (lit) Even a dog has [its share of] three bushels of rice husks. (fig) Each and every one should have a share of the food available. [Note: a *shēng* is a unit of dry measure for grain equal to one liter.]

103 **Gǒu zǒu qiān lǐ chī shǐ; láng zǒu qiān lǐ chī rén.** 狗走千里吃屎, 狼走千里吃人。 (lit) [Although] a dog [may] travel a thousand leagues, [it will still] eat excrement; [and although a] wolf [may] travel a thousand leagues, [it will still] eat people. (fig) People cannot overcome their basic natures. "A leopard cannot change its spots." [Cf. *Érnǚ Yīngxióng Zhuàn*, chap. 31; note: the order of the two halves may be reversed; see also *gǒu chī shǐ* and *gǒu gǎi bùliǎo* above.]

104 **Gǒu zuǐ lǐ tǔ bù chū xiàngyá.** 狗嘴里吐不出象牙。 (lit) Out of a dog's mouth [will] never come ivory tusks. (fig) A filthy mouth cannot utter decent language. [See also *dúshé zuǐ lǐ* above.]

105 **Guǎ bù dí zhòng; ruò bù dí qiáng.** 寡不敌众, 弱不敌强。 A few are no match for the many [and the] weak are no match for the strong. [Cf. *JW*, chap. 32; note: the first half is used as a *chengyu*: *guǎbùdízhòng*; originally: *guǎ bù shèng zhòng* from *Hán Fēizǐ: Nán Sān*.]

106 **Guā dì tiāo guā, tiāo de yǎnhuā.** 瓜地挑瓜, 挑得眼花。 (lit) [When one is] choosing melons in a melon field, [one has so many] to choose [from that one's] eyes [are] bedazzled. (fig) Too many choices make one indecisive. A "kid in a candy store" doesn't know which way to turn. [Rhyme.]

107 **Guǎfu mén qián, shìfēi duō.** 寡妇门前, 是非多。 (lit) In front of a widow's gate troubles are many. (fig) In front of a widow's house is a sure spot for trouble. [Note: in traditional China widows were often the occasion of quarrels and trouble.]

108 **Guāi de yě shì téng; dāi de yě shì téng.** 乖的也是疼, 呆的也是疼。 (lit) Well behaved [children] are loved, [and] stupid [children] are also loved. (fig) Parents love their children alike whether they are quick to catch on or stupid. [Rhyme; cf. *Érnǚ Yīngxióng Zhuàn*, chap. 26.]

109 **Guài rén bù zhī lǐ, zhī lǐ bù guài rén.** 怪人不知理, 知理不怪人。 [One who] blames others does not understand reason/how things are, [while one who] understands reason(s) doesn't blame others. [Note: *zhī lǐ* means "to understand reason or (the reasons) why things are the way they are." The two halves are also used in the reverse order (q.v.).]

110 **Guāi rén kàn yī yǎn; dāizi kàndào wǎn.** 乖人看一眼, 呆子看到晚。 [A] smart person [understands everything at] one glance, [while a] dullard [won't know anything even by] looking all day long.

111 **Guài rén xū zài fù; xiāngjiàn yǒu héfáng?** 怪人须在腹, 相见有何妨? (lit) [If you] bear a grudge [against] someone, [you must] keep [it inside your] belly; [if you have to] meet each other, what harm is there? (fig) One should not avoid meeting a person against whom one harbors a grudge. [Cf. *Fēngshén Yǎnyì*; chap. 59.]

112 **Guān bù chāi bìngrén.** 官不差病人。 [An] official [should] not send [a] sick person on an errand.

113 **Guān bù lí yìn; huò bù lí shēn.** 官不离印, 货不离身。 (lit) [Just as an] official is never without his [official] seal [of office, so a businessman's] goods are never far from his person. (fig) One always carries with one things of vital importance. [See also *chuán bù lí duò* above.]

114 **Guān bùróng zhēn; sī kěróng chē.** 官不容针, 私可容车。 (lit) Officially [one can]not permit a needle, [but] privately [one] may let in a carriage. (fig) Officially no exceptions should be made, but privately rules may be greatly stretched. [Cf. *Jīngshì Tōngyán*, chap. 36; see also *guān jǐn, sī bù jǐn* below.]

115 **Guāncai tóu biān nǎ yǒu zhòu sǐ guǐ?** 棺材头边哪有咒死鬼? (lit) Where was there [ever a case of] someone in a coffin from being cursed to death? (fig) No one has ever died from being cursed at. One should not get upset at being cursed at. [Cf. *Píng Yāo Zhuàn*, chap. 9.]

116 **Guàn céng wéi lǚ, piān lián kè.** 惯曾为旅, 偏怜客。 (lit) [One who is] used to constant traveling is inclined to have compassion for [other] travelers. (fig) People who have gone through similar experiences have sympathy for each other.

117 **Guān chà, lì chà; láirén bù chà.** 官差吏差, 来人不差。 (lit) [That] official [may be] wrong [or this] mandarin [may be] wrong, [but] the messenger who [actually] comes [sent by the superiors] is not wrong. (fig) Right or wrong, people just [have to) follow orders or do their jobs; they're not to blame. [Cf. *JW*, chap. 3; *Hé Diǎn*, chap. 9.]

118 **Guān chuán lòu; guān mǎ shòu; guān yǎng de lǎodiē bù zhǎng ròu.** 官船漏, 官马瘦, 官养的老爹不长肉。 (lit) Official ships leak; official horses grow thin; old fathers who are cared for in rotation [in their children's homes] won't grow fat. (fig) No one takes care of public property or interests; what belongs to everybody belongs to nobody. [Rhyme; see also *guān fáng lòu* below.]

119 **Guān chūyú mín; mín chūyú tǔ.** 官出于民, 民出于土。 (lit) Officials come from the people, [just as] the people come from the land. (fig) Officials depend upon the people, just as the people depend upon the land.

120 **Guān dà, bù yā xiānglín.** 官大不压乡邻。 [When an] official [assumes] high [office, he should] not oppress [his] hometown neighbors. [See also *fùguì bù yā* above.]

121 **Guān dà yī jí, yā sǐ rén.** 官大一级, 压死人。 [An] official one rank higher [can] control a person [one rank lower.]

122 **Guǎn de sān céng mén lǐ; guǎnbude sān céng mén wài.** 管得三层门里, 管不得三层门外。 [One should only] care about affairs within [one's] family, not those outside of it. [Cf. *JPM*, chap. 7; note: *sān céng mén*, (lit) "three layers of doors"; in traditional China, well-to-do extended families usually had three parallel rows of buildings within the walls of the compounds of their homes.]

G

123 **Guān duàn, shí tiáo lù.** 官断十条路。(lit) Officials judging [a case have] ten different ways. (fig) It's difficult to anticipate the outcome of a law case [in traditional China] as every one is settled differently. Going to court is a "crap shoot"; there's no way to predict what will happen. [Cf. *Xǐngshì Yīnyuán Zhuàn*, chap. 81.]

124 **Guān fáng lòu; guān mǎ shòu; guān zhòng tángwū jī shǐ chòu.** 官房漏, 官马瘦, 官众堂屋鸡屎臭。(lit) Public buildings leak, public horses are thin, [and in the] public meeting halls [there are] stinking chicken droppings. (fig) No one takes care of public property. [Rhyme; compare with *guān wū lòu* below.]

125 **Guānfǔ bù dǎ sònglǐ de /Guān bù dǎ sònglǐ rén.** 官府不打送礼的 / 官不打送礼人。(lit) Officials don't whip those who offer presents. (fig) Those who send bribes to the magistrate are sure to escape punishment. [Cf. *Sān Xiá Wǔ Yì*, chap. 111; see also *zāngguān bù dǎ* below.]

126 **Guān gāo bì xiǎn; shì dà bì qīng.** 官高必险, 势大必倾。(lit) Officials [of] high [rank] must [face] danger, [and those whose] power is great [sooner or later] must collapse. (fig) The higher one's position is the more risk one faces. "The bigger they are, the harder they fall."

127 **Guǎng gǔ chuízi dǎ bù xiǎng.** 光鼓锤子打不响。(lit) A drumstick alone can't make much noise. (fig) It's impossible to accomplish much alone.

128 **Guǎnggùn bù chī yǎnqián kuī.** 光棍不吃眼前亏。(lit) A smart guy won't suffer a loss right under his nose. (fig) A clever person usually retreats or compromises under unfavorable conditions. [Cf. *Wǔ Sōng*, chap. 2; also said *hǎohàn bù chī*, etc.]

129 **Guǎnggùn dǎ jiǔ jiǔ; bù dǎ jiā yī.** 光棍打九九, 不打加一。(lit) A smart guy hits ninety-nine, [but] not one more [i.e., one hundred]. (fig) A clever person knows to stop before going too far.

130 **Guǎnggùn dù lǐ yǒu bǎ chèng.** 光棍肚里有把秤。(lit) A smart guy has a steelyard [measure] in his heart. (fig) A clever person knows what's what. [Cf. *Wǔ Sōng*, chap. 2.]

131 **Guǎnggùn huítóu, èsǐ gǒu.** 光棍回头饿死狗。(lit) [If] a "smart guy" [can] turn over a new leaf, [then] dogs [can] starve to death [i.e., something impossible]. (fig) It is very unlikely that (such) scoundrels can mend their ways. [Cf. *gǒu bù chī shǐ* above.]

132 **Guǎnggun shū zài tuǐ shàng; bù néng shū zài zuǐ shàng.** 光棍输在腿上, 不能输在嘴上。A "smart guy" may lose by running away [from a fight, etc., but he] will never admit that he lost. [Rhyme.]

133 **Guǎng jiāo bùrú zéyǒu.** 广交不如择友。Better to choose [one's] friends [with care] than to make friends indiscriminately. [Cf. *Lìjì: Xué Jì*.]

134 **Guǎng jì bùrú dàn mò.** 广记不如淡墨。(lit) A broad memory is not as [good as] pale ink. (fig) Written notes are always better than memory alone. [See also *hǎo jìxìng bùrú* and *xīn jì bùrú* below.]

135 **Guǎn gōng de, gōng wān; guǎn jiàn de, jiàn zhí.** 管弓的弓弯, 管箭的箭直。(lit) [Those who are] in charge of [making] bows [should make them] curved, [and those who are] in charge of [making] arrows [should make them] straight. (fig) Each should do his or her own duty or mind his or her own business. "You do your job and I'll do mine."

136 **Guāng shuō bù liàn, wǎng xué bǎinián.** 光说不练, 枉学百年。(lit) All talk [but] no practice [is to] waste [one's] effort [though it be for one] hundred years. (fig) Talk without actual practice will come to nothing.

137 **Guān guān xiānghù,* (yǒu qiānlián).** 官官相护, (有牵连)。Officials protect each other, ([as they all] have ties [between them]). [Note: *guānguān-xiānghù* is used as a *chengyu*; cf. *Xǐngshì Héngyán*, chap. 20; *Lǎo Cán Yóujì*, chap. 5.]

138 **Guāngyīn shì jiàn, rìyuè rú suō.** 光阴是箭, 日月如梭。(lit) Time [flies] like an arrow [and] the days and nights [as fast] as a shuttle. (fig) Time flies quickly. [Note: *rìyuè-rúsuō* is used as a *chengyu*; cf. *Gǔ-Jīn Xiǎoshuō*, chap. 26; *Xǐngshì Héngyán*, chap. 5; note: *guāng-yīn*, (lit) "light and shadow" means "time"; *rì-yuè*, (lit) "sun and moon," means "days and nights."]

139 **Guāngyīn sì jùnmǎ jiābiān; fú shì sì luòhuā / liúshuǐ.** 光阴似骏马加鞭, 浮世似落花 / 流水。Time gallops by like a swift horse being whipped, [and] worldly affairs pass like flowers falling [or] water flowing away.

140 **Guāngzhe jiǎo bù pà chuān xié de hàn.** 光着脚不怕穿鞋的汉。(lit) [Those who are] barefoot are not afraid of guys wearing shoes. (fig) The poor [who have nothing to lose] are not afraid of the rich. Desperate people have nothing to lose.

141 **Guān jǐng bùrú tīng jǐng.** 观景不如听景。(lit) Going sightseeing is not as [good as being] told by others. (fig) Descriptions are often better than the actual scene itself. [Rhyme.]

142 **Guān jìn, sī bù jìn.** 官禁私不禁。Officially, [some things are] prohibited, [but] privately [they are] not. [See also *guān bùróng zhēn* above.]

143 **Guān jiǔ, zì fù.** 官久自富。[When one has been in an] official [position for a] long time, [one will] naturally [become] wealthy. [See also *yī rén qīng zhèng fù* below.]

144 **Guàn kǒu hǎo wǔ; rén kǒu nán wǔ.** 罐口好捂, 人口难捂。(lit) The mouths of jars may be stopped up, [but] the mouths of people [can] not be stopped. (fig) You cannot squelch public opinion. [See also *fáng mín zhī kǒu* above.]

145 **Guānmén dǎ gǒu; sāwǎng bǔyú.*** 关门打狗, 撒网捕鱼。(lit) Close the door [when you] beat a dog [so it can't get away]; cast the net wide [to] catch fish. (fig) Different matters require different tactics. [Note: *guānmén dǎ gǒu* is a set phrase usually referring to bottling up an enemy to prevent his escape; *sāwǎng bǔyú* is also a military expression meaning to deploy one's forces widely.]

146 **Guānmén yǎng hǔ; hǔ dà shāngrén.** 关门养虎, 虎大伤人。(lit) [If you] raise a tiger [secretly] behind closed doors, [when the] tiger grows up [it will] harm you [or others]. (fig) If one helps bad people, one will suffer the consequences later. [Cf. *Shuō Yuè Quán Zhuàn*, chap. 40.]

147 **Guān qí bù yǔ, zhēn jūnzǐ; luò zǐ wú huǐ, dàzhàngfu.** 观棋不语真君子, 落子无悔大丈夫。[One who while] watching a chess [game] keeps silent [is] a true gentleman; [one who] makes a move, [and does] not regret, [i.e., change] it [later, is a] good sportsman. [Said, e.g., by chess players.]

148 **Guān qīng, mín zì ān; (fǎ zhèng, tiān xīn shùn).** 官清民自安, (法正天心顺)。[When] officials [are] "clean," [i.e., honest and upright], the people [will] naturally be peaceful; ([if] justice prevails, Heaven [will] respond favorably. [From a play by the Yuan dynasty playwright Xuan Hanqing.]

149 **Guān qíng rú zhǐ báo.** 官情如纸薄。Feelings [between] officials [are as thin] as paper, [i.e., when one is in trouble, the others won't support him]. [Cf. *Xǐngshì Héngyán*, chap. 27; note: *rénqíng* "relations; feelings"; *qíngmian*, "feelings; sensibilities"; see also *rénqíng zǐ zhǐ* below.]

150 **Guān qīng, yámen shòu.** 官清衙门瘦。[When] officials are "clean," [i.e., honest and upright], [their subordinates in the] magistrate's office [will be] thin, [i.e., won't be rich]. [Also said *guān qīng, sìlǐ shòu*; ". . . the runners are thin"; note: *yámén* refers to the local magistrate's office in imperial China, usually in the county seat; see also *dāngchāi de* above and *yamen de qián* and *yǒu guān, bù chóu zàolì* below.]

151 **Guān qí yǒu, zhī qí rén.** 观其友, 知其人。(lit) To look at [someone]'s friends [is to] know that person. (fig) People are known by the company they keep.

152 **Guān rén rú guān yù; zhuō yǎn xǐ jī píng.** 观人如观玉, 拙眼喜讥评。Judging people['s characters] is like] judging jade; the incompetent like to criticize.

153 **Guānr méile shāmào; wēnshén méile língguāng.** 官儿没了纱帽, 瘟神没了灵光。(lit) [An] official [who] has lost [his] black gauze cap [is like a] God of Plagues without [his] halo. (fig) No one is afraid of an official who has lost his office.

154 **Guǎn shān chī shān; guǎn shuǐ chī shuǐ.** 管山吃山, 管水吃水。(lit) [Those who are] in charge of mountain [areas] eat [off the] mountains [and those who are] in charge of water [areas] eat [off the] waters. (fig) People in charge get different kinds of benefits depending on what they are in charge of. [Cf. *Rúlín Wàishǐ*, chap. 41; see also *dáyú de bù lí* above and *jìn shān shǐ mù* and *kào shān, chī shān* below.]

155 **Guǎn sháo de, guǎn bùliǎo shāohuǒ.** 管勺的, 管不了烧火。(lit) [The] cook cannot be in charge of stoking the fire. (fig) One should not interfere with other people's business.

156 **Guān wū lòu; guān mǎ shòu.** 关屋漏, 关马瘦。(lit) A house [which has been] closed up [for a long time will] leak, [and a] horse [which has been] shut up [for a long time will be] thin. (fig) People and things which are not used go into a decline. [Rhyme; these characters may be a misinterpretation of *guān fáng lòu* above.]

157 **Guān wú sān rì jǐn.** 官无三日紧。(lit) Officials are not strict for [even] three days. (fig) An official won't strictly enforce the rules for long. [Cf. *Èr Kè Pāi'àn Jīngqí*, chap. 17; see also *fǎ wú sān rì yán* above.]

158 **Guān xiàng guān; mín xiàng mín; (qióngrén xiàng de shì qióngrén).** 官向官, 民向民, (穷人向的是穷人)。Officials are partial to officials, common people support common people, ([and] it's poor people who help each other). (fig) Like helps like. [Rhyme; the last part is often omitted, or may vary, as *guāngjiǎo de xiàngde shì qióngrén*, "Those who are barefoot help the poor."]

159 **Guǎnxiánshì, luò bùshi.** 管闲事, 落不是。"Poking one's nose into other people's business" [will] result in being blamed.

160 **Guān xíng hǎo guò; sīxíng nán ái.** 官刑好过, 私刑难挨。Official punishment [in a law court may] be borne, [but] illegal punishments are hard to bear. [Said of punishments by landlords, money lenders, etc. in traditional China.]

161 **Guān yú hǎi zhě nán wéi shuǐ.** 观于海者难为水。(lit) One [who has] seen the sea [is] hard [put] to care about rivers. (fig) Having seen the greater world, one is beyond caring about trifles. To a sophisticated person, there is nothing new under the sun. [From Mencius (*Méngzi: Jìn Xīn Shàng*); cf. *Érnǚ Yīngxióng Zhuàn*, chap. 15; see also *céng jīng cānghǎi* above.]

162 **Guǎn zhōng kuī bào, kě jiàn yī bān.** 管中窥豹, 可见一斑。(lit) Peek [at a] leopard through [a bamboo] tube, [and you] can [only] see one spot. (fig) Even though one has only a limited knowledge of something, one can imagine the entire thing. [Cf. *Jìn Shū: Wáng Xiàn Zhī Zhuàn*; note: *guǎnzhōng-kuībào* is used as a *chengyu* meaning "having a limited view or knowledge of something."]

163 **"Guān" zì, liǎng zhāng kǒu.** "官"字, 两张口。(lit) [The Chinese character for] "official" [looks like it contains] two [characters for] "mouth" (口). (fig) Government officials often "speak out of both sides of their mouths," (i.e., say one thing at one time and something else at another) and do not keep their promises. [This is an orthographic pun.]

164 **Guàn zǐ rú shā zǐ.** 惯子如杀子。(lit) To spoil a child is like killing a child. (fig) Children must learn discipline in order to survive. [Also said *jiāo zǐ, shā zǐ*; note: *jiāoguàn*, "to spoil (someone)."]

165 **Guā shóu yào zhāi; guǒ shú yào cǎi.** 瓜熟要摘, 果熟要采。(lit) [When they are] ripe, melons [and] fruit should be picked. (fig) Grasp the opportunity when conditions are favorable; "*carpe diem*." [Rhyme.]

166 **Guā shú zì luòdì; shuǐ dào zì chéng chuān.** 瓜
熟自落地，水到自成川。(lit) [When] melons
are ripe, [they will] naturally fall to the ground,
[just as when] water comes, [it] naturally forms
[into] rivers. (fig) Don't be impatient; things (will)
happen naturally in their own time.

167 **Guā tián bù nà lǚ; lǐ xià bù zhèng guān.*** 瓜田
不纳履，李下不正冠。(lit) Don't tie your
shoes in a melon patch, [and] don't adjust your
hat under a plum tree. (fig) Don't engage in any
behavior which might appear suspicious.

168 **Guā wú gǔnyuán; rén wú shíquán.** 瓜无滚圆，
人无十全。[Just as] no melon is fully round,
[so] no person is 10[0 percent] perfect. [Rhyme;
see also rén wú wánrén below.]

169 **Guāzǐ bù bǎo, shì rénxīn.** 瓜子不饱，是人心。
(lit) Melon seeds do not satisfy one's hunger completely, [but they at least] represent sincerity. (fig)
(Like entertaining a guest with melon seeds: it's
nothing much, but) it's the thought that counts.
[Usually said politely by a host.]

170 **Gǔ bù dǎ, bù xiǎng; huà bù shuō, bùmíng.** 鼓不
打不响，话不说不明。(lit) [A] drum won't
make sound unless [it's been] beaten; words not
spoken [can]not be understood. (fig) One must
speak up in order to be understood by others.
[Compare with the following two entries; cf. Èr
Kè Pāi'àn Jīngqí, chap. 38; see also rén bù shuō
below.]

171 **Gǔ bù dǎ, bù xiǎng; lǐ bù biàn, bùmíng.** 鼓不打
不响，理不辩不明。[Just as] without being
beaten, drums won't sound, [so] without being
debated over, the truth won't come clear. [See
also huà bù shuō, bùmíng below.]

172 **Gǔ bù dǎ, bù xiǎng; zhōng bù zhuàng, bù míng.**
鼓不打不响，钟不撞不鸣。(lit) [A] drum
won't make sound unless [it's been] beaten, nor
will a bell unless [it's been] struck. (fig) People
won't make comments unless there is some reason. [Cf. Èr Kè Pāi'àn Jīngqí, chap. 38; compare
with the preceding two entries.]

173 **Gūdān zhě nán qǐ; zhòng xíng zhě yì qū.** 孤单者
难起，众行者易趋。(lit) A single person can
hardly get started [while] a group going together
can easily advance. (fig) Many people make a job
easier. "Many hands make light work."

174 **Gū dú chù rǔ; jiāozǐ mà mǔ.** 孤犊触乳，骄子
骂母。(lit) [Just as an] only calf will butt [up
against its mother's] udders, [so a] spoiled child
curses [at its] mother. (fig) Children should not
be spoiled (especially by their mothers). [Rhyme;
note: calves bump their mother's udders when
they wish to nurse.]

175 **Gǔ duō, chōng chū mǐ; rén duō, jiǎng chū lǐ.** 谷
多舂出米，人多讲出理。(lit) [Just as when
there is] more grain, [it's easier to] husk the rice,
[so when there are] more people, [it's easier to]
reason out the truth. (fig) Public opinion or discussion will expose the truth. [Rhyme; see also
gōngpíng chūyú above.]

176 **Guǐ bù zhāo, bù lái.** 鬼不招，不来。(lit) Devils
don't come unless [they are] invoked. (fig) Bad
people don't come unless they are invited. Bad
behavior invites others of a similar ilk.

177 **Guì de bù guì; jiàn de bù jiàn.** 贵的不贵，贱
的不贱。Expensive goods are not really expensive [because they are of high quality, and] cheap
goods are not really cheap [because they are usually of low quality]. [See also piányi wú hǎo huò
and hǎo wù bù jiàn and yī fēn jiàqian below.]

178 **Guǐhuǒ bù gǎn jiàn zhēn huǒ.** 鬼火不敢见真
火。(lit) Fox fire dares not meet real fire. (fig) The
crooked fear the upright. Uprightness can always
overcome heterodoxy.

179 **Guì jīng, bù guì duō.** 贵精，不贵多。(lit) Value
quality; do not value quantity. (fig) It's quality, not
quantity, that counts. [Cf. Lao She's Zhèng Hóng
Qí Xià.]

180 **Guìrén bù tà xiǎndì.** 贵人不踏险地。(lit) A
person of high rank does not go to dangerous
places. (fig) Rich (or noble) people don't (have
to) take risks. [A traditional Chinese belief; see
also jiā lěi qiānjīn below.]

181 **Guìrén duō wàng shì.** 贵人多忘事。(lit) Noble
people [tend to] forget things more [because they
are so busy]. (fig) A person of (your) eminence
has so many important matters to deal with that
some may become forgotten. [Said either flatteringly or ironically; cf. DRC, chap. 6.]

182 **Guìrén huàyǔ chí.** 贵人话语迟。A person [who
assumes himself to be] important [deliberately]
speaks slowly.

183 **Guìrén tái yǎnkàn, biànshì fúxīng lín.** 贵人抬
眼看，便是福星临。[If a] noble person casts
a [favorable] eye [on you], that's [your] lucky star
drawing nigh.

184 **Guī shī wù yǎn qióngkòu mò zhuī.** 归师勿掩，
穷寇莫追。(lit) [One should] not attack a re-
treating enemy [and] not pursue a hard-pressed
foe; (fig) One should not press a defeated enemy so hard that they turn and fight in desperation. Don't force people into a corner (as they
may fight back desperately like cornered rats).
[Cf. R3K, chap. 95; Sunzi: Jūn Zhēng; vs. yí jiāng
shèng yǒng below.]

185 **Guǐ (yě) pà èrén.** 鬼（也）怕恶人。(Even)
ghosts are afraid of evil people. [Cf. JW, chap. 36;
Xǐngshì Yīnyuán Zhuàn, chap. 39.]

186 **Guì yì jiāo; fù yì qī.** 贵易交，富易妻。[When a
man] rises in status, [he] changes [his old] friends,
[and when a man becomes] rich, [he] changes
[his] wife, [i.e., takes an additional wife and neglects or abandons the first one]. [See also pínjiàn
zhī zhī below.]

187 **Gǔ kōng, shēng gāo; rén kuáng, huà dà.** 鼓空，
声高；人狂，话大。[Just as] empty drums
[make the] loudest sound, [so] proud and self-
conceited people talk big. [See also hǎo māo bù
jiào and kōng guànzi and shuǐ jìng zé and zhěng
píng bù yáo below.]

188 Gǔlái cún lǎo mǎ, bùbì qǔ chángtú. 古来存老马，不必取长途。 (lit) Since time immemorial [people have] kept old horses, not chosen [for their ability to go] long distances, [but because they know the routes from long experience]. (fig) Value older people for their experience and knowledge, rather than for their physical strength. [From a Tang dynasty poem "Jiāng Hàn" by Du Fu; see also *lǎo mǎ shí tú* below.]

189 Gǔlái fāng ěr xià, shéi néng bù tūn gōu? 古来芳饵下，谁能不吞钩？ (lit) Since time immemorial, [whenever there has been] fragrant bait [hung out], underneath [there has always been] someone unable [to resist] swallowing the hook. (fig) Where there are benefits to be got, there will always be people willing to take risks or die to get them. [See also *rén wèi cái sǐ* and *zhòngshǎng zhīxià* below.]

190 Gūniang xián sǎo chǒu. 姑娘嫌嫂丑。 (lit) A sister [says she] dislikes [her] elder brother's wife [for her] ugliness. (fig) One should not complain about things which are none of their business. [Note: Traditionally the relation between gū-sǎo (brother's sister and brother's wife) is a troubled one.]

191 Gùnzi shāng ròu; èyǔ shāng gǔ. 棍子伤肉，恶语伤骨。 A club hurts the flesh, [but] evil words hurt the bone. [See also *biān zhī shāng ròu* above.]

192 Guó bùkě yī rì wú jūn. 国不可一日无君。 [A] nation cannot [afford even] one day without [its] ruler. [Cf. *R3K*, chap. 3 and 85; see also *cháotíng bùkě* above.]

193 Guō bù rè, bǐng bù tiē. 锅不热，饼不贴。 (lit) [If the] wok [frying pan] is not hot, the cakes won't stick [to it]. (fig) Wait until the time is right before taking action.

194 Guò ěr zhī yán bùkě tīng xìn. 过耳之言不可听信。 (lit) Words overheard are not to be trusted. (fig) Hearsay is not reliable. [Cf. *JW*, chap. 10.]

195 Guǒ guā shīdì zé bù róng; yú lóng shī shuǐ zé bùlíng. 果瓜失地则不荣，鱼龙失水则不灵。 (lit) Fruit [and] melons without land won't grow; [and] fish [and] dragons without water can't function. (fig) No one can be divorced from the support of the masses. [From a biography written by the Song dynasty poet Su Shi; note: dragons are believed to live in water.]

196 Guò hé mò wàng dāqiáo rén. 过河莫忘搭桥人。 (lit) [When you] cross a river, don't forget the people [who] built the bridge. (fig) (After one has succeeded,) one should not forget the people who have helped one in the past. [Note: *dāqiáo*, (lit) "to build bridges," has the figurative meaning of "to act as a go-between"; see also *chīshuǐ bù wàng* above.]

197 Guójiā xīng-wáng, pǐfū yǒu zé. 国家兴亡，匹夫有责。 (lit) [For] the rise and fall of the nation, [every] common man (sic) has a responsibility. (fig) All men (sic) share a common responsibility for the fate of their country. [Cf. *Yuè Fēi Zhuàn*, chap. 8.]

198 Guòle zhège cūn, méi zhège diàn. 过了这个村，没这个店。 (lit) Past this village there'll be no [more] inns [like this one]. (fig) Don't pass up a good (or last) chance, as it will not come again. [Cf. *Érnǚ Yīngxióng Zhuàn*, chap. 9; see also *jī bù kě shī* below.]

199 Guō lǐ yǒu, wǎn lǐ cái yǒu. 锅里有，碗里才有。 Only if [the collective] pot has [food in it will] there be [food] in [one's individual] bowl. [This was a communist slogan in the 1950s; see also *dà hé lǐ yǒu shuǐ* above.]

200 Guó luàn chū zhōngchén.* 国乱出忠臣。 [When the] country [is] in turmoil, [it will] come out [who] the loyal court officials [are]. [Originally *guójiā hūnluàn, yǒu zhōngchén* from *Lǎozǐ*, chap. 18; see also *jífēng zhī jìncǎo* and *rén dào nánchù* and *shì biàn zhī rénxīn* below.]

201 Guòqù, wèilái, bùrú xiànzài. 过去未来，不如现在。 Neither past nor future are as good as the present. [Rhyme.]

202 Guòtóu fàn bié chī; guòtóu huà bié jiǎng. 过头饭别吃，过头话别讲。 (lit) Don't eat excessive [amounts of] food, [and] don't talk excessive talk. (fig) Don't eat too much food [and] don't brag or exaggerate or say anything that will hurt or offend others. [See also *huà bùyào shuō* below.]

203 Guó yǐ mín wéi běn; mín yǐ shí wéi tiān. 国以民为本；民以食为天。 A country depends on [its] people as [its] base, [just as] the people depend on food [to survive]. [Cf. *Dōng Zhōu Lièguó Zhì*, chap. 81.]

204 Guó yǒu guófǎ; jiā yǒu jiāguī. 国有国法，家有家规。 [Just as a] country has [its] laws, [so a] family·has [its] rules. [See also *jiā yǒu jiāguī* below.]

205 Guò zé wù dàn gǎi. 过则勿惮改。 [If you] have faults, do not fear to change [them]. [Cf. the Confucian Analects: *Lúnyǔ: Xué Ér.*]

206 Gǔ zhōng yú gōng, shēng wén yú wài. 鼓钟于宫，声闻于外。 (lit) [If one] strikes the bell in the palace [the] sound [is] heard outside. (fig) Inside stories always leak out. [Cf. *Niè Hǎi Huā*, chap. 16; see also *zhōng zài sìyuàn* below.]

207 Gǔ zuò, gǔ dǎ; luó zuò, luó qiāo. 鼓作鼓打，锣作锣敲。 (lit) Beat drums [as they were] made [to be] beaten; beat gongs [as they were] made [to be] struck. (fig) Different problems should be dealt with in different appropriate ways.

G

H

1 **Hǎi kuò cóng yú yuè; tiān kōng rèn niǎo fēi.** 海阔从鱼跃，天空任鸟飞。(lit) The sea is so broad [that] fish may swim freely, [and] the sky so vast [that] birds may fly as they will. (fig) The world is full of boundless opportunities. "The sky's the limit." [Cf. *JW*, chap. 84, and the *chengyu*: *hǎikuò-tiānkōng*, from a poem by the Tang dynasty monk Xuan Lan.]

2 **Hǎi kū zhōng jiàn dǐ; rén sǐ bù zhīxīn.** 海枯终见底，人死不知心。[When the] sea runs dry, [you can] see [its] bottom, [but even when a] person dies, [you] won't [ever] know [his or her true] mind. [Cf. *Fēngshén Yǎnyì*, chap. 21; see also *zhī rén, zhī miàn* below.]

3 **Hǎinèi cún zhījǐ, tiānyá ruò bǐlín.** 海内存知己，天涯若比邻。(lit) In this world, [as long as one] has a true friend, the remotest corner of the earth [is as close] as [one's] next door neighbor. (fig) Great distances cannot separate close friends. [Said when parting or in letters; originally from a Tang dynasty poem "Sòng Dù Shào Fù Zhī Rèn Shǔ Chuān" by Wang Bo; used by Mao Zedong to describe the close relationship between China and Albania in the 1960s.]

4 **Hàirén zhī xīn, bùkě yǒu; fáng rén zhī xīn, bùkě wú.** 害人之心不可有，防人之心不可无。(lit) An intention to harm others [one] should not have, [but] an intention to [be on] guard [against] others [one] cannot do without. (fig) One should never intend to do harm to others, but should always guard against the harm others might do to oneself.

5 **Hàirén zhōng hài jǐ.** 害人终害己。[Those who] harm others ultimately harm themselves. [Cf. the *píngshū: Shuō Táng*, chap. 62.]

6 **Hǎishàng wú yú, xiā zìdà.** 海上无鱼，虾自大。(lit) [When] there are no fish in the seas, the shrimp are arrogant. (fig) When there are no people of true ability about, lesser people will naturally become leaders. [See also *shān zhōng wú lǎohǔ*.]

7 **Hǎi shēn bùpà yú dà.** 海深不怕鱼大。(lit) The sea [is so] deep [that it can hold all] fish, however big [they are]. (fig) Broad-minded people can be tolerant toward others with a variety of differing opinions.

8 **Hǎishuǐ bùkě dǒu liáng.** 海水不可斗量。(lit) The water in the sea cannot be measured with a bushel. (fig) A great person cannot be judged by ordinary standards. [Often preceded by *rén bù kě mào xiàng* below.]

9 **Hǎi yuè shàng kě qīng; kǒu nuò bù kě yí.** 海岳尚可倾，口诺不可移。(lit) Even seas [and] mountains may be overturned, [but] oral promises can't be changed. (fig) One must keep one's word at all costs. [See also *xǔ rén yī wù* and *yī yǔ wéizhòng* below.]

10 **Hǎi zài shēn yǒu dǐ; shān zài gāo yǒu dǐng.** 海再深有底，山再高有顶。(lit) The sea has a bottom, however deep; [and] the mountain has a top, however high. (fig) Everything has a limit.

11 **Háma tiào sān tiào, háiyào xiē yīxiē.** 蛤蟆跳三跳，还要歇一些。(lit) [After] three leaps, even a frog needs a rest. (fig) Everyone needs time to rest or to collect one's thoughts.

12 **Hángháng chū zhuàngyuán.** 行行出状元。See *qíshí'èr háng, hángháng* below.

13 **Hángjiā kàn méndao; wàiháng kàn rènao.** 行家看门道，外行看热闹。An expert knows what to look for [in a performance, while] a layman [just] watches the show. [Rhyme; cf. *Yuè Fēi Zhuàn*, chap. 93; *Wǔ Sōng*, chap. 3; note: *méndào* refers to "tricks of the trade."]

14 **Hángjiā mò shuō lìba huà.** 行家莫说力八话。(lit) An expert [should] never [pretend to] speak lay language. (fig) An expert should not pretend to be a layman (in order to avoid extra work, etc.) as he will be found out. [Cf. *Érnǔ Yīngxióng Zhuàn*, chap. 11; note: *lìba* is colloquial for "layman; non-specialist."]

15 **Hángjiā shēnshen shǒu, biàn zhī yǒu méiyǒu.** 行家伸伸手，便知有没有。(lit) [As soon as an] expert extends his hand [to a job], he [immediately] knows what is and what is not. (fig) An expert knows what's what as soon as he "rolls up his sleeves" and puts his hand to it. A specialist can size up a situation at a glance. [Rhyme; see also *yǎn qiǎo hé xū* below.]

16 **Hān guā zhǎng de dà.** 憨瓜长得大。Simpletons [who do not take things too seriously] grow healthy. [Note the colloquial expression: *xīnkuān tǐ pàng* "(One whose) heart (is) carefree grows fat."]

17 **Hán māo bù zhuō shǔ.** 寒猫不捉鼠。(lit) A cat [that is afraid of] cold won't [go out to] catch mice. (fig) A person who is afraid of hardships won't accomplish anything in life.

18 **Hánmén chū cáizǐ; gāoshān chū jùn niǎo.** 寒门出才子，高山出俊鸟。Poor families [can] produce talented people, [just as] the high [remote] mountains [can] produce beautiful birds. [Vs. *gǒuwō lǐ* above; see also *shēnshān chū jùn niǎo* below.]

19 **Hànqíng jí rú huǒ.** 旱情急如火。(lit) A drought is as urgent as a fire. (fig) Sending relief to a drought-stricken area is as urgent as putting out a fire.

20 **Hán róng zhōng yǒuyì; rènyì shì shēng zāi.** 含容终有益，任意是生灾。Yielding [to others] in the end brings benefits, [while] being willful is to invite disaster. [Cf. *Xǐngshì Héngyán*, chap. 34; see also *ráorén bù shì* below.]

21 **Hān tóu lángr, zēng fú, zēng shòu.** 憨头郎儿，增福增寿。 Fools [always] get lucky [and] live long. [Cf. the classical novel *Jìnghuā Yuán*, chap. 93.]

22 **(Hán Xìn jiàng bīng,) duōduō-yìshàn.** (韩信将兵，)多多益善。 (lit) ([Just as with] Han Xin commanding troops,) the more [there are], the better. (fig) The more one has, the better. [Han Xin was a general who helped Liu Bang in the early Han period; cf. *Shǐ Jì: Huái Yīn Hóu Lièzhuàn*; also quoted in Mao Zedong's *Collected Works* (*Máo Zédōng Xuǎnjí*), vol. 5, p. 116; the second half is often omitted when this is used as a *xiehouyu*.]

23 **Hào chá zhě bù rù jiǔlóu.** 好茶者不入酒楼。 (lit) Tea-drinkers don't enter wine shops. (fig) Each person has his or her own individual interests and tastes.

24 **Hǎo dì bù zhòng, cǎo chéng wō.** 好地不种，草成窝。 (lit) [Even on] cultivated land, [if] not sown, weeds [will] grow [so tall that wild animals will] nest [in it]. (fig) Even given favorable conditions, one must invest some effort in order to achieve anything. [Also said *hǎo tián bù chù, cǎo chéng wō*.]

25 **Hǎo duòshǒu néng shǐ bā miàn fēng.*** 好舵手能使八面风。 (lit) A good helmsman can take advantage of winds from any direction. (fig) A good leader can deal with any situation which arises and/or can bring into full play the talents of all his subordinates.

26 **Hǎo ér, hǎo nǚ, yǎnqián huā.** 好儿，好女，眼前花。 (lit) Good sons [and] daughters [are like] flowers in season; [i.e., they will soon disappear]. (fig) (Even good) sons and daughters will eventually leave their parents.

27 **Hǎo fàn bùpà wǎn, (qù huà bù xián màn).** 好饭不怕晚，(趣话不嫌慢)。 (lit) [As long as it's a] good meal, [it] doesn't matter [if it's] late; ([as long as it's an] interesting [story, it] doesn't matter [if it's told] slowly). (fig) The best food takes time to prepare, (and the best stories are told slowly). As long as one has great achievements, it doesn't matter if they come slowly or late in one's life or career. [Rhyme; see also *chí huā màn fā* above.]

28 **Hǎo gǒu bù lánlù /dǎnglù.** 好狗不拦路/挡路。 (lit) A good dog does not block the road. (fig) A good person should not act as an obstacle to others' progress. One should not be a "dog in the manger."

29 **Hǎo gǒu hù sān lín; hǎohàn hù sān cūn.** 好狗护三邻，好汉护三村。 (lit) [Just as a] good dog protects [its] three neighbors [so a] hero protects [his] three [neighboring] villages. (fig) A good man should protect his neighbors from danger. [See also *hǎohàn hù sān lín* below.]

30 **Hǎo guān yì zuò; hǎorén nán zuò.** 好官易做，好人难做。 (lit) [To be a] good official is easy, [but⊙ to be a] good person is difficult. (fig) It is (even) harder to be a good person than to be a good government official. [Cf. *R3K*, chap. 14; note: *zuò (hǎo) rén*, "to be a good person."]

31 **Hǎohàn bù chī yǎnqián kuī.** 好汉不吃眼前亏。 (lit) A hero [will] not suffer a loss [right] under his nose. (fig) A smart person never deliberately puts himself at a disadvantage or "butts his head against a brick wall." A wise person doesn't put up a fight when the odds are against him. "Discretion is the better part of valor." [Cf. *Wǔ Sòng*, chap. 2; Mao Dun's *Zǐyè* (Midnight); see also *guānggùn bù chī* above.]

32 **Hǎohàn bù dǎ, bùcéng xiāngshí.** 好汉不打，不曾相识。 (lit) [If two] heroes never fight [they can] never know each other well [enough to be] friends]. (fig) Some people have to fight before they can become friends. "From an exchange of blows, friendship grows." [See also *bù dǎ, bù (chéng)* above.]

33 **Hǎohàn bù gǎn fá tùr.** 好汉不赶乏兔儿。 (lit) A good [hunts]man doesn't chase tired hares. (fig) A decent person doesn't take unfair advantage of others. "Don't shoot sitting ducks." [Cf. *JW*, chap. 71.]

34 **Hǎohàn bùpà chūshēn dī.** 好汉不怕出身低。 [If one is] a good person, it doesn't matter [if one has] humble origins. [Cf. *Érnǚ Yīngxióng Zhuàn*, chap. 11.]

35 **Hǎohàn bù tí dāngnián yǒng.** 好汉不提当年勇。 (lit) A [true] hero doesn't bring up [his] past bravery. (fig) A hero never brags about his past glories. [Cf. *Yuè Fēi Zhuàn*, chap. 87; also said *hǎohàn bù kuā dāng nián yǒng*.]

36 **Hǎohàn hù sān lín.** 好汉护三邻。 A good man [should] protect [his] neighbors [from danger]. [Cf. *Yuè Fēi Zhuàn*, chap. 90; see also *hǎo gǒu hù sān lín* above.]

37 **Hǎohàn liúxuè, bù liúlèi.** 好汉流血，不流泪。 (lit) A hero sheds blood [but] not tears. (fig) A brave man would rather shed blood than to show weakness by crying. [See also *zhàngfu yǒu lèi* below.]

38 **Hǎohàn pà lǎnhàn; lǎnhàn hái pà wāi sǐ chán.** 好汉怕懒汉，懒汉还怕歪死缠。 [Even] heroes are afraid of rascals, [and] even rascals are afraid of [the kind of lazy fools who talk nonsense and] pester [one] to death. (fig) Never waste your time arguing with fools and rascals. [Rhyme.]

39 **Hǎohàn shàngchǎng, yī rén dǐng liǎ.** 好汉上场，一人顶俩。 (lit) When a hero comes out [to do battle], [he] alone is equal to two [in the fight]. (fig) One well-trained person can do the job of two. [Rhyme; see also *lǎojiàng chūmǎ* below.]

40 **Hǎohàn shí hǎohàn; (xīngxīng xī xīngxīng).** 好汉识好汉，(星星惜星星)。 (lit) [Just as one] hero [can] recognize [another] hero, ([so] clever people are attracted to [other] clever people). (fig) Good people appreciate each other's abilities; "like attracts like." [Also said *hǎohàn xī hǎo hàn*, "good people are attracted to each other"; the two halves may be reversed; see also *yīngxióng shí yīngxióng* below.]

41 **Hǎohàn shuō zuò, jiù zuò.** 好汉说做就做。 (lit) [As soon as a] hero says [he will] do [something], then [he] does [it]. (fig) A gentleman always keeps his word. [See also the following entry.]

H

H

42 **Hǎohàn yī yán, kuài mǎ yī biān.** 好汉一言，快马一鞭。(lit) A good man [need only give his] one word [just as a] swift horse [needs only] one [touch of the] whip. (fig) A good man always keeps his word. [Rhyme; also said *jūnzǐ yī yán* below; see also the preceding entry.]

43 **Hǎohàn zhǐpà bìng lái mó.** 好汉只怕病来磨[/魔]。(lit) A hero fears [nothing] but illness [wearing him down]. (fig) Even a brave person cannot avoid illness. [Note: in the original source *Wǔ Dài Shǐ Yǎnyì*, chap. 57, the character for *mó*, "demon / magic" was used.]

44 **Hǎohàn zuòshì, hǎohàn dāng.** 好汉做事，好汉当。(lit) [What a] hero does, a hero bears [the consequences of]. (fig) A good person takes responsibility for the consequences of his or her own actions ("like a man").

45 **Hǎohàn zuòshì, zuòdào tóu; hǎo mǎ dēngchéng, pǎodào tóu.** 好汉做事做到头，好马登程跑到头。[Whenever a] true man does a job, [he] does [it] thoroughly, [just as when a] good horse sets out, [it always] completes [its] journey. [Rhyme.]

46 **Hǎo hé bùrú hǎo sàn.** 好合不如好散。[Even] more important than a friendly meeting is a friendly parting.

47 **Hǎohuà bù bèirén, bèirén méi hǎohuà.** 好话不背人，背人没好话。Good [things need] not [be] said behind people's backs; [any] words [said] behind someone's back must be bad. [See also *hǎoshì bù mán* below.]

48 **Hǎohuà bù zài duō, jǐ jù chéng zhījǐ.** 好话不在多，几句成知己。Agreeable speech lies not in quantity; a few [such] words can make bosom friends. [Rhyme.]

49 **Hǎohuà néng chuān tiě.** 好话能穿铁。(lit) Reasonable speech can penetrate iron. (fig) (1) Reason is a strong force. (2) Sincere words can move people.

50 **Hǎo hǔ jià bu zhù qún láng.** 好虎架不住群狼。(lit) A strong tiger is no match for a pack of wolves. (fig) One is no match against many. [See also *gǒu duō, bù pà láng* above.]

51 **Hǎo huò wúxū zhāolái; (hǎo jiǔ bùyòng guà zhāopái).** 好货无须招徕，(好酒不用挂招牌)。(lit) Goods of fine quality have no need [of promotion to] attract [customers, (and) good wine does not need to hang [out a] sign). (fig) High quality goods and people of talent need no promotion. "Good wine needs no bush." [The two parts of this rhymed couplet are often used separately with the same meaning; see also *hǎo jiǔ bùyòng* and *jiǔ hǎo, rén zì lái* below.]

52 **Hǎo jiādàng pà sān fèn fēn.** 好家当怕三份分。A good estate should not be divided.

53 **Hǎo jiè hǎo huán; zài jiè bù nán.** 好借好还，再借不难。(lit) [If] well-borrowed [and] well-returned, [then] borrowing again [will] not be difficult. (fig) Return what you borrow promptly and you will be welcome to borrow again. [Rhyme; cf. *JW*, chap. 16.]

54 **Hǎo jiǔ bùpà xiàngzi shēn.** 好酒不怕巷子深。(lit) A good wine fears not the depth of a lane [i.e., the place where it is sold being "off the beaten track"]. (fig) Good quality or ability will attract customers, no matter how remote they are. [See also *jiǔ hǎo, rén zì lái* below and the following entry.]

55 **Hǎo jiǔ bùyòng guà zhāopái.** 好酒不用挂招牌。(lit) Good wine does not require hanging [out a] sign [to attract customers]. (fig) Goods of fine quality or people of ability have no need of promotion to attract customers. "A good wine needs no bush." [See also *hǎo huò wúxū* above and the preceding entry.]

56 **Hǎo jiǔ shuō bù suān; suān jiǔ shuō bù tián.** 好酒说不酸，酸酒说不甜。(lit) Good wine won't become sour, however it is downplayed; sour wine won't become sweet, however it is praised. (fig) Good people are good, and bad people are bad, no matter what others say about them. [See also *hǎorén shuō bù huài* below.]

57 **Hǎo jìxing bùrú làn bǐtóu.** 好记性不如烂笔头。(lit) A good memory is not as good as the ragged tip of a [brush] pen. (fig) It is much better to take written notes than to rely on one's memory. [See also *xīn jì bùrú* below.]

58 **Hǎole shāngbā, wàngle tòng.** 好了伤疤望了痛。(lit) Once the wound is healed, one forgets the pain. (fig) One forgets the bitter past when one has become better off.

59 **Hǎo mǎ bù chī huítóu cǎo.** 好马不吃回头草。(lit) A good horse will never [return to] graze on grass [it has already] passed by. (fig) A gentleman will not return to a position or offer which he has previously declined. [See also *měnghǔ bù chī* below.]

60 **Hǎo māo bù jiào; hǎo gǒu bù tiào.** 好猫不叫，好狗不跳。(lit) Good cats don't mew [and] good dogs don't jump about. (fig) People of ability never show off. [Rhyme; see also *gǔ kōng, shēng gāo* above and *hǔ bào bù wài* and *kōng guànzi* and *shuǐ jìng zé* below.]

61 **Hǎo mǎ yá qián bù dītóu.** 好马崖前不低头。(lit) A fine horse won't lower its head [i.e., give up] before a cliff. (fig) A strong-willed person won't succumb to difficulties.

62 **Hǎo mèng nán cháng; cǎiyún yì sàn.** 好梦难长，彩云易散。(lit) Sweet dreams are short-lived, [and] rosy clouds are easily dispersed. (fig) Good times don't last long. [Cf. *Míng Shǐ Yǎnyì*, chap. 37; see also *hǎo wù bù jiānláo* below.]

63 **Hǎo nán bù chī hūn shí fàn; hǎo nǚ bù chuān jià shí yī.** 好男不吃婚时饭，好女不穿嫁时衣。(lit) A good man does not eat [his] wedding food, [and] a good woman does not wear [her] wedding clothes. (fig) Men and women who have high aspirations do not live on the property they get from their parents when they marry. [Cf. *JPM*, chap. 85; also said *hǎo nán bù chī fēnjiā fàn*; etc., "A good man never depends on the property he receives as a family inheritance, etc." in *Rúlín Wàishǐ*, chap. 11.]

64 **Hǎo nán bù gēn nǚ dòu.** 好男不跟女斗。(lit) Good men do not fight with women. (fig) No decent man will fight a woman [Cf. Lao She's play *Lóng Xū Gōu* (Dragon Beard Ditch).]

65 **Hǎo péngyou qín suànzhàng.** 好朋友勤算帐。(lit) Good friends are diligent about settling accounts. (fig) Prompt payments of loans makes for good friendships. "Short reckonings make long friends." [See also *qīnxiōngdì míng* below.]

66 **Hǎo quán bù yíng tóu sān shǒu; zìyǒu gāozhāo zài hòutou.** 好拳不赢头三手, 自有高招在后头。(lit) A good boxer doesn't (try to) win [with his] first three blows; [his] high skill [in martial arts in fact won't be seen until] the end. (fig) A superior fighter holds back at first, to give his opponent time to reveal his weaknesses, so he can evaluate and take advantage of them.

67 **Hǎo qǔzi bù chàng sān biàn.*** 好曲子不唱三遍。(lit) A good tune [should] not be sung three times. (fig) People get tired of repetition even of something basically good. [Also said *hǎo qǔzi chàng sān biàn, yě yào kǒu chòu*, "A good tune sung three times will make one's mouth stink"; vs. *hǎoxì nàikàn* below; see also *huà shuō sān biàn* below.]

68 **Hǎorén bù chángshòu; huòhai yīqiān nián.** 好人不长寿, 祸害一千年。(lit) Good people don't always live long [while] bad people [may last] a thousand years. (fig) It's fate that decides. [Cf. *JPM*, chap. 73; here *huòhai*, "calamities," refers to bad people.]

69 **Hǎorén hái děi kào yī zhuāng.** 好人还得靠衣装。Even fine people need fine clothes [to present themselves properly]. [See also *rén kào yī zhuāng* below.]

70 **Hǎorén pà kuā; huàirén pà bā.** 好人怕夸, 坏人怕疤。Good people [should] beware of praise, [while] evil people are wary of exposure.

71 **Hǎorén shuō bù huài; hǎo jiǔ jiǎo bù suān.** 好人说不坏, 好酒搅不酸。(lit) Good people cannot [be made] bad [by] talk, [just as] good wine won't [become] sour [by being] stirred. (fig) Slander can't harm a truly upright person. [See also *gēn shēn bùpà fēng* and *hǎo jiǔ shuō bù suān* above.]

72 **Hǎorén xiāngfēng, èrén yuǎnlí.** 好人相逢, 恶人远离。[When] good people get together, evil people keep their distance.

73 **Hǎorén xiāngféng, èshì xiāng lí.** 好人相逢, 恶事相离。(lit) [When] good people meet, evil doings leave. (fig) When bad people get together, no good can come of it.

74 **Hǎoshì bùchūmén; èshì chuán qiān lǐ.** 好事不出门, 恶事传千里。Good news [about someone] never gets past the door; [but] bad news [about someone] is transmitted a thousand leagues away. [Cf. *JW*, chap. 73; *WM*, chap. 24; compare Mark Twain's "A lie gets halfway around the world before truth puts on its boots"; the order of the two halves may be reversed (q.v.).]

75 **Hǎoshì bù mán rén; mán rén méi hǎoshì.** 好事不瞒人, 瞒人没好事。[One's] good deeds, [one does]n't keep secret [from] others, [and anything that is] kept secret [from] others is [always] not good. [Cf. *Wǔ Sōng*, chap. 6; see also *hǎohuà bù bèirén* above.]

76 **Hǎoshì bù zài máng lǐ.** 好事不在忙里。(lit) Good deeds do not exist in haste. (fig) One can't accomplish anything (good) by hurrying.

77 **Hǎoshì duō mó.** 好事多磨。(lit) [Accomplishing] great things [has] many hardships. (fig) In accomplishing anything worthwhile, one is bound to encounter setbacks. [Note: originally *hǎoshì* referred to a successful marriage or engagement, so "it takes many twists and turns to accomplish a good marriage" is sometimes equated with "The course of true love never did run smooth." Cf. *JW*, chap. 28; *DRC*, chap. 1; *Èr Kè Pāi'àn Jīngqí*, chap. 9.]

78 **Hǎoshì guòtóu fǎn chéng huàishì.** 好事过头反成坏事。(lit) [If a] good thing [is carried] to excess, [it will] rather become a bad thing. (fig) A good thing overdone turns into a bad thing. There's such a thing as too much of a good thing. [See also *fēi jī bù xiàdàn* above.]

79 **Hǎoshì méi xiàshāo.** 好事没下梢。(lit) Good deeds [sometimes] have no [good] ending. (fig) Good deeds sometimes come to nothing. [*Xiàshāo*, literally the thin end of a pole, log, etc., here refers to an ending.]

80 **Hǎo shí shì tārén; è shí shì jiārén.** 好时是他人; 恶时是家人。[In] good times, [people regard their relatives as] being strangers, [but in] bad times, [people regard them as] being family. [Rhyme; see also *pínjiàn, qīnqi lí* and *pín jī nàoshì* below.]

81 **Hǎoshǒu bù dí shuāng quán; shuāng quán nán dí sì shǒu.** 好手不敌双拳, 双拳难敌四手。(lit) [One] good hand is no match for two fists, [and] a pair of fists is no match for four hands. (fig) Even a good fighter can't fight two at once, nor can two fight four. [Cf. *JW*, chap. 77; *Xīngshì Héngyán*, chap. 29; note: *hǎoshǒu*, (lit) a "good hand," means an experienced hand or expert.]

82 **Hǎo sǐ bùrú è huó.** 好死不如恶活。(lit) A good death is not as good as a terrible life. (fig) A poor life is better than a good death. [Cf. *JW*, chap. 63; see *hǎo sǐ bù làn huózhe* in *Yuè Fēi Zhuàn*, chap. 23 and Lao She's play *Cháguǎn* ("Teahouse"); see also *zài shēng yī rì* below.]

83 **Hǎo sǔn chū zài líba wài.** 好笋出在篱笆外。(lit) Good [bamboo] shoots grow outside the fence. (fig) Good products come from remote places and talented people may come from poor regions. [See also *shēnshān chū jùn niǎo* below.]

84 **Hǎo tiě bù dǎ dīng; hǎo nán bù dāngbīng.*** 好铁不打钉, 好男不当兵。[Just as] good iron won't be hammered [into] nails, [so] good men [should] not be made [into common] soldiers. [Rhyme; a pre-1949 saying.]

H

85 **Hào wèn jìnhū zhì; zhī chǐ jìnhū yǒng.** 好问近乎智，知耻近乎勇。Inquisitiveness is close to wisdom; [and] shame is close to bravery. [Cf. *Shǐ Jì: Píng Jìnhóu Zhǔfù Lièzhuàn.*]

86 **Hǎo wù bù jiàn; jiàn wù bù hǎo.** 好物不贱，贱物不好。(lit) Good goods are not cheap, and [cheap] goods are not good. (fig) Goods of high quality are not cheap, and inexpensive goods are (usually) not good. [Cf. *Xīngshì Yīnyuán Zhuàn.* chap. 85; see also *guì de bù guì* above; and *yī fēn jiàqian* below.]

87 **Hǎo wù bù jiānláo.** 好物不坚牢。(lit) Bcautiful things are not durable. (fig) Happy times do not last long. [Cf. *Gǔ-Jīn Xiǎoshuō*, chap. 29; see also the following entry.]

88 **Hǎo wù nán quán; hóng luó chǐ duǎn.** 好物难全，红罗尺短。(lit) Anything good can hardly be kept intact; [expensive] red silk is measured [in] short [lengths]. (fig) "The good die young." [Cf. *JPM*, chap. 89; see also the preceding entry.]

89 **Hǎo xié bù tà chòu gǒu shǐ.** 好鞋不踏臭狗屎。(lit) Fine shoes don't step in stinking dog excrement. (fig) Decent people don't condescend to arguing with scoundrels. [Cf. *Xīngshì Yīnyuán Zhuàn*, chap. 52.]

90 **Hǎoxì nàikàn; hǎo qǔ zhōngtīng.** 好戏耐看，好曲中听。(lit) A good opera bears [many] watchings, [and] a good tune deserves [many] hearings. (fig) One never gets tired of a good opera or a good song. [Vs. *hǎo qǔzi bù chàng* above.]

91 **Hǎoxīn bù dé hǎo bào.** 好心不得好报。Good-heartedness does not [always] receive a good recompense. [Cf. *JPM*, chap. 97; vs. the following entry.]

92 **Hǎoxīn yǒu hǎo bào.** 好心有好报。(lit) Good-heartedness meets with good recompense. (fig) One's charity is or will be rewarded. [Also said *hǎoxīn zì yǒu hǎo bào*; see the preceding entry and *shàn yǒu shànbào* below.]

93 **Hǎo yǒu hǎo bào; è yǒu èbào.** 好有好报，恶有恶报。(lit) Goodness is repaid with goodness [and] evil is repaid with evil. (fig) One should do good and not do evil; those who do evil things suffer themselves sooner or later. [See also *shàn yǒu shànbào* and *xíngshàn, dé shàn* below.]

94 **Hǎo yǔ, tiān liúkè.** 好雨，天留客。[By such a] good rain, Heaven has detained the guest. [Said by a host when a guest is unable to part because of bad weather. This is a shorter version of a longer written sentence: *xià yǔ(,) tiān(,) liú kè(;) tiān(;) liú(,) wǒ bù liú*, often cited as a humorous ambiguity, where the punctuation marks in parenthesis indicate the possible pause junctures in reading. The alternative reading means: "When it rains, Heaven detains the guest(s); Heaven detains them, not I." See also *rén liú, sānfēn jiǎ* below.]

95 **Hǎo zhàng bùrú wú.** 好帐不如无。(lit) A good debt [i.e., where terms are favorable] is [still] not as good as not having [any debt at all]. (fig) It is better not to be in debt, no matter how favorable the terms of a loan.

96 **Hàozi jíle yě yǎo māo.** 耗子急了也咬猫。(lit) A rat [when] cornered [will] even bite [a] cat. (fig) In a desperate situation one can do anything. [See also *ègǒu bù pà* above and *tùzi jíle* and *zhí xiàng gǎn gǒu* below.]

97 **Hǎo zǐ wù yòng duō; yī gè dǐ shí gè.** 好子勿用多，一个抵十个。One doesn't need many sons; one [good son] is equal to ten [ordinary sons].

98 **Hébāo shí gè dòng, zhuànqián bùgòu yòng.** 荷包十个洞，赚钱不够用。(lit) [If your] purse [has] ten holes [in it, however much] money [you] earn, [you will] never have enough. (fig) If one has too many expenditures or if one is not economical, no money will ever be accumulated. [Rhyme; note: *hébāo* originally referred to a purse; it now refers to a pocket.]

99 **Hēguànle de shuǐ; shuōguànle de zuǐ.** 喝惯了的水，说惯了的嘴。[Just as one is] used to drinking water, [so one is also] used to speaking [the truth].

100 **Hé hé, shítou zài.** 河涸，石头在。(lit) The river [may] run dry, [but] the stones remain. (fig) Even though one may fail, one's aspirations remain.

101 **Héhuā suī hǎo, yě yào lǜ yè fúchí.** 荷花虽好，也要绿叶扶持。(lit) Although the lotus is beautiful, [it] completely depends on the support [of its] green leaves. (fig) Everyone needs the support of others. [Also said *hé huā hái děi lǜ yè fú*; often quoted by Mao Zedong; see also *mǔdan suī hǎo* and *qī fēn luó-gǔ* and *yī gè lǐba* below.]

102 **Hēi fà bù zhī qínxué zǎo; báishǒu fāng huǐ dúshū chí.** 黑发不知勤学早，白首方悔读书迟。(lit) [When one has] black hair [and one does] not know [how important it is to] study hard early [in life, then] only [later when one has a] white head will [one] regret [that it is] too late to study. (fig) If one doesn't study hard when young, then one will regret it later, when one is too old to learn. [See also *lǎo bù xiēxīn* and *qián sānshí nián shuì* and *shàozhuàng bù nǔlì* below.]

103 **Hēi guō lǐ zhǔchū xiāng mǐfàn.** 黑锅里煮出香米饭。(lit) Tasty rice is cooked out of a black pot. (fig) People or things are not to be judged by their superficial appearances. "Don't judge a book by its cover."

104 **Hēixīn rén dào yǒu mǎ'ér qí.** 黑心人到有马儿骑。(lit) A black-hearted person may in fact have a horse to ride. (fig) Contrary to our expectations, evil people may lead happy, prosperous lives.

105 **Hé lǐ méi yú, shì shàng kàn.** 河里没鱼，市上看。(lit) [One can see whether there are] fish in the river [or] not [by] looking in the market. (fig) One can judge things by inference. [See also *mǐ liáng zài shì shàng* below.]

106 **Hé lǐ wú yú, shì shàng zhǎo.** 河里无鱼市上找。(lit) [When] there are no fish in the river, seek in the market. (fig) One has to look in the right place if one wants to find something.

107 **Hé lǐ wú yú, xiā yě guì.** 河里无鱼, 虾也贵。(lit) [When] there are no fish in the river, shrimp [becomes] expensive. (fig) When there are no products of good quality available, even products of poorer quality will sell at higher prices. [See also *lǎn huò děng hángshì* below.]

108 **Hé lǐ yānsǐ shuǐ yāzi.** 河里淹死水鸭子。(lit) [Even] ducks may be drowned in the river. (fig) People of ability sometimes fail out of negligence or over-confidence. [See also *shàn yóu zhě nì* below.]

109 **Hé lǐ yǒu xiā, shuǐ zé jìng.** 河里有虾, 水则净。(lit) [If] there are shrimp in the river, the water will be clear. (fig) There is always one thing which can overcome another. [See also *lǎoshǔ zài dà* and *yī wù xiáng yī wù* below.]

110 **Hèngcái bù fù mìng qióngrén.** 横财不富命穷人。Ill-gotten gains won't enrich one [who is] destined to be poor. [Cf. *Xǐngshì Héngyán*, chap. 18.]

111 **Hèn xiǎo fēi jūnzǐ; wú dú bù zhàngfu.** 恨小非君子, 无毒不丈夫。(lit) [One who] hates little is not a great man; [one who] has no viciousness, is not a hero. (fig) Great men harbor deep hatreds and heroes must be ruthless. [Cf. *WM*, chap. 120; the second half is often used independently as a set phrase, as in *JPM*, chap. 92; vs. *liàng xiǎo fēi jūnzi* below.]

112 **Hěnxīn zuò cáizhu.** 狠心做财主。[It requires a] cruel heart to be a wealthy person. [Note: *cáizhǔ* originally referred to the rural gentry.]

113 **Héqi xiū tiáo lù; rě rén zhù dǔ qiáng.** 和气修条路, 惹人筑堵墙。(lit) Amiability builds roads, [while] offending [people] builds walls. (fig) Amiability makes friends, while hurting people makes enemies.

114 **Héshang jiàn qián, jīng yě mài.** 和尚见钱, 经也卖。(lit) [When a] monk sees money [he will] even sell [his books of Buddhist] scriptures. (fig) Some people will sell their souls for money.

115 **Héshang wú ér, xiàozǐ duō.** 和尚无儿, 孝子多。[Although] monks have no children, [yet they may have] many filial sons [because others respect and support them]. [Cf. *DRC*, chap. 85.]

116 **Héshang zài, bōyú zài.** 和尚在, 钵盂在。(lit) [Where] there's [a] monk, there's [his] alms bowl. (fig) As long as one is alive, one's relationships to others continue to exist.

117 **Hé shēn, shuǐliú jìng; xī qiǎn, shuǐ shēng xuān.** 河深水流静, 溪浅水声喧。(lit) [If the] river is deep, the water flows quietly; [if the] stream is shallow, the water sounds noisy. (fig) People of great knowledge are usually modest and quiet, whereas people of little knowledge often do a lot of empty talking or boasting. [See also *gǔ kōng, shēng gāo* above and *kōng guànzi* and *zhěng píng bù yáo* below.]

118 **Hé shì bù biǎo lǐ.** 和事不表理。[If you want to] settle [a] matter peacefully, don't discuss [who is] right or wrong.

119 **Héshuǐ bù fàn jǐngshuǐ.** 河水不犯井水。(lit) River water does not intrude into well water. (fig) No one should encroach upon the precincts of another. [More commonly said *jǐngshuǐ bù fàn héshuǐ* above.]

120 **Héshuǐ bù zhǎng, xiān jià qiáo; yǔshuǐ wèi luò, xiān dā péng.** 河水不涨先架桥, 雨水未落先搭棚。(lit) Build the bridge first, [when] the river [has] not [yet] risen; build the shed first before it rains. (fig) Always make preparations well in advance. [See also *píngshí duō dǎ jǐng* below.]

121 **Héshuǐ gān, jǐngshuǐ gān.** 河水干, 井水干。(lit) [When the] river [runs] dry, [the] wells [will also be] dry. (fig) There are always connections or causes between phenomena. Things are interrelated.

122 **Hé shuǐ wú yú; hé guān wúsī?** 何水无鱼, 何官无私? (lit) What water is without fish, [and] where are there officials without selfishness? [I.e., there aren't any.] (fig) Officials are always interested in their own personal gain. [Note: *sīxīn*, "seeking personal gain."]

123 **Huó sī chéng yī lǚ; jī cùn chéng yī chǐ.** 和丝成一缕, 积寸成一尺。(lit) Mixed silk fibers become one thread; accumulated inches make one foot. (fig) To accomplish anything one has to make consistent efforts over time.

124 **Hè suǒ lóng zhōng, zhǎnchì nán.** 鹤锁笼中, 展翅难。(lit) A crane locked in a cage has difficulty spreading [its] wings. (fig) A person of intelligence or talent cannot bring his or her full potential into play under adverse conditions.

125 **Hé yǒu hédào; shān yǒu shānlù.** 河有河道, 山有山路。(lit) Rivers have their courses, [and] mountains have their roads. (fig) (1) Everything has its own ways. (2) Everyone has his or her own way of life.

126 **Hé yǒu jiǔ qū bā wān; rén yǒu sān huí liù zhuǎn.** 河有九曲八弯, 人有三回六转。[Just as] rivers have nine twists [and] eight bends, [so] people [also frequently] have changes [of attitude, mind, or character over time]. [Rhyme.]

127 **Hé yǒu liǎng àn; shì yǒu liǎngmiàn.** 河有两岸, 事有两面。[Just as a] river has two banks, [so] every matter has two sides.

128 **Hóng pí luóbo, zǐ pí suàn; yǎng liǎn lǎopo, dītóu hàn.** 红皮萝卜紫皮蒜, 仰脸老婆低头汉。[Just as] red radishes [and] purple garlic [are spicy], [so] women [who walk with their] faces looking up [and] men [who walk with their] heads down [are hard to deal with]. [Note: In traditional China, women who walked with their faces not lowered were thought to be assertive or aggressive, and men who walked with their heads facing down were said to be scheming and cunning.] [Rhyme.]

129 **Hòu chā yī rì yāng; wǎnshōu shí tiān gǔ.** 后插一日秧, 晚收十天谷。(lit) Transplant rice seedlings one day late [and your] harvest [will be] ten days late. (fig) One will suffer losses if one puts things off or lets opportunities slip by. [See also *jíjié bù ràng rén* below.]

130 **Hóu mén shēn sì hǎi.** 侯门深似海。(lit) Noblemen's doors [are as] deep as the sea. (fig) It's difficult to visit a noble person's home. The mansions of the nobility are inaccessible to the common people. [Cf. *DRC*, chap. 6, and the *chengyu*: *hóumén-sìhǎi*.]

131 **Hòumǔ de quántou; yún lǐ de rìtóu.** * 后母的拳头，云里的日头。[A] stepmother's fists [are a hidden menace, like] the sun in the clouds. [Originally *Wǎn niáng de quántou* . . . in *Rúlín Wàishǐ*, chap. 5; see also *gé chóng dùpí* above and *pí lǐ shēng de* below.]

132 **Hòu wèi bì xī dú.** 厚味必腊毒。(lit) [The most] delicious food is always the most poisonous. (fig) The most enjoyable things in life are often harmful to one's health. "The best things in life are either illegal or fattening." [A common belief; cf. *Guó Yǔ: Zhōu (Xià)*]

133 **Hóuzi bù zuān quān, duō qiāo jǐ biàn luó.** 猴子不钻圈，多敲几遍锣。(lit) [If the trained circus] monkey [is] not [willing to] jump through the hoop, [one only needs to] strike the gong a few more times. (fig) If one trick doesn't work, one will have to try another. "There's more than one way to skin a cat."

134 **Hóuzi jīnglíng, guāng gǔtou.** 猴子精灵，光骨头。(lit) Monkeys [may be] "clever" [but they nevertheless are] only [skin and] bones [i.e., not fat, despite their cleverness]. (fig) Cleverness isn't everything. There is such a thing as being too smart. [Note: *jīnglíng*, used of children, means "clever, smart"; see also *cōngming fǎn bèi* above.]

135 **Huà bù shuō, bùmíng; mù bù zuān, bù tòu.** 话不说不明，木不钻不透。(lit) Words not spoken [can]not be understood, [just as] wood not drilled [can]not be penetrated. (fig) You can't make yourself understood if you don't speak up. [See also *gǔ bù dǎ* above and *zhōng bù dǎ* below.]

136 **Huà bù tóujī, bàn jù duō.** 话不投机，半句多。(lit) [If the] talk is disagreeable, [then another] half sentence is too much. (fig) It's a waste of breath to continue to talk with someone with whom one does not agree. [Note: *huàbùtóujī* is used as a set phrase meaning "to be at loggerheads"; see also *jiǔ féng zhījǐ* below.]

137 **Huà bùyào shuōsǐ; lù bùyào zǒu jué.** 话不要说死，路不要走绝。(lit) Don't say anything absolutely [and] don't walk too far. (fig) In saying or doing anything, one should allow for unseen circumstances. Never "paint yourself into a corner"; always leave yourself some room to maneuver. [Note: *zǒu juélù* means "to get into an impasse"; see also *guòtóu fǎn bié chī* above.]

138 **Huācǎo shēng zì shān zhōng; yànyǔ chūzì xīnzhōng.** 花草生自山中，谚语出自心中。[Just as] flowers [and] grass grow in the mountains, [so] proverbs come from the hearts [of the people]. [See also *qiézi bù kǎi xū* below.]

139 **Huà chū yuānjia kǒu; lì chū yǒu biāo niú.** 话出冤家口，力出有膘牛。(lit) [Critical] words ☺ come from the mouths of those who love [one], [just as] strength comes from oxen [which are]

fat. (fig) (Only) those who have one's best interests at heart will (take the trouble to) criticize one. [Rhyme; note: *yuānjia* (lit) "rival" is also a term of affection used to mean "lover," "sweetheart," and is often used to refer to one's spouse or child.]

140 **Huā dào chūntiān, zìrán kāi.** 花到春天，自然开。(lit) [When] spring comes, flowers [will] naturally bloom. (fig) Things develop naturally in their own time.

141 **Huà dào shéjiān, liú bàn jù.** 话到舌尖，留半句。(lit) [When] words [come] to the tip of [your] tongue, hold [back] half [of them]. (fig) Don't say everything you think. It is not always wise to tell the whole truth. "(Speech is silver;) silence is gold."

142 **Huā duì huā, liǔ duì liǔ; pò běnjī duì shé tiáozhou.** 花对花柳对柳，破畚箕对折笤帚。(lit) [Just as] flowers are matched to flowers [and] willows are matched to willows, [so a] broken dust pan is matched to a rotten broom. (fig) Somewhere there is a woman for every man. "Every Jack has his Jill." [Cf. *Shí Diǎn Fóu*, chap. 6; also said . . . *pò fèn jī duì làn sàozhou* "a broken dung-carrying basket matches a rotten broom"; see also *zhèng guǒ pèi hǎo zào* below.]

143 **Huà duō, méi rén xìn; yǔ dà, làole tián.** 话多没人信，雨大涝了田。Too many words, people won't believe, [just as] too much rain [will] flood a field. [Rhyme.]

144 **Huà duō yì shī; xiàn cháng yì duàn.** 话多易失，线长易断。Too much talk [makes it] easy [to] slip, [just as] too long [a] thread is easy to break.

145 **Huā féng shí fā.** 花逢时发。(lit) Flowers bloom when their time comes. (fig) People have good luck when fortune decrees. [Cf. *Fēngshén Yǎnyì*, chap. 15; see also *huā luò, huā kāi* below.]

146 **Huà guǐ róngyì; huà rén nán.** 画鬼容易，画人难。(lit) [It is] easier to draw a devil than to draw people; [i.e., if it is harder to portray familiar things like people, dogs and horses accurately, because they are familiar to everyone, while it is easier to portray ghosts and spirits because they are rarely seen, and they often change their appearances, so there is no set standard to judge by.] (fig) It is easier to do things in an individualistic, idiosyncratic way than to follow fixed procedures according to a set standard. [Originally from *Hán Fēizǐ*.]

147 **Huāhuā jiàozi, rén tái rén.** 花花轿子，人抬人。[Even if one sits in a] beautifully decorated sedan-chair, [one still needs] others to lift one up. (fig) Everyone relies on "mutual backscratching." [This is often used in two parts as a *xiehouyu*.]

148 **Huàishì chuán qiān lǐ; hǎoshì bùchūmén.** 坏事传千里，好事不出门。See *hǎoshì bùchūmén* above.

149 **Huái shàn rú zhēn; tuō è rú lǚ.** 怀善如珍，脱恶如履。[One should] hold onto [one's] virtue as [one would] a treasure, [and one should] throw off [one's] bad habits as [one would discard] old shoes.

150 **Huàjiàng bù gěi shén zuòyī.** 画匠 不给 神作
揖。 (lit) Artisan-painters [who make the statues
of gods] don't bow to them. (fig) Those who know
the backgrounds of famous people don't always
respect them. [See also *jìn sì rénjiā* below.]

151 **Huà jīng sān zhāng zuǐ; chángchong yě zhǎng
tuǐ.** 话 经 三 张 嘴; 长 虫 也 长 腿。 (lit)
[After] words [have] passed [through] three⊙
mouths, even snakes [will be believed to have]
grown legs. (fig) Rumors exaggerate everything, (so don't believe them). [Rhyme; note:
chángchong (lit) "long worm" means "snake";
see also *dōngmén shī tiáo* above.]

152 **Huā kāi, tiānxià nuǎn; huā luò, tiānxià hán.** 花
开天下暖，花落天下寒。 (lit) [When] flow-
ers bloom, it's warm everywhere; [when] flowers wither, it's cold everywhere. (fig) People are
warm toward those who are rich or in power
and cold to those who are poor or out of power.
[Rhyme.]

153 **(Huà lóng, huà hǔ, nán huà gǔ;) zhī rén, zhī
miàn, bù zhīxīn.** (画龙画虎，难画骨;) 知
人知面，不知心。 (lit) ([Although when one]⊙
draws a dragon [or] a tiger, it is difficult to draw
their bones; [so] one can) know a person's figure [or] face [but] not his heart. (fig) It is difficult to know people's true nature. [Cf. *WM*, chap.
45; also said *huà hǔ, huà pí gǔ*, etc., as in *Gǔ-Jīn
Xiǎoshuō*, chap. 1; *JPM*, chap. 80. The first part
may be omitted, as in *JPM*, chap. 51; see also *hǎi
kū zhōng jiàn* above and *suī yǒu qīn fù* and *zhī rén,
zhī miàn* below.]

154 **Huā luò, huā kāi, zì yǒu shí.** 花落花开，自有
时。 (lit) Flowers bloom [and] fade naturally at
their [appointed] times. (fig) People's fortunes are
all determined by fate. [See also *huā fēng shí fā*
above.]

155 **Huā mùguā, kōng hǎokàn.** 花木瓜，空好看。
(lit) The prettiest papaya are the emptiest [in-⊙
side]. (fig) "Beauty is only skin deep." [Cf. *WM*,
chap. 24.]

156 **Huángdì yě yǒu cǎoxié qīn.** 皇帝也有草鞋
亲。 (lit) Even the emperor has straw-sandal relatives. (fig) Everyone has poor relations. [See also
cháotíng hái yǒu qióng below.]

157 **Huángguā páo bù guòlái, páo húzǐ.** 黄瓜刨不
过来，刨瓠子。 (lit) [Those who] can't skin
cucumbers, skin soft-skinned gourds. (fig) Those
who can't bully the powerful, bully the weak.
[Note the *chengyu*: *qīruǎn-pàyìng*, "bullying the
weak but fearing the strong."]

158 **Huángjīn bù dǎ, bù chéngqì.** 黄金不打，不成
器。 (lit) Gold without being hammered won't
become [useful] utensils. (fig) Without education
or training one will not (grow up to) be a useful person. [Note: *chéngqì*, (lit) "become an instrument," means to grow up to be a useful person; *bùchéngqì* is also an idiom meaning "good-
for-nothing; worthless."]

159 **Huángjīn wèi wéi guì; ānlè zhíqián duō.** 黄金
未为贵，安乐值钱多。 Gold is not the only
[thing which is] valuable; peace [and] happiness

are worth more [than] money. [Cf. *WM*, chap. 55;
also said *xiū dào huángjīn guì, ānlè zuì zhíqián*.]

160 **Huángjīn wú jiǎ; xìfǎ wú zhēn.** 黄金无假，戏法
无真。 (lit) There is no false gold [and] there are
no true magic tricks. (fig) Truth is truth and falsehood is falsehood. [See also *shì zhēn, nán jiǎ* and
shì zhēn, nán miè and *zhēn de, jiǎ bùliǎo* below.]

161 **Huángjīn yǒu jià; rén wú jià.** 黄金有价，人无
价。 Gold has a price [but] people are priceless.
[From the Qing dynasty *sǎn qǔ* verse; *Jì Shēng
Cǎo*.]

162 **Huánglián jiù rén, wú gōng; rénshēn shārén, wú
guò.** 黄连救人无功，人参杀人无过。 (lit)
Chinese goldthread [root] cures people, [but it
is] not praised [because it is bitter]; ginseng [root
sometimes] kills people [but it is] not condemned
[because it is widely believed to have beneficial
medicinal properties.] (fig) People do not always
get the credit or blame they truly deserve. [Note:
huángliánmù, Chinese pistache or "goldthread,"
is a bitter medicinal herb.]

163 **Huánglián shù, gēn pán gēn; qióngkǔ rén, xīn-
liánxīn.** 黄连树根盘根，穷苦人心连心。
(lit) [Just as the] roots of the Chinese goldthread
tree entwine around one another, [so] hearts of
the poor are linked one to another. [Rhyme; note:
the Chinese goldthread tree is used to produce
an extremely bitter medicine, and is a common
image for the bitterness of poverty; see also the
preceding entry.]

164 **Huáng lí, hēi lí; dé shǔ zhě xióng.** 黄狸黑狸，
得鼠者雄。 [It doesn't matter if a] leopard cat
[is] yellow or black; [as long as it can] catch mice,
[it's] great. [Cf. *Liáo Zhāi Zhì Yì: Xiùcái Qū Guài*;
see also *bái māo, hēi māo* above.]

165 **Huángnián dàdùzi.*** 荒年大肚子。 (lit) [In]
famine years [people have] greater appetites.
(fig) The less people have, the more they want.

166 **Huángnián wú liùqīn.** 荒年无六亲。 [In] famine
years [people try to survive], ignoring [even their]
relatives. [Note: *liùqīn*, (lit) "the six relations" (i.e.,
father, mother, elder brothers, younger brothers,
wife, children), more generally refers to any kin;
see also *rén qióng duàn liùqīn* below.]

167 **Huángniú guò hé, gè gù gè; bānjiū shàng shù,
gè jiào gè.** 黄牛过河个顾个，斑鸠上树
个叫个。 (lit) [When] oxen cross a river, each
takes care of itself, [and when] turtledoves are in
the trees, each sings its own tune. (fig) (It's a fact
that) everyone looks after himself or herself without concern for others.

168 **Huángquán lùshàng wú lǎoshào.** 黄泉路上无
老少。 (lit) On the road to the netherworld,
there is no [difference between the] young [and
the] old. (fig) Death may befall both old and
young alike.

169 **Huángshǔláng bù xián xiǎo jī shòu.** 黄鼠狼
不嫌小鸡瘦。 A yellow weasel doesn't care
whether chickens are thin [or not]. (fig) Some
chiselers try to exploit as much advantage as possible, no matter how small it may be.

170 **Huángshǔláng zhuān tiāo bìng yāzi yǎo.** 黄鼠狼专挑病鸭子咬。 (lit) Weasels specifically look for sick ducks to bite. (fig) Evil doers always target the most vulnerable. [Also said *huángshǔláng dǎn yǎo bìng yāzi*.]

171 **Huáng tiān bù fù hǎoxīn rén.** 皇天不负好心人。 Heaven will not disappoint kindhearted persons.

172 **Huáng tiān bù fù kǔxīn rén.** 皇天不负苦心人。 (lit) Heaven does not disappoint people who take pains. (fig) Providence doesn't let down those who do their best. "Heaven helps those who help themselves." [Cf. Mao Dun's novel *Zǐyè* (Midnight).]

173 **Huānxǐ pòcái, bù zài xīn shàng.** 欢喜破财, 不在心上。 (lit) [If one] loses money (or property) [when one is] happy, [one] won't take it to heart. (fig) Happiness is more important than money. [Cf. *Èr Kè Pāi'àn Jīngqí*, chap. 11; see also *cái qù, shēn ānlè* above and *pòcái shì dǎng zāi* below.]

174 **Huānyú xián yè duǎn; jìmò hèn gēng cháng.** 欢娱嫌夜短, 寂寞恨更长。 (lit) [When one is] happy [one] feels [that the] nights are short, [but when one is] lonely, [one hates the] night hours [being] long. (fig) Happy nights are short and lonely nights are long. [Cf. *WM*, chap. 21; note: traditionally nights in China are divided into five two-hour periods called *gēng*; see *sān gè wǔgēng* below.]

175 **Huà pà sān tóu duìmiàn; shì pà wāgēn jué màn.** 话怕三头对面, 事怕挖根掘蔓。 (lit) [One's] speech [should be able to] withstand three person['s] bearing witness, [and one's] deeds [should be able to] withstand tracing [to their] root causes. (fig) What one says and does should always be able to bear the scrutiny of outsiders.

176 **Huāqián nán mǎi huítóu kàn.** 花钱难买回头看。 (lit) Spending money cannot buy hindsight. (fig) Looking back and summing up one's experience is priceless.

177 **Huà shì kāi xīn de yàoshi.** 话是开心的钥匙。 (lit) Words are the keys to (opening) the heart. (fig) The proper words can (en)lighten people's minds. [Note: *kāixīn*, normally one word meaning "to make happy," here has the sense of "getting through to."]

178 **Huà shuō sān biàn dàn rú shuǐ.** 话说三遍淡如水。 (lit) Words spoken three times [are] bland as water. (fig) Gossip or anything else repeated over and over is boring. [See also *hǎo qǔzi bù chàng* above.]

179 **Huà shuō wéi kōng; luòbǐ wéi shí.** 话说为空, 落笔为实。 (lit) Words spoken are empty, [but] putting pen to paper is real. (fig) Talk is empty, but a written record is binding. [A line from the modern play *Bái Máo Nǚ* (The White-Haired Girl).]

180 **Huā wú bǎi rì hǎo; shítou yě yǒu fānzhuǎn shí.** 花无百日好, 石头也有翻转时。 (lit) No flower ever blossoms for a hundred days, [and] there will be a day when even stones will turn over. (fig) You will not always be in a superior

position and I will not always be in a disadvantageous one. "Every dog will have his day."

181 **Huā wú qiān rì hóng.** 花无千日红。 (lit) No flower blooms for a thousand days. (fig) Nothing beautiful or good lasts forever. [See also *rén wú qiān rì hǎo* below.]

182 **Huà xū tōngsú, fāng chuán yuǎn.** 话须通俗, 方传远。 (lit) Speech must be colloquial if it is to spread far. (fig) Only sayings which have become popular spread far and wide.

183 **Huā yǒu chóng kāi rì; rén wú zài shàonián.** 花有重开日, 人无再少年。 (lit) Flowers have a time to reblossom, [but] human beings are never young again. (fig) One is only young once.

184 **Hǔ bào bù wài qí zhǎo.** 虎豹不外其爪。 (lit) Tigers [and] leopards don't show their claws. (fig) People of real ability don't show off vainly. [Cf. *Huái Nán Zǐ: Bīng Lüè Xùn*; see also *hǎo māo bù jiào* above and *shuǐ jìng zé* below.]

185 **Hǔ bēi shì; lí bēi shēn.** 虎卑势, 狸卑身。 (lit) Tigers and foxes lower [their] bodies [in order to attack, instead of to yield, as it might first appear]. (fig) Some people pretend to yield when in fact they are preparing to attack. [See also *jiǎng fēi zhě yì fú* below.]

186 **Hù chuāng, hù de yī bāo nóng.** 护疮, 护得一包脓。 (lit) [If one] hides [a] sore, [one will] get a pustule. (fig) If one covers up one's mistakes, one may suffer greater losses later on.

187 **Hǔ dú, bù shí ér /zǐ.** 虎毒, 不食儿/子。 (lit) Tigers [although] fierce, never eat [their own] cubs. (fig) Even wild animals don't harm their own kind. [Cf. *JW*, chap. 27; *Fēngshén Yǎnyì*, chap. 83.]

188 **Hǔ fù wú quǎnzǐ.** 虎父无犬子。 (lit) A tiger father [i.e., courageous] won't have a dog son [as incapable as a puppy]. (fig) A brave father won't have a good-for-nothing son. [Cf. *R3K*, chap. 83; see also *hǔ mén wú quǎn zhǒng* below.]

189 **Hú-Guǎng shú, tiānxià zú.** 湖广熟, 天下足。 [When the two] Hu provinces [(Hunan and Hubei)] have a bumper harvest, the whole country will be free from hunger. [Rhyme; note: in the Ming dynasty *Hú-guǎng* was the name of the region which included the present provinces of Hunan and Hubei; see also *liǎng Guǎng shú*, etc., and *Sū-Hú shú* below.]

190 **Huì dǎ, huì suàn, qián-liáng bù duàn; xì shuǐ cháng liú, chī-chuān bù chóu.** 会打会算钱粮不断, 细水长流吃穿不愁。 (lit) [If one] knows how to figure and reckon, [one's] money [and] food won't run out; [just as a] fine [steady trickle of] water [will] flow [for a] long [time, so one will] not [have to] worry about eating and clothing. (fig) Good bookkeeping means good housekeeping; a long-term budget ensures plenty of food and clothing. [Rhyme; note: *xìshuǐ chángliú* is an idiom meaning "to economize to avoid a shortage."]

191 **Huìgū bù zhī chūnqiū.** 蟪蛄不知春秋。(lit) Summer cicadas don't know [either] spring [or] autumn. (fig) Those who know little of the world are shortsighted. [Note: cicadas live mainly in the summer and die in early autumn; cf. *Zhuāngzǐ: Xiāo Yáo Yóu;* see also *jǐngwā bù kěyǐ* and *xià chóng bù kě* below.]

192 **Huì jià, jià duìtóu; bù huì jià, jià ménlóu.** 会嫁嫁对头，不会嫁嫁门楼。(lit) [A woman who] knows how to marry [well will] marry one [she] loves; [a woman who does] not know how to marry well [will] marry [for] a big house. (fig) It is better for a woman to marry for love than for property, power, or position. [Rhyme; cf. *Xǐngshì Héngyán,* chap. 20; note: *ménlóu* refers to a house with a gate with a roof on it, found only in rich people's homes; see also *huì xuǎn de xuǎn* below.]

193 **Huì jiào de gǒu bù xiōng.** 会叫的狗不凶。(lit) Dogs who bark are not fierce. (fig) People who shout usually don't resort to violence. "Barking dogs don't bite." [See also *ài jiào de máquè* above.]

194 **Huì jiāo péngyou, jiāo xiē tiějiàng, mùjiàng; bù huì jiāo péngyou, jiāo xiē dàoshì, héshang.** 会交朋友，交些铁匠木匠；不会交朋友，交些道士和尚。(lit) [One who is] good at choosing friends makes friends with blacksmiths [and] carpenters; [one who is] not, makes friends with Taoists and [Buddhist] monks. (fig) It is better to make friends with people who can be of practical use to one. [Rhyme.]

195 **Huì shuō de, liǎngtóu mán; bù huì shuō de, liǎngtóu chuán.** 会说的两头瞒，不会说的两头传。(lit) Those [who really] know how to talk [successfully] hide [things from] both sides, [while] those who do, do not pass [rumors] to both sides. (fig) Good mediators are selective in what they repeat. [Rhyme.]

196 **Huì shuō de rě rén xiào; bù huì shuō de rě rén tiào.** 会说的惹人笑，不会说的惹人跳。[One who is] good at talking stirs others [to] laugh; [one who is] not stirs others [to] jump [up in anger]. [Rhyme; see also *sān jù huà néng* below.]

197 **Huì xuǎn de xuǎn érláng; bù huì xuǎn de xuǎn tiánzhuāng.** 会选的选儿郎，不会选的选田庄。[Parents who] choose well [for their daughter to marry] choose [on the basis of the] young man; [parents who do] not choose well [for their daughter] choose [on the basis of the size of the] country estate [of the prospective in-laws]. [Rhyme; see also *huì jià, jià duìtóu* above.]

198 **Huì yán ruò huángjīn.** 惠言若黄金。Wise and sincere words are as precious as gold. [A line from a Tang dynasty poem by Chǔ Guāngxì.]

199 **Huìyǎn shí yīngxióng.** 慧眼识英雄。(lit) Discerning eyes [can] distinguish a hero [from the common crowd]. (fig) Discerning eyes can tell greatness [from mediocrity]. [Note: *huìyǎn* was originally a Buddhist term referring to eyes which can see the past and the future.]

200 **Huǐ-yù cónglái bùkě tīng.** 毁誉从来不可听。Slanders [and] praises [should] never be taken to heart. [Cf. *Jǐngshì Tōngyán,* chap. 4.]

201 **Huì zhuō lǎoshǔ de māor bù jiào.** 会捉老鼠的猫儿不叫。(lit) A cat which knows how to catch mice doesn't mew. (fig) One who has real skill doesn't show it off.

202 **Huì zǒu, zǒu bu guò yǐngzi; huì shuō, shuō bu guò zhēnlǐ.** 会走走不过影子，会说说不过真理。[Just as even a] good walker can never catch up with his shadows, [so even a] good talker can never argue with truth or reason.

203 **Hù jiā zhī gǒu, dàozéi suǒ wù.** 户家之狗，盗贼所恶。(lit) Dogs which guard the house are deeply hated by robbers. (fig) Those who wish you ill will dislike those who remain loyal to you. [Cf. *Sòng Shǐ: Zhào Fàn Zhuàn.*]

204 **Hǔláng tóngxí, gè huái díyì.** 虎狼同席，各怀敌意。(lit) Tigers [and] wolves [may] sit together, [but they] each harbor enmity [for the other]. (fig) Sometimes people are forced into (superficial) alliances (e.g., Mao Zedong and Chiang Kaishek during the Sino-Japanese War). [Rhyme note: *hǔláng,* (lit) "tigers and wolves," also refers to robbers and bandits.]

205 **Húli bù zhī wěiba chòu.** 狐狸不知尾巴臭。(lit) [A] fox doesn't know [its] tail stinks. (fig) One cannot see one's own shortcomings. [See also *lú bù zhī* below.]

206 **Húli kān jī, yuè kān yuè xī.** 狐狸看鸡，越看越稀。(lit) [If you let a] fox watch chickens, the chickens will become fewer and fewer. (fig) If one appoints the wrong person to a task or position, things will get worse. "Don't set a fox to guard a chicken coop." [See also *mò jiào hóuzi* below.]

207 **Húli shuōjiào, yìzài tōu jī.** 狐狸说教，意在偷鸡。(lit) [While] a fox [may] preach religion, [its] intention lies in stealing chickens. (fig) Whatever sweet words the wicked may utter, their true intentions are still evil.

208 **Húli wěiba cáng bu zhù.** 狐狸尾巴藏不住。(lit) A fox cannot hide [its] tail. (fig) One's evil character, deeds, or intentions cannot be covered up. [Note: *húli wěiba,* "fox's tail," here means "something which gives away a person's true character or evil intent."]

209 **Húli zài jiǎohuá, yě dòu bu guò hǎo lièshǒu.** 狐狸再狡猾，也斗不过好猎手。(lit) [The] fox, [no matter] how cunning, still cannot outsmart a skilled hunter. (fig) A tricky person may be clever, but the one who catches or exposes him or her is even more clever.

210 **Húli zuòmèng, yě xiǎng jī.** 狐狸做梦，也想鸡。(lit) Even [when a] fox is dreaming, [it] thinks about chickens. (fig) Bad people are incorrigible. "A leopard cannot change its spots." [See also *zéirén ǎn de* below.]

211 **Hǔ luò píng yáng bèi gǒu (/quǎn) qī.** 虎落平阳被狗(/犬)欺。(lit) A tiger, [when leaving the hill and] descending to the flatlands, [will be] insulted by dogs. (fig) Out of one's normal position or situation, one is at a disadvantage. [See also *lóng yóu qiánshuǐ* below.]

H

212 **Hú mǎ yī běifēng; Yuè niǎo cháo nán zhī.** 胡马依北风，越鸟巢南枝。 (lit) Horses in the north face the north wind [and] birds in the south make their nests [on the] south [facing] branches. (fig) All people suffer from homesickness. [Originally from the poem "Kǒngquè Dōng Nán Fēi" in the Han dynasty yuèfǔ style; cf. Xǐngshì Héngyán, chap. 19. Hú here refers to (the land of) minorities to the north and west of China in ancient times; Yuè was the name of a kingdom in present day Zhejiang during the Spring and Autumn period. See also hú sǐ bì shǒu qiū below.]

213 **Hǔ mén chū bàozi.** 虎门出豹子。 (lit) [From within] a tiger's gates leopards are produced. (fig) Courageous fathers have courageous offspring. [See also the following entry.]

214 **Hǔ mén wú quǎn zhǒng.** 虎门无犬种。 (lit) [In] a tiger's gates there are no puppy dogs. (fig) Courageous fathers have courageous offspring. [Cf. Mao Dun's novel Zǐyè (Midnight); see also hǔ fù wú quǎnzǐ above.]

215 **Húnshēn shì tiě, dǎ de duōshao dīngr?** 浑身是铁，打得多少钉儿? (lit) [If your] entire body were [made of] iron, how many nails could be made [of it]? (fig) One person alone has not that much strength or power. [Cf. JPM, chap. 14; Yuè Fēi Zhuàn, chap. 24.]

216 **Hūnyīn quàn lǒng; huò suì quàn kāi.** 婚姻劝拢；祸祟劝开。 (lit) [One should try to] bring together estranged couples [and to] drive away the spirits of misfortune. (fig) One should try to promote good and drive away misfortune. [See also nìng chāi qiān zuò miào below.]

217 **Huò bēi bù bèn jīngjì; rén qióng bù bèn qīnqi.** 货卑不奔经纪，人穷不奔亲戚。 (lit) [Just as one] should not show poor-quality goods to traders, [so one should] not go to [one's] relations [for help when one is] poor. (fig) Just as poor-quality goods are looked down upon by traders, so poor people are looked down upon by their relatives. [Rhyme.]

218 **Huò bǐ huò děi rēng; rén bǐ rén děi sǐ.** 货比货得扔，人比人得死。 (lit) [If some] goods [are] compared with others, [then the inferior ones] ought to be thrown out; [if some] people [are] compared with others, [then the inferior ones ought to] die. (fig) One should not compare goods or people; just be content with what you have or can afford. "Comparisons are odious." [See also rén bǐ rén below.]

219 **Huò bù dān xíng.** 祸不单行。 Misfortunes never come singly. [Cf. JW, chap. 15; WM, chap. 37; this usually follows fú wú shuāng zhì above (q.v.); note: huòbùdānxíng has become a set phrase.]

220 **Huò bù hào, bù néng wéi huò.** 祸不好，不能为祸。 [If one is] not fond [of things that are likely to invite] disaster, [then one's life] cannot become a disaster.

221 **Huò bù rù shèn jiā zhī mén.** 祸不入慎家之门。 (lit) Misfortune [does] not enter the door of a prudent family. (fig) Misfortune won't befall a family whose members are cautious [in their words and deeds].

222 **Huǒ cóng xiǎo shí jiù; shù cóng xiǎo shí xiū.** 火从小时救，树从小时修。 (lit) Put out the fire when [it is] small; prune the tree when [it is] young. (fig) (1) Try to solve problems as soon as they appear. (2) Educate children when they are young and malleable. [Rhyme.]

223 **Huò dào dìtóu sǐ.** 货到地头死。 (lit) [When] goods [arrive at their] destination [they become] dead [i.e., they then must be sold for whatever price they can fetch]. (fig) Regardless of how much you paid for something, it is only worth what the market will currently bear.

224 **Huó dào lǎo, xué dào lǎo.** 活到老，学到老。 (lit) [If one] lives to an old age, [one will continue to] learn until old age. (fig) You're never too old to learn. It's never to late to learn. [See also xué dào lǎo and zuò dào lǎo below.]

225 **Huò dào líntóu, huǐ hòu chí.** 祸到临头，悔后迟。 [When] disaster is upon [one's] head, [then it is] too late for regret. [Now more commonly said huò dào líntóu hòuhuǐ chí.]

226 **Huò dào zhūtóu làn; qián dào gōngshì bàn.** 火到猪头烂，钱到公事半。 (lit) [Just as] cooking makes a pig's head tender, [so] money [applied to a matter gets it] done. (fig) Bribery is the ultimate arbitrator of official decisions. [Rhyme; cf. JPM, chap. 47; Rúlín Wàishǐ, chap. 13; note: huǒhou refers to the degree and duration of heating or cooking.]

227 **Huò fú jiē yóu zì shēngchéng.** 祸福皆由自生成。 Fortune [and] misfortune both are produced by [one's own] conduct. [Cf. Zuǒ Zhuàn: Xiāng Gōng 23 Nián.]

228 **Huò hǎo, kè zì lái.** 货好，客自来。 (lit) [If the] goods are good, customers [will] come as a matter of course. (fig) "Good wine needs no bush." [See also hǎo huò wúxū zhāolái above and jiǔ hǎo, rén zì lái below.]

229 **Huò jiàn běn zhǔ, huì shuōhuà.** 货见本主，会说话。 (lit) [When] goods see [their] original owner [they] will talk. (fig) Every owner recognizes his or her own wares.

230 **Huò mài yǔ shí jiā.** 货卖与识家。 Goods [should be] sold to those [who] can appreciate [their true value]. [See also mài jīn xū xiàng below.]

231 **Huó máng jiǎn kuàidāo.** 活忙拣快刀。 (lit) [When] things are busy, choose [a] sharp knife. (fig) When there are many problems to solve, choose an able person who can "cut to the heart of the matter" and grasp the key issue(s).

232 **Huǒ shāo bājiāo, xīn bù sǐ.** 火烧芭蕉，心不死。 (lit) The banana [tree] is burnt [but its] core remains. (fig) Some people do not give up easily, or are not easily reconciled to defeat.

233 **Huǒ shāo dào shēn, gè zì qù sǎo; fēng chài rù huái, suíjí jiěyī.** 火烧到身，个自去扫；蜂虿入怀，随即解衣。 (lit) [When] fire approaches [one's own] body, one naturally goes for a broom [to beat out the fire]; [when] a bee or a poisonous insect gets into [one's] clothes, [one] disrobes at once. (fig) When disasters come, each person runs for his own life. [Cf. WM, chap. 17; Jǐngshì Tōngyán, chap. 28; Rúlín Wàishǐ, chap. 13.]

234 **Huǒ shāo méimao, qiě gù yǎnqián.** 火烧眉毛，且顾眼前。(lit) [When] fire approaches [your] eyebrows, just mind [what's] before [your] eyes. (fig) In extremely urgent situations, one has to take care of the immediate problem, regardless of the long-term consequences. [Note: *zànqiě*, "temporarily"; *huǒshāo-méimao* is used as a set phrase meaning a desperate or urgent situation.]

235 **Huò shì cǎo; kè shì bǎo.** 货是草，客是宝。(lit) Goods are straw, [but] customers are treasure. (fig) Goods are as worthless as straw unless there are customers to buy them. [Rhyme.]

236 **Huò wú dàxiǎo, quē zhě biàn guì.** 货无大小，缺者便贵。It doesn't matter whether the goods are large or small; what is scarce is expensive. [Cf. *Xǐngshì Héngyán*, chap. 35.]

237 **Huò xī fú suǒ yǐ; fú xī huò suǒ fú.** 祸兮福所倚，福兮祸所伏。(lit) Good fortune lies within bad fortune, [and] bad fortune hides within good fortune. (fig) People's luck changes; whether something is good luck or bad is not always clear. [A citation from *Lǎozǐ* (*Dào Dé Jīng*), chap. 58, quoted in Mao Zedong's *Máo Dùn Lùn* (On Contradiction); see also *fú zhōng fú huò* above and *huò zhōng yù fú* and *Sài wēng shī mǎ* below.]

238 **Huò yào mài dāngshí.** 货要卖当时。(lit) Goods should [be] sold in season [i.e., when they are in fashion or demand]. (fig) "Strike while the iron is hot." "Timing is all." [Note: *dāngshí* equals *dānglìng*, "in season"; *dānglìng shāngpǐn*, "seasonal goods."]

239 **Huò yóu è zuò; fú zì dé shēng.** 祸由恶作，福自德生。Misfortunes [come] from [one's] evil doings; good fortune [results] from [one's] virtue.

240 **Huò yǒu gāodī sān děng jià; kè wú yuǎnjìn yībān kàn.** 货有高低三等价，客无远近一般看。Goods come in different grades [which are sold at different] prices, [but all] customers whether [they come from] near [or] far [should be] treated the same. [Cf. *JW*, chap. 84.]

241 **Huò yǔ fú wéi lín.** 祸与福为邻。(lit) Disaster and good fortune are [close] neighbors. (fig) Fortune and misfortune are closely related. [Cf. *Dōng Zhōu Lièguó Zhì*, chap. 81; see also *fú zhōng fú huò* above.]

242 **Huò zhě zhī fǎn, mí dào bù yuǎn.** 祸者知返，迷道不远。(lit) [If] one who gets lost knows [enough] to turn back, [(s)he] won't go too far in the wrong direction. (fig) One who knows to correct his or her mistakes in time won't get into serious trouble. [Rhyme.]

243 **Huò zhōng yù fú; fú zhōng fú huò.** 祸中寓福，福中伏祸。In calamity lies good fortune, [and] in good fortune hides calamity. [See also *fú zhōng fú huò* and *huò xī fú suǒ yǐ* and *huò yǔ fú wéi lín* above.]

244 **Hǔ shēng sān zǐ, bì yǒu yī biāo.** 虎生三子，必有一彪。(lit) [If a] tiger has three cubs, there must be one [which is most] ferocious. (fig) A strong or capable person must have at least one strong, capable child.

245 **Hǔ shé róngyì; qiǎn shé nán.** 呼蛇容易，遣蛇难。(lit) Calling a snake out is easier than driving it away. (fig) It's easier to get people to come than to ask them to leave. [Cf. *Jǐngshì Tōngyán*, chap. 16.]

246 **Hǔ shòu, xióngxīn zài.** 虎瘦，雄心在。(lit) [A] tiger, [although] thin, still has ambitions. (fig) A person, although old, weak, or in distress, may still have ambitions. [Cf. *JW*, chap. 33.]

247 **Hú sǐ bì shǒu qiū.** 狐死必守丘。(lit) [When a] fox dies, [it] must face [its] den. (fig) Everyone gets homesick sometimes. [Part of a line from an ancient poem by Qu Yuan in *Chǔ Cí: Jiǔ Zhāng: Āi Yǐng*, cited in *Xǐngshì Héngyán*, chap. 19; see also *hú mǎ yī běifēng* below.]

248 **Hǔ sǐ, bù luò jià.** 虎死，不落架。(lit) A tiger [may] die, [but it does] not lose [its majesty]. (fig) A dead tiger is still a tiger. Although someone powerful dies, his influence remains. [Note: *jiàzi*, "skeleton; haughty manner"; cf. *Wǔ Sōng*, chap. 1; see also *fènghuáng luò jià* above.]

249 **Hǔ sǐ liú pí; rén sǐ liúmíng.** 虎死留皮，人死留名。(lit) [When a] tiger dies, [it] leaves its skin; [when a] person dies, (s)he leaves [his or her] reputation. (fig) A person's good name is the most important thing in life. [Also said *bào sǐ liú pí*, etc., "When a leopard dies, etc."; see also *rén de míng* and *rén guò liúmíng* below.]

250 **Hútúzhàng hǎo suàn; jiāwù shì nánchán.** 糊涂帐好算，家务事难缠。(lit) [It's] easier to clear up muddled account [books] than to deal with a family's affairs. (fig) Relations among family members are extremely complex and hard to deal with. [See also *qīngguān nán duàn* and *wàirén nán guǎn* below.]

251 **Hǔ zài ruǎn dìshang yì shīzú; rén zài tián yán lǐ huì shuāijiāo.** 虎在软地上易失足，人在甜言里会摔交。(lit) [Just as it is] easy for a tiger to lose its footing on soft ground, [so it is] easy for people to get tripped [up] in sweet words. (fig) People are often deceived by flattery.

252 **Hú zhōng wú jiǔ, nán liúkè.** 壶中无酒，难留客。(lit) [When] there's no wine in the pot [it's] difficult [to expect one's] guests to stay. (fig) If one has no money, one will have no friends.

H

J

1 **Jiā bù hé, wàirén qī.** 家不合, 外人欺。 A family in disharmony [will] be bullied by outsiders. [Also said *jiā bù hé, bèi rén qī*; note: *qīwǔ*, "to bully"; see also *jiā hé wànshì xīng* below.]

2 **Jiāchǒu bùkě wài yáng.*** 家丑不可外扬。 (lit) Family scandals should not be raised outside [the home]. (fig) "Don't wash your (family's) dirty linen in public." Internal matters should not be discussed in front of outsiders. [Cf. *Èr Kè Pāi'àn Jīngqí*, chap. 5; see also *chòu yú bù jiàn* and *gēbó shé le* above.]

3 **Jià chūqu de nǚ'ér; pō chūqu de shuǐ.*** 嫁出去的女儿, 泼出去的水。 (lit) [A] daughter married off [is like] water poured out [on the ground]. (fig) Once a girl is married off (in traditional China), she has no more ties to her natal family. [Cf. *DRC*, chap. 81.]

4 **Jià fū, suí fū.** 嫁夫随夫。 Marry [a] husband [and] follow [him] forever. [See also *jià jī, suí jī* below.]

5 **Jiā fù, xiǎo'ér jiāo.** 家富, 小儿娇。 [If] the family is rich, the child(ren) will be spoiled. [See also *jiào fù chūlái* and *jiāozǐ bùxiào* below.]

6 **Jià gāo, zhāo yuǎnkè.** 价高, 招远客。 [One who pays] high prices [i.e., a wholesale buyer] will get sellers from afar.

7 **Jiā hé wànshì xīng.** 家和万事兴。 A family [in] harmony [will] prosper in everything. [Cf. the Qing dynasty novel: *Èrshí Nián Mùdǔ Zhī Guài Xiànzhuàng*, chap. 87; see also *jiā bù hé* above and *jiā yǒu yīxīn* below.]

8 **Jiājiā de guōzi yǒu hēi wū.** 家家的锅子有黑污。 (lit) Every family's cooking pot has one black spot. (fig) Every family has a "skeleton in the cupboard." [See also the following entry.]

9 **Jiājiā dōu yǒu yī běn nán niàn de jīng.*** 家家都有一本难念的经。 (lit) Every family has one sutra [which is] hard to chant. (fig) Each family has its own problems. Every family has a "skeleton in the cupboard." [See also *shéi jiā zào tǔ* and *yī jiā bù zhī* below and the preceding entry.]

10 **Jiājiā mài suān jiǔ; bù fàn shì gāoshǒu.** 家家卖酸酒, 不犯是高手。 (lit) [When] every [wine] shop is selling sour wine, [the ones who] don't [appear] to be top notch [by comparison]. (fig) Small cheats get caught, but the master criminals get away. [Rhyme.]

11 **Jiājiào suī yán, chǒushì nánmiǎn.** 家教虽严, 丑事难免。 (lit) Although a family's teaching [may be] strict, scandals are hard to avoid. (fig) Scandals will happen, even in the best regulated families. [Rhyme.]

12 **Jiā jī dǎ de tuántuánzhuàn; yějī dǎ de tiē tiān fēi.** 家鸡打得团团转, 野鸡打得贴天飞。 (lit) Domestic fowl [when] beaten [will just] run around in circles [in their coop, but] wild fowl, [when] beaten, [will] fly away. (fig) A family member has to stay with the family even though suffering abuse, while an outsider would certainly leave. [Cf. *JPM*, chap. 12.]

13 **Jià jī, suí jī; jià gǒu, suí gǒu.*** 嫁鸡随鸡, 嫁狗随狗。 (lit) [A woman] married to a cock follows the cock, [and a woman] married to a dog follows the dog. (fig) Whatever a woman's husband is, she is committed to follow him forever (in traditional China). [Cf. *DRC*, chap. 81; *Chū Kè Pāi'àn Jīngqí*, chap. 38; see also *jià fū, suí fū* above.]

14 **Jiā lěi qiānjīn, zuò bù chuí táng.** 家累千金, 坐不垂堂。 (lit) [Those whose] families [have] accumulated a lot of money never sit under eaves [where they might be hit by falling tiles]. (fig) Wealthy people are (able to be) more cautious about their own safety. [Cf. *Shǐ Jì: Sīmǎ Xiàngrú Lièzhuàn*; note: *qiānjīn*, (lit) "[a] thousand [ounces of] gold," is a metaphor for "a lot of money"; *zuòbùchuítáng* is a set phrase meaning "stay of harm's way"; see also *guìrén bù tà xiàndǐ* above.]

15 **Jiā lǐ shì, jiā lǐ liǎo.** 家里事, 家里了。 Family matters [should be] settled at home.

16 **Jiàn ān sī mǎ; dǔwù-sīrén.** 见鞍思马, 睹物思人。 Seeing a saddle [makes one] think of a horse, [and] seeing [his or her] belongings [makes one] think of [a dear] one. [Cf. *DRC*, chap. 44; note: *dǔwù-sīrén* is a *chengyu* meaning "seeing something reminds one of someone"; see also *jiàn jǐng shēng qíng* below.]

17 **Jiàn cù suī lì, bù shè bù fā; rén suī cōngming, bù xué bù zhī.** 箭簇虽利, 不射不发; 人虽聪明, 不学不知。 Although the head of an arrow is sharp, [if it is] not discharged [it will] not fly; [similarly,] although a person [may be] intelligent, [if (s)he does] not study, [(s)he will] not be knowledgeable.

18 **Jiǎn dào piányi chái; shāopò jiā dǐ guō.** 拣到便宜柴, 烧破夹底锅。 (lit) Picking up cheap firewood [is not worth it if you] burn up [your] thick [((lit) double]-bottomed cooking pot. (fig) By exploiting petty advantages, one often suffers great losses. [Note the colloquial expression: *dé bù shǎng shī*, "the gain is not worth the loss."]

19 **Jiāng fēi zhě yì fú.** 将飞者翼伏。 (lit) [Birds which are] getting ready to fly lower [their] wings. (fig) (1) One should prepare before making one's move. (2) Don't be misled by quiet appearances. [See also *hǔ bēi shì* above.]

20 **Jiāng hǎi bù jù xì liú, Tài Shān bù jù tǔ shí.** 江海不拒细流, 泰山不拒土石。 (lit) Rivers [and] seas do not reject small [streams] joining [them]; Mount Tai does not refuse to receive earth [and] stones. (fig) People of virtue are always willing to learn from anyone. [See also *dàhǎi bù xián shuǐ* above.]

21 **Jiānghé bù qū, shuǐ bù liú.** 江河不曲，水不流。 (lit) [If the] rivers do not bend, the water [will] not flow forward. (fig) Setbacks and hardships spur one to forge ahead.

22 **Jiānghú yuè lǎo, yuè hánxīn.** 江湖越老，越寒心。 (lit) The older a wayfarer gets, the more disappointed [he becomes]. (fig) The more one sees of life and the world, the more disillusioned one becomes. [Note: *jiānghú* refers to those who lead a vagrant life, sometimes to tramps and gypsies, but here refers to those who are worldly-wise.]

23 **Jiàng mén bì yǒu jiàng; xiàng mén bì yǒu xiàng.** 将门必有将，相门必有相。 (lit) [In a] general's family there must be [more] generals, [and in a] prime minister's family there must be [more] prime ministers. (fig) Like breeds like. [Cf. *Shǐ Jì: Mèng Cháng Jūn Lièzhuàn*; see also *fēng shēng fēng* above.]

24 **Jiāngshān yì gǎi, běnxìng nán yì.** 江山易改，本性难易。 It's easier to move mountains or rivers [than to] change [a person's] basic nature. "A leopard cannot change its spots." [Cf. *Xǐngshì Héngyán*, chap. 35; see also *gǒu chī shǐ* above and *shé rù zhú dòng* and *tōu shí (de) māor* and *yī rén, yī xiàng* below.]

25 **Jiàngshuài wúnéng, lèisǐ sān-jūn.** 将帅无能，累死三军。 (lit) [If a] general is incompetent, [he may] wear out three armed forces. (fig) An incompetent leader can cause great harm to his subordinates. [See also *bīng xióng* above; note: technically *sān-jūn* referred to combined forces of infantry, charioteers, and cavalry, and now refers to the three branches of the armed services: army, navy, and air force.]

26 **(Jiāng) Tàigōng diàoyú, yuàn zhě shànggōu.*** (姜)太公钓鱼，愿者上钩。 (lit) [When the] Heavenly Master (Jiang) Taigong went fishing, [only] willing fish took the hook. (fig) Only willing victims let themselves be caught. [Jiang Ziya or Jiang Taigong ("Heavenly Master Jiang"), a premier in the Western Zhou dynasty noted for his eccentricities, always went fishing by holding a straightened unbaited hook suspended above the water. Cf. *Wǔ Wáng Fá Zhòu Pínghuà* (King Wuwang's Expedition against King Zhou) and *Fēng Shén Yǎnyi* (The Romance of the Deification of the Gods), chap. 23. This popular saying was used by Mao Zedong to describe those Chinese intellectuals taking American relief aid in an essay praising one who did not, Zhu Ziqing.]

27 **Jiàn guài bù guài; qí guài zì bài.** 见怪不怪，其怪自败。 [When you see] strange [things] don't be afraid, [and] their fearful [aspect] will naturally disappear. [Rhyme; cf. *DRC*, chap. 94.]

28 **Jiàn guān, sānfēn zāi.** 见官，三分灾。 [When one] meets with a [government] official, [one has at least a] thirty percent [chance of] calamity. [Said in traditional China.]

29 **Jiànguo guǐ, pà hēi.** 见过鬼，怕黑。 (lit) [After] having seen a ghost, [one] is afraid of the dark. (fig) "Once bitten, twice shy." [See also *yīzhāo bèi shé yǎo* below.]

30 **Jiàng xiàng běn wú zhǒng; nán'ér dāng zìqiáng.** 将相本无种，男儿当自强。 (lit) Generals [and] prime ministers are not born; heroes must themselves work hard [to achieve greatness]. (fig) People are not born to greatness; rather they must achieve it by their own efforts. [Cf. *Fēngshén Yǎnyì*, chap. 24; *Shǐ Jì: Chén Shè Shì Jiā*; *Gǔ-Jīn Xiǎoshuō*, chap. 21.]

31 **Jiàng xiàng chū hánmén.** 将相出寒门。 Generals [and] prime ministers (can) come from poor families. [Cf. *Xīxiāng Jì*, Act 5, Scene 3; vs. *jiàng mén bì yǒu jiàng* above.]

32 **Jiāngyīn mò dòngshǒu; Wúxī mò kāikǒu.** 江阴莫动手，无锡莫开口。 (lit) Don't fight [with people from] Jiangyin [in Jiangsu province, as they are generally believed to be physically belligerent], [and] don't argue with [people from] Wuxi [also in Jiangsu province, as they are believed to be quarrelsome]. (fig) Don't (try to) compete with experts. [Rhyme.]

33 **Jiāng yù qǔ zhī, bì xiān yǔ zhī.** 将欲取之，必先与之。 (lit) [If in the] future [one] desires to get something, [one] must first give something. (fig) In order to get, one must first give. [Cf. *Lǎozǐ*, chap. 33, paraphrased by Mao Zedong in reference to the nationalization of private enterprises; see his Collected Works *Máo Zédōng Xuǎnjí*, vol. 4.]

34 **Jiàng zài móu ér bù zài yǒng; bīng zài jīng ér bù zài duō.** 将在谋而不在勇，兵在精而不在多。 [The quality of a] general lies in [his] strategy, rather than in [his] courage, [and the effectiveness of] soldiers lies in [their] quality, rather than in [their] number. [Cf. *Gǔ-Jīn Xiǎoshuō (Yù Shì Míng Yán)*, chap. 21; the second half may be used alone (q.v.).]

35 **Jiàn zàiwài, jūn mìng yǒusuǒ bù shòu.** 将在外，君命有所不受。 (lit) [When a] general is out [in battle], [even] the emperor's orders [may] some[times] not be obeyed. (fig) A field commander must decide even against the king's orders. The person responsible on the spot sometimes has to make decisions contrary to his (original) orders. [Cf. *Shǐ Jì: Sūnzǐ Wú Qǐ Lièzhuàn*; *Shǐ Jì: Sīmǎ Ráng Jū Lièzhuàn*; *R3K*, chap. 103; see also *chūbīng bù yóu jiàng* above.]

36 **Jiàn huǒ bù miè, huǒ shāo shēn; jiàn shé bù dǎ, shé yǎo rén.** 见火不灭，火烧身；见蛇不打，蛇咬人。 (lit) [When one] sees a fire [and does] not put [it] out, the fire [will] burn him; [if one] sees a snake [and does] not strike [it], the snake [will] bite him. (fig) One should nip trouble in the bud or (be prepared to) suffer the consequences. [Rhyme.]

37 **Jiàn jǐng shēng qíng.** 见景生情。 Seeing [certain] places or sights arouses [one's] feelings. [Cf. *Xǐngshì Héngyán*, chap. 35; this rhyme is a colloquial version of the chengyu: *chùjǐng-shēngqíng*; note: *jǐngxiàng*, "scene, sight, circumstances"; see also *jiàn ān sì mǎ* above.]

38 **Jiàn lǎo wú máng; rén lǎo wú gāng.** 剑老无芒，人老无刚。 (lit) [When] swords [get] old, [they] have no edge; [when] people [get] old, [they]

have no strength. (fig) When people get older, they lose their strength of will. [Rhyme; cf. *Dōng Zhōu Lièguó Zhì*, chap. 32; note: *fēngmáng*, "cutting edge"; "abilities."]

39 **Jiàn lǐ mǎi lái, jiàn lǐ mài; róngyì de lái, róngyì shě.** 贱里买来贱里卖，容易得来容易舍。 Cheaply bought, cheaply sold; easy come, easy go. [Cf. *JPM*, chap. 76.]

40 **Jiàn pín xiū xiào, fù xiū kuā; shéi shì cháng pín jiǔ fù jiā?** 见贫休笑富休夸，谁是常贫久富家? (lit) [If you] see poor [people] don't idly laugh; [if you are] rich, don't idly boast; whose family will be always poor or always rich? (fig) Don't laugh at the poor and don't boast of your wealth; no one will be poor or rich all his or her life. [Rhyme.]

41 **Jiàn rén bù shīlǐ; duō zǒu èrshí lǐ.** 见人不施礼，多走二十里。 (lit) [If when you] meet someone [you do] not greet [them] politely [when asking for directions, you may] walk an extra twenty miles. (fig) If one is not willing to approach others correctly and learn from them, one will not succeed. [Rhyme; note: *shīlǐ* or *xínglǐ*, "to salute; to greet politely, e.g., by bowing"; see also *rén shēnglù bù shú* below.]

42 **Jiàn rén bù shì, zhū è zhī gēn; jiàn jǐ bù shì, bǎi shàn zhī mén.** 见人不是诸恶之根，见己不是百善之门。 Seeing [only other] people's problems [is the] root of all kinds of evils; seeing [one's] own mistakes [is the] door to goodness. [Rhyme.]

43 **Jiàn rén tiāodàn bù chīlì.** 见人挑担不吃力。 (lit) [One who only] watches others carrying burdens does not get tired. (fig) No one can truly know the weight of another's burden. If one has not done something oneself, one can't know what it's like. [Cf. *Hé Diǎn*, chap. 5; see also *kàn rén tiāodàn* below.]

44 **Jiǎn rì bùrú zhuàng rì.** 拣日不如撞日。 (lit) Choosing a day is not as good as chancing upon a day. (fig) Chancing upon an opportune time is even better than planning in advance. [Said when one encounters a good opportunity.] [Cf. *Hé Diǎn*, chap. 1; see also *lái de zǎo bùrú* below.]

45 **Jiàn shàn, zé xué; yǒu guò, zé gǎi.** 见善则学，有过则改。 (lit) [If you] see goodness, learn [from it]; [if you] have faults, reform [them].

46 **Jiàn shé bù dǎ, sānfēn zuì.** 见蛇不打，三分罪。 (lit) [If one] sees a snake [and] does not strike [it, one is] thirty percent guilty. (fig) Not to oppose evil whenever one sees it is wrong.

47 **Jiàn shí bù qiǎng, dào lǎo bù zhǎng.** 见食不抢，到老不长。 [If when you] see food [you] don't take [it], [when you] get old [you will] not be healthy. [A rhyme said humorously to one's guests at banquets to encourage them to eat more.]

48 **Jiàn tù fàngyīng; yù zhāng fā jiàn.** 见兔放鹰，遇獐发箭。 (lit) [When you] see the hare, loose the falcon; [when you] see the river deer, loose your arrow. (fig) (1) Seize the opportunity when it presents itself. (2) Take aim at your target before you act. [See also *bù jiàn tùzi* above.]

49 **(Jiàn tù gù quǎn wèi wéi wǎn;) wáng yáng bǔ láo wèi wéi chí.** (见兔顾犬未为晚;)亡羊补牢未为迟。 (lit) (It is not too late to set the dog on the hare after you see it [run by]), nor is it too late to mend the fold after [some of the] sheep have been lost. (fig) "Better late than never." [Cf. *Zhànguó Cè: Chǔ Cè Sì*; the first half is often omitted, and the second part used alone (q.v.).]

50 **Jiàn xián, bù jiàn yú.** 荐贤，不荐愚。 Recommend [the] talented, not [the] stupid. [Cf. *Wǔ Sòng*, chap. 6.]

51 **Jiàn yì bù wéi, wú yǒng.** 见义不为无勇。 (lit) [One who] knows what is right, [but] doesn't fight [for it is] not brave. (fig) One who does not have the courage to oppose injustice is a coward. [Cf. *Shǐ Jì: Yàn Zhì Lièzhuàn*; note the chengyu: *jiànyì-yǒngwéi*, "bravely fight for justice."]

52 **Jiàn yī shì; zhī shí shì.** 见一事，知十事。 (lit) See one thing [and you will] know ten. (fig) A clever person learns or generalizes from what (s)he already knows or sees. [See also the following entry.]

53 **Jiàn yī shì; zhī yī shì.** 见一事，知一事。 (lit) See one thing [and you will] learn [another] one [from it]. (fig) A clever person learns something from experience.

54 **Jiàn zài xián shàng, bùdé bù fā.** 箭在弦上，不得不发。 (lit) [Once the] arrow is (fitted) on the bow string, one cannot but shoot [it]. (fig) Once things have reached a certain point, there is no turning back. The only way to go is forward. [Cf. *R3K*, chap. 32; note: *jiànzàixiánshàng* is a set phrase meaning "everything is ready and there can be no turning back"; see also *kāigōng, méiyǒu* below.]

55 **Jiànzhèng, jiànzhèng; bù jiàn, bù zhèng.** 见证，不见不证。 (lit) [What one] witnesses, [one can bear] witness to; [if you did] not see it, don't bear witness. (fig) Never bear witness in a law court if you didn't see something with your own eyes. [Cf. *Wǔ Sòng*, chap. 2.]

56 **Jiàn zhě yì; xué zhě nán.** 见者易，学者难。 (lit)
• One who [only] *sees* [things thinks they are] easy, [but] one who *studies* [them knows they are] difficult. (fig) Seeing is easy; learning is difficult.

57 **Jiāo bù yán, shī zhī duò.*** 教不严，师之惰。 [If the] teaching is not strict, [it's because] the teacher is lazy. [From the classical primary textbook *Sān Zì Jīng* (The Three Character Classic); see also the line which precedes this one: *yǎng bù jiào, fù zhī guò*, "If one raises a child without discipline, it's an error by its father" (q.v.) below.]

58 **Jiáo de cài gēn, bǎi shì kě zuò.** 嚼得菜根，百事可做。 (lit) [One who has] chewed vegetable roots [for lack of anything better to eat] can accomplish anything. (fig) One who has gone through hardships can do anything.

59 **Jiāo duōle bù nián; huà duōle bù tián.** 胶多了不粘，话多了不甜。 Too much glue won't stick, [and] many words won't be sweet [to the ears]. (fig) Don't talk too much. [Rhyme.]

60 **Jiào fù chūlái; jiào ér yīnghái.** 教妇初来，教儿婴孩。(lit) Teach [your] wife [when she first arrives at her husband's family's home, and] train [your] child [when it's] an infant. (fig) It is best to begin disciplining wives and children to behave correctly as early as possible. [Rhyme; cf. *Yán Shì Jiā Xùn: Jiào Zǐ*; note: *jiàoyǎng*, "raise; train; educate"; see also *dāngmiàn jiào zǐ* above.]

61 **Jiàohuāzi yě yǒu sān gè qióng péngyou.** 叫花子也有三个穷朋友。(lit) Even beggars have three poor friends. (fig) Everyone has some friends (to help out).

62 **Jiàohuì túdi, èsǐ shīfu.** 教会徒弟，饿死师傅。(lit) [After he has] taught all [his skills to his] apprentice, the master [will] starve to death. (fig) Don't teach people everything you know. [Note the colloquial expression: *liú yīshǒu*, "to hold back a trick or two."]

63 **Jiào rén bù shíběn; shétou dǎ gè gǔn.** 叫人不蚀本，舌头打个滚。(lit) Greeting someone doesn't cost you anything [except] a roll of your tongue. (fig) It doesn't cost one anything to be civil to others. [Rhyme; cf. *Wǔ Sōng*, chap. 5; see also *qīngjiào biérén* below.]

64 **Jiāo rén, jiāoxīn; jiāo huā, jiāo gēn.** 交人交心，浇花浇根。(lit) To communicate [with] people, open [your] heart, [just as when] watering flowers [you should] water [their] roots. (fig) To make friends, frankness and sincerity are the most important things. [Technically a rhyme; the order of the two halves may be reversed.]

65 **Jiǎo shàng de pào, zìjǐ zǒu de; shēnshang de chuāng, zìjǐ rě de.** 脚上的泡自己走的，身上的疮自己惹的。(lit) Blisters raised on [one's] feet [are due to one's] own walking, [and] boils growing on [one's] body [are of one's own doing. (fig) The cause of the problem lies with oneself. "As one makes one's bed, so one must lie in it."

66 **Jiàoshòu, jiàoshòu; yuè jiāo, yuè shòu.** 教授教授，越教越瘦。Professor(s), professor(s); the more they profess, the thinner they get. [Pun; a satirical comment on the low salaries of academics in China, originally criticizing the inflationary policies of the late 1940s, resurrected in the 1990s; cf. *sòutóu* "stupid person" is Wu dialect.]

67 **Jiàoshū sān nián, jiāo zìshēn.** 教书三年，教自身。(lit) To teach [students for] three years [is to] teach oneself. (fig) A teacher learns more by teaching others. To teach is to learn. [See also *jiào-xué xiāng zhǎng* below.]

68 **Jiǎo tà liǎng chuán bì luòshuǐ.** 脚踏两船必落水。[One who] straddles two boats is bound to fall [into the] water. (fig) Fence-straddlers will eventually get into trouble.

69 **Jiǎo tù sǐ, liáng gǒu pēng; gāo niǎo jìn, liánggōng cáng.** 狡兔死，良狗烹；高鸟尽，良弓藏。(lit) [When] the wiliest hare is caught, the good [hunting] dog is [killed and] cooked; [when] the high [flying] birds are all [shot], the fine bow/archer is put away. (fig) When victory is won, those who have performed meritorious service

are eliminated or ignored. [Rhyme; cf. *Shǐ Jì: Huái Yīn Hóu Lièzhuàn*; note: *liánggōng*, (lit) "fine bow," can also refer to a fine archer.]

70 **Jiǎo tù yǒu sān kū.*** 狡兔有三窟。(lit) A wily hare has three burrows. (fig) A clever person always makes alternative, "back-up" plans. [Originally from *Zhànguó Cè: Qí Cè Sì*; as a chengyu: *jiǎotù-sānkū*.]

71 **Jiào-xué xiāng zhǎng.** 教学相长。(lit) Teachers [and] students mutually benefit. (fig) Teaching benefits teacher and students alike. [This is sometimes treated as a chengyu; see also *jiàoshū sān nián* above.]

72 **Jiāoyǎng bùrú lì jiān.** 娇养不如历艰。Better let [one's children] go through hardships than to spoil [them]. [Note the chengyu: *jiāoshēng-guànyǎng*, "pampered since childhood."]

73 **Jiāoyì bù chéng, rényì zài.** 交易不成，仁义在。[Although the] business transaction did not go through, the feeling of friendship remains. [Now more commonly said *mǎi-mài bù chéng, qíngyì zài*. (q.v.)]

74 **Jiāoyǒu mǎn tiānxià, zhīxīn yǒu jǐ rén?*** 交友满天下，知心有几人？[One may] have friends all over the world, [but] there are [very] few people [who] truly understand [one's] heart. [The two halves are often used separately.]

75 **Jiǎo zhèng bùpà xié wāi.** 脚正不怕鞋歪。(lit) A straight foot is not afraid of a crooked shoe. (fig) An upright person need not fear slander or rumors. A clear conscience laughs at false accusations. [See also *gēn shēn bùpà* above and *xīn zhèng bùpà* below.]

76 **Jiāo zhě yú; yú zhě jiāo.** 骄者愚，愚者骄。The proud [are] foolish; the foolish [are sure to be] proud.

77 **Jiāozǐ bùxiào.** 骄子不孝。[A] spoil[ed] child is unfilial. [Cf. *Shǐ Jì: Liáng Xiào Wáng Shì Jiā*; see also *jiā fù, xiǎo'ér jiāo* above.]

78 **Jiā pín bù bàn sùshí; cōng rǒng bùxiá cǎoshū.** 家贫不办素食，匆冗不暇草书。(lit) [If you are] poor, don't [think you can] entertain [your guests with] vegetarian food; [if] in a hurry, [you're] too busy to write in a fancy running hand. (fig) Don't attempt to take (what might appear to be) shortcuts. If you're going to do something, you have to do it right. One has to observe the proper forms if one wants to do something successfully.

79 **Jiā pín, bù shì pín; lù pín, pín shā rén.** 家贫不是贫，路贫贫杀人。Poverty at home is not poverty, [but] poverty on the road [can] kill one. [Cf. *Rúlín Wàishǐ*, chap. 24; also said *zàijiā bù shì pín . . .* etc.; see also *qióng jiā, fù lù* below.]

80 **Jiā pín chū xiàozǐ.*** 家贫出孝子。Poor families produce dutiful sons.

81 **Jiā pín sī liáng qī.** 家贫思良妻。[When the] family is poor, [they will] think [of getting a] good wife [to help out]. [Cf. *Shǐ Jì: Wèi Shì Jiā*.]

82 **Jiāshū dǐ wàn jīn.*** 家书抵万金。A letter from home is worth ten thousand [ounces of] gold. [A line from the Tang dynasty poet Du Fu's poem: "Chūn Wàng."]

J

83 **Jiāsī bù lùn zūn-bēi.** 家私不论尊卑。Family property [should be shared by all the family members], no matter how high or low in seniority. [Cf. *Gǔ-Jīn Xiǎoshuō*, chap. 10.]

84 **Jiā wú èr zhǔ; guó wú èr wáng.*** 家无二主，国无二王。A family [can]not have two masters, [just as] a country [can]not have two kings. [Cf. *Lǐjì: Fāng Xì*; *Xǐngshì Yīnyuán Zhuàn*, chap. 95; *JW*, chap. 39; see also *yī shān bù néng*.]

85 **Jiā wú quán fàn.** 家无全犯。(lit) [An entire (extended)] family does not commit crimes. (fig) An entire (extended) family cannot be held responsible for the crimes by one or a few of its members. [Cf. *Jǐngshì Tōngyán*, chap. 40; *JW*, chap. 63; see also *xiǎo'ér fànzuì* and *yī rén zuò zuì* below.]

86 **Jiā wú shēnghuó jì, bùpà liáng jīn.** 家无生活计，不怕斗量金。[If] a family has no [long-term] plan for making a living, even bushels of gold won't help. [Cf. *Jǐngshì Tōngyán*, chap. 24; *JPM*, chap. 96; see also *jī cái qiānwàn* and *jiā yǒu qiānjīn* below.]

87 **Jiā wú zhǔ, wū dǎo shù.** 家无主，屋倒竖。[If a] home has no one in charge, [the house will] turn upside down. [A rhyme often said after the mistress of the house dies; cf. *Chū Kè Pāi'àn Jīngqí*, chap. 16; *Niè Hǎi Huā*, chap. 14; *JPM*, chap. 3.]

88 **Jiā yán, ér xuéhǎo; zǐ xiào, fù xīnkuān.** 家严儿学好，子孝父心宽。[When] the family/home is strict, the children learn from good example; [when] the sons are filial, the father['s heart is] carefree. [Note: *kuānxīn*, "carefree"; *jiāyán* is also used as a respectful term to refer to one's father.]

89 **jià yī bù zé zhǔ.** 价一不择主。(lit) [With] one [set] price, [the seller] doesn't [have to] solicit any particular customers. (fig) If a business sets one fixed price, then customers will come to them naturally. [Cf. *Jǐngshì Tōngyán*, chap. 22; note: *zhǔgù*, "customer."]

90 **Jiā yǒu cháng yè, suī jī bù è; guó yǒu cháng fǎ, suī wēi bù wáng.** 家有常业虽饥不饿，国有常法虽危不亡。[Just as a] family with an established profession won't go hungry in times of famine, [so a] country governed by laws [rather than by men] won't be conquered in times of danger. [Cf. *Hán Fēizǐ: Shì Xié*.]

91 **Jiā yǒu huángjīn; wài yǒu dǒu chèng.** 家有黄金，外有斗秤。(lit) [If you] have gold at home, other [people can] gauge [it to the] bushel. (fig) Outsiders are able to estimate one's wealth. [Note: a *dǒu* (= one deciliter) is a standard measure for grain.]

92 **Jiā yǒu huànnán; lín bǎo xiāngzhù.** 家有患难，邻保相助。[If] misfortune befalls a family, neighbors help one another. [Cf. *JPM*, chap. 14.]

93 **Jiā yǒu jiāguī; jūn yǒu jūnfǎ.** 家有家规，军有军法。A family has [its] family rules, [just as] the army has military regulations. [See also *guó yǒu guófǎ* above.]

94 **Jiā yǒu jiā zhǔ; miào yǒu miàozhǔ.** 家有家主，庙有庙主。(lit) Every house has its master, [just as] every temple has its head [priest]. (fig) Every organization has a leader. [Rhyme; see also *jiā yǒu qiān kǒu* below.]

95 **Jiā yǒu qiānjīn bùrú rì jìn fēnwén.** 家有千金不如日进分文。Having a thousand [ounces of] gold at home is not as [good as having a] daily (i.e., steady) income of [one] single penny. [See also *jiā wú shēnghuó jì* above.]

96 **Jiā yǒu qiān kǒu; zhǔshì yī rén.** 家有千口，主事一人。[Although there may be] many people in a family [there can only be] one master. [Cf. *Èr Shí Zǎi Fán Huá Mèng*, chap. 12; see also *jiā wú èr zhǔ* above and *jiā zhōng bǎi shì* below.]

97 **Jiā yǒu qiānwàn; xiǎo chù bùkě bù suàn.** 家有千万，小处不可不算。[Even if your] family has a large fortune, small expenditures must still be carefully calculated.

98 **Jiā yǒu sān dǒu liáng, bù dāng háizi wáng.** 家有三斗粮，不当孩子王。[If you] have three bushels of grain at home, never be a teacher of children. [A rhyme; used before 1949 to comment on the low status of primary and high school teachers; cf. *Dàxué Chūnqiū*, Book 30; note: a *dǒu* (equals one deciliter) is a standard measure of grain.]

99 **Jiā yǒu wànguàn cái bùrú yīshēn jiàn.** 家有万贯财不如一身健。(lit) [Even if one's] family has ten thousand strings of [one thousand copper cash] coins, it's not as good as a healthy body. (fig) "Health is better than wealth." [Note: *guàn* literally refers to a string of one thousand copper coins or "cash" used in dynastic China; *wànguàn* means "wealthy"; see also the *chengyu: yáochǎn-wànguàn*, "having great wealth."]

100 **Jiā yǒu wútóng, zhāo fènghuáng; jiā yǒu guāng-gùn, zhāo guānggùn.** 家有梧桐招凤凰，家有光棍招光棍。(lit) [Just as] a Chinese parasol tree at [one's] home [will] attract [Chinese] phoenixes, [so] a [poor] bachelor in [one's] home [will] attract others [of his kind]. (fig) "Birds of a feather flock together." [Note: *guānggun* here refers to men who are too poor to marry; see also *méiyǒu wútóng shù* below.]

101 **Jiā yǒu yī lǎo; huángjīn huó bǎo.*** 家有一老，黄金活宝。[If a] family has an old person, [he or she is] a golden living treasure. (fig) An old person in the family is a living treasure [who will always offer good advice]. [Rhyme; see also *bù tīng lǎorén* above.]

102 **Jiā yǒu yīxīn, yǒuqián mǎi jīn; jiā yǒu èr xīn, wú qián mǎi zhēn.** 家有一心有钱买金，家有二心无钱买针。(lit) [If the whole] family [is of] one mind, [they will] have money to buy gold; [if the whole] family [is of] two minds, [they will] not have [enough] money to buy [even] a needle. (fig) Family unity is of paramount importance in ensuring a family's success. [Note: *èrxīn* as one word means "disloyal"; see also *jiā hé wànshì xīng* above.]

103 **Jiā zéi nán fáng.** * 家贼难防。 A thief inside [one's] home is difficult to guard against. [Note: *jiāzéi-nánfáng* is also treated as a *chengyu*; see also *méi(yǒu) jiā zéi* and *yuàn zéi bì yǒu* and *zéi wú lì dǐ* below.]

104 **Jiā zhōng bǎi shì xīng, quán kào zhǔrén mìng.** 家中百事兴，全靠主人命。 The prosperity of a family depends completely on its master's fate. [Rhyme; cf. *Jǐngshì Tōngyán*, chap. 22.]

105 **Jī bù chī wú gōng zhī shí.** 鸡不吃无工之食。 (lit) Chickens do not eat food [that they] have not earned. (fig) One should not take anything from others which one does not deserve. [Cf. *JW*, chap. 47; see also *jūnzǐ bù chī* and *wú gōng, bù shòu* below.]

106 **Jī bù kě shī; shí bùzài lái.** * 机不可失，时不再来。 Don't let slip an opportunity; time [passed will] never come again. "Carpe diem." [Cf. *Shǐ Jì: Huái Yīn Hóu Lièzhuàn*; note: *jībùkěshī* is also treated as a set phrase; see also *guòle zhège cūn* above.]

107 **Jī bù mì, huò xiān zhāo.** 机不密，祸先招。 (lit) [If one's] plans are not kept [secret], misfortunes [will be] encountered first [i.e., before the plans can be implemented]. [Cf. *Xǐngshì Héngyán*, chap. 20; note: *jīmì de shì*, "secret matter(s)."]

108 **Jī bù zé shí; hán bù zé yī; huāng bù zé lù; pín bù zé qī.** 饥不择食，寒不择衣，慌不择路；贫不择妻。 (lit) A hungry person finds no fault with the food; a cold person is not choosy about clothing; one who is fleeing never considers the path, [and one who is] poor can't be choosy in [his choice of a] wife. (fig) People who are in need cannot afford to be choosy. "Beggars can't be choosers." [Rhyme: cf. Mencius, *Mèngzǐ: Jìn Xīn Shàng*; WM, chaps. 3 and 61; note: *jībù-zéshí* is also used as a *chengyu*; see also *jī zhě yì wéi shí* below.]

109 **Jī cái qiānwàn bùrú bójì zài shēn.** 积财千万不如薄技在身。 (lit) Hoarding a large fortune is not as good as [being] in possession of some slight [technical] skill. (fig) One can always make one's living if one has a skill. [Cf. *Yán Shì Jiā Xùn: Miǎn Xué*; see also *jiā wú shēnghuó jì* below.]

110 **Jī dù bù zhī yā dù shì.** 鸡肚不知鸭肚事。 (lit) The chicken's belly doesn't know what's going on in the duck's belly. (fig) One never knows what's going on in others' minds.

111 **Jī duō bù xiàdàn; rén duō chī xiánfàn.** 鸡多不下蛋，人多吃闲饭。 [If there are] too many hens, [they] won't lay eggs, [and if there are] too many people, [they just] sit idle. [Note: *chī xiánfàn*, (lit) "eat idle food," means "to lead an idle life."]

112 **Jì dú wú guò duànliáng.** 计毒无过断粮。 The most damaging strategy is to cut off [one's enemies' supplies of] food. [Cf. *Yuè Fēi Zhuàn*, chap. 90.]

113 **Jièchuāng yào shǎo bu liǎo chòu liúhuáng.** 疥疮药少不了臭硫磺。 (lit) Scabies medicine must contain stinky sulfur. (fig) Sometimes things can't be accomplished without involving some unpleasant person(s).

114 **Jiēdǐ jiù pà lǎo xiāngqīn.** 揭底就怕老乡亲。 (lit) [If one is afraid of having one's] secret(s) exposed, [those] to fear [most are one's] fellow townsmen. (fig) People from one's home town are most likely to know or reveal one's background.

115 **Jiē guǒ de shù yì zāo dǎ.** 结果的树易遭打。 (lit) Trees that bear fruit are often beaten. (fig) People of accomplishment are always envied or attacked. [See also *shù dà zhāofēng* and *yáoyáo zhě yì zhé* below.]

116 **Jiè jiǔ xiāochóu, chóu gèng chóu;** * (chōu dāo duàn shuǐ, shuǐ gèng liú). 借酒消愁，愁更愁；(抽刀断水，水更流)。 Drowning [one's] sorrows in drink [only] makes them worse; ([just as when one] draws [one's] sword to stop the water, the water [will] flow even more [when the sword is removed]). [The order of the two halves may be reversed (q.v.).]

117 **Jiè lái de shuǐ bù jiěkě.** 借来的水不解渴。 (lit) Water borrowed [from others] won't satisfy [your] thirst. (fig) You can't always rely on other people's help to solve your own problems.

118 **Jiè lái de yīshang bù hétǐ.** 借来的衣裳不合体。 (lit) Clothes borrowed from others won't fit. (fig) Borrowed items or glory will not improve one's own appearance, and in fact will make one appear worse for having borrowed them.

119 **Jiélìng bù dào, bù zhī lěngnuǎn; rén bù xiāngchǔ, bù zhī hòubáo.** 节令不到，不知冷暖；人不相处，不知厚薄。 [When the] season [has] not arrived, [one can]not know [whether it is going to be] warm [or] cold; [similarly, when] people do not deal with each other [regularly], [they do] not know [whether their relationship is] close or not.

120 **Jiě líng háishi xì líng rén.** 解铃还是系铃人。 (lit) [The one who should] untie the bell [is the very] person [who] tied [it on]. (fig) The only one who can solve the problem is the one who created it in the first place. [Cf. *DRC*, chap. 90; based on a Chan (Zen) fable about removing a bell from a tiger's neck.]

121 **Jiè wú gòu; sī wú rǔ.** 戒无诟，思无辱。 (lit) [If one always] admonishes oneself, [one will] not be sullied; [if one always] thinks [before acting, one will] not be disgraced. (fig) If one always thinks carefully and watches one's own behavior, one will avoid disgrace. [Cf. *Shuō Yuàn: Jìng Shèn*.]

122 **Jiéyù shì zuìhǎo de yàopǐn.** 节欲是最好的药品。 Restraint from [one's] desires is the best medicine [for one's well being]. [Note: *liùyù*, the "six desires" listed in the Buddhist scriptures: sex, appearance, posturing, language, smoothness, longing.]

123 **Jièzhài bù shì jiācái.** 借债不是家财。 (lit) Borrowed money is not [one's] own property. (fig) Never depend on borrowing for a living.

124 **Jiè zhài huánzhài; kūlong cháng zài.** 借债还债，窟窿长在。 [If one] borrows money [to] pay [one's] debts, the deficit is still there. [Rhyme; originally *jiè* (揭) *zhài* . . . etc.]

J

125 **Jièzhài yào rěn; huánzhài yào hěn.** 借债要忍, 还债要狠。 [In] contracting debts [one] must be self-restraining as much as possible, [but in] repaying debts [one] must be resolute [until] they are completely paid off. [Rhyme]

126 **Jífēng zhī jìncǎo; bǎn dàng jiàn zhōngchén.** 疾风知劲草，板荡见忠臣。 (lit) [From a] strong wind, [one may] know the strength of the grass, [and from] troubled times [one may] see the loyalty of officials. (fig) It is in hard times that people's true characters are revealed. [Cf. *Hòu Hàn Shū: Wáng Bà Zhuàn*; note: *bǎn dàng*, (lit) "wayward [and] unscrupulous," alludes to two poems in the Poetry Classic: *Shījīng: Dà Yǎ*; see also *guó luàn chū zhōngchén* above and *rén dào nánchù* and *shì biàn zhī rénxīn* below.]

127 **Jīhán qǐ dào xīn.*** 饥寒起盗心。 Hunger and cold tempt [people] to steal.

128 **Jìjié bù ràng rén.** 季节不让人。 (lit) The seasons do not yield to anyone. (fig) The seasons do not wait for (farming) people. One must do things at the appropriate time. "Time waits for no man." [See also *hòu chā yī rì yǎng* above.]

129 **Jì lái zhī, zé ān zhī.*** 既来之，则安之。 (lit) Since [you] are here, just be content with it [i.e., the environment or circumstances, no matter how undesirable they are]. (fig) It is best to make the best of things (or) take things as they come. [Cf. the Confucian Analects: *Lúnyǔ: Jì Shì; Xīxiāng Jì*, Act 2, Scene 2.]

130 **Jīmáo shàng bùliǎo tiān.** 鸡毛上不了天。 (lit) A chicken feather cannot ascend to heaven. (fig) Common people cannot accomplish anything great. [See also the following entry.]

131 **Jīmáo yě néng fēi shàngtiān.** 鸡毛也能飞上天。 A chicken feather *can* fly up to heaven. [*Jī máo shàng tiān* is an expression used by Mao Zedong in 1958 to describe the realization of the poor peasants' People's Communes in contrast to the negative thinking expressed in the traditional saying *jī máo shàng bù liǎo tiān*, "A chicken feather cannot ascend to heaven"; see the preceding entry.]

132 **Jìn chú, dé shí; jìn mín, dé lì.** 近厨得食，近民得力。 [Stay] close to the kitchen [and you will] have food; [stay] close to the people [and you will] have power. [This is a reversed revision of an older proverb: *jìn guān dé lì; jìn chú de shí*, "stay close to officials and you will have power; stay close to the kitchen, and you will have food"; see also *jìn shuǐ lóutái* below.]

133 **Jǐnfáng nù lǐ xìng; màn fā xǐ zhōng yán.** 谨防怒里性，慢发喜中言。 (lit) [One must] guard against losing [one's] temper in anger, [and be] slow in speech when happy. (fig) One should be temperate in one's speech at all times, and avoid saying things in anger or in the joy of the moment which one might regret later. [Note: *shǐ xìngzi*, "to get into a temper."]

134 **Jīngāng-nùmù bùrú púsà dī méi.** 金刚怒目不如菩萨低眉。 (lit) A Buddha's warrior attendant's fierce stare is not as [useful as a] Buddha with [his] eyes lowered. (fig) Kind advice is more effective than angry criticism. "You will catch more flies with honey than you will with vinegar." [Cf. *Tài Píng Guǎng Jì*, chap. 174; note: *jīngāng-nùmù* is a *chengyu* meaning "to be fierce of visage"; see also *duō zāihuà* above.]

135 **Jīngāng sīdǎ, fó yě lǐ bù xià.** 金刚厮打，佛也理不下。 (lit) [When the] Buddha's warrior attendants fight [with each other], even the Buddha can do nothing. (fig) When people in a family or group quarrel or fight, even their elders can't judge who is to blame, who started it, etc. [Rhyme.]

136 **Jīngchéng suǒ zhì, jīnshí-wéikāi.*** 精诚所至，⊙金石为开。 (lit) Wherever [there is] sincerity, metal [and] stone [can] be parted. (fig) No difficulty is insurmountable if one is sincere. [Note *jīnshí*, (lit) "metal and stone" is used as a literary metaphor for hardness; *jīnshí-wéikāi* is a *chengyu* meaning "sincerity can make metal and stone crack"; see also *zhìchéng suǒ zhì* below.]

137 **Jǐng gān cái zhī shuǐ kěguì.** 井干才知水可贵。 (lit) Not until the well [goes] dry [does one] know the value of water. (fig) One does not appreciate the true value of things until they are gone. [See also *chuān wà bù zhī* above and *yǒu mǎo, bù zhī* below.]

138 **Jīng gōng zhī niǎo shāng qū mù.** 惊弓之鸟伤曲木。 (lit) The bird [who has been] frightened by a bow is [also] afraid of bent twigs. [Note: *jīnggōngzhīniǎo* is often used alone as a *chengyu* meaning "a badly frightened person"; see also *yīzhāo bèi shé yǎo* below.]

139 **Jìngle fùmǔ, bù pà tiān; jiǎole zūshuì, bù pà guān.** 敬了父母，不怕天；缴了租税，不怕官。 (lit) [If you] respect [your] parents, [you need] not be afraid of Heaven; [if you have] paid [your] taxes, [you need] not be afraid of [government] officials. (fig) If one behaves properly, one need never fear punishment, either here or in the hereafter. [Note: *zūshuì*, "land taxes and other levies."]

140 **Jīng rén bù guì yù; jiāo rén bù guì zhū.** 荆人不贵玉；蛟人不贵珠。 (lit) Those who are engaged in [the production of] jade and pearls don't regard them as precious. (fig) Rich people who are born into a comfortable life simply take it for granted. [Rhyme; note: *Jīng* originally referred to Bian He, who discovered jade at Jing mountain in the kingdom of Chu in Hubei province; *jiāo* refers to a mythical sea creature.]

141 **Jīng rén jù, tiānwài dé.** 惊人句，天外得。 (lit) Amazing phrases come from beyond the heavens. (fig) Memorable lines (e.g., epigrams, aphorisms, poetry, etc.) just "come" to people, purely through inspiration; "it just came to me."

142 **Jīngshǒu sānfēn féi.*** 经手三分肥。 (lit) [Whenever anything] passes through [one's] hands, [one is bound to get at least] thirty percent "greased." (fig) When one is in an official position, one can always get some personal benefit out of it.

143 **Jǐngshuǐ bù fàn héshuǐ.** 井水不泛河水。(lit) Well water does not interfere with river water. (fig) One should not interfere with the business of others. [Cf. DRC, chap. 69; see also héshuǐ bù fàn above.]

144 **Jǐngshuǐ bù wàiliú; mìshì bù wàichuán.** 井水不外流，秘事不外传。[Just as] well water does not leak out, [so] secrets [should] not [be allowed to] leak out [either].

145 **Jǐngshuǐ wú dà yú; xīn lín wú cháng mù.** 井水无大鱼，新林无长木。(lit) [In] well water there are no big fish, [and in] a new[ly planted] forest there are no tall trees. (fig) Talented people can't be produced under unfavorable conditions or without proper education. [Rhyme; cf. Lǚ Shì Chūnqiū: Yǒu Shǐ Lán; Yù Dà; see also tǔ bì zé cǎomù below.]

146 **Jǐng táo sān biàn, chī tiánshuǐ; rén cóng sān shī, wǔyì gāo.** 井淘三遍吃甜水，人从三师武艺高。[Just as a] well dredged three times gives fresh water, [so] a person who has followed [i.e., learned a trade from] three masters is most skilled. [See also jǐng yào táo below.]

147 **Jìng tā yī zhàng bùrú gào tā yī zhuàng.** 敬他一丈不如告他一状。(lit) [In dealing with] bullies, deferring to them is not as [good as] suing them. (fig) It's better to take the initiative and stand up to bullies than to submit to them.

148 **Jīngtōng zàiyú yùnyòng.** 精通在于运用。(lit) Mastery lies in application. (fig) "Practice makes perfect."

149 **Jǐngwā bù kěyǐ yǔ hǎi.** 井蛙不可以语海。(lit) [To] frogs [in a] well, [one] may not speak [of the] sea. (fig) There is little point in discussing with narrow-minded people things beyond their understanding. [Cf. Zhuāngzǐ: Qiū Shuǐ; in Zhuāngzǐ this is followed by xià chóng bù kěyǐ yǔ bīng (q.v.); note also the chengyu: jǐngdǐzhīwā, (lit) "frog(s) in the bottom of a well," and the word jǐngwā, both meaning "person(s) with limited outlooks"; see also huìgū bù zhī above.]

150 **Jīngyàn dà sì xuéwen.** 经验大似学问。Experience is superior to learning.

151 **Jǐng yào táo; rén yào jiāo.** 井要淘；人要教。[Just as] wells must be [repeatedly] dredged, [so] people must be [repeatedly] taught. [Rhyme; see also jǐng táo sān biàn above.]

152 **Jīng yī shì, zhǎng yī zhì.** 经一事，长一智。(lit) Have an experience, grow in knowledge. (fig) Wisdom comes from experience. [See also bù jīng yī shì and chī yī qiàn below.]

153 **Jìn hé mò wǎng shǐ shuǐ; jìn shān mò wǎng shāo chái.** 近河莫枉使水，近山莫枉烧柴。(lit) [Even if you are] close to the river don't waste water; [even if you are] close to the mountain don't waste fire wood. (fig) Be economical even in times of plenty.

154 **Jīn jiāng huǒ shì fāng zhī sè; rén yòng cái jiāo shǐ jiàn xīn.** 金将火试方知色，人用财交始见心。[Just as it is only when] gold is tested in fire [can one] know [its relative] purity, [so it's only when you] deal with people about money matters [that you] begin to know [their] hearts. [Note:

chéngsè, "relative purity (of gold or silver)"; see also zhēn jīn bùpà huǒ below.]

155 **Jìnle miào mén, jiù suí héshang.** 进了庙门，就随和尚。(lit) Having entered the temple, then follow the [Buddhist] monks. (fig) "When in Rome, do as the Romans do." [See also rùjìng wèn jìn below.]

156 **Jìnle Sānbǎodiàn dōu shì shāoxiāng rén.** 进了三宝殿都是烧香人。(lit) Having entered the worship hall [of a Buddhist temple], all are [there to] burn incense. (fig) If people come together, it must be for some (common) reason or object. In the temple all are pilgrims. [Rhyme; note: Sān Bǎo Diàn usually refers to the main worship hall of a Buddhist temple; see also jì zài fó huì xià above.]

157 **Jīnqián rú fèntǔ; rénpǐn zhí qiān jīn.** 金钱如粪土，人品值千斤。Gold and money are [worthless as] dung [and] dirt, [while one's] integrity is as valuable as gold.

158 **Jìn rén lì; tīng tiānmìng.** 尽人力，听天命。Do your best [and] resign yourself to fate. [Cf. DRC, chap. 48; see also móushì zài rén below.]

159 **Jīnrì bù zhī láirì shì.*** 今日不知来日事。(lit) Today [one does] not know what will come tomorrow. (fig) One can't predict the future. One never knows what's going to happen next in life.

160 **Jīnrì shì, jīnrì bì.*** 今日事，今日闭。(lit) Today's affairs [should be] finished today. (fig) "Don't put of until tomorrow what you can do today."

161 **Jìn shān duō yǔ; jìn hǎi duō fēng.** 近山多雨，近海多风。(lit) Close to the mountains [there is] more rain; close to the sea [there is] more wind. (fig) One is always influenced by one's surroundings.

162 **Jǐnshàng-tiānhuā cháng shíyǒu; xuězhōng-sòngtàn néng jǐ rén?** 锦上添花常时有，雪中送炭能几人？(lit) There are sometimes [people who] "add flowers onto brocade," [but] how many people "send charcoal in snowy weather"? (fig) There will always be people who come to flatter you when you are successful, but no one will come to help you when you are in need; the world is full of "fair weather friends," but "nobody knows you when you're down and out." [Cf. Chū Kè Pāi'àn Jīngqí, chap. 20; also said zhǐyǒu jǐnshàng-tiānhuā; nǎ dé xuězhōng-sòngtàn (q.v.); note: jǐnshàng-tiānhuā, "adding flowers to brocade" and xuězhōng-sòngtàn "sending charcoal in snowy weather" are commonly used fused phrase literary idioms (chengyu); note: shíyǒu, "to happen now and then."]

163 **Jìn shān shǐ mù; jìn shuǐ shí yú.** 近山使木，近水食鱼。(lit) Close to the mountains, [one may have] wood to use; close to the water, [one may have] fish to eat. (fig) Make full use of whatever favorable conditions or resources you may have. [Rhyme; see also dǎyú de bù lí above and kào shān, chī shān below.]

J

164　**Jīnshēng bù yǔrén-fāngbiàn; niànjīng Mítuó zǒngshì kōng.** 今生不与人方便, 念经弥陀总是空。 [If one] doesn't help others in this life, [even if one] chants all of the names of the Buddhas, it will be of no use. [Note: *Mítuó* is short for *Āmítuófó*, a name for the Buddha often chanted by Buddhist monks in China; *yǔrén-fāngbiàn* is a set phrase meaning "to make things easy for others."]

165　**Jìn shuǐ lóutái, (xiān dé yuè).*** 近水楼台, 先得月。 (lit) The balconies [or towers] nearest the water (get the moon[light] first). (fig) Those with "connections" to an organization (or a person with power) get preferential treatment. [A quotation from *Qīng Yè Lù* by the Song dynasty poet Yu Wenbao; this has become a set idiom, written *jìnshuǐ-lóutái-xiāndéyuè*, meaning "to be in a favored position"; the last three words are often omitted, as in a *xiēhòuyǔ*, making the first four characters appear to be a *chengyu* with the same meaning.]

166　**Jìn shuǐ zhī yú xìng; jìn shān shí niǎo yīn.** 近水知鱼性, 近山识鸟音。 [One who lives] near the river knows the habits of fish, [and one who lives] near the mountains knows the songs of birds. (fig) People are most familiar with their immediate surroundings. [Rhyme.]

167　**Jìn sì rénjiā bù zhòng sēng.** 近寺人家不重僧。 (lit) People [who live] close to a temple don't hold monks in great respect. (fig) People pay no attention to talented people or unusual happenings in their immediate environment. "Familiarity breeds contempt." [See also *huàjiàng bù gěi* above and *yuǎn lái de héshang* below.]

168　**Jīn wō, yín wō bùrú zìjiā de cǎo wō.*** 金窝, 银窝不如自家的草窝。 (lit) Gold or silver mansions are not as good as one's own thatched house. (fig) "There's no place like home." [Also said . . . *bùrú zìjiā de qióng wō.*]

169　**Jīn wú zúchì; rén wú wánrén.*** 金无足赤, 人无完人。 [Just as] gold [can]not be pure, [so] people [can]not be perfect. [Often quoted by Mao Zedong; the two halves are often reversed (q.v.); see also *shì ruò qiúquán* below.]

170　**Jīn xiānglín; yín qīnjuàn.** 金乡邻, 银亲眷。 Neighbors [are as precious as] gold [whereas] relatives [are only as precious as] silver. [See also *yuǎnqīn bùrú* and *yuǎnqīn, jìnlín* below.]

171　**Jǐn xíng wú hǎo bù.** 紧行无好步。 (lit) [In] hurried going there are no good steps. (fig) Haste makes for missteps. "Haste makes waste." [Cf. *R3K*, chap. 74; *Hé Diǎn*, chap. 3; see also *jí xíng wú shàn jì; jí zhōng yǒu shī; tān kuài chū chācuò* and *yù sù zé bù dá* below.]

172　**Jìn xìn shū bùrú wú shū.** 尽信书不如无书。 (lit) Completely believing books is not as [good as] not having any books [at all]. (fig) It is better not to have any books at all than to believe in them implicitly. [Cf. *Mencius*, *Mèngzǐ: Jìn Xīn Xià* and *Lǎo Cán Yóujì*, chap. 14.]

173　**Jǐn yán shèngyú fúyào.** 谨言胜于服药。 (lit) Prudent speech is better than taking medicine. (fig) An once of prudence in one's speech is worth "a pound of cure" if one is not prudent in speech.

174　**Jīn-yín bù guòshǒu.** 金银不过手。 (lit) Gold [and] silver [should] not pass through [someone else's] hands. (fig) Money dealings should be done face-to-face by the two parties directly involved, and not through some third party, in order to avoid misunderstandings later.

175　**Jīn-yín bù lòubái.** 金银不露白。 (lit) [One's] gold [and] silver [should] not be revealed. (fig) Never display (all) your assets. [See also *cái bù lòubái* above and *qiáncái bù lòu* and *zhēn yínzi* below.]

176　**Jīn zānzi diào zài jǐng lǐtou; yǒu nǐ de cái shì nǐ de.** 金簪子掉在井里头, 有你的才是你的。 (lit) [A] gold pin [may] fall into a well, [but if it's] yours, then [it's] yours. (fig) If one is destined to get something one will get it eventually, against all odds. [Cf. *DRC*, chap. 30.]

177　**Jīnzhāo yǒu jiǔ, jīnzhāo zuì.** 今朝有酒, 今朝醉。 (lit) Today [we] have wine [so] today [let us get] drunk. (fig) Enjoy the present; "gather ye rosebuds while ye may"; *carpe diem.* [A line from the Tang dynasty poet Luo Yin's poem "Zì Qiǎn," ("Dispelling One's Sorrows").]

178　**Jǐn zhuāngjia; màn mǎi-mài.** 紧庄稼, 慢买卖。 [One has to be] urgent [in doing] farm work [i.e., to catch the seasons, weather, etc., but] unhurried [in doing] business [in order to maximize profit].

179　**Jìn zhū zhě chì; jìn mò zhě hēi.*** 近朱者赤, 近墨者黑。 (lit) One [who is] near vermilion [will take on a] red[dish hue], [and] one [who is] near ink [will become] black[ened]. (fig) One is influenced by one's surroundings and/or the company one keeps. [Cf. *JW*, chap. 22; see also *ǎi jìn sì jìn.*]

180　**Jīnzi háishì jīnzi huàn.** 金子还是金子换。 (lit) Gold must be exchanged for gold. (fig) Nobility must be matched with nobility. [Cf. *DRC*, chap. 46; also said *jīnzi zōng děi jīnzi huàn.*]

181　**Jírén zìyǒu tiān xiàng.** 吉人自有天相。 (lit) Virtuous people naturally have Heaven's help. (fig) Heaven rewards the good. [Cf. *Xǐngshì Héngyán*, chap. 25; *JW*, chap. 27; also said *jírén zìyǒu tiān bǎoyòu*, "Heaven protects the good"; *jírén* is sometimes *shànrén.*]

182　**Jī shàn féng shàn; jī è féng è.** 积善逢善, 积恶逢恶。 [One who] accumulates good [deeds will] encounter good[ness]; [one who] accumulates evil [deeds will] meet with evil. [Cf. *Gǔ-Jīn Xiǎoshuō*, chap. 26.]

183　**Jī shàn wú rén jiàn; cúnxīn yǒu tiān zhī.** 积善无人见, 存心有天知。 (lit) [When one] does good deeds, [even though] no one sees, [one's] good intentions are seen by Heaven. (fig) The truly virtuous do good regardless of whether anyone knows about it or not.

J

184 **Jī shàn zhī jiā bì yǒuyú qìng.** 积善之家必有余庆。(lit) A family [which] accumulates [many] good deeds will have a surplus of blessings. [Cf. *Zhōu Yì: Kūn.*]

185 **Jī shǎo chéng duō; jí yè chéng qiú.** 积少成多, 集腋成裘。(lit) [If one] accumulates [many] small [amounts, they will] become a lot; the smallest, finest fragments of fox fur, sewn together, will make a fine robe. (fig) "Many a little makes a mickle." [Both halves are used separately as chengyu; cf. *Hàn Shū: Dǒng Zhòng Shū Zhuàn* and *Shèn Zǐ: Zhī Zhōng*; see also *jī yǔ chén zhōu* below.]

186 **Jī shí dé yīkǒu, qiángsì bǎo shí dé yī dǒu.** 饥时得一口, 强似饱时的一斗。A mouthful of food in times of hunger is better than a bushel of grain in times of fullness. [Rhyme; cf. *Xǐngshì Héngyán*, chap. 37; note: a *dǒu* is a unit of dry measure for grain equal to one deciliter.]

187 **Jí shuǐ bù yǎngyú.** 急水不养鱼。(lit) [In] rapid[ly flowing] water, [one can]not raise fish. (fig) Short-tempered people can't get along with others.

188 **Jí shuǐ yě yǒu huítóu làng.** 急水也有回头浪。(lit) A rushing torrent also makes backward waves. (fig) One will sometimes meet with setbacks even when everything is going smoothly.

189 **Jǐ suǒ bù yù, wù shī yú rén.** 己所不欲, 勿施于人。(lit) That which oneself does not want, [one should] not do to [other] people. (fig) Do not unto others what you would not like yourself. [Cf. the Confucian Analects: *Lúnyǔ: Wèi Líng Gōng*; this is sometimes referred to as "The Silver Rule."]

190 **Jiǔ bìng chéng liángyī.** 久病成良医。(lit) Prolonged illness makes [a patient] a good doctor. (fig) Experience is a good teacher. [See also *chī yào sān nián* above and *sān zhé gōng zhī* below.]

191 **Jiǔ bìngchuáng qián méi xiàozǐ.** 久病床前没孝子。There are no filial children beside the bed [of a parent who has been] sick for [too] long. [See also *bǎi rì chuáng qián* and *chuángtóu yǒu luó gǔ* above.]

192 **Jiùbīng rú jiùhuǒ.** 救兵如救火。[Sending] relieving troops [i.e., reinforcements] is as [urgent as] fighting a fire. [Cf. *Hé Diǎn*, chap. 10.]

193 **Jiǔ bù jiě zhēn chóu.** 酒不解真愁。Liquor cannot dispel real sorrows. [See also *jiè jiǔ xiāochóu* and *yào bù néng zhì* below; vs. *jiǔ xiāo bǎi chóu* and *pòchú wànshì* below.]

194 **Jiǔ bù yán gōng.** 酒不言公。[While drinking] wine, don't talk [about] public [business]. [See also *chī jiǔ bù yán gōngwù* above.]

195 **Jiǔ bù zuì rén, rén zì zuì; sè bù mí rén, rén zì mí.** 酒不醉人人自醉, 色不迷人人自迷。Wine does not intoxicate people, [but] people get [themselves] drunk; lust does not lead men astray, [but] men lead [themselves] astray. [Cf. *Jǐngshì Tōngyán*, chap. 24; *WM*, chap. 21; *Érnǚ Yīngxióng Zhuàn*, chap. 23; see also *jiǔ sè huò zhī méi* below.]

196 **Jiǔ céng zhī tái qǐ yú lěi tǔ.** 九层之台起于垒土。(lit) (Even) a nine-storied terrace [must be] built up layer by layer. (fig) Great achievements are the result of continued accumulated efforts. [See also *qiān lǐ zhī xíng* below.]

197 **Jiǔ chén, wèi chún; rén lǎo, shí shēn.** 酒陈味醇, 人老识深。(lit) [As] wine matures, [its] flavor mellows; [as] people get older, [their] understanding is deeper. (fig) Both wine and judgment mature with age.

198 **Jiǔ dào zhēnxìng.** 酒道真性。(lit) [When drinking] wine, [one] speaks [and reveals one's] true nature. (fig) In vino veritas. [Cf. *Ér Kè Pāi'àn Jīngqí*, chap. 38; see also *jiǔ hòu tù zhēnyán* and *jiǔ rù, shé chū* and *zuì shì xǐng shí yán* below.]

199 **Jiù de bù qù; xīn de bù lái.** 旧的不去, 新的不来。[If] the old doesn't go away, the new won't come. [Said of housecleaning, governments, etc.]

200 **Jiǔ duō shāng shēn, qì dà shāngrén.** 酒多伤身, 气大伤人。[As too] much wine harms the health, [so too] great anger hurts [other] people.

201 **Jiǔ dǔ, shénxiān shū.** 久赌, 神仙输。[After] a long time gambling, [even a] god [will] lose. [Cf. *Wǔ Sōng*, chap. 6; see also *jiǔ dǔ wú shèng jiā* below.]

202 **Jiǔ dǔ wú shèng jiā.** 久赌无胜家。(lit) [With] constant gambling there's no winner. (fig) A constant gambler will inevitably lose. [Cf. *Wǔ Sōng*, chap. 6; see also the preceding entry.]

203 **Jiǔ féng zhījǐ qiān zhōng shǎo; huàbùtóujī, bàn jù duò.** 酒逢知己千盅少; 话不投机, 半句多。[When sharing] liquor [among] close friends, a thousand cups are too few, [but when people] talk at cross purposes, a half a sentence [can be too] much. [Cf. *Sān Xiá Wǔ Yì*, chap. 70; now more commonly *qiān bēi shǎo . . .*; note: *huàbùtóujī*, "to be at loggerheads," is treated as a set phrase; see also *huà bù tóujī* above.]

204 **Jiù hán mòrú zhòng qiú; zhǐ bàng mòrú zìxiū.** 救寒莫如重裘, 止谤莫如自修。(lit) To protect [one against] cold, there is nothing better than a heavy fur coat; to put a stop to slander there is no better way than to improve [one's] behavior. [Rhyme; cf. *Sān Guó Zhì: Wèi Shū: Wáng Chǎng Zhuàn*]

205 **Jiǔ hǎo, rén zì lái.** 酒好, 人自来。(lit) [If the] wine is good, people [will] come as a matter of course. (fig) Goods of quality or people of ability will attract notice without promotion. "Good wine needs no bush." "If a man builds a better mouse trap, the world will beat a path to his door." [See also *hǎo huò wúxū* and *hǎo jiǔ bùpà* and *hǎo jiǔ bùyòng* above.]

206 **Jiǔ hòu tù zhēnyán.** 酒后吐真言。(lit) After [drinking] liquor, [one] spits out true words. (fig) "In wine there is truth"; in vino veritas. [Cf. Cao Yu's modern play *Wáng Zhāojūn*, Act 4; see also *jiǔ dào zhēnxìng* above and *jiǔ rù, shé chū* and *zuì shì xǐng* below.]

207 **Jiǔ hòu wú dé.** 酒后无德。(lit) After [too much] liquor, there is no virtue. (fig) After one drinks too much, one has no manners. [Cf. *DRC*, chap. 45.]

J

208 **Jiùhuǒ xū jiù miè; jiù rén xū jiù chè.** 救火需救灭, 救人需救彻。 To put out a fire, [one] must put [it] out thoroughly; to help a person, [one] must help [him] out completely. [Cf. *WM*, chap. 9; *Érnǚ Yīngxióng Zhuàn*, chap. 8; see also *jiù rén, jiù dàodǐ* below.]

209 **Jiùjí, bù jiù qióng.** 救急不救穷。 (lit) [One may] help [others in an] emergency, [but do] not help [those who are in constant] poverty. (fig) One can help others (occasionally) in emergencies, but one cannot (be expected to) help others all·the time. [Also said as *jiùjí, jiù bùliǎo qióng*.]

210 **Jiùle luòshuǐgǒu, huítóu yǎo yīkǒu.** 救了落水狗, 回头咬一口。 [If you] save a drowning dog, [you'll be] bitten by it later. (fig) If you help bad people, you'll be harmed by them later. [Rhyme; note: *luòshuǐgǒu*, (lit) "a dog in the water," is a metaphor for "one who is in trouble"; also note: *dǎ luòshuǐgǒu*, (lit) "to beat a dog in the water"; (fig) "to exterminate bad people completely," was used in an essay in "Fén" by Lu Xun entitled "'Fèi'è Bōlài' Yīnggāi Huǎnxíng" below; see also *yǐ jiāng shèng yǒng* below.]

211 **Jiǔlìng dà rú jūnlìng.*** 酒令大如军令。 Drinking games are [to be observed even] more seriously than military orders. [Cf. *DRC*, chap. 40; note: *(xíng) jiǔ lìng*, "(to play) drinking games"; *cāi quán xíng lìng*, "finger games played when drinking."]

212 **Jiǔliú rě rén xián.** 久留惹人嫌。 (lit) Staying [too] long makes people tire of one. (fig) Never overstay your welcome. [See also *jiǔ zhù lìngrén jiàn* below.]

213 **Jiùmìng rú jiùhuǒ.** 救命如救火。 Saving a life [is] as [urgent as] putting out a fire.

214 **Jiǔ néng chéngshì; jiǔ néng bài shì.** 酒能成事, 酒能败事。 (lit) Liquor can accomplish things [and] liquor can ruin things. (fig) Affairs can be either settled or ruined by wine. [Cf. *WM*, chap. 4.]

215 **Jiǔ péng, fàn yǒu; méi qián, fēnshǒu.** 酒朋饭友, 没钱分手。 [The kind of] friends [who join one only for] wine and food, [when there is] no more money, [will] leave [you]. [Rhyme; note: *jiǔròu-péngyou*, "fair weather friends"; see also the following entries.]

216 **Jiǔ péng, fàn yǒu; nándé chángjiǔ.** 酒朋饭友, 难得长久。 [The kind of] friendship [based on] wine and food seldom lasts long. [Rhyme; see also the preceding entry and following entries.]

217 **Jiǔqián, jiǔqián; jiǔ hòu wú yán.** 酒钱酒钱, 酒后无言。 (lit) Wine money, wine money; after drinking there's no [coherent] talking. (fig) [It's better to] pay for your drinks first, as after you're drunk, there'll be no talking to you. [Rhyme.]

218 **Jiù rén, jiù dàodǐ; sòng rén, sòng dàojiā.** 救人救到底, 送人送到家。 (lit) [If you are going to] help someone, help [him] thoroughly, [and if you are going to] see someone off, see [him all the way] home. (fig) If you're going to help someone or do something, do it thoroughly. [See also *bāng rén, bāng dàodǐ* and *jiùhuǒ xū jiù miè* above and *sòng rén, sòng dàojiā* below.]

219 **Jiù rén xū jiù jí.** 救人须救急。 [To really] help a person, [one] must help [him] in [times of] emergency. [Cf. *Xǐngshì Héngyán*, chap. 10; see also *jūnzǐ zhōu rén* below.]

220 **Jiù rén yī mìng, shèng zào qī jí fútú.** 救人一命, 胜造七级浮屠。 To save one human life is better than building a seven-storied pagoda [to the Buddha]. [Cf. *Xǐngshì Héngyán*, chap. 22; *JW*, chap. 80; *Hé Diǎn*, chap. 5; note: *fútú*, originally a transliteration of the Sanskrit word for Buddha, here means "pagoda"; see also *diǎn tǎ qī céng* above and *zàijiā jìng fùmǔ* below.]

221 **Jiǔròu-péngyou duō duō yǒu, luònán zhīzhōng bàn gè wú.** 酒肉朋友多多有, 落难之中半个无。 There are many, many "friends" [who come just to enjoy] good wine and food, [but when you] fall into difficulty, not even half [a] one [will come to help]. [Note: *jiǔròu-péngyou*, "fair weather friends"; see also the preceding and following entries.]

222 **Jiǔròu-péngyou hǎo zhǎo; huànnànzhījiāo nán féng.** 酒肉朋友好找, 患难之交难逢。 [It's] easy to make friends [who come only for] wine and food, [but] difficult to meet friends [who will] share hardships [with you]. [Note: *huànnànzhījiāo* is a set phrase meaning "a friend in adversity"; see also the preceding three entries.]

223 **Jiǔ rù, shé chū.** 酒入舌出。 (lit) [When] wine [is] in, [the] tongue [is] out. (fig) It is easy to make indiscreet remarks under the influence of alcohol, (so beware!). [Rhyme; see also *jiǔ dào zhēnxìng* above.]

224 **Jiǔ sè huò zhī méi.** 酒色祸之媒。 Wine [and] sexual desire [are the] agents of disaster. [See also *jiǔ bù zuì rén* above.]

225 **Jiùshēng, bù jiù sǐ.** 救生, 不救死。 (lit) Save the living; not the dead. (fig) The living can be saved, but the dead cannot. Save or concentrate your efforts where they can do some good. [Cf. *Guānchǎng Xiànxíng Jì*, chap. 23.]

226 **Jiǔ xiāng, bùpà jià gāo.** 酒香, 不怕价高。 (lit) [If the] wine smells good, it doesn't matter how high the price [is]. (fig) (Any) goods of high quality may command a high price.

227 **Jiǔ xiāo bǎi chóu.** 酒消百愁。 Wine destroys all worries. [See also *yī zhǎn néng xiāo* below; vs. *jiǔ bù jiě* above.]

228 **Jiǔ zhù lìngrén jiàn.** 久住令人贱。 (lit) One who lives [under another's roof] too long [will be] looked down upon. (fig) Never overstay your welcome. [See also *jiǔliú rě rén xián* above.]

229 **Jiǔ zhù línjū wéi yī zú.** 久住邻居为一族。 Long-standing neighbors become [like] clan-relatives. [See also *duōnián línjū* above and *yuǎnqīn bùrú jìnlín* below.]

230 **Jiǔ zǐ bù wàng méi.** 九子不忘媒。 (lit) [Even after having had] nine sons, [a married couple] should not forget the matchmaker [who first introduced them]. (fig) One should always be grateful to one's benefactor(s).

231 **Jiǔ zǐ bù zàng fù, yī nǚ dǎ jīng guān.** 九子不葬父，一女打荆官。 [Even if] nine sons were unwilling [to pay for the] burial of their father, one daughter still would weave a coffin out of bush branches. [Daughters were sometimes believed to be even more filial than sons in traditional China.]

232 **Jiǔzuì zǒng yǒu yī xǐng; cáimí yǒng wú zhǐjìng.** 酒醉总有一醒；财迷永无止境。 Drunkenness always has an awakening, [but] a money-grubber['s desire] knows no limits.

233 **Jìwǎng-bùjiù.** 既往不咎。 See *chéngshì bù shuō* above.

234 **Jí xíng wú hǎo bù.** 急行无好步。 (lit) [In] hurried going there are no good steps. (fig) Haste makes for missteps. "Haste makes waste." [See also *jǐn xíng wú hǎo bù* above and *xìngjí diàobude* and *yù sù zé bù dá* below.]

235 **Jí xíng wú shàn jì.** 疾行无善迹。 (lit) Hasty walking leaves no good traces. (fig) "Haste makes waste." [See also *jǐn xíng wú hǎo bù* above.]

236 **Jí-xiōng xiāng jiù; huànnàn xiāng fú.** 吉凶相救，患难相扶。 Victims of misfortune aid each other [and] those in distress support each other. [Rhyme; cf. *R3K*.]

237 **Jī yǔ chén zhōu; qún qīng zhé zhóu.** 积羽沉舟，群轻折轴。 (lit) [An] accumulation of feathers [can] sink a boat, [and] many light [things can] break an axle. (fig) Many small problems can lead to great disasters. Tiny things can become a mighty force. [Cf. *Zhànguó Cè: Wèi Cè Yī*; the first part may be used alone as a *chengyu*.]

238 **(Jì) zài ǎi yán xià, zěn gǎn bù dītóu?** (既)在矮檐下，怎敢不低头？ (lit) [Since] [one stands] under low eaves, how can one dare not to lower one's head? (fig) When one depends on others (for food, pay, support, etc.), one must do whatever they say. [Cf. *WM*, chap. 28; *JPM*, chap. 90; *Dōng Zhōu Lièguó Zhì*, chap. 90; note the *chengyu*: *jì rén líxià*, (lit) "to live under another's roof"; (fig) "to depend on someone for a living."]

239 **Jì zài fó huì xià, dōu shì yǒu yuán rén.** 既在佛会下，都是有缘人。 (lit) Since [we are all] in the Buddhist brotherhood, [we must] all have been destined [to meet] by fate. (fig) If people come together, it must be because they share a common destiny. [Cf. *JW*, chap. 36; note: *yuánfèn*, "fate which brings people together"; see also *gèrén yǒu gèrén* and *jìnle Sānbǎodiàn* above and *xiāngféng hébì* below.]

240 **Jī zhě yì wéi shí; kě zhě yì wéi yǐn.** 饥者易为食，渴者易为饮。 The hungry are not choosy about food, [and] the thirsty are not choosy about drink. [Cf. *Xǐngshì Héngyán*, chap. 10; see also *jī bù zé shí* above.]

241 **Jí zhōng yǒu shī.*** 急中有失。 (lit) In haste there is loss. (fig) It is easy to make mistakes when one is in a hurry. "Haste makes waste." [See also *jǐn xíng wú hǎo bù* and *yù sù zé bù dá* below and the preceding entry.]

242 **Jí zǒu bīng; màn zǒu ní.** 急走冰，慢走泥。 (lit) [One has to] walk fast [on] ice [and] walk slowly [on a] mud[dy road]. (fig) Different problems should be dealt with in different ways.

243 **Juānjuān bù sāi, jiāng wéi jiānghé.** 涓涓不塞，江为江河。 [If] small trickles are not stopped, [they] will become rivers. [Cf. *Liù Tāo: Shǒu Tǔ Xù Niè Hǎi Huā*, chap. 56; see also *jī yǔ chén zhōu* above.]

244 **Jǔ dàshì zhě bì yǐ rén wéi běn.** 举大事者必以人为本。 (lit) One who would pursue a great cause must take human beings as the basis. (fig) The success of any great enterprise depends on the people involved. [Cf. *R3K*, chap. 41.]

245 **Jūnlìng rú shān (dǎo).** 军令如山（倒）。 (lit) A military order is like a mountain (falling). (fig) Military orders carry great weight and must be obeyed without question. [Cf. *Míng Shǐ Yǎnyì*, chap. 16.]

246 **Jūn shǎng bù yú yuè.** 军赏不踰月。 Soldiers' [monthly] payments [should] not be overdue [or they'll revolt]. [A warning to leaders; cf. *Hàn Shū: Chén Tāng Zhuàn*; also said *bīng shǎng bù yú rì* "Soldiers' pay should not be a day late."]

247 **Jūnwáng fākuáng, bǎixìng zāoyāng.** 君王发狂，百姓遭殃。 [When] kings go mad, the common people suffer disasters. [Rhyme; note: *(lǎo) bǎixìng*, "common people."]

248 **Jūn wú méi, zhōng dào huí.** 军无媒，中道回。 [If an] army has no guide [in its march], [it will have to] turn back half way along. [Rhyme; cf. *Xīn Táng Shū: Gāo Lì Zhuàn*.]

249 **Jūn yǒu tóu; jiàng yǒuzhǔ.** 军有头，将有主。 (lit) Soldiers have [their] leaders [and] generals have their masters. (fig) At all levels of an organization everyone has someone to answer to. [Cf. *Gǔ-Jīn Xiǎoshuō*, (*Yù Shì Míng Yán*), chap. 21.]

250 **Jūn yǒu zhèng chén; fù yǒu zhèng zǐ.** 君有诤臣，父有诤子。 (lit) Princes [may] have ministers [who] remonstrate [with them and] fathers [may] have sons who oppose [them]. (fig) Sometimes it is necessary for subordinates to criticize their superiors. [Cf. *Dōng Zhōu Lièguó Zhì*, chap. 89.]

251 **Jūnzhōng wú xìyán.** 军中无戏言。 (lit) In military [affairs] there is no joking. (fig) Military orders must be carried out. [Cf. *R3K*, chap. 95; this has become an idiomatic phrase.]

252 **Jūnzǐ bàochóu, shí nián bù wǎn.*** 君子报仇，十年不晚。 [For a] gentleman [to] take [his] revenge, ten years is not too late. [Cf. *Yuè Fēi Zhuàn*, chap. 31; see also the following entry.]

253 **Jūnzǐ bàochóu, zhídài sān nián; xiǎorén bàochóu, zhǐ zài yǎnqián.** 君子报仇直待三年，小人报仇只在眼前。 A gentleman, to take his revenge, [will] wait for three years, [while] a base person takes [his] revenge immediately. [Cf. *Xǐngshì Héngyán*, chap. 34; see also the preceding entry.]

254 **Jūnzǐ bù chī wú míng zhī shí.** 君子不吃无名之食。 A gentleman never eats food which he doesn't deserve. [Cf. *JPM*, chap. 34; see also *jī bù chī* above, and *wú gōng, bù shòu* below.]

255 **Jūnzǐ bù gēn niú shǐ qì.** 君子不跟牛使气。A gentleman never argues with an ox [i.e., a brute; a base person].

256 **Jūnzǐ bù jiàn xiǎorén guò.*** 君子不见小人过。(lit) A gentleman does not begrudge a base person's trespasses. (fig) A gentleman never pays attention to the wrongs which base people commit. [Cf. *Érnǚ Yīngxióng Zhuàn*, chap. 32; see also *chéng dàshì* and *dàrén bù jì* above.]

257 **Jūnzǐ bù niàn jiù è.** 君子不念旧恶。A gentleman does not bear grudges. [Cf. *JW*, chap. 31; note: *bùniàn-jiù'è* has become a set phrase meaning "to forgive and forget"; see also *jūnzǐ jì ēn*, below.]

258 **Jūnzǐ bù qī ànshì.** 君子不欺暗事。A gentleman never does bad things in secret [i.e., things against his conscience]. [Originally *fú qī ànshì, qī kuàng sān guāng*, from *Jiǎn Wén Dì Jì: Tǐ Bì Zī Xù*; see also *míngrén bù zuò* below.]

259 **Jūnzǐ bù xiū dāngmiàn.** 君子不羞当面。A gentleman does not cause [another] embarrassment to [his] face [or in front of others]. [Cf. *Xīngshì Yīnyuán Zhuàn*, chap. 81, *JPM*, chap. 47.]

260 **Jūnzǐ chéng rén zhī měi.*** 君子成人之美。A gentleman [always helps] others attain [their] desires. [Cf. the Confucian Analects: *Lúnyǔ: Yán Yuān*; note: *chéngrénzhīměi* has become a set phrase meaning "to help someone to fulfill his wishes."]

261 **Jūnzǐ chéng rén zhī měi, (bù chéng rén zhī è).** 君子成人之美，(不成人之恶)。A gentleman helps others in [doing] good, [but does] not help others in [doing] evil. [From the Confucian Analects: *Lúnyǔ: Yán Yuān*; the second half is usually omitted; see the preceding entry.]

262 **Jūnzǐ dòng kǒu, bù dòngshǒu.** 君子动口，不动手。Gentlemen move [their] mouths [but] not [their] fists. [See Lu Xun's short story *A Q Zhēn Zhuàn* (The True Story of Ah Q); see also the following entry.]

263 **Jūnzǐ dòng kǒu; xiǎorén dòngshǒu.** 君子动口，小人动手。(lit) A gentleman uses [his] mouth, [while only] a base person uses [his] fists. (fig) Gentlefolk settle their differences verbally, not with brute force. [Cf. *Guānchǎng Xiànxíng Jì*, chap. 44; also said *jūnzǐ kāi kǒu; xiǎorén kāi quán*; see also the preceding entry.]

264 **Jūnzǐ fáng huàn wèi rán.** 君子防患未然。A gentleman tries to prevent disaster before it befalls. [Cf. *Guānchǎng Xiànxíng Jì*, chap. 56, and the *chengyu*: *fánghuàn-wèirán*, "to take preventative measures"; see also *fáng huàn yú wèirán* above and *jūnzǐ wèn zāi* below.]

265 **Jūnzǐ fáng wèirán, bù chù xiányí jiàn.** 君子防未然，不处嫌疑间。(lit) [A] gentleman guards against the unforeseen, [and does] not put [himself] under suspicion. (fig) A wise man is cautious and avoids the appearance of wrong-doing. [Cf. the Han dynasty *yuèfǔ* (song poem) "Jūnzǐ Xíng"; see also *fáng huàn yú wèirán* above and the preceding entry.]

266 **Jūnzǐ hé ér bùtóng.** 君子合而不同。A gentleman gets along [with others], but is not like [them].

267 **Jūnzǐ huái xíng; xiǎorén huái huì.** 君子怀刑，小人怀惠。Gentlemen think of the law, [while] base persons think of favors [they may receive]. [Note: *yōuhuì*, "benefits"; see also *yì dòng jūnzǐ* below.]

268 **Jūnzǐ jì ēn, bù jìchóu.** 君子记恩，不记仇。A gentleman remembers others' favors to him [but does] not remember enmity [over wrongs others have done to him]. [Cf. *Yuè Fēi Zhuàn*, chap. 51; see also *jūnzǐ bù niàn jiù è* above.]

269 **Jūnzǐ jīn rén zhī è; xiǎorén lì rén zhī wēi.** 君子矜人之扼，小人利人之危。A gentleman pities people's distress, [while] a base person takes advantage of people's difficulties. [Cf. *Dōng Zhōu Lièguó Zhì*, chap. 55.]

270 **Jūnzǐ juéjiāo bù chū èshēng.** 君子绝交不出恶声。A gentleman terminates a friendship without making any complaint. [Cf. *Zhànguó Cè: Hán Cè 2*; *Shǐ Jì: Yuè Yì Lièzhuàn*; also said *jūnzi jiāo jué, bù yuànyán*; see also the following entry.]

271 **Jūnzǐ juéjiāo, bù jìchóu.** 君子绝交，不记仇。A gentleman ends a friendship without any grudges. [See also the preceding entry.]

272 **Jūnzǐ qiān yán yǒu yī shī; xiǎorén qiān yán yǒu yī dàng.** 君子千言有一失，小人千言有一当。[Even a] gentleman [may] make one slip in a thousand words, [and even a] base person [may occasionally] get one in a thousand right. [A line from the famous Yuan dynasty playwright Guan Hanqing's play *Lǔ Zài Láng*.]

273 **Jūnzǐ tǎndàngdàng; (yǒu huà dāng miàn jiǎng).** 君子坦荡荡，(有话当面讲)。A gentleman [is] straightforward and frank; ([whatever he] has to say, [he says] to one's face). [Rhyme; the first part is from the Confucian Analects: *Lúnyǔ: Shù Ér*; the second part is a modern addition.]

274 **Jūnzǐ wèn zāi, bù wèn fú.** 君子问灾，不问福。A gentleman is concerned about [future] adversities, [so as to be well prepared], [but] not about [future] blessings. [Cf. *WM*, chap. 61; also said *jūnzǐ wèn huò, bù wèn fú*, in *Xīyáng Jì*, chap. 3 and *Sān Xiá Wǔ Yì*, chap. 69; see also *jūnzǐ fáng huàn* above.]

275 **Jūnzǐ yán xiān, bù yán hòu.** 君子言先，不言后。(lit) A gentleman speaks before [the fact, but] not after. (fig) A gentleman makes everything clear beforehand. [Cf. *Wǔ Sōng*, chap. 6.]

276 **Jūnzǐ yī yán, kuài mǎ yī biān.*** 君子一言，快马一鞭。(lit) A gentleman [need only give his] word, [just as a] swift horse [needs only] one [touch of the] whip. (fig) A gentleman's word, once given, cannot be retracted. A gentleman always keeps his word. [Cf. *JPM*, chap. 53; see also *hǎohàn yī yán* above; vs. *kuàimǎ yī biān* below.]

277 **Jūnzǐ yī yán, sìmǎ-nánzhuī.** 君子一言，驷马难追。(lit) Once a gentleman [has given his] word, a team of four horses cannot overtake it. (fig) A gentleman never goes back on his word.

[Note: *sìmǎ-nánzhuī* is used as a *chengyu* meaning "What has been said cannot be unsaid"; see also *yī yán jì chū* below.]

278 **Jūnzǐ yù yú yì; xiǎorén yù yú lì.** 君子欲于义，小人欲于利。A gentleman desires according to righteousness, [while] a base person desires according to [personal] profit. [Rhyme; see also *yǐ dòng jūnzǐ* below.]

279 **Jūnzǐ zài dé, bù zài yī.** 君子在德，不在衣。[The worth of a] gentleman resides in [his] virtue, not in [his fine] clothing.

280 **Jūnzǐ zhēng lǐ; xiǎorén zhēngzuǐ.** 君子争理，小人争嘴。Gentlemen strive [to observe] proper etiquette, [while] lowly persons strive [with their] mouths [i.e., eating and drinking]. [Cf. *Xíngshì Yīnyuán Zhuàn*, chap. 78; note: *zhēngzuǐ* is a colloquial expression meaning either to "talk back" or to "hog food."]

281 **Jūnzǐ zhī jiāo, dàn rú shuǐ.*** 君子之交，淡如水。(lit) Friendship between gentlemen [is] clear as water. (fig) Although the friendship between (upper class) gentlefolk may appear distant, the friendship is still very much there, untainted by shallow self-interest. [Often followed by *xiǎorén zhī jiāo, tián rú mì* (q.v.); cf. *Zhuāngzǐ: Shān Mù* and *Shǐ Jì: Biǎo Jì*; note: *dàn*, (lit) "insipid; tasteless," has Taoist connotations of purity.]

282 **Jūnzǐ zhī zé, wǔ shì ér zhǎn.** 君子之则，五世而斩。(lit) The virtue of good men will not last [more than] five generations. (fig) The good influence of righteous people cannot last much longer than their lifetimes. [Note: the ideal traditional Chinese family would have "five generations under one roof."]

283 **Jūnzǐ zhōu jí [/jì], bù jì fù.** 君子周急／济，不继富。A man of virtue helps [people in] distress, rather than adding to [those who are] well-off. [Cf. the Confucian Analects: *Lúnyǔ: Yōng Yě*; note: *zhōujì*, "to help out the needy."]

284 **Jūnzǐ zhōu rén zhī jí.** 君子周人之急。A gentleman helps people [in] urgent [need]. [See the Confucian Analects: *Lúnyǔ: Yōng Yě*.]

285 **Jǔshǒu bù dǎ wú niáng zǐ; kāikǒu bù mà péilǐ rén.** 举手不打无娘子，开口不骂赔礼人。Never raise your hand to strike a motherless child; never open your mouth to swear at one [who] offers an apology.

K

1 **Kāigōng, méiyǒu huítóu jiàn.** 开弓没有回头箭。(lit) [Once the] bow is pulled, the arrow will never return. (fig) Once action has been initiated, one should carry it through to the end. There's no turning back. [See also *jiàn zài xián shàng* above.]

2 **Kāikai mén lái, qī jiàn shì: chái-mǐ-yóu-yán-jiàng-cù-chá.** 开开门来七件事，柴米油盐酱醋茶。Everyday at the outset [(lit) once one opens the door], [one has to deal with the] seven [daily necessities of life]: fuel, rice, oil, salt, [soy] sauce, vinegar, [and] tea. (fig) First and foremost everyone has to make sure that one has the basic necessities of daily life. [Note: *chái-mǐ-yóu-yán*, (lit) "fuel, rice, oil and salt," and *yóu-yán-jiàng-cù*, "oil, salt, soybean sauce, and vinegar," are common expressions meaning "the chief daily necessities of life."]

3 **Kāitóu fàn hǎochī; kāitóu huà nánshuō.** 开头饭好吃，开头话难说。[To] start a meal is easy, [but to] start a conversation is difficult.

4 **Kāi yú háng bùguǎn biē shì.** 开鱼行不管鳖市。(lit) A fish-seller doesn't concern himself with the market [price of] soft-shelled turtles. (pun) (fig) One should not stick one's nose into things which don't concern one. [Note: *biē shì*, "market (price of) soft-shelled turtles" is a pun on *biē (rén de) shì*, "other (people's) affairs."]

5 **Kǎn bù dǎo dà shù, nòng bù duō cháihuo.** 砍不倒大树，弄不多柴火。(lit) [If you] don't chop down the big trees, [you] can't get much firewood. (fig) If one doesn't invest great capital, effort, or risk, one cannot expect great profits. [See also *yào dé fù* below.]

6 **Kàn cài chīfàn; liángtǐ-cáiyī.** 看菜吃饭，量体裁衣。(lit) [The amount of] rice [one] eats depends on [how well] the [accompanying] dishes [are prepared], and one's [clothes [are] cut [by] measuring [one's] body. (fig) One adjusts oneself to circumstances. [Quoted by Mao Zedong in *Fǎnduì Dǎng Bāgǔ*; note: *liángtǐ-cáiyī* is used as a *chengyu* meaning "to act according to actual circumstances"; see also *chīfàn, chuān yī* above and *kào shān, chǐ shān* and *kèzhe tóu* and *yǒu chǐ shuǐ* below.]

7 **Kàn de pò; rěn bu guò.** 看得破，忍不过。(lit) [Although one] can see through it, [one] can [hardly] endure [it]. (fig) Although one can understand something philosophically, (sometimes) one just can't stand it. [Cf. *Érnǚ Yīngxióng Zhuàn*, chap. 40; cf. the (Buddhist) *chengyu: kàn pò hóngchén*, "to see through the emptiness of the material world."]

8 **Kàn de rén zhòng, dédào rén yòng.** 看得人重，得到人用。[One who gives proper] respect [to] others [will] be employed [by] others. [Rhyme.]

9 **Kàn huā róngyì; zāihuā nán.** 看花容易，栽花难。(lit) To look at flowers is easy, [but to] grow flowers is difficult. (fig) It's easy to observe something, but harder to do it oneself. [See also *kàn shí róngyì* below.]

10 **Kǎnle nǎodài, bùguò wǎn dà bāla.** 砍了脑袋，不过碗大疤瘌。(lit) [Even if one is] beheaded, [it will] only [leave a] scar [as big] as a bowl. (fig) I don't care even if you chop off my head. True heroes do not fear death. [Cf. *Sān Xiá Wǔ Yì*, chap. 75.]

11 **Kàn rén, kàn xīn; tīng huà, tīngyīn.** 看人看心，听话听音。 To [truly] understand a person, look at his heart; to [truly] understand [someone's] speech, listen to the tone [i.e., the underlying implicit message]. [Rhyme; note: *tīngyīn* is a colloquial expression meaning to "take a hint"; vs. *luógǔ tīng yīn* and *yào zhī xīnfūshì* below.]

12 **Kàn rén tiāodàn bù chīlì.** 看人挑担不吃力。 (lit) To watch [another] person carrying a load does not require any exertion. (fig) No one knows the weight of another's burden. [See also *jiàn rén tiāodàn* above.]

13 **Kàn shí róngyì; zuò shí nán.** 看时容易，做时难。 When [one is] watching [it seems] easy, [but] when [one has to] do [it oneself, it is] difficult. [See also *kàn huā róngyì* above.]

14 **Kǎn yī zhī, sǔn bǎi zhī.** 砍一枝，损百枝。 (lit) [If you] chop off one branch, [you] harm a hundred branches. (fig) If you hurt one person, you harm many. [Cf. *JPM*, chap. 64; *Érnǚ Yīngxióng Zhuàn*, chap. 21.]

15 **Kào lìliang néng jǔ qiānjīn; kào zhìhuì néng jǔ wàn jīn.** 靠力量能举千斤，靠智慧能举万斤。 (lit) Using [brute] strength, [one can] hold a thousand catties, [but] using wisdom, [one can] hold ten thousand. (fig) Brain power is stronger than muscle power. [Note: literally, one *jīn* or "catty" is equal to one-half kilogram, but *qiānjīn* is figuratively taken to mean "a ton, very heavy, weighty"; see also *zhì dí qiān jūn* below.]

16 **Kào rén fú, zǒu bùliǎo cháng lù.** 靠人扶，走不了长路。 (lit) [If one] relies on others' support, [one] cannot walk a long way. (fig) One should depend on oneself in doing everything. [Rhyme; see also the following entry.]

17 **Kào rén, kào pǎo le; kào qiáng, kào dǎo le.** 靠人靠跑了，靠墙靠倒了。 (lit) [If you always] depend on others, [others will] run away; [if you always] lean against a wall, [the wall] will collapse. (fig) One should depend on oneself in doing everything. [See also the preceding entry.]

18 **Kào shān, chī shān; kào shuǐ, chīshuǐ.*** 靠山吃山，靠水吃水。 (lit) [If one lives] beside a mountain, [one's living] depends on [the resources of] the mountain; [if one lives] close to water, [one is] dependent on [the resources of] the water. (fig) One must make a living according to one's given circumstances. [Cf. *Rúlín Wàishǐ*, chap. 41; see also *guǎn shān chī shān* and *jìn shān shǐ mù* and *kàn cài chīfàn* above and the following entry.]

19 **Kào shān, shān dǎo; yǐ qiáng, qiáng tā.** 靠山山倒，依墙墙塌。 (lit) [If one] depends on the mountain [for a living for too long, the] mountain [will] collapse; [if one always] leans against a wall [for support, the] wall will collapse. (fig) One should always depend on oneself. [Note: *kàoshān* is also used with the idiomatic meaning of a patron or backer; see also the following entry.]

20 **Kàozhe dà hé, yǒu shuǐ chī; kàozhe dà shù, yǒu chái shāo.** 靠着大河有水吃，靠着大树有柴烧。 (lit) [Those who live] by a river [always] have water to drink [and those who live] near big trees [always] have firewood to burn. (fig) If one allies oneself with powerful people, one always benefits from their largesse. [See the preceding entry.]

21 **Kèbó bù zhuànqián; zhōnghòu bù shéběn.** 刻薄不赚钱，忠厚不折本。 Sharpness [does] not earn [one] money, [and] honesty [will] not lose money. [Cf. *Xǐngshì Héngyán*, chap. 3.]

22 **Kèbó chéng jiā, lǐ wú jiǔ xiǎng.** 刻薄成家，理无久享。 [One who] exploits [others in order to] make [his] fortune, [by] reason [will] not enjoy [his] riches for long.

23 **Kě bù jí yǐn; è bù jí wèi.** 渴不急饮，饿不急喂。 [When] thirsty, don't drink too fast, [and when] hungry, don't eat too fast. (fig) Always remain coolheaded in times of emergency.

24 **Kè bù sòngkè.** 客不送客。 A guest [need] not see off [another] guest. [Said by a departing guest to another guest; cf. *Wǔ Sōng*, chap. 10.]

25 **Kè dà, qī háng; háng dà, qī kè.** 客大欺行，行大欺客。 [When the] customer is richer, [(s)he] bullies the business[person]; [when the] business[person] is richer, (s)he bullies the customer(s).

26 **Kè lái, zhǔrén huān; kè zǒu, zhǔrén kuān.*** 客来主人欢，客走主人宽。 [When the] guests come, the host is happy; [when the] guests are gone, the host is at ease. [Rhyme.]

27 **Kèmǎ shàng bùliǎo zhèn.** 骒马上不了阵。 (lit) A mare can't be ridden into battle. (fig) Women cannot cope with great affairs or appear on grand occasions.

28 **Kěn xué zhī rén rú hé dào; bù xué zhī rén rú hāo cǎo.** 肯学之人如禾稻，不学之人如蒿草。 (lit) People [who are] willing to learn are [as useful as] rice seedlings, [while] people [who are] not [willing to] learn are as [useless as] wormwood grass. [Note: *hāocǎo*, artemisca or bitter fleabane, is a worthless weed that looks like rice seedlings.]

29 **Kè sàn, zhǔrén kuān. / Kè qù zhǔ ān.** 客散主人宽。/客去主安。 [When] guests have left, the host is at peace.

30 **Kě shí yī dī rú gānlù; yào dào zhēn fāng, bìng jí chú.** 渴时一滴如甘露；药到真方，病即除。 (lit) [When] thirsty, one drop [of water is] like sweet dew; [when the] medicine [is formulated] according to the proper prescription, the illness is eradicated. (fig) In order to solve a problem, one must find exactly the right solution. [See also *mǎ'ér zhuā zōng* below.]

31 **Kè suí zhǔ biàn.** 客随主便。 (lit) Guest(s) [should act] according to the host's convenience. (fig) It is only right to do as one's host sees fit.

32 **Kě yù ér bù kě qiú.*** 可遇而不可求。 (lit) [(Sometimes it happens by chance that) one] may come by [something by sheer luck], but not by searching [for it]. (fig) Sometimes things just "fall into one's lap." [See also *qiúzhī-bùdé* and *tàpò tiě xié* and *yǒuyì zhònghuā* below.]

K

33 **Kězhe tóu, zuò màozi.** 可着头，做帽子。(lit) Before making a hat, measure the head. (fig) Live within your means. "Cut your coat according to your cloth." [Cf. *DRC*, chap. 75; see also *chīfàn, chuān yī* and *kàn cài chīfàn* above and *shǒuzhe duōdà* below.]

34 **Kōng guànzi, huíshēng xiǎng.** 空罐子，回声响。(lit) The empty jar makes the loudest echo. (fig) Those with the least accomplishments usually boast the loudest. [See also *gǔ kōng, shēng gāo* above and *shuǐ shēn bù xiǎng* and *zhěng píng bù yáo* below.]

35 **Kōnghuà suí fēng sìchù piāo; yànyǔ rù xīn jìde láo.** 空话随风四处飘，谚语入心记得牢。Empty words are scattered in all directions by the wind, [but] proverbs learned by heart are fixed in the mind.

36 **Kǒngquè àixī yǔmáo; hǎorén zhēnxī míngyù.** 孔雀爱惜羽毛，好人珍惜名誉。[Just as] peacocks treasure [their] feathers, [so] good people treasure [their] reputations.

37 **Kōngxīn dà shù bù chéngcái.** 空心大树不成材。(lit) Trees with hollow cores can't become fine wood. (fig/pun) One who has no education can accomplish nothing. [Note: *mùcái*, "wooden material" and *réncái*, "talented people"; *chéngcái*, (1) "grow into useful timber"; (2) "become a useful person"; *bùchéngcái* is also an idiomatic expression meaning "good-for-nothing"; see also *shù bù xiū* below.]

38 **Kǒu bù'èrjià.** 口不二价。[An honest (business) person] never says two prices. [Note: *bù'èrjià* is a set phrase meaning "(having a) single / fixed price."]

39 **Kǒu rú jiōng, yán yǒuhéng; kǒu rú zhù, yán wú jù.** 口如扃，言有恒；口如注，言无据。[If one's] mouth [is] like a door-bolt, [one's] words have credence; [if one's] mouth [runs on] like a wine pot, [one's] words are unreliable. [Note: *zhù* here refers to an ancient wine pot in use between the Tang and the Yuan dynasties; this proverb was quoted by the Ming dynasty empress dowager *Rén Xiào Wén* in her essay in *Nèi Xùn: Shèn Yán Zhāng*.]

40 **Kǒu shé cónglái shì huò jī.** 口舌从来是祸基。[The] mouth [and] tongue have always been the roots of disaster. [Cf. *Xǐngshì Héngyán*. chap. 33; note: *kǒushé* as a single word (cí) means "quarrel, dispute"; see also the following entry.]

41 **Kǒu shì huò zhī mén; shé wéi zhǎn shēn dāo.** 口是祸之门，舌为斩身刀。[Your] mouth is the door to disaster; [your] tongue is the knife [that will] kill you. [Cf. *Gǔ-Jīn Xiǎoshuō*, chap. 3; see also *bìng cóng kǒu rù* and *chūkǒu xū chéngshí* above and the preceding entry.]

42 **Kuàidāo bù mó shì kuài tiě.** 快刀不磨是块铁。Sharp knives [that are] not [kept] sharpened are [mere] pieces [of] iron. (fig) Talented people must be challenged to sharpen their wits and prevent them from becoming "rusty."

43 **Kuàidāo bù xiāo zìjǐ de bǐng.** 快刀不削自己的柄。(lit) A sharp knife doesn't cut its own handle. (fig) One shouldn't harm one's own self, family, or group. [Cf. *Dàng Kòu Zhì*, chap. 122; but see also *càidāo bù néng* above.]

44 **Kuàidāo xiàmiàn wú yìng mù.** 快刀下面无硬木。(lit) Under a sharp knife there is no hard wood. (fig) So long as one is resolute and strong-willed, there are no obstacles that cannot be overcome.

45 **Kuàihuo guāngyīn róngyì guò.** 快活光阴容易过。(lit) Happy times pass by easily. (fig) Happy days fly fast. "Time flies when one is having fun." [Cf. *Niè Hǎi Huā*, chap. 31.]

46 **Kuàimǎ bùyòng biān cuī; xiǎng gǔ bùyòng zhòng chuí.** 快马不用鞭催，响鼓不用重槌。(lit) A swift horse needs no whipping [and] a good drum needs no heavy beating. (fig) An intelligent person needs only a hint (or rigorous training). [Rhyme; see also *míngrén bùyòng* below.]

47 **Kuàimǎ pǎo duàn tuǐ.** 快马跑断腿。(lit) [A] fast horse [will be] run [till its] legs [are] broken. (fig) People of ability are usually given more work. [Said either as a compliment or as a complaint; see also *néng zhě duō láo* below.]

48 **Kuàimǎ yě yào xiǎngbiān cuī; xiǎng gǔ yě yào zhòng chuí léi.** 快马也要响鞭催，响鼓也要重槌擂。(lit) Even a fast horse needs the crack of the whip to urge [it on]; even a loud drum needs a heavy stick to beat [it]. (fig) Greater demands are laid on people of intelligence so that they will produce more or do better. Certain people perform better under pressure.

49 **Kuàimǎ yī biān; kuài rén yī yán.** 快马一鞭，快人一言。(lit) [Just as a] fast horse [needs only] one [touch of the] whip, [so a] straightforward person needs only a word [in order to understand or to make a decision.] [Cf. *JPM*, chap. 53; note *shuǎngkuài*, "straightforward"; note: *kuài rén, kuài shì*, "a straightforward person [does] things straightforward[ly] (without first weighing the pros and cons)" and *kuài rén, kuài yǔ*, "A straightforward person speaks frankly"; see also *jūnzǐ yī yán, kuài mǎ yī biān* above.]

50 **Kuān dǎ dìjiǎo, zhǎi lěi qiáng.** 宽打地脚，窄垒墙。(lit) [In building a wall,] the foundation [should be] laid wide [and the] wall [should be] built up narrow. (fig) In studying, one's fundamental knowledge should be solid.

51 **Kuángfēng bù jìngrì; bàoyǔ bù zhōngzhāo.** 狂风不竟日，暴雨不终朝。(lit) Fierce winds don't last the day; hailstorms don't last the morning. (fig) Raging storms don't last long. Difficult times will come to an end sooner or later.

52 **Kǔhǎi wúbiān, huítóu shì àn.*** 苦海无边，回头是岸。(lit) The "bitter sea" is boundless; if you "turn around" [i.e., repent and believe in the Buddha], there's the shore [i.e., salvation]. (fig) If one commits any mistakes, fix them as soon as possible. [Note: *kǔhǎi* is a Buddhist term referring to the "Sea of Woes," i.e., the bitterness of earthly life; cf. the *chengyu: kǔhǎi yú shēng*, "surviving in the bitter sea of life"; *huítóu-shì'àn* is used as a

K

Buddhist *chengyu* with the meaning "repent and be saved"; see also *yǒu chóu jiē kǔhǎi* below.]

53 **Kǔnbǎng bù chéng fūqī.** 捆绑不成夫妻。 (lit) [One can]not bind [a man and a woman together] to make [them] husband [and] wife. (fig) Force alone cannot accomplish anything. [Cf. Mao Zedong's speech: "Zài Zhōngguó Gòngchǎndǎng Dì-Bā Jiè Zhōngyáng Wěiyuánhuì Dì-Èrcì Quántǐ Huìyì Shàng de Jiǎnghuà" ("Speech to the Second Plenary Session of the Central Party Committee of the Eighth Party Congress"); see also *qiǎngpò bù chéng* below.]

54 **Kùn lóng yì yǒu shàngtiān shí.** 困龙亦有上天时。 (lit) Even a dragon in difficulty [may] soar to

the sky [some]time. (fig) A person who is in difficult straits at present may nevertheless succeed later on.

55 **Kūshù bù jiē guǒ; kōnghuà bù zhíqián.** 枯树不结果，空话不值钱。 [Just as] withered trees don't bear fruit, [so] empty words are worthless.

56 **Kǔ yán yào; gānyán jí.** 苦言药，甘言疾。 (lit) Bitter words [are like] medicine [that cures diseases]; [it's] sweet words [that bring] illness. (fig) Accept well meant criticism and beware of flattery. [Cf. *Shǐ Jì: Shāng Jūn Lièzhuàn.*]

57 **Kǔ yè de háizi duō chīnǎi.** 哭夜的孩子多吃奶。 (lit) Babies [who] cry [at] night get more milk. (fig) Those who speak out or complain get more help. "The squeaky wheel gets the oil."

L

1 **Lā bù kāi yìnggōng, shè bù sǐ èláng.** 拉不开硬弓，射不死饿狼。 (lit) [If one is] unable to draw a strong bow, [one will] not be able to shoot the evil wolf to death. (fig) One must (be able to) take strong measures to deal with a powerful or dangerous enemy.

2 **Lādào cháng lǐ yībàn, shōudào dùn lǐ cái suàn.** 拉到场里一半，收到囤里才算。 (lit) [When the harvest of grain has been] carried to [the threshing] ground, [you only have] half [of it]; only when [it has] entered the granary, [can one] count [on it all]. (fig) Things half-done are not done. [Rhyme.]

3 **Lái de yì, qù de yì.*** 来得易，去得易。 "Easy come, easy go." [Cf. *Jǐngshì Tōngyán*, chap. 31; also said *lái de róngyì, qù de kuài*.]

4 **Lái de zǎo bùrú lái de qiǎo.*** 来的早不如来的巧。 Coming early is not as good as to come just at the right moment. [Rhyme; see also *jiàn rì bùrú* above.]

5 **Lái ér bù wǎng, fēilǐ yě.*** 来而不往非礼也。 (lit) Taking and not giving is not polite. (fig) It's impolite not to reciprocate a gift. [Cf. *Lǐjì: Qū Lǐ Shàng*; now sometimes used ironically to justify striking back, like "One good turn deserves another."]

6 **Làiháma xiǎng chī tiān'é ròu.** 癞蛤蟆想吃天鹅肉。 (lit) Toads want to eat swan's flesh. (fig) People often engage in wishful thinking. [Often said of a man hopelessly desiring a woman; cf. *Rúlín Wàishǐ*, chap. 3; *DRC*, chap. 11.]

7 **Lái shì rénqíng; qù shì zhài.** 来是人情，去是债。 To receive [a] present or favor is to incur [a] debt.

8 **Lái shì shìfēi rén; qù shì shìfēi zhě.** 来是是非人，去是是非者。 [As] the source [of the trouble] is a troublemaker, [the one to] get rid [of the trouble should be] the troublemaker. (fig) Since he caused the trouble it's up to him to fix it. [Cf. *DRC*, chap. 68; see also *jiě líng háishì* above.]

9 **Lái shuō shìfēi zhě, jiùshì shìfēi rén.** 来说是非者，就是是非人。 One who comes to gossip (or sow dissension) is [usually] involved in the trouble. [Cf. *JW*, chap. 29.]

10 **Lái zài huā shù xià, bì shì cǎi huā rén.** 来在花树下，必是采花人。 (lit) [Anyone who] comes under the flower tree must be one [who intends to] pick flowers. (fig) People do not go somewhere without a motive. [See also *wú shì, bù dēng* below.]

11 **Láizhě bù jù; jù zhě bù lái.** 来者不惧，惧者不来。 Those who come [are surely] not afraid; those who are afraid won't come. [Cf. *Dōng Zhōu Lièguó Zhì*, chap. 46; *Xǐngshì Héngyán*, chap. 34.]

12 **Láizhě bùshàn; shàn zhě bù lái.*** 来者不善，善者不来。 (lit) Those who come are not good, [and] those [who are] good don't come. (fig) Only those with evil or ulterior motives will come to trouble one. [Cf. *Yuè Fēi Zhuàn*, chap. 12; see also *dàizhě bù lái* above.]

13 **Lá kǒuzi yào jiàn xuè.** 拉口子要见血。 (lit) [When a] wound is made, blood should be seen. (fig) Anything one does should show a result. [Cf. *Érnǚ Yīngxióng Zhuàn*, chap. 19.]

14 **Làn bíkǒng púsà, xǐ wén chòu zhūtóu.** 烂鼻孔菩萨，喜闻臭猪头。 (lit) A Buddha [with a] festering nose likes to smell a stinking pig's head. (fig) "Birds of a feather flock together." [Note the *chengyu: chòu wèi xiāng tóu*, "Evil doers congregate together."]

15 **Làn chuán piān yù dāngtóu làng.** 烂船偏遇当头浪。 (lit) Broken ships always sail against adverse tides. (fig) Misfortunes always befall unlucky people. "Misfortunes never come singly." [See also *pò chuán piān yù* and *wū lòu gèng zāo* below.]

16 **Lǎnduò de mǎ, lùchéng yuǎn; lìnsè de rén, péngyou yuǎn.** 懒惰的马路程远，吝啬的人朋友远。 [Just as a] horse [which is] lazy [will make one feel that] the journey [is a] long [distance]; [so a] person [who is] cheap [will find his

friends keep a] long [distance from him as well].
[Rhyme.]

17 **Lǎnduò, tǎofàn gùn.** 懒惰讨饭棍。 (lit) Laziness [is a] beggar['s] stick. (fig) The root cause of beggary is laziness.

18 **Lǎnduò yīshí; sǔnshī yīshēng.** 懒惰一时, 损失一生。 (lit) Be lazy for one time [and you will] lose [for your] whole life. (fig) One should be diligent at all times; don't waste time idly.

19 **Làng cóng fēng lái; cǎo cóng gēn lái.** 浪从风来, 草从根来。 (lit) Waves come from wind; grass comes from roots. (fig) There's a cause for everything. [Rhyme; see also *fēng bù chuī* above.]

20 **Làn guō zìyǒu làn guōgài; chǒu rén zìyǒu chǒurén ài.*** 烂锅自有烂锅盖, 丑人自有丑人爱。 (lit) [Just as a] worn-out pot naturally has a worn-out lid, [so one] ugly person naturally has [another] ugly person to love. (fig) An ugly man or woman will always have another woman or man to love them. "There's no pot so ugly it can't find a lid." [Rhyme; see also *huā duì huā* above and *zhèng guō pèi hǎo zào* below.]

21 **Láng wú géyè ròu; shǔ wú géyè liáng.** 狼无隔夜肉; 鼠无隔夜粮。 (lit) Wolves never keep meat overnight; rats never keep [their] grain overnight. (fig) Some people seem to be congenitally shortsighted. [The second half is also used alone (q.v.).]

22 **Lángzhōng yī bù hǎo zìjǐ de bìng.*** 郎中医不好自己的病。 (lit) A doctor can't cure [his] own sickness. (fig) Some people criticize others, but not themselves. [Cf. "Physician, heal thyself."]

23 **Làngzǐ dāngjiā, èsǐ quánjiā.** 浪子当家, 饿死全家。 [When a] prodigal son [takes] charge of the family, the whole family [will] starve to death.

24 **Làngzǐ-huítóu, jìnbuhuàn.** 浪子回头金不换。 A prodigal son [who] reforms [can]not be exchanged [for] gold. [Cf. *Érnǚ Yīngxióng Zhuàn*, chap. 15; also said *bàizǐ huítóu . . .*; note: *làngzǐ-huítóu* is treated as a *chengyu* meaning "return of a prodigal son," and *jìnbuhuàn* has become an idiomatic phrase meaning "invaluable; priceless."]

25 **Láng zǒu qiān lǐ chī rén; gǒu dào tiānbiān chī shǐ.** 狼走千里吃人, 狗到天边吃屎。 [Even if a] wolf travels a thousand miles, [it will still] eat people [and even if a] dog gets as far as the horizon, [it will still] eat excrement. (fig) People cannot change their basic character. "A leopard cannot change its spots." [See also *gǒu chī shǐ* and *gǒu zǒu qiān lǐ* and *jiāngshān yì gǎi* above and *shé zuān de kūdòng* and *yī rén, yī xiàng* below.]

26 **Lǎnhàn píng zuǐqín; hǎohàn píng tuǐqín.** 懒汉凭嘴勤, 好汉凭腿勤。 (lit) Lazybones rely on [their] mouths, [while] diligent people rely on [their] legs. (fig) Lazy people are fond of talking, while diligent people work tirelessly.

27 **Lǎn huò děng hángshì.** 懒货等行市。 (lit) Goods of poor quality [have to] wait for [a rise in] market prices [caused by scarcity]. (fig) If conditions are not favorable at the present time, wait for an opportunity later. [See also *hé lǐ wú yú* above.]

28 **Lā niú bù shàng shù; lā gǒu bù shàng péng.** 拉牛不上树, 拉狗不上棚。 (lit) [One can]not pull [an] ox onto [a] tree, nor [can one] pull [a] dog onto [the roof of a] shed. (fig) You can't do anything by going against the objective realities of nature.

29 **Lǎn lǘ shàng mò, (shǐ niào duō).** 懒驴上磨, ⊙(屎尿多)。 [When a] lazy donkey turns a grindstone, ([it] takes lots of [time off for] shitting [and] pissing). [A joking description of one who works slowly or delays; also used as a *xiehouyu*.]

30 **Lánlù shítou yǒu rén bān.** 拦路石头有人搬。 (lit) Stones blocking the road [will sooner or later be] removed by someone. (fig) Obstacles will always be overcome sooner or later.

31 **Làn má nǐng chéng shéng, lìliàng dà qiānjīn.** 烂麻拧成绳, 力量大千斤。 (lit) [Even] rotten hemp twisted into a rope [will have a] strength [as] great [as] a thousand pounds. (fig) In unity there is strength. [Note: literally, one *jīn* or "catty" is equal to one-half kilogram, but *qiānjīn* is figuratively taken to mean "a ton; a great weight."]

32 **Lǎn māo dǎi bu zhù sǐ lǎoshǔ.** 懒猫逮不住死老鼠。 (lit) A lazy cat can't [even] catch a dead mouse. (fig) Lazy people won't do even the simplest of things.

33 **Lǎn rén huítóu, lì dà rú niú.** 懒人回头, 力大如牛。 [If a] lazybones mends [his] ways, [his] strength is as [that of a] bull. [Rhyme.]

34 **Lǎn rén zuòshì yī dàn tiāo.** 懒人做事一担挑。
  • (lit) Lazy people work [by] carrying [everything all on] one shoulder pole. (fig) Lazy people do everything at once, at the last minute, rather than according to a set plan.

35 **Lǎo bàng chū míngzhū.*** 老蚌出明珠。 (lit) ⊙Older [freshwater] mussels [may] produce bright pearls. (fig) An older couple may give birth to a fine son or daughter. [Cf. *Chū Kè Pāi'àn Jīngqí*, chap. 32; see also *lǎogua wō lǐ* and *pò jiǎn chū* below.]

36 **Lǎo bù jūlǐ; bìng bù jūlǐ.** 老不拘礼, 病不拘礼。 [Both] the old and the sick need not observe the [usual polite] courtesies. [Rhyme; cf. *Rúlín Wàishǐ*, chap. 12.]

37 **Lǎo bù lǎo, zìjǐ xiǎo.** 老不老, 自己晓。 (lit) Old [or] not, oneself knows [best]. (fig) One is only as old as one feels oneself to be. [Rhyme; compare the common *suyu* expression: *Rén lǎo; xīn bù lǎo*, "old in body, (but) not in spirit."]

38 **Lǎo bù líjiā shì guìrén; shào bù líjiā shì fèirén.** 老不离家是贵人, 少不离家是废人。 [An] ⊙old "stay-at-home" is fortunate; [a] young "stay-at-home" is a good-for-nothing. [Rhyme.]

39 **Lǎo bù xiēxīn, shào bù nǔlì.** 老不歇心, 少不努力。 [If one's] mind [can]not rest [when one is] old, [it is because one was] lazy [when one was] young. [Cf. *xīnlì*, "mental and physical labor"; see also *hēi fà bù zhī* above and *shàozhuàng bù nǔlì* below.]

40 **Lǎo bù yǐ jīngǔ wéi néng.** 老不以筋骨为能。(lit) The old cannot exhibit their ability using [their] muscles. (fig) Older people cannot compete with younger people in physical strength, (although they may have superior abilities in other areas).

41 **Lǎogua wō lǐ chū fènghuáng.** 老鸹窝里出凤凰。(lit) A phoenix [may] come out of a crow's nest. (fig) Talented people may come from an ordinary family, or beautiful girls from a poor family. [Cf. DRC, chap. 65; see also *lǎo bàng chū míngzhū* above.]

42 **Lǎohǔ háiyǒu gè dǎdǔnr de shíhou.** 老虎还有个打盹儿的时候。(lit) There are times when even tigers take a nap. (fig) Even the most alert people will sometimes slacken their vigilance. "Even Homer sometimes nods."

43 **Lǎohǔ jiè zhū; yǒu jìn, méi chū.** 老虎借猪, 有进没出。(lit) [When] a tiger borrows a pig, [it] goes in [but does] not come out. (fig) When a powerful person "borrows" something, do not expect to have it returned. [Rhyme.]

44 **Lǎohǔ jīnqiánbào; gè zǒu gè de dào.** 老虎金钱豹, 个走个的道。(lit) A tiger [and] a leopard each takes its own road. (fig) People should mind their own business. [Rhyme.]

45 **Lǎohǔ pìgu mōbude.** 老虎屁股摸不得。(lit) A tiger's backside [no one] dares to touch. (fig) A person who thinks him or herself above criticism puts on airs. [Used sarcastically by Mao Zedong to describe cadres who thought they were "untouchable," i.e., immune from criticism; a popular slogan used during the Cultural Revolution.]

46 **Lǎohǔ yī gè néng lánlù; hàozi yī wō dé wèi māo.** 老虎一个能拦路, 耗子一窝得喂猫。(lit) One tiger alone can block the road, [but] one [whole] nest of rats [can only] make a meal for a cat. (fig) One person of high ability is worth more than a whole group of people of low ability.

47 **Lǎo jiàn chūnhán, qiūhòu rè.** 老健春寒, 秋后热。(lit) [An] old [person, although] healthy, [is like a chilly] spring or a warm autumn [i.e., cannot last long]. [Cf. DRC, chap. 57.]

48 **Lǎojiàng chūmǎ, yī gè dǐng liǎ.*** 老将出马, 一个顶俩。(lit) [When] an old general goes into action, alone [he] can fight two [at a time]. (fig) An experienced hand can get twice as much done. [Rhyme; see also *hǎohàn shàngchǎng* above.]

49 **Lǎolao jiā de gǒu; chīwánle jiù zǒu.** 姥姥家的狗, 吃完了就走。Granny's dog leaves as soon as it finishes eating its food. [This rhyme is a common teasing endearment said lovingly by grandparents when their grandchildren leave after visiting.]

50 **Lǎo mǎ shí tú.*** 老马识途。(lit) [An] old horse knows the road. (fig) Older people are more experienced. [Cf. *Hán Fēizǐ: Shuō Lín Shàng;* this is often mistaken as being a chengyu; see also *gǔlái cún lǎo mǎ* above and *chēngjiāng shì lǎo* below.]

51 **Lǎo mǐfàn niē shā bù chéng tuán.** 老米饭捏⊘杀不成团。(lit) Steamed stale rice, [even if] squeezed very hard, [just] won't stick together. (fig) People who don't get along well will not cooperate or work well together, no matter how hard you try to force them. [Cf. *Wǔ Sōng,* chap. 6.]

52 **Lǎorén bù jiǎng gǔ, hòushēng huì shī pǔ.** 老人不讲古, 后生会失谱。[If] the old don't recall the [values of the] past [for the young, their] descendants will go against [traditional moral] standards. [Rhyme; note: here *shī pǔ* or *lípǔ,* (lit) "to lose the family lineage records" or "departing from the standard"; "beyond reasonable limits" is a colloquial expression for a lapse in moral standards.]

53 **Lǎorén hào shù yuǎn shì.** 老人好述远事。Old people are fond of talking about the distant past.

54 **Lǎoshǔ guò jiē, rénrén hǎn dǎ.** 老鼠过街, 人人喊打。(lit) [When a] rat crosses the street, everyone shouts [and] beats [it]. (fig) Evil people are hated by everyone. [Cf. Mao Zedong's essay: "Fǎnduì Dǎng Bāgǔ"; in *Máo Zédōng Xuǎnjí,* vol. 4: 77; this is often used as a political slogan against "counter-revolutionary elements" in society; also said *guò jiē lǎoshǔ* etc.]

55 **Lǎoshǔ zài dà yě pà māo.** 老鼠再大也怕猫。(lit) However big a rat is, it still fears a cat. (fig) There's always somebody bigger or stronger. [See also *yī wù xiáng yī wù,* "One thing can conquer another."]

56 **Lǎotóu yào qǐng; xiǎohái yào hǒng.** 老头要请, 小孩要哄。[One should] be polite to the old [and] coaxing to children. [Cf. *hǒng háizi,* "to coax, 'con', or humbug; to tell 'white lies' to."]

57 **Láoxīn bùrú láolì.** 劳心不如劳力。(lit) Racking [one's] brains (or worrying) is not as good as serious labor (or action). (fig) Better set to work than just sit thinking or worrying. [Cf. the Song dynasty author Lu Juren's *Guān Zhēn.*]

58 **Láoxīn zhě zhì rén; láolì zhě zhì yú rén.*** 劳心者治人, 劳力者治于人。Those who labor with their minds rule others [and] those who labor physically are ruled by others. [A quotation from Mencius, *Mèngzǐ: Téng Wén Gōng Shàng.*]

59 **Lǎo yào diānkuáng, shào yào wěn.** 老要癫狂, 少要稳。The old may be a bit unconventional (or unrestrained), [but] the young should be steady. [Cf. *Érnǚ Yīngxióng Zhuàn,* chap. 22.]

60 **Lǎo yī, shào bǔ.** 老医少卜。(lit) Old doctors [and] young diviners [are the best]. (fig) The best doctors are old and the best diviners are young. [Cf. *Xǐngshì Héngyán,* chap. 28.]

61 **Lǎozi fàngpì, xiǎozi pǎo èr lǐ dì.** 老子放屁, 小子跑二里地。(lit) [When] the superior breaks wind, [his] subordinates [have to] run two *lǐ.* (fig) Subordinates have to remain at their superiors beck and call, often running around on (what they consider to be) "fool's errands." [See also *shàngsi fàng gè pì* below.]

62　**Lǎozi tōu guā, dào guǒ; érzi shārén, fànghuǒ.** 老子偷瓜盗果, 儿子杀人放火。 [If] the father steals melons [and] pilfers fruit [i.e., commits petty theft], the son [will] commit murder and arson. (fig) One must set a good example for one's offspring in deeds as well as in words. [Rhyme; see also *fù yù xíngjiè* above.]

63　**Làyuè shuǐtǔ guì sānfēn.** 腊月水土贵三分。 (lit) [In the] twelfth lunar month water [and] land are more expensive. (fig) Everything is more expensive in the depths of winter.

64　**Léishēng dà, yǔdiǎn xiǎo.** 雷声大, 雨点小。 (lit) [When the] thunder is loud, [the] raindrops are small. (fig) (It is often the case that) those who engage in a lot of talk about (doing) something in fact take very little or no action on the matter. "Much talk, little action." "Much cry and little wool." [Cf. *JPM*, chap. 20.]

65　**Lè jí shēng bēi; pǐ jí tài lái.*** 乐极生悲, 否极泰来。 Extreme happiness begets sorrow; [from] extreme misery good [fortune] springs. [This is a combination of two common *chengyu* which appears in *WM*, chap. 24; note: *pǐ*, here "misfortune," and *tài*, here "good fortune," are terms from the *Yìjīng* (Book of Changes); note: *lèjíshēngbēi* and *pǐjí-tàilái* may be used as *chengyu*.]

66　**Lè mò lèyú hào shàn, kǔ mò kǔyú duō tān.** 乐莫乐于好善, 苦莫苦于多贪。 [As to] happiness, [there is] no happiness [greater] than doing good [to others]; [as to] bitterness, [there is] no bitterness [greater] then greed. [Rhyme; see the *chengyu*: *hàoshàn-lèshī*, "doing good and helping others."]

67　**Lěng liàn "sānjiǔ"; rè liàn "sānfú."** 冷练"三九", 热练"三伏"。 (lit) [One must] train in the coldest days of winter [and in] the hottest days of summer. (fig) Only in situations of extreme hardship can one train oneself to be strong. [Note: *sānjiǔ(tiān)* refers to the third nine-day period following the winter solstice, and *sānfú* refers to the three ten-day periods of the hot season.]

68　**Lěng pà fēng qǐ; qióng pà qiànzhài.** 冷怕风起, 穷怕欠债。 (lit) [Just as when] cold, [one is] afraid of a rising wind, [so when] poor, [one is] afraid of getting into debt. (fig) When one is in unfortunate circumstances, one dreads unfavorable happenings even more. [See also *wú fēng*, *hán yěhǎo* below.]

69　**Lěng shì yī gè rén lěng; rè shì dàjiā rè.** 冷是一个人冷, 热是大家热。 (lit) [When it's] cold [one is] cold alone, [but when it's] hot, everyone is hot [together]. (fig) Cold, sorrow, or privation are suffered individually, but warmth is shared by everyone.

70　**Lěng shǒu nán zhuā rè mántou.** 冷手难抓热馒头。 (lit) A cold [bare] hand is hard put to grasp a hot steamed bun. (fig) Sometimes it's hard to know where to start (in dealing with somebody or something).

71　**Lěngshuǐ yào rén tiāo; rèshuǐ yào rén shāo.** 冷水要人挑, 热水要人烧。 (lit) Cold water needs people to carry [it and] hot water needs people to heat [it]. (fig) Without people doing things, nothing can get done. [Rhyme; see also *tiānshàng wú yún* below.]

72　**Lěng tāng, lěng fàn hǎochī; lěng yán, lěng yǔ nántīng.** 冷汤冷饭好吃, 冷言冷雨难听。 Cold soups [and] cold rice are all right to eat, [but] cold words [and] cold remarks grate on the ear.

73　**Lěngtiān mò zhē huǒ; rètiān mò zhēfēng.** 冷天莫遮火, 热天莫遮风。 (lit) [In] cold weather, don't block the fire [from others]; [in] hot weather, don't block the wind [from others]. (fig) One should always take others' interests into consideration instead of only considering one's own.

74　**Liǎn chǒu, guài bù zháo jìngzi.** 脸丑, 怪不着镜子。 (lit) [If one's] face is ugly, [one] cannot blame the mirror. (fig) If one misbehaves, one cannot blame others for the results.

75　**Liáng cái bù zhōng xiǔ yú yán xià; liáng jiàn bù zhōng mì yú xiá zhōng.** 良材不终朽于岩下, 良剑不终秘于匣中。 (lit) Good lumber won't end up rotting at the foot of a cliff [in the mountains where it was cut, and a] fine sword won't end up hidden in its case. (fig) Able persons will not remain unknown and unemployed forever. [Cf. *Dōng Zhōu Lièguó Zhì*, chap. 87.]

76　**Liàng dà, fú yě dà; (jī shēn, huò yì shēn).** 量大福也大, (机深祸亦深)。 The greater [one's] magnanimity [toward others], the greater [one's] good fortune [will be]; (the more complex [one's] schemes [are], the greater the disaster [to follow]). [Cf. *Shuǐhǔ Quán Zhuàn*, chap. 19; *Èr Kè Pāi'àn Jīngqí*, chap. 36; note: *dùliàng dà*, "magnanimous"; the first part is usually used alone.]

77　**Liǎng Guǎng shú, tiānxià zú.*** 两广熟, 天下足。 See *Hú-Guǎng shú, tiānxià zú* above.

78　**Liǎng guó jiāozhàn, bù zhǎn láishǐ.*** 两国交战, 不斩来使。 (lit) [When] two countries are at war, [their] envoys [should] not be killed. (fig) [Now used to mean:] "Blame not the bearer of bad tidings." "Don't blame me; I'm just the messenger." [Also said *liǎng guó xiāng zhèng bù zhài lái shǐ.*]

79　**Liáng gǔ shēn cáng ruò xū.** 良贾身藏若虚。 (lit) A good businessman hides [his goods] in secret places as [if he had] nothing, [just as a talented man hides his talent]. (fig) It is unwise to show off (one's assets or talents) in public. [Cf. *Shǐ Jì: Lǎozǐ Hán Fēi Lièzhuàn.*]

80　**Liǎng gū zhījiān nán wéi fù.** 两姑之间难为妇。 (lit) [Caught] between [her] two sisters-in-law [i.e., her husband's two unmarried sisters], it's hard to be a [good] wife. [In a traditional Chinese extended family, familial in-fighting made life difficult for daughters-in-law.]

81　**Liǎng hài quánhéng, dāng qǔ qí qīng.** 两害权衡, 当取其轻。 (lit) [When] two harms [are being] weighed, [one] should choose the lighter of them. (fig) Of two evils, choose the lesser one.

L

82 **Liǎng hǔ xiāng dòu, (bì yǒu yī shāng).** 两虎相斗，必有一伤。 (lit) [When] two tigers fight, one must be wounded. (fig) When two (strong) parties fight, one is sure to lose. [Cf. *R3K*, chap. 62; also said *liǎng hǔ xiāng zhèng*, etc.; note: *liǎnghǔ-xiāngdòu* is often used as a *chengyu* or as a *xiehouyu*, both with the meaning of the latter part, which is suppressed; see also *èr hǔ xiāng dòu* above.]

83 **Liáng jī nán zài.** 良机难再。 (lit) Good opportunities hard[ly come] again. (fig) Opportunity only knocks once.

84 **Liǎng jūn xiāngyù, yǒng zhě shèng.** 两军相遇，勇者胜。 (lit) When two armies meet [i.e., fight], the braver [will] win. (fig) Bravery can be more important than sheer strength or numbers.

85 **Liáng nóng bù wèi shuǐ-hàn bù gēng; liáng gǔ bù wèi shé yuè bù shì.** 良农不为水旱不耕，良贾不为折阅不市。 [Just as a] good farmer won't stop farming because [there's] flood [or] drought, [so a] good merchant won't stop doing business from fear of going broke. [Cf. *Xúnzǐ: Xiū Shēn*; note: *shé yuè*, "to lose one's capital."]

86 **Liáng qín xiàng mù ér qī; xiánchén zé zhǔ ér shì.** 良禽相木而栖，贤臣择主而侍。 [Just as a] wise bird looks over a tree before alighting, [so a] wise minister chooses the master he will serve. [Cf. *R3K*, chap. 14; as a *chengyu*: *liáng qín zé mù*.]

87 **Liángsǎn suī pò, gǔ gé shàng zài.** 凉伞虽破，骨格尚在。 Although the umbrella is broken, the frame still exists. (fig) Some people even under adverse conditions will maintain their integrity.

88 **Liángshàn bèi rén qī; cíbēi shēng huàn hài.** 良善被人欺，慈悲生患害。 Benevolent [people] get bullied by others [and the] tenderhearted invite disaster. [Cf. *JPM*, chap. 38; see also *rén shàn, dé rén qī* below.]

89 **Liàng xiǎo fēi jūnzi.** 量小非君子。 (lit) [One who] judges [others] small[-mindedly] is no gentleman. (fig) A person with little tolerance is no gentleman. [Note: *qìliàng xiǎo*, "low tolerance," see also *hèn xiǎo fēi jūnzǐ* above.]

90 **Liǎng xióng bù bìnglì.** 两雄不并立。 (lit) Two heroes can't co-exist [on one place]. (fig) Two strong (willed) people cannot co-exist.

91 **Liáng yán yī jù, sān dōng nuǎn; liùyuè hán.*** 良言一句三冬暖，恶语伤人六月寒。 A kind word [will] warm [one for] three winter [months], [while] a harsh word can wound [one] coldly [even in the heat of] summer. [Rhyme; note: *sān dōng*, "three winter months"; see also *lì rén zhī yán* below.]

92 **(Liángyào kǔkǒu (lìyú bìng);) zhōngyán nì'ěr (lìyú xíng).** (良药苦口利于病，)忠言逆耳利于行。 ([Just as] good medicine [which is] bitter in the mouth [is] good for [one's] illness, [so] sincere advice [which] offends the ear [is] beneficial to [one's] conduct. [Rhyme; cf. *R3K*, chap. 60; *Kǒngzǐ Jiā Yǔ: 6 Běn*; the second part may be used alone, and both *liángyào-kǔkǒu* and *zhōngyán nì'ěr* may be used as *chengyu* with the meaning of "the truth hurts"; see also *yào kǔ zhìbìng* below.]

93 **Liángyī mén qián bìngrén duō.** 良医门前病人多。 (lit) There are more patients in front of the door of a good doctor. (fig) People will search out the services of a talented person. "If a man builds a better mousetrap, the world will beat a path to his door."

94 **Liáng yuán suī hǎo, bù shì jiǔ liàn zhī jiā.** 梁园虽好，不是久恋之家。 (lit) Although the Liang Garden is fine, it is not a home [one can be] attached to for a long time. (fig) Although this place is very nice, it is not (the) home for me. "There's no place like home." [Note: *Liáng yuán* refers to a garden built by the Han dynasty Emperor Liang Xiao Wang (Liu Wu); cf. *WM*, chap. 6; see also *Cháng'ān suī hǎo* above.]

95 **Liàn tǔ nán yí.** 恋土难移。 A place [one is] attached to, [one is] reluctant to leave. [Cf. *WM*, chap. 31.]

96 **Liǎn wū yì xǐ; xīn wū nán chú.** 脸污易洗，心污难除。 (lit) It's easy to wash dirt [from one's] face; [but] difficult to remove dirt [from one's] mind. (fig) It's hard to reform one's evil nature.

97 **Líba zhá de jǐn, yěgǒu zuān bù jìn.** 篱笆扎得紧，野狗钻不进。 [Rhyme; see *lí láo, quǎn bù rù* below.]

98 **Lǐ bù duǎn, zuǐ bù ruǎn.** 理不短，嘴不软。 (lit) [If] reason is not short, [one's] mouth is not soft. (fig) When one has reason on one's side, one usually speaks forcefully. [Rhyme; vs. *xīn lǐ yǒu bìng* below.]

99 **Lì dāo shāng tǐ, chuāng yóu hé; è yǔ shāngrén, hèn bù xiāo.** 利刀伤体疮犹合，恶语伤人恨不消。 [When] sharp knives cut [one's] person, the wounds may heal, [but when] evil words hurt someone, [his] hatred [will] not disappear [so be careful of what you say about people]. [See also *biǎn zhī shāng ròu* above and *lì rén zhī yán* below.]

100 **Lì dà wéi wáng.** 力大为王。 [As long as one's] power is great, one can be king [regardless of one's ability or lack thereof.]

101 **Lǐ duō, rén bù guài.** 礼多人不怪。 (lit) [For an] excess of courtesy, no one [will] blame [you]. (fig) One will never be blamed for being too polite. Civility costs nothing (and may gain you something). [Cf. *Guānchǎng Xiànxíng Jì*, chap. 31; *lǐduō-rénbùguài* is now treated as a set phrase.]

102 **Lièhuǒ jiàn zhēnjīn.** 烈火见真金。 (lit) A fierce fire shows true gold. (fig) True gold stands the test of fire. A person's true worth is revealed under difficult conditions. Trials test character. [See also *shuǐ shēn jiàn cháng rén* and *zhēn jīn bùpà* below.]

103 **Lièrén jìn shān, zhǐjiàn qínshòu; yàonóng jìn shān, zhǐjiàn yàocǎo.** 猎人进山只见禽兽，药农进山只见药草。 (lit) [When] hunters enter the mountains, [they] only see game, [and when] medicinal herb collectors enter the mountains, [they] only see medicinal herbs. (fig) People usually focus their attention on things they have an interest in.

104 **Lièshì mùnián, zhuàngxīn bù yǐ.** 烈士暮年, 壮心不已。 (lit) [When a] person of high endeavor [is in his] sunset [years], [his] ambition is not finished. (fig) A noble hearted person may retain high aspirations or ambitions even in old age. [This is a line from a poem by Cáo Cāo.]

105 **Lì jiàn dé rén jìng; kǒu jiàn dé rén zēng.** 力贱得人敬, 口贱得人憎。 (lit) Cheap labor gets respect; a "cheap mouth" gets dislike (i.e., [one whose] labor is inexpensive [i.e., not overpriced] gets other['s] respect, while [one who] "bad-mouths" [others] gets people['s] dislike.) (fig) Those who deal with others fairly are respected, while those who engage in vicious slander are disliked. [Note: jiànzuǐ, (lit) "cheap-mouth," (fig) "to 'bad mouth'; to gossip or slander."]

106 **Líjiā sān lǐ yuǎn, bié shì yī xiāng fēng.** 离家三里远, 别是一乡风。 (lit) Three miles away from home is another land [in terms of] customs. (fig) The customs of others always seem different from what one is used to at home. [Cf. JW, chap. 15.]

107 **Líjiā yī lǐ bùrú wū lǐ.** 离家一里不如屋里。 (lit) Being a mile from home is never as [easy as being] at home. (fig) "There's no place like home." "East or west, home is best." [Rhyme; cf. WM, chap. 61.]

108 **Lí láo, quǎn bù rù.** 篱牢犬不入。 (lit) [When a] fence is strong, no dogs [can] get in. (fig) Strict precautions within can stop one's enemy from intruding. [Cf. WM, chap. 24; the modern rhymed version is líba zhá de jǐn, yěgǒu zuān bù jìn.]

109 **Lì néng shèng pín; jǐn néng shèng huò.** 力能胜贫; 谨能胜祸。 Diligence can overcome poverty [and] prudence can avert misfortune. [Note: jǐnshèn, "prudence."]

110 **Lín fán zé fǔ zhì, zhū měi zé bàng liè.** 林繁则斧至, 珠美则蚌裂。 (lit) A flourishing [grove of] trees [invites] axes to come; beautiful pearls [cause] shells [to be] broken open. (fig) High talent or beauty may invite disaster, (so one should avoid ostentatious displays). [Cf. Xúnzǐ: Quàn Xuě; see also jiē guǒ de shù above and shù dà zhāofēng below.]

111 **Línjū hǎo, sài jīn bǎo.** 邻居好赛金宝。 A good neighbor [is as] precious [as] gold [and] treasure. [Rhyme; cf. Wǔ Sōng, chap. 2; see also jīn xiānglín above.]

112 **Línjū shīhuǒ, bù jiù, zì wēi.** 邻居失火, 不救自危。 (lit) [If one's] neighbor['s house] catches fire [and one does] not help [to put it out, one also] endangers oneself.

113 **Línjū yǎnjing liǎngmiàn jìng; jiēfang xīntóu yī gǎn chèng.** 邻居眼睛两面镜, 街坊心头一秆秤。 (lit) Neighbors' eyes [are as clear as] two-sided mirrors; [the] hearts [of the people on one's] street [are as accurate as] scales. (fig) One's neighbors see clearly what is right and what is wrong and can make an accurate judgment on the scales of justice. [See also gōngpíng chǔyú above and lùshang xíngrén and rén yǎn shì and tiānxià qiányǎnr and zhīdǐ mò guò and zhòngrén (yǎnjing) below.]

114 **(Lín yá lì mǎ, shōu jiāng wǎn;) chuán dào jiāng xīn, bǔ lòu chí.** (临崖立马收缰晚,) 船到江心补漏迟。 (lit) ([When the] horse comes to [the edge of] the cliff, [it is] too late to draw rein); [when the] boat reaches mid-stream, [it is] too late to plug the leaks. (fig) Don't wait until problems arise to deal with them; use some foresight. [Cf. Xǐngshì Héngyán, chap. 17; the second part is more commonly used alone; also said mǎ lín xuán yá (q.v.).]

115 **Línyuān-xiànyú bùrú guī ér jié wǎng.*** 临渊羡鱼不如归而结网。 (lit) [Standing] by the water and longing for fish [is] not as good as going home and weaving a net. (fig) One should take practical steps to achieve one's goals rather than merely daydreaming. [Cf. Huái Nán Zǐ: Shuō Lín Xùn; Hàn Shū: Lǐ Yuè Zhì; línyuān-xiànyú is used as a chengyu with this meaning.]

116 **Lín zhōng bù mài xīn; hú shàng bù yù yú.** 林中不卖薪, 湖上不鬻鱼。 (lit) Don't peddle firewood in the forest [and] don't sell fish on the lake. (fig) Don't "carry coals to Newcastle."

117 **Lín zhōng yǒu wān shù; shìshàng wú wánrén.** 林中有弯树, 世上无完人。 (lit) [Just as] there are crooked trees in the forest, [so] there are no perfect people in the world. (fig) No one is perfect. [See also rén wú wánrén below.]

118 **Lǐ qīng, qíngyì zhòng.*** 礼轻情意重。 (lit) The gift is light, [but] the feeling is profound. (fig) It's nothing much, but it's the thought that counts. [As a chengyu: lǐ qīng yì zhòng; see also qiān lǐ sòng émáo below.]

119 **Lìqì rùshǒu, bùkě jiè rén.** 利器入手, 不可借人。 (lit) [Once a] sharp sword [has] come into [your] hands, [it] may not be lent to others. (fig) Power once gained should not be given to others. [Cf. Dōng Zhōu Lièguó Zhì, chap. 7.]

120 **Lí qún de miányáng, chízǎo yào wèi láng.** 离群的绵羊, 迟早要喂狼。 (lit) A sheep separated from the flock will feed a wolf sooner or later. (fig) Anyone who is separated from his or her group will suffer sooner or later.

121 **Lì rén zhī yán, nuǎn rú bùbó; shāngrén zhī yán, tòng rú dāo jǐ.** 利人之言, 暖如布帛; 伤人之言, 痛如刀戟。 Words beneficial to others [are] as warm as cloth and silk; words harmful to others hurt as hurtful as a swords and halberds. [See also liáng yán yī jù above.]

122 **Lí shān shí lǐ, chái zài wūlǐ; lí shān yī lǐ, chái zài shān lǐ.** 离山十里柴在屋里, 离山一里柴在山里。 (lit) Ten miles away from the mountains, [there is] firewood at home; one mile away from the mountains, [there is] firewood in the mountains. (fig) Adverse conditions make people forge ahead, while overly favorable conditions make people lazy. [Based on a popular Ming dynasty folk story.]

123 **Lì shēng wú bàng bù yīngxióng.** 历生无谤不英雄。 [One who in his] entire life has not been [at sometime enviously] slandered is not [to be considered an] able person. [See also shù dà zhāofēng below.]

124 **Liù cì liáng yī, yī cì cái.** 六次量衣，一次裁。(lit) Take measurements six times [before you] cut a dress once. (fig) One must do all one's investigations, analyses, and/or preparations before one makes the decision to act.

125 **Liú de qīngshān zài, bùpà méi chái shāo.*** 留得青山在，不怕没柴烧。(lit) As long as green hills remain, do not fear a shortage of firewood to burn. (fig) "While there's life, there's (still) hope." [Cf. *Chū Kè Pāi'àn Jīngqí*, chap. 22; *DRC*, chap. 82; see also *liúxià húlu zǐ* below.]

126 **Liú de zài; luòde guài.** 留得在，落得怪。[As a guest, when asked to] stay, [one should] stay; [otherwise] the blame [of offending one's host will] fall on one. [A rhyme said of guests persuaded to stay longer. Cf. *JW*, chap. 96.]

127 **Liú jūn qiān rì, zhōng xū yī bié.** 留君千日，终须一别。(lit) [Even if a guest is persuaded to] stay a thousand days [by a hospitable host], [there] must finally come a parting. [Said when one wants or has to leave; cf. *Jǐngshì Tōngyán*, chap. 24; see also *qiān lǐ dā cháng péng* and *shèngyàn bì sàn* and *sòng jūn qiān lǐ* and *tiānxià wú bù sàn* below.]

128 **Liúqíng bù jǔshǒu; jǔshǒu bù liúqíng.** 留情不举手，举手不留情。[If you] have [any] forgiveness, don't strike [someone, but when you finally do] strike [someone], put all your forgiveness aside. [Cf. *JW*, chap. 21.]

129 **Liùqīn hé yī yùn.** 六亲和一运。All relatives share the same fate. [Cf. *Xǐngshì Héngyán*, chap. 18; *DRC*, chap. 108; note: *liù qīn*, (lit) "the six relations," refers to one's father and sons, older and younger brothers, wife, and children.]

130 **Liùshí nián fēngshuǐ lúnliú zhuàn.*** 六十年风水轮流转。(lit) In [a calendrical cycle of] sixty years, the omens come full circle in turn. (fig) Every life will have its ups and downs. "Every dog will have his day." [See also *sānshí nián hé* below.]

131 **Liúshuǐ bù fǔ; hù shū bù lóu /dù.** 流水不腐，户枢不蝼／蠹。(lit) Running water is never stale, [and] door hinges never get worm-eaten. (fig) Things which are in constant use do not get rusty. If one keeps active, one's mind and body will not become infirm. [Cf. *Lǚ Shì Chūnqiū: Jìng Shù*; note: *liúshuǐ bù fǔ* and *húshū-bùdù* have become set phrases; see also *tiě bù mó, shēngxiù* below.]

132 **Liúxià dǒu hé chèng, wèi de shì gōngpíng.** 留下斗和秤，为的是公平。[The reason our ancestors] left [us] bushels and steelyard scales was for fairness [in trade]. [Note: *dǒu*, is a Chinese unit of dry measure for grain equal to one deciliter, here refers to a measuring container which holds that amount of grain.]

133 **Liúxià húlu zǐ, nǎ pà méiyǒu piáo.** 留下葫芦籽，哪怕没有瓢。(lit) [As long as there are some] gourd seeds left over, do not fear [that you will] be without gourds [to use as ladles for water]. (fig) As long as there are still some resources left, there's still a chance. "Where there's life, there's hope." [See also *liú de qīngshān* above.]

134 **Liúyán zhǐyú zhī zhě.** 流言止于知者。(lit) Rumors [will] stop [when they come to] the wise. (fig) A wise person does not believe or repeat rumors. [Cf. *Xúnzǐ: Dà Lüè*.]

135 **Lì wēi xiū fùzhòng; yán qīng mò quàn rén.** 力微休负重；言轻莫劝人。Don't take heavy burdens upon yourself if you are not strong enough [and] don't give advice to others if your words carry little weight. [Cf. the *chengyu: rén wēi, yán qīng*, "the words of a person of no consequence carry little weight."]

136 **Lǐ xià yú rén, bì yǒu suǒ qiú.** 礼下于人，必有所求。[When someone] humbles him or herself before a person, [(s)he] must have some favor to ask [of that person]. [Cf. *Wǔ Sōng*, chap. 2.]

137 **Lǐyú zhǎo lǐyú; jìyú zhǎo jìyú.** 鲤鱼找鲤鱼，鲫鱼找鲫鱼。(lit) Carp seek carp, [and] crucian carp seek crucian carp. (fig) People seek company of their own kind. "Birds of a feather flock together."

138 **Lǐ zhèng bùpà guān; xīn zhèng bùpà tiān.** 理正不怕官，心正不怕天。[If one's] reasons are just, [one need] not fear [government] officials; [if one's] heart is [honest and] upright, [one need] not fear Heaven. [See also *xīn zhèng bùpà* below.]

139 **Lóng bù lí hǎi; hǔ bù lí shān.*** 龙不离海，虎不离山。(lit) A dragon won't leave the sea [and] a tiger won't leave the mountain. (fig) The powerful won't give up their power or position. [Vs. *fèng bù lí cháo* above; see also *lóng guī cānghǎi* below.]

140 **Lóng duō bù zhìshuǐ; jī duō bù xiàdàn.** 龙多不治水，鸡多不下蛋。(lit) [When there are] too many dragons, the waters can't be controlled [and when there are] too many hens, [they] don't lay eggs. (fig) "Too many cooks spoil the broth." [Note: in traditional mythology dragons were supposed to control rivers and flooding; see also *rén duō, shǒu zá* below.]

141 **Lóng guī cānghǎi; hǔ rù shēnshān.** 龙归沧海，虎入深山。(lit) A dragon returns to the great seas [and] a tiger goes into the deep mountains. (fig) People go to places where there's plenty of scope for their talents. [See also *lóng bù lí hǎi* above.]

142 **Lóng hǔ xiāng zhēng, xiǎo lù zāoyāng.** 龙虎相争，小鹿遭殃。(lit) When a tiger and a dragon quarrel, the young stag has to suffer. (fig) Innocent people have to suffer when their leaders come into conflict. [Also said *lóng jǔ xiāng dòu, yú xiā zāo yāng*.]

143 **Lóng pà jiē lín; hǔ pà chōujīn.** 龙怕揭鳞，虎怕抽筋。(lit) Dragons are [most] afraid of [their] scales being scraped off [and] tigers are [most] afraid of pulling a tendon. (fig) Everyone has a weakness which (s)he fears will be exposed; everyone has an "Achilles' heel." [Rhyme; cf. *Fēngshén Yǎnyì*, chap. 13.]

144 **Lóng pèi lóng; fèng pèi fèng; bógū duì bógū; wūyā duì wūyā.** 龙配龙，凤配凤，鹁鸪对鹁鸪，乌鸦对乌鸦。(lit) A dragon matches a dragon, a phoenix a phoenix, a wood pigeon a wood pigeon, [and] a crow a crow. (fig) Marriage

partners should be well-matched in their social and economic statuses.

145 **Lóng shēng lóng; fēng shēng fēng; lǎoshǔ yǎng ér huì dǎ dòng.** 龙生龙，凤生凤，老鼠养儿会打洞。Dragons beget dragons, phoenixes beget phoenixes, [and] the son of a mouse can dig holes; (fig) "Like begets like"; "like father, like son." [This rhyme was often cited during the Cultural Revolution to support the theory of *xuètǒnglùn* "blood inheritance" of class characteristics; also said *fēng shēng fēng*, etc., above.]

146 **Lóng yǎn shí zhū; fēng yǎn shí bǎo; niú yǎn shí qīngcǎo.** 龙眼识珠，凤眼识宝，牛眼识青草。(lit) A dragon's eyes can recognize pearls, a phoenix's eyes can see treasures, [and] an ox's eyes know what kind of grass is edible. (fig) A person of excellent judgment is able to tell superior goods from bad ones, as opposed to an ordinary person who can only distinguish ordinary things. [Note: *shíhuò*, "to be able to evaluate merchandise; to have an eye for quality."]

147 **(Lóng yóu qiǎnshuǐ, zāo xiā xì;) hǔ luò píngyuán, bèi quǎn qī.** (龙游浅水遭虾戏，)虎落平原被犬欺。(lit) (A dragon in the shallows falls victim to shrimps [and]) a tiger [down] on the plain can be set upon by dogs. (fig) The powerful in an unfavorable situation can be insulted by the weak. Out of one's element or position, one can be bullied, just like everyone else. [Cf. *JW*, chap. 28; note: tigers are believed to live mostly in the mountains in China; note: *píngyuán* may also be *píngyáng*; see also *hǔ luò píng yáng* above.]

148 **Lòu chǒu bùrú cángzhuō.** 露丑不如藏拙。(lit) Better to hide one's clumsiness than to expose [it to the world]. (fig) If you're not competent, don't try to show off.

149 **Luànshì chū yīngxióng.*** 乱世出英雄。Troubled times produce heroes. [See also *fēngxiǎn lǐ chū* above.]

150 **Lǔ Bān wú mù, nán zuò wū.** 鲁班无木，难做屋。(lit) [Even] Lu Ban [the master carpenter] without wood would be hard put to build a house. (fig) It is difficult to accomplish anything without adequate materials or conditions. It is difficult or impossible to "make bricks without straw." [Note: the chengyu: *Bān mén nòng fǔ*, (lit) "to flourish an axe in front of the gate of Lu Ban, the master carpenter"; (fig) "to display one's inferior skill before an expert."]

151 **Lù bùpíng, yǒu rén cǎi.*** 路不平，有人踩。(lit) [If the] road is uneven, someone [will] trample [it flat]. (fig) People are sensitive to injustice. [Note: *bùpíng*, (lit) "uneven," also means "unjust"; see also *dàolù bùpíng* above; see also the colloquial *suyu* expression: *lù jiàn bùpíng, bá dāo xiāng zhù*, (lit) [Whenever one] sees injustice on the road, [he will] draw his sword in mutual assistance.]

152 **Lǘ bù zhī zì chǒu, hóu bù xián liǎn shòu.** 驴不知自丑，猴不嫌脸瘦。(lit) [A] donkey doesn't know [its] own ugliness, [and a] monkey doesn't worry [about its] thin face. (fig) People usually can't recognize their own shortcomings, and may

even regard them as good points. [Rhyme; compare Robert Burns: "Oh, the gift the gods would give us, to see ourselves as others see us"; see also *děngtài zhào rén* and *húli bù zhī* above and *niú bù zhī jiǎo wān* and *rén guàn shè jǐ guò* below.]

153 **Lù cháng, bù dān zǒu; huái cái, bù gūxíng.** 路长不单走，怀财不孤行。Never go a long distance alone, [and] never travel carrying [a large amount of] money [on your person].

154 **Lù dāng xiǎn chù nán huíbì; shì dàotóu lái, bù zìyóu.** 路当险处难回避，事到头来，不自由。(lit) When [one] reaches the perilous section of a road, it is difficult to avoid risk; when things come up, one can't help it. (fig) When things happen in life, one just has to deal with them. [Cf. *Sān Xiá Wǔ Yì*, chap. 78.]

155 **Lù jí wú jūnzǐ.** 路急无君子。(lit) [In] emergencies [out on the] road, there are no gentlemen. (fig) When the chips are down, it's every man for himself. Desperate people will resort to anything. [See also *lù sǐ, bù zé yīn* and *shì jí wú jūnzǐ* below.]

156 **Luóbo shú, tàiyī kū.*** 萝卜熟，太医哭。(lit) [When] turnips are in season, the doctors cry [i.e., are out of work]. (fig) Vegetables such as turnips and carrots are good for one's health. "An apple a day keeps the doctor away." [Rhyme; note: *tàiyī* originally referred to the imperial physician, but here refers to any doctor.]

157 **Luòcháo zǒng yǒu zhǎngcháo rì.** 落潮总有涨潮日。(lit) [When there is] ebbing, there is always a day of rising. (fig) The pendulum always swings back the other way. Bad times can't last forever. [See also *gōng tài mǎn* above and *rén yǒu qī pín* and *rì zhōng zé yí* below.]

158 **Luó-gǔ chángle, wú hǎoxì.** 锣鼓长了，无好戏。[If the] gong [and] drum [accompaniment go on] too long, there will be no good performance. (fig) Things can't be done satisfactorily if they are put off too long. [See also *yè cháng, mèng duō* below.]

159 **Luó-gǔ tīng yīn; shuōhuà tīng shēng.** 锣鼓听音，说话听声。(lit) [When listening to] gongs [and] drums, [one] listens for the music, [so when listening to] speech, [one] listens for the [tone of] voice. (fig) One must listen carefully to the speaker's tone of voice to catch the true message behind the words. [Note: *tīngyīn* also means to "take a hint"; note the colloquial *suyu* expression *xiánwàizhīyīn*, (lit) "the sound beyond the strings"; (fig) "overtones; implication"; see also *kàn rén, kàn xīn* above and *yào zhī xīnfùshì* below.]

160 **Luó lǐ jiǎn guā, jiǎn de yǎnhuā.** 锣里拣瓜，拣得眼花。(lit) Choosing [a] melon [from] a [big] basket[ful] makes one bedazzled. (fig) Having to choose one from among many makes one indecisive or overwhelmed by too many choices. [Cf. *Wǔ Sōng*, chap. 6; *Xǐngshì Yīnyuán Zhuàn*, chap. 18.]

161 **Lùshang shuōhuà, cǎo lǐ yǒu rén.** 路上说话，草里有人。(lit) What [one] says on the road [may well be overheard by] someone [hidden] in the grass [along the roadside]. (fig) What one says in private may be overheard. "The walls have ears."

L

[Cf. *JPM*, chap. 23; see also *gé qiáng yǒu ěr* above and *méiyǒu bù tòufēng* below.]

162 **Lùshang xíngrén kǒu sì bēi.** 路上行人口似碑。 (lit) [What the average] passerby on the street says is like [words graven on] stone tablets. (fig) Ordinary people can make a fair judgment about most people or things. [Cf. *Shí Diǎn Tóu*, chap. 8; *Fēngshén Yǎnyì*, chap. 56; see also *gōngpíng chūyú* and *línjú yǎnjing* above and *rén yǎn shì* and *tiānxià qiányǎnr* and *zhīdǐ mò guò* and *zhòngrén yǎnjing* below.]

163 **Lù shì rén zǒu chūlái.** 路是人走出来。 (lit) Roads were trampled out by people. (fig) One need not "stick to the beaten path." Create your own way. Be a "trail blazer."

164 **Lùshui-fūqī bù chángjiǔ.*** 露水夫妻不长久。 (lit) Illicit lovers won't last long. (fig) Brief liaisons or summer romances don't last long. [Note: *lùshui-fūqī*, (lit) "dew drop couple," refers to an unmarried couple living together.]

165 **Lùsī bù chī lùsī ròu.** 鹭鸶不吃鹭鸶肉。 (lit) An egret doesn't eat the flesh of [other] egrets. (fig) Do not harm your own kind. Like does not harm like. [Cf. *JW*, chap. 24; see also the following entry.]

166 **Lùsī bù dǎ jiǎoxià táng.** 鹭鸶不打脚下塘。 (lit) [An] egret does not strike the pond beneath ⊙ [its] feet. (fig) One does not do harm to one's neighbors. "Don't foul your own nest." [See also *měnghǔ bù chī* and *tùzi bù chī* below and the preceding entry.]

167 **Lù sǐ, bù zé yīn.** 鹿死不择音。 (lit) A dying deer is not selective [about whether its] cries [sound good or not]. (fig) A desperate person will resort to anything. [Cf. *Zuǒ Zhuàn: Wén Gōng 17 Nián*; note: *lùsǐ-bùzéyīn* is sometimes treated as a set phrase; see also *lù jí wú jūnzǐ* above.]

168 **Lù yào yī bù, yī bù de zǒu; fàn yào yīkǒu, yīkǒu de chī.** 路要一步一步的走，饭要一口一口的吃。 (lit) [On the] road [one] has to walk step by step, [and one's] food has to be eaten one

mouthful at a time. (fig) One has to learn or do things step by step.

169 **Lù yáo zhī mǎlì; rì jiǔ jiàn rénxīn.** 路遥知马力，日久见人心。 [Just as a] long journey [lets one] know [a] horse's strength, [so a] long time [lets one] know a person's mind. [Cf. *Fēngshén Yǎnyì*, chap. 20; *JW*, chap. 26; also said . . . *shì jiǔ jiàn rénxīn*, ". . . [so a] long task [lets one] know a person's mind."] [Both halves may be used independently.]

170 **Lù yuǎn méi qīng zài.*** 路远没轻载。 (lit) [On a] long road there are no light burdens. (fig) Light burdens, when carried for a long time, grow heavy. [See also *yuǎnlù méi qīng zài* below.]

171 **Lù yù bù shì bàn.*** 路遇不是伴。 [Strangers] met on the road are not companions. [Vs. *tóngxíng wú shū bàn* below.]

172 **Lù zài zuǐ biān.*** 路在嘴边。 (lit) The road is beside [one's] mouth. (fig) If one is willing to ask for directions, one will never lose one's way. [See also *dàlù shēng* above and *zuǐ dǐxià* below.]

173 **Lǔ zì mài qiú ér bù shòu; shì zì yù biàn ér bù xìn.** 虏自卖裘而不售，士自誉辩而不信。 (lit) [Just as a non-Han Chinese] minority person won't [be able to] sell a fur coat [even if he boasts of its quality], [so] a scholar who praises himself won't be believed. (fig) Self-recommendation will come to nothing. [Cf. *Hán Fēizǐ: Shuō Lín Xià*; note: here *lǔ* is an old term previously used to refer to ethnic minorities from China's border areas.]

174 **Lǘzi néng gēngtián, huángniú bù zhíqián.** 驴子能耕田，黄牛不值钱。 (lit) [If] donkeys ⊙ could plow fields, oxen would be worthless. (fig) If persons of no ability were to assume positions of power, people of real ability would be unemployed. [Rhyme.]

175 **Lǘzi shì gè guài; qí zhe fǎn bǐ qiān zhe kuài.** 驴子 ⊙ 是个怪，骑着反比牵着快。 (lit) The donkey is a strange [beast]; [it walks] faster [when] ridden than [when] led. (fig) Some people are lazy and must be pressured to perform. [Rhyme.]

M

1 **Mǎ chí xián biān qīng; xīnjí xián chē màn.** 马迟嫌鞭轻，心急嫌车慢。 (lit) [When the] horse [is] slow, [one] complains that the whip is too light; [when one is] impatient, [one] complains that the cart [is too] slow. (fig) When one is impatient, time seems to pass too slowly. [See also *děng rén yì lǎo* above and *xīnjí, mǎ xíng chí* below.]

2 **Mǎ'ér zhuā zōng, niú qiān bí.** 马儿抓鬃，牛牵鼻。 (lit) Grasp a horse [by its] mane, [and] lead an ox [by its] nose. (fig) In solving a problem one must address the crucial element. [See also *kě shí yī dǐ* above.]

3 **Mǎ féng Bólè ér sī; rén yù zhījǐ ér sǐ.** 马逢伯乐而嘶，人遇知己而死。 (lit) [Just as] horses [al-

ways] neigh in recognition of Bo-le [the supreme judge of horses, [so when] one meets [someone who] understands him, [he] would die [for him]. (fig) People will gladly serve a superior who treats them well. [Cf. *R3K*, chap. 60; Bólè was a legendary judge of horses in the Spring and Autumn Period; see also *shì wèi zhījǐ* below.]

4 **Mǎi bù lái, yǒuqián zài; mài bù chū, yǒu huò zài.** 买不来有钱在，卖不出有货在。 (lit) [If you can]not buy [something, you still] have [your] money remaining; [if you can]not sell [something, you still] have [your] goods remaining. (fig) When one has nothing to lose, one might as well try; no loss is involved either way. [Rhyme.]

5 **Mài bǔ, mài guà; zhuǎn huí shuōhuà.** 卖卜卖卦，转回说话。(lit) [Those who] tell fortunes talk in circumlocutions. (fig) Fortunetellers speak in riddles. [Rhyme; cf. WM, chap. 61; see also ruò xìn bù below.]

6 **Mài fàn de bùpà dàdùhàn; mài jiǔ de bùpà hǎiliàng.** 卖饭的不怕大肚汉，卖酒的不怕海量。A rice-seller welcomes men with big bellies, [and] a wine-seller welcomes heavy drinkers. [Note: hǎiliàng (lit) "ocean capacity," refers to drinkers with a great capacity for liquor.]

7 **Mài guā de shuō guā tián; mài huā de shuō huā xiāng.** 卖瓜的说瓜甜，卖花的说花香。(lit) Melon sellers say their melons are sweet, [and] flower sellers say their flowers are fragrant. (fig) Everyone praises his own talents or wares. [See also mài guā, shuō guā below.]

8 **Mǎi guā kàn pí; mǎi zhēn kàn kǒng.** 买瓜看皮，买针看孔。(lit) [When] buying melons, look at [their] skins; [when] buying needles, look at [their eye-]holes. (fig) One must focus on the key points in making observations.

9 **Mài guā, shuō guā tián; mài cù, shuō cù suān.** 卖瓜说瓜甜，卖醋说醋酸。(lit) A melon-seller says [his] melons are sweet, [and] a vinegar-seller says [his] vinegar is sour. (fig) Everyone boasts of his own wares. [See also mài guā de shuō above.]

10 **Mài jīn xū xiàng shí jīn jiā.** 卖金须向识金家。(lit) [When] selling gold, [you] must [go] to [those who] know [all about] goldware. (fig) Only experts can appreciate or assess the true worth of fine things. [See also huò mài yǔ shí jiā above.]

11 **Mǎi-mài bù chéng, qíngyì zài.** 买卖不成，情意在。[Even if a] business [deal is] not successful, the relationship [between the two people still continues to] exist. (fig) In the interests of a long-term relationship, one should be civil even if the immediate business deal falls through. [Also said jiāoyì bù chéng, rényì zài (q.v.); see also qù shí liú rénqíng below.]

12 **Mǎi-mài, mǎi-mài; héqì shēngcái.*** 买卖买卖，和气生财。(lit) Buying [and] selling, buying [and] selling; [it's] politeness [and] amiability [that] makes money. (fig) In doing business, being able to get along with people is the real key to success and wealth. [Rhyme; note that mǎi-mài (sic) means "business."]

13 **Mǎimairén, yǒu sānfēn nàixìng.** 买卖人，有三分耐性。(lit) A businessperson has three parts patience. (fig) Anyone who does business must have patience. [Note: mǎi-mài means "business" and mǎimai, "small business."]

14 **Mǎi piányi shì shàngdàng de hòumén.** 买便宜是上当的后门。(lit) A cheap price is a quick route to being cheated. (fig) Be wary of "good deals." [Cf. Wǔ Sōng, chap. 1; see also guì de bù guì above.]

15 **Màizuǐ lángzhōng méi hǎo yào.** 卖嘴郎中没好药。(lit) A doctor [who] boasts of [(the effectiveness of) his] medicine has no good medicine. (fig) People who brag usually have no real ability. [Also said: shuōzuǐ . . . etc. (q.v.); note: lángzhōng is a colloquial term for a physician in traditional

herbal medicine; see also gǔ kōng, shēng gāo and hǎo māo bù jiào and kōng guànzi above and shuǐ jìng zé and zhěng píng bù yáo below.]

16 **Mǎ kàn yá bǎn; rén kàn yánxíng.** 马看牙板，人看言行。[Just as] horses [are judged by] looking at [their] teeth, [so] people [are judged by looking at their] words [and] deeds. [Note: yá bǎn is colloquial for yá kǒu, "age of an animal judged by its teeth."]

17 **Mǎ kào ān zhuāng; rén kào yīshang.** 马靠鞍装，人靠衣裳。(lit) [It's the] saddle [that] makes the horse, [and the] tailor [that] makes the man. (fig) "Fine feathers make fine birds." "Clothes make the man." [See also fó yào jīn zhuāng above.]

18 **Mǎ lǎo, wú rén qí; rén lǎo, jiù shòu qī.** 马老无人骑，人老就受欺。[When] horses get old no one rides them [and when] people get old [they] get bullied. [Rhyme.]

19 **(Mǎ lín xuányá shōu jiāng wǎn;) chuán dào jiāngxīn, bǔ lòu chí.** (马临悬崖收缰晚，)船到江心补漏迟。[When the] horse comes to the edge of the cliff, [it is] too late to draw rein;) [when a] boat reaches midstream, [it is] too late to stop the leaks. (fig) Don't wait until problems arise to deal with them; use some foresight. [Also said lín yá lì mǎ (q.v.), note the chengyu: xuányá-lèmǎ, to "rein in at the last moment"; and the idiom jiāngxīn-bǔlòu, to "try to avoid disaster when it's too late."]

20 **Mámiàn gūniang ài cā fěn; lài lì gūniang hào dài huā.** 麻面姑娘爱擦粉，癞痢姑娘好戴花。(lit) [A] pock-marked girl loves to powder [her] face, [and a] young woman [affected with] favus of the scalp likes to wear flowers. (fig) People with defects try to hide them from others.

21 **Màn chuán pǎo sǐ mǎ.** 慢船跑死马。(lit) A slow boat can run a horse to death. (fig) Even a slow boat, aided by wind or current behind it, is faster than a fast horse, which will eventually become tired. It is better to get help from others than simply to depend on oneself alone.

22 **Mán de guò rén; mán bu guò shén.** 瞒得过人，瞒不过神。[One] can hide [the truth from other] people, [but one can]not hide [the truth from the] gods. (fig) One's misdeeds cannot be covered up forever. "Truth will (come) out in the end." [See also bèitóu lǐ zuòshì and chái duī lǐ cáng above and shuǐ luò shítou and zhǐ bāo bu zhù huǒ below.]

23 **Máng bù zé jià.** 忙不择价。(lit) Busy [people are] not choosy [about] price. (fig) One is not choosy when one is in a hurry or in dire need. [Cf. Jīngshì Tōngyán, chap. 15.]

24 **Máng jiā bù huì; huì jiā bù máng.** 忙家不会，会家不忙。(lit) The ones [who are running around] busily [do] not know how, [and] those who know how [do] not [appear to be] busy. (fig) Those who do not know how run around madly [because they don't know what they're doing, while] the experienced do not appear to be busy [because they know what they're doing]. [Cf. JW, chap. 21; see the chengyu: shǒu máng jiǎo luàn, "busy in a disorganized way."]

M

25 **Máng lǐ yào zhēnzhuó; dān chí, bù dān cuò.** 忙里要斟酌, 担迟, 不担错。 [When] in haste, [one] must think carefully; [it is better to] be late, [and] not to be wrong. [Rhyme; see also *dān chí, bù dān cuò* above.]

26 **Màn gōng chū qiǎo jiàng.*** 慢功出巧将。 Slow work produces skilled craftsmen. [See also the following entry.]

27 **Màn gōng chū xìhuó/ xì huò.*** 慢功出细活/ 细货。 Slow work produces fine work/goods. ⌐ [Note: *xìhuó*, "a job requiring fine workmanship or meticulous care; skilled work."]

28 **Máng póniang jià bù dào hǎo hànzi.** 忙婆娘嫁不到好汉子。 (lit) A hasty [i.e., impatient] girl won't get a good man for a husband. (fig) Hastiness or impatience can bring no good results.

29 **Mángrén wú zhì.** 忙人无智。 (lit) Busy people have no wisdom. (fig) One can't think clearly when one is in a rush. [Cf. *Wǔ Sōng*, chap. 2; see also *jí xíng wú hǎo bù* above.]

30 **Mángrén xī rì duǎn.** 忙人惜日短。 (lit) Busy people begrudge the days [being] short. (fig) Diligent people always feel that time is too short to accomplish all they want to do.

31 **Máng shí yòngzhe, xiánshí jiǎng.** 忙时用着闲时讲。 (lit) [Policies and measures] to be used in emergency [should be] discussed in times of peace. (fig) One should make one's preparations against the unforeseen well in advance.

32 **Máng zhōng (duō) yǒu cuò.** 忙中(多)有错。 (lit) In haste, there are more mistakes. (fig) "Haste makes waste." [Cf. *Gǔ-Jīn Xiǎoshuō*, chap. 12; see also *jí xíng wú hǎo bù* above.]

33 **Màn lǔ yáochuán, zhuō zuì yú.** 慢橹摇船, 捉醉鱼。 (lit) Row the boat slowly [if you want to] catch beguiled fish. (fig) If you're out to get someone or something, it's best to move in a slow and apparently relaxed manner so as to lull your prey into a false sense of security. [Cf. *Èr Kè Pāi'àn Jīngqí*, chap. 38.]

34 **Mán shàng, bù mán xià.** 瞒上, 不瞒下。 [One can] conceal [the true state of affairs from those] above [but] never [from those] below. [Cf. *Rúlín Wàishǐ*, chap. 4; see also *mán tiān, mán dì* below.]

35 **Mán tiān, mán dì; mán bu liǎo gébì línjū.** 瞒天瞒地, 瞒不了隔壁邻居。 [One may be able to] hide the truth from heaven [and] earth, [but one] cannot hide the truth from [one's] neighbors. [See also *línjū yǎnjing* above and *shuōhuǎng bù mán* below.]

36 **Màntiān yàojià; jiùdì huán qián.*** 漫天要价, 就地还钱。 (lit) [As] high [as the] sky [is the] asking price, [and as] low [as the] earth [is the] money [offered] in return. (fig) Sellers (may) ask a sky-high price, [but] buyers (can) make a down-to-earth offer. [Note: *jiùdì* means "on the spot"; cf. *Rúlín Wàishǐ*, chap. 14, and Lu Xun's *Zhōngguó Xiǎoshuō Jí*.]

37 **Mán zhài bì qióng; mán bìng bì sǐ.** 瞒债必穷, 瞒病必死。 (lit) [One who tries to] hide [his] debts is bound [to suffer from] poverty, [just as one who tries to] hide [his] illness is doomed to die. (fig) It can be dangerous to pretend to be more well off than one really is.

38 **Mǎn zhāo sǔn; qiān shòuyì.*** 满招损, 谦受益。 ⊙ (lit) [Self] satisfaction summons losses, [while] modesty receives benefits. (fig) One loses by pride and gains by modesty. [Cf. *Jǐngshì Tōngyán*, chap. 3.]

39 **Màn zǒu, diē bù dǎo; xiǎoxīn, cuò bùliǎo.** 慢走跌不倒, 小心错不了。 (lit) Walk slowly [and you] won't fall down; act carefully [and you] won't go wrong. (fig) One can't be too careful. [Rhyme.]

40 **Màn zǒu qiáng rú xiē.** 慢走强如歇。 (lit) [A] slow walk[er] is faster than [someone who walks fast but always has to stop and] rest. (fig) Persistence is important in learning or doing anything. "Slow and steady wins the race." [See also *bùpà màn* above.]

41 **Māo bù jí, bù shàng shù; tù bù jí, bù yǎo rén.** 猫不急不上树, 兔不急不咬人。 (lit) [If] cats are not under duress, [they] will not climb trees, [and if] rabbits are not pressed, [they will] not bite people. (fig) If pressed too hard, people will eventually rise in revolt. "Even a worm will turn." [See also *tùzi jíle* below.]

42 **Māo'er, gǒu'er, shí wēncún.** 猫儿狗儿识温存。 (lit) (Even) cats and dogs appreciate kindness and consideration. (fig) Everyone appreciates human kindness. [Cf. *Érnǚ Yīngxióng Zhuàn*, chap. 25.]

43 **Māo'er kǒu zhōng wā bù chū shí.** 猫儿口中挖不出食。 (lit) Food cannot be retrieved from inside a cat's mouth. (fig) Things lost can't be regained. [Cf. *Xǐngshì Héngyán*, chap. 5.]

44 **Máomáoyǔ dǎ shī yīshang; bēi bēi jiǔ chī bài jiādàng.** 毛毛雨打湿衣裳, 杯杯酒吃败家当。 [Just as] little drops of rain will [eventually] soak through [one's] clothes, [so] cup [after] cup of liquor will [eventually] eat away [all] one's property.

45 **Mào mù zhīxià wú fēng cǎo; dà kuài zhījiān wú měi miáo.** 茂木之下无丰草, 大块之间无美苗。 (lit) Under thick trees there's no luxuriant grass [and] among the vast [expanse of virgin] land there are no fine seedlings. (fig) Without a suitable environment, one cannot develop fully. [Rhyme.]

46 **Māozi lāshǐ, zìjǐ gài.** 猫子拉屎, 自己盖。 (lit) A cat covers up its excrement by itself. (fig) One should clean up one's own mess.

47 **Mǎ pà qí; rén pà bī.** 马怕骑, 人怕逼。 [Just as] a horse does not like to be ridden, [so] people don't like to be pressed. [Rhyme.]

48 **Máquè fēiguò dōu yǒu gè yǐngzi.** 麻雀飞过都有个影子。 (lit) [Even] a sparrow makes a shadow when it flies by. (fig) Whoever does something bad or commits a crime will inevitably leave some trace behind. [See also *měngchóng fēiguò* and *yǒu chē jiù yǒu zhé* below.]

49 **Máquè suī xiǎo, wǔzàng jùquán.*** 麻雀虽小, 五脏俱全。 (lit) Although [a] sparrow [is] small, [it has] all five of the vital organs. (fig) Although something may be small, it may have all the necessary parts [e.g., in miniature, a small organization or an essay]. [Cited in Mao Zedong's speech "Nóng Yè Hézuòhuà de Yīchǎng" in volume five of his Collected Works *Máo Zédōng Xuǎnjí*.]

50 **(Mǎ shàng bù zhī mǎ xià kǔ); bǎo hàn bù zhī è hàn jī.** (马上不知马下苦); 饱汉不知饿汉 饥。 (lit) ([One] on horseback doesn't know the suffering of [one who] walks [and]) a guy [who is] full doesn't know the bitterness a hungry guy suffers. (fig) It is difficult to fully appreciate the suffering of others unless one has endured it oneself. [The second part is also used alone (q.v.); see also *jiàn rén tiāodàn* above and *shì fēi jīngguò* below.]

51 **Mǎ shàng shuāisǐ yīngxióng hàn; hé zhōng yānsǐ huìshuǐ rén.** 马上摔死英雄汉, 河中淹死 会水人。 The good rider may fall to death from horseback [and] a good swimmer may drown in the river [so don't be over-confident]. [See also *sānshí nián nòng mǎ qí* and *shàn yóu zhě nì* below.]

52 **Mǎ xíng qiān lǐ, wú rén bù néng zì wǎng.** 马行千 里, 无人不能自往。 (lit) [Though] it may run a thousand leagues, a horse won't go forward without someone [leading it]. (fig) Talented people can't accomplish anything unless someone with connections recommends them for a position or advancement. [Cf. *JW*, chap. 80.]

53 **Mǎyǐ lěi wō, tiān jiàng yǔ.** 蚂蚁垒窝, 天将 雨。 [When] ants build up their nests, it is going to rain. [A common folk belief phrased as a *qìxiàng yànyǔ*, "weather proverb"; see also *wūyā zhī fēng* below.]

54 **Mǎ yǒu sān féi, sān shòu; rén yǒu sān qǐ, sān luò.** 马有三肥三瘦, 人有三起三落。 [Just as in their lives] horses [experience] three [times getting] thinner [and] three [times] getting fatter, [so] people [in life will also experience] three rises [and] three falls. (fig) Life is full of "ups and downs." One should be able to experience adversity in one's life with a philosophical attitude.

55 **Měi bù měi, xiāng zhōng shuǐ; qīn bù qīn, gùxiāng rén.*** 美不美乡中水, 亲不亲故乡 人。 (lit) Sweet or not, [it is] water from home; related or not, [(s)he is] a fellow countryman. (fig) One is always attached to one's native place. [Cf. *JW*, chap. 5; *Érnǚ Yīngxióng Zhuàn*, chap. 23; see also *zuò yǐn jiāxiāng* below.]

56 **Méi chīguo zhūròu, hái méi jiànguo zhū pǎo.** 没 吃过猪肉, 还没见过猪跑。 (lit) [Even if you] have never eaten pork [before], still [have you] not [at least] seen a pig run? (fig) Even if one has had no direct experience in a matter, common everyday knowledge and experience should give one some idea about how things are done.

57 **Měi fú rén zhǐ; měi zhū rén gū.** 美服人指, 美珠人估。 (lit) Beautiful clothes invite comment, [and] beautiful pearls invite judgments [of

their value]. (fig) Anything unusual will be noticed and commented upon, (so do not do anything to draw attention to yourself).

58 **Méi jiǔ, méi jiāng; zuò shénme dàochǎng?** 没 酒没浆, 做什么道场? (lit) Without wine or liquor, how can one perform Taoist rites? (fig) Without the necessary facilities or conditions one cannot accomplish anything. [Rhyme; cf. *WM*, chap. 21; see also *méi tǔ, dǎ bù* below.]

59 **Méile Wáng tú, lián máo chī zhū.** 没了王屠, 连毛吃猪。 (lit) Without Wang the butcher, [one would have to] eat pork with hair [on it]. (fig) Without the help or participation of a professional, one cannot get the job done well. [Cf. *JPM*, chap. 73; see also the popular reversal of this proverb by Mao Zedong below: *sǐle Zhāng túfū, bù chī hún máozhū*.]

60 **Méi qiǎo bù chéng huà.** 没巧不成话。 Without coincidence(s), there would be no story (to tell). [Cf. *WM*, chap. 24; a colloquial version of a phrase commonly found in classical novels: *wú qiǎo bù chéng shū*.]

61 **Méiren bù tiāodàn; bǎoren bù huán qián.** 媒 人不挑担, 保人不还钱。 [A] matchmaker doesn't shoulder responsibility [for what she says, just as a] guarantor does not pay the debts [of those he vouches for].

62 **Méiren kǒu, sì mì bō.** 媒人口, 似蜜钵。 (lit) [A] matchmaker's tongue is as [sweet as a] honey jar. (fig) Marriage matchmakers will say anything in order to arrange a marriage and earn their fee.

63 **Méiren kǒu, wúliàng dǒu.** 媒人口, 无量斗。 (lit) [A] matchmaker's words [can]not be measured [in] bushels. (fig) A matchmaker's words can't be believed. [Rhyme; cf. *Shí Diǎn Tóu*, chap. 12; note: a *dǒu* is a unit of dry measure for grain equal to one deciliter.]

64 **Méi shuǐ bù shā huǒ.** 没水不杀火。 (lit) Without water, [one] cannot put out fires. (fig) Nothing can be accomplished without money. [Cf. *Xīngshì Yīnyuán Zhuàn*, chap. 64.]

65 **Méi tǔ, dǎ bù chéng qiáng.** 没土, 打不成墙。 (lit) Without earth [one] cannot build a wall. (fig) Nothing can be accomplished without appropriate materials or conditions. [See also *méi jiǔ, méi jiāng* above.]

66 **Méiyǒu bù sàn de yánxí.** 没有不散的 筵席。 (lit) There is no feast which does not end. (fig) "All good things must come to an end." [Also said *tiānxià wú bù sàn de yánxí* (q.v.); see also *qiān lǐ dā cháng péng* below.]

67 **Méiyǒu bù tòufēng de qiáng.** 没有不透风的 墙。 (lit) There is no wall which does not have a crack. (fig) There are people listening everywhere, (so be careful what you say)! "The walls have ears." [See also *gé qiáng yǒu ěr* and *lùshang shuōhuà* above.]

68 **Méiyǒu dǎ hǔ jiàng, guòbude Jǐngyánggǎng.** 没 有打虎将, 过不得景阳岗。 (lit) Without a leader with the strength and skill to kill a tiger, [one] cannot cross over Jingyang Ridge [where Wu Song killed a tiger in *WM*]. (fig) Only people of ability can solve problems.

M

69 **Méiyǒu dǎ hǔ yì, bù gǎn shàng shān gǎng; méiyǒu qín lóng shù, bù gǎn xià shēnyuān.** 没有打虎艺, 不敢上山岗; 没有擒龙术, 不敢下深渊。(lit) Without the [strength and] skill to kill tigers, [one] dare not go up the hill; without the [strength and] skill to catch a dragon, one dare not go down into the deep abyss. (fig) If someone is not competent, (s)he should not take on the job. [Note: tigers are traditionally believed to live in the hills, and dragons in water.]

70 **Méiyǒu gāoshān, bù xiǎn píngdì.*** 没有高山, 不显平地。(lit) Without mountains [one would] not see the plains. (fig) Differences are only revealed by comparison. [Cf. *Xǐngshì Yīnyuán Zhuàn,* chap. 96.]

71 **Méiyǒu gōngláo, háiyǒu kǔ láo; (méiyǒu kǔ láo, yě yǒu píláo).** 没有功劳还有苦劳, (没有苦劳也有疲劳)。[Although one] did not accomplish anything great, at least [one tried and] made [some] effort; ([and even if one] did not make [great] efforts, at least [one should get credit for trying at all and] tiring [oneself out trying]). [Rhyme; cf. *Yuè Fēi Zhuàn,* chap. 26; the second part is a contemporary addition, usually used to defend oneself when one is criticized.]

72 **Méiyǒu guòbuqù de hé.** 没有过不去的河。(lit) There is no river which cannot be crossed. (fig) There's always a way to solve a problem. [See also *méiyǒu shàng bù qù de yá* below.]

73 **Méi(yǒu) jiā zéi, yǐn bù chū wài guǐ lái.** 没(有)家贼, 引不出外鬼来。(lit) Unless there's a thief inside the family, devils from outside won't be lured in. (fig) Outsiders cannot harm a family unless some family member(s) cooperate. [Cf. *DRC,* chap. 72; also said *méi jiā qīn, yǐn bù chū wài guǐ lái;* see also *jiā zéi nán fáng* above and *yuǎn zéi bì yǒu* and *zéi wú lǐ dǐ* below.]

74 **Méiyǒu shàng bù qù de yá.** 没有上不去的崖。(lit) There's no precipice that cannot be scaled. (fig) There's always a way to solve a problem. [See also *méiyǒu guòbuqù de hé* above.]

75 **Méiyǒu wútóng shù, yǐnbude fènghuáng lái.** 没有梧桐树, 引不得凤凰来。(lit) [If] there is no Chinese parasol tree, the phoenix cannot be enticed to come. (fig) No one of ability will come without favorable conditions. [This is a reversal of *jiā yǒu wútóng, zhāo fènghuáng* (q.v.) above.]

76 **Méiyǒu xiū chéng fó, shòu bùliǎo yī lú xiāng.** 没有修成佛, 受不了一炉香。(lit) [If one] has not become a Buddha by self-cultivation, [one is] not entitled to receive burning incense. (fig) A person of no ability is not entitled to receive respect or take on heavy responsibility.

77 **Měiyù chūzì chǒu shí.** 美玉出自丑石。(lit) Fine jade is produced out of ugly stone. (fig) People of talent are produced through training and education.

78 **Méi zuò kuīxīnshì, bù pà guǐ jiàomén.*** 没做亏心事, 不怕鬼叫门。(lit) [If one] has not done anything to be ashamed of, [one] need not fear devils calling at the door. (fig) "A quiet conscience sleeps in thunder." [See also *báitiān bù zuò,* and *bù zuò kuīxīnshì* above and *rén néng kèjǐ* and *rìjiān bù zuò* below.]

79 **Měngchóng fēiguò, dōu yǒu yǐng.** 蠓虫飞过, 都有影。(lit) Even [when] midges fly past, [they] all make a shadow. (fig) Whatever has been done, some evidence of it can be found. [See also *máquè fēiguò* above and *yǒu chē jiù yǒu zhé* below.]

80 **Měnghǔ bù chī huítóu shí.** 猛虎不吃回头食。(lit) [A] fierce tiger never returns to food [it has previously given up]. (fig) A person of aspirations will never turn back to take up a position (s)he has previously quit or declined. [See also *hǎo mǎ bù chī* above.]

81 **Měnghǔ bù chī wō páng shí.** 猛虎不吃窝旁食。(lit) [Even a] fierce tiger [will] not eat the game near [its] lair. (fig) Even a scoundrel will not do evil things in his own neighborhood. Don't foul your own nest. [See also *lùsī bù dǎ* above and *tùzi bù chī* below.]

82 **Měng jiāngjūn wú dāo shābude rén.** 猛将军无刀杀不得人。(lit) [Even a] valiant general, without a sword, cannot kill anyone. (fig) Even a competent person can't handle things successfully without certain conditions or tools. "One can't make bricks without straw." [See also *qiǎofù nánwéi* below.]

83 **Mèng shì xīntóu xiǎng.** 梦是心头想。Dreams evolve out of one's thoughts. [Cf. *Fēngshén Yǎnyì,* chap. 14; *JPM,* chap. 78; see also *rì yǒusuǒsī* below.]

84 **Měngshòu bùrú qún hú.** 猛兽不如群狐。(lit) [One] fierce beast is no match for a pack of foxes. (fig) One individual, however strong, cannot overcome a group of people acting in concert.

85 **Měng shòu yì fú; rénxīn nán xiáng.** 猛兽易服, 人心难降。Fierce beasts [are] easy to tame, [in comparison to] people's minds, [which can] hardly be controlled.

86 **Ménmén tōng, yàngyàng sōng.** 门门通, 样样松。(lit) [One who claims to have the] knack of doing everything [in fact is] slack [in doing] everything. (fig) To "know everything" is to know nothing. [Rhyme; note: *méndao,* "knack of doing things."]

87 **Mén nèi yǒu jūnzǐ; mén wài jūnzǐ zhì.** 门内有君子, 门外君子至。(lit) [If] there's a gentleman inside [one's] house, outside [there will] come other gentlemen. (fig) One good man will attract others of his kind. [Cf. *Jīngshì Tōngyán,* chap. 1; see also *jiā yǒu wútóng* above.]

88 **Mén qián jié qǐ gāo tóu mǎ, bù shì qīn lái yě shì qīn.** 门前结起高头马, 不是亲来也是亲。(lit) [If there are] tall horses tied in front of one's house, even non-relatives will come [to claim themselves] as relatives [of the master]. (fig) When one comes to power, people will flock to seek benefits from him. [Cf. *Wǔ Sōng,* chap. 3.]

89 **Mén qián shuānzhe bójiǎo lǘ, jiùshì zhìqīn yě bù qīn.** 门前拴着跛脚驴, 就是至亲也不亲。 (lit) [When one has a] lame donkey tied in front of [one's] door, even close relatives become like strangers. (fig) When you are poor, even your close relatives won't visit you. "Nobody knows you when you're down and out." [See also *jǐnshàng-tiānhuā* above and *pín jū nàoshì* and *qián jìn, qíngyì jué* and *yǒuqián shíde guǐ* and *yǒuqián yǒu jiǔ* below.]

90 **Ménshén lǎole bù zhuō guǐ.** 门神老了不捉鬼。 (lit) Old door gods can't catch ghosts. (fig) When one grows old, one is no longer useful. [See also *rén lǎo wúnéng* below.]

91 **Mēntou gǒu, dǒu xià kǒu.** 阿头狗, 陡下口。 (lit) A silent dog bites suddenly. (fig) Beware of quiet people who do not indicate what they are thinking. [Rhyme; see also *jiàng fēi zhě yì fú* above.]

92 **Miànruǎn de shòuqióng.** 面软的受穷。 (lit) [One who has a] "soft face" [will] suffer [from] poverty. (fig) One cannot be overly soft-hearted. One has to be "thick-skinned" in order to survive.

93 **Miàn xiàng bùrú xīn xiàng.** 面相不如心相。 [Better to judge people by their] hearts rather than [by their] appearance. [Cf. *Gǔ-Jīn Xiǎoshuō*, chap. 9; note: *kànxiàng*, "to practice physiognomy; tell fortunes by looking at the face."]

94 **Miào dà, shén jiù líng.** 庙大, 神就灵。 (lit) The bigger the temple, the more powerful [its] god. (fig) People in higher positions have more power.

95 **Miè chán sān zhuàn jǐn; huà shuō sān biàn wěn.** 篾缠三转紧, 话说三遍稳。 Binding an article three [times] around with bamboo slips [makes it] tight; repeating what [one means] three times [makes it] clear[ly understood].

96 **Mìfāng zhì dà bìng.*** 秘方治大病。 (lit) A secret prescription [may] cure a serious illness. (fig) Sometimes "home remedies" can be more effective than specialized medicines or treatments. Do not overlook simple solutions. [See also *cǎoyào yī wèi* above and *piānfāng zhì dà bìng* below.]

97 **Mǐ liáng zài shì shàng; hángqíng zài lùshang.** 米粮在市上, 行情在路上。 (lit) Grain is [sold] on the market, [but its] market price [is available] on the road [from those who have traveled to the market]. (fig) One has to make investigations among the people in order to find out the true conditions. [See also *hé lǐ méi yú* above.]

98 **Mín bù wèi sǐ, nàihé yǐ sǐ jù zhī.** 民不畏死, 奈何以死惧之。 (lit) [As] the common people do not fear death, why threaten them with it? (fig) Once the common people have risen in rebellion there's no way to suppress them. [Cf. *Lǎozǐ (Dào Dé Jīng)*, chap. 74; often quoted by Mao Zedong.]

99 **Mín bù yù guān dòu.** 民不与官斗。 (lit) Common people [should] not struggle with [government] officials. (fig) Ordinary people have no chance of success in conflicts with official bureaucracy. "You can't fight City Hall."

100 **Míng bù zhèng; yán bù shùn.** 名不正, 言不顺。 [If the] name is not right, the word(s) [can]not be appropriate. [From the Confucian Analects: *Lúnyǔ: Zǐ Lù*; note also the Confucian concept of the "rectification of names" (*zhèng míng*).]

101 **Mìngdìng yīnggāi bā hé mǐ; zǒubiàn tiānxià bù mǎn shēng.** 命定应该八盒米, 走遍天下不满升。 [If one is] fated to have [only] eight ounces of rice, [even if one] travels all over the world [trying], [one] won't get one pound. [Note: *gě* and *shēng* are units of dry measure for grain: ten *gě* equal one *shēng*, which is equal to one liter; see also the following entry.]

102 **Mìng hǎo, xīn yě hǎo; fùguì zhídào lǎo.** 命好心也好, 富贵直到老。 [If one has a] good fate and a kind heart, [one will] enjoy riches and honor throughout one's life. [Rhyme.]

103 **Míngjìng suǒyǐ zhào xíng; gǔ shì suǒyǐ zhī jīn.** 明镜所以照形, 古事所以知今。 [Just as a] bright mirror [may be] used to reflect images, [so] ancient events may be used to understand the present.

104 **Mìng lǐ yǒu shí zhōng xū yǒu; mìng lǐ wú shí mò qiǎngqiú.** 命里有时终须有, 命里无时莫强求。 [If it is] decreed by fate, [one] will certainly have [something]; [if one is] fated not to have [it], one need not seek hard [for it]. [Rhyme; cf. *JPM*, chap. 14; see also *yī yǐn, yī zhuó* below and the preceding entry.]

105 **Míng qiāng yì duǒ; ànjiàn nán fáng.*** 明枪易躲, 暗箭难防。 (lit) [An] open spear [thrust is] easy to dodge [but an] arrow [in the] dark is hard to guard against. (fig) Open attacks are easier dealt with than surprise attacks or hidden innuendo. [Cf. *Dàng Kòu Zhì*, chap. 108; see also *bùpà hóngliǎn* and *bùpà míngchù* above and *zhǐ rènde zhēngyǎn* below.]

106 **Míngrén bù shuō àn huà.** 明人不说暗话。 An honest person does not resort to insinuation. [See also *míngrén bù zuò* below.]

107 **Míngrén bùyòng xìshuō.*** 明人不用细说。 A discerning person needs no detailed explanation. [Also said *míngrén bù xū xìshuō* and *míngrén bù dài xìshuō*; cf. *Érnǚ Yīngxióng Zhuàn*, chap. 19; see also *kuàimǎ bùyòng* above and *xiǎng gǔ bùyòng* and *yī yán qǐ zhìzhě* below.]

108 **Míngrén bù zuò ànshì.*** 明人不做暗事。 [An] honest person does not do underhanded things. [Cf. *JW*, chap. 84; *Gǔ-Jīn Xiǎoshuō*, chap. 28; see also *jūnzǐ bù qī* above and *míngrén bù shuō* below.]

109 **Míngrén diǎntóu, jí zhī; chī rén quán dǎ, bù xiǎo.** 明人点头即知, 痴人拳打不晓。 (lit) [A] clever person understands at a nod, [while a] stupid person won't understand [even when] beaten. (fig) "A nod is as good as a wink (to a blind horse)." [See also the following entry.]

110 **Míngrén yī diǎn jiù tòu; yúrén bàng dǎ bù huí.** 明人一点就透, 愚人棒打不回。 (lit) [A] clever person [given] a nod will understand, [while a] stupid person [even when] beaten [with a] stick won't. (fig) "A nod is as good as a wink (to a blind horse)." [See also the preceding entry.]

M

M

111 **Míngrén zì duàn; yúrén guān duàn.** 明人自断，愚人官断。Intelligent people [realize their own mistakes and] correct themselves; foolish people [won't realize their own mistakes and will be] sentenced by judges.

112 **Mìng ruò qióng, jué dé huángjīn, huāzuò tóng; mìng ruò fù, shí de bái zhǐ, biànchéng bù.** 命若穷，掘得黄金，化作铜；命若富，拾得白纸，变成布。[If one is] destined to be poor, [even] the gold [one] digs up becomes copper; [if one is] destined to be rich, the white paper [one] picks up becomes cloth. [Rhyme; cf. *Chū Kè Pāi'àn Jīngqí: Zhuǎn Yùn Hàn . . .*]

113 **Míngshī chū gāotú.** 名师出高徒。A famous teacher produces talented students. [Said by others as a compliment to a teacher; see also *yánshī chū gāotú* below.]

114 **Míng yǒu wángfǎ; àn yǒu shénlíng.** 明有王法，暗有神灵。(lit) [In] public there are earthly laws; [in] private there are gods. (fig) One's good and bad behavior will ultimately be judged by heaven, if not by earthly laws. [Cf. *WM*, chap. 15.]

115 **Míng zhī bù shì bàn; shì jí qiě xiāngsuí.** 明知不是伴，事急且相随。[Although one] clearly understands [that someone] is not good company, in times of emergency [one] has to follow [such people]. [Cf. *Xǐngshì Héngyán*, chap. 33.]

116 **Mó dāo bù wù kǎn chái gōng.** 磨刀不误砍柴工。(lit) Sharpening [one's] knife [before one] cuts wood is not a waste of time. (fig) Time spent on the preparation for a task will not delay its progress.

117 **Módāo, hèn bùlì; dāo lì, shāng rén zhǐ.** 磨刀恨不利，刀利伤人指。(lit) [When you] grind [your] knife, [you] complain [the knife is] not sharp enough; [when the] knife [becomes] sharp, [it will] cut your fingers. (fig) There are two sides to everything.

118 **Mò dào rén xíng zǎo; gèng yǒu zǎo xíng rén.** 莫道人行早，更有早行人。Don't say [you are] going early; there are people [who are] starting even earlier. [Cf. *Sān Xiá Wǔ Yì*, chap. 30.]

119 **Mò fàn rén huì, mò chù rén tòng.** 莫犯人讳，莫触人痛。(lit) Don't violate [other] people's taboos [and] don't touch on [other] people's hurts. (fig) Don't bring up "taboo subjects" or speak of things which might hurt other's feelings. "Don't speak of halters in the house of a hanged man." [See also *āizi miànqián* and *dāngzhe āirén* above.]

120 **Mò jiào hóuzi qù kān guǒ; mò jiào shuǐtǎ qù shǒu yú.** 莫叫猴子去看果，莫叫水獭去守鱼。(lit) Don't ask a monkey to watch a fruit [garden, and] don't let an otter protect a fish [pond]. (fig) Don't invite trouble by asking untrustworthy people for help. "Don't set a fox to guard a chicken coop." [See also *húli kān jī* above.]

121 **Mò kàn qiángdào chī ròu; yào kàn qiángdào shòuzuì.** 莫看强盗吃肉，要看强盗受罪。(lit) Don't [just] consider [that] robbers [get to] eat meat [i.e., live "high on the hog"]; [you] must [also] consider [that] they get punished. (fig)

When looking at an issue, one has to consider the "down" side as well as the good side.

122 **Mò tì gǔrén dān yōu.** 莫替古人耽忧。(lit) Don't worry on behalf of the ancients. (fig) Don't worry about things which don't concern you. [Cf. *JW*, chap. 78.]

123 **Móushì zài rén; chéngshì zài tiān.*** 谋事在人，成事在天。(lit) Planning affairs lies with humans; accomplishing things lies with Heaven. (fig) "Man proposes; God disposes." [Rhyme; compare: "*L'homme propose, Dieu dispose.*" "*La gente pone y Dios dispone.*" "*Der Mensch denkt's, Gott lenkt's.*" cf. *R3K*, chap. 103; *DRC*, chap. 6; vs. *shì zài rén wéi*; see also *qiān suàn, wàn suàn* and *shì dà, shì xiǎo* and *tiān suàn bù yóu* below.]

124 **Mò wèn shōuhuò; dàn wèn gēngyún.** 莫问收获，但问耕耘。(lit) Do not ask [about the] harvest; rather ask [about the] plowing. (fig) One should be more concerned about taking action than (worrying) about the results of taking action.

125 **Mò xiǎng qīngshān niǎo; yǎng hǎo lóng zhōng jī.** 莫想青山鸟，养好笼中鸡。(lit) Don't think about [trying to catch] birds in the green hills; [better] to raise chickens in the cage. (fig) Don't indulge in fantasy; be practical instead.

126 **Mò xìn zhí zhōng zhí; xū fáng rén bùrén.** 莫信直中直，须防人不仁。(lit) Don't believe [people are] absolutely frank and straightforward; [one] must [always] guard against [other] people's ill-intentions. [Cf. *Fēngshén Yǎnyì*, chap. 21.]

127 **Mù bù lí gēn; shuǐ bù tuō yuán.** 木不离根；水不脱源。(lit) Trees can't leave their roots; waters can't be separated from their sources. (fig) Nothing should be done without (adhering to) basic principles. [See also *mù wú běn bì kū* below.]

128 **Mù bù zuān, bù tòu; rén bù jī, bù fā.** 木不钻不透，人不激不发。(lit) [Just as] wood cannot be penetrated [all the way] through without drilling, [so] people won't act without being aroused. [Cf. *Gǔ-Jīn Xiǎoshuō*, chap. 5.]

129 **Mǔdan suī hǎo, quán píng lù yè fúchí.*** 牡丹虽好，全凭绿叶扶持。(lit) Although the peony is beautiful, [it] completely depends on the support [of its] green leaves. (fig) Everyone needs help. [Cf. *JPM*, chap. 76; *DRC*, chap. 110; *Xǐngshì Yīnyuán Zhuàn*, chap. 32; *Érnǚ Yīngxióng Zhuàn*, chap. 19; also said *héhuā suī hǎo, yě yào . . .* (q.v.); see also *dà shítou bù lí* above and *yī gè líba* below.]

130 **Mǔ gǒu bù chū pìgu, gōng gǒu nán shàng.** 母狗不出屁股，公狗难上。(lit) [If] female dogs [did] not present [their] posteriors, [it would be] difficult for male dogs to mount [them]. (fig) Men can't misbehave with women unless the women are willing.

131 **Mùjiang dài jiā; zì zuò zì shòu.** 木匠戴夹，自作自受。(lit) [When a] carpenter [ends up] wearing a cangue [i.e., a wooden yoke], [it's a case of] getting what [he] himself made. (fig) One will suffer the consequences of one's own actions. "As a man sows, so shall he reap." "As you make your bed, so you must lie in it." "Hoist with one's own petard." [This is also used as a *xiehouyu*, with the

second part delayed or suppressed; *zìzuò-zìshòu* is also a set phrase with the same meaning.]

132 **Mùjiang pà qījiang; qījiang pà guāngliàng.*** 木匠怕漆匠，漆匠怕光亮。 (lit) [Just as the] carpenter fears the lacquerer [who can find defects in the work while lacquering it, so the] lacquerer fears bright light, [under which the defects of his own work will be exposed]. (fig) There is always someone bigger or better (to be afraid of). [Rhyme; see also *yī wù xiáng yī wù* below.]

133 **Mù'ǒu bù huì zìjī tiào; mùhòu dìng yǒu qiānxiàn rén.** 木偶不会自己跳，幕后定有牵线人。 (lit) Puppets can't dance by themselves; there must be someone behind the curtain pulling the strings. (fig) There is always someone behind the scenes "pulling the strings."

134 **Mù wú běn bì kū; shuǐ wú yuán bì jié.** 木无本必枯；水无源必竭。 (lit) Trees without

roots will wither [and] waters without sources will run dry. (fig) Things go bad when they lose (contact with) their roots or basic principles. [Cf. *Dōng Zhōu Lièguó Zhì*, chap. 38; see also *mù bù lí gēn* above.]

135 **Mù xiǔ chóng shēng; qiáng xià yǐ rù.** 木朽虫生，墙罅蚁入。 (lit) Rotten wood produces worms [and] cracked walls let in ants. (fig) Disasters come from defects within.

136 **Mù yǐ chéng zhōu.** 木已成舟。 (lit) The wood is already made into a boat. (fig) What is done cannot be undone. "The die is cast." [See also *shēng mǐ chéngle* below.]

137 **Mù yǒu běn; shuǐ yǒu yuán.** 木有本，水有源。 (lit) Water has its sources; trees have their roots. (fig) All things have their causes or foundations. [See also *shì yǒu yīn* and *wú fēng bù qǐ* and *yǒu fēng fāng qǐ* below.]

N

1 **Nǎ chù huángtǔ bù mái rén?** 哪处黄土不埋人？ (lit) [In] what place [will] earth not bury a person? (fig) One may find a place to be buried wherever one dies. [Said to encourage people to leave home to seek a living elsewhere; see also *shù nuó, sǐ* below.]

2 **Ná de zhù de shì shǒu; yǎn bu zhù de shì kǒu.** 拿得住的是手，掩不住的是口。 (lit) [One] can control [other people's] hands, [but one] can't shut [other people's] mouths. (fig) One cannot stop others from talking. People will talk. Secrets will come out sooner or later. [Rhyme.]

3 **Ná fǔ de dé cháihé; zhāng wǎng de dé yú-xiā.** 拿斧的得柴禾，张网的得鱼虾。 [One] who wields an axe gets firewood, [and one] who casts a net gets fish [and] shrimp. (fig) You will get benefits according to the kind of effort you invest. "As ye sow, so shall ye reap." [See also *zhòng guā, dé guā* below.]

4 **Nǎge hàozi bù tōu yóu?** 哪个耗子不偷油？ (lit) What rat doesn't steal oil? (fig) It's difficult to alter one's basic character. "A leopard can't change his spots." [Cf. *DRC*, chap. 91; see also *gǒu chī shǐ* and *gǒu zǒu qiān lǐ* and *jiāngshān yì gǎi* above and *shé zuān de kūdòng* and *yī rén, yī xiàng* below and the following entry.]

5 **Nǎge māor bù chī xīng?*** 哪个猫儿不吃腥？ (lit) What cat doesn't eat fish? (fig) It's difficult to alter one's basic character. "A leopard can't change his spots." [Cf. *WM*, chap. 21; see also the preceding entry.]

6 **Nǎ gēn zhǐtou yě shì zìjǐ de ròu.** 哪根指头也是自己的肉。 (lit) Every finger is of one's own flesh. (fig) Children born of the same parents should all be treated equally. [See also *shí gè zhǐtou* and *shǒubèi yě shì ròu* below.]

7 **Nǎge yú bù shí shuǐ?** 哪个鱼不识水？ (lit) What fish doesn't know how to swim? (fig) An

expert knows his trade. [Note: *shí shuǐ xìng*, "to know how to swim."]

8 **Nán dà dāng hūn; nǚ dà dāng jià.*** 男大当婚，女大当嫁。 (lit) [When a] male grows to adulthood [he] ought to take a wife, [and when a] female grows up [she] ought to get married. (fig) Men and women all should marry; it's only natural. [Cf. *Shuǐhǔ Hòu Zhuàn*, chap. 39; *Wǔ Sōng*, chap. 6; *R3K*, chap. 54.]

9 **Nándé zhě, xiōngdì; yì dé zhě, tiándì.** 难得者兄弟，易得者田地。 [It's even] harder [to have friendship as close as] brothers than it is to get [good] farmland. [Rhyme; cf. *Gǔ-Jīn Xiǎoshuō*, chap. 10.]

10 **Nán'ér fēi wúlèi; bù yīn biélí liú.** 男儿非无泪，不因别离流。 [It's not that true] men have no tears, [but only that they do] not shed [them] over parting. [Said when parting; see also *nán'ér yǒu lèi* below.]

11 **Nán'ér xī xià yǒu huángjīn.** 男儿膝下有黄金。 (lit) There's [something as precious as] gold beneath a true man's knees. (fig) A true man should not easily go down on both knees to surrender or beg for mercy. [Cf. *Chū Kè Pāi'àn Jīngqí*, chap. 21.]

12 **Nán'ér yǒu lèi, bù qīng tán; (zhǐ yīn wèi dào shāngxīn shí).** 男儿有泪不轻弹，(只因未到伤心时)。 (lit) A man has tears [but does] not lightly shed [them]; ([it's] only because [he has] not yet encountered an instance of deep sorrow). (fig) Men only weep when deeply hurt. [Originally *zhàngfu yǒu lèi* . . .; the second part may be omitted.]

13 **Náng lǐ chéng zhuī, zì chū jiān.** 囊里盛锥，自出尖。 (lit) [An] awl in [a] bag [will] naturally stick out. (fig) Talent will naturally distinguish itself.

14 **Nán jiāng yī rén shǒu, yǎn dé tiānxià mù.** 难将一人手，掩得天下目。(lit) It's impossible for one person's hand to cover everyone's eyes. (fig) It's impossible to deceive everyone. [See the colloquial *suyu* expression: *yī shǒu zhē tiān*, "to (try to) hoodwink everyone"; see also *yī shǒu bù néng* and *zhī shǒu nán zhē* below.]

15 **Nán pà rù cuò háng; nǚ pà jià cuò láng.** 男怕入错行，女怕嫁错郎。(lit) Men [should] worry about entering the wrong trade, [and] women [should] worry about marrying the wrong husband. (fig) A man should be careful in choosing his trade, and a woman should be careful about choosing her husband. [Rhyme.]

16 **Nán rén bù mèng tuó; běi rén bù mèng xiàng.** 南人不梦驼，北人不梦象。(lit) Southerners don't dream of camels [and] northerners don't dream of elephants. (fig) One's dreams always have some relationship to reality or locality.

17 **Nánrén wú gāng bùrú cū kāng.** 男人无刚不如粗糠。A man without "steel" [i.e., staunchness] is as worthless as crude chaff. [Rhyme; see *gāngqiáng*, "staunch, firm."]

18 **Nánshì bì zuò yú yì; dàshì bì zuò yú xì.** 难事必作于易，大事必作于细。(lit) Difficult tasks must be done [starting] from the easy [part, and] big tasks must be done [starting] from the small [parts]. (fig) In undertaking large or difficult tasks, it is often better to start with the easy parts first. [Rhyme.]

19 **Nán yào qiào, yīshēn zào; (nǚ yào qiào, yīshēn xiào).** 男要俏一身皂，(女要俏一身孝)。[If a] man [wants to] look handsome, [he should dress] completely [in] black; (if a woman wants to look pretty, she should dress completely in white). [Rhyme; often used in classical novels.]

20 **Nán yào qín, nǚ yào qín; sān shí cháfàn bù qiúrén.** 男要勤，女要勤，三食茶饭不求人。(lit) If the man is hard-working [and] the woman is [too], [they will] never [need to] ask others for [their] three [daily] meals. (fig) If both husband and wife are hard-working, they need never ask for help to get by.

21 **Nán zhě bù huì; huì zhě bù nán.** 难者不会，会者不难。[For] those who cannot, it's difficult, [and for] those who can, it's easy. [Colloquially *nán de bù huì; huì de bù nán*.]

22 **Nánzǐ chī, yīshí mí; nǚzǐ chī, méi yào yī.** 男子痴一时迷，女子痴没药医。[If a] man falls in love, [his] infatuation will pass sooner or later, [but for a] woman there's no cure [for her passion]. [Rhyme; note: *chīmí*, "infatuated."]

23 **Nánzǐ sānshí yīzhīhuā; nǚzǐ sānshí lǎorenjia.** 男子三十一枝花，女子三十老人家。A man of thirty [is like] a flower, [while] a woman of thirty [is considered] old. [Rhyme; note: *yīzhīhuā*, (lit) "a flower," colloquially means "a fine thing."]

24 **Nǎo yī nǎo, lǎo yī lǎo; xiào yī xiào, shí niánshào.*** 恼一恼老一老，笑一笑十年少。(lit) The more one worries, the older one gets; if one laughs, one feels ten years younger. (fig) Worry or irritation makes one old and laughter makes one young. [Rhyme; see also *xiào yī xiào* below.]

25 **Nǎr diēdǎo, nǎr pá qǐ.** 哪儿跌倒，哪儿爬起。(lit) Wherever [you] fall down, that's the place where [you should] get back up. (fig) Wherever you've made mistakes, that's just the place to remedy them; don't just run away! [See also *cǎo lǐ shí zhēn* above.]

26 **Ná yú mò fàng xiā.** 拿鱼莫放虾。(lit) [When] catching fish, don't let the shrimp get away. (fig) Don't neglect minor gains or profit.

27 **Néng bá chū nóng lái, cái shì hǎo gāoyao.** 能拔出脓来，才是好膏药。(lit) Only if it can draw out pus is it a good medicinal plaster. (fig) One can judge a truly good method only by its results. "The proof of the pudding is in the eating."

28 **Néng chǎn zhě bì néng jiāo.** 能谄者必能骄。Those who are capable of flattering [their supervisors] must [also] be arrogant [toward their subordinates].

29 **Néng chī fēiqín yīkǒu, bù shí zǒushòu bàn jīn.** 能吃飞禽一口，不食走兽半斤。(lit) [It is better to be] able to eat one mouthful of fowl than to eat half a catty of beast [meat]. (fig) Birds are much more tasty than other meats. [Note the *chengyu*: *fēiqín-zǒushòu*, "birds and beasts"; also said *nìng chī fēiqín sì liǎng, bù chī zǒushòu bājīn* (q.v.).]

30 **Néng láo bù néng jiǎn, dàotóu méi jīzǎn; néng jiǎn bù néng láo, dàotóu děngyú líng.** 能劳不能俭，到头没积攒；能俭不能劳，到头等于零。[If one] can be diligent [but] not economical, in the end [one] won't collect any savings; [if one] can be economical, [but] not diligent, in the end [it will all] come to nothing.

31 **Néngrén shì bèn rén de núlì.** 能人是笨人的奴隶。Able people are the slaves of fools [because they can do things that others cannot or will not]. [See also *néng zhě duō láo* below.]

32 **Néngrén zhīwài yǒu néngrén.** 能人之外有能人。(lit) Behind an able person, there is an abler person. (fig) There's always someone better. No one is superior to all others. [Also said *néngrén bēihòu yǒu néngrén*; see also the following entry and *qiáng zhōng háiyǒu* and *shān wài yǒu shān* and *shé tūn shǔ* below.]

33 **Néngrén zìyǒu néngrén fú.** 能人自有能人伏。[For every] able person there is always an[other] able [person able] to conquer [him/her]. [Cf. *Fēngshén Yǎnyì*, chap. 74; see also the preceding entry and *qiáng zhōng háiyǒu* and *rén wài yǒu rén* and *shān wài yǒu shān* and *shé tūn shǔ* and *yī wù zhì yī wù* below.]

34 **Néng shū bù zé bǐ.*** 能书不择笔。(lit) An able calligrapher is not [particular in] choosing [his] writing brush. (fig) A true expert can do a good job under less than ideal conditions.

35 **Néng zhě duō láo.** 能者多劳。Those [who are] able (should) do more [(extra)] work. [Said, e.g., when asking someone to do something (extra); this is often mistakenly taken to be a *chengyu*; see also *gàn jǐng bì xiān jié* and *kuàimǎ pǎo duàn tuǐ* and *néngrén shì bèn rén* above and *qiǎo zhě duō láo* below.]

36 **Niáng hǎo, nān hǎo; yāng hǎo, dào hǎo.*** 娘好
团好，秧好稻好。 Good mothers (or parents)
[raise] good children, [just as] healthy seedlings
[grow into] good grain. [Rhyme; note *nān* is Wu
dialect for "boy"; *Wú Xià Yàn Lián*, vol. 3.]

37 **Niánjì bù ráorén.** 年纪不饶人。 Age pardons
no one. [Note: *ráo shè*, "to forgive."]

38 **(Niánnián fáng jiǎn;) yè yè fáng zéi.** (年 年 防
俭，) 夜 夜 防 贼。 (Be prepared for crop failure every year [and]) guard against burglars every night. [Advice to household heads; cf. *Xǐngshì
Yīnyuán Zhuàn*, chap. 90; also said *niánnián fáng
qiàn*, etc.; note that *jiǎn nián* is colloquial for
qiànnián, "a year of poor harvests."]

39 **Niántóu yī jiāo, zāihuò quán xiāo.** 年头一跤，
灾祸全消。 A fall [at the] beginning of the year
[will] dispel all the disasters [for the remainder of
the year]. [A rhyme said as a charm to dispel any
impression of starting off the year "on the wrong
foot" whenever any misfortune occurs at the beginning of the year.]

40 **Niǎo guì yǒu yì; rén guì, yǒu zhì.** 鸟贵有翼，
人贵，有智。 [Just as the] value of birds [is that
they] have wings, [so the] value of humans [is that
they have] wisdom.

41 **Niǎo lái tóu lín; rén lái tóu zhǔ.** 鸟来投林，人来
头主。 [Just as] birds come into the woods, [so]
people come to [seek help and protection from
powerful] patrons. [Cf. *Xǐngshì Héngyán*, chap.
25.]

42 **Niǎo měi zài yǔmáo; rén měi zài qínláo.** 鸟美
在羽毛，人美在勤劳。 [Just as] the beauty
of birds lies in [their] plumage, [so] the beauty of
human beings lies in [their] diligence. [Rhyme.]

43 **Niǎo shòu, máo cháng; rén pín, zhì duǎn.** 鸟
瘦毛长，人贫智短。 [Just as when] birds
[get] thin, [their] feathers [seem] longer [by com-
parison], [so when] people [are] poor, [they are]
short of ideas [as to how to get along]. [Cf. *Jǐngshì
Tōngyán*, chap. 31; see also *rén pín, zhì duǎn* below.]

44 **(Niǎo yào fēi,) tiān yào xiàyǔ, niáng yào jiàrén.***
(鸟要飞,) 天要下雨，娘要嫁人。 (lit) (Birds
will fly,) the heavens will rain, and [widowed]
mothers will [re-]marry; [there's nothing to be
done about it]. (fig) Some things are inevitable.
[Cf. *Wú Xià Yàn Lián*, vol. 2; this is a Ningbo *yanyu*
supposedly quoted by Mao Zedong concerning
the flight of Lin Biao, his then heir apparent, to
Mongolia in 1971 while trying to escape to the
Soviet Union after his plot to usurp power was
discovered.]

45 **Nìfēng diǎnhuǒ, zì shāo shēn.** 逆风点火，自
烧身。 (lit) [If one] lights a fire against the wind,
[one will] burn oneself. (fig) If one goes against
accepted practices, one may get hurt. "Play with
fire and you may get burned."

46 **Nǐ jìng wǒ yī chǐ; wǒ jìng nǐ yī zhàng.** 你敬我一
尺，我敬你一丈。 You respect me one foot
[and] I'll respect you ten feet. (fig) (1) Respect
should be mutual. (2) Retaliate against your opponent using tactics ten times stronger than his.

47 **Nìng chāi qiān zuò miào; bù chāi yī duì hūn.**
宁拆千座庙，不拆一对婚。 Rather destroy
a thousand temples than to harm one couple's
marriage. [See also *hūnyīn quàn lǒng* above.]

48 **Nìng chī fēiqín sì liǎng, bù chī zǒushòu bàn jīn.**
宁吃飞禽四两，不吃走兽半斤。 (lit) [It is]
better to eat four ounces of fowl than to eat half
a catty of beast [meat]. (fig) Birds are much more
tasty than other meats. [Note the *chengyu*: *fēiqín-
zǒushòu*, "birds and beasts"; this is a modern version of *néng chī fēiqín yīkǒu, bù shí zǒushòu bàn
jīn* (q.v.); one *jīn* or "catty" (now equal to one-
half kilogram) contains eight *liǎng*.]

49 **Nìng chī guòtóu fàn; mò shuō guòtóu huà.** 宁吃
过头饭，莫说过头话。 It is better to overeat
than to overstate.

50 **Nìng chī xiān táo yìkǒu; bù chī làn xìng yī kuāng.**
宁吃仙桃一口，不吃烂杏一筐。 (lit) It is
better to have [only] one mouthful of the celestial
peach than to eat a basket of rotten apricots. (fig)
It is better to have fewer and better than to have
more but worse; quality is more important than
quantity.

51 **Nìng cóng yī ér shēnzào; wú fàn shè ér liǎng shī.**
宁从一而深造，毋泛涉而两失。 Better to
follow one [thing] and master [it] deeply than to
be lightly involved [in two things] and master neither.

52 **Nìng gěi jī rén yīkǒu; bù gěi fùrén yī dǒu.** 宁给
饥人一口，不给富人一斗。 (lit) It is better
to give one mouthful of food to a hungry person
than to give a bushel of grain to a rich man. (fig)
It is better to give help to those in need. [Rhyme;
cf. *Sān Xiá Wǔ Yì*, chap. 100.]

53 **Nìng gēn yàofàn de niáng; bù gēn zuòguān de
diē.** 宁跟要饭的娘，不跟做官的爹。 (lit) [A
child would] rather [stay] with a mother [who is
a] beggar than with a father [who is a rich] official. (fig) Mothers treat their children better than
fathers do.

54 **Nìng guǎn qiān jūn; mò guǎn yī fū.** 宁管千军，
莫管一夫。 It is better to command [an army of]
a thousand soldiers than to direct one [common]
man [who is untrained or undisciplined].

55 **Nìng hē kāi-méi zhōu; bù chī zhòu-méi fàn.** 宁
喝开眉粥，不吃皱眉饭。 (lit) Better to drink
"unfurrowed-brow" porridge than to eat "knit-
ted-brow" rice. (fig) It is better to be poor and
happy than to be rich and have worries.

56 **Nìng jiāo shuāngjiǎo tiào; bù jiāo mīmī xiào.** 宁
交双脚跳，不交咪咪笑。 [It is] better to make
friends with [honest people who] stamp both feet
[i.e., forthright, outspoken people] than to make
friends with [tricky] people [who] smile with narrow[ed eyes]. [Rhyme.]

57 **Nìng jiào zuòguò; mò yào cuòguò.** 宁叫做过，
莫要错过。 It is better to have attempted to do it
than to have missed [the opportunity]. [Also said
nìngkě zuòguò, . . . etc.]

N

58 **Nìng jìn yī cùn sǐ; wú /wù tuì yī chǐ shēng.** 宁进一寸死，毋/勿退一尺生。Better to advance an inch and die than to retreat a foot alive. (fig) Never give up; never retreat. [See also *nìngkě zhànzhe sǐ* below.]

59 **Nìng jiù bǎi zhī yáng; bù jiù yī tiáo láng.** 宁救百只羊，不救一条狼。It is better to save a hundred sheep than to save one wolf [i.e., a bad person]. [Rhyme.]

60 **Nìngkě càiyuán huāng; bùkě líba dǎo.** 宁可菜园荒，不可篱笆倒。(lit) Better to let the vegetable garden [lie] barren than to let the fence fall down. (fig) The most important thing is to protect one's property.

61 **Nìngkě pín hòu fù; bùkě fù hòu pín.*** 宁可贫后富，不可富后贫。It is better to be rich after [having been] poor than to be poor after [having been] rich. [See also *nìngkě wúle yǒu* and *yóu jiǎn rù shē* below.]

62 **Nìngkě shéběn; xiūyào jī sǔn.** 宁可折本，休要饥损。(lit) It is better to lose money [in business transactions] than to suffer harm [from hunger]. (fig) One's health is more important than one's business. [Cf. *JPM*, chap. 62.]

63 **Nìngkě shuō de bù tòu; bù kě guòfèn kuākǒu.** 宁可说得不透，不可过分夸口。(lit) [It is] better not to express oneself fully than to boast. (fig) Better to understate than to overstate. [Rhyme.]

64 **Nìngkě wúle yǒu; bùkě yǒule wú.** 宁可无了有，不可有了无。It is better to go from poverty to riches than from riches to poverty. [Cf. *Chū Kè Pāi'àn Jīngqí*, chap. 22; see also *nìngkě pín hòu fù* above and *yóu jiǎn rù shē* below.]

65 **Nìngkě xìn qí yǒu; bùkě xìn qí wú.** 宁可信其有，不可信其无。(lit) It is better to believe it is [true] than to believe it is not. (fig) Just to be on the safe side, you'd be better off to believe it. [E.g., a fortuneteller's prediction of bad luck; cf. *Dàng Kòu Zhì*, chap. 82; *WM*, chap. 60; *Chū Kè Pāi'àn Jīngqí*, chap. 20.]

66 **Nìngkě yī bù shì; bùkě liǎng wúqíng.** 宁可一不是，不可两无情。(lit) Better that [only] one [party] be wrong than that both [parties] lose [their] affection [for each other]. (fig) Just because one person is unfriendly, it's not necessary to reciprocate. [Said by the second party.]

67 **Nìngkě yǔ rén bǐ zhòngtián; bùkě yǔ rén sài guònián.** 宁可与人比种田，不可与人赛过年。(lit) [It is] better to compete with others in farming than to compete with others in celebrating the New Year. (fig) Diligence is more important than ostentatious display.

68 **Nìngkě yùsuì, bùkě wǎquán.** 宁可玉碎，不可瓦全。(lit) Rather be a shattered jade [vessel] than an unbroken [piece of] pottery. (fig) It is better to die in glory than to live in dishonor. [Also said as *nìng wéi yùsuì, bù zuò wǎquán* (q.v.); cf. *Zàishēng Yuán*, chap. 62; *Běi Qí Shū*; note: *yùsuì*, (lit) "shattered jade," is a literary phrase meaning "death before dishonor."]

69 **Nìngkě zhànzhe sǐ; juébù guìzhe shēng.** 宁可站着死，绝不跪着生。(lit) [It is] better to die standing, absolutely [better] than living [while] kneeling. (fig) Better to die resisting than to live in submission. [As a *chengyu*: *nìngsǐ-bùqū*, "rather die than submit"; see also *nìng jìn yī cùn sǐ* above.]

70 **Nìng là yīqún; bù là yī rén.** 宁落一群，不落一人。(lit) [It is] better to neglect a group [of people] than to reject a single person. (fig) One person left out will complain bitterly, while a group left out will not feel individually discriminated against.

71 **Nìng rén fù wǒ; wú wǒ fù rén.** 宁人负我，毋我负人。Rather let others be ungrateful to me, [but] not I to others. [An ancient rule for behavior toward others; contradicted in *R3K*, chap. 4, by Cáo Cāo, who was therefore branded as a *jiān chén* ("bad minister").]

72 **Nìng shēn fú rén shǒu; mò kāi xiàn rén kǒu.** 宁伸扶人手，莫开陷人口。[It is] better to extend [your] hand to support others than to open [your] mouth to slander others. [Rhyme.]

73 **Nìng shě qiānjīn xiàn zhēn fó; bù bá yī máo chā zhū shēn.** 宁舍千金献真佛，不拔一毛插猪身。(lit) It is better to contribute a thousand [ounces of] gold to a real Buddha than to stick a "feather" onto a pig's body. (fig) It is better to spend more on something worthwhile than to waste [even] a dime on something which is not worth it. [Note: *máo* means both "feather" and "ten cents."]

74 **Nìng shě shí mǔ dì; bù chī yǎbakuī.** 宁舍十亩地，不吃哑巴亏。(lit) It is better to give up ten *mǔ* of land than to swallow a bitter pill in silence. (fig) It is better to suffer losses that are known to everybody than to suffer losses that are kept to oneself only. [Note: one *mu* equals 0.0667 hectares; *yǎbakuī*, (lit) "mute suffering," means "bottled-up grievances."]

75 **Nìng tiāo qiān jīn dàn; bù bào ròu gēda.** 宁挑千斤担，不抱肉疙瘩。(lit) It is easier to carry a thousand catties [of stuff] than to hold a "precious lump of flesh" in one's arms. (fig) Holding a (squirming) baby is more difficult than carrying a load of heavy things. [Cf. *Wǔ Sōng*, chap. 7; note: literally, one *jīn* or "catty" is equal to one-half kilogram, but *qiānjīn* is figuratively taken to mean "a ton; a great weight."]

76 **Nìng wéi jī kǒu/tóu; wú wéi niú hòu/wěi.** 宁为鸡口/头，毋为牛后/尾。(lit) Better be the head of a chicken than the tail of an ox. (fig) It is better to be the head of a small group than to hold a less powerful position in a large one; "better to be a big frog in a little pond, than a small frog in a big one"; "better to be the head of a dog than the tail of a lion." [The original rhymed version is from *Zhàn Guó Cè*; the second pair of alternatives is the modern colloquial version.]

77 **Nìng wéi tàipíng quǎn; mò zuò luànlí rén.** 宁为太平犬，莫做乱离人。Better to be a dog in [times of] peace than to be a human being wandering in [times of] chaos. [Cf. *Xǐngshì Héngyán*,

chap. 3; note: *luànlí*, "to be separated or rendered homeless by war."]

78 **Nìng wèi yǔ ér chóumóu.** 宁未雨而绸缪。(lit) Better to [start] weaving [one's silk rain cloak] before it rains. (fig) It is better to make one's preparations early; provide for a rainy day. [This is an expansion of the *chengyu*: *wèi yǔ chóumóu*.]

79 **Nìng wéi yùsuì; bù wéi wǎquán.** 宁为玉碎；不为瓦全。(lit) Rather be a shattered jade [vessel] than to be a complete [piece of] pottery. (fig) It is better to die in glory than to live in dishonor. [Note: *yùsuì*, (lit) "shattered jade," is a literary phrase meaning "death before dishonor"; see also *nìngkě yùsuì* above.]

80 **Nìng xǔ rén; mò xǔ shén.** 宁许人，莫许神。It is better to make a promise to a person than to make a vow to a god. (fig) It is dangerous to break vows made to the gods. [Cf. *Hé Diǎn*, chap. 1; note: *xǔyuàn*, "to make a vow (to a god)."]

81 **Nìng yǎng wán zǐ; mò yǎng dāizi.** 宁养顽子，莫养呆子。It is better to raise a naughty boy than an idiot. [Said to comfort the parents of naughty children.]

82 **Nìng yào xiān nán hòu yì; wú shǐ xiān yì hòu nán.** 宁要先难后易，毋使先易后难。It is better to do something difficult first and then to do something easy than to do something easy first and then to do something difficult.

83 **Nìngyuàn dùndùn quē; bù yuàn yī dùn wú.** 宁愿顿顿缺，不愿一顿无。[It is] better to not have enough [for] every meal than to miss one meal [entirely].

84 **Nìng yú qiān rén hǎo; mò yǔ yī rén chóu.** 宁与千人好，莫与一人愁。[It is] good to be on good terms with a thousand people; don't be on bad terms with one.

85 **Nìng zài zhí zhōng qǔ; bù xiàng qǔ zhōng qiú.** 宁在直中取，不向曲中求。It is better to get something by straightforward means than to seek it by crooked means. [Cf. *Fēngshén Yǎnyì*, chap. 23.]

86 **Nìng zhuàng jīn zhōng yīxià; bù dǎ pò gǔ sānqiān.** 宁撞金钟一下，不打破鼓三千。(lit) It is better to strike a golden bell [only] once than to beat a broken drum three thousand times. (fig) It is better to ask for help just once from someone with courage and insight than to ask a thousand times of someone without those qualities. [Cf. *DRC*, chap. 72.]

87 **Nìng zǒu shí bù yuǎn; bù zǒu yī bù xiǎn.** 宁走十步远，不走一步险。(lit) It is better to walk ten [extra] steps around than to take one step into danger. (fig) "Better (to be) safe than sorry." [Cf. *Sān Xiá Wǔ Yì*, chap. 110.]

88 **Níqiū xiān bù qǐ dà làng; tiàozao dǐng bù qǐ bèi wō.** 泥蚯掀不起大浪，跳蚤顶不起被窝。(lit) A loach [fish] cannot stir up great waves [and] a flea cannot hold up a bed quilt. (fig) A weak and powerless person cannot accomplish anything great.

89 **Nìshuǐ-xíngzhōu, bù jìn zé tuì.** 逆水行舟，不进则退。(lit) [When] sailing against the current, [one] must forge ahead or be driven back. (fig) One must constantly forge ahead (in study, life, etc.), or one will fall behind. [Often quoted by Mao Zedong; note: *nìshuǐ-xíngzhōu* is a *chengyu* meaning "to go against the current"; see also *xué rú nìshuǐ* below.]

90 **Nǐ shuōbude wǒ tóu tū; wǒ xiàobude nǐ yǎn xiā.** 你说不得我头秃，我笑不得你眼瞎。(lit) You should not talk about my bald head, [and] I should not laugh at your blind eyes. (fig) Everyone has his or her own shortcomings. Don't talk about other people's defects. [Cf. *Xǐngshì Yīnyuán Zhuàn*, chap. 91.]

91 **Nítāi biàn bù chéng huófó.** 泥胎变不成活佛。(lit) [An unpainted] clay figure cannot be changed into a living Buddha. (fig) A person of bad character or poor ability cannot be changed into a person of good character or ability. "You can't make a silk purse out of a sow's ear." [Note: *nítāi*, (lit) "clay embryo," refers to an unpainted or ungilded clay figurine.]

92 **Niú bù hē shuǐ, nán àn jiǎo.** 牛不喝水，难按角。(lit) [If an] ox doesn't want to drink water, [it's] difficult to press down its horns. (fig) You can't force others to do what they don't want to do; "you can lead a horse to water, but you can't make it drink." [Note also the colloquial *suyu* expression: *niú bù hē shuǐ, qiáng àn tóu*, "trying to press an ox's head down when it doesn't want to drink" in *DRC*, chap. 46, and *àn niú tóu* above.]

93 **Niú bù zhī jiǎo wān; mǎ bù zhī liǎn cháng.** 牛不知角弯，马不知脸长。(lit) An ox doesn't know [it has] crooked horns; nor does a horse know [it has a] long face. (fig) One doesn't know one's own shortcomings. [See also *dēngtái zhào rén* and *húli bù zhī* above and *rén guàn shè jǐ guò* below.]

94 **Niú bù zhī lì dà; rén bù zhī jǐ guò.** 牛不知力大，人不知己过。[Just as an] ox doesn't know [its own] strength, [so] people don't know [their] own mistakes.

95 **Niú chī qīngcǎo, jī chī gǔ; gèrén zìyǒu gèrén fú.*** 牛吃青草鸡吃谷，个人自有个人福。(lit) Oxen eat grass [and] chickens eat grain; each one has its own blessings. (fig) Individuals have their own lot or luck in life. [Rhyme; also said *niú chī dàocǎo, yā chī gǔ* etc.; see also *yā chī tiánluó* below.]

96 **Niú dà, yā bù sǐ shīzi.** 牛大压不死虱子。(lit) [An] ox [is] big, [but it] can't crush [a] louse. (fig) Big or small, each has its own strengths and limitations.

97 **Niúpí bù shì chuī de; Tài Shān bù shì lěi de.*** 牛皮不是吹的，泰山不是垒的。(lit) Cowhides are not [removed by] blowing, [just as] Mount Tai was not formed by piling up [earth]. (fig) It's no use bragging. [Rhyme; note: *chuīniú(pí)*, (lit) "to blow (off) a cow('s skin)" means "to boast; to brag"; Mt. Tai in Shandong province, one of the five sacred mountains of Buddhism, is traditionally taken as an image of greatness.]

98 **Niú yǒu qiānjīn zhī lì; rén yǒu dào niú zhī fāng.** 牛有千斤之力，人有倒牛之方。 (lit) No matter how strong bulls are, humans have ways of overturning them. (fig) However strong one's opponent is, one can find a way to conquer him. Wisdom can overcome brute force. [Cf. *Xīyáng Jì*, chap. 31; note: literally, *qiānjīn* means "one thousand catties," but *qiānjīn* is figuratively taken to mean "a ton; a great weight."]

99 **Nǐ yǒu nǐ de guān mén jì; wǒ yǒu wǒ de tiào qiáng fǎ.** 你有你的关门计，我有我的跳墙法。 (lit) You have the close-the-door tactics, [and] I have the jump-over-the-wall method. (fig) One adopts an appropriate policy in response to an opponent's tactics.

100 **Nìzǐ, wán qī, wú yào kě zhì.** 逆子顽妻，无药可治。 (lit) [For] an unfilial son [or] a stubborn wife, there is no medicine [which] can cure [them]. (fig) One can do nothing with an unfilial son or a stubborn wife. [Cf. *Xǐngshì Héngyán*, chap. 27.]

101 **Nǐ zǒu nǐ de yángguāndào; wǒ zǒu wǒ de dúmùqiáo.*** 你走你的阳关道，我走我的独木桥。 (lit) You [may] walk the main road [and] I'll take the single plank bridge. (fig) You go your way and I'll go mine. [You look after your business and I'll look after mine. [Rhyme; note: *yángguān dào*, "broad road; thoroughfare"; *dúmùqiáo*, (lit) "single-plank bridge," (fig) "difficult path."]

102 **Nóng shuāng piān dǎ wú gēn cǎo; huò lái zhǐ bèn fú qīng rén.** 浓霜偏打无根草，祸来只奔福轻人。 [Just as] severe frost only harms rootless grass, [so] disasters only hasten to [fall on] people of little luck. [Cf. *Chū Kè Pāi'àn Jīngqí*, chaps. 11 and 22; see also *yánshuāng piān dǎ* below.]

103 **Nǚ dà, bùzhōng liú; liúle, jié yuānchóu.** 女大不中留，留了结冤仇。 A grown-up girl should not be kept [at home (i.e., unmarried) by her parents]; [if she] is, [she will] harbor hatred for them. [Cf. *Jǐngshì Tōngyán*, chap. 38; note: *bù zhōng* is northern dialect for "not all right."]

104 **Nǚ dà shíbā biàn; (línshí shàng jiào, biàn sān biàn).*** 女大十八变，（临时上轿，变三变）。 (lit) A girl changes eighteen times [in physical appearance before] reaching womanhood; (near the time she gets married, she'll change three times more). [Cf. *DRC*, chap. 78; also said *máotou gūniang* . . . etc.]

105 **Nǚ dà zì qiǎo; gǒu dà zì yǎo.** 女大自巧，狗大自咬。 When girls grow up, they will naturally become skillful or clever, [just as] when dogs grow big, they will naturally [learn to] bite [so, unlike with boys, there is no need to teach them at home]. [Note: unmarried girls in traditional China were often not taught any skills at home, leaving the task to their future mothers-in-law.]

106 **Númǎ liànzhàn dòu.** 驽马恋栈豆。 (lit) A slow-running horse is reluctant to leave [its] stable fodder. (fig) An incapable person with limited vision only sees small immediate benefits. [Note: *númǎ*, (lit) "inferior horse," is also used to refer to dull, incompetent people.]

107 **Númǎ qiān lǐ, gōng zài bù shě.** 驽马千里，功在不舍。 (lit) [If] an inferior horse [travels one] thousand miles, [its] achievement is [only due to] perseverance. (fig) Often accomplishment is not the result of brilliance, but only of hard work. [Often said modestly of oneself; note: technically one *lǐ* equals one-half of a kilometer; see also the preceding entry and *bèn niǎo xiān fēi* above.]

108 **Nùqì shāng gān.** 怒气伤肝。 (lit) Anger harms [one's] liver. (fig) Anger is harmful to one's health. [Cf. *Hòu Hàn Yǎnyì*, chap. 85.]

109 **Nǚrén shì zhěntou biān de fēng; bù tīng yě děi tīng.** 女人是枕头边的风，不听也得听。 (lit) Women are [like] the wind blowing by the pillow: like it or not, [one] has to listen [to them]. (fig) Men are influenced by their wives at night. [Cf. the colloquial *súyǔ* expression: *chuī zhěn biān fēng*, "to be influenced by one's wife at night"; see also *zhěn biān gàozhuàng* below.]

110 **Nǚshēng wàixiàng.** 女生外向。 (lit) Women are born with an outward orientation. (fig) (1) Girls from birth are destined to be married off to other families. (2) Women will inevitably side with their husbands, rather than with their natal families.

111 **Nǚ wèi yuè jǐ zhě róng.** 女为悦己者容。 A woman will beautify herself for one who pleases her. [See also *shì wèi zhījǐ zhě* below.]

112 **Nǚxu yǒu bànzǐ zhī láo.** 女婿有半子之劳。 A son-in-law has [i.e., should perform] half the duties of a son. [In traditional patrilineal China, sons were expected to support parents and perform rites. If a family had no son, real or adopted, a son-in-law was "married in" for these purposes.]

113 **Nǚzǐ wú cái biànshì dé.** 女子无才便是德。 An unschooled girl is a virtuous one. [A common belief in traditional China; cf. *DRC*, chap. 4.]

O

1 Ŏurán fàncuò jiàozuò guò; cúnxīn fàncuò jiàozuò è. 偶然犯错叫做过，存心犯错叫做
恶。An occasional mistake is called an error; a
deliberate mistake ıs called an evil. [See also *shì
bù guò sān* below.]

P

1 Pá de gāo, diē de zhòng. 爬得高，跌得重。(lit)
The higher [one] climbs, the heavier [one] falls.
(fig) The higher the official position one holds, the
greater disaster one invites. "The bigger they are,
the harder they fall." [Cf. *DRC*, chap. 13; *Lǎo Cán
Yóujì*, chap. 3.]

2 Pà de lǎohǔ, wèibude zhū. 怕得老虎，喂不得
猪。(lit) [If one is too] afraid of tigers, one won't
raise pigs. (fig) If one is too full of fears, one won't
be able to accomplish anything at all.

3 Pà jiàn de shì guài; nán duǒ de shì zhài. 怕见的
是怪，难躲的是债。(lit) [Just as one wants to]
avoid seeing demons, [so it's] hard to hide from
creditors. [Rhyme; cf. *Chū Kè Pāi'àn Jīngqí*, chap.
15.]

4 Pà láng, pà hǔ; bié zài shān shàng zhù. 怕狼
怕虎，别在山上住。(lit) [If you are] afraid
of tigers and wolves, don't live in the mountains.
(fig) Don't take the risk unless you are willing to
face the danger. [Rhyme.]

5 Pàngzi bù shì yīkǒu chī de.* 胖子不是一口吃
的。(lit) Fatties don't get [fat by] eating [only]
one mouth[ful]. (fig) One doesn't get to be a certain way overnight, but as the result of long-term
behavior. [Cf. *DRC*, chap. 84; see also *yīkǒu chī
bù chéng* below.]

6 Pǎole héshang, pǎo bùliǎo miào.* 跑了和尚，
跑不了庙。(lit) [The] monks [may] run away,
[but the] monastery cannot. (fig) One can never
(completely) escape (the consequences of one's
actions).

7 Pèile qiān gè bùrú xiān gè. 配了千个不如先
个。(lit) [Although] mated to a thousand [hus-
bands], none [is] as good as the first one. (fig) The
first husband is always the best, however many
times a woman may get married.

8 Péngyou qiān gè shǎo; chóurén yī gè duō. 朋友
千个少，仇人一个多。A thousand friends
[are] too few, [and] one enemy [is] too many.

9 Piānfāng zhì dà bìng. 偏方治大病。Folk prescriptions [(or home remedies) can] cure serious
illnesses. [See also *cǎoyào yī wèi* and *mìfāng zhì*
above and *xiǎo yào zhì* below.]

10 Piányi bù guò dàng jiā. 便宜不过当家。(lit)
Discounts [should] not [go] outside one's family. (fig) Benefits should be kept within the family. "Charity begins at home." [Cf. *DRC*, chap. 65;
JPM, chap. 35; see also *fěi shuǐ bù guò* above.]

11 Piányi wú hǎo huò; (hǎo huò bù piányi). 便宜
无好货，(好货不便宜)。No cheap goods
are good, ([and] good goods aren't cheap). [Cf.
Guānchǎng Xiànxíng Jì, chap. 49; see also *guì de
bù guì* above.]

12 Pīchái bù zhào wén, lèisǐ pīchái rén. 劈柴不照
纹，累死劈柴人。(lit) Splitting logs not along
the grain will tire the wood cutter to death. (fig)
One should grasp the essentials in solving problems and not "go against the grain."

13 Pīchái, kàn chái shì; rù mén, kàn rén yì. 劈柴
看柴势，入门看人意。(lit) [Just as when]
cutting wood, [one should] pay attention to [its]
grain, [so upon first] entering [someone's] door,
[one should] consider [one's] host's wishes. (fig)
One should always take the situation and people's feelings into account. [Note: *rùmén* is also
a verb-object compound word meaning "to begin to learn the fundamentals," so this could also
be interpreted as "when one is just starting out at
something"; see also *chūmén guān tiānsè* above.]

14 Pǐ jí tài lái. 否极泰来。[From] extreme misery good fortune springs. [Note: *pǐ*, here "misfortune," and *tài*, here "good fortune," are terms
from the *Yijīng* (Book of Changes); note: this is
also used as a chengyu; see also *lè jí shēng bēi*
above.]

15 Pí lǐ shēng de, pí lǐ rè; pí lǐ bù shēng, lěng sì tiě.
皮里生的皮里热，皮里不生冷似铁。To
one's own flesh and blood [children], one's heart
is warm, [but] to [stepchildren] not one's flesh
and blood, one's heart is cold as iron. [See also
gé chóng dùpí and *hòumǔ de quántou* above.]

16 Pín bù xué jiǎn; fù bù xué shē. 贫不学俭，富
不学奢。The poor don't [have to] learn [to
be] economical, [while the] rich don't [have to]
learn [to be] extravagant; [they both just do it nat-
urally].

17 Pín bù yōuchóu; fù bù jiāo. 贫不忧愁，富不
骄。Do not be worried in poverty nor arrogant
in wealth.

18 Pín bù yǔ fù dí; jiàn bù yǔ guì zhēng. 贫不与富
敌，贱不与贵争。(lit) The poor [should] not
oppose the rich; the lowly [should] not contend
with nobles. (fig) The poor and the common people don't stand a chance [in traditional China].
[Cf. *Jīngshì Tōngyán*, chap. 7.]

19 Píng'ān jiùshì fú.* 平安就是福。Peace [and]
security are blessings.

P

20 **Píngshēng bù zuò zhòu méi shì; shìshàng yīng wú qièchǐ rén.** 平生不做皱眉事，世上应无切齿人。 [If you] do nothing in [your] whole life [which causes others to] knit their brows, [then] there [should] be no one on earth [who] greatly hates [you]. [Cf. *Jǐngshì Tōngyán*, chap. 8; note: *qièchǐ*, (lit) "to gnash one's teeth."]

21 **Píngshí bù shāoxiāng; línshí bào fójiǎo.** 平时不烧香，临时抱佛脚。 (lit) [It is unwise to] never burn joss sticks in ordinary times, [but only] embrace the foot of the Buddha in times of need. (fig) Make preparations well in advance and don't put things off until it's too late. [Originally *xiánshí bù shāoxiāng; jí lái bào fó jiǎo*; see WM, chap. 17; note: *línshí bào fójiǎo* is a colloquial *suyu* expression meaning "to seek help at the last minute."]

22 **Píngshí duō dǎ jǐng, tiānhàn bù qiú shén.** 平时多打井，天旱不求神。 (lit) [In] ordinary times, dig more wells [and in] times of drought [you will] not need to ask gods [for water]. (fig) It is wise to make preparations against possible times of hardship well in advance. "Save for a rainy day." [See also *héshuǐ bù zhǎng* above.]

23 **Pín jiā, bǎi shì bǎi nán zuò; fù jiā, chāi de guǐ tuīmò.** 贫家百事百难做，富家差得鬼推磨。 [For a] poor family everything is difficult, [but a] rich family can make a ghost turn a mill stone. [Cf. *Gǔ-Jīn Xiǎoshuō*, chap. 4; see also *yǒule qián* and *yǒuqián néng shǐ guǐ* below.]

24 **Pínjiàn, cháng sī fùguì; fùguì, yòu lǚ wēijī.** 贫贱常思富贵，富贵又屡危机。 (lit) [When poor, [one] longs [to be] rich, [but when one becomes] rich, then [one will] encounter misfortune. (fig) Too much fortune will bring one misfortune. One should be content with what one has. [Cf. *Jǐngshì Tōngyán*, chap. 17.]

25 **Pínjiàn fūqī bǎi shì āi.** 贫贱夫妻百事挨。 A poor couple in poverty [has to endure] all sorts of hardship.

26 **Pínjiàn, qīnqi lí; fùguì, tārén hé.** 贫贱亲戚离，富贵他人合。 (lit) [When one is] poor, relatives [will] distance [themselves, but when one is] rich, strangers [will] come. [Cf. *Gǔ-Jīn Xiǎoshuō*, chap. 22; see also *hǎo shí shì tārén* above and *pín jū nàoshì* below.]

27 **Pínjiàn zhī zhī [/jiāo] bù kě wàng; zāokāngzhīqī bù xià táng.** 贫贱之知[/交]不可忘，糟糠之妻不下堂。 Friends [that were] known [when one was] in poverty, should not be forgotten, [and one's] wife [who shared] hardships [with you] should not be abandoned. [Cf. *Gǔ-Jīn Xiǎoshuō* (*Yù Shì Míng Yán*), chap. 27; note: *zāokāngzhīqī*, "a wife who has shared husband's hardships," has become a set noun phrase; see also *guì yì jiāo* above.]

28 **Pín jū nàoshì wú rén wèn; fù zài shēnshān yǒu yuǎnqīn.** 贫居闹市无人问，富在深山有远亲。 [If a] poor [person] lives [in the] busy city center, no one [will] visit [him], [but if you're] rich [and live] deep [in the] mountains, [you'll] have relatives [coming from] afar [to visit you and ask you for favors]. [See also *fùguì tārén* and *pínjiàn,*

qīnqi lí above and *qián jù rúxiōng* and *shí lái, shéi bù lái* below.]

29 **Pín wú běn; fù wú gēn.** 贫无本，富无根。 (lit) Poverty has no stem [and] wealth has no root. (fig) No one is born poor or rich. [Rhyme.]

30 **Pīnzhe yīshēn guǎ, gǎn bǎ huángdì lā xiàmǎ.** 拼着一身剐，敢把皇帝拉下马。 (lit) [One who is] willing to risk death by a thousand cuts [will] dare to unhorse the emperor. (fig) A determined person is capable of doing anything. [Cf. *DRC*, chap. 68; now more commonly said as *shěde yīshēn guǎ*, etc. (q.v.), as used by Mao Zedong during the Cultural Revolution to encourage the Red Guards to attack his rivals and other high level party officials; see also *shěde yīshēn guǎ* and *sǐle lóngpáo* below.]

31 **Pǐ xiāng chū hǎo jiǔ.** 僻乡出好酒。 [The] remote countryside [can] produce good wine. (fig) Talented people can be produced in remote places. [See also *hánmén chū cáizǐ* above and *shēnshān chū jùn niǎo* below.]

32 **Pí zhī bù cún, máo jiāng yān fù.** 皮之不存，毛将焉附。 (lit) With the skin gone, what can the hair adhere to? (fig) A thing cannot exist without its basis. [Originally from the *Zuǒ Zhuàn: Xī Gōng 14 Nián*; quoted by Mao Zedong to mean that the intellectuals, having no independent class status of their own, must attach themselves to the proletariat once the bourgeois class was destroyed.]

33 **Pòcái shì dǎng zāi.** 破财是挡灾。 Losing money will ward off [other] disasters [that might happen to one]. [A superstitious belief; said as (self) consolation; also said *pòcái xiāo zāi*; see also *cái qù*, *shēn ānlè* and *huānxǐ pòcái* above.]

34 **Pò cháo zhīxià, ān yǒu wán luǎn.** 破巢之下，安有完卵。 (lit) Beneath a broken nest, how [can] there be any whole [i.e., unbroken] eggs? (fig) If the base is destroyed, things which depend on it cannot survive. If the group is harmed, the individual can hardly survive. [See also *fù cháo zhīxià* above.]

35 **Pò chē hào lǎn zài.** 破车好揽载。 (lit) [One who drives a] broken cart [always] hopes to take on [more] loads. (fig) There are always people who want to do things beyond their ability.

36 **Pò chuán piān yù dǎtóufēng.** 破船偏遇打头风。 (lit) A leaky boat meets with a head wind. (fig) "Misfortunes never come singly." "It never rains but it pours." [See also *làn chuán piān yù* above and *wū lòu gèng zāo* below.]

37 **Pòchú wànshì wú guò jiǔ.** 破除万事无过酒。 To drive away all [worrisome] matters, there is nothing [which] can surpass wine. [Cf. *JW*, chap. 60; vs. *jiǔ bù jiě* above.]

38 **Pò gǔ, wàn rén chuí.** 破鼓万人捶。 (lit) [A] broken drum [will be] beat[en by] thousands upon thousands of people. (fig) When one is in difficult circumstances, one will be bullied by everyone. [Quoted in *Lǎo Shè Wénjí: Zhào Zǐ Yuè*.]

39 **Pò jiǎn chū jùn é.** 破茧出俊蛾。 (lit) From a damaged cocoon flies out a beautiful moth. (fig) A homely woman may give birth to a handsome child. [See also *lǎo bàng chū míngzhū* above.]

40 **Pò jiā xiànlìng; mièmén cìshǐ.** 破家县令, 灭门刺史。 (lit) A county magistrate [may] ruin a family, [but] a provincial governor [may] execute [an entire] clan. (fig) The higher the official, the more powerful or vicious they are. [Cf. *Xǐngshì Héngyán*, chap. 29; *Rúlín Wàishǐ*, chap. 1.]

41 **Pò jiā zhí wànguàn.** 破家值万贯。 (lit) [Even a] tumbledown home is worth ten thousand strings of cash. (fig) "Be it ever so humble, there's no place like home." [Note: *guàn* refers to a "string" of one thousand copper coins or "cash" strung through the square holes in the middle, used in traditional China.]

42 **Pò mào zhīxià, duō hǎorén.** 破帽之下, 多好人。 (lit) Under shabby hats [are found] many good people. (fig) Don't judge people by their appearances only.

43 **Pò qiáng luàn rén tuī; pò gǔ luàn rén léi.** 破墙乱人推, 破鼓乱人擂。 (lit) A broken wall is pushed by every passerby, [and] a broken drum is beaten by everyone who cares to. (fig) A person who is down and out gets kicked by everyone. [Rhyme; see also *qiáng dǎo zhòngrén tuī* below.]

44 **Pò rén mǎimai yī fàn, rú shā fùmǔ qī-zǐ.** 破人买卖衣饭, 如杀父母妻子。 To destroy [someone's] business [and means of making a] living is like killing [his] parents [and] wife [and] children. [Cf. *WM*, chap. 21; note: *mǎi-mài* means "business" and *(zuò) mǎimai* means "(to do) small business."]

Q

1 **Qiān bān yì xué; qiān qiào nán tōng.** 千般易学; 千窍难通。 It's easy to study a thousand trades, [but] hard to be good at them all. [Vs. *qiān zhāo yào huì* below.]

2 **Qián bù suàn; hòu yào luàn.** 前不算, 后要乱。 Without advance planning, later [things] will be in chaos. [Rhyme.]

3 **Qiáncái bù lòu (yǎn).** 钱财不露 (眼)。 (lit) Never show off [your] wealth ([to the] eyes [of others]). (fig) Don't show off your money. [Also said as *qiáncái bù lòu bái*; see also *cái bù lòubái* and *jīn-yín bù lòubái* above and *zhēn yínzi* below.]

4 **Qiáncái rú fèntǔ; rényì zhí qiānjīn.** 钱财如粪土, 仁义值千金。 Wealth is as [worthless as] dung [and] dirt, [while] benevolence [toward others] is worth a thousand [ounces of] gold. [Cf. *Xǐngshì Héngyán*, chap. 17.]

5 **Qiáncái shì tǎng lái zhī wù.** 钱财是倘来之物。 Money is something that comes by chance.

6 **Qián chē (zhī) fù, hòu chē (zhī) jiàn/jiè.** 前车 (之) 覆, 后车 (之) 鉴/诫。 (lit) The overturned cart ahead [is a] warning [to the] cart behind. (fig) One should learn from the mistakes of others. [Cf. *Fēngshén Yǎnyì*, chap. 80; as a *chengyu: qiánchēzhījiàn*, "lessons drawn from other's mistakes," in *Xúnzǐ: Chéng Xiàng*; see also *qiánrén shìjiǎo* and *qiánrén zhì* and *qián shì bù wàng* and *qián yǒu chē* below; note: *jiànjiè*, "warning, object lesson."]

7 **Qiān chǐ de shuǐ, kàn de qīng; cùn hòu de xīn, kànbutòu.** 千尺的水看得清, 寸厚的心看不透。 (lit) Water [a] thousand feet [deep] can be seen through, [but a] heart [only an] inch thick can't be seen through. (fig) It's difficult to know other people's minds.

8 **Qiān chuān wàn chuān; mǎpì bù chuān.*** 千穿万穿; 马屁不穿。 (lit) Many things [can be seen] through, [but] flattery won't be. (fig) All kinds of pretense can be seen through, but not flattery. Flattery will get you everywhere. [Note: *pái mǎpì*, "to flatter."]

9 **Qiān chuí chéng lìqì; bǎi liàn biàn chún gāng.** 千捶成利器, 百炼变纯钢。 (lit) A sharp weapon must be struck a hundred blows [and] pure steel must be tempered a hundred times. (fig) An able person has to steel and temper himself over and over again. [Note the *chengyu: bǎiliàn-chénggāng*; "be tempered into steel."]

10 **Qiān chuí dǎ luó; yīchuí-dìngyīn.** 千锤打锣, 一锤定音。 (lit) A thousand [people may] beat gongs, [but] the tune is set by one [person only]. (fig) Many may take part in the discussion, but the decision will be made by one person only. [Note: *yīchuí-dìngyīn*, is a set phrase meaning "to have the final word."]

11 **Qiān duǒ táohuā, yī shù shēng.** 千朵桃花, 一树生。 (lit) A thousand peach flowers bloom on one tree. (fig) Children of the same mother should be kind to each other. [Cf. *JPM*, chap. 78.]

12 **Qiān fāng yì dé; yī xiào nán qiú.** 千方易得, 一效难求。 [A] thousand prescriptions are easy [to] get, [but] one effective [one] is difficult to find. (fig) Different problems require different solutions. One cannot simply apply ready-made formulas to every problem.

13 **Qiān fū suǒ zhǐ, wú jí ér sǐ.*** 千夫所指, 无疾而死。 (lit) [If one is] pointed at [by a] thousand people, [although one is] not sick, [one will] die. (fig) It is hard to withstand public opinion. [Note: *qiānfū-suǒzhǐ* is a *chengyu* meaning "(to be) universally condemned"; see also *rén bù jīng bǎi yǔ* below.]

14 **Qiān gāo chēngchuán; yī gāo kào'àn.** 千篙撑船; 一篙靠岸。 (lit) [It may take a] thousand pushes [to] pole [a] boat [forward], [but it still needs] one [final] push to get [it] to shore. (fig) The last effort in the final stages of a project is most important. [Rhyme.]

15 **Qiáng bīn bù yā zhǔ.** 强宾不压主。 (lit) [A] strong guest does not outshine [his] host. (fig) A gentleman does not ride roughshod over others

Q

on their own home territory. [Cf. *R3K*, chap. 13; *WM*, chap. 20.]

16 **Qiāng dǎ chūtóuniǎo.** 枪打出头鸟。(lit) The leading bird is the first to be shot. (fig) Those who stand out are usually the first to be attacked. [Note: *chūtóuniǎo* has become a colloquial expression meaning "outstanding person"; see also *chūtóu chuánzi* and *chū lín sǔnzi* above.]

17 **Qiángdào yánjiē zǒu, wú zāng bù dìngzuì.** 强盗沿街走，无赃不定罪。(Lit) [Even if a] bandit walks along the street, without goods [he stole], [you can]not declare [him] guilty. (fig) Without concrete proof, people cannot be convicted. [See also *dà dào yánjiē* above.]

18 **Qiáng dǎo zhòngrén tuī.** 墙倒众人推。(lit) [When a] wall [is] collapsing, everybody [comes to give it a] push. (fig) Everyone wants to kick someone who is down. [Said of those losing or out of power; cf. *DRC*, chap. 69; see also *pò qiáng luàn rén tuī* above.]

19 **Qiáng jiàng shǒuxià wú ruò bīng.** 强将手下无弱兵。(lit) Under an able general there are no cowardly troops. (fig) An able leader inspires or only employs able followers. [Cf. *Èr Kè Pāi'àn Jīngqí*, chap. 9; *Sān Xiá Wǔ Yì*, chap. 82.]

20 **Qiángjì bùrú shàn wù.** 强记不如善悟。A good memory [or "rote memorization"] is not as [good as] a good [ability to] understand. [Note: *lǐngwù*, "comprehend," and *wùxing*, "power of comprehension; insight."]

21 **Qiáng lǐ kāihuā; qiáng wài xiāng.*** 墙里开花，墙外香 (lit) Flowers bloom inside the walls [but their] fragrance [spreads] outside the walls. (fig) People who are not appreciated in their own place are known and respected in other places. "A prophet is not without honor save in his own country." [Vs. *yuǎn lái de héshang huì niànjīng* below.]

22 **Qiáng lóng bù yā dìtóushé.*** 强龙不压地头蛇。(lit) [A] mighty dragon [can]not crush [a] local snake. (fig) A local despot is difficult to subdue. [Cf. *JW*, chap. 45; see also *è lóng nán dòu* above.]

23 **Qiáng niǔ de guā bù tián.*** 强扭的瓜不甜。(lit) [An unripe] melon forcibly picked [off the vine] is not sweet. (fig) If one forces something, no good result will come of it. Wait until the time is right. [See also *qiǎngpò bù chéng* below.]

24 **Qiǎngpò bù chéng mǎi-mài; qiǎngqiú bù chéng fūqī.*** 强迫不成买卖，强求不成夫妻。No forced business [dealings] can be successful, [just as] no forced marriages will succeed [either]. [See also *kǔnbǎng bù chéng* above.]

25 **Qiáng pò, máquè duō; rén qióng, zāinàn duō.** 墙破麻雀多，人穷灾难多。[Just as] in a broken wall there are more sparrows, [so when] people are poor, [they suffer] more misfortunes.

26 **Qiángtóu lúwěi; tóu zhòng, jiǎo qīng, gēn dī qiǎn.** 墙头芦苇；头重，脚轻，跟低钱。(lit) [When] bullrush reeds grow atop a wall, [they have] heavy tops, light bases, [and their] roots are shallow. (fig) Some people have impressive

sounding titles, but in fact they are not qualified for their positions.

27 **Qiángtóu yī kē cǎo; fēng chuī liǎngbiāndǎo.** 墙头一棵草，风吹两边倒。(lit) A tuft of grass atop a wall, [when the] wind blows, sways in both directions. (fig) One who has no principles just follows the prevailing (political) winds. [Rhyme; note: *qiángtóu cǎo* refers to an indecisive "fence-sitter"; *liǎngbiāndǎo* is now a colloquial expression meaning "to waver between sides."]

28 **Qiáng yǒu fèng; bì yǒu ěr.** 墙有缝，壁有耳。(lit) Walls have cracks [and] walls have ears. (fig) Secret things will eventually leak out. [Cf. *JPM*, chap. 26; see also *gé qiáng yǒu ěr* above.]

29 **Qiáng zhōng háiyǒu qiáng zhōng shǒu; néngrén bèihòu yǒu néngrén.*** 强中还有强中手，能人背后有能人。(lit) Among the strong, there are even stronger ones, [and] behind able people there are [even] abler people. (fig) No matter how good one is, there is always someone better. [Cf. *JW*, chap. 14; *Yuè Fēi Zhuàn*, chap. 46. Note: the two halves are often used independently. The first part is also said as *qiáng zhōng zì yǒu qiáng zhōng shǒu*; see also *néngrén zhīwài* above and *rén wài yǒu rén* and *shān wài yǒu shān* and *shé tūn shǔ* and *yǐ wù xiáng yǐ wù* below.]

30 **Qiānjīn bù sǐ; bǎi jīn bù xíng.** 千金不死，百金不刑。[Pay a] thousand [ounces of] gold, [and you will] not die; [pay a] hundred [ounces of] gold, [and you will] not [be] punish[ed]. [Refers to the corruptibility of judges in traditional China.]

31 **Qiānjīn de gǔniú, yě yào dītóu hē shuǐ.** 千斤的牯牛，也要低头喝水。(lit) Even a bull of a thousand catties has to lower its head to drink water. (fig) However able a person may be, one sometimes has to "lower oneself" to ask others for help. [Note: literally, one *jīn* or "catty" is equal to one-half kilogram, but *qiānjīn* is figuratively taken to mean "a ton; a great weight."]

32 **Qiānjīn mǎi chǎn; bābǎi mǎi lín.*** 千金买产，八百买邻。(lit) [If you spend one] thousand catties [of gold to] buy [real] estate, eight hundred [of them should be spent on] obtaining good neighbors. (fig) Good neighbors are most important. [Note: *fángdi chǎn*, "real estate"; technically one *jīn* or "catty" equals one-half kilogram, but here *qiānjīn* means "a lot of money"; see also *bǎiwàn mǎi zhái* and *fángzi hǎo zhù* above and *qiān qián mǎi lín* and *xuǎnzé fángwū* below.]

33 **Qiānjīn nán mǎi huítóu kàn.** 千金难买回头看。(lit) A thousand [ounces of] gold cannot purchase [the benefits of] hindsight. (fig) Experience is most valuable. [Note: see the preceding entry.]

34 **Qiānjīn nán mǎi lǎolái shòu.** 千金难买老来瘦。(lit) A thousand [ounces of] gold cannot buy slenderness in old age. (fig) Slenderness in old age is a blessing.

35 **Qiānjīn nán mǎi liǎng tóngxīn.** 千金难买两同心。(lit) A thousand [ounces of] gold can hardly purchase two people of the same mind. (fig) A kindred spirit is hard to find. [Cf. *Xǐngshì Héngyán*,

chap. 9; see also *qián qián nán mǎi yī gè yuàn* below.]

36 **Qiānjīn nán mǎi wáng rén bǐ.** 千金难买亡人笔。 A thousand [ounces of] gold can hardly purchase the calligraphy of one's dear departed [which is most precious]. [Cf. *Gǔ-Jīn Xiǎoshuō*, chap. 10.]

37 **Qiānjīn nán mǎi yīkǒuqì.** 千金难买一口气。 (lit) A thousand [ounces of] gold cannot buy one breath of life. (fig) Life is the most precious thing.

38 **Qiānjīn nán mǎi yī xiào.*** 千金难买一笑。 (lit) A thousand [ounces of] gold can hardly purchase a smile. (fig) A fair lady's smile is most precious. Beautiful women are hard to please. [Originally referring to the concubine of the last emperor of the Shang dynasty Zhou Wang; cf. *Dōng Zhōu Lièguó Zhì*, chap. 2; *DRC*, chap. 31; also said *yī xiào zhí qiān jīn*.]

39 **Qián jìn, qíngyì jué.*** 钱尽，情义绝。[When] money is used up, friendship ends. [See also *qián jù rúxiōng* below.]

40 **Qiānjīn zhī qiú, fēi yī hú zhī yè.** 千金之裘，非一狐之腋。 (lit) A [fox fur] robe worth a thousand [ounces of] gold is not [made from the fur of just] one fox's armpit. (fig) The success of a great cause depends on the cooperation of many people. [Cf. *Shǐ Jì: Liú Jìng Shū Sǔn Tōng Lièzhuàn*; see also *qiān yáng zhī pí* below.]

41 **Qiān jūn yì dé; yī jiàng nán qiú.*** 千军易得，一将难求。 It is easy to get a thousand soldiers, but hard to find one good general. [Cf. *Dōng Zhōu Lièguó Zhì*, chap. 46; *R3K*, chap. 70.]

42 **Qián jù rúxiōng; qián sàn rú bēn.** 钱聚如兄，钱散如奔。 (lit) [When one has] money, [people] flock [to one] like brothers; [when one's] money is gone, [people] flee [from one]. (fig) When you are rich, people flock to you and respect you; when you are poor, people flee when you come. "Nobody knows you when you're down and out." [Note: *rúxiōng*, "elder sworn brother"; see also *mén qián shuānzhe* and *pín jū nàoshì* and *qián jìn, qíngyì jué* above and *yǒuqián yǒu jiǔ* below.]

43 **Qián kě tōng shén.*** 钱可通神。 (lit) Money can get through to the gods. (fig) With money one can accomplish anything. "Money makes the mare go." [Also said *qián néng tōng shén* in *Xǐngshì Yīnyuán Zhuàn*, chap. 1; see also *cái dòng rénxīn* above and *qián tōng shén lù* and *yǒuqián néng shǐ guǐ* below.]

44 **Qiān lǐ dā cháng péng, méiyǒu bú sàn de yánxí.** 千里搭长棚，没有不散的筵席。 (lit) [Even if you] put up [temporary] pavilions [to entertain guests stretching] for a thousand miles, [nevertheless] no feast will last forever. (fig) "All good things must come to an end." [See also *liú jūn qiān rì* above and *shèngyàn bì sàn* and *sòng jūn qiān lǐ* and *tiānxià wú bù sàn* below.]

45 **Qiānlǐmǎ yě yǒu yī juě.** 千里马也有一蹶。 (lit) Even a horse [which can run a] thousand leagues [per day] may stumble once. (fig) However able one may be, one may sometimes make mistakes; "even Homer sometimes nods." [Note: *qiānlǐmǎ*

is equivalent to "winged steed"; one *lǐ* technically equals one-half kilometer.]

46 **Qiān lǐ sòng émáo; lǐ qīng, rén yì (/ qíngyì) zhòng.*** 千里送鹅毛，礼轻仁意(/情意)重。 (lit) [When] a goose feather is sent a thousand miles, the gift is light, but the sentiment is heavy. (fig) A gift itself may be small, but the goodwill (or sentiment) it represents is heavy. [Often said by the giver of a gift; cf. *Érnǚ Yīngxióng Zhuàn*, chap. 38; *Jìnghuā Yuàn*. chap. 50; also said as a chengyu: *qiān lǐ é máo, (lǐ qīng, yì zhòng)*.]

47 **Qián liú sān bù, hǎo zǒu; hòu liú sān bù, hǎo xíng.** 前留三步好走，后留三步好行。 (lit) Leave three steps [space] both in front and behind, [and you'll] walk more freely. (fig) It is best to leave some leeway in everything one does.

48 **Qiān lǐ yīnyuán, yī xiàn qiān.*** 千里姻缘一线牵。 (lit) [Two beings] destined to marry each other, [though] a thousand miles apart, are joined by a single string. (fig) A thousand miles can't keep apart a couple that are fated to wed: their lives and destinies are tied by a long and invisible thread. [Cf. *DRC*, chap. 57; *JW*, chap. 54; see also *shì yīnyuán* and *yīnyuán, yīnyuán* below.]

49 **Qiān lǐ zhī dī; kuì yú yíxué.*** 千里之堤，溃于蚁穴。 (lit) A thousand-league long dike [can] collapse because of an ant hole. (fig) Slight negligence may lead to great disaster; "a small leak can sink a great ship." [Cf. *Hán Fēizǐ: Yù Lǎo*; note: traditionally one *lǐ* equals approximately one-half of a kilometer.]

50 **Qiān lǐ zhī xíng, shǐ yú zú xià.** 千里之行，始于足下。 (lit) [A] thousand league's journey begins from under [one's] foot. (fig) The most difficult part of any task is getting started. "A journey of a thousand miles begins with a single step." [Cf. *Lǎozǐ*, *Dào Dé Jīng*, chap. 64, in which this line follows the line *jiǔ céng zhī tái qǐ yú lěi tǔ* (q.v.); one *lǐ* equals approximately one-half kilometer.]

51 **Qiān mài, wàn mài; shéběn bù mài.** 千卖万卖，折本不卖。 [One can] sell [something under virtually] any circumstances, except selling at a loss.

52 **Qiān nián de yězhū, lǎohǔ de shí.** 千年的野猪，老虎的食。 (lit) A thousand-year-old boar [is] a tiger's meal. (fig) Sooner or later, the weaker fall prey to the more powerful. [Cf. *Dàng Kòu Zhì*, chap. 104.]

53 **Qiān nián tiándì, bābǎi zhǔ.** 千年田地，八百主。 (lit) [There have been] eight hundred owners of the land in a thousand years. (fig) The owners (or farmers) of the land keep changing. [Cf. *JPM*, chap. 71; see also *tián shì zhǔrén* below.]

54 **Qiān nián wényuē huì shuō huà.** 千年文约会说话。 (lit) A thousand-year-old contract will speak [the truth]. (fig) Contracts are valid proof, however long ago they were signed; written documents are good proof. [Note: *wénzì de píngyù*, "written proof," and *qìyuē*, "contract."]

Q

55 **Qiānniú, yào qiān bí/niúbízi.** 牵牛，要牵鼻/牛鼻子。 (lit) To lead an ox, [you] have to lead [it by the] nose. (fig) In order to solve a problem, one must seize it at a vital point. [See also *chī lì yào bōpí* above.]

56 **Qiān qián mǎi lín; bābǎi mǎi shè.** 千钱买邻，八百买舍。 (lit) One thousand cash buys a [good] neighbor, [while it only takes] eight hundred to buy a house. (fig) When buying a house, choosing one's neighbors is more important than choosing the house itself. [Note: *qián* refers to copper coins or "cash" used in traditional China; see also *bǎiwàn mǎi zhái* and *qiānjīn mǎi chǎn* above and *xuǎnzé fángwū* below.]

57 **Qiān qián nán mǎi yī gè yuàn.** 千钱难买一个愿。 (lit) A thousand cash cannot purchase the same mind. (fig) A kindred spirit is hard to find. [See also *qiānjīn nán mǎi liǎng* above and the previous entry.]

58 **Qiān qián shē bùrú bābǎi xiàn.** 千钱赊不如八百现。 (lit) Better eight hundred in hand than a thousand on credit. (fig) "A bird in the hand is worth two in the bush." [Cf. *Xǐngshì Héngyán*, chap. 20; see also *duō dé bùrú* above.]

59 **Qián qiàn wèi qīng; miǎn kāi zūn kǒu.** 前欠未清，免开尊口。 [While] former debts still [are] not cleared, [one should] not open [one's] "venerable mouth" [to ask for another loan]. [Said sarcastically; note: *miǎnkāizūnkǒu* has become an idiom meaning something like "no comments, please."]

60 **Qián qīn; rén bù qīn.** 钱亲，人不亲。 (lit) Money is dear; people are not. (fig) Money is dearer than relatives.

61 **Qiān qiú bùrú yī xià.** 千求不如一吓。 A thousand pleas are not as [effective as] one threat.

62 **Qiān rén nuònuò bùrú yī shì è'è.** 千人喏喏不如一士咢咢。 Better to have one [scholar] argue [with you] than a thousand people agree [with you]. [Advice to a wise ruler; cf. *Shǐ Jì: Shāng Jūn Lièzhuàn*.]

63 **Qiān rén qiān píqì; wàn rén wàn múyàng.** 千人千脾气，万人万模样。 [In] one thousand people, each one [has a different] temperament; [and in] ten thousand people, each one [has a different] appearance.

64 **Qiánrén sǎ tǔ, míle hòurén yǎn.** 前人洒土，迷了后人眼。 (lit) The dirt scattered by [one's] forebears blurs the sight of [the] descendants. (fig) Later generations must bear the consequences of the wrongs done by their ancestors. [Cf. *DRC*, chap. 72; *Érnǚ Yīngxióng Zhuàn*, chap. 12.]

65 **Qiánrén shījiǎo; hòurén bǎ huá.** 前人失脚，后人把滑。 (lit) [If the] one in front loses [his] footing, the one behind [will] mind his step. (fig) It is wise to draw a lesson from others' mistakes. [Cf. *Gǔ Yáoyàn*, chap. 49; see also *qián chē zhī fù* above and *qiánrén zhì* below.]

66 **Qiān rén suǒ zhǐ, wú bìng ér sǐ.** 千人所指，无病而死。 (lit) When everybody points their fingers at a [bad] person, [he or she], although not sick, will die. (fig) If one commits bad acts or goes against social conventions one will not have a happy life.

67 **Qiánrén tiántǔ; hòurén shōu.** 前人田土, 后人收。 (lit) [The] ancestors farm lands; [their] descendants harvest. (fig) Wealth acquired by ancestors is enjoyed by their descendants. [See also *qiánrén zāishù* below.]

68 **Qiánrén zāishù; hòurén chéngliáng.*** 前人栽树，后人乘凉。 (lit) The forebears plant the trees, [and] their descendants enjoy the shade. (fig) One generation plants the trees under which another takes its ease. Later generations (will) reap the benefits of their forebears' efforts. [Now also said *qiánrén zhòng shù*, etc.; see also *qiánrén tiántǔ* above.]

69 **Qiánrén zhì; hòurén jiè.** 前人踬，后人戒。 (lit) [If the] one in front stumbles, the one behind takes heed. (fig) It is wise to learn a lesson from others' mistakes. [Cf. *Gǔ Yáoyàn*, chap. 35; see also *qián chē zhī fù* and *qiánrén shījiǎo* above.]

70 **Qiān rì kǎnchái, yī rì shāo.** 千日砍柴，一日烧。 (lit) Collect firewood for a thousand days, [but] burn it in one day. (fig) Long preparations are necessary against one day's use. [Also said *qiān tiān kǎnchái . . .*, or *qiān rì dǎchái . . .* etc.; see also *yǎngbīng qiān rì* below.]

71 **Qián sānshí nián shuì bù xǐng; hòu sānshí nián shuì bù zháo.** 前三十年睡不醒，后三十年睡不着。 (lit) [If during one's] first thirty years [one] sleeps too much, [then during one's] last thirty years [one will] not be able to sleep. (fig) If one wastes the first thirty years of one's life, it will be too late to accomplish anything in the second thirty years. One should be diligent during one's youth. [See also *hēi fà bù zhī* above and *shàozhuàng bù nǔlì* below.]

72 **Qián shēng qián; lì gǔn lì.** 钱生钱，利滚利。 Money begets money; interest compounds interest.

73 **Qián shì bù wàng; hòushì zhī shī.*** 前事不忘，后事之师。 (lit) [If] previous experiences are not forgotten, [they can be] teachers for later matters. (fig) Past experience, if not forgotten, is a guide for the future. [Cf. *Zhànguó Cè: Zhào Cè Yī*; *Shǐ Jì: Qín Shǐ Huáng Běn Jì*; see also *qián yǒu chē* below.]

74 **Qián shì rén zhī dǎn; cái shì fù zhī miáo.** 钱是人之胆，财是富之苗。 (lit) Money is a person's courage; assets are the source of riches. (fig) A person with money is bold; a person of means will get richer. [Cf. *Sān Xiá Wǔ Yì*, chap. 96.]

75 **Qiǎn shuǐ yānsǐ rén; píng lù diē sǐ mǎ.** 浅水淹死人，平路跌死马。 (lit) Shallow water drowns people, [and] flat roads [can] trip [up and] kill horses. (fig) One should always be careful, so as not to suffer the unexpected. [See also *quàn jūn mò dǎ* and *zǒu píng lù* below.]

76 **Qiān suàn, wàn suàn bùrú lǎotiān yī suàn.** 千算万算不如老天一算。 (lit) Thousands upon thousands [of human] plans are not equal to one of Heaven's plans. (fig) Whatever human minds intend, it's Heaven that decides the end; "man proposes, heaven disposes." [Rhyme; also said qiān suàn, wàn suàn, bùjì tiān suàn; see also móushì zài rén above and shì dà, shì xiǎo and tiān suàn bù yóu below.]

77 **Qián tōng shén lù.** 钱通神路。 (lit) Money opens the way to heaven. (fig) Money will move the gods. "Money makes the mare go." [See also qián kě tōng shén above and tiānxià wú nánshì below.]

78 **Quántou shàng wú yǎn.** 拳头上无眼。 (lit) On fists there are no eyes. (fig) In fights someone may be seriously hurt (by accident).

79 **Qiān xū bù dǐ yī shí.** 千虚不抵一实。 A thousand empty [promises] are not worth one true [deed]. [Cf. Jīngshì Tōngyán, chap. 3.]

80 **Qiān yáng zhī pí, bùrú yī hú zhī yè.** 千羊之皮不如一狐之腋。 (lit) A thousand pieces of sheep's skin are not worth one [special piece of] fox's fur. (fig) A thousand ordinary people are not worth one able person. [Cf. Shǐ Jì: Zhào Shì Jiā; note: yè refers to the fur taken from the armpits of foxes, highly prized and used to make hú pí dàyī, coats made from strips of this fur; see also qiānjīn zhī qiú above.]

81 **Qiān yán hǎo gè rén; yī yán nǎo gè rén.** 千言好个人，一言恼个人。 (lit) [It takes a] thousand words [to] make a friend, [but only] one word [to] offend someone. [Rhyme; see nǎonu, "to be angry, offended."]

82 **Qián (yào) yòng zài dāokǒu shàng.** 钱(要)用在刀口上。 (lit) Money [should be] used on the edge of the knife. (fig) One should spend one's money where it counts; don't be stingy on important matters. [Cf. Guānchǎng Xiànxíng Jì, chap. 25; see also yǒu gāng shǐ zài below.]

83 **Qiān yī fà ér dòng quánshēn.*** 牵一发而动全身。 (lit) Pull one hair and the whole body moves. (fig) Touching one small part will affect the whole. One slight move can affect the whole situation. [Originally a line by the Qing dynasty poet Gong Zizhen; qiānyīfà ér dòngquánshēn has become a fixed phrase.]

84 **Qián yǒu chē; hòu yǒu zhé.*** 前有车，后有辙。 (lit) [If in] front there is a cart, behind [it] there [must] be tracks. (fig) One can learn from the previous example of others. [See also qián chē zhī fù above and qián shì bù wàng below.]

85 **Qiān zhàng máshéng zǒng yàoyǒu yī gè jié.** 千丈麻绳总要有一个结。 (lit) However long it may be, a rope needs a knot. (fig) (pun) Everything eventually has an ending, no matter how long it lasts. [Cf. Zàishēng Yuán, chap. 58; jié means both "knot" and "ending."]

86 **Qiān zhāo yào huì; yī zhāo yào hǎo.** 千招要会，一招要好。 [One] should be a jack-of-all-trades as well as a master of one. [Vs. qiān bān yì xué above.]

87 **Qiān zhōng yǒu tóu; wàn zhōng yǒu wěi.** 千中有头，万中有尾。 (lit) In a thousand [things] there is a beginning; in ten thousand [things] there is an end. (fig) (1) Everything has a beginning and an ending. (2) In every group there must be a leader (and followers).

88 **Qiān zhǔzhāng, wàn zhǔzhāng; huángjīn nán mǎi zì zhǔzhāng.** 千主张，万主张；黄金难买自主张。 (lit) [There may be] thousands upon thousands of opinions, [but forming one's] own opinions [upon which to make a decision is as] difficult [as getting] gold. (fig) Forming one's own opinions is difficult but necessary. [Rhyme.]

89 **"Qiàn" zì yā rén tóu.** "欠"字压人头。 (lit) The word "owe" weighs on a person's head. (fig) If one is in debt, one can't hold one's head up. [Cf. Wǔ Sōng, chap. 2; note: the Chinese character 欠 qiàn "owe" has the character 人 rén "person" as its lower component.]

90 **Qiāo bīng, shuǐ yě dòng; dǎshuǐ, yú tóutòng.** 敲冰水也动，打水鱼头痛。 (lit) [When one] breaks the ice, the water [beneath will] also move; [when one] draws water, the fish [will get] headaches. (fig) There are interconnections between things which mutually influence one another. [Rhyme; note: dǎshuǐ, (lit) "to hit water," means "to draw water."]

91 **Qiǎo cáifeng shǒuxià wú suì bù.** 巧裁缝手下无碎布。 (lit) Under the hands of a skilled tailor, there are no leftover [pieces of] cloth. (fig) A true expert can make full use of everything without wasting anything.

92 **Qiǎofù nánwei wú mǐ zhī chuī.*** 巧妇难为无米之炊。 (lit) [Even] the clever[est] housewife is hard pressed to cook a meal without rice. (fig) You can't make something out of nothing; "one can't make bricks without straw." [Said of the clever wife Wang Xihong in DRC, chap. 24; cf. Gǔ-Jīn Xiǎoshuō; chap. 8; note: wúmǐzhīchuī has become a set expression equivalent to "make bricks without straw." See also měng jiāngjūn wú above.]

93 **Qiǎogàn néng bǔ xióngshī; mángàn nán zhuō xīshuài.** 巧干能捕雄狮，蛮干难捉蟋蟀。 [If one] works skillfully, [one] can catch [a] lion, [but if one] acts rashly, it is difficult to catch [even a] cricket.

94 **Qiáo guī qiáo; lù guī lù.*** 桥归桥，路归路。 (lit) A bridge is a bridge [and] a road is a road. (fig) Different matters should be dealt with according to their categories. Don't "confuse apples with oranges."

95 **Qiāoluó dǎ zhōng; gè guǎn yī gōng.** 敲锣打钟，各管一工。 [One] beats the gong [and the other] tolls the bell; individuals have their own duties. [Rhyme.]

96 **Qiāoluó, mài táng; gè gàn yī háng.** 敲锣卖糖，各干一行。 (lit) [You] beat [your] gong [and I will] sell [my] candies. (fig) People should stick to their own duties and responsibilities and not stick their noses into others' affairs. "You do your job and I'll do mine." [Rhyme.]

Q

97 **Qiàomén mǎn dì pǎo; kàn nǐ zhǎo bù zhǎo.** 窍门满地跑，看你找不找。(lit) The key [to any problem maybe] found anywhere; it's up to you to find it. (fig) There's always a way to solve a problem, it all depends on whether one has the knack of finding it or not. [Rhyme.]

98 **Qiǎo qī cháng bàn zhuō fū mián.*** 巧妻常伴拙夫眠。A clever wife often [gets] paired up sleeping [with a] clumsy husband. [Cf. WM, chap. 24.]

99 **Qiǎoshǒu nán shǐ liǎng gēn zhēn.** 巧手难使两根针。(lit) [Even a] skilled tailor can't use two needles [at one time]. (fig) There are limits to everyone's abilities, no matter how clever he or she may be.

100 **Qiào suǒ dào mǎ shǔ cáizhì; diàotóu bùgù shì cōngming.** 撬锁盗马属才智，掉头不顾是聪明。Prying open locks [and] stealing horses [may be] reckoned as smart, [but to] turn [one's] head [away and] ignore [such things] is [truly] intelligent.

101 **Qiǎoyán bùrú zhídào.** 巧言不如直道。Beating around the bush is not as good as straight talk. [Cf. Sān Kè Pāi'àn Jīngqí, chap. 26; note: qiǎoyán, "cunning (or deceitful) talk."]

102 **Qiǎo zhà bùrú zhuō chéng.** 巧诈不如拙诚。(lit) It is better to be simplistically honest than cleverly deceitful. (fig) One shouldn't try to "play games" with people. [Cf. Hán Fēizǐ: Shuō Lín Shàng.]

103 **Qiǎo zhě duō láo, zhuō zhě xián.** 巧者多劳，拙者闲。The able always do more [while] the incompetent stay idle. [Cf. JW, chap. 46; see also néng zhě duō láo above.]

104 **Qiǎo zhōng shuōhuà; qiǎo zhōng yǒu rén.** 巧中说话，巧中有人。[It often happens that] just when you're speaking [derogatorily about someone] by coincidence that person appears [and hears what you are saying]. (fig) "Speak of the devil (and he appears)." [Cf. Wǔ Sōng, chap. 2; see also shuōdào Cáo Cāo below.]

105 **Qí bù kàn sān bù, bù niē zǐr.** 棋不看三步，不捏子儿。(lit) [In a] chess [game] [if you can]not see [ahead] three moves, don't touch the chess pieces. (fig) Before one takes any action, one should think through the consequences thoroughly. [Note: qízǐ, "chess pieces"; see also the following entry.]

106 **Qí cuò yī zhāo; mǎnpán jiē shū.*** 棋错一招，满盘皆输。[In a] chess [game] one wrong move [and the] whole game [will be] lost. (fig) One wrong step can cause complete failure or serious loss. [Cf. Gǔ-Jīn Xiǎoshuō, chap. 2; see also yī zhāo bùshèn below.]

107 **Qī dà liǎng, huángjīn rìrì zhǎng; qī dà sān, huángjīn jī rú shān.** 妻大两，黄金日日长，妻大三，黄金积如山。[If the] wife is two years older [than her husband], gold accumulates with each passing day; [if the] wife is three years older, gold piles up as high as a hill. [Cf. JPM, chap. 7; this pair of rhymed couplets expresses a traditional belief that older women are more prudent.]

108 **Qiézi bù kāi xū huā; yànyǔ dōu shì shíhuà.** 茄子不开虚花，谚语都是实话。(lit) [Just as] eggplants do not have non-bearing blossoms, [so] all proverbs are true [to life]. (fig) Every proverb is rooted in experience and has practical application. [See also huācǎo shēng above.]

109 **Qī fēn luó-gǔ, sānfēn chàng.** 七分锣鼓，三分唱。(lit) [A good Chinese opera performance is] seventy percent [accompanying] gongs [and] drums [and] thirty percent singing. (fig) One cannot accomplish anything without the support of others. [Compare sānfēn luó-gǔ below; see also héhuā suī hǎo above and yī gè líba below.]

110 **Qí gāo yī zhāo, fù shǒu fù jiǎo.** 棋高一着，缚手缚脚。(lit) A better chess player [can] bind [his opponent] hand and foot. (fig) Someone superior in skill can stymie his or her opponent. [Cf. Èr Kè Pāi'àn Jīngqí, chap. 2; note: gāo yī zhāo, (lit) "better (by) one move."]

111 **Qí hǔ zhě, shìbude xià.*** 骑虎者，势不得下。(lit) [One who] rides a tiger is hard put to dismount. (fig) Once one is in a difficult situation, it is difficult to extricate oneself. [More commonly as a chengyu: qí hǔ nán xià.]

112 **Qì kě gǔ ér bùkě xiè.** 气可鼓而不可泄。Morale should be boosted, not dampened. [Mao Zedong said this to guide communist propaganda work.]

113 **Qī kǒuzi dāngjiā; bā kǒuzi zhǔshì.** 七口子当家，八口子主事。(lit) Seven people [act as] family heads [and] eight people [act as] leaders (in an organization). (fig) "Too many cooks spoil the broth." [See also rén duō, shǒu zá below.]

114 **Qí lǘ bù zhī gǎnjiǎo de kǔ.** 骑驴不知赶脚的苦。(lit) [One who] rides a donkey [does] not know the hardship of the donkey driver [who] follows along on foot. (fig) One in a favorable situation has no idea of the hardships of one who is not. [See also bǎo hàn bù zhī above.]

115 **Qīn bāng qīn; lín bāng lín; (héshang wéihù chūjiā rén).** 亲帮亲，邻帮邻，(和尚维护出家人)。(lit) Relatives help relatives, neighbors help neighbors, ([and] monks protect monks). (fig) People help their own kind. [Note: chūjiā, (lit) "leave home," means to become a Buddhist monk or nun; the second part is usually omitted.]

116 **Qīn bù guò fùmǔ; jìn bù guò fūqī.*** 亲不过父母，近不过夫妻。No one is as dear as [one's] parents, nor as close as husband [and] wife.

117 **Qīn bù jiàn shū; hòu bù jiàn xiān.** 亲不间疏，后不僭先。Close relatives and friends [can]not be separated [by] distant ones, [and] new [friends can]not replace old [ones]. (fig) Close relatives and friends come before distant ones, and old friendships before new ones. One must always observe traditional social protocol in dealing with people and things. [Cf. DRC, chap. 20; more commonly shū bù jiàn qīn, etc. (q.v.); note: jiàn is a verb, "to create a gap"; see jiàngé, "separate"; see also qīn zhě gé zhī below.]

118 **Qīn bù qīn, shì xiāngdǎng.** 亲不亲，是乡党。 [Whether they are] relatives or not, people from the same province [are dear to each other]. [See also *qīn xiàng qīn* and *rén bù qīn* below.]

119 **Qīn bù zé gǔròu; hèn bù jì jiù chóu.** 亲不择骨肉，恨不记旧仇。 (lit) [In] loving, [do] not distinguish between [your] dear ones; [in] hating [do] not remember old enmities. (fig) All [one's] relatives are dear [and] all personal enemies are forgivable. [Vs. *jūnzǐ bù niàn*.]

120 **Qīngchūn bù zài.*** 青春不再。 [One's] youth never returns. [See also the following entry.]

121 **Qīngchūn yì guò; báifà nán ráo.*** 青春易过，白发难饶。 (lit) [The] springtime [of one's life] passes quickly [and] gray hair is hard to avoid. (fig) Youth passes quickly and old age comes all to soon. [See also *rénshēng jǐ jiàn* below and the preceding entry.]

122 **Qīng chūyú lán ér shèngyú lán.*** 青出于蓝而胜于蓝。 (lit) Indigo comes from blue, but it surpasses blue. (fig) The student (often) excels his teacher. The younger generation surpasses the older generation. [Cf. *Xúnzǐ: Quàn Xué Piàn*; note: *qīngchūyúlán* has become a set phrase idiom with the metaphorical meaning of "the pupil surpasses the teacher."]

123 **Qíng dài yǔsǎn; bǎo dài gānliáng.** 晴带雨伞，饱带干粮。 (lit) [When setting out on a trip, even when the weather is] fine, carry an umbrella [with you, and even when you are] not hungry, carry dried food [with you]. (fig) Always be prepared for the unpredictable.

124 **Qíng dài yǔsǎn, bǎo dài jī liáng.** 晴带雨伞，饱带饥粮。 (lit) Take an umbrella when [the weather is] fine and extra rations when you are full. (fig) Where there is precaution, there is no danger; preparedness prevents peril. [See also *qíng gān kāi shuǐdào* below.]

125 **Qīngdí bì bài.** 轻敌必败。 [One who] underestimates the enemy is doomed to failure. [Cf. *Wǔ Sōng*, chap. 6.]

126 **Qìngfǔ bù sǐ, Lǔ nàn wèi yǐ.** 庆父不死，鲁难未已。 (lit) Until Qingfu is done away with, the crisis in the state of Lu will not be over. (fig) There will always be trouble until the one who stirs it up is removed. [Cf. *Zuǒ Zhuàn: Míng Gōng Yuán Nián*; note: *Qìngfǔ* refers to an usurper in the state of Lu in the Spring and Autumn period.]

127 **Qíng gān bùkěn zǒu, zhǐ dài yǔ lín tóu.** 晴干不肯走，只待雨淋头。 (lit) [It is unwise] not to leave [when it is] clear and dry, [but to] wait [and get] drenched in the rain. (fig) If one does not act appropriately at the right time, one will encounter difficulties later. [Rhyme; cf. *Fēngshén Yǎnyì*, chap. 33; *Gǔ-Jīn Xiǎoshuō*, chap. 1; see also *tiān qíng bùkěn* below.]

128 **Qíng gān kāi shuǐdào, xū fáng bàoyǔ shí.** 晴干开水道，须防暴雨时。 (lit) [When it's] clear [and] dry digging drainage ditches is necessary [in order to] guard against times of downpour. (fig) One should make preparations early against disasters later on. [See also *qíng dài yǔsǎn* above and *tiān qíng bù kāi gōu* below.]

129 **Qīngguān nán chū huá lì shǒu.** 清官难出猾吏手。 Honest officials can't avoid [being deceived and fooled by their] sly subordinates' (hands). [Cf. *Hé Diǎn*, chap. 5; see also *shàngmíng bù zhī* below.]

130 **Qīngguān nán duàn jiāwù shì.*** 清官难断家务事。 (lit) [Even an] honest official is hard put to adjudicate domestic cases. (fig) Family disputes are the hardest to resolve. [Cf. *DRC*, chap. 80; see also *hútuzhàng hǎo suàn* above and *wàirén nán guǎn* below.]

131 **Qǐng guǐ róngyì; sòng guǐ nán.** 请鬼容易，送鬼难。 (lit) To invoke devils is easy, [but to] get rid of them is difficult. (fig) It is easier to invite trouble than it is to get rid of it. [Also said *qǐng shén róngyì; sòng shén nán*, "To invoke spirits is easy," etc.]

132 **Qǐng jiàng bùrú jījiàng.** 请将不如激将。 (lit) Inviting a warrior is not as [effective as] provoking him. (fig) To a warrior a provocation is more effective than an invitation. If you really want to arouse people, get them angry. [Said by Piggy in *JW*, chap. 31; note the expression *jījiàngfǎ*, "goading someone into action by ridicule, sarcasm, etc."; see also *quàn jiàng bùrú* below.]

133 **Qǐngjiào biérén bù shíběn; shétou dǎ gè gǔn.** 请教别人不蚀本，舌头打个滚。 (lit) To consult others costs [one] nothing [but the effort of] rolling [one's] tongue. [Technically a rhyme; see also *jiào rén bù shíběn* above.]

134 **Qìngjia péngyou yuǎn lái xiāng.** 亲家朋友远来香。 (lit) Friends [and] relatives [kept] at a distance smell better. (fig) Relationships go smoother if one preserves some distance from one's relatives and friends. [See also *qīnqi yuǎnlí xiāng* and *xiāngjiàn yì dé* below.]

135 **Qīng jiǔ hóng rén miàn; cáibó dòng rénxīn.** 清酒红人面，财帛动人心。 [Just as] clear liquor [can] redden people's faces, [so] wealth [can] influence people's minds. [Cf. *Xǐngshì Yīnyuán Zhuàn*, chap. 12; *Èr Kè Pāi'àn Jīngqí*, chap. 28.]

136 **Qǐngkè chī jiǔ, liáng jiādàng.** 请客吃酒，量家当。 [When] entertaining guests with food and drink, [do so] according [to your] economic conditions. [Cf. *Xǐngshì Yīnyuán Zhuàn*, chap. 18.]

137 **Qīngmíng bù chāi xù, dào lǎo bùchéngqì.** 清明不拆絮，到老不成器。 [Anyone who has] not taken off [his] cotton [padded winter] clothing [(for regular spring cleaning), and not gone out to begin working in the fields by the time of] Qing Ming [Festival, usually the fourth or fifth lunar month in spring], is [obviously spoiled or lazy and will] accomplish nothing great in later life. [Note: *bùchéngqì* is an idiom for "good-for-nothing; worthless."]

138 **Qíng mò duō wàng; kǒu mò duō yán.** 情莫多妄；口莫多言。 (lit) [One's] affections should not be overly indulged in; [just as one's] mouth [should] not be overly talkative. (fig) One should be reserved in both behavior and speech.

Q

139 **Qīng ná níqiu, zhòng zhuō yú.** 轻拿泥鳅，重捉鱼。(lit) [In catching a] loach, hold [it] lightly; [in catching a] fish, hold [it] tightly. (fig) Different problems should be dealt with in different ways. [Note: a loach is an eel-like fish.]

140 **Qīng rén hái zì qīng.** 轻人还自轻。To show no respect for others is to show no respect for oneself. [See also *yǔ rén fāngbiàn* below.]

141 **Qíng shēn, gōngjìng shǎo; zhījǐ tánxiào duō.** 情深恭敬少，知己谈笑多。(lit) [When] friendship [is] deep, formalities are few; [for] close confidants, chats [and] laughter are many. (fig) Intimate friends don't stand on ceremony.

142 **Qǐng yī, xū qǐng liáng; chuán yào, xū chuán fāng.** 请医须请良，传药须传方。(lit) [When you] need a doctor, get a good one, [when you] need medicine, get the prescription [for it as well so you'll be able to get more of it later]. (fig) Don't just do or study things by rote, but learn the principles or reasons behind them. [Rhyme; cf. *JPM*, chap. 49.]

143 **Qíng yuè shū, lǐ yuè duō.** 情越疏，礼越多。The more distant the relationship [between two people], the more formality [is required].

144 **Qín Huì háiyǒu sān gè xiānghǎode.** 秦桧还有三个相好的。(lit) Even Qin Kui, [the traitor minister of the Song dynasty] had three good [friends]. (fig) Even evil people have friends. [Note: the name of *Qín Kuì* (1090–1155), the execrated capitulationist of the Song dynasty, has become, like that of Quisling, synonymous with treachery.]

145 **Qín hǔ yì; zòng hǔ nán.** 擒虎易，纵虎难。(lit) Capturing [a] tiger is easy, [but] releasing one [may cause] difficulties (because it will take revenge). (fig) Before one releases an enemy, one had better consider the consequences. [Also said *zhuō hǔ róngyì; fàng hǔ nán* and *fú hǔ zé yì; zòng hǔ zé nán*; see also *fānghǔ-guīshān* above.]

146 **Qín mā dài chū lǎn érzi.** 勤妈带出懒儿子。(lit) A diligent mother brings up a lazy son. (fig) Often because the mother is hardworking, her children are lazy and spoiled.

147 **Qīnqīn-gùgù yuǎn lái xiāng.** 亲亲故故远来香。Relatives and old friends from afar [are always] most welcome. [Note: gùjiù, "old friends and acquaintances."]

148 **Qīnqi yuǎnlí xiāng; línjū gāo dǎ qiáng.** 亲戚远离香，邻居高打墙。[Just as] relatives separated by long distances [have] better [relationships, so] neighbors (should) build high walls [between themselves]. [Vs. *yuǎnqīn bùrú* below; see also *qìngjia péngyou* above.]

149 **Qín shì yáoqiánshù; jiǎn shì jùbǎopén.** 勤是摇钱树，俭是聚宝盆。(lit) Diligence is [what] shakes the money tree; frugality is the treasure bowl. (fig) Hard work will bring one money, and thrift will accumulate property. [See *qínjiǎn*, "hardworking and thrifty"; *yáoqiánshù*, "ready source of money"; *jùbǎopén*, "cornucopia."]

150 **Qīn suī qīn, cáibó fēn.** 亲虽亲，财帛分。(lit) Although relatives [may be] relatives, [nevertheless their] finances [should be] separate. (fig) Between relatives accounts should be clearly settled. [See also *qīnxiōngdì* below.]

151 **Qīn wàng qīn hǎo; lín wàng lín hǎo.** 亲望亲好，邻望邻好。Relatives wish each other well [and] neighbors do too. [See also *qīn wèi qīn hǎo* below.]

152 **Qīn wèi qīn hǎo; lín wèi lín ān.** 亲为亲好，邻为邻安。Relatives wish each other well, [and] neighbors wish each other peace. [See also *qīn wàng qīn hǎo* above.]

153 **Qīn xiàng qīn; gù xiàng gù.** 亲向亲，故向故。Relatives are partial to relatives, [and] old friends are partial to each other. [Note: gùyǒu, "old friends"; see also *qīn bù qīn* above.]

154 **Qīnxiōngdì míng suànzhàng.*** 亲兄弟明算帐。(lit) [Even] blood brothers keep careful accounts. (fig) Clear reckoning makes long friends. [See also *hǎo péngyou qín* and *gōngpíng suànzhàng* and *qīn suī qīn* above and *xiōngdì suī hé* below.]

155 **Qín yǒugōng; xī wúyì.** 勤有功，嬉无益。Diligence leads to success; idle play brings no benefits.

156 **Qīn yǒu yuǎnjìn; lín yǒu lǐ-wài.** 亲有远近，邻有里外。[Just as] there are close relatives [as well as] distant [ones, so] there are close neighbors [as well as] distant [ones].

157 **Qīn zé bù xiè; xiè zé bù qīn.** 亲则不谢，谢则不亲。(lit) [If people have] close relations, then no thanks [are necessary]; [if] thanks [are expressed] then [the relationship is] not close. (fig) If you are close relatives, there is no need for formality between you; otherwise the relationship is distant. [Note: Chinese traditionally do not express thanks to immediate family members in their daily life.]

158 **Qín zéi xiān qín wáng.*** 擒贼先擒王。(lit) [To] catch bandits, first catch [their] king. (fig) To disable a group, first eliminate their (ring) leaders. [See also *dǎ shé xiān dǎ tóu* above and *qún yàn wú shǒu* below.]

159 **Qīn zhě gē zhī bù duàn; shū zhě xù zhī bù jiān.** 亲者割之不断，疏者续之不坚。It is impossible to break [the relationship between] close friends and relatives, [and] mere acquaintances' connections cannot be strong. [Cf. *Míng Shǐ: Gāo Wēi Zhuàn*; see also *shū bù jiàn qīn* below.]

160 **Qióng bù yǔ fù dòu; fù bù yǔ guān dòu.*** 穷不与富斗，富不与官斗。The poor [should] not struggle with the rich, [and] the rich [should] not struggle with [government] officials [because they'll both lose]. [Cf. *Suí Táng Yǎnyì*, chap. 5; see also *mín bù yù guān dòu* above.]

161 **Qióng cūn yǒu fù hù; fù cūn yǒu qióngrén.** 穷村有富户，富村有穷人。(lit) In a poor village there are rich families, and in a rich village there are poor families. (fig) There are (relative differences between) rich(er) and poor(er) people everywhere.

162 **Qióng fù bù rèn qīn.** 穷富不认亲。 (lit) Rich [and] poor won't acknowledge [each other as] relatives. (fig) Some rich won't acknowledge their poor relatives, and some poor [who have moral integrity] won't make claims on their rich relatives.

163 **Qióng jiā, fù lù.** 穷家富路。 (lit) [Be] poor [at] home [and] rich [on the] road. (fig) When at home, be economical; when on the road, bring extra money with you. [Cf. *Sān Xiá Wǔ Yì*, chap. 23; see also *jiā pín, bù shì pín* above.]

164 **Qióng jiā nán shě; gùtǔ nán lí.** 穷家难舍, 故土难离。 (lit) [Even] a shabby home is hard to leave [behind]; [one's] native soil is hard to leave. (fig) No one likes to leave his home and native place, however poor they may be. [Also said *qióng jiā nán shě, rè tú nán lí.*]

165 **Qióng lái bùyào pèi gāo qīn.** 穷来不要配高亲。 [Those who have] come from poor [families should] not be matched [in marriage] with rich families. [Note: *pèi qīn* is a colloquial expression for "joining in marriage."]

166 **Qióng pà qīn; fù pà zéi.** 穷怕亲, 富怕贼。 The poor fear [meeting their] friends and relatives [and losing face, as much as] the rich fear thieves.

167 **Qióngrén jiē qián wú rén wèn; fùrén qiā lǐ jié bīn péng.** 穷人街前无人问, 富人千里结宾朋。 [A] poor person [even if he lives on a] main street won't be visited; [while a] rich person [even if he lives a] thousand miles [away in a remote place] will meet guests [and] friends. [See also *pínjiàn, qīnqi lí* and *pín jū nàoshì* above.]

168 **Qióngrén wú zāi jí shì fú.** 穷人无灾即是福。 [For] poor people just having no disasters [befalling them] is a blessing. [Cf. *Wǔ Sōng*, chap. 2.]

169 **Qióngrén yǒu gè qióng púsà.** 穷人有个穷菩萨。 (lit) Poor people have a poor Buddha. (fig) The poor have their own blessings. [Cf. *Wǔ Sōng*, chap. 6.]

170 **Qióng suànmìng; fù shāoxiāng.*** 穷算命, 富烧香。 (lit) The poor have their fortunes told [so as to know the future, and] the rich burn incense [to the Buddha]. (fig) While the poor hope for fortune, the rich protect theirs.

171 **Qióng suī qióng, háiyǒu sān dàn tóng.** 穷虽穷, 还有三担铜。 (lit) Poor as one [who was once wealthy] has become, [(s)he] still has three *dan* of copper left. (fig) A rich family, even when going bankrupt, will still have some property left. [Rhyme; one *dàn* is a unit of weight equal to fifty kilograms; see also *dà chuán lànle* and *fùle pín* above and *shòu sǐ de luòtuo* and *tóng pén lànle* below.]

172 **Qióng yǒu qióng chóu; fù yǒu fù chóu.** 穷有穷愁, 富有富愁。 The poor have the poor's worries [and] the rich have the worries of the rich.

173 **Qióng zé biàn, biàn zé tōng.** 穷则变, 变则通。 [When one has] run out [of everything], then change [becomes necessary]; [once] changed, then a solution [will emerge]. [Cf. the *chengyu*: *qióng zé sì biàn*, "When one is impoverished,

one thinks of change"; a line from the Book of Changes (*Yìjīng/Zhōu Yì*).]

174 **Qì qiáng qiān zhāo; chāi wū yī rì.** 砌墙千朝, 拆屋一日。 (lit) [To] build walls takes a thousand days, [but to] topple down a house takes [only] one day. (fig) Constructive work is difficult, while destruction is easy.

175 **Qì qiáng, xiān dǎ jī; chī dàn, xiān yǎngjī.** 砌墙先打基, 吃蛋先养鸡。 (lit) [To] build [a] wall, first lay the foundation; [to] eat eggs, first raise the chickens. (fig) In any task, one must lay the foundations first. [Rhyme.]

176 **Qī shān, mò qī shuǐ; qī shuǐ, biàn shuǐ guǐ.** 欺山莫欺水, 欺水变水鬼。 (lit) [Better to] fool around with mountains than to fool around with water; [if one] fools around with water, [one may] become a "drowned ghost." (fig) Although in nature water (courses) may not appear as imposing as mountains are, in fact if (hydraulics are) not handled correctly, water can be extremely dangerous to people. [Here *qī*, (lit) "to cheat" or "to bully," means "to fool around with."]

177 **(Qīshí'èr háng,) hángháng chū zhuàngyuan.** (七十二行,) 行行出状元。 (lit) ([There are] seventy-two professions, [and]) every profession produces its own leading authority. (fig) Every field has its "stars" or experts. If one works hard and perfects one's skill, one may become an expert in one's field, whatever it may be. [Cf. *Érnǚ Yīngxióng Zhuàn*, chap. 11; *Wǔ Sōng*, chap. 3; note: *zhuàngyuan* was a title for the highest-ranked successful candidate in the highest-level examination under the old imperial system; the first part may be omitted; also said *sānbǎi liùshí háng*, etc. (q.v.)]

178 **Qīshíèr háng, zhuāngjia wéi qiáng.** 七十二行, 庄稼为强。 [Of all the] seventy-two trades, farming is the most important.

179 **Qí shū, háiyǒu qízǐ zài.** 棋输, 还有棋子在。 (lit) [Although one may] lose [at] chess, [the chessboard and] chessmen still exist. (fig) Though one may fail, the basic conditions to continue or start over still exist. [See also *liú de qīngshān zài* above.]

180 **Qǐtóu róngyì; jié shāo nán.*** 起头容易, 结梢难。 (lit) Starting is easy, [but] concluding is difficult. (fig) It is easier to start something than to conclude it satisfactorily. [Cf. *JW*, chap. 96.]

181 **Qiú, biàn qiú Zhāng Liáng; bài, biàn bài Hán Xīn.** 求便求张梁, 拜便拜韩信。 (lit) [If you're going to] ask for help, then ask [it of a wise man like] Zhang Liang or [an able general like] Han Xin. (fig) If one is going to seek help, seek it from the right person, (i.e., a person of great ability or one who can really help you). [Cf. *JPM*, chap. 7; Han Xin was a famous general of the early Han dynasty who served first under Xiang Yu and later under Liu Bang; Zhang Liang was Liu Bang's most important strategist; see also *qiúrén xū qiú* and *zǒu sān jiā* below.]

Q

182 **Qiúrén bùrú qiú jǐ.*** 求人不如求己。 [It is] better to seek help from oneself than from outsiders. [Cf. *DRC*, chap. 72; Mao Dun's *Chūn Cán Jí* (Spring Silkworms); *qiúrén bùrú qiújǐ* has become a set colloquial expression.]

183 **Qiú rén mèng shè; kě rén mèng jiāng.** 囚人梦赦, 渴人梦浆。 (lit) A prisoner dreams of amnesty [and] a thirsty person dreams of [drinking] liquids. (fig) One dreams of what one desires. [Cf. *Gǔ-Jīn Xiǎoshuō*, chap. 16.]

184 **Qiúrén xū qiú dàzhàngfu; jì rén xū jì jíshí wú.** 求人须求大丈夫; 济人须济及时无。 [If you have to] ask someone for help, [it is] best to ask a real man, [who can help you, and if you are going to] help someone [at all, it is] best to help [them in their true] time of need. [Rhyme; cf. *JPM*, chap. 56 and 60; note: *dàzhàngfu*, "a real man; a man of fortitude and courage"; see the *chengyu*: *jìrénzhíjí*, "to relieve someone in need"; see also *qiú*, *biàn qiú Zhāng Liáng* below.]

185 **Qiúzhī-bùdé, bù qiú zì lái.** 求之不得, 不求自来。 [It often happens that if you] seek something, [you will] not get [it, but if you do] not seek [it, it] will just come [to you]. [Both halves are used independently as *chengyu*; see also *kě yù ér bù kě qiú* above and *tàpò tiě xié* below.]

186 **Qī xián, fū huò shǎo.** 妻贤, 夫祸少。 [If the] wife is virtuous, the husband [will meet with] fewer disasters. [Cf. *DRC*, chap. 68.]

187 **Qì xiǎo, yì yíng.** 器小易盈。 (lit) A small container is easy to fill. (fig) A small-minded person is always self-satisfied. [Cf. *Jìnghuā Yuán*, chap. 12.]

188 **Qǐ xīn bùrú mǎi jiù.** 起新不如买旧。 Better to buy old than to build new [e.g., houses].

189 **Qíxīn de mǎyǐ néng chī hǔ.** 齐心的蚂蚁能吃虎。 (lit) Ants in unison can eat a tiger. (fig) "In unity there's strength." [See also *qún yǐ néng xiáng dúshé* below.]

190 **Quán bù lí shǒu; qǔ bù lí kǒu.*** 拳不离手, 曲不离口。 (lit) [To practice] martial arts [one can] not do without [one's] hands; [to practice] songs [one can] not do without one's mouth. (fig) If you want to perfect your skill, you must practice everyday. "Practice makes perfect." [See also *bùpà liàn bù chéng* above and *sān rì bù tán* below.]

191 **Quǎn fèi bù ài rén xíng lù.** 犬吠不碍人行路。 (lit) [A] barking dog doesn't prevent people [from] walking on the road. (fig) Evil people's clamoring won't prevent people from getting on with their work, so it should be ignored.

192 **Quàn jiàng bùrú jījiàng.** 劝将不如激将。 (lit) Better to challenge a general [into battle] than to [try to] persuade [him into battle]. (fig) If you really want to arouse people, get them angry. [See also *qǐng jiàng bùrú jījiàng* above.]

193 **Quàn jūn mò dǎ sān chūn niǎo, zǐ zài kē zhōng pàn mǔ guī.** 劝君莫打三春鸟, 子在窠中盼母归。 (lit) [It is] advisable [for] gentlemen [i.e., one] not to shoot birds in spring, [as their] offspring are in the nest expecting [their] mother's return. (fig) People should protect parents who are raising young children. [Note: *sān chūn* refers either to the first three lunar months, usually February—April, or to the third lunar month, *jì chūn*, alone; the modern word for "nest" *cháo* is sometimes substituted for *kē*.]

194 **Quàn jūn píngdì shàng, hái sì guò pō shí.** 劝君平地上, 还似过坡时。 (lit) [It is] advisable [for] gentlemen [i.e., one] [when walking] on flat land [to be as careful as] when traversing a slope. (fig) Even when things are going smoothly one (still) can't be too careful; one should never slacken one's vigilance. [See also *qiǎn shuǐ yānsǐ* above and *zǒu píng lù, fáng shuāijiāo* below.]

195 **Quǎnmǎ yóu zhī liàn zhǔ.** 犬马尤知恋主。 (lit) [Even a] dog [or a] horse feels an attachment to its master. (fig) Servants are emotionally attached to their masters. [Cf. *Xǐngshì Héngyán*, chap. 35.]

196 **Quàn rén chūshì piān zhī yì; zì dào líntóu shǐ jué nán.** 劝人出世偏知易; 自到临头始觉难。 To exhort others to "hold aloof from the world" [people] always think is easy, [but when they] actually come to doing it themselves, [they] begin to realize it's not so easy. [Note: *chūshì* is a Buddhist expression meaning to "renounce the world."]

197 **Quàn rén róngyì; zhù rén nán.** 劝人容易, 助人难。 (lit) Giving advice to people is easy, [but actually] helping them is difficult. (fig) "Talk is cheap." "Actions speak louder than words."

198 **Quàn rén xū xià wúqíng kǒu.** 劝人须下无情口。 [In] advising (or criticizing) people, [one] must speak without favor [i.e., straightforwardly, so that it will really help]. [Note: *xià kǒu* means "to speak."]

199 **Quǎn shǒuyè; jī sī chén.** 犬守夜, 鸡司晨。 (lit) A dog watches at night [and] a cock crows at dawn. (fig) Each one has his own duty to perform. [Cf. Qin Jiwen's *Zàishēng Yuán*, chap. 11.]

200 **Quánshuǐ zuì qīng; yànyǔ zuì jīng.** 泉水最清, 谚语最精。 [Just as] spring water [is] most clear, [so] proverbs [are] the most concise. [Rhyme.]

201 **Quántou cháo wài dǎ; gēbo wǎng lǐ wān.*** 拳头朝外打, 胳膊往里弯。 (lit) Fists [naturally] strike outward [and] arms [naturally] bend inward. (fig) One should fight against outsiders and protect one's own people. [See also *gēbo zǒngshì* above.]

202 **Quántou dà shì gēge; gètóu zhuàng shì qiáng liáng.** 拳头大是哥哥, 个头壮是强梁。 (lit) Those with big fists are elder brothers [and those with] stout bodies are powerful. (fig) "Might makes right."

203 **Qǔ dào de qī, mǎi dào de mǎ; rèn rén qí lái, rèn rén dǎ.** 娶到的妻, 买到的马; 任人骑来, 任人打。 A wife [one has] married [is like a] horse [one has] bought: one may ride [them] or beat [them as one pleases]. [Rhyme.]

204 **Qǔdé jīng lái Táng Sēng shòu; rěxia huò lái Xíngzhě dān.** 取得经来唐僧受，惹下祸来行者担。(lit) [The credit for] bringing back the [Buddhist] scriptures [on the Pilgrimage to the West is] given to [the Monk] Tang Seng, [while the responsibility for any] disasters encountered [on that trip is] shouldered by [his] disciple Xingzhe [i.e., Sun Wukong, the Monkey King]. (fig) Successes are always credited to superiors, while failures are blamed on his or her subordinates. [Allusions to the principal characters in *JW*; see also *sān rén tóngxíng* below.]

205 **Què bǔ tángláng, rén bǔ què; àn sòng Wú Cháng, sǐ bù zhī.** 雀捕螳螂，人捕雀；暗送吴常，死不知。(lit) The oriole catches the mantis, who [in turn] is caught by a human; [neither] knows [of their] approaching death. (fig) Don't covet gains ahead without being aware of the dangers behind. People who plot evil deeds may suffer the same fate. [Cf. *Érmǔ Yīngxióng Zhuàn*, chap. 5; note: *Wú Cháng* is the Chinese equivalent of the Grim Reaper of Death, sent by the King of the Underworld. This is a variation of the more common *tángláng bǔ chán* below.]

206 **Qué láng nán dòu.** 瘸狼难斗。(lit) [A] lame wolf is [even] more difficult to deal with [than an ordinary one]. (fig) The worse people are, the harder they are to deal with.

207 **Què zhī fēng; yǐ zhī shuǐ.** 鹊知风，蚁知水。(lit) The magpie [is the first to] feel the wind [and the] ant [to] know [the coming] rain. (fig) If one lives in a particular environment for long, one can usually predict what will happen next. [Note: *xǐquè*,

"magpie"; see also *mǎyǐ lěi wō* above and *wūyā zhī fēng* below.]

208 **Qǔ fǎ hū shàng, jìng dé hū zhōng; (qǔ fǎ hū zhōng, jìn dé hū qí xià).*** 取法乎上，竟得乎中；（取法乎中，仅得乎其下）。(lit) [If one] takes as a model the best, [one can] make only a mediocre [copy]; ([if one] takes as [one's] model mediocrity, [one will] get something inferior [to that]). (fig) Aim high or you'll fall below average. [Also said *gǔ fǎ hū shàng, dé hū qí zhōng; qǔ fǎ hū; and fǎ hū shàng, jìn dé qí zhōng; fǎ hū qí zhōng, zé dé qí xià* (q.v.).]

209 **Qū mù wù zhí shéng; zhòng fá wù míng zhèng.** 曲木恶直绳，重罚恶明正。[Just as] a crooked board hates [a carpenter's] straight [plumb] line, [so one who] deserves severe punishment hates clear proof [of his or her guilt.]

210 **Qún yàn wú shǒu nán chéng xíng.** 群雁无首难成行。(lit) Wild geese without [their] leader [find it] difficult to fly in formation. (fig) If a group loses its leader, they will be in disarray. [See also *qín zéi xiān qín wáng* above and *shé wú tóu* and *yàn fēi qiān lǐ* below.]

211 **Qún yǐ néng xiáng dúshé.** 群蚁能降毒蛇。(lit) A horde of ants can conquer a poisonous snake. (fig) "In unity lies strength." [See also *qíxīn de mǎyǐ* above.]

212 **Qù shí liú rénqíng; zhuàn lái hǎo xiāngjiàn.** 去时留人情，转来好相见。[If you] part on friendly terms, you can come back to see one another again. [Cf. *Suí Táng Yǎnyì*, chap. 14; see also *mǎi-mài bù chéng* above and *shānshuǐ shàng yǒu* below.]

R

1 **Ràng lǐ yī cùn; dé lǐ yī chǐ.** 让礼一寸，得礼一尺。(lit) Yield an inch [and] gain a foot. (fig) If one makes a small concession, one may make a greater gain later on. [Note: *lǐràng*, "to give precedence to someone out of courtesy or thoughtfulness."]

2 **Rànglù bù shì chī hàn.** 让路不是痴汉。[One who] yields to others is not [a] fool. [See also *chī hàn bùkěn* above and *ráorén bù shì* below and the following three entries.]

3 **Ràng rén bù wéi dī.** 让人不为低。[One who] yields to others is not considered inferior [to others]. [See also the preceding and following entry.]

4 **Ràng rén sānfēn bù wéi shū.** 让人三分不为输。[One who] concedes thirty percent is not considered [to have] lost. [See also the preceding and the following entries.]

5 **Ràng rén yī zhāo, tiān kuān dì kuò.** 让人一着，天宽地阔。(lit) One who [deliberately] retreats one move [in chess has] broad scope [for advance or retreat later]. (fig) Those who give precedence out of courtesy or who make concessions are allowing themselves broader scope for advance or retreat. [Note: *zhāoshù* refers to

a move in Chinese chess; see also *ráorén bù shì* below and the preceding four entries.]

6 **Ràng yī, ràng èr; bù néng ràng sān, ràng sì.** 让一让二，不能让三让四。(lit) One may make a concession once or twice, [but] not three or four times. (fig) There is a limit to one's accommodation. [See also *shì bù guò sān* below.]

7 **Ráorén bù shì chī; chī hàn bù ráorén.** 饶人不是痴，痴汉不饶人。[To] forgive others is not stupid; [it's a] stupid person [who] does not forgive others. [See also *ránglù bù shì* above.]

8 **Ráorén bù shì chī; guòhòu dé piányi.** 饶人不是痴，过后得便宜。To forgive others is not foolish; later [one will] benefit. [See also *chī hàn bùkěn* and *hán róng zhōng yǒuyì* and *ránglù bù shì* above.]

9 **Ráorén shì fú; qīrén shì huò.** 饶人是福，欺人是祸。To forgive others is a blessing; to bully others is a misfortune.

10 **Rè jí shēng fēng; lè jí shēng bēi.** 热极生风，乐极生悲。[Just as] extreme warmth brings about winds, [so] extreme pleasure brings about sorrow.

R

11 **Rén ài fù de; gǒu yǎo qióng de.*** 人爱富的，狗咬穷的。 Everyone respects the rich, [while] dogs bite the poor.

12 **Rén bǎ liǎn bù yào, bǎi shì dōu kě wéi.** 人把脸不要，百事都可为。 A person [who has] lost all sense of shame may do anything [bad].

13 **Rén bàn xiánliáng, zhì zhuǎn gāo.** 人伴贤良，智转高。 Whoever keeps company with a virtuous person [will himself] become virtuous.

14 **Rén bèn, yuàn dāo dùn.*** 人笨，怨刀钝。 (lit) A person [who is] clumsy complains about [his] knife [being] blunt. (fig) Incompetent people often try to shift the blame for their failures to other causes. "A poor workman blames his tools."

15 **Rén bǐ rén děi sǐ; huò bǐ huò děi rēng.** 人比人得死，货比货得扔。 (lit) [When] people are compared to [other] people [they] will die; [just as when] goods are compared to [other] goods [they] will be thrown out. (fig) It's comparison that makes people miserable, just as comparison makes some goods appear to be of poorer quality than others. [See also *rén bǐ rén, qì sǐ rén* below.]

16 **Rén bǐ rén, qì sǐ rén.*** 人比人，气死人。 It is comparison that makes men miserable; one should not compare oneself with others. [Cf. *Zàishēng Yuán*, chap. 68; see also *huò bǐ huò* above and the previous entry.]

17 **Rén bì zì wǔ, ér hòu rén wǔ.** 人必自侮，而后人侮。 If you are dishonored, it must be because you dishonored yourself first. [Cf. Mencius, *Mèngzǐ: Lí Lóu, Shàng*.]

18 **Rén bù chū míng, shēn bù guì; huǒ bù shāo shān, dì bù féi.** 人不出名身不贵，火不烧山地不肥。 A person who is not well-known won't be valued highly [by others], [just as on] hills [which have] not been burned over, the soil is not [as] fertile. [Rhyme.]

19 **Rén bù cí lù; hǔ bù cí shān.** 人不辞路，虎不辞山。 (lit) Human beings cannot be separated from roads, [just as] tigers cannot be separated from mountains. (fig) Everyone has to leave home and travel sometimes.

20 **Rén bù jīng bǎi yǔ; chái bù jīng bǎi fǔ.** 人不经百语，柴不经百斧。 (Even a good) person cannot [withstand] a hundred [people] speaking [ill of him or her, just as] firewood cannot [withstand] a hundred [strokes of an] axe. [Rhyme; note: *jīng bù qǐ* "cannot withstand"; see also *qiān fū suǒ zhǐ* above.]

21 **Rén bù kě mào xiàng; hǎishuǐ bù kě dǒu liáng.*** 人不可貌相，海水不可斗量。 (lit) People cannot be judged [by their] looks, [just as the] sea cannot be measured in bushels. (fig) Do not judge people by their appearances. [Rhyme; cf. *Xǐngshì Héngyán*, chap. 3; note: one *dǒu* equals one deciliter; see also *hǎishuǐ bùkě* above and *rénxīn nán cè* below.]

22 **Rén bù kě wàngběn.** 人不可忘本。 (lit) One should not forget one's roots. (fig) (1) One should not forget one's (class) origins. (2) One should not forget one's past (sufferings). (3) One should not forget one's benefactor(s). [Cf. *Chū Kè Pāi'àn Jīngqí*, chap. 21.]

23 **Rén bùlùn dàxiǎo; mǎ bùlùn gāodī.** 人不论大小，马不论高低。 [One should] no more judge people by their age than [one would] judge horses by their height.

24 **Rén bù qīn, tǔ hái qīn.** 人不亲，土还亲。 People from the same place feel close even if they aren't related to each other. [See also *qīn bù qīn* and *qīn xiàng qīn* above.]

25 **Rén bù qiú rén, yībān dà; shuǐ bù xià tān, yī zhǎng píng.** 人不求人一般大，水不下滩一掌平。 (lit) [If] one doesn't ask others [for anything, one stands] equal [to everybody else, just as if] water doesn't encounter shoals, [it remains all] at the same level. (fig) It is best not to be indebted or beholden to others.

26 **Rén bù shuō, bù tōng; mù bù zuān, bù tòu.** 人不说，不通；木不钻，不透。 [If you] don't try to speak [i.e., reason with] others, [they] won't understand [you, just as] without drilling, [you can]not get through a wood[en board]. [See also *gǔ bù dǎ* above.]

27 **Rén bù wèi jǐ, tiānzhū-dìmiè.*** 人不为己，天诛地灭。 (lit) [If] people do not look out for themselves first, Heaven and Earth will destroy [them]. (fig) People must look out for their own interests first. [The second half is a *chengyu*. This traditional saying was revised into a rhymed communist slogan *rén bù wèi jǐ, dǐng tiān lì dì*, "If one is selfless, one fears nothing," created by substituting the *chengyu: dǐngtiān-lìdì*: "fearing neither heaven nor earth," for the second part.]

28 **Rén bùyí hǎo; gǒu bùyí bǎo.** 人不宜好，狗不宜饱。 (lit) [It is] not advisable [for] people [to be too] well-off, [just as it is] not advisable [for] dogs [to be too] well-fed. (fig) People become avaricious if they are too well-off, just as watchdogs become lazy if they are too well-fed. [Rhyme.]

29 **Rén chuàn ménzi rě shìfēi; gǒu chuàn ménzi ái bàng chuí.** 人串门子惹是非，狗串门子挨棒锤。 [If] one goes from door to door [gossiping], [one will just] stir up trouble, [just as when a] dog goes from door to door, it gets beaten with (laundry) clubs. [Rhyme; note: *chuàn ménzi*, "to visit people's homes casually."]

30 **Rén dào wǔshí, zhī tiānmìng.** 人到五十，知天命。 [By the time] one is fifty, [one] knows [one's] fate in life. [A paraphrase of part of a famous quotation from the Confucian Analects: *Lúnyǔ: Wéi Zhèng*; see also *rén nián wǔshí* below.]

31 **Rén dǎoméi, hē kǒu liángshuǐ yě yào sāi yá.** 人倒霉，喝口凉水也要塞牙。 (lit) [When] bad luck [comes to] people, [even] a mouthful of cool water will get stuck between [their] teeth. (fig) "Misfortunes never come singly." "It never rains but it pours." [See also *yùn qù, huángjīn* below.]

32 **Rén dào nánchù cái jiàn xīn.*** 人到难处才见心。 (lit) [It is] only when a person gets into difficulty that one can [truly] see his heart. (fig) It is only when we see how someone behaves in a difficult situation that we can see his or her true character. [See also *jífēng zhī jìncǎo* above and *shì biàn zhī rénxīn* and *zhǐ zhī wǒ wàimiàn* below.]

R

33 **Rén dào nánchù jiù rú hǔ luò shēn kēng.** 人到难处就如虎落深坑。 A person in a tight difficult situation is just like a tiger fallen into a deep pit [i.e., (s)he can do nothing].

34 **Rén dào shì jí chù, jiù yǒu chūqí chù.** 人到事急处，就有出奇处。 [When a] person gets into a desperate situation, that's [when (s)he will] show remarkable resourcefulness. [Note the *chengyu: jízhōng-shēngzhì*, "showing resourcefulness in an emergency"; see also *rén jí, zhì shēng* below.]

35 **Rén dào shì zhōng mí, jiù pà bù tīng quàn.** 人到事中迷，就怕不听劝。 [When] a person becomes deeply involved in something, [the thing to] fear is [that he will lose his objectivity and] not listen to reason.

36 **Rén dào sìshíwǔ, zhèngrú chū shān hǔ.** 人到四十五，正如出山虎。 [When] one reaches [the age of] forty-five, [he is] just as [energetic as a] tiger coming out of the mountains. [A rhyme, said of men.]

37 **Rén dào wúqíng, qièmò xiāngjiāo.** 人到无情，切莫相交。 [If some]one no [longer] shows [any] friendship [for you], be sure not to continue the relationship.

38 **Rén dào wú qiú, pǐn zì gāo.** 人到无求，品自高。 [If one] arrives [at a point where s/he] has nothing to ask for [from others, one's moral] character [will] naturally be higher. [Note: *pǐndé*, "moral character."]

39 **Rén dào zhōngnián, wànshì xiū.** 人到中年，万事休。 (lit) [When] people get to middle age, everything comes to a halt. (fig) After middle age, nothing great can be accomplished. [Cf. *Gǔ-Jīn Xiǎoshuō*, chap. 33; see also *yuè guò shíwǔ* below.]

40 **Rén dà, xīn dà.** 人大，心大。 [As] people grow up, [their] will [also] grows. [Usually refers to children having grown up and wanting to make their own decisions; cf. *DRC*, chap. 28.]

41 **Rén de míng; shù de yǐng.** 人的名，树的影。 [Just as] a tree [casts] its shadow, a person [car-]ries] a reputation. [Rhyme; cf. *JPM*, chap. 86; also said *rén yǒu míng, shù yǒu yǐng*; see also *hǔ sǐ liú pí* above and *rén guò liúmíng* below.]

42 **Rěn dé yīshí fèn, zhōngshēn wú nǎomèn.** 忍得一时忿，终身无恼闷。 [One who can] bear one's indignation for short periods of time [will] have no anxiety for one's whole life. [Rhyme; cf. *DRC*, chap. 9; see below *rěn rǔ zhì sān gōng* below.]

43 **Réndīng shàng bǎi, wǔyì jiē quán.** 人丁上百，武艺皆全。 [In] a population reaching a hundred, all sorts of skills and talents [can be found]. [Note: *réndīng*, "a population," usually refers to adult males.]

44 **Rén dìng shèng tiān.*** 人定胜天。 People can conquer nature; humans are the masters of their own fate. [Cf. *Shǐ Jì: Wú Zǐxū Lièzhuàn*; often used by Mao Zedong.]

45 **Rén duō, bù pà hǔ; gǒu duō, bù pà láng.** 人多不怕虎，狗多不怕狼。 (lit) Many people [together] won't fear [a] tiger, [and] many dogs [together] won't fear [a] wolf. (fig) There is strength in numbers.

46 **Rén duō, chéng wáng.** 人多，成王。 (lit) Many people [under you] make [you] a king. (fig) The more people one controls, the greater is one's power. [Cf. *Xīyáng Jì*, chap. 77; Ding Ling's modern novel *Tàiyáng Zhào Zài Sānggān Hé Shàng*, chap. 39.]

47 **Rén duō chī láng; láng duō chī rén.** 人多吃狼，狼多吃人。 (lit) Many people [together can] eat a wolf, [just as] many wolves [together can] eat a man. (fig) In unity there is strength.

48 **Rén duō, chū Hán Xìn.*** 人多出韩信。 The more people [there are, the more likely it is that an able person such as] Han Xin will appear. [Han Xin was a famous general under Liu Bang, the founding emperor of the Han dynasty.]

49 **Rén duō, hǎo zhòngtián; rén shǎo, hǎo guònián.** 人多好种田，人少好过年。 (lit) Many people are better for planting fields, [but] fewer people [to feed] are better at [Chinese] New Year's. (fig) Many hands make the farming work lighter, but fewer mouths to feed make life easier. [Rhyme; note: *guò niánguān*, "to settle all one's outstanding debts by the end of the year."]

50 **Rén duō, hǎo zuògōng; yǐ duō, kùnsǐ chóng.** 人多好做工，蚁多困死虫。 (lit) Many people are better for work, [just as] many ants are better to wear down [an] insect. (fig) "Many hands make light work"; "there is strength in numbers." [Rhyme; see also the following entry.]

51 **Rén duō, hǎo zuòhuó; (rén shǎo, hǎo chīfàn).** 人多好做活，(人少，好吃饭)。 "Many hands make light work," ([but if there are] fewer people [it's] easier [to get enough] to eat). [Cf. *Émǔ Yīngxióng Zhuàn*, chap. 21; the first part is also said *rén duō hǎo bànshì*: cf. *Yuè Fēi Zhuàn*, chap. 84; the second part is added as a humorous contrast; see also the preceding entry.]

52 **Rén duō, lìliàng dà; chái duō, huǒyàn gāo.** 人多力量大，柴多火焰高。 There is strength in numbers, [just as] more wood makes a bigger fire. [See also *zhòngrén shíchái* below.]

53 **Rén duō luàn lóng duō hàn, (mǔjī duōle bù xiàdàn, xífù duōle pópo zuòfàn).** 人多乱，龙多旱，(母鸡多了，不下蛋，媳妇多了，婆婆做饭)。 (lit) [If there are] more people, [there will be more] confusion; [if there are] more dragons, [there will be] drought; ([if there are] more hens, no one lays eggs; [if there are] more daughters-in-law, the mothers-in-law [will have to] do the cooking). (fig) "Everybody's business is nobody's business." "Too many cooks spoil the broth." [Rhyme; note: in traditional China the first part was commonly used alone; note: dragons were believed to control water courses. See also *rén duō, shǒu zá* below.]

54 **Rén duō, méi hǎo tāng; zhū duō, méi hǎo kāng.** 人多没好汤，猪多没好糠。 (lit) [If there are] too many people, [there] won't be good soup [to eat and if there are] too many pigs, there won't be enough chaff [to eat]. (fig) Benefits divided among too many people become insignificant. [Rhyme.]

R

55 **Rén duō, shì zhòng.*** 人多势重。The more people there are, the greater the strength one can muster.

56 **Rén duō, shǒu zá.*** 人多手杂。(lit) [When there are too] many people [involved in a matter], [their] hands [get] entangled. (fig) "Too many cooks spoil the broth." [See also *lóng duō* and *qí kǒuzi* and *rén duō luàn* above and *shāogōng duōle* and *zuò shě dào biān* below.]

57 **Rén duō, xīn bù qí; éluǎnshí jǐ, diào pí.** 人多心不齐，鹅卵石挤掉皮。(lit) [When there are] too many people, [there can be] no unanimity of minds, [just as when] cobblestones are crowded together, [their] surfaces are worn away. (fig) It's inevitable that there is friction in a group and concerted effort becomes impossible. [Vs. *rénxīn qí* below.]

58 **Rén duō yì jì yǒuyì; wù yù yī bèi yǒuyòng.** 人多一技有益，物裕一倍有用。Learning another skill will always benefit one, [just as] having a spare of something [always] comes in handy. [See also *yì bù yà shēn* below.]

59 **Rén duō, zuǐ zá.*** 人多嘴杂。(lit) [When there are] many people [gossiping], [their] mouths [get] tangled. (fig) Just let people say and think whatever they want; don't pay attention to gossip. [This is often mistaken as a *chengyu*.]

60 **Rén è, lǐ bù è.** 人恶礼不恶。[Although other] people may be rude, courtesy [dictates that one] not be rude [in return]. [Cf. *JPM*, chap. 80.]

61 **Rén ér wú héng, bù kěyǐ zuò wūyī.** 人而无恒，不可以作巫医。(lit) [If] one has no persistence of purpose, [he] may not [even qualify to] be a witch doctor. (fig) If one has no perseverance, one can accomplish nothing. [Originally a quotation from the Confucian Analects: *Lúnyǔ: Zǐ Lù, Dì 13*.]

62 **Rén fēi cǎomù, qǐnéng wúqíng?*** 人非草木，岂能无情？ Humans are not grass [or] trees, [so] how can they avoid emotion? [Originally from an essay "Qiū Shēng Fù" by Ouyang Xiu in the Northern Song dynasty; cf. *WM*, chap. 13.]

63 **Rén fēi shèngxián; shú néng wú guò?*** 人非圣贤，孰能无过？ People are not saints, [so] how can they be faultless? "To err is human." [Cf. *Sān Xiá Wǔ Yì*, chap. 109; see also *shì ruò qiúquán* below.]

64 **Rén gēn shì zǒu; gǒu gēn pì zǒu.** 人跟势走，狗跟屁走。(lit) People follow along with [those who have] power, [just as] dogs follow [the smell of] flatulence. (fig) Some people want to associate themselves with powerful people. [See also *gǒu bù chī shǐ* above and *rén jìng fù de* below.]

65 **Rén gè yǒu xīn.** 人各有心。(lit) People each have [their own] hearts. (fig) (1) Everyone has his or her own intentions. (2) All people have consciences. [Cf. *Sān Guó Zhì: Wèi Shū: Sān Shào Dì Jì*.]

66 **Rén gè yǒu zhì, (bùkě xiāngqiǎng.)** 人各有志，(不可相强)。Different people have different aspirations, ([and] cannot be forced to do things [that they don't want to do]). [Cf. *Érnǚ Yīngxióng*

Zhuàn, chap. 40; the first part is commonly used alone as a set phrase; see the preceding entry.]

67 **Rén guàn shè jǐ guò; jìng bù yǎn rén cī.** 人惯赦己过，镜不掩人疵。(lit) People tend to forgive [their] own mistakes [but the] mirror [will] not hide their defects. (fig) People's shortcomings are more apparent to others than to themselves. [See also *lú bù zhī* above.]

68 **Rén guì jiàn jī.** 人贵见机。(lit) People value seeing opportunities. (fig) To see an opportunity is precious. When opportunity knocks, seize it!

69 **Rén guò liúmíng; yàn guò liú shēng.** 人过留名，雁过留声。A person leaves a reputation behind, [just as] a wild goose leaves its sound [lingering after it's gone]. [Cf. *Érnǚ Yīngxióng Zhuàn*, chap. 32; see also *hǔ sǐ liú pí* and *rén de míng* above.]

70 **Rén guò sānshí bù xuéyì.** 人过三十不学艺。(lit) [A] person over thirty cannot learn [new] skills. (fig) "You can't teach an old dog new tricks."

71 **Rén gù yǒu yī sǐ, huò zhòngyú Tài Shān, huò qīng yú hóngmáo.** 人固有一死，或重于泰山，或轻于鸿毛。(lit) [Although] death certainly befalls [all] people [alike], [it may be] weightier than Mount Tai [or] lighter than goose feather. (fig) Some people's deaths are more consequential than others. [Originally from Sima Qian's *Bào Rén Ān Shū* (or *Bào Rén Shàoqīn Shū*) in the Han dynasty; quoted by Mao Zedong in his essays "Jìniàn Zhāng Sīdé" and "In Memory of Dr. Norman Bethune," two of the "Three Constantly Read Essays" during the Cultural Revolution; Mount Tai, a large mountain in Shandong province and one of the five sacred mountains, is commonly used as a symbol of great weight or import. *Zhòngyútàishān*, (lit) "(to be) weightier than Mount Tai"; (fig) "(to be) of greatest significance," and *qīngyú-hóngmáo*, (lit) "(to be) lighter than goose feather"; (fig) "without the least significance," are *chengyu*.]

72 **Rén hǎo, shuǐ yě tián.** 人好，水也甜。(lit) [When] people['s company is] good, even water tastes sweeter. (fig) Even the water tastes sweeter to the guests if the host shows sincere hospitality. [Usually said by guests.]

73 **Rén hǒng dìpí, dì hǒng dùpí.*** 人哄地皮，地哄肚皮。(lit) [If] people cheat the land, the land [will] cheat [people's] bellies. (fig) If people don't work hard on the land, the land won't produce enough to feed the people.

74 **Rén jiàn lì ér bù jiàn hài; yú jiàn shí ér bù jiàn gōu.** 人见利而不见害，鱼见食而不见钩。People see advantages rather than seeing disadvantages, [just as] fish see the bait rather than the hook. [Cf. *Jìnghuā Yuán*, chap. 92.]

75 **Rén jiàn mùqián; tiān jiàn jiǔyuǎn.** 人见目前，天见久远。Human beings [can only] see the present, [while] Heaven sees far and wide. (fig) Human beings are usually shortsighted. [See *Gǔ Jīn Xiǎoshuō*, chap. 31.]

76 **Rénjiān sīyǔ, tiān wén ruò léi; àn shì kuīxīn, shén mù rú diàn.** 人间私语，天闻若雷；暗室亏心，神目如电。 Secret whisperings are heard in heaven like thunder; evil [done in] dark places is seen by the gods like lightning. [Cf. *Érnǚ Yīngxióng Zhuàn*, chap. 4.]

77 **Rén jí, bàn bu liǎo hǎoshì; māo jí, dài bu zhù hàozi.** 人急办不了好事，猫急逮不住耗子。 People can't do anything well in haste, [just as] an impatient cat can't catch mice.

78 **Rén jí, jì shēng.** 人急计生。 In a moment of desperation one can always hit upon a good idea. [Cf. *Xǐngshì Héngyán*, chap. 33; note the *chengyu: jízhòng-shēngzhì*; see also *rén dào shì jí chù* above.]

79 **Rén jí, lì dà.** 人急力大。 [When one] is desperate, [one's] strength grows.

80 **Rén jìng fù de; gǒu yǎo pò de.** 人敬富的，狗咬破的。 (lit) People respect the wealthy, [while] dogs bite the ragged. (fig) People are snobbish. [See also *rén gēn shì zǒu* above.]

81 **Rén jí zàofǎn; gǒu jí tiào qiáng.** 人急造反，狗急跳墙。 Desperation will drive people to rebel [just as] it will drive a dog to jump over a wall. [Cf. *DRC*, chap. 27; note: *gǒu jí tiào qiáng*, "a cornered beast acts desperately," is a colloquial expression used to describe people driven to desperate actions.]

82 **Rén jí, zhì shēng.** 人急智生。 (lit) [When a] person [is in an] emergency, wisdom is born. (fig) Necessity produces invention. "Necessity is the mother of invention." [Cf. *WM*, chap. 6; *Érnǚ Yīngxióng Zhuàn*, chap. 8; as a *chengyu: jí zhōng shēng zhì*; see also *rén dào shì jí* above.]

83 **Rén kàn zhìqì; shù kàn cái.** 人看志气，树看材。 [In judging a] person, [one] looks at [his or her] aspirations, [just as in judging trees, one] looks at [the quality of its] timber.

84 **Rén kào yī zhuāng; fó kào jīn zhuāng.** 人靠衣装，佛靠金装。 (lit) People need clothes to wear, [just as] Buddhas need gold to look good. (fig) A person's good appearance depends very much on what he or she wears. Appearances are important. [Also said *rén yào*, etc.; see also *fó yào jīn zhuāng* and *mǎ kào ān zhuāng* above.]

85 **Rén kǒu kuài guò fēng.** 人口快过风。 (lit) Human mouths are faster than the wind. (fig) Rumors can spread faster than the wind.

86 **Rén kǔ, bù zhīzú; dé Lǒng, fù wàng Shǔ.** 人苦不知足，得陇复望蜀。 (lit) [It's a] shame [that] people are never satisfied; [having] acquired [the kingdom of] Lǒng, [they] look toward (acquiring) [the kingdom of] Shǔ. (fig) The more people get, the more they want. [*Lǒng* and *Shǔ* are two traditional names for parts of ancient China, now located in modern Gansu and Sichuan provinces, respectively; from a poem by the Tang dynasty poet Li Bai, entitled "Gǔ Fēng," verse 23; as a *chengyu: délǒng-wàngshǔ*, "having insatiable desires"; see also *rénshēng bù zhīzú* below.]

87 **Rén kǔ, bù zìzhī.** 人苦，不自知。 People suffer [from] not knowing [their] own [limitations].

88 **Rén kùn mài wū; zhū kùn zhǎng ròu.** 人困卖屋，猪困长肉。 [When] people [are] lazy, [they must] sell [their] houses, [but when] pigs [are] lazy, [they] become fat. [Note: *kùn* is dialect for "lazy"; see also *xìnle dù* below.]

89 **Rén lǎo, jiān; mǎ lǎo, huá.** 人老奸，马老滑。 People [when] old, [become] wily, [just as] horses [with] age [become] cunning. [Note: *jiānhuá*, "crafty"; compare the following entry.]

90 **Rén lǎo, jīng; jiāng lǎo, là.** 人老精，姜老辣。 An older person is shrewder, [just as] old ginger is more pungent. [Note: the adjective *lǎolà*, "(1) experienced; (2) determined; drastic; ruthless"; see also *shēngjiāng shì lǎo de là* below; compare the preceding entry.]

91 **Rén lǎo wúníng; shén lǎo wú líng.** 人老无能，神老无灵。 [When] people [grow] old, [they become] incapable, [just as when] gods [grow] old they are no longer efficacious. [Note: *língyàn*, "efficacious"; see also *ménshén lǎole* above and the following entry.]

92 **Rén lǎo, zhū huáng, bù zhíqián.*** 人老珠黄，不值钱。 [When] people [get] old, [like old,] yellowed pearls, [they] lose their value. [Note: *rénlǎo-zhūhuáng*, is used as a set expression meaning "youth's splendor has faded"; see also *shù lǎo, shēng chóng* below and the preceding and following entries.]

93 **Rén lǎo, zhū huáng, méi yào yī.** 人老珠黄，没药医。 (lit) People [grow] old, [just as] pearls [grow] yellow [with age]; there is no medicine which can cure [it]. (fig) Old age is inevitable. [See the preceding entry.]

94 **Rèn lǐ, bù rèn rén; bùpà bù liǎoshì.** 认理不认人，不怕不了事。 [If one acts or makes decisions] based on reason, [and] not based on person[al relationships], [then there is] no need to worry that things cannot be resolved.

95 **Rén liú, sānfēn jiǎ; yǔ liú, shífēn zhēn.** 人留三分假，雨留十分真。 (lit) [If] someone [politely] detains [a guest, it's] thirty percent false, [but if] rain detains [a guest from departing, it's] one hundred percent true. [See also *hǎo yǔ, tiān liúkè* above.]

96 **Rén líxiāng jiàn.** 人离乡贱。 (lit) [When] one leaves [one's] native place, [one feels] worthless. (fig) One feels worthless in a strange land. [Cf. *JW*, chap. 36.]

97 **Rén máng; shén bùmáng.** 人忙，神不忙。 (lit) Humans get agitated, [but] gods do not. (fig) Those who seek help (in life) get agitated, but those who are asked for help do not (so there's no point in getting upset about life's vicissitudes).

98 **Rén miàn xiāngsì; rénxīn bùtóng.** 人面相似，人心不同。 (lit) People's appearances are similar [but] their hearts are different. (fig) "Appearances can be deceiving." [Cf. *Xǐngshì Héngyán*, chap. 10.]

99 **Rén miàn zhǐchǐ, xīn gé qiān lǐ.** 人面咫尺，心隔千里。 [Although] people may stand face to face, [their] minds [may be a] thousand miles apart. [Cf. *JPM*, chap. 81; note also the *chengyu: zhǐchǐ-*

tiānyá, "only a short distance away, yet poles apart."]

100 **Rénmìng dà rú tiān.** 人命大如天。Human life is as important as heaven. [Said, e.g., of murder; cf. *WM*, chap. 22; see also the following entry.]

101 **Rénmìng guān tiān.** 人命关天。(lit) [A case involving] human life concerns heaven. (fig) To kill a person is a crime as high as heaven. [Cf. *Chū Kè Pāi'àn Jīngqí*, chap. 15; note: *rénmìng-guāntiān* is also used as a *chengyu* meaning "a matter of life and death."]

102 **Rén mò zhī qí zǐ zhī è, mò zhī qí miáo zhī shuò.** 人莫知其子之恶，莫知其苗之硕。(lit) People don't know the evil of their children, nor see the growing of the seedlings they plant. (fig) One naturally can't see the shortcomings of one's favorites. [Cf. Confucius' *Lǐjì: Dà Xué* (The Book of Rites: Great Learning).]

103 **Rén néng bǎi rěn zì wú yōu.** 人能百忍自无忧。(lit) Those [who] can endure everything naturally [will] have no worries. (fig) Endurance drives worries away. [Cf. *Xǐngshì Héngyán*, chap. 34.]

104 **Rén néng kèjǐ, shēn wú huàn; shì bù qī xīn, shuì zì ān.** 人能克己，身无患；事不欺心，睡自安。If one can control oneself, one will never invite trouble; if one never does anything deceitful, one will sleep soundly. [Rhyme; note the *chengyu: kèjǐ-fùlǐ*, "to restrain oneself and restore the ancient rites"; see also *méi zuò kuīxīnshì* above.]

105 **Rén nián wǔshí bù wéi yāo.** 人年五十不为夭。One [who is] fifty years old cannot [be said to] die young. [Saying dating from before 1949; see also *rén dào wǔshí* above.]

106 **Rén pà chūmíng; zhū pà zhuàng.*** 人怕出名，猪怕壮。Fame portends trouble for humans [just as] fattening does for pigs. [Cf. *DRC*, chap. 83; often used by Mao Zedong.]

107 **Rén pà diūliǎn; shù pà bōpí.*** 人怕丢脸，树怕剥皮。Losing face is as important to people as losing bark is to a tree. [See also *rénrén yǒu miàn* below.]

108 **Rén pà è; dì pà huāng.** 人怕饿，地怕荒。Hunger is [as] fearsome to people [as] lying barren is to the land.

109 **Rén pà lǎolái pín.** 人怕老来贫。[What] people fear [most is] poverty in old age. [See also *tián pà qiūrì hàn* below.]

110 **Rén pà lǎolái qióng; hé pà Hánlù fēng.** 人怕老来穷，禾怕寒露风。[What] people fear most [is being] poor in old age, [just as] rice [about to sprout] can't stand the [cold] wind late in autumn. [Rhyme; note: *Hànlù*, "Cold Dew" refers to the seventeenth solar term.]

111 **Rén pà lǎo xīn; shù pà lǎo gēn.** 人怕老心，树怕老根。The worst thing for people is to feel [themselves] old, [just as] the worst thing for trees is withering roots.

112 **Rén pà luò dàng; tiě pà luò lú.** 人怕落荡，铁怕落炉。(lit) People are [as] afraid of falling into a marsh [as] iron is of falling into a stove. (fig) Falling into traps set by others is as dangerous to people as iron falling into a furnace and melting. [Cf. *WM*, chap. 61.]

113 **Rén pà niánlǎo; hé pà gān.** 人怕年老，河怕干。People are afraid of old age [just as] rivers fear dry[ing up].

114 **Rén pà qíxīn; hǔ pà chéngqún.** 人怕齐心，虎怕成群。People united in a common cause [are just as dangerous as tigers] united in a pack.

115 **Rén pà sānfēn guǐ; guǐ pà qīfēn rén.** 人怕三分鬼，鬼怕七分人。(lit) People fear ghosts thirty percent, [while] ghosts fear people seventy percent. (fig) Evildoers are more afraid of the just than the other way around (because they know that justice will always triumph in the end). [Also said *rén yǒu sānfēn pà guǐ, guǐ yǒu qīfēn pà rén*; see also *rén yǒu sānfēn pà hǔ* below.]

116 **Rén pà shàngchuáng; zì pà shàng qiáng.** 人怕上床，字怕上墙。[Just as] people are afraid to be on [their death] beds, [so people] fear having [their Chinese] characters [displayed] on the wall [where their faults of their calligraphy can plainly be seen]. [Usually said modestly of one's own calligraphy.]

117 **Rén pà shāngxīn; shù pà bōpí.** 人怕伤心，树怕剥皮。Having their feelings hurt is as important to people as losing bark is to trees.

118 **Rén pěng xì; xì pěng rén.** 人捧戏，戏捧人。(lit) [If] audiences praise the play, the play [will] make the actors famous. (fig) (1) If an actor gives a good performance in a play, that play will make him or her famous. (2) Whether something is successful or not ultimately depends on its reception with critics, powerful people and/or the masses. [See also *shí nián pùzi* below.]

119 **Rén píng bù yǔ; shuǐ píng bù liú.** 人平不语，水平不流。(lit) People [who have been treated on the level] do not speak, [just as] water [which is held] level does not flow. (fig) People who have been treated fairly don't complain. [Rhyme; cf. *Xǐngshì Héngyán*, chap. 17; two halves also occur in the reverse order: see *shuǐ píng bù liú* below.]

120 **Rén píng zhìqì; hǔ píng wēi.** 人凭志气，虎凭威。People['s success] depends on [their] determination [just as a] tiger['s ability to frighten] depends on [its] imposing appearance.

121 **Rén pín, zhì duǎn; mǎ shòu, máo cháng.** 人贫志短，马瘦毛长。(lit) [When] people are poor, [their] ambitions are reduced, [just as when] horses get thin, [their] hair [appears to be] longer. (fig) Poverty stifles ambition. [See also *niǎo shòu, máo cháng* above.]

122 **Rén qiǎo bùrú jiāshi qiǎo; jiāshi zài qiǎo shì rén zào.** 人巧不如家什巧，家什再巧是人造。(lit) People's ingenuity [may] not [be as good] as ingenious tools, [but no matter] how ingenious the tools [are, they are] made by people. (fig) Human beings are ultimately the decisive factor in success.

123 **Rén qī bù shì rǔ; rén pà bù shì fú.** 人欺不是辱，人怕不是福。To be bullied is not an insult; to be feared is not a blessing. [Rhyme; cf. Lin Baitong's *Gǔ Yàn Jiàn*, a Qing dynasty proverb collection.]

124 **Rénqíng bù shì zhài; hébì dǐng guō mài.** 人情不是债，何必顶锅卖。(lit) Human relationships are not [like a money] debt; it is not necessary to mount [your] cooking pot on [your] head and sell [it to repay them]. (fig) If you can repay a favor, do so; otherwise forget it. [This rhyme is a humorous denial of the following entry.]

125 **Rénqíng dà sì shèngzhǐ.** 人情大似圣旨。People will do more out of personal favoritism than [they would on the] emperor's edict. [Cf. *JW*, chap. 53.]

126 **Rénqíng dàyú fǎdù.*** 人情大于法度。(lit) People will do more based on personal favoritism than according to the law. (fig) Personal relationships are more important than the law in deciding a case.

127 **Rénqíng guī rénqíng; gōngdào guī gōngdào.** 人情归人情，公道归公道。Private relationships are one thing [and] public justice is [quite] another [so the former should not interfere in the latter]. [See also *gōng shì gōng* above.]

128 **Rénqíng jí rú zhài, tóu dǐng guō'ér mài.** 人情急如债，头顶锅儿卖。(lit) [Repaying a] favor is as urgent as [repaying a] debt; [if necessary one will have to] put [one's] cooking pot [on one's] head [and] sell [it in order to repay it].

129 **Rénqíng, rénqíng; zài rén qíngyuàn.** 人情人情，在人情愿。(lit) True affection lies in a person's willingness. (fig) Only gifts and favors given willingly are a sign of true affection. [Cf. *WM*, chap. 38.]

130 **Rénqíng Sānxiá shuǐ; shìshì yīpánqí.** 人情三峡水，世事一盘棋。(lit) Human affections [are like] water rushing through the Three [Yangtse] Gorges; the ways of the world [are like] a game of chess. (fig) Human affections are transient and human affairs are a constant contest. [The Three Gorges of the Yangtse River in Sichuan province are famous for their beauty and turbulence; see also *rénshēng yīpánqí* below.]

131 **Rénqíng sì zhǐ zhāngzhāng báo; shìshì rú qí jújú xīn.** 人情似纸张张薄，世事如棋局局新。[Each instance of] human affection is as thin as a [separate] sheet of paper; life's situations are each as different as each [new] game of chess. [See also *guān qíng rú zhǐ báo* above and *rénshēng yīpánqí* below.]

132 **Rén qīn, gǔròu xiāng.** 人亲，骨肉香。(lit) [When] people are related, [their] flesh [and] blood [ties are] strong. (fig) "Blood is thicker than water." [See also *xuè bǐ shuǐ nóng* below.]

133 **Rénqíng yī bǎ jū; nǐ bù lái, wǒ bù qù.** 人情一把锯；你不来，我不去。Human relationships [are like the movement of a] saw; if there's no "to," there's no "fro." [Rhyme.]

134 **Rén qióng, dāngjiē màiyì; hǔ shòu, lánlù shāngrén.** 人穷当街卖艺，虎瘦拦路伤人。(lit) [When (s)he is] poor, a person [will] make a living as a street-performer [just as when it is] hungry, a tiger [will] attack people on the road. (fig) When poor, one must resort to any means to make a living.

135 **Rén qióng duàn liùqīn.** 人穷断六亲。[When] one is poor, [even one's close] relatives break [off relations]. [Note: *liùqīn*, the "six relations," refers to father, mother, elder brothers, younger brothers, wife and children; see also the colloquial expression: *liùqīn bù rèn*, "not recognizing one's relations"; see also *huāngnián wú liùqīn* above.]

136 **Rén qióng, péngyou shǎo; yī pò, shīzi duō.** 人穷朋友少，衣破虱子多。[When] one is poor, [one] has fewer friends, [just as when one's] clothes [get] ragged, [there are] more lice.

137 **Rén qióng, qióng zài zhài; tiān lěng, lěng zài fēng.*** 人穷穷在债，天冷冷在风。(lit) People are poor because of debts, [just as] the weather feels cold because of the wind. (fig) Indebtedness leads to poverty (so avoid it).

138 **Rén qióng, quǎn yě qī.** 人穷，犬也欺。[When] people are poor, even dogs will bully [them]. [See also *rén ruǎn bèi gǒu qī* below.]

139 **Rén qù, bùzhōng liú.** 人去不中留。[If] someone [wants to] leave, it's not OK [to try to persuade him to] stay [i.e., because his heart is not here]. [Cf. *DRC*, chap. 46; see also *xīn qù, yì nán liú* below.]

140 **Rénrén tóu shàng dǐng kuài tiān.** 人人头上顶块天。(lit) There is a patch of heaven over everyone's head. (fig) Every individual has an equal potential to bring his or her potential into full play. [See also *gè rén tóushang* above.]

141 **Rénrén yǒu miàn, shùshù yǒu pí.** 人人有面，树树有皮。(lit) Every person has a face [just as] every tree has bark. (fig) "Face" [i.e., self-esteem] is as important to a human being as bark is to a tree. [Cf. *JPM*, chap. 76; see also *rén pà diūliǎn* above.]

142 **Rén ruǎn bèi gǒu qī; niǎo ruǎn bèi māo qī.** 人软被狗欺，鸟软被猫欺。A person [of] weak [character] will be bullied by dogs [just as a] weak bird will be bullied by cats. [See also *rén qióng, quǎn yě qī* above.]

143 **Rén ruòbù kuākǒu, xiūchǐ bù líntóu.** 人若不夸口，羞耻不临头。If one doesn't boast, shame won't come upon [one's] head. [Rhyme.]

144 **Rěn rǔ zhì sān gōng.** 忍辱至三公。[One who can] swallow insults [will] rise to high official position. [Note: *sān gōng* refers to the three highest officials in the Western Han dynasty, *chéngxiàng*, "prime minister," *tàiwèi*, "supreme commander," and *yùshǐ dàfu*, "imperial secretary"; see also *rěn dé yīshí fēn* below.]

145 **Rén shàn, dé rén qī; mǎ shàn, dé rén qí.** 人善得人欺，马善得人骑。An honest person [will always] be imposed upon [just as] an obedient horse [will always] be ridden. [Also said *rén shàn, yǒu rén* ... etc.; cf. *JPM*, chap. 76; see also *liángshàn bèi rén qī* above.]

R

146 **Rén shàng yībǎi, xíngxíng-sèsè.** 人上一百，形形色色。(lit) In [a group of] one hundred people, [there are] every [imaginable] sort. (fig) "It takes all sorts (of people) to make a world." [Note: *xíngxíng-sèsè* is a *chengyu* meaning "of every shade and description."]

147 **Rén shǎo, chùsheng duō.** 人少，畜生多。(lit) There are fewer human beings than animals. (fig) There are more bad people (in the world) than good ones.

148 **Rénshēng bǎisuì, zǒng yǒu yī sǐ.** 人生百岁，总有一死。(lit) [Although] one may live to one hundred, there is always one death. (fig) Everyone has to die sooner or later. [Cf. *Xǐngshì Héngyán*, chap. 27.]

149 **Rénshēng bù dé xíng xiōngyì, suī huó bǎisuì yóu wéi yāo.** 人生不得行胸臆，虽活百岁犹为夭。(lit) [If in] one's life [one] cannot realize [one's] ambitions, although [one may] live [to be a] hundred years old, [it's] like dying young. (fig) One who cannot realize his aspirations dies young, though he may live to be a hundred years old.

150 **Rénshēng bù zhīzú, dé Lǒng yòu wàng Shǔ.** 人生不知足，得陇又望蜀。(lit) Humans [are] born never [to] know satisfaction; [as soon as one] occupies Long, [one] also looks toward Shu [as well]. (fig) Humans are greedy; they will never be satisfied with what they have. [Note: *dé Lǒng wàng Shǔ*, a *chengyu* meaning "to have insatiable desires," refers to a famous episode in *R3K*, in which Zhuge Liang helped Liu Bei to occupy the small country of Long (near present day Gansu province), as part of his larger scheme to invade Shu, in modern day Sichuan province; see also *rénxīn bùzú* and *rénxīn gāo guò tiān* below.]

151 **Rénshēng dàn jiǎng qián sānshí.** 人生但讲前三十。(lit) [In evaluating] someone's life, only discuss the first thirty [years]. (fig) You can judge a person's accomplishments in life by his first thirty years.

152 **Rénshēng jǐ jiàn yuè dāngtóu?** 人生几见月当头？(lit) [In] one's life how many [times can one] see the moon overhead? (fig) How many times can a person look up at the moon in his life? How many good times can one have in one's life? How brief life is! [See also *qīngchūn yì guò* above.]

153 **Rén shēnglù bù shú, suíchù jiào "Āshū."** 人生路不熟，随处叫"阿叔"。(lit) [When] one [is on an] unfamiliar road [and] lost, wherever [one goes, one should] address everyone [one meets as] "uncle." (fig) Be polite and modest whenever you come into a new place or situation. [Rhyme; note: *shūshu*, (lit) "father's younger brother," is a child's polite form of address toward a male of a generation older than oneself; *Ā* is a familiar, rustic prefix; see also *jiàn rén bù shílǐ* above.]

154 **Rénshēng qīshí gǔlái xī.*** 人生七十古来稀。Since ancient times, people have rarely lived to the age of seventy. [A line from a poem, "Qǔ Jiāng," by the Tang dynasty poet Du Fu.]

155 **Rénshēng rú báijū-guòxì.** 人生如白驹过隙。Human life is [as short as the time it takes for a] small white horse to pass through a crevice. [Cf. *R3K*, chap. 107; note: *báijū-guòxì* is used as a *chengyu* with the sense of "How time flies!"; originally from *Zhuāngzǐ: Zhī Běi Yóu*, in which *bái jū* is a metaphor for the sun.]

156 **Rénshēng sàng jiā wáng shēn, yányǔ zhàn le bāfēn.** 人生丧家亡身，言语占了八分。In life the ruin of families [and] the death of individuals [results] eighty percent [i.e., primarily] from imprudent talk. [See also *bìng cóng kǒu rù* above.]

157 **Rénshēng yīpánqí.** 人生一盘棋。(lit) Human life is [constantly changing like] a chess game. (fig) Life has vicissitudes. [See also *rén yǒu qí pín* and *shìshì yǒuchéng* and *suī yǒu xiōngsuì* below.]

158 **Rénshēng yīshì; cǎo shēng yī qiū.** 人生一世，草生一秋。(lit) People [only] live one lifetime, [just as] grass [only] grows for one autumn. (fig) People only live their allotted time, just as grass dies in autumn. [Cf. *Píng Yāo Zhuàn*, chap. 10.]

159 **Rén shì dì xíng xiān; (yī tiān bùjiàn, zǒu yīqiān).** 人是地行仙，(一天不见，走一千)。(lit) People are [like] gods wandering on earth, ([if you do] not see [them, they may have] traveled a thousand [miles away]). (fig) (1) People are wanderers; (here today, (but) gone tomorrow). (2) Human beings are powerful. [Rhyme; cf. *DRC*, chap. 87; the second half may be omitted.]

160 **Rén shì dí zāixīng.** 忍事敌灾星。(lit) [One who can] endure things [will be able to] resist the disaster star. (fig) One who can control himself and suppress his indignation will avoid disasters. [Note: *zāixīng* refers to an omen of disaster in Chinese astrology; compare "ill-starred"; see also *rěn yī shí* below.]

161 **Rénshì kěyǐ bǔ tiāngōng.** 人事可以补天工。(lit) Human actions can supplement nature's work. (fig) Humans can create what nature can't. [Note the *chengyu*: *qiǎoduó-tiāngōng*, "superb craftsmanship, excelling nature"; see also *tiāngōng, rén kě dài* below.]

162 **Rénshì nán féng kāikǒu xiào.** 人世难逢开口笑。In life it is rare to encounter [happy things that make one] laugh heartily. [A line from a Tang dynasty poem by Du Mu entitled "Jiǔ Rì Qí Shān Dēng Gāo," later quoted by Mao Zedong in a poem entitled "Hè Xīnláng: Dú Shǐ."]

163 **Rén shì tiě; fàn shì gāng;* (yī dùn bù chī, è de huāng).** 人是铁，饭是钢；(一顿不吃，饿得慌)。(lit) People are [like] iron; food is [like] steel; (if one misses a meal, one will become weak from hunger). (fig) Humans are like (naturally occurring) iron; food makes them like steel; (even a strong and healthy person will become weak from lack of food). [Rhyme; the first half is a very popular saying; the second half may be omitted; cf. *Yuè Fēi Zhuàn*, chap. 31.]

164 **Rén shì yīfu, mǎ shì ān.** 人是衣服，马是鞍。(lit) Clothing is to people [what] a saddle is to a horse. (fig) "Clothes make the man." [Cf. *Yuè Fēi*

Zhuàn, chap. 90; see also *mǎ kào ān zhuāng* and *rén kào yī zhuāng* above.]

165 **Rén shú, hǎo bànshì.** 人熟，好办事。 (lit) [When] people are close, matters are easily handled. (fig) It is easier to take care of matters when one is on good terms with the other party. [See also *rén shú shì yī bǎo* below.]

166 **Rén shú, lǐ bù shú.** 人熟，礼不熟。 (lit) People may be familiar, [but] courtesy [should] not be familiar. (fig) Even when one is on good terms with someone, courtesies should still be observed and gifts should still be presented. [Cf. *Wǔ Sōng*, chap. 2.]

167 **Rén shú shì yī bǎo.** 人熟是一宝。 (lit) Familiarity between people is a treasure. (fig) Friends and acquaintances are most valuable when you want to have business done. [See also *rén shú, hǎo bànshì* above.]

168 **Rén sǐ rú dēng miè.** 人死如灯灭。 (lit) People die just as [oil] lamps go out. (fig) Life is like a candle flame; all is vanity. [Cf. *Wǔ Sōng*, chap. 2; *Érnǚ Yīngxióng Zhuàn*, chap. 9; *JPM*, chap. 62.]

169 **Rén sǐ zhàng làn.** 人死帐烂。 (lit) [When a] person dies [his] account is canceled. (fig) Death cancels all debts.

170 **Rén sú bù kě yī.** 人俗不可医。 [A] person['s] vulgar [taste] cannot be cured. [Note: *yōngsú*, "vulgar; philistine."]

171 **Rén suí wángfǎ, cǎo suí fēng.** 人随王法，草随风。 People must abide by the law (of the land), [just as] grass bows before the wind. [See also *wángzǐ fànfǎ* below.]

172 **Rén tái, rén gāo.** 人抬，人高。 [By flattering one another], people raise each other higher. [Cf. *Wǔ Sōng*, chap. 6.]

173 **Rén tóng cǐ xīn, xīn tóng cǐ lǐ.** 人同此心，心同此理。 (lit) People all share this mind, [and their] minds all share this principle. (fig) A sense of justice is common to all people. [Cf. *Érnǚ Yīngxióng Zhuàn*, chap. 9.]

174 **Rěn tòng yì; rěn yǎng nán.** 忍痛易，忍痒难。 (lit) It is easier to endure pain [than to] endure an itch. (fig) People are easily tempted. [From an essay by the Song dynasty poet Su Dongbo.]

175 **Rén tuōrén, jiē shàngtiān.** 人托人，接上天。 (lit) [If] people [keep on] asking for help [on behalf of] others, [eventually one can] connect up to Heaven. (fig) In order to achieve one's goal, one has to work slowly through layers of connections. [Note: *běnshi tōng tiān*, "the ability to contact the top people"; *guānxi wǎng*, "network of connections."]

176 **Rén wài yǒu rén; tiān wài yǒu tiān.** 人外有人，天外有天。 There are always more talented people who can be found, [just as] there are even higher heavens beyond the sky, [so don't be conceited]. [Cf. *Yuè Fēi Zhuàn*, chap. 81; note: *tiānwài-yǒutiān* is used as a set phrase meaning "knowledge/capability is limitless"; see also *qiáng zhōng háiyǒu* above and *shān wài yǒu shān* below.]

177 **Rén wǎng gāochù zǒu; shuǐ wǎng dīchù liú.** 人往高处走，水往低处流。 People [naturally] tend to rise [in social position, just as] water [naturally] tends to flow down[hill]. [Rhyme.]

178 **Rén wàng rén hǎo; yánwàng wàng guǐ hǎo.** 人望人好，阎王望鬼好。 (lit) Humans wish their own kind well [just as] Yan Wang [the King of Hell] wishes his devils well. (fig) Each group cares about its own kind.

179 **Rén wàng xìngfú; shù wàng chūn.** 人望幸福，树望春。 Humans hope for happiness [just as] trees look forward to spring.

180 **Rén wèi cái sǐ; niǎo wèi shí wáng.*** 人为财死，鸟为食亡。 (lit) Human beings die in the pursuit of wealth [just as] birds die in the pursuit of food. (fig) The wages of avarice is death. [See also *gǔlái fāng ěr* above.]

181 **Rén wéi qiú jiù; wù wéi qiú xīn.** 人惟求旧，物惟求新。 (lit) [In] people, only seek old [friends]; [in] things [only] seek new [ones]. (fig) Old friends are better, just as new things are better. [Cf. *Shāng Shū: Pán Gēng*; see also *yīfu shì xīn de hǎo* below.]

182 **Rén wèi shāngxīn bùdé sǐ; huā cán yè luò shì gēn kū.** 人未伤心不得死，花残叶落是根枯。 People don't die unless their hearts are broken; [just as] flowers and leaves don't fall unless the roots are withered. [Cf. *JW*, chap. 66.]

183 **Rén wú bǎinián zhuō.** 人无百年拙。 (lit) People can't be foolish [for one] hundred years [i.e., all their lives]. (fig) People become wiser as they get older. [Note: *bǎinián*, (lit) "a hundred years" also means "a lifetime."]

184 **Rén wú gāngqiáng, ānshēn bù láo.** 人无刚强，安身不牢。 A person cannot secure a position in society if (s)he is not strong enough. [Cf. *JPM*, chap. 1 and *WM*, chap. 24; see also *rénxīn wú gāng* below.]

185 **Rén wú hài hǔ xīn; hǔ yǒu shāngrén yì.** 人无害虎心，虎有伤人意。 (lit) People have no desire to harm tigers, [but] tigers want to hurt people. (fig) We have no intention to harm others, but others may try to hurt us [so be careful].

186 **Rén wú hèngcái, bù fù; mǎ wú yè liào, bù féi.** 人无横财不富，马无夜料不肥。 A person cannot get rich without a windfall or ill-gotten gains [just as] a horse won't grow strong without eating fodder at night. [Also said . . . *mǎ wú yě cǎo* . . . "without [eating] wild grasses"; vs. *wài cái bù fú rén* and *xiǎng shí hèngcái* below.]

187 **Rén wú hòu yǎn.** 人无后眼。 (lit) People do not have eyes in the back of their heads [so they cannot avoid treachery, deceit, etc.]. (fig) Be careful. [Cf. *JPM*, chap. 25; see also *shǒuzhǎng zěnyàng* below.]

188 **Rén wú liánchǐ; wángfǎ nán zhì.** 人无廉耻，王法难治。 [If a] person has no sense of shame, [even] the law will hardly control him.

189 **Rén wú lì jǐ, shéi kěn zǎoqǐ.** 人无利己，谁肯早起。 No one gets up early [to work] if it is not in his or her own interest. [Rhyme; cf. *Jǐngshì Tōngyán*, chap. 21; see also *bù tú lì* above.]

R

190 **Rén wú qiān rì hǎo; huā wú bǎi rì hóng.** 人无千日好，花无百日红。 People cannot always be fortunate, or get along smoothly, [just as] flowers do not bloom forever. [Cf. *Xīngshì Héngyán*, chap. 1; the second part is also used alone; see also *huā wú qiān rì* above.]

191 **Rén wú qiān rì jì, lǎo zhì yīchǎngkōng.** 人无千日计，老至一场空。 If one does not have a long-term plan, [when one becomes] old, [one will have] nothing at all.

192 **Rén wú tóu bù zǒu; niǎo wú tóu bù fēi.** 人无头不走，鸟无头不飞。 (lit) People without heads [can]not walk, [just as] birds without heads [can]not fly. (fig) People cannot do things without a leader. [See also *bīng wú jiàng* above and *shé wú tóu* below.]

193 **Rén wú wánrén; jīn wú zúchì.** * 人无完人，金无足赤。 People cannot be perfect [just as] gold cannot be pure. [Also said *rén wú wánrén; jīn wú zújīn*; often used by Mao Zedong; the two halves are more usually said in the reverse order (q.v.); see also *shì ruò qiúquán* below.]

194 **Rén wú xiàoliǎn xiū kāi diàn.** 人无笑脸休开店。 (lit) A person [who can]not smile had better not open up a store. (fig) (The appearance of) friendliness is necessary to being a successful businessperson.

195 **Rén xiāng, qiān lǐ xiāng.** 人香，千里香。 (lit) [If a] person [smells] fragrant, [the fragrance will] waft a thousand miles. (fig) A good reputation will spread far and wide. [Cf. the Yuan dynasty stage version of *JW*, vol. 6, act 23, by Yang Jinxian; note: one *lǐ* equals one-half kilometer.]

196 **Rén xián shēngbìng; shí xián shēng tái.** 人闲生病，石闲生苔。 [When] people are idle, [they] become sick, [just as when] stones are [left] idle, moss grows [on them].

197 **Rén xià rén, xià sǐ rén.** 人吓人，吓死人。 [Only] people can frighten other people to death, [not ghosts].

198 **Rénxīn bù sì shuǐ cháng liú.** 人心不似水长流。 (lit) People's minds are not like rivers [which] flow constantly. (fig) People are inconstant and change their minds. [Cf. *Dòu É Yuán*, Act 1, by the Yuan dynasty classical playwright Guan Hanqing.]

199 **Rénxīn bù tóng, gè rú qí miàn.** 人心不同，各如其面。 (lit) People's hearts differ [just as] their faces do. (fig) People have different minds [just as] they have different looks. [Cf. *Ěrnǚ Yīngxióng Zhuàn*, chap. 7; see also *rénxīn rú miàn* below.]

200 **Rénxīn bùzú, shé tūn xiàng.** * 人心不足，蛇吞象。 People are [sometimes] as greedy as a snake trying to swallow an elephant. [Cf. *Jīngshì Tōngyán*, chap. 25; a line of poetry by the Ming dynasty poet Luó Hóngxiān, alluding to an image in the ancient text *Shān Hǎi Jīng*; see also *rén kǔ, bù zhīzú* and *rénshēng bù zhīzú* above and *rénxīn gāo guò tiān* and *zhè shān wàngjiàn* below.]

201 **Rénxīn dōu shì cháo shàng zhǎng.** 人心都是朝上长。 (lit) All human hearts grow upwards. (fig) Everyone has high aspirations.

202 **Rénxīn (dōu) shì ròu zhǎng de.** 人心(都)是肉长的。 (lit) People's hearts are made of flesh. (fig) All human beings have tender feelings.

203 **Rénxīn dōu zài rénxīn shàng.** 人心都在人心上。 (lit) Sincerity is always [recalled or recognized] in the hearts of others. (fig) Sincerity will be returned with sincerity. [Cf. Lao She's play: *Lóng Xū Gōu* (Dragon Beard Ditch), Act 3; see also *rénxīn huàn rénxīn* below.]

204 **Rénxīn gāo guò tiān; zuòle huángdì, xiǎng chéng xiān.** 人心高过天；做了皇帝，想成仙。 (lit) The human heart is higher than Heaven; [when one has] become [an] emperor, [one] wants to become a god. (fig) Humans are never content. [See also *rénshēng bù zhīzú* and *rénxīn bùzú* above.]

205 **Rénxīn gé dùpí.** * 人心隔肚皮。 (lit) People's hearts are separated [(i.e., hidden) behind their] belly skins. (fig) It's hard to see into another person's heart. [Cf. *Ěrnǚ Yīngxióng Zhuàn*, chap. 40; *Xīngshì Héngyán*, chap. 43.]

206 **Rén xíng yǒu jiǎoyìn; niǎo guò yǒu luò máo.** 人行有脚印，鸟过有落毛。 (lit) [When] a person walks by, he leaves his footmarks behind, [just as] when a bird passes by, it leaves feathers on the ground. (fig) One cannot completely cover one's tracks; truth will out in the end.

207 **Rénxīn huàn rénxīn.** 人心换人心。 (lit) Human hearts repay human hearts [in kind]. (fig) If you are kind and honest, others will be kind and honest to you. [Cf. *Zàishēng Yuán*, chap. 69; see also *rénxīn dōu zài* above.]

208 **Rénxīn nán cè; hǎishuǐ nán liáng.** * 人心难测，海水难量。 People's minds are hard to fathom, [just as] ocean water cannot be measured. [Cf. *Èr Kè Pāi'àn Jīngqí*, chap. 20; *Xīngshì Héngyán*, chap. 22; see also *rén bù kě mào xiàng* above.]

209 **Rénxīn qí, Tài Shān yí.** * 人心齐，泰山移。 (lit) When people are of one mind, Mount Tai can be moved. (fig) When people are of one mind, they can move mountains. "In unity there is strength." [Rhyme; Mount Tai, a large mountain in Shandong province and one of the five sacred mountains, is commonly used as a symbol of great weight or import.]

210 **Rénxīn rú miàn.** 人心如面。 (lit) People['s] hearts are like [their] faces. (fig) People have different minds just as they have different appearances. [Cf. *Zuǒ Zhuàn: Xiāng Gōng 31 Nián*; see also *rénxīn bù tóng* above.]

211 **Rénxīn sì tiě, guān fǎ rú lú.** 人心似铁，官法如炉。 (lit) [Even] if a person's will is [as hard as] iron, the law is [as fierce as] a furnace. (fig) Just as iron will melt in a furnace, so no person can resist the law. [Cf. *Jǐngshì Tōngyán*, chap. 14.]

212 **Rénxīn wèi mǐn, gōng lùn nán táo.** 人心未泯，公论难逃。 [As long as] the people's sense of justice has not disappeared, public judgment [will be] difficult to avoid.

213 **Rénxīn wú gāng, yīshì qióng.** 人心无刚，一世穷。 If one is not strong-willed, one will remain poor all one's life. [See also *rén wú gāngqiáng* above.]

214 **Rén yăn nán hŏng.*** 人眼难哄。 (lit) People's eyes are hard to cheat. (fig) Public opinion is hard to deceive. [See also the following entry.]

215 **Rén yăn shì bă chèng.** 人眼是把秤。 (lit) People's eyes are like a scale. (fig) Public opinion can judge good from bad just as a scale can accurately assess weight. [See also *gōngpíng chūyú* and *línjū yǎnjing* above and *tiānxià qiányǎnr* and *zhīdǐ mò guò* and *zhòngrén yǎnjing* below and the preceding entry.]

216 **Rén yán wèibì zhēn; tīng yán tīng sānfēn.** 人言未必真, 听言听三分。 People do not always speak the truth, [so] believe [only] thirty percent of what you hear. [Rhyme; see also *féng rén qièshuō* above.]

217 **Rén yào cháng jiāo; zhàng yào duăn suàn.** 人要长交, 帐要短算。 Friends [should be] kept [for a] long [time]; accounts [should be] settled [in a] short [time].

218 **Rén yào zhōngxīn; huŏ yào kōngxīn.** 人要忠心, 火要空心。 [In] people, [one] needs loyal hearts, [just as in] fires, [one] needs ventilation. (fig) If one has loyal people, they will serve the country well, just as fires which have ventilation will burn well. [Rhyme; cf. *Wŭ Sōng*, chap. 8.]

219 **Rén yī, jĭ băi.** 人一己百。 [If] others [succeed by exerting] one [ounce of effort], I [will exert] one hundred [times as much effort]. [Confucius' *Lĭjì : Zhōng Yŏng* (The Golden Mean).]

220 **Rěn yīshí, yānxiāo-yúnsàn; rěn piànkè, hăikuò-tiānkōng.** 忍一时, 烟消云散; 忍片刻, 海阔天空。 (lit) [If one can] endure [things for] a short time, [one's problems will] "vanish like mist and smoke"; [if one can] endure [things for] a short while, [one's life will be] "as boundless as the sea and sky." (fig) If one can be patient in life and endure life's difficulties and indignities, one can have far greater chances of success in life. [Note: *yānxiāo-yúnsàn* and *yānxiāo-yúnsàn* are commonly used fixed literary *chengyu* expressions; see also *rěn shì dí zāixīng* above.]

221 **Rén yòng qián shì; jīn yòng huŏ shì.** 人用钱试, 金用火试。 People are tested by money, [just as] gold is tested by fire. [See also *zhēn jīn bùpà huŏ* below.]

222 **Rén yŏu gé xiŭ zhī zhì.** 人有隔宿之智。 (lit) People have wisdom [which comes] overnight. (fig) Sometimes it's necessary to "sleep on it" overnight. Things which aren't clear may become clearer after long and careful consideration.

223 **Rén yŏu liángxīn, gŏu bù chī shĭ.** 人有良心, 狗不吃屎。 (lit) [When] people have good consciences, [then] dogs [will] no [longer] eat excrement. (fig) People are usually not good-hearted. [See also *gŏu bù chī shĭ* and *gŏu găi bùliăo* above.]

224 **Rén yŏu liăng zhī jiăo; yínzi yŏu bā zhī jiăo.** 人有两支脚, 银子有八支脚。 (lit) People have two feet, [but] silver has eight (i.e., is faster). (fig) People cannot chase after luck; it happens or it doesn't.

225 **Rén yŏu qiánhòu yăn; fùguì yīqiān nián.** 人有前后眼, 富贵一千年。 (lit) If a person has eyes in front and in back of his head, he will remain wealthy for a thousand years. (fig) If one behaves cautiously at all times, he will enjoy a life of great wealth and high position. [Rhyme; see also *rén wú hòu yăn* below.]

226 **Rén yŏu qī pín, bā fù.** 人有七贫八富。 (lit) One may be poor at one time and rich at another. (fig) Life is full of ups and downs. [See also *rénshēng yīpánqí* above and *shìshì yŏuchéng* below.]

227 **Rén yŏu rén yán; shòu yŏu shòu yŭ.** 人有人言, 兽有兽语。 (lit) Human beings have their languages [and] wild animals have theirs. (fig) Good people and bad people have different ways of talking. [Note: *gěshòu*, (lit) "wild animals," here refers to bad people; see also *rén shăo, chùsheng duō* above.]

228 **Rén yŏu sānfēn pà hŭ; hŭ yŏu qīfēn pà rén.** 人有三分怕虎, 虎有七分怕人。 (lit) Tigers are more afraid of people than people are afraid of tigers. (fig) Bad people are more afraid of good people than good people are afraid of bad ones. [See also *rén pà sānfēn guĭ* above.]

229 **Rén yŏu shànyì, tiān bì cóng zhī.** 人有善意, 天必从之。 [If] one has good intentions, Heaven will [help to] realize them. [Also said . . . *bì yòu zhī*, ". . . Heaven will protect him."]

230 **Rén yŏu shīshŏu; mă yŏu lòu tí.*** 人有失手, 马有漏蹄。 Every person makes mistakes [sometimes, just as] every horse stumbles. [Cf. *Yuè Fēi Zhuàn*, chap. 28.]

231 **Rén yŏu tóng mào rén; wù yŏu tóngxíng wù.** 人有同貌人, 物有同形物。 There are people with the same appearance, [just as] there are things of the same shape.

232 **Rén yuàn, yŭ shēng gāo.** 人怨, 语声高。 (lit) [When one] complains, [one's] voice is louder. (fig) When people have complaints about unjust treatment, they naturally raise their voices. [Vs. *yŏu lĭ bù zài* below.]

233 **Rén zài, rénqíng zài; (rén wáng, liăng wú jiāo).** 人在人情在, (人亡两无交)。 Affection [among friends and relations] continues as long as the person is alive, [but] the parties lose touch when their common contact dies). [Said of family or social relations.]

234 **Rén zài shí zhōng, chuán yù shùnfēng.** 人在时中, 船遇顺风。 [When] things are going well for someone, [it's like sail] boat[ing] with a favorable wind.

235 **Rén zài wūyán xià, bùdé bù dītóu.** 人在屋檐下, 不得不低头。 (lit) [When a] person is under low eaves, [one has] no choice but to lower [one's] head. (fig) When one depends on others (for food, pay, support, etc.), one must do whatever they say. [Also said (jī) zài . . . (q.v.); see also *chángzi zhù zài* above.]

236 **Rén zào yŏu huò; tiān zào yŏu yŭ.** 人躁有祸, 天燥有雨。 [When a] person is hot-tempered there [will] be trouble, [just as when] the sky is hot and dry, there [will] be rain. [Note: this is a

pun on *zào*, "hot-tempered" and *zào*, "hot and dry (weather)."]

237 **Rén zhě jiàn rén; zhìzhě jiàn zhì.** 仁者见仁，智者见智。(lit) The benevolent see benevolence [and] the wise see wisdom. (fig) Different people have different views. "Let's agree to disagree." [Cf. *Yìjīng: Xì Cí.*]

238 **Rén zhēngqì; huǒ zhēng yàn.** 人争气，火争焰。People strive to rise to a challenge, [just as] fire aspires to [create a] flame. [See also the following entry.]

239 **Rén zhēng yīkǒuqì; fó shòu yī lú xiāng.** 人争一口气，佛受一炉香。(lit) People [will] rise to challenges, [just as] Buddhas [will] have incense [burned to them]. (fig) People will naturally stand up to challenges or bullying in life. [Cf. *JPM*, chap. 76; note: *zhēng (yī) kǒu qì*, "rise to a challenge; win credit for oneself; protect one's dignity"; see also the preceding entry.]

240 **Rén zhí, bù fù; gǎng zhí, bù shēn.** 人直不富，港直不深。A person [who is] straight [i.e., honest] won't get rich, [just as] a harbor [that is] straight [i.e., not curved] won't be deep [i.e., won't make a good harbor].

241 **Rén zhī bùxìng mòguòyú zìzú.** 人之不幸莫过于自足。No one is more unfortunate than those who are self-conceited.

242 **Rén zhī xiāngqù rú jiǔ niúmáo.** 人之相去如九牛毛。The differences between people [are] as [numerous as] the [total] number of hairs on nine oxen. [Note the chengyu: *xiāngqù-shènyuǎn*, "a world of difference".]

243 **Rén zhí, yǒu rén hé; lù zhí, yǒu rén xíng.** 人直有人合；路直有人行。[When] people are "straight" [i.e., upright and honest], other people [want to be] near them, [just as when] roads are straight, there are people walking [on them]. [See also *shù zhí, yòngchù duō* below.]

244 **"Rěn" zì, jiā zhōng bǎo.** "忍"字，家中宝。(lit) The word "forbearance" [is a] family's treasure. (fig) The family whose members can get along with each other and make concessions will live in harmony and prosper.

245 **"Rěn" zì tóu shàng, yī bǎ dāo.** "忍"字头上，一把刀。[The Chinese character] rěn 忍 ["forbearance," is written with a character for] "knife" 刀 [positioned] above [the character for "heart" 心]. (fig) If one is not patient, the sword will drop into one's heart; impatience invites disaster. [Cf. *Wǔ Sòng*, chap. 5; this may be said to be an example of Chinese character word-play or orthographic pun, as in a *zìmí*, "character riddle"; also said "*rěn" zì xīn shàng yī bǎ dāo.*]

246 **Rén zǒushí qì, mǎ zǒu biāo; (héshang dān zǒu dúmùqiáo).** 人走时气，马走膘，(和尚单走独木桥)。(lit) [Some] people get lucky, [just as some] horses get fat; [while many Buddhist] monks cross single plank bridges alone [i.e., tread their lonely, famililess way]). (fig) Some people get lucky and are successful, (while others do not;) that's just how life is. [Cf. *Yuè Fēi Zhuàn*, chap. 30; note: *zǒushí* means *zǒuyùn*, "to get lucky"; *dúmùqiáo*, (lit) "single-plank bridge," (fig)

"difficult path"; the optional second part is simply added as ə rhyme.]

247 **Rèxīnrén zhāolǎn shìfēi duō.** 热心人招揽是非多。An enthusiastic person invites trouble. [See also the following entry.]

248 **Rèxīn xián guǎn zhāo fēi; lěngyǎn wú xiē fánnǎo.** 热心闲管招非，冷眼无些烦恼。(lit) The enthusiastic invite trouble, [while] bystanders have no anxiety. (fig) Those who get involved with others' problems (may) bring trouble upon themselves, while those who remain aloof do not run that risk. [See also the preceding entry.]

249 **Rè zào nǎpà shī chái shāo.** 热灶哪怕湿柴烧。(lit) [If the] stove is hot, even wet firewood will burn. (fig) An able person won't be afraid to take up a challenging task. [Cf. *Hé Diǎn*, chap. 6.]

250 **Rì cháng, shì duō; yè cháng, mèng duō.** 日长事多，夜长梦多。(lit) The longer the day, the more things [come up], [just as] the longer the night, the more dreams [one has]. (fig) The longer you wait to do something, the more likely it is that something else will come up, so better not put things off. [The second part (q.v.) is often used alone as a *chengyu* with the meaning "long delays cause many hitches."]

251 **Rì chū wàn yán, bì yǒu yī shāng.** 日出万言，必有一伤。(lit) [If] ten thousand words are spoken in a day, there must be someone [who is] harmed. (fig) "Silence is golden."

252 **Rìjiān bù zuò kuīxīnshì; bànyè qiāomén bù chījīng.** 日间不作亏心事，半夜敲门不吃惊。(lit) [If one] doesn't do anything with a bad conscience in the daytime, [one] need not be afraid when [one hears] knocking at the door in the middle of the night. (fig) "A quiet conscience sleeps in thunder." [See also *báitiān bù zuò* and *bù zuò kuīxīnshì* and *méi zuò kuīxīnshì* above.]

253 **Rì jì bùzú; suì jì yǒuyú.** 日计不足；岁计有余。[Although in a] daily calculation [what one saves may] not be much, [over the] years [it will add up to] having surplus. [Rhyme; cf. *Zhuāngzǐ: Gēng Sāng Chǔ*; see also *jī shǎo chéng duō* above.]

254 **Rì jiǔ jiàn rénxīn.** 日久见人心。[See *lù yáo zhī mǎlì* above.]

255 **Rì lǐ jiǎng dào yèlǐ, púsà hái zài miào lǐ.** 日里讲到夜里，菩萨还在庙里。(lit) [Monks] preach from day to night, [but the image of the] Buddha still remains in the temple. (fig) Empty talk comes to nothing; one must do something!

256 **Rì lǐ mò shuō rén; yèlǐ mò shuō guǐ.** 日里莫说人，夜里莫说鬼。(lit) In the daytime, don't talk about [other] people [or they will come]; at night, don't talk about ghosts [or they will appear]. (fig) [A superstitious warning similar to:] "Speak of the devil (and he will appear)." [See also *shuōdào Cáo Cāo* below.]

257 **Rìrì xíng, bùpà wàn lǐ lù; shíshí zuò, bùpà shì bù chéng.** 日日行，不怕万里路；时时做，不怕事不成。However long the distance is, you will cover it if you walk every day; however much the work is, you will finish it if you work all the time.

258 **Rì yǒusuǒsī; yè yǒu suǒ mèng.*** 日有所思, 夜有所梦。[What you] think about in the daytime, [you will] dream about at night. [See also *mèng shì xīntóu* above.]

259 **Rì yǒu yīn-qíng; yuè yǒu yíng-kuī.*** 日有阴晴, 月有盈亏。(lit) The sun shines and disappears; the moon waxes and wanes. (fig) One may be well-off at one time and poor at another. [See also *luòcháo zǒng yǒu* and *rén yǒu qī pín* above and *rì zhōng zé yí* below.]

260 **Rì yuǎn rì shū; rì qīn rì jìn.** 日远日疏, 日亲日近。(lit) The longer [one is] separated [from someone], the more estranged [one will be]; the longer [people are] together, the closer [they will] grow. (fig) Remoteness begets neglect, while nearness brings about intimacy. [Originally from *WM*, chap. 2; sometimes said *rì shū, rì yuǎn*, etc.]

261 **Riyuè suī míng, bù zhào fù pén zhīnèi.** 日月虽明, 不照覆盆之内。(lit) However bright the sun or the moon may be, [their light] cannot reach [a spot] inside an inverted basin. (fig) It is common that there are unrighted wrongs or unredressed injustices in the world. [Cf. *Hòu Xīyóu Jì*, chap. 21.]

262 **Rì zhōng zé yí; yuè mǎn zé kuī.** 日中则移, 月满则亏。(lit) The sun rises to its zenith and then moves on; the moon waxes to its fullest and then wanes. (fig) Things will naturally go back in the opposite direction when they have reached an extreme. "The pendulum will swing back again." [Cf. *DRC*, chap. 13; see also *luòcháo zǒng yǒu* and *rén yǒu qī pín* and *rì yǒu yīn-qíng* above.]

263 **Ròu chī qiān rén kǒu; zuì luò yī rén shēn.** 肉吃千人口, 罪落一人身。The meat [may be] eaten by a thousand people, [but the] punishment falls on one person [only, so no one individual will dare to take the risk].

264 **Róuruǎn shì lì shēn zhī běn; gāngqiáng shì rěhuò zhī tāi.** 柔软是立身之本, 刚强是惹祸之胎。[To be] flexible is essential for getting along in the world; to be unyielding is the embryo of disaster. [Cf. *Shuǐhǔ Quán Zhuàn*, chap. 24.]

265 **Ruǎndāozi shārén bù jiàn xuè.** 软刀子杀人不见血。(lit) Killing with a "soft sword" sees no blood [shed]. (fig) It's difficult to detect the source of false charges cleverly fabricated. [Note: *ruǎndāozi*, (lit) "soft knife," means "harming by imperceptible means"; see also *shé shàng yǒu* below.]

266 **Rú bù zhīzú, zé shī suǒ yù.** 如不知足, 则失所欲。If [you're] not content [with what you've got], [you'll] lose what you desire. [Cf. *Sān Guó Zhì: Wèi Shū*; note the chengyu: *zhīzú (zhě) chánglè*, "(one) who knows how to be satisfied will always be happy"; see also *zhīzú, shēn cháng lè* below.]

267 **Rù háng sān rì wú liè.** 入行三日无劣。(lit) [Even if one has] engaged in a trade [for only] three days, [one] won't [be too] bad [at it]. (fig) One can learn something (just) by associating with specialists. [Cf. *Érnǚ Yīngxióng Zhuàn*, chap.

33; see also *gēnzhe wǎjiang* above and *sān tiān zhù zài* below.]

268 **Rùjìng wèn jìn; rù guó wèn sú.*** 入境问禁, 入国问俗。(lit) [Upon] crossing a border, ask [what is] forbidden; [on] entering a country, ask [about the local] customs. (fig) On arriving in a new place, inquire about the local taboos and customs; "when in Rome, do as the Romans do." [Originally from the Confucian *Lǐjì: Qū Lǐ Shàng*; now sometimes abbreviated as *rùjìng suí sú*; see also *dào shénme shān* and *jìnle miào mén* above.]

269 **Rùmén wèn róngkū shì; guānzhe róngyán biàn dézhī.** 入门问荣枯事, 观着容颜便得知。[When you] come in, don't ask [someone] how he's getting on; [just] look at [his] facial expression [and you'll] know [whether he's happy or sad]. [See also *chūmén guān tiānsè* and *pīchái, kàn chái* above and *shàng shān kàn shānshì* below.]

270 **Ruòbù yǔ rén xíng fāngbiàn, niàn jìn Mítuó zǒngshì kōng.** 若不与人行方便, 念尽弥陀总是空。Unless [one] helps [other] people [in life], chanting all the Buddhist [scriptures] is totally useless. [Note: *Mítuó* is short for *Āmítuófó*, the name of Amida Buddha, often chanted aloud by Buddhists; see also *diǎn tǎ qī céng* above.]

271 **Ruò jiāng róngyì dé, biàn zuò děngxián kàn.** 若将容易得, 便作等闲看。If [one] thinks [that something was] obtained [too] easily, then [one will] regard it lightly. [Cf. *JW*, chap. 22.]

272 **(Ruò xìn bǔ, màile wū;) mài guà kǒu, méi liàng dǒu.** (若信卜卖了屋,) 卖卦口没量斗。(If [you] believe in divination, [you will end up] selling [your] house [to pay diviners];) fortunetellers' mouths [are like] bottomless bushel-baskets [i.e., fraudulent and useless]. [Rhyme; cf. *Jīngshì Tōngyán*, chap. 13; note: a *dǒu* is a measure for grain equal to one deciliter; see also *mài bǔ, mài guà* above and *yīnyáng bù kěxìn* below.]

273 **Ruò yào duàn jiǔ fǎ, xǐng yǎnkàn zuì rén.** 若要断酒法, 醒眼看醉人。If [you] want to [find a] way to quit drinking [just] look at a drunkard [when you're] sober. [Also said *ruò yào bù hē jiǔ*, etc.; see also *tiānzǐ shàngqiě* below.]

274 **Ruò yào fā, qióngrén tóu shàng guā.** 若要发, 穷人头上刮。(lit) If [one] wants to get [rich], [one needs to] shave poor people's heads. (fig) One cannot get rich without exploiting the poor. [Rhyme; note: *fācái*, "to get rich"; *guā*, (lit) "to shave," is colloquial for "exploit whatever one can from others"; see also *shābude pín jiā* below.]

275 **Ruò yào fù, shǒu dìng Xíngzài mài jiǔ cù; ruò yào guān, shārén fànghuǒ shòu zhāo'ān.** 若要富, 守定行在卖酒醋; 若要官, 杀人放火受招安。If [you] want [to get] wealthy, stay in [the city of] Xingzai [and] sell wine [and] vinegar; if [you] want [to become an] official, [then be a bandit] killing and burning, [and then] get amnesty and enlistment. [This rhymed couplet is a cynical comment about traditional China made by Zhang Zhifu in his *Kě Shū* in the Song dynasty; *Xíngzài* refers to the "imperial residence" or "temporary capital" of the Southern Song emperor in

R

Ling'an (now Hangzhou), the "Kinsai" described by Marco Polo in his book, during the Mongol occupation of northern China (A.D. 1127–1279).]

276 **Ruò yàohǎo, dà zuò xiǎo.** 若要好, 大做小。 (lit) If [one] wants [to do] well, [the] big [must] make [itself] small. (fig) If you want to get along smoothly, you will have to humble yourself when necessary. [Rhyme; cf. *JW*, chap. 87.]

277 **Ruò yàohǎo, wèn sān lǎo.** 若要好, 问三老。 If [you] want [to get things done] well, ask the old [for advice]. [Rhyme; technically *sān lǎo* refers to *xià shòu*, ages 60–79, *zhuāng shòu*, ages 80–99; and *shàng shòu*, above 100 years old.]

278 **Ruò yào jīng, rén qián tīng.** 若要精, 人前听。 If [you] want [to be] wise, listen [more] to [other] people. [Rhyme.]

279 **Ruò yào rén bù zhī, chúfēi jǐ mò wéi.*** 若要人 不知, 除非己莫为。 (lit) If [you] don't want others to know [about something], the only way is [for you your]self not to do [it]. (fig) The only sure way to remain blameless is not to do anything for which you could be blamed. [Cf. *JPM*, chap. 12; *Wǔ Sōng*, chap. 2; a paraphrase from the *Hàn Shū Mù Chéng Zhuàn*; see also *tiānxià de huàishì* and *yào rén zhī* and *zhǐpà bù zuò* and *zuò zhě bù bì* below.]

280 **Ruò yào yǒu qiánchéng, mò zuò méi qiánchéng.** 若要有前程, 莫做没前程。 If [you] want to have a [bright] future, never do [anything that will] hinder [your] future. [Cf. *JW*, chap. 8.]

281 **Ruò yī fófǎ, lěngshuǐ mò xiā.** 若依佛法, 冷水 莫呷。 (lit) If [one strictly] observes [all of the (dietary)] regulations of Buddhism, [even] cold water [may] not be held in [one's] mouth. (fig) (1) Living a good life is more important than blindly following dogma. (2) One need not take (dietary) restrictions too seriously. [Cf. *Xǐngshì Héngyán*, chap. 26.]

282 **Rú rén yǐnshuǐ, lěngnuǎn-zìzhī.** 如人饮水, 冷 暖自知。 (lit) As [when] someone drinks water, [one] knows oneself [whether it's] cold or warm. (fig) One cannot know the essence of something until one has experienced it oneself. [Note: *lěngnuǎn-zìzhī*, is a *chengyu* meaning "to know something without being told."]

283 **Rù shān bù pà shāngrén hǔ; jiù pà rénqíng liǎng-miàn dāo.** 入山不怕伤人虎, 就怕人情两 面刀。 (lit) Do not fear tigers in the mountains, [rather] fear people who are two-faced in their dealings with others. [See also *bùpà hóngliǎn* above.]

284 **Rù shuǐ jiàn cháng rén.** 入水见长人。 (lit) [When they] enter the water [then we'll] see [who are the] tall people. (fig) At the critical moment one can see who the talented or capable people are. [See also *tiān tā*, *zìyǒu* below.]

285 **Rù tián guān jià; cóng xiǎo kàn dà.** 入田观稼, 从小看大。 Go to the fields and inspect the crops [if you want to know how the harvest will be]; observe the child if you want to know [how he or she will be as an] adult. "The child is the father to the man." [Rhyme; note the colloquial expression *sān suì zhī lǎo*, "By age three, one can know the adult."]

S

1 **Sāhuǎng de rén zǒng hào fāshì.** 撒谎的人总 好发誓。 People who lie always make vows easily.

2 **Sài wēng shī mǎ, ān zhī fēi fú.** 塞翁失马, 安知 非福。 (lit) [When] the old man on the frontier lost his horse, who could have known it was a blessing [in disguise]! (fig) A loss may turn out to be a gain. [Based on a popular fable in *Huái Nán Zǐ: Rén Jiān Xùn*.]

3 **Sānbǎi liùshí háng, hángháng chī fàn, zhuó yīshang.** 三百六十行, 行行吃饭, 着衣裳。 [In all the] three hundred and sixty [i.e., various] professions, the reason people engage in them [is] to earn food and clothing. [Rhyme; cf. *Hé Diǎn*, chap. 6; note: *chuānzhuó*, "dress; apparel"; *sānbǎiliùshíháng* is a colloquial expression meaning "all trades and professions."]

4 **(Sānbǎi liùshí háng,) hángháng chū zhuàng-yuán.** (三百六十行,) 行行出状元。 (lit) ([In all of the] three hundred and sixty professions,) each trade produces [its own] "Number one Scholar." (fig) (1) Every profession produces its own leading authority. Every trade has its master(s). (2) If one works hard and perfects one's skill, one may become an expert in one's field, whatever it may be. [Used as advice to encourage individuals to persevere in their profession; note: *zhuàngyuan* literally refers to a title conferred on the one who came in first in the highest level of the imperial examinations; also said *qīshíèr háng*, etc. (q.v.); see the preceding entry.]

5 **Sān bēi hé wànshì; yī zuì jiě qiān chóu.** 三杯和 万事, 一醉解千愁。 Three cups [of wine may] pacify many matters; once drunk, all worries are forgotten. [See also *jiǔ xiāo bǎi chóu* above.]

6 **Sān bù niù liù.** 三不拗六。 (lit) Three are no match for six. (fig) The majority have the final say. [See also *sān quán diébude* and *shuāng quán nán dí* and *sì bù niù liù* below.]

7 **Sān cháng bǔ yī duǎn; sān qín jiā yī lǎn.** 三长 补一短, 三勤夹一懒。 [Just as] three good points make up for one shortcoming [in a person, so] three diligent [people will] influence a lazy [one].

8 **Sān cì bānjiā děngyú yī cì shīhuǒ.** 三次搬家 等于一次失火。 Moving [one's] home three times is as bad as a fire [i.e., in terms of disruption, losing things, etc.]. [A popular saying.]

9 **Sān cùn shé hàizhe qī chǐ shēn.** 三寸舌害着七尺身。 (lit) A tongue of three inches [can] harm a seven foot [tall] body. (fig) Trouble comes out of people's mouths. [Note: one Chinese "foot" or *chǐ* equals one-third of a meter; see also *bìng cóng kǒu rù* above.]

10 **Sānfēn jiàngrén, qīfēn zhǔrén.** 三分匠人，七分主人。 (lit) A craftsman [is] thirty percent [free], [and] seventy percent [beholden to his] employer. (fig) One has to do what one's employer(s) tell(s) one. [Cf. *Érnǚ Yīngxióng Zhuàn*, chap. 2.]

11 **Sānfēn luó-gǔ; qīfēn chàng.** 三分锣鼓，七分唱。 (lit) [The success of an opera performance depends only] thirty percent [on the accompanying] gongs and drums [and] seventy percent [on the] singing [of the actors and actresses]. (fig) In any endeavor, success depends primarily on those who play the major role(s). [Compare *qī fēn luó-gǔ* above.]

12 **Sān fēn réncái; qīfēn dǎbàn.*** 三人才，七分打扮。 [Women are] three-tenths natural [appearance and] seven-tenths makeup. [Note: here *réncái* is a colloquial expression meaning "beautiful appearance."]

13 **Sānfēn rénshì; qīfēn tiān.** 三分人事，七分天。 [In farming, the harvest depends only] thirty percent on human effort, [and] seventy percent [on] the weather.

14 **Sānfēn tiāncái; qīfēn xué.** 三分天才，七分学。 [Success depends] thirty percent [on one's] talent [and] seventy percent [on one's hard work and] study.

15 **Sān gè bù kāikǒu, shénxiān nán xiàshǒu.** 三个不开口，神仙难下手。 [If you] keep [your] mouth shut [even] the gods can do nothing with you. [See also *bù gān jǐ shì* above and *yī wèn sān bù zhī* below.]

16 **Sān gè chòu píjiàng, dǐng gè Zhūgé Liàng.*** 三个臭皮匠，顶个诸葛亮。 (lit) Three smelly cobblers [with their wits combined] equal Zhuge Liang, [the master mind]. (fig) Three fools are the equal of one wise man; "Two heads are better than one." [Zhuge Liang was the archetypal master strategist in *R3K*. This *yanyu* was paraphrased as *sān ge chòupíjiang, héchéng yī gè Zhūgé Liàng* by Mao Zedong in his essay: "Dǎng Nèi Tuánjiède Biànzhèng Fàngfǎ"; also said *sān gè chòu píjiang sài guò Zhūgé Liàng*.]

17 **Sān gè wǔgēng dǐ yī gōng.** 三个五更抵一工。 Three early risings equal one [day's] work. [Note: in traditional China the day was divided into twelve two-hour periods or *gēng*; *wǔgēng* refers to the time period between 3:24 and 5:24 A.M., the fifth night watch; see also *zǎoqǐ sān zhāo* below.]

18 **Sāng tián biàn cānghǎi; cānghǎi biàn sāng tián.** 桑田变沧海，沧海变桑田。 (lit) Mulberry fields change into seas [and] the seas turn into mulberry fields. (fig) Time brings great changes to the world. Life is full of vicissitudes. [Cf. *Gǔ-Jīn Xiǎoshuō*, chap. 18; as a *chengyu*: *cānghǎi-sāngtián*; see also *rénshēng yīpánqí* and *rén yǒu*

qī pín above and *shìshì yǒuchéng* and *suī yǒu xiōngsuì* below.]

19 **Sān jiān wǎ bàndǎo rén.** 三尖瓦绊倒人。 (lit) A piece of pointed [i.e., broken] tile [can] trip a person up. (fig) A petty person can make a greater one suffer.

20 **Sān jù hǎohuà bùrú yī mǎ bàng.** 三句好话不如一马棒。 (lit) Three pieces of good advice are not so good as one good blow with the stick. (fig) Hard tactics are (sometimes) more effective than soft ones. [See also the following entry.]

21 **Sān jù hǎohuà bùrú yī quántou.** 三句好话不如一拳头。 (lit) Three pieces of good advice are not as good as one blow with [your] fist. (fig) Hard tactics are (sometimes) more effective than soft ones. [See also the previous entry.]

22 **Sān jù huà néng bǎ rén shuōxiào qǐlai; yī jù huà jiù jiāng rén shuō tiào qǐlai.*** 三句话能把人说笑起来，一句话就将人说跳起来。 Three words may set one laughing, [while sometimes only] one word may set one jumping [in anger, so be careful!]. [See also *huì shuō de rě* above.]

23 **Sān nián bù fēi, fēi jiāng chōng tiān; sān nián bù míng, míng jiāng jīngrén.** 三年不飞，飞将冲天；三年不鸣，鸣将惊人。 [If] birds have not flown for three years, [they] will soar into the clouds; [if they] have not sung for three years, their songs will take everyone by surprise. [This rhyme is usually said of an author, artist, or scholar who comes out with a work after a long silence.]

24 **Sān nián bù shàngmén, dāng qīn yě bù qīn.** 三年不上门，当亲也不亲。 (lit) [If you] don't visit [your] relatives for three years, they will forget about you. (fig) "Out of sight, out of mind." [Cf. *JW*, chap. 40.]

25 **Sān nián qīng zhīfǔ, shíwàn xuěhuā yín.** 三年清知府，十万雪花银。 (lit) [Even after being an] "honest and clean" official for three years, [one still garners one] hundred thousand ounces of snow-white silver. (fig) Even self-professed honest and clean officials fleece(d) the people [in traditional Chinese society]. [Cf. *Rúlín Wàishǐ*, chap. 8.]

26 **Sān nián shí mǎ xìng; wǔ nián dǒng rénxīn.** 三年识马性，五年懂人心。 It takes three years to get to know a horse's nature, [but] five years to get to know a person's heart/mind. [Rhyme; see also *rén dào nánchù* above.]

27 **Sān nǚ, yī é chéng shì.** 三女一鹅成市。 (lit) Three women [and] one goose make a [noise like an entire] market. (fig) Women are noisy.

28 **Sānqiān yǔ wǒ hǎo; bābǎi yǔ tā jiāo.** 三千与我好，八百与他交。 Three thousand are on good terms with me [and] eight hundred are his friends. (fig) I have my friends and he has his; each person has his or her own friends. [Rhyme.]

29 **Sān quán diébude sì shǒu.** 三拳迭不得四手。 (lit) Three fists are no match for four hands. (fig) A minority cannot overcome a majority. [Cf. *JPM*, chap. 13; see also *sān bù niù liù* above and *sì bù niù liù* and *shuāng quán nán dí* below.]

S

30 **Sān rén chéng hǔ.** 三人成虎。(lit) [If] three people [say there is a] tiger, [it will] become [accepted as truth]. (fig) Rumors repeated will be believed. [Cf. *Zhànguó Cè: Qín Cè 3*; see also *chányán sān zhì* above.]

31 **Sān rén, liù yàng huà.** 三人，六样话。(lit) Three people [will have] six different opinions. (fig) Everyone has his own opinion. [Cf. Mao Dun's novel *Zǐyè* (Midnight), chap. 16; see also *sān rén shuōzhe* and *shí jiā guō zào* below.]

32 **Sān rén shuōzhe, jiǔ tóu huà.** 三人说着九头话。(lit) [When] three people [are] speaking [the result is] nine [different] opinions. (fig) Each of three people has his or her own opinions. [Cf. *Hé Diǎn*, chap. 5; see also *sān rén, liù yàng huà* above.]

33 **Sān rén tái bù guò gè "lǐ" qù.** 三人抬不过个"理"去。Even a majority can't overcome reason. [Cf. *DRC*, chap. 65.]

34 **Sān rén tóngxíng, bì yǒu wǒ shī.*** 三人同行必有我师。[If we] three people are walking together, [at least one of the other two] will be my teacher. (fig) One can always learn something from others. [A famous maxim *(géyán)* from the Confucian Analects: *Lúnyǔ: Shù Ér.*]

35 **Sān rén tóngxíng, xiǎode kǔ.** 三人同行，小的苦。(lit) [When there are] three partners, the smallest [shoulders] the hardships. (fig) The third of three partners is always the one to suffer. [Said by Piggy in *JW*, chap. 76, distorting the famous saying of Confucius (see the preceding entry); note: *xiǎode*, (lit) "small one"; (fig) a polite, self-deprecating term for "I; me"; see also *qǔdé jīng lái* above.]

36 **Sān rén wù dàshì; liù ěr bù tōng móu.** 三人误大事，六耳不通谋。(lit) Three people will foul up any affair; six ears cannot keep a secret. (fig) Nothing can be kept a secret if more than two people know about it. [See also *sān rén zhī* below.]

37 **Sān rén yītiáoxīn, huángtǔ biànchéng jīn.** 三人一条心，黄土变成金。(lit) When three persons are of the same mind, yellow earth becomes gold. (fig) When many people are of one mind and pull together, great things can be accomplished. [Rhyme; see also *xiélì shān chéng* and *yī jiā tóngxīn* and *zhòngrén yìxīn* below.]

38 **Sān rén zhī, tiānxià xiǎo.** 三人知，天下晓。(lit) [If] three people know [a secret], the whole world will know [it]. (fig) Not more than two people can keep a secret. [See also *sān rén wù dàshì* above.]

39 **Sān rì bù jiànmiàn, bù zuò jiùshí kàn.** 三日不见面，不作旧时看。(lit) [After] three day['s] not seeing [someone], [one can]not look [at him or her] the same old way. (fig) One can hardly imagine what changes will occur after not seeing someone for some time. [Usually said flatteringly to one whom one has not seen for some time; see also *shì bié sān rì* below.]

40 **Sān rì bù tán, shǒushēng jīngjí.** 三日不弹，手生荆棘。(lit) Three days without playing [one's instrument and one's] hands sprout brambles. (fig) If one does not practice regularly, one gets out of practice. [Cf. *DRC*, chap. 86; see also *quán bù lí shǒu* above and *yì rì liàn* below.]

41 **Sān rì jiānbǎng, liǎng rì tuǐ.** 三日肩膀，两日腿。[If one carries things on one's] shoulders [for] three days, [and] walks [for] two days [one will become accustomed to hard work].

42 **Sān rì wú liáng bù jù bīng.** 三日无粮不聚兵。[If the soldiers] have not [had] food for three days, [one can]not muster an army. [See also *bīngmǎ wèi dòng* and *cháotíng bù chāi* above.]

43 **Sānshíliù jì, zǒu wéi shàng jì.*** 三十六计，走为上计。(lit) [Of the] thirty-six stratagems, running [away] is best. (fig) (When a difficult situation has reached the point beyond any solution, then) the best thing to do is to run away. [Originally "thirty-six" simply implied "many"; this expression is now often reinterpreted to mean that running away is the best solution to all problems.]

44 **Sānshí nián fēngshuǐ lúnliú zhuàn.*** 三十年风水轮流转。Fortunes and misfortunes come in thirty-year cycles. [See also *sānshí nián hé dōng* below.]

45 **(Sān)shí nián hé dōng; (sān)shí nián hé xī.*** (三)十年河东，(三)十年河西。(lit) [For] thirty [/ten] years [people] east of the river [prosper], [then] for [another] thirty [/ten] years those on the west bank [prosper]. (fig) Fortune (and misfortune) comes in cycles. [Cf. *Rúlín Wàishǐ*, chap. 46; see also *liùshí nián* and *sānshí nián fēngshuǐ* above.]

46 **Sānshí nián nòng mǎ qí, jīnrì bèi lǘ pū.** 三十年弄马骑，今日被驴扑。(lit) [After] having ridden horses for thirty years, one can be thrown off a donkey. (fig) Even an old hand can be taken in. [See also *mǎ shàng shuāisǐ* above.]

47 **Sānshí shì gāng; sìshí shì tiě.** 三十是钢；四十是铁。(lit) [A man at] thirty is [as strong as] steel, [but at] forty is [like] iron. (fig) One becomes physically weaker after forty.

48 **Sānshí wǎnshang qiāo luó-gǔ, bù zhī qióngrén kǔ bù kǔ.** 三十晚上敲锣鼓，不知穷人苦不苦。(lit) [Those who] beat gongs and drums on Lunar New Year's Eve do not know whether the poor are suffering. (fig) Those who are well off do not understand the hardships of the poor. [Rhyme; see also *bǎo hàn bù zhī* above.]

49 **Sān tiān bù dǎ, shàngfáng jiē wǎ.** 三天不打，上房揭瓦。[There are some people so bad that if] not beaten [every] three days, [they'll be] up stealing the tiles off [your] roof. [Rhyme; note: *shàngfáng*, the main rooms in a traditional Chinese house compound where the master's quarters were located.]

50 **Sān tiān zhù zài shíjiàng jiā, bù huì qì wū, huì dǎ qiáng.** 三天住在石匠家，不会砌屋会打墙。(lit) [After] living three days with a mason, [even if one] can't build a house, [at least one will] know how to lay bricks. (fig) If one spends

time with experts, one will inevitably learn something. [See also *gēnzhe wǎjiang* and *rù háng sān rì* above.]

51 **Sān zhé gōng zhī wéi liángyī.** 三折肱知为良医。 [If you] break your arm three times, [you'll naturally] become a good doctor. (fig) Prolonged illness makes a patient a good doctor. Experience is a good teacher. [See also *chī yào sān nián* and *jiǔ bìng chéng liángyī* above.]

52 **Sè bù mí rén; rén zì mí.** 色不迷人，人自迷。 Sex does not ensnare men; men ensnare themselves. [Usually preceded by *jiǔ bù zuì rén* above (q.v.); also said *huā bù mí rén* etc.; see also the following entry.]

53 **Sēng lái, kàn fó miàn.*** 僧来，看佛面。 (lit) [When a] monk comes [begging], look at the Buddha's "face" [behind him]. (fig) Regardless of what you think of a person who asks for help, you had better consider the "face" of any powerful people he or she may be connected with. [Cf. *Guānchǎng Xiànxíng Jì*, chap. 2.]

54 **Sè shì shārén dāo.** 色是杀人刀。 (lit) Sexual lust is a murderous sword. (fig) Lust can lead to ruin. [Cf. *Hòu Hàn Yǎnyì*, chap. 75; note: *hàosè*, "lustful," is usually said of men only.]

55 **Shābude pín jiā, zuòbude fù jiā.** 杀不得贫家，做不得富家。 [If one does] not kill [i.e., oppress or exploit] the poor, [one] cannot get rich. [From traditional China; cf. the *chengyu*: *wéi fù bù rén*, "be rich and cruel"; see also *ruò yào fā* above and *shā dé qióngrén* below.]

56 **Shā dé qióngrén; zuò dé fù hù.** 杀得穷人，做得富户。 [One] must oppress [or exploit] the poor [in order to] become rich. [See also *shābude pín jiā* above.]

57 **Shā fù zhī chóu, bù gòng dài tiān.*** 杀父之仇，不共戴天。 (lit) [With] the enemy who has slain one's father [one can]not [live] together under the same sky. (fig) One must avenge one's father's murder. [Cf. Confucius' *Lǐjì: Qū Lǐ*; note: *bùgòngdàitiān*, is a set phrase meaning "absolutely irreconcilable."]

58 **Shā jī yān yòng niú dāo?** 杀鸡焉用牛刀？ (lit) How can one use an ox-slaughtering knife to kill chickens? (fig) A small job does not require a big operation or a great talent. One should not engage in overkill. [Cf. Confucian Analects: *Lúnyǔ: Yáng Huò*; *WM*, chap. 15.]

59 **Shāle tóu, wǎn dà de bā.*** 杀了头，碗大的疤。 (lit) [Even if one is] beheaded, [it's nothing but a] scar as big as a bowl. (fig) One should not be afraid to die. [Usually said by those sentenced to die in *wǔ xiá xiǎoshuō* (sword-fighting novels) and communist propaganda literature.]

60 **Shāmào dǐxia wú qióng hàn.** 纱帽底下无穷汉。 (lit) Beneath [a black] cotton gauze cap there are no poor fellows. (fig) One who holds an official post will never be poor (as he can make money from presents, bribes, etc.). [Note: *shāmào* refers to a black cotton gauze cap with paddle-like ornaments attached to the back, worn by officials in imperial times.]

61 **Shān bù ài lù; lù zì tōng shān.** 山不碍路，路自通山。 (lit) Mountains do not block roads; roads naturally go through mountains. (fig) There will always be a way (out). [Cf. *JW*, chap. 80; see also *shān gāo zì yǒu* and the following entry.]

62 **Shān bù zhuǎn, lù zhuǎn; (hé bù wān, shuǐ wān).** 山不转路转，(河不弯水弯)。 (lit) If the mountains don't turn, the roads [will] turn; ([if] the rivers don't bend, the water bends). (fig) Things are always changing or accommodating. There will always be a way (out). [See also *tiān bù zhuàn* below and the preceding entry.]

63 **Shàn è dàotóu zhōng yǒu bào; zhǐ zhēng lái zǎo yǔ lái chí.** 善恶到头终有报；只争来早与来迟。 Good [and] evil in the end [will] be recompensed; [it is] only a question of sooner or later. [Cf. *JW*, chap. 11; *Èr Kè Pāi'àn Jīngqí*, chap. 28; see also *hǎo yǒu hǎo bào* above and *shàn yǒu shànbào* below.]

64 **Shān gāo pà màn shàng.** 山高怕慢上。 (lit) High mountains fear slow climbing. (fig) However high the mountains are, people can climb to the top of them if they persevere. However difficult a task, people can succeed if they persevere. [See also *bùpà màn, jiù pà zhàn* above.]

65 **Shān gāo yǒu dǐng; shuǐ shēn yǒu dǐ; lù cháng yǒu tóu.** 山高有顶，水深有底，路长有头。 (lit) [However] high the mountain [is, it] has a top; [however] deep the water [is, it] has a bottom; [however] long the road [is, it] has an end. (fig) There are limits to everything.

66 **Shān gāo zhē bu zhù tàiyáng.** 山高遮不住太阳。 (lit) However high a mountain may be, it cannot block the sun. (fig) No matter how powerful someone may be, (s)he cannot hide the truth. [Cf. *DRC*, chap. 24; see also *nán jiāng yī rén shǒu* above.]

67 **Shān gāo zì yǒu kè xíng lù; shuǐ shēn zì yǒu dùchuán rén.** 山高自有客行路，水深自有渡船人。 (lit) However high the mountains may be, there are paths for people who traverse them; however deep the rivers may be, there are people who ferry across them. (fig) However difficult the journey, there is bound to be a way. [Cf. *JW*, chap. 74; see also *shān bù ài lù* above.]

68 **Shàng bù jǐn, zé xià màn.** 上不紧则下慢。 [If the] superiors are not strict, then [the] inferiors [will be] slack. [Cf. *WM*, chap. 17.]

69 **Shǎng bù ràng yuānchóu; fá bù lùn gǔròu.** 赏不让冤仇，罚不论骨肉。 Awards [should be granted] regardless of [whether one has done] wrong [to you, and] punishment [given] regardless of [whether someone is a] flesh and blood [relation to you]. [Rhyme; cf. *Sān Guó Zhì: Wèi Shū: Wǔ Wén Shì Wáng Gōng Zhuàn*.]

70 **Shàngchǎng róngyì; xiàchǎng nán.** 上场容易；下场难。 (lit) It's easier to get onto the stage than to get down off it. (fig) It's easier to get into situations than to get out of them. [See also *shàngshān róngyì* and *shàng zéichuán yì* below.]

S

71 **Shàng guà bùlíng, xià guà líng.** 上卦不灵，下卦灵。 (lit) [If] the first divinatory symbol doesn't work, the next one will. (fig) If the first time you fail, the next time you will succeed; "if at first you don't succeed, try, try again." [Note: *bǔguà*, "to divine by the Eight Trigrams"; *língyàn*, "divinely efficacious."]

72 **Shàng huí dàng; xué huí guāi.** 上回当，学回乖。 (lit) Taken in [one] time; learn [one] lesson. (fig) One can learn valuable lessons from setbacks. "A fall into the pit, a gain in wit." [Cf. *Wǔ Sōng*, chap. 2; see also *chī yī huí kuī* and *chī yī qiàn* above.]

73 **Shàngliáng bù zhèng, xià liáng wāi.*** 上梁不正，下梁歪。 (lit) [If the] main [roof] beam is not upright, the lower ones [will be] crooked. (fig) If those in authority do not behave properly, their subordinates will follow suit. [Cf. *JPM*, chap. 26.]

74 **Shàngmén de mǎi-mài hǎo zuò.** 上门的买卖好做。 (lit) It's easier to do business [with people who] come to you. (fig) It's easier to deal with others on one's own turf. [Cf. *JW*, chap. 28.]

75 **Shàngmíng bù zhī xià àn.** 上明不知下暗。 (lit) An enlightened superior doesn't know his subordinates' darkness. (fig) An honest superior cannot know the wicked behavior of his subordinates. [See also *qīngguān nán chū* above.]

76 **Shàng rén bù hào, xià rén bù yào.** 上人不好，下人不要。 [If the] superior doesn't like [it], [his] subordinates don't want [it]. [Rhyme; cf. *Dōng Zhōu Lièguó Zhì*, chap. 23.]

77 **Shāngrén zhī yán qiáng yú máo jǐ.** 伤人之言强于矛戟。 Words that hurt people [are] sharper than spears. [See also *gùnzi shāng ròu* and *lì dāo shāng tǐ* above.]

78 **Shàng shān dǎchái; guò hé tuō xié.** 上山打柴，过河脱鞋。 (lit) [While] in the mountains cut wood, [and while] crossing a river take off your shoes. (fig) Always be flexible and adapt yourself to circumstances. [Rhyme.]

79 **Shàng shān diào bù zháo yú; xià shuǐ dǎ bù zháo chái.** 上山钓不着鱼，下水打不着柴。 (lit) It's impossible to catch fish in the mountains or to gather firewood in the river. (fig) One must do things appropriate to the surrounding conditions. [Note the *chengyu*: *yuán mù qiú yú*, (lit) "climbing a tree to catch fish"; (fig) "a fruitless approach."]

80 **Shàng shān gǎn dǎ hǔ; xiàhǎi gǎn qín lóng.*** 上山敢打虎；下海敢擒龙。 (lit) Dare to go up into the mountains to hunt tigers, [and] down to the sea to catch dragons. (fig) Do not fear any difficulty. [Cf. *Érnǚ Yīngxióng Zhuàn*, chap. 9.]

81 **Shàng shān kàn shānshì; rù mén kàn rényì.** 上山看山势，入门看人意。 (lit) [While] climbing a hill, pay attention to the hill's terrain; [when you] enter a door, pay attention to people's wishes or expectations. [Note: *dìshì*; *xíngshì* "terrain"; see also *chūmén guān tiānsè* above.]

82 **Shàng shān qín hǔ yì; kāikǒu qiúrén nán.*** 上山擒虎易，开口求人难。 It's easier to go up into the mountains to catch a tiger than [to bring oneself] to ask others for help. [Also said … *kāi kǒu gào rén nán*.]

83 **Shàngshān róngyì; xiàshān nán.** 上山容易，下山难。 (lit) It's easier to go up a hill than it is to go down the hill. (fig) It's easier to get into situations than to get out of them. Mind your step. [A caution to remind people to be careful in doing things which appear to be easy; see also *shàngchǎng róngyì* above.]

84 **Shàngsi fàng gè pì, xiàshǔ chàng tái xì.** 上司放个屁，下属唱台戏。 (lit) [When] the superior breaks wind, his subordinates sing an opera. (fig) One word from the superior makes everybody busy. [Rhyme; see also *lǎozi fàngpì* above.]

85 **Shàngtào de hóuzi yóu rén shuǎ.** 上套的猴子由人耍。 (lit) The tied-up monkey is played with by others. (fig) One who has fallen into another's trap will be controlled by that person. [Note: *shuǎ hóuzi*, "to play with a monkey."]

86 **Shǎng yǐ quàn shàn; fá yǐ chéng'è.** 赏以劝善，罚以惩恶。 Awards [are granted in order] to encourage [people to do] good, [and] punishments [are given in order] to punish [those who do] evil.

87 **Shàng yǒu tiāntáng; xià yǒu Sū-Háng.*** 上有天堂，下有苏杭。 Above there is paradise; below [on earth] there are [the two beautiful cities of] Suzhou [and] Hangzhou. [Rhyme; cf. *Gǔ-Jīn Xiǎoshuō*, chap. 1; see also *Sū-Háng bù dào* below.]

88 **Shàng yǒu zhèngcè; xià yǒu duìcè.** 上有政策，下有对策。 [Those] above have [official] policies; [those] below have an appropriate [counter] policy [which allows them to get around the official policy by observing its letter, but not its spirit]. [A popular saying in use since the Cultural Revolution.]

89 **Shàng zéichuán yì; xià zéichuán nán.** 上贼船易，下贼船难。 (lit) It's easier to get onto a thief's boat than to get off it. (fig) It's easier to get involved with bad people than to get disentangled from them. [See also *shàngchǎng róngyì* above.]

90 **Shān lǐ háizi bù pà láng; chénglǐ háizi bù pà guān.** 山里孩子不怕狼，城里孩子不怕官。 (lit) Children in the mountains are not afraid of wolves; those in the cities are not afraid of officials. (fig) One grows accustomed to things with which one is in constant proximity.

91 **Shān mù wěizi zuò bùliǎo zhèngliáng.** 杉木尾子做不了正梁。 (lit) Wood from the top part of the China fir [tree] can't be made into a main roof beam. (fig) Ordinary people cannot fulfill the role of talented people. [Said of people of little ability, or modestly of oneself; the China fir has a wood of poor quality.]

92 **Shānshān yǒu lǎohǔ; chùchù yǒu qiángrén.** 山山有老虎，处处有强人。 [Just as] there are tigers on every mountain, there are able people everywhere.

93 **Shànshū bù zé bǐ.** 善书不择笔。 (lit) [One who is] good at calligraphy is not [fussy about] choosing a brush pen. (fig) A good calligrapher can write beautifully even with an inferior pen. A truly

talented person can be successful even with inferior tools or help.

94 **Shānshuǐ shàng yǒu xiāngféng zhī rì.** 山水尚有相逢之日。(lit) The mountains and the rivers will meet sooner or later. (fig) Always part as friends, as you never know when you'll meet again. [Cf. *Rúlín Wàishǐ*, chap. 14; see also *dàhǎi fúpíng* and *qù shí liú rénqíng* above.]

95 **Shān wài yǒu shān; tiān wài yǒu tiān.** 山外有山，天外有天。(lit) Beyond the mountains there are [more] mountains, [and] beyond heaven there are [more] heavens. (fig) There is always someone or something greater or better. No one thing or person can claim to be the greatest or best. [Note: *tiānwài-yǒutiān* is used as a set phrase meaning "knowledge/capability is limitless"; see also *néngrén zhīwài* and *qiáng zhōng háiyǒu* and *rén wài yǒu rén* above and *shé tūn shǔ* and *yī wù xiáng yī wù* below.]

96 **Shàn yǒu shànbào, è yǒu èbào; (bù shì bù bào, shíchen wèi dào).** 善有善报，恶有恶报；(不是不报，时辰未到)。(lit) Goodness is repaid with goodness, [and] evil is repaid with evil; (it is not that there is no recompense; [it is only that] the time has not [yet] come). (fig) There is justice in the world, sooner or later. [Note that the first two parts of the first half of this rhyme are often used together or separately, without the second half; see also *hǎo yǒu hǎo bào* and *shàn è dàotóu* above.]

97 **Shān yǒu shānshén; miào yǒu miàozhǔ.** 山有山神，庙有庙主。(lit) Mountains have mountain gods [and] temples have head abbots. (fig) In every place there is someone in charge.

98 **Shàn yóu zhě nì; shàn qí zhě zhuì.** 善游者溺，善骑者坠。(lit) [Even a] good swimmer [can] drown [and a] good rider [can] be thrown. (fig) Over-confidence may lead to carelessness or failure. [Cf. *Sān Xiá Wǔ Yì*, chap. 88; *Huái Nán Zǐ: Yuán Dào Xùn*; see also *mǎ shàng shuāi* above.]

99 **Shān yǔ yù lái, fēng mǎn lóu.** 山雨欲来，风满楼。(lit) [When the] mountain rains are about to come, the wind fills the tower. "The wind sweeping through the tower heralds a rising storm in the mountains." "The rising wind forebodes the coming storm." (fig) Coming events cast their shadows before them. [A line from the poem "Xiányáng Chéng Dōng Lóu" by the Tang dynasty poet Xǔ Hún, later became proverbial.]

100 **Shān zhōng cháng yǒu qiān nián shù; shìshang bìng wú bǎisuì rén.** 山中常有千年树，世上并无百岁人。(lit) In the mountains there are always trees a thousand years old, [but] in the world there are hardly any people one hundred years old. (fig) People rarely live to the age of one hundred.

101 **Shān zhōng wú lǎohǔ, hóuzi chēng dàwáng.*** 山中无老虎，猴子称大王。(lit) [When] there's no tiger on the mountain, the monkey becomes king. (fig) When authority is absent, those in lesser positions try to take over. When there are no truly able leaders, one must be content with less able people. "In the land of the blind, the one-eyed man is king." [See also *hǎishàng wú yú* above and *shǔ zhōng wú dàjiàng* and *yánwáng bù zài* below.]

102 **Shān zhōng yǒu zhí shù; shìshang wú zhí rén.** 山中有直树，世上无直人。(lit) In the mountains, there are straight trees, [but] in the world there are no "straight" [i.e., upright and honest] people.

103 **Shàn zhū, è ná.** 善猪恶拿。(lit) [Even when catching a] docile pig, [one must] use a firm hand. (fig) When you are out to catch someone, don't let down your guard. [Cf. *JW*, chap. 19; see also *fú hǔ, xiū kuān* above.]

104 **Shào bù xīlì; lǎo bù xièxīn.** 少不惜力，老不歇心。[When] young, don't spare [your] energy; [when] old, don't spare [your] mind.

105 **Shào chéng ruò tiānxìng.** 少成若天性。[A habit acquired when one is a] child becomes [like a] natural instinct. [Cf. *Hàn Shū: Jiǎ Yì Zhuàn*; see also *xíguàn chéng zìrán* below.]

106 **Shǎo chī, duō zīwèi; duō chī, huài dùpí.*** 少吃多滋味，多吃坏肚皮。Eat little [and you'll] enjoy the flavor more; eat too much [and you'll] spoil your stomach.

107 **Shǎo chī, xiāng; duō chī, shāng.** 少吃香，多吃伤。Eat less [and you will find the food] tasty; eat more [and you will] harm [your health]. [Rhyme.]

108 **Shǎo chī xiányú, shǎo kǒugān.** 少吃咸鱼，少口干。(lit) [If one does] not eat too much salted fish, [one will] not feel thirsty. (fig) One won't invite trouble if one doesn't poke one's nose into other's affairs.

109 **Shāo de zhǐ duō, rě de guǐ duō.** 烧的纸多，惹的鬼多。(lit) The more paper [spirit-money one] burns, the more ghosts [one] attracts. (fig) The more you give, the more people come to you for help. [Rhyme; note: burning paper "spirit money" to gods is a traditional way of asking for help from heaven.]

110 **Shāogōng duōle, dǎ làn chuán.** 艄公多了，打烂船。(lit) Too many steersmen [will] wreck the boat. (fig) "Too many cooks spoil the broth." [See also *rén duō, shǒu zá* above.]

111 **Shàonián fūqī, lǎolái bàn; yī tiān bùjiàn, wèn sān biàn.** 少年夫妻老来伴，一天不见问三遍。[If] married young, a couple [will become] good company when old; [when they] don't see each other, they inquire about each other three times a day. [Rhyme.]

112 **Shàonián mùjiang; lǎo lángzhōng.** 少年木匠，老郎中。Young carpenters [and] old doctors [are better qualified].

113 **Shǎo (suǒ) jiàn; duō (suǒ) guài.** 少(所)见，多(所)怪。[Things (which are)] seldom seen [are felt to be] strange. [Cf. the preface to *Chǔ Kè Pāi'àn Jīngqí*; now more commonly said *shǎo jiàn, duō guài*; see also the following entry.]

114 **Shǎo suǒ jiàn, duō jiànguài; dǔ tuótuó wèi mǎ zhǒng bèi.** 少所见多见怪，睹橐驼谓马肿背。(lit) [One who has] seen little regards many things as strange; [(s)he] sees a camel [and] calls [it a] horse with a hunchback. [Cf. *Jìnghuā Yuán*, chap. 9; see also the preceding entry.]

S

115 **Shàozhuàng bù nǔlì; lǎodà tú shāng bēi.*** 少壮
不努力，老大徒伤悲。(lit) [If one does] not
work hard [when young and] strong, [when one
is] old, [one will have to] lead a miserable life. (fig)
"An idle youth, a needy old age." [A line from the
Han dynasty *yuèfǔ* poem: "Cháng Gē Xíng"; see
also *hēi fà bù zhī* and *lǎo bù xiēxīn* above.]

116 **Shārén bùguò tóu diǎn dì.** 杀人不过头点地。
(lit) Killing someone is the same as [having his]
head touch the ground. [When someone "kow-
tows," (i.e., kneels and touches one's head to
the ground in respect or submission), his head
touches the ground, just as it would if one killed
him.] (fig) When an enemy has yielded, his life
should be spared; a wrongdoer who admits his
wrong should be forgiven. [Cf. *Érnǚ Yīngxióng
Zhuàn*, chap. 16; *Xǐngshì Yīnyuán Zhuàn*, chap.
87; *DRC*, chap. 9.]

117 **Shārén, chángmìng; qiànzhài, huán qián.*** 杀人
偿命，欠债还钱。A murderer must pay with
his life, [just as] a debtor must pay his debt. "An
eye for an eye." [Cf. *Chū Kè Pāi'àn Jīngqí*, chap.
33.]

118 **Shārén kě shè, tiānlǐ nán róng.*** 杀人可赦，天
理难容。(lit) [If] murder is pardoned, Heaven's
justice will find it hard to bear. (fig) If murder
were pardoned, there would be no reason in human affairs. [See also the preceding entry.]

119 **Shārén, kě shù; qíng lǐ nán róng.** 杀人可恕，情
理难容。[If] murder is forgiven, reason cannot accept it. [Note: *qínglǐ-nánróng*, "incompatible with the accepted codes of human conduct,"
is used as a *chengyu* meaning "unreasonable; pre-
posterous"; see also the following entry.]

120 **Shārén mièkǒu; sǐ wú duìzhèng.** 杀人灭口，
死无对证。(lit) Dead people's mouths are
destroyed; the dead [can]not bear witness. (fig)
"Dead men tell no tales." [Note: *sǐwúduìzhèng*,
"the dead cannot bear witness," is treated as a
set phrase; see also *sǐrén tóu shàng* below.]

121 **Shārén xū jiàn xuè; jiù rén xū jiù chè.** 杀人须
见血，救人须救彻。[In] killing a person [you]
must see blood; [in] saving a person [you] must
save him completely. [Cf. *WM*, chap. 9; the order
of the two parts may be reversed; see also *sòng
rén, sòng dàojiā* below.]

122 **Shārén yīwàn; zì sǔn sānqiān.** 杀人一万，自损
三千。(lit) To kill ten thousand [of the enemy, it
is inevitable that you will] lose three thousand of
your own. (fig) One cannot win without sacrifice.
There are inevitably losses on both sides in any
struggle.

123 **Shěbude háizi, tào bu zhù láng.*** 舍不得孩子，
套不住狼。(lit) [One who is] not willing to risk
[his] child will not catch the wolf. (fig) If one is
unwilling to take great risks, one cannot achieve
great things. [See also the following entry.]

124 **Shěbude jīn dànzi, dǎ bùliǎo fènghuáng lái.** 舍
不得金弹子，打不了凤凰来。(lit) [One
who] begrudges [using] gold bullets will never
shoot a phoenix. (fig) If you are not ready to make
big sacrifices, you will never achieve great results.
[See also the preceding entry.]

125 **Shé cháng, shì duō.** 舌长事多。(lit) The longer
the tongue, the more trouble. (fig) Those who talk
too much or gossip invite trouble.

126 **Shěde yìshēn guǎ, gǎn bǎ huángdì lā xiàmǎ.** 舍
得一身剐，敢把皇帝拉下马。(lit) [One
who is] willing to risk death by a thousand cuts
[will] dare to unhorse the emperor. (fig) A determined person is capable of doing anything. [Cf.
DRC, chap. 68; *JW*, chap. 25; Mao Zedong used
this proverb to encourage the Red Guards to attack "Capitalist Roaders" in the Chinese Communist party during the Cultural Revolution; see also
pīnzhe yìshēn guǎ above and *sǐle lóngpáo* below.]

127 **Shè hǔ bùchéng, chóng liàn jiàn; zhǎn lóng
bùduàn, chóng mó dāo.** 射虎不成重练箭，
斩龙不断重磨刀。(lit) [If you] shoot at a
tiger [and] miss, practice [your] archery more; [if
you] hack at a dragon continuously [and don't kill
it], sharpen [your] knife again. (fig) "If at first you
don't succeed, try, try again."

128 **Shéi dǎ luó, shéi chīfàn.** 谁打锣，谁吃饭。(lit)
Who[ever] beats the gong [may] have a meal.
(fig) Whoever works has the right to enjoy the
benefits. [Cf. *JPM*, chap. 86.]

129 **Shéi jiā zào tū bù màoyān; shéi jiā guōdǐ méiyǒu hēi?** 谁家灶突不冒烟，谁家锅底没有
黑？(lit) Whose family's chimney does not send
off smoke, [and] whose family's cooking pot is not
black at the bottom? (fig) Every family has its own
troubles. Every family has its "skeleton in the cupboard." [See also *jiājiā dōu yǒu* above and *yī jiā
bù zhī* below.]

130 **Shéi rén bèihòu wú rén shuō; nǎge rén qián bù
shuō rén?** 谁人背后无人说，哪个人前
不说人？Who is never gossiped about behind
[his or her] back [and] who never talks about
people to others? [Cf. Liu Shaoqi's book: *Lùn
Gòngchǎndǎng Yuán de Xiūyǎng* ("How to Be a
Good Communist").]

131 **Shéi shì cháng pín jiǔ fù jiā?** 谁是长贫久富
家？Who[se] family [will remain] forever rich
[or] poor?

132 **Shéi shǒu lǐ yǒu liáng, shéi shì cūnlǐ wáng.** 谁
手里有粮，谁是村里王。Whoever has [the
largest (store of)] grain on hand, [that's] who is
the king of the village. (fig) The richest have the
final say. [Rhyme.]

133 **Shéizhī pán zhōng cān, lìlì jiē xīnkǔ?** 谁知盘中
餐，粒粒皆辛苦？(lit) Who knows [that in] the
food in [our] bowls, every grain [of rice that one
eats is the fruit of] intensive toil? (fig) One should
not waste food. [This is a famous line from a Tang
dynasty poem entitled "Mǐn Nóng" by Li Shen.]

134 **Shéi zhòng kuángfēng, shéi shòu bàoyǔ.** 谁
种狂风，谁受暴雨。(lit) Whoever
sows gale winds will harvest hail storms. (fig) Evil will
be recompensed with evil. [See also *shàn yǒu
shànbào* above.]

135 **Shéjiān suī ruǎn, néng shì rén.** 舌尖虽软，能
螫人。The tip of the tongue, although soft, can
sting people.

136 **Shēn ān dǐ wàn jīn.** 身安抵万金。A peaceful life is as precious as ten thousand [ounces of] gold.

137 **Shén bàng yǒuqián de; guǐ qī kuà lán de.** 神傍有钱的，鬼欺挎篮的。Gods protect those [who] have money, [while] ghosts bully those [who] carry baskets [over their arms; i.e., "bag persons"; beggars, the poor].

138 **Shēngcún huáwū; língluò shānqiū.** 生存华屋，零落山丘。[lit] [One may] live in a magnificent house, [but end up] withered and fallen [i.e., buried] on a [barren] hill. (fig) One never knows how one will end up in life. [Note: *shānqiū*, (lit) "hill," in a literary term for "tomb."]

139 **Shēn dà, lì bù kuī.*** 身大力不亏。[lit] [If one's] body is big, [his] strength [will] not [be] lacking. (fig) A stout person will certainly be physically strong.

140 **Shén duō, yào shè miào; miào duō, yào shāoxiāng.** 神多要设庙，庙多要烧香。[lit] [If there are] more gods, more temples have to [be] built; [if there are] more temples, more incense has to [be] burnt. (fig) If there are more bureaucrats, more and more offices or departments will be set up, so that when one wants to have something done, one will have to go to even more offices. Bureaucracy multiplies itself.

141 **Shèng-bài nǎi bīngjiā chángshì.*** 胜败乃兵家常事。[lit] [Both] victory [and] defeat are ordinary affairs for [military] commanders. (fig) One encounters both successes and failures in life. "You win some and you lose some." [Cf. WM, chap. 55; JW, chap. 5.]

142 **Shèng bù jiāo; bài bù něi.*** 胜不骄，败不馁。[In] victory [be] not proud; [in] defeat [be] not depressed. [Also said *shèn mò jiāo; bài mò něi*.]

143 **Shēng bù rù guān mén; sǐ bù rù dìyù.** 生不入官门，死不入地狱。[lit] [When] alive do not enter the doors of officialdom, [and when] dead, do not enter Hell. (fig) Avoid any dealings with government officials as you would the Devil himself.

144 **Shēng chái diǎn bù zháo, quán píng sìmiàn fēng.** 生柴点不着，全凭四面风。[lit] Fresh[ly] cut green] firewood [which usually] cannot catch fire, completely depends on the four winds [to burn]. (fig) Even if one's ability is not great, given the right conditions, one can succeed. Favorable conditions can compensate for what one lacks in ability.

145 **Shēngchéng de luòtuo gǎi bù chéng xiàng.** 生成的骆驼改不成象。[lit] A natural-born camel can't be changed [into an] elephant. (fig/pun) One's looks cannot be changed. [Pun: *gǎi bù chéng xiàng*, (lit) "can't be changed into an elephant," is a pun on *gǎi bù chéng zhǎngxiàng*, "can't change/improve one's looks."]

146 **Shēngchéng pí; zhǎngchéng gǔ.** 生成皮，长成骨。[lit] [His or her] skin was born like that, [and his or her] bones [just] grew like that. (fig) Some people are just born a certain way and can't be changed.

147 **Shēng, dǎ tóng; shú, dǎtiě.** 生打铜，熟打铁。Strike copper [while it is] cold; strike iron [while it is] hot. (fig) Different problems should be dealt with in different ways.

148 **Shēng Dōng Wú; sǐ Dāntú.** 生东吴，死丹徒。[One should] live [in] Suzhou [a place of rice and fish, and] die [in] Dantu [in the southwest of Jiangsu province, south of the Yangtse River, where the earth is dry and good for burying the dead]. [A rhyme from the collection of Tang poetry: *Quán Táng Shī: Dāntú Yàn*.]

149 **Shēngjiāng shì lǎo de là.*** 生姜是老的辣。(lit) Old ginger is hotter than new. (fig) Old people are more experienced. "There is many a good tune played on an old fiddle." [Cf. Wǔ Sòng, chap. 2; often said in praise of older people; note: the adjective *lǎolà*, "(1) experienced; (2) determined; drastic; ruthless"; see also *lǎo mǎ shí tú* and *rén lǎo, jīng* above.]

150 **(Shéng jù, mù duàn;) shuǐ dī, shí chuān.** (绳锯木断，) 水滴石穿。(lit) (A rope [can] saw [through] wood, [and]) water [continuously] dripping [can] pierce a stone. (fig) Anyone can carry out a difficult task if (s)he persists. Persistence overcomes all difficulties. [This rhyme is from the Song dynasty Luo Dajing's *Hè Lín Yù Lù*, chap. 10; the second part, originally from the *Hàn Shū: Méi Chéng Zhuàn*, may also appear as *dī shuǐ chuān shí*; both halves are used independently as chengyu.]

151 **Shēng, kàn yīshang; shú, kàn rén.** 生看衣裳，熟看人。[When you meet] a stranger, you [can only] judge [him] by his clothes, [but someone you] know well, [you can] judge by [his] personality. [See *wéirén*, "conduct."]

152 **Shēng mǐ chéngle shú fàn.** 生米成了熟饭。(lit) The raw rice has [already] been cooked. (fig) "What is done is done" (and can't be undone). "The die is cast." [Cf. DRC, chap. 62; Xǐngshì Yīnyuán Zhuàn, chap. 91; see also *mù yǐ chéng zhōu* above and *shǐ zài xián shàng* below.]

153 **Shèngrén nù fā bù shàng liǎn.** 圣人怒发不上脸。(lit) [When a] sage is angry, [it] never shows on [his] face. (fig) One should not reveal one's emotions openly. [Cf. Fēngshén Yǎnyì, chap. 75.]

154 **Shèngrén yě yǒu (sānfēn) cuò.*** 圣人也有(三分)错。(lit) [Even] a wise man makes mistakes (thirty percent [of the time]). (fig) Everyone makes mistakes sometimes. "Even Homer sometimes nods." [See also *cōngming yīshì* above and *zhìzhě qiān lǜ* below.]

155 **Shěngshì, wú shì.** 省事无事。(lit) Doing less [in the end will] save trouble. (fig) The less one does, the less potential for trouble there is for problems arising later on. [Cf. Wǔ Sòng, chap. 6; see also *duō zuò, duō cuò* above.]

156 **Shénguǐ pà léng rén.** 神鬼怕楞人。(lit) [Even] gods [and] ghosts are afraid of those [who] speak their minds. (fig) People who speak their minds straightforwardly are usually not popular with others. [Cf. WM, chap. 36; also said as *shén guǐ pà è rén* in WM, chap. 36; note: *léng*, (lit) "sharp-edged," here has the sense of *léngjiǎo*, "daring to

S

differ with others"; see also *zhí gōu diào bùliǎo yú* below.]

157 **Shèngyàn bì sàn.** 盛宴必散。 (lit) [Even the] grandest feast must come to an end. (fig) Good times cannot last forever. [Cf. *DRC*, chap. 13; see also *liú jūn qiān rì* and *qiān lǐ dā cháng péng* above and *sòng jūn qiān lǐ* and *tiānxià wú bù* below.]

158 **Shēngyì hǎo zuò; huǒji nán kào.** 生意好做, 伙计难靠。 It's easy to do business, [but] difficult to depend on [one's] employees. [Said by employers.]

159 **Shēng yǒu yá; zhī wúyá.** 生有涯, 知无涯。 Life has limits [but] knowledge has no bounds. *Ars dura; vita brevis.* [Cf. *Zhuāngzǐ: Yǎng Shēng Zhǔ*.]

160 **Shèng zhě wéi wáng; bài zhě wéi kòu.** 胜者为王, 败者为寇。 (lit) [If] one wins, [he becomes a] king; [if one] loses, [he becomes a] bandit. (fig) Winners are always right, and losers are always in the wrong. [Also said *shèng zhě wáng hóu; bǎi zhě kòu*.]

161 **Shēnhòu shí Fāng Gān.** 身后识方干。 (lit) [Not until] after [his] death was Fang Gan recognized. (fig) Many talented people are not appreciated until after they have died. [Note: Fang Gan was a talented scholar in the Tang dynasty.]

162 **Shēnjiào zhòngyú yánjiào.** 身教重于言教。 (lit) Personal example [carries] more weight than [mere] preaching. (fig) Example is better than precept. [Also said *shēnjiào shèngyú yánjiào*.]

163 **Shén pà jìng; guǐ pà sòng.** 神怕敬, 鬼怕送。 (lit) Gods don't want to be worshiped [just as] ghosts fear [being] exorcised. (fig) Truly good people don't want admiration [just as] bad people don't want to be driven off.

164 **Shēnshān cáng hǔ bào; kuàngyě, nì qílín.** 深山藏虎豹, 旷野匿麒麟。 (lit) The mountains hide tigers and leopards, [and the] wilderness conceals unicorns. (fig) There may be people of talent hidden in remote places. [Cf. the *píngshū: Yuè Fēi Zhuàn*, chap. 43; see also the following two entries.]

165 **Shēnshān chū jùnmǎ; píngdì chū dāi lǘ.** 深山出骏马, 平地出呆驴。 (lit) [From the] far mountains come strong horses, [while the] flatlands produce stupid donkeys. (fig) Talented people are produced by difficult conditions, while an easy life produces good-for-nothings.

166 **Shēnshān chū jùn niǎo.** 深山出俊鸟。 (lit) [From] deep [in the] mountains come beautiful birds. (fig) Beautiful ladies and gifted scholars are (sometimes) produced in remote places. [See also *hánmén chū cáizǐ* and *pì xiāng chū hǎo jiǔ* above and *yáng qún chū luòtuo* below and the preceding two entries.]

167 **Shēnshǒu bù dǎ chuí wěi gǒu.** 伸手不打垂尾狗。 (lit) Don't stretch out [your] arm to beat dogs [with their] tails between [their] legs. (fig) Treat leniently those who show signs of repentance.

168 **Shēnshǒu bù dǎ xiàoliǎn rén.*** 伸手不打笑脸人。 (lit) An extended hand [will] not hit someone with a smiley face. (fig) No one will strike a smiling face.

169 **Shēnshǒu sānfēn lì; bù gěi yě gòuběn.** 伸手三分利, 不给也够本。 (lit) [If one just] sticks out [one's] hand, [one will usually get] thirty percent profit; [but even if one is] not given anything, [at least one] loses nothing. (fig) As long as one at least takes action, one may get some benefit, whereas if one just sits idle, one will certainly get nothing at all. "Don't just sit there; do something!" [See also *xíngdòng yǒu sānfēn* below.]

170 **Shénxiān dǎgǔ yǒu cuò diǎn.** 神仙打鼓有错点。 (lit) [Even] gods make slips [when] beating a drum. (fig) "To err is human."

171 **Shénxiān nán diào wǔ shí yú.** 神仙难钓午时鱼。 (lit) [Even] gods [find it] difficult to catch fish [at] noontime. (fig) Nothing can be done if the time is not right. [Note: *wǔshí*, the time period between 11 A.M. and 1 P.M.; see *sān gè wǔgēng* above.]

172 **Shénxiān nán shí wán sǎn.** 神仙难识丸散。 [Even] gods are hard put to tell [what's inside the] medicines in traditional Chinese] pills [and] powders. [Cf. *Wǔ Sōng*, chap. 3.]

173 **Shénxian xiàfán, xiān wèn tǔdì.** 神仙下凡, 先问土地。 (lit) [When] celestial beings descend [from Heaven] to earth, [they have to] first enquire of the local Earth God. (fig) Upon entering another's territory, it is essential to pay one's respects to the local authorities. [Note: *xiàfán* is a Buddhist term referring to gods descending to earth from Heaven; see also *xíng kè bài zuò kè* below.]

174 **Shēn xiū érhòu jiā qí.** 身修而后家齐。 [When a] person purges [himself of] error, then [his] family [will be] well-behaved. [Cf. *Rúlín Wàishǐ*, chap. 11.]

175 **Shēn zài fú zhōng, bù zhī fú.** 身在福中, 不知福。 (lit) [When] one is in the midst of happiness, [one may] not know [what] happiness [is]. (fig) One may not appreciate a good thing when one has it.

176 **Shēn zhèng, bùpà yǐngr wāi (/xié).** 身正不怕影儿歪(/斜)。 (lit) [If one's] body is upright, [one has] no [need to] fear [one's] shadow [being] crooked. (fig) If one's behavior is always correct, one need never fear slanderous accusations. [See also *jiǎo zhèng bùpà* above and *xīn zhèng bùpà* below.]

177 **Shè rén xiān shè mǎ; qín zéi xiān qín wáng.*** 射人先射马, 擒贼先擒王。 (lit) ([When] shooting a person, first shoot [his] horse;) [when] catching robbers, first catch their leader. (fig) In attacking people or a problem, concentrate on the key points. [Originally a couplet from Du Fu's poem: "Qián Chū Sài"; cf. *DRC*, chap. 55.]

178 **Shé rù zhú dòng, qū xīn hái zài.** 蛇入竹洞, 曲心还在。 (lit) [Even though a] snake enters [a straight] bamboo tube, [its] inclination to wiggle still exists. (fig) An evil doer cannot change his basic nature. "A leopard cannot change its spots." [Also said *shé zuān zhú dòng*, etc.; see also *gǒu chī shǐ* and *jiāngshān yì gǎi* above and *tōu shí (de) māor* and *yī rén, yī xiàng* below.]

179 **Shē sān bùdí xiàn èr.** 赊三不敌见二。(lit) [Getting] a promise for three is not as good as actually seeing two [in hand]. (fig) "A bird in the hand is worth two in the bush." [Cf. *JW*, chap. 3; also said *qiān qián shē bùrú bābǎi xiàn* in *Xǐngshì Héngyán*, chap. 20; *Hé Diǎn*, chap. 4; note: *shēqiàn* "to give or get credit"; see also *duō dé bùrú* above and *shí shē bùrú* below.]

180 **Shé shàng yǒu lóng quán; shārén bù jiàn xuè.** 舌上有龙泉，杀人不见血。(lit) On the tongue, there is a [sharp] sword; [it] kills people without a drop of blood being seen. (fig) Words (of a sharp-tongued person) can do serious harm. [Note: *Lóng Quán* refers to a city in southern Zhejiang province where famous *Lóng Quán* swords are made; see also *ruǎndāozi* above.]

181 **Shétou dǎ gè gǔn, zhīshi jì yī běn.** 舌头打个滚，知识记一本。(lit) Give [your] tongue a roll [and your] knowledge [will] increase [by] one book. (fig) If you are willing to ask people what you don't know, your knowledge will increase. [Rhyme.]

182 **Shétou dǐxia yāsǐ rén.** 舌头底下压死人。People [can be] crushed to death under the tongue. (fig) Rumors and gossip can seriously injure people.

183 **Shé tūn shǔ, yīng diāo shé; yī wù xiáng yī wù.** 蛇吞鼠，鹰叼蛇，一物降一物。(lit) Snakes swallow rats [and] eagles hold snakes in their mouths; there is always one thing to conquer another. (fig) Everything has its vanquisher. [Note: this entire proverb may be used as a *xiehouyu*; the second part is commonly used alone; see also *néngrén zhīwài* and *qiáng zhōng háiyǒu* and *rén wài yǒu rén* and *shān wài yǒu shān* above and *yī wù xiáng yī wù* below.]

184 **Shé wéi lì-hài běn; kǒu shì huò-fú mén.** 舌为利害本，口是祸福门。[One's] tongue is the root [cause of both] benefits [and] harm; [one's] mouth is [like] a door [open to either] disaster [or] blessings. [Rhyme; cf. *Xǐngshì Héngyán*, chap. 29; see also *bìng cóng kǒu rù* above.]

185 **Shé wú tóu ér bù xíng; niǎo wú chì ér bù fēi.** 蛇无头而不行，鸟无翅而不飞。(lit) [A] snake without a head [can]not crawl [and a] bird without wings [can]not fly. (fig) A group cannot act without a leader. [Cf. *JW*, chap. 77; see also *bīng wú jiàng* and *rén wú tóu* above.]

186 **Shē zhě, fù bùzú; jiǎn zhě, pín yǒuyú.** 奢者富不足，简者贫有余。One [who lives in] luxury [will always feel he] want of money [even if he is] wealthy; one [who lives] frugally [will always feel there is] enough [even if he is] poor. [Rhyme.]

187 **Shé zhě ménhù zhī guān yuè.** 舌者门户之关钥。(lit) The tongue [is like the] door key [which] shuts the mouth. (fig) Be prudent in speech. "Be a guardian, not an usher, at the portal of thy thought."

188 **Shé zǒu wúshēng; jiānjì wúxíng.** 蛇走无声，奸计无形。[Just as] snakes move silently, [so] evil plots are invisible.

189 **Shé zuān de kǔdòng, shé zhīdào.** 蛇钻的窟洞，蛇知道。(lit) The snake knows the hole into which it crawls. (fig) One who has done some mischief knows very well what (s)he has done. [Cf. *JPM*, chap. 86.]

190 **Shíbā, èrshísān, dǐ guò mǔdān.** 十八，二十三抵过牡丹。(lit) [A girl between] eighteen [and] twenty-three [years old] is [as beautiful] as a peony. (fig) Young women are beautiful. "Sweet sixteen."

191 **Shì bài, nú qī zhǔ; shí shuāi, guǐ nòng rén.** 势败奴欺主，时衰鬼弄人。[When] circumstances defeat [one], [one's] servants [will] bully [their] master; [when you have had] bad luck, devils [will] "do" you. [Cf. *Chū Kè Pāi'àn Jīngqí*, chap. 11.]

192 **Shì biàn zhī rénxīn.** 事变知人心。(lit) [Only when the] situation changes [does one] know a person's [true] mind. (fig) One only gets to know another's true loyalty, sincerity or friendship in times of adversity or emergency. [Note: *shìbiàn* as a noun means "emergency"; see also *guó luàn chū zhōngchén* and *rén dào nánchù* above.]

193 **Shì bié sān rì, guā mù xiāng kàn.** 士别三日，刮目相看。(lit) A scholar who has been away three days must be looked at with new eyes. (fig) One can hardly imagine what changes will occur after a period of separation. [Usually said to one whom one has not seen for some time; originally *guā mù xiàng dài* in *Sān Guó Zhì: Wǔ Shū: Lǚ Méng Zhuàn*; note: *guāmù-xiàngkàn* is used as a *chengyu* meaning "to treat someone with increased respect"; see also *sān rì bù jiàn* above.]

194 **Shì bù guò sān.*** 事不过三。(lit) Never do anything more than three [times]. (fig) One may be forgiven once, and maybe twice, but not a third time. [Cf. *JW*, chap. 27; this is also sometimes understood to mean "things happen in threes"; see also *ràng yī, ràng èr* above.]

195 **Shí bù kě shī; (jī bù zài lái).** 时不可失，(机不再来)。(lit) The time [should] not be lost; (the opportunity [may] not come again). (fig) "There is no time like the present." "Opportunity doesn't knock twice."

196 **Shì bù néng bàn de tài jué; huà bù néng shuō de tài sǔn.*** 事不能办得太绝，话不能说得太损。(lit) Affairs cannot be handled too uncompromisingly, [and] words cannot be spoken too cuttingly. (fig) Do not go to extremes or excess: Never force others' backs to the wall, nor be overly insulting to others.

197 **Shì bù sānsī, zhōng yǒu hòuhuǐ.** 事不三思，终有后悔。[If one does] not think things over three [times before doing anything], eventually there will be [a day of] regret. [Cf. *Yù Shì Míng Yán*, chap. 2; see also *shì yào qián sī* below.]

198 **Shí bù yán; qǐn bù yǔ.** 食不言，寝不语。[When] eating or [when] in bed, don't talk too much. [Note: Chinese were traditionally taught that this was injurious to health; originally from the Confucian Analects: *Lúnyǔ: Xiāng Dǎng Piàn*; see also *qǐnshí*, "sleeping and eating."]

S

199 **Shí bù zhīnèi, bì yǒu fāngcǎo.** 十步之内，必有芳草。 (lit) Within ten steps there must be fragrant grass. (fig) Though a small place, there must be heroes there. There are able people everywhere. [As a chengyu: *shí bù fāng cǎo*; see also *shí shì zhī yì* below.]

200 **Shì cǎo yǒu gēn; shì huà yǒu yīn.** 是草有根，是话有因。 [Just as] every [blade of] grass has [its] roots; [so behind] every word there is a reason. [See also *shì yǒu yīn* below.]

201 **Shì cóng huǎn lái.** 事从缓来。 Things [should be] done in a slow and unhurried manner. [Cf. *JW*, chap. 85; see also *shì kuān zé yuán* below.]

202 **Shí dào, huā jiù kāi.** 时到花就开。 (lit) [When the] time is right, the flowers will bloom. (fig) In doing anything, wait for the right time. [See the chengyu: *shuǐ dào gú chéng*, "when conditions are ripe success will follow"; see also *shíjiān zú* and *yùn dào shí lái* below.]

203 **Shí dào tiānliàng fāng hǎo shuì; rén dào lǎolái cái xuéguāi.** 时到天亮方好睡，人到老来才学乖。 [Just as it is] not until [just before] dawn [that people] sleep best, [so it is] not until people are old [that they] learn to be wise. [Note: *guāiqiǎo*, "clever."]

204 **Shì dàotóulái, bù zì yóu.** 事到头来，不自由。 In the end, [it's] not up to one [to decide]. [Cf. *Sān Xiá Wǔ Yì*, chap. 78; note: *dàotóulái*, "after all; in the long run; in the end"; see also *móushì zài rén* and *qiān suàn, wàn suàn* above and *tiān suàn bù yóu* below.]

205 **Shì dà, shì xiǎo; jiàn guān jiù liǎo.** 事大事小，见官就了。 [No matter whether the] matter is large or small, once [one] sees the magistrate, [it will] be resolved. [Rhyme.]

206 **Shī duōle, bù yǎng; zhài duōle, bù chóu.*** 虱多了不痒，债多了不愁。 [Just as when one has] too many lice, [one] doesn't itch, [so when one has] too many debts, [one] stops worrying. [Cf. *Hé Diǎn*, chap. 4.]

207 **Shí duō, wú zīwèi.** 食多，无滋味。 (lit) Eating (too) much, there is no flavor. (fig) Over-indulgence dulls one's appetite.

208 **Shī ēn mò wàng bào; wàng bào mò shī'ēn.** 施恩莫望报，望报莫施恩。 [If you] do [others a] favor, don't expect [to be] rewarded; [if you] expect [to be] rewarded, don't do [others any] favors. [Cf. *Rúlín Wàishǐ*, chap. 32, and *Érnǚ Yīngxióng Zhuàn*, chap. 27.]

209 **Shì ér bù sǐ; shì cái bù sàn.** 是儿不死，是财不散。 (lit) [If one] is [destined to have a] son, [the son will] not die; [if one] is [destined to have] wealth, [it will] not be lost. (fig) What is destined to be, will be. "*Que será, será.*"

210 **Shí fǎng jiǔ kōng, yěhǎo shěng qióng.** 十访九空，也好省穷。 (lit) [Even if] nine out of ten [relatives or friends you] visit refuse [you, you] can still [borrow enough to] get by [on]. (fig) Even if you are refused nine out of ten times, don't give up hope; keep trying. [Cf. *Xǐngshì Yīnyuán Zhuàn*, chap. 25.]

211 **Shì fēi jīngguò, bù zhī nán.** 事非经过不知难。 Unless [one] has experienced something oneself, [one can]not know its difficulties. [See also *jiàn rén tiāodàn* above.]

212 **Shìfēi lái rù ěr, bù tīng zìrán wú.** 是非来入耳，不听自然无。 [When] gossip comes to [your] ear, [if you do] not listen [to it, it will] naturally disappear. [Cf. *JPM*, chap. 85.]

213 **Shìfēi zhǐ wèi duō kāikǒu; fánnǎo jiēyīn qiáng chūtóu.** 是非只为多开口，烦恼皆因强出头。 Troubles only [come about] as [a result of] too much opening of the mouth; worries [are] all because of deliberately showing off. [Rhyme; see also *bìng cóng kǒu rù* above.]

214 **Shìfēi zhōngrì yǒu; bù tīng zìrán wú.** 是非终日有，不听自然无。 Troubles and disputes occur all day long, [but] if [you just] don't listen, of course there aren't any. [Cf. *JPM*, chap. 83; *Wǔ Sōng*, chap. 1.]

215 **Shìfēi zì yǒu gōnglùn.*** 是非自有公论。 (lit) Rights and wrongs are [subject to] public opinion. (fig) Public opinion is the best judge of who's right and who's wrong. Public opinion is the best judge. [Cf. *Shì Shuō Xīn Yǔ: Pǐn Zǎo*; also said *shìfēi qūzhí zì yǒu gōnglùn*; see also *gōngpíng chǔyú zhòng yì* and *lùshang xíngrén* and *rén yǎn shì bǎ chèng* above and *tiānxià qiányǎnr* and *zhīdǐ mò guò* and *zhòngrén yǎnjing* below.]

216 **Shífēn xīngxing, shǐ jiǔfēn.** 十分惺惺，使九分。 (lit) [Of] all [your] wisdom and intelligence, use [only] ninety percent. (fig) Use your wisdom sparingly. Don't "put all your cards on the table." Don't "show off" or "come on too strong" at first. Always hold back a bit, and leave yourself some room to maneuver later. [Note the colloquial expression *liú yìshǒu*, "to hold back a trick or two"; see also *shí gè chúzi* below.]

217 **Shì fú, bù shì huò; shì huò, duǒ bu guò.** 是福不是祸，是祸躲不过。 (lit) [If it] is a blessing, [it will] not be[come] misfortune; [if it] is misfortune, [it] cannot be avoided. [Rhyme.]

218 **Shīfu lǐng jìnmén; xiūxíng zài gèrén.** 师傅领进门，修行在个人。 The master leads [the student] into the door [i.e., teaches the trade], [but] the perfection [of the apprentice's skill] lies in the individual [apprentice's own efforts]. [Note: *xiūxíng*, "practice" (of Buddhism).]

219 **Shí gè chúzi, jiǔ gè dàn.** 十个厨子，九个淡。 (lit) [Out of] ten cooks, nine [leave their dishes a little] bland. (fig) A good chef always holds back on the salt. Don't go all-out, don't stick your neck all the way out; always allow for unforeseen circumstances; leave room to maneuver. [See also *shífēn xīngxing* above.]

220 **Shí gè piányi, jiǔ gè ài.** 十个便宜，九个爱。 (lit) [If there are] ten [opportunities to take] petty advantage, nine [people will] love [to do so]. (fig) Nine out of ten people like to get things on the cheap or to gain petty advantages.

221 **Shí gè qián yào huā; yī gè qián yào shěng.** 十个钱要花，一个钱要省。 (lit) Spend ten coins [when it's] necessary, [but] save [every] one [when it's not needed].

S

222 **Shí gè rén, shí yàng xìng.** 十个人，十样性。 Ten persons [have] ten different characters. [Cf. *Hé Diǎn*, chap. 2.]

223 **Shí gè zhǐtou bù néng yìbān qí.*** 十个指头不能一般齐。 (lit) [Even one's] ten fingers are unequal in length. (fig) All people are not all the same [e.g., equally talented, capable, etc.; said, e.g., of one's children; see also *nǎ gēn zhǐtou* above.]

224 **Shì gǒu, gǎi bùliǎo chī shǐ; shì láng, gǎi bùliǎo chī ròu.** 是狗改不了吃屎，是狼改不了吃肉。 (lit) [If it] is a dog, [it] cannot change [its habit of] eating excrement, [and if it] is a wolf, [it can]not change [its habit of] eating meat. (fig) An evil person cannot change his or her nature. "A leopard cannot change his spots." [See also *gǒu chī shǐ* and the following entry.]

225 **Shì gǒu jiù huì chī shǐ; shì shé jiù yào yǎo rén.** 是狗就会吃屎，是蛇就要咬人。 (lit) [If it] is a dog, then [it] will eat excrement, [and if it] is a snake, then [it] will bite people. (fig) Evil people always do evil things. [See also *gǒu zǒu qiān lǐ* above and the preceding entry.]

226 **Shí jiā guō zào, jiǔ bùtóng.** 十家锅灶，九不同。 (lit) In [any] ten homes, nine kitchens are different. (fig) Different people have different ideas. [See also *sān rén, liù yàng huà* below.]

227 **Shíjiān jiǎzǐ xūyú shì.** 世间甲子须臾事。 (lit) In [the earthly] world, sixty years [are but the] matter of a moment. (fig) Time flies like an arrow. [From a Tang dynasty poem by Xu Hun: "Sòng Chùshī Guī Shān."]

228 **Shìjiān kǔshì mòruò kū; wú yán zhī kū zuìwéi kǔ.** 世间苦事莫若哭；无言之哭最为苦。 Nothing on earth is more bitter than crying, [but] crying without words is the most bitter. [Rhyme.]

229 **Shìjiān méi gè zǎo zhīdao.** 世间没个早知道。 No one on earth [can] predict [what will happen in the] future. [Cf. *Érnǚ Yīngxióng Zhuàn*, chap. 35.]

230 **Shíjiān zú, guǒzi shú.** 时间足，果子熟。 [When the] time is ripe, the fruit will mature. [Rhyme; see also *shí dào, huā jiù kāi* above.]

231 **Shí jìn, niǎo tóu lín.** 食尽鸟投林。 (lit) [When the] food is gone, [city] birds seek the forest. (fig) Those who cannot support themselves in one place will try someplace else. [Cf. *DRC*, chap. 5.]

232 **Shì jí wú jūnzǐ.** 事急无君子。 (lit) In times of emergency there are no gentlemen. (fig) Courtesies are neglected in times of emergency. [Cf. *Suí Táng Yǎnyì*, chap. 7; see also *lù jí wú jūnzǐ* above.]

233 **Shí jù yànyǔ, wǔ jù zhēn.** 十句谚语，五句真。 (lit) [Out of] ten proverbs, five [are] true. (fig) Not all proverbs are correct.

234 **Shǐkelàng zuò bù chū mì lái.** 屎壳郎做不出蜜来。 (lit) Dung beetles don't produce honey. (fig) Evil persons never do anything good.

235 **Shì kě shā ér bùkě rǔ.** 士可杀而不可辱。 A gentleman prefers death to humiliation. [Cf. *Xǐngshì Héngyán*, chap. 29.]

236 **Shǐ kǒu rú bí, zhì lǎo bù shī.** 使口如鼻，至老不失。 (lit) Use [your] mouth as [you use your] nose [i.e., for not speaking] [and you'll] never have trouble in all [your] life. (fig) Be prudent in speech.

237 **Shì kuān zé yuán.** 事宽则圆。 (lit) [Handling one's] affairs in a calm and unhurried manner will [result in] success. [Cf. *Érnǚ Yīngxióng Zhuàn*, chap. 25; note: *yuánmǎn*, "satisfactory"; see also *shì cóng huǎn lái* above.]

238 **Shí lái, fú còu.** 时来福凑。 When luck is with one, blessings follow. [Cf. *Chū Kè Pāi'àn Jīngqí*, chap. 35.]

239 **Shí lái, shéi bù lái; shí bù lái, shéi lái?** 时来谁不来，时不来谁来？ (lit) [When] fortune smiles on one, everyone comes; when bad luck befalls one, everyone goes away. (fig) "Nobody knows you when you're down and out." [Cf. *JPM*, chap. 30; see also *pín jū nàoshì* and *qián jù rúxiōng* above.]

240 **Shí lái, wán tiě yě shēng guāng.** 时来，顽铁也生光。 (lit) [When] luck comes, even dull iron becomes bright. (fig) When things are going well everything seems to go right. [Cf. *Jīngshì Tōngyán*, chap. 31; see also *yùn qù, huángjīn shīsè* below.]

241 **Shí lǐ bùtóng sú.** 十里不同俗。 (lit) Ten miles [apart] the customs are quite different. (fig) Different districts have different customs. [See also *gèchù gè xiāngsú* above.]

242 **Shí lǐ bù wèn fàn; èrshí lǐ bù wèn diàn.** 十里不问饭，二十里不问店。 (lit) [When traveling,] don't ask about food [for the first] ten leagues, [and] don't ask about inns [for the first] twenty leagues. (fig) When starting to do anything, don't concern yourself about the end, otherwise you will just slacken your efforts; concentrate on the task at hand. [Note: one *lǐ* equals one-half kilometer.]

243 **Shí lǐ wú zhēn xìn.** 十里无真信。 (lit) [After traveling] ten *lǐ*, there are no true words. (fig) After a story or message is repeated several times, it will become completely distorted. [One *lǐ* equals one-half of a kilometer.]

244 **Shīluò huángjīn yǒu chù zhǎo; shīluò guāngyīn wú chù xún.** 失落黄金有处找，失落光阴无处寻。 Gold lost may be found somewhere, [but] time lost is nowhere to be found. [More commonly said *yī cùn guāngyīn* below.]

245 **Shì mǎ, jiù chōng bùliǎo qílín.** 是马就充不了麒麟。 (lit) [If it] is a horse, then it cannot pass as a Chinese unicorn. (fig) An ordinary person can't be passed off as an outstanding one.

246 **Shì mǎ, yǒu sānfēn lóng gǔ.** 是马有三分龙骨。 (lit) [Even if it] is a horse, [it] has one-third dragon's bones. (fig) There's something uncommon in everything common.

247 **Shí mó, jiǔ nàn chū hǎorén.** 十磨九难出好人。 Hardships produce outstanding persons. [Note: *mónàn*, "hardships."]

S

248 **Shí nián chuāng xià wú rén wèn; yījǔ chéngmíng tiānxià zhī.** 十年窗下无人问, 一举成名天下知。 [After persevering] in obscurity for ten years in [one's] study, [one may] become famous overnight. [Used in traditional China to encourage children to study hard. Note: *yījǔ-chéngmíng* has become a set phrase meaning "to become famous overnight"; see also *shū zhōng zìyǒu* below.]

249 **Shí nián hé dōng; shí nián hé xī.*** 十年河东, 十年河西。 See *sānshí nián hé dōng; sānshí nián hé xī* above.

250 **Shí nián jī tóu, shēng pīshuāng.** 十年鸡头, 生砒霜。 The head of a ten-year[-old] chicken [is as poisonous as] fresh arsenic [so don't eat it]. [This is a common Chinese belief.]

251 **Shí nián pùzi, rén pěng zìhao; bǎinián pùzi, zìhao pěng rén.** 十年铺子, 人捧字号; 百年铺子, 字号捧人。 [In a] ten-year[-old] shop, [it's] customers [who] make the name famous, [but with a] hundred-year[-old] shop, [it's] the name [which makes] the people [who own the shop] famous. [See also *rén pěng xì* above.]

252 **Shí nián shù mù, bǎi nián shù rén.*** 十年树木, 百年树人。 (lit) [It takes] ten years to grow trees, [but] a hundred years to rear people. (fig) It takes ten years to grow a tree and a hundred years to cultivate (a generation of) good people. [Cf. *Gǔnzi: Quán Xiū*; note: *bǎinián-shùrén* has become a set phrase meaning "it takes a century to rear talented people"; see also *yī nián shù gǔ* below.]

253 **Shípò rénqíng biànshì xiān.** 识破人情便是仙。 [One who can] see through [and ignore] worldly entanglements is [like a] god [i.e., detached and free].

254 **Shìqián yào dǎnxiǎo; shìhòu yào dǎndà.** 事前要胆小, 事后要胆大。 Before something [happens], be cautious; after something [has happened], [(then) you can be] bold.

255 **Shì qīn, bì gù.** 是亲必顾。 [If someone] is a relative, [one] must show [special] consideration. [See also *shì yī qīn* below and the following entry.]

256 **Shìqíng kàn lěngnuǎn; rén miàn zhú gāodī.** 世情看冷暖, 人面逐高低。 (lit) The ways of the world depend on hot and cold, [and other] people's faces follow [one's] ups [and] downs. (fig) The feelings of people toward one alter with one's rise and fall in social position. [Cf. *Gǔ-Jīn Xiǎoshuō*, chap. 40.]

257 **Shì qīn, sānfēn xiàng; shì huǒ, rè guò kàng.** 是亲三分向, 是火热过炕。 (lit) [If people] are relatives, [they're at least] thirty-percent inclined [to favor one another], [just as surely as] a fire [is] hotter than a [heated] tile sleeping platform. (fig) "Blood is thicker than water." [Rhyme; see also *rén qīn, gǔròu xiāng* above and *xuè bǐ shuǐ nóng* below and the preceding entry.]

258 **Shí qióng, jié nǎi jiàn.** 时穷, 节乃见。 [In] times [of] poverty, [moral] integrity is seen. [Note: *qìjié*, "integrity; moral courage."]

259 **Shīqù yī è, rì zhǎng shí shàn.** 失去一恶, 日长十善。 Eliminating one evil counts [as the equivalent of] developing virtues [in a day].

260 **Shì ruò qiúquán, hé suǒ lè?** 事若求全, 何所乐? If [you] want everything perfect, how [can there be] any happiness? [Cf. *DRC*, chap. 76; see also *fǎng mùtou* and *rén fēi shèngxián* and *rén wú wánrén* above.]

261 **Shìshàng wú nánshì, zhǐpà yǒuxīnrén.*** 世上无难事, 只怕有心人。 (lit) Nothing in the world is difficult for one who sets his mind to it. (fig) "Where there's a will, there's a way." [Cf. *JW*, chap. 2; *Érnǚ Yīngxióng Zhuàn*, chap. 16; see also *tiānxià wú nánshì* and *yǒuzhìzhě* below.]

262 **Shì shàng wú yú, háma guì.** 市上无鱼, 蛤蟆贵。 (lit) [If] on the market there is no fish, frogs [will] be expensive. (fig) If there are no goods of fine quality available, the price of poor quality goods will rise. [See also *hé lǐ wú yú* above.]

263 **Shí shē bùrú yī xiàn.** 十赊不如一现。 (lit) Ten credits are not as good as one in ready cash. (fig) One shouldn't risk losing something sure for something that is not sure. "A bird in the hand is worth two in the bush." [See also *shē sān bùdí* above.]

264 **Shí shì bàn tōng bùrú yī shì jīngtōng.** 十事半通不如一事精通。 [To have] half-knowledge of ten things is not as good as [having a] thorough knowledge of one thing. [See also *bùpà qiān zhāo* above and *yàngyàng jīngtōng* below.]

265 **Shìshí shèngyú xióngbiàn.** 事实胜于雄辩。 (lit) Facts are stronger than eloquence. (fig) Facts speak louder than words. [This was used as the title of an essay in Lu Xun's *Rè Fēng*.]

266 **Shíshíwùzhě wéi jùnjié.*** 识时务者为俊杰。 (lit) Those [who are] attuned to the tide of the times are people of outstanding talent. (fig) A wise person knows when to bow to circumstances. Realists succeed. [Originally from *Sān Guó Zhì*; also cf. *R3K*, chap. 76; see also *dàzhàngfu néng qū* above.]

267 **Shìshì yǒuchéng bì yǒu bài; wéirén yǒu xīng bì yǒu shuāi.** 世事有成必有败, 为人有兴必有衰。 [In life's] affairs [one] must have failures as well as successes; to conduct one['s life] is to have rises as well as declines. [Rhyme; see also *rén yǒu qī pín* above and *suī yǒu xióngsuì* below.]

268 **Shíshì zào yīngxióng.*** 时势造英雄。 (lit) Situations create heroes. (fig) The times produce great men. [Vs. *yīngxióng zào shíshì* below.]

269 **Shí shì zhī yì, bì yǒu zhōng xìn.** 十室之邑必有忠信。 [Even in] a town of ten households, there must be loyal and honest people. [Cf. *Jīngshì Tōngyán*, chap. 1; see also *shí bù zhīnèi* above.]

270 **Shí shuāi, guǐ nòng rén.** 时衰, 鬼弄人。 (lit) [When one's] luck is in decline, devils [come to] bully you. [Cf. *Jīngshì Tōngyán*, chap. 28; note: *zuònòng*, "to play tricks on."]

271 **Shí wǎng, jiǔ kōng; yī wǎng chénggōng.** 十网九空, 一网成功。 (lit) [Cast a] net ten [times, you will have] nine empty [and only] one success. (fig) Success comes only after setbacks and failures. [Rhyme.]

272 **Shì wèi zhījǐ zhě sǐ; (nǚ wèi fēijǐ zhě róng).** 士为知己者死，（女为悦己者容）。 A scholar [is willing to] die for a convivial friend, ([just as] a woman will beautify herself for the one who loves her). [See also *mǎ féng Bólè* above.]

273 **Shì wú bù kě duì rén yán.** 事无不可对人言。 (lit) [One's] doings [should] not contain any [words that can]not be said in front of others. (fig) Nothing should be hidden from others. [Cf. *Sòng Shǐ: Sīmǎ Guāng Zhuàn.*]

274 **Shì wú sān, bùchéng.** 事无三不成。 (lit) Affairs without three [tries will] not succeed. (fig) One will not succeed without making repeated efforts. "Third try never fails." "Third time's a charm." [Cf. *JW,* chap. 83.]

275 **Shì wú shàn wéi; xíng wú dú chū.** 事无擅为，行无独出。 (lit) Things [can]not be done at will; actions [can]not be independently produced. (fig) People cannot do things or just act in any way that they wish to. [Cf. *Jǐngshì Tōngyán,* chap. 6.]

276 **Shǐ xīn, yòngxīn; fǎn hài qí shēn.** 使心用心，反害其身。 [One who] has [ulterior] motives [to harm others] in fact [will] harm himself. [Cf. *Xǐngshì Héngyán,* chap. 5; note: *xīnjì,* "scheming."]

277 **Shì yào qián sī; miǎn láo hòuhuǐ.** 事要前思，免劳后悔。 Thinking before doing things [will] save one regretting later. [See also *shì bù sānsī* above.]

278 **Shí yè zhūmén, jiǔ bù kāi.** 十谒朱门九不开。 (lit) [Of] ten visits [paid] to the vermilion gate [of an official mansion], nine are [sure to be] rejected. (fig) It's not easy to get access to an official.

279 **Shì yì bù kuī rén.** 事艺不亏人。 (lit) [If there] is a skill, [it will] not harm anyone. (fig) Having (mastered) a skill never did anyone any harm. [See also *cì zǐ qiānjīn* above.]

280 **Shì yīnyuán, bàng dǎ bù huí.** 是姻缘，棒打不回。 (lit) [If they] are destined to be together, [then] clubs could not beat [them] apart. (fig) Those fated to be married cannot be separated. [Cf. *DRC,* chap. 90; see also *qiān lǐ yīnyuán* above.]

281 **Shì yī qīn, guà yī xīn.** 是一亲，挂一心。 (lit) [If it] is a relative, one's heart is involved. (fig) One is always concerned about one's relatives. [Rhyme; see also *shì qīn, bì gù* above.]

282 **Shì yǒu dòuqiǎo; wù yǒu gù rán.** 事有斗巧，物有故然。 (lit) [In some] matters there are coincidences, [just as some] objects are [the way they are] naturally. (fig) Sometimes coincidences just happen, and some things just turn out the way they do. [Cf. *Xǐngshì Héngyán,* chap. 31; note: *dòuqiǎo* is colloquial for *còuqiǎo,* "coincidences"; see also *wú qiǎo, bù chéng shū* below.]

283 **Shì yǒu yīn; huà yǒu yuán.*** 事有因，话有缘。 [Just as] things have causes, [so] words have reasons. [See also *shì cǎo yǒu gēn* above.]

284 **Shì zài rén wéi.*** 事在人为。 (lit) [Every]thing [depends] on human effort. (fig) People make things happen. [Note: *shìzàirénwéi* is treated like a fixed phrase idiom; vs. *móushì zài rén* above.]

285 **Shǐ zài xián shàng, bùdé bù fā.** 矢在弦上，不得不发。 (lit) [Once] the arrow is [fitted] to the bowstring, [it] cannot but be shot. (fig) Some things, once started, can't be stopped. "The die is cast." [Note: *shǐzàixiánshàng* is used as a set phrase meaning "imminent; unstoppable"; see also *shēng mǐ chéngle* above.]

286 **Shí zhàng shēnshuǐ yì cè; yī rén xīnsī nán liáng.** 十丈深水易测，一人心思难量。 Water thirty-three feet deep is easily measured, [but a] person's thoughts are hard to fathom.

287 **Shì zhēn, nán jiǎ; shì jiǎ, nán zhēn.*** 是真难假，是假难真。 (lit) [If it] is true, [it is] difficult to falsify; [if it] is false, [it is] difficult to [make it] true. (fig) Truth and falsehood are hard to confuse. [Cf. *Èr Kè Pāi'àn Jīngqí,* chap. 17.]

288 **Shì zhēn, nán miè; shì jiǎ, yì chú.** 是真难灭，是假易除。 [If it] is truth, [it is] hard to destroy; [if it] is false, [it is] easy to eradicate. [Cf. *WM,* chap. 62; see also *huángjīn wú jiǎ* above.]

289 **Shī zhī háolí, chà yǐ qiān lǐ.** 失之毫厘，差以千里。 (lit) A miscalculation of a millimeter [causes] a discrepancy of a thousand *lǐ.* (fig) An error the breadth of a single hair can lead one a thousand leagues astray; a small discrepancy can lead to a great error. [Cf. *Shǐ Jì: Tài Shǐ Gōng Zìxù;* see also *chà zhī háolí* above; one *lǐ* equals one-half of a kilometer.]

290 **Shǒubèi yě shì ròu; shǒuxīn yě shì ròu.*** 手背也是肉，手心也是肉。 Both the back of one's hand and the palm of one's hand are of one's own flesh. (fig) All of one's children and family members are dear to one; one should love and treat all one's family members equally. [Cf. *Zàishēng Yuán,* chap. 71; see also *nǎ gēn zhǐtou* above.]

291 **Shòubude yān xūn, chéngbude fó.** 受不得烟熏，成不得佛。 [If one] can't endure [incense] smoke, [one] can't become a Buddha. (fig) Everything has a cost. If one is not willing to invest some effort or pay some price, one cannot attain one's goals. "If you can't take the heat, get out of the kitchen."

292 **Shòu bù yā zhí.** 寿不压职。 (lit) Age [should] not outweigh official rank. (fig) Mere age should not be considered more important than (high) official rank (in observing courtesies or formalities). [Note: *guān zhí* "official position."]

293 **Shǒu cháng, shān xiù duǎn; rén qióng, yánsè dī.** 手长衫袖短，人穷颜色低。 (lit) When the arms are long, [one's] gown sleeve seems short; if a person is poor [(s)he has to put on a] humble countenance. (fig) Poverty makes one feel inferior.

294 **Shǒu chā yú lán, bìbude xīng.** 手插鱼篮避不得腥。 (lit) One can't avoid the smell of fish when one puts one's hand into a fish-basket. (fig) If one engages in bad behavior, one will certainly get a bad reputation. [Cf. *JW,* chap. 86.]

S

295　**Shōu chuán hǎo zài shùnfēng shí.** 收船好在顺风时。(lit) Gather in [your] sails when the wind is favorable. (fig) Quit while things are going well. "Quit while you are ahead." [Cf. *Érnǚ Yīngxióng Zhuàn*, chap. 15; note also the *chengyu: jiànfēng-shǐduò*, "trim one's sails to the wind."]

296　**Shǒu dào yún kāi, yuè zìmíng.** 守到云开，月自明。(lit) Wait until the clouds disperse [and the] moon will [be] bright/evident. (fig) Wait for the right opportunity and things will go well. [Note: *zìmíng*, (lit) "become bright"; (fig) "be self-evident."]

297　**Shòu gǒu, mò tī; bìng mǎ, mò qī.** 瘦狗莫踢，病马莫欺。(lit) Don't kick a thin dog [and] don't mistreat a sick horse. (fig) Don't bully the poor and weak. [Rhyme.]

298　**Shòu kǒu rú píng; fáng yì rú chéng.** 守口如瓶，防意如城。Keep [your] mouth [shut as tightly as a] bottle [and] restrain [your] desires as [closely as a fortress] wall. [Note: *shǒukǒu-rúpíng* is used as a *chengyu* meaning "(be) tight-mouthed."]

299　**Shòu luòtuo qiáng sì xiàng.** 瘦骆驼强似象。(lit) [A] lean camel [is as] strong as [an] elephant. (fig) The rich, though in decline, are still better off than ordinary working people. [Cf. *Jīngshì Tōngyán*, chap. 25; see also *shòu sǐ de luòtuo* below.]

300　**Shòu rén yī fàn, tīng rén shǐhuan.** 受人一饭，听人使唤。[If you] accept a meal [from] someone, [then you must be prepared to] accept orders from him (or her). [Cf. Lu Xun's essay "Guānyu Fùnǚ Jiěfàng" in *Nán Chāng Běi Diào Jí*; see also *chī rénjiā wǎn* above.]

301　**Shòu rén zhī tuō, zhōng rén zhī shì.** 受人之托，终人之事。(lit) [If one] agrees to do something [for] someone, [then one should] see it through to the end. (fig) If one promises to do something, one should fulfill one's promise. [Note: *wěituō*, "entrust"; *shòurénzhītuō* has become an idiom meaning "to receive a request to do something."]

302　**Shǒushēn rú zhí yù.** 守身如执玉。[One should] preserve [one's] honor (or chastity) as [one] holds [a treasured] jade. [Note: *shǒushēn*, "to keep oneself flawless"; *shēnfèn*, "dignity."]

303　**Shòu sǐ de luòtuo bǐ mǎ dà.** 瘦死的骆驼比马大。(lit) A starved camel is [still] bigger than a horse. (fig) A rich person in decline is still better off than an ordinary working person. [Cf. Lao She's play: *Lóng Xū Gōu* ("Dragon Beard Ditch") Scene I, Act 2; *DRC*, chap. 6; see also *bǎi zú zhī chóng* and *qióng suī qióng* above and *shòu luòtuo* above.]

304　**Shòuxiáng rú shòudí.** 受降如受敌。[One should be as vigilant in] accepting a surrender as [in] engaging an enemy (i.e., it may be a trick).

305　**Shòuyī duōle, zhìsǐ niú.** 兽医多了，治死牛。(lit) [If there are] too many veterinarians, [they will] "cure" the ox to death. (fig) "Too many cooks spoil the broth."

306　**Shǒuzhǎngr zěnyàng kàn de jiàn shǒubèir?** 手掌儿怎样看得见手背儿？(lit) How can the palm see [what] the back of the hand [is doing]? (fig) One doesn't have eyes in the back of one's head; one can't be aware of everything that's going on behind the scenes. [See also *rén wú hòu yǎn* above.]

307　**Shǒuzhe duōdà de wǎn, chī duōdà de fàn.** 守着多大的碗，吃多大的饭。(lit) Eat [your] meals according to the size of the bowl [you] hold. (fig) Keep expenditures within the limits of income. [Cf. *DRC*, chap. 6; see also *chīfàn, chuān yī* and *kèzhe tóu* above.]

308　**Shǒu zhōng méi bǎ mǐ, jiào jī, jī bù lái.** 手中没把米，叫鸡鸡不来。(lit) Without a handful of rice in your hand, [when you] summon chickens, they won't follow [you]. (fig) You can't get anything done if you give no benefits to others.

309　**Shuǎngkǒu wù duō, zhōng zuò jí; kuài xīn shì guò, bì wéi yāng.** 爽口物多终作疾，快心事过必为殃。[One who eats too] many tasty things [will] end up falling ill, [and one who indulges in] too much pleasure must invite disaster. [Cf. *Gǔ-Jīn Xiǎoshuō*, chap. 3; note the *chengyu: lèjí-shēngbēi*, "extreme joy begets sorrow."]

310　**Shuāng mù qiáo hǎo zǒu; dúmùqiáo nán xíng.** 双木桥好走，独木桥难行。(lit) [It is] easy to walk [across a] double-plank bridge, [but] difficult to walk [across a] single-plank one. (fig) It is difficult to do anything single-handedly. [Note: *dúmùqiáo*, (lit) "single-plank bridge," (fig) "difficult path."]

311　**Shuāng quán nán dí sì shǒu.** 双拳难敌四手。(lit) Two fists are no match for four hands. (fig) A few are no match against the many. [Cf. *Xǐngshì Héngyán*, chap. 29; see also *sān bù niù liù* above and *sì bù niù liù* below.]

312　**Shuāngrì bù zháo, dānrì zháo.** 双日不着，单日着。(lit) [If we] don't meet on even-numbered days, [we are] bound to] meet on odd-numbered days. (fig) People are bound to run into each other again. [Cf. *WM*, chap. 21; see also *chuántóu bù yù* and *dàhǎi fúpíng* above.]

313　**Shuānzhe bózi de gǒu dǎ bù chéng liè.** 拴着脖子的狗打不成猎。(lit) A dog leashed by the neck cannot hunt. (fig) One who is restricted or controlled cannot do a good job.

314　**Shuān zhù lǘ zuǐ, mǎ zuǐ; shuān bu zhù rén zuǐ.** 拴住驴嘴马嘴，拴不住人嘴。(lit) [One can] muzzle the mouth of a donkey [or] a horse, [but] not the mouths of people. (fig) You can't silence people; they will be heard. [See also *tán kǒu hǎo fēng* below.]

315　**Shū bù jiàn qīn.*** 疏不间亲。(lit) Distant [relations should] not interfere [between] close relatives. (fig) Outsiders should not sow discord among close relatives or friends. [Cf. *Hán Shī Wàizhuàn*, chap. 3; *Xǐngshì Héngyán*, chap. 2; note: *jiàn* is a verb, "to create a gap"; see *líjiàn*, "to sow discord"; note: *shūbùjiànqīn* is used as a set phrase meaning "blood is thicker than water"; see also *qīn bù jiàn shū* and *qīn zhě gē zhī* above and *xuè bǐ shuǐ nóng* below.]

316 **Shù bù xiū, bù chéngcái; ér bù yù, bù chéngrén.** 树不修不成材，儿不育不成人。[Just as] trees not trimmed won't become good timber, [so] children not educated won't grow up [properly]. [Pun/note: *mùcái*, "wooden material" and *réncái*, "talented people"; *chéngcái*, (1) "grow into useful timber"; (2) "become a useful person"; *bùchéngcái* is also an idiomatic expression meaning "good-for-nothing"; see also *kōngxīn dà shù* above and the following entry.]

317 **Shù bù xiū, guǒ bù shōu.** 树不修，果不收。(lit) [If] trees are not pruned, fruit cannot be harvested. (fig) Young people won't become useful adults without discipline and education. [Rhyme; see also the preceding entry.]

318 **Shù dà, fēn chà; rén dà, fēnjiā.** 树大分叉，人大分家。[Just as a] tree will produce branches [when it] grows taller, [so a traditional extended] family will divide up the family property and live apart [when the children] grow up. [Rhyme; see also *fēn jiā sān nián* above.]

319 **Shù dǎo, húsūn sàn.*** 树倒猢狲散。(lit) [When the] tree falls, the monkeys scatter. (fig) When one's family or patron falls from power, those who have been supported or protected will disperse. [Cf. *DRC*, chap. 13; *Chū Kè Pāi'àn Jīngqí*, chap. 22; note: *shù-dǎo-húsūn-sàn* is a colloquial expression meaning "when the mighty fall, their hangers-on disperse."]

320 **Shū dào yòng shí fāng hèn shǎo; (shì fēi jīngguò bù zhī nán).*** 书到用时方恨少，(事非经过不知难)。[One will] not regret having done too little reading until [one is required to] apply [what one has studied, and one will] not know the difficulty of the work until one begins to do it [oneself]. [The first half is most commonly used alone.]

321 **Shù dà, yǒu kūzhī.** 树大有枯枝。(lit) [When] a tree [gets] big, [it always] has [some] withered twigs. (fig) There will always be a few bad people in any large group of people.

322 **Shù dà zhāofēng; (guān dà zhāo huò).** 树大招风，(官大招祸)。(Lit) [Just as a] tall tree invites the wind, ([so a] high official invites disasters). (fig) A person in a high social position is likely to be attacked. [Cf. *JW*, chap. 33; the first part is usually used alone, often as a *chengyu*, with the meaning of the second part understood, as in a *xiehouyu*; see also the following entry.]

323 **Shù dà, zhāofēng; (míng dà, zhāo jì).*** 树大招风，(名大招忌)。(lit) Great trees invite the wind, ([and] great fame invites envy). (fig) Detraction pursues the great. [Cf. *JW*, chap. 35; the second part is usually omitted; see also the preceding entry.]

324 **Shú dú Tángshī Sānbǎi Shǒu, bù huì yínshī, yě huì yín.*** 熟读唐诗三百首，不会吟诗，也会吟。[If one has] thoroughly read the *Three Hundred Poems of the Tang*, [even if one really does] not know how to compose/recite poetry, [one will] still [be able to] compose/recite. [From the preface to the most popular edition of the *Three Hundred Poems of the Tang*, by the Qing dynasty editor who called himself *Héng Táng Jù Shì* (Heng Tang, the Lay Buddhist); note: *yínshī* means to recite or compose poetry; see also *āizhe tiějiang* above.]

325 **Shú dú Wáng Shūhé bùrú lín zhèng duō.** 熟读王叔和不如临症多。(lit) Thoroughly reading [medical books by] Wang Shuhe, [a famous doctor of the Jin dynasty,] is not as good as [having] treated a lot [of cases; i.e., clinical experience]. (fig) Actual experience is better than abstract knowledge. [Cf. *Rúlín Wàishǐ*, chap. 31; note: *línchuáng; lín zhèng* "clinical experience."]

326 **Shù gāo qiān zhàng, yè luò guī gēn.*** 树高千丈，叶落归根。(lit) A tree [may grow a] thousand feet tall, [but when its] leaves fall, [they] return to [its] roots. (fig) People residing far from home will eventually return to their native soil. [Cf. *Xǐngshì Yīnyuán Zhuàn*, chap. 96; *Érnǚ Yīngxióng Zhuàn*, chap. 19; as a *chengyu*: *yèluò-guīgēn*; note: one *zhàng* equals 3.33 meters; see also *shuǐ liú qiān zāo* and *tùzi mǎn shān* below.]

327 **Shù gāo qiān zhàng zǒng yǒu gēn; héliú wàn lǐ zǒng yǒu yuán.** 树高千丈总有根，河流万里总有源。(lit) A tree a thousand feet tall always has roots; a river ten thousand leagues long always has a source. (fig) One can trace everything to its origins, causes or reasons. [Note: one *lǐ* equals one-half kilometer.]

328 **Shuǐ bù jī bù yuè; rén bù jī bù fèn.** 水不激不跃，人不激不奋。[Just as] water not dammed won't rise, [so] people not stimulated won't exert [themselves]. [Cf. *Gǔ-Jīn Xiǎoshuō*, chap. 5.]

329 **Shuǐ dà, màn bu guò yāzi qù.** 水大，漫不过鸭子去。(lit) However high the river rises, it cannot rise over the ducks. (fig) However hard one tries, one can never surpass everyone; you'll never catch up with everyone.

330 **Shuǐdī jī duō, chéng mǎn pén; yànyǔ jī duō, chéng xuéwen.** 水滴积多盛满盆，谚语积多成学问。[Just as] water drops accumulated fill up a basin, [so] many proverbs become knowledge.

331 **Shuǐ dī, shí chuān.** 水滴石穿。See *shéng jù, mù duàn* above. [As a *chengyu*: *shuǐdī-shíchuān*.]

332 **Shuǐ gāo, chuán qù jí; shā xiàn, mǎ xíng chí.** 水高船去急，沙陷马行迟。(lit) [When the] river rises, boats sail fast [and when] the sand sinks, horses run slowly. (fig) One can only do what the situation allows. [Cf. *JW*, chap. 55.]

333 **Shuǐhuǒ bù liúqíng.*** 水火不留情。(lit) Floods [and] fire show no mercy. (fig) Everyone is equally liable to fires and floods. [Note: *shuǐhuǒ*, (lit) "water and fire," also "flood and conflagration," is a metaphor for "extreme misery"; *liúqíng*, "to show mercy or forgiveness."]

334 **Shuǐhuǒ bùtóng lú.** 水火不同炉。(lit) Fire [and] water can't [coexist in the] same stove. (fig) (Some people are) incompatible as fire and water. [Note: *shuǐhuǒ*, (lit) "water and fire," is here a metaphor for "opposites"; see also the following entry.]

S

335 **Shuǐhuǒ bù xiāngróng.*** 水火不相容。(lit) Fire and water are incompatible. (fig) (Some people are) as incompatible as fire and water. [See also the preceding entry.]

336 **Shuǐ jìng zé bù shēn.** 水径则不深。(lit) Straight-running water doesn't [run] deep. (fig) One who tries to show off his or her abilities or talents is shallow. [Cf. *Hán Shī Wàizhuàn*, chap. 1; see also *gǔ kōng*, *shēng gāo* and *hǎo mǎo bù jiào* and *kōng guànzi* above and *zhěng píng bù yáo* below.]

337 **Shuǐ jí yú; yú jí shuǐ. / Shuǐ bàng yú; yú bàng shuǐ.** 水籍鱼，鱼籍水。/ 水傍鱼，鱼傍水。(lit) Water is interdependent with fish [and] fish with water. (fig) People and or things are all interdependent. [Note also the communist slogan: *jūn mín yú shuǐ qíng*, "the [People's Liberation] army [and] the people [are as] close [as] fish [and] water."]

338 **Shuǐ kuān, yú dà.** 水宽鱼大。(lit) Wide rivers contain big fish. (fig) Talented people come from or stay in places where there are excellent conditions and scope for their talents. [See also *shuǐ qīng, yǎngbude yú* below.]

339 **Shuǐ lái hé zhǎng; fēng lái shù dòng.** 水来河涨，风来树动。(lit) [When the] water approaches, the river rises [and when the] wind blows, the trees stir. (fig) There must be a cause behind every result. [See also *mù yǒu běn* above and *wú fēng bù qǐ* and *yǒu fēng fāng qǐ* below.]

340 **Shuǐ lái, tǔ yǎn; bīng dào, jiàng yíng.** 水来土掩，兵到将迎。(lit) [When the] water rises, [we use] earth to resist [it]; [when] soldiers come [we use] generals to deal with [them]. (fig) Different situations require different measures. [Cf. *WM*, chap. 20; *R3K*, chap. 73.]

341 **Shuǐ liú qiān zāo, rào huí dàhǎi.** 水流千遭，绕回大海。(lit) However long a distance the water flows, it [eventually] returns to the sea. (fig) However far away people travel, they will eventually come back (home) where they started from. [See also *shù gāo qiān zhàng* above and *tùzi mǎn shān* below.]

342 **Shuǐ liú shī; huǒ jiù zào.** 水流湿，火就燥。(lit) Water flows toward to wet [lower places, and] fire [burns] toward dry [places]. (fig) "Like seeks like." [Cf. *Lǎo Cán Yóujì*, chap. 11.]

343 **Shuǐ luò shítou xiàn; shìhòu jiàn rén xīn.** 水落石头现，事后见人心。[Only after the] water [has] receded [do the] stones appear; [only] after things [happen can one] see people['s] true natures. [Note the *chengyu*: *shuǐluò-shíchū*, (lit) "When the water recedes, the stones appear," (fig) "Truth will out"; see also *bèitóu lǐ zuòshì* and *chái duī lǐ cáng* above and *zhǐ bǎo bu zhù huǒ* below.]

344 **Shuǐ néng chuān shí; rén néng bān shān.** 水能穿石，人能搬山。[Just as dripping] water [can] wear through rock; [so] people can remove mountains. [Note the *chengyu*: *shuǐdī-shíchuān*, (lit) "Dripping water wears through stones." (fig) "Constant effort brings success."]

345 **Shuǐ píng bù liú; rén píng bù yán.** 水平不流，人平不言。(lit) Water won't flow [if the surface is] level [and] people won't complain [if they are treated] "on the level" [i.e., fairly]. [Cf. *Xǐngshì Héngyán*, chap. 17; the two halves also occur in the reverse order: see also *yǐ wǎn shuǐ* below.]

346 **Shuǐ píng bù liú; rén píng bù yǔ.** 水平不流，人平不语。[Just as] water [held] level doesn't flow, [so] people [treated on the] level [i.e., fairly; equally] don't talk [i.e., complain]. [Cf. *Xǐngshì Héngyán*, chap. 17.]

347 **Shuǐ qiǎn bùróng dà zhōu.** 水浅不容大舟。(lit) Shallow waters [can]not hold big boats. (fig) (1) Limited by conditions, one cannot accomplish anything great. (2) Talented people cannot work under a leader of little ability.

348 **Shuǐ qiǎn, yǎng bu zhù dà yú.** 水浅养不住大鱼。(lit) [When the] water is too shallow, big fish cannot be kept. (fig) Small places cannot attract or keep people of talent. [See also *shuǐ kuān, yú dà* above and *xiǎo shuǐ bùróng* below.]

349 **Shuǐ qīng, shí zì jiàn.** 水清，石自见。(lit) [When the] water becomes clear, the stones will be seen. (fig) The truth will come out by itself when things clear up. [Note the *chengyu*: *shuǐluò-shíchū*, "Truth will out."]

350 **Shuǐ qīng, wú dà yú.** 水清无大鱼。(lit) [If the] water is [too] clear and clean, there are no big fish. (fig) If you are too particular about trifling matters, people of talent will not stay around you or work under you. [See also *shuǐ zhì qīng zé* below and the following entry.]

351 **Shuǐ qīng, yǎngbude yú.** 水清养不得鱼。(lit) [If the] water is [too] clear, fish cannot be raised. (fig) If one is to clear or frank about things, people won't be happy. [Often used in the sense of "leave sleeping dogs lie"; see also *shuǐ zhì qīng* above and the preceding entry.]

352 **Shuǐ shēn bù xiǎng; xiǎng shuǐ bù shēn.** 水深不响，响水不深。(lit) Deep water doesn't [make a] sound, [and] water [that makes a] sound isn't deep. (fig) Learned people are modest, while shallow people brag. [See also *gǔ kōng*, *shēng gāo* and *kōng guànzi* and *shuǐ jìng zé* above and *zhěng píng bù yáo* below.]

353 **Shuǐ shēn jiàn cháng rén.** 水深见长人。(lit) [If the] water is deep [one can] see [who's a] tall person. (fig) Difficult problems reveal people's true abilities. [Also said *rù shuǐ jiàn cháng rén*; see also *lièhuǒ jiàn zhēnjīn* above.]

354 **Shuì shí shǎo yǐnshuǐ; shuì qián bù yǐnchá.** 睡时少饮水，睡前不饮茶。When sleeping, drink less water [and] don't drink tea before going to bed [and you'll sleep through the night].

355 **Shuǐ tài qīng zé wú yú; rén tài jǐn zé wú zhì.** 水太清则无鱼，人太紧则无智。Too-clear water [can]not hold fish [and] overly harsh or demanding people have no wisdom. [See also *shuǐ zhì qīng* below.]

356 **Shuǐ zhì qīng zé wú yú; rén zhì chá zé wú tú.** 水 至清则无鱼, 人至察则无徒。 (lit) [If] water is too clear, there will be no fish [in it, and if] a person is too discerning [in his or her observations], (s)he'll have no followers. (fig) People who insist on being too precise about things will not have any followers or friends. [See also *shuǐ qīng, wú dà yú* and *shuǐ qīng, yǎngbude yú* and *shuǐ tài qīng* above.]

357 **Shūjí hǎobǐ héliú, shǐ rén sìtōng-bādá.** 书籍好 比河流, 使人四通八达。 Books are like flowing rivers, [which can] carry one in all directions. [Note: *chengyu: sìtōng-bādá*, "extending in all directions."]

358 **Shù jīngjí, dé cì; shù táolǐ, dé yīn.** 树荆棘得 刺, 树桃李得荫。 (lit) [If you] plant brambles, [you'll] get thorns; [if you] plant peach [and] plum [trees], [you'll] get shade. (fig) Good-heartedness often meets with like recompense, while evil will be recompensed with evil. "As ye sow, so shall ye reap." [Cf. *Jīngshì Tōngyán*, chap. 18; see also *shàn yǒu shànbào* above.]

359 **Shù lǎo, bàn xīn kōng; rén lǎo, shìshì tōng.** 树老 半心空, 人老事事通。 [When] trees [get] old, [they have] half-empty trunks, [but when] people [get] old, [they are full of] knowledge [about how to] get things done. [Rhyme; see also the following entry.]

360 **Shù lǎo, gēn duō; rén lǎo, huà duō.** 树老根多, 人老话多。 [Just as when] trees get older, [they] have more roots, [so when] people get older, [they] talk more. [Rhyme.]

361 **Shù lǎo, gēn duō; rén lǎo, jiànshi duō.** 树老根 多, 人老见识多。 Old trees have more roots [and] old people [have had] more experience.

362 **Shù lǎo, shēng chóng; rén lǎo, wúyòng.** 树老生 虫, 人老无用。 [Just as when] trees get old [they become] full of worms, [so when] people get old [they are] useless. [Rhyme; see also *rén lǎo, zhū huáng* above.]

363 **Shù lǎo, xīn kōng; rén lǎo, diān dōng.** 树老心 空, 人老颠东。 [Just as when] trees get old they become hollow at the core, [so when] people get old, they become muddle-headed. [Rhyme; note: *diān sān dǎo sì*, "incoherent; confused."]

364 **Shù lǎo, zhāofēng; rén lǎo, zhāo jiàn.** 树老招 风, 人老招贱。 (lit) [Just as when] trees get old, [they] invite [attack by the] wind, [so when] people get old [they] invite contempt [from others]. [Cf. *Jīngshì Tōngyán*, chap. 6; see also *mǎ lǎo, wú rén qí* above.]

365 **Shúlù fānchē.** 熟路翻车。 (lit) Familiar roads overturn vehicles. (fig) Mistakes can easily occur when one is not cautious due to overfamiliarity. [See also *shùnshuǐ zhōu* below.]

366 **Shū náng wú dǐ.** 书囊无底。 (lit) Book bags have no bottoms. (fig) One cannot read every book on earth.

367 **Shùn dài bù wéi tōu.** 顺带不为偷。 [Accidentally] walking off with [something] is not [to be] regarded as stealing. [Cf. *Wǔ Sōng*, chap. 8.]

368 **Shùn dé gū lái, shī sǎo yì.** 顺得姑来, 失嫂 意。 (lit) [If you] please older brother's sister, [you'll] offend older brother's wife. (fig) If you please one person, you'll offend another. It's difficult to please everyone.

369 **Shùnqíng shuō hǎohuà, miǎnde tǎorénxián.** 顺 情说好话, 免得讨人嫌。 [It is better to] speak fairly and reasonably [in accordance with others' feelings], [so as to] avoid being [considered] disagreeable.

370 **Shùnshuǐ zhōu, duō kuánglán.** 顺水舟, 多狂 澜。 (lit) A ship that sails with the wind meets more big waves. (fig) People under favorable conditions may get themselves in danger (out of negligence). [See also *shúlù fānchē* above.]

371 **Shùn tiān zhě chāng; nì tiān zhě wáng.** 顺天者 昌, 逆天者亡。 Those who obey [the will of] heaven [will] prosper, [while] those who oppose heaven [will] perish. [A rhyme; cf. *Qíng Shǐ Yǎnyì*, chap. 46; also said *shùn tiān zhě cún; nì tiān zhě wáng*, "those who obey the will of heaven will survive, etc."; see also the following entry.]

372 **Shù nuó, sǐ; rén nuó, huó.** 树挪死, 人挪活。 [When] trees move, [they] die, [but when] people move, [it will enable them to] survive. [Note: *nuówō*, "to move to another place"; see also *nǎ chù huángtǔ* above.]

373 **Shùn zhī zhě chāng; nì zhī zhě wáng.** * 顺之者 者昌, 逆之者亡。 Those who obey it [will] prosper, [while] those who oppose it [will] perish. [Said, e.g., of the rule of a tyrant; also said *shùn wǒ zhě cháng; nì wǒ zhě wáng* and *shùn zhī zhě cún; nì zhī zhě wáng*, "those who obey will survive, etc."; see also the preceding entry.]

374 **Shuōdào Cáo Cāo, Cáo Cāo jiù dào.** 说到曹操, 曹操就到。 (lit) Speak of Cáo Cāo, [and] Cáo Cāo arrives. (fig) "Speak of the devil (and he shall appear)." [Cf. *Niè Hǎi Huā*, chap. 29; and Mao Dun's novel, *Zǐyè* (Midnight); see also *qiǎo zhōng shuōhuà* and *rì lǐ mò shuō rén* above and *shuōzhe hóngliǎn de* below.]

375 **Shuō dào nǎli, zuòdào nǎli.** 说到哪里, 做到 哪里。 Whatever [one] says, [one should] do it. [See also *shuō yī shì yī* below.]

376 **Shuō de hǎo bùrú zuò de hǎo.** 说得好不如做 得好。 (lit) Good talk is not as good as good work. (fig) "Actions speak louder than words."

377 **Shuō de hǎotīng, zhǐ tīng bāfēn.** 说的好听, 只 听八分。 (lit) [When someone] speaks pleasing [words], only listen to eighty percent. (fig) Believe only eighty percent of pleasing words. [See also *tián yán duó zhì* below.]

378 **Shuōhuà bùmíng, yóurú hūn jìng.** 说话不明, 犹如昏镜。 (lit) [When one] speaks unclearly, [it is] just like a murky mirror. (fig) Ambiguous speech is like a cloudy mirror. [Rhyme; cf. *Érnǚ Yīngxióng Zhuàn*, chap. 23.]

379 **Shuōhuà méi jiǎo, zǒu qiān lǐ.** 说话没脚, 走 千里。 (lit) Spoken words have no feet, [but they] travel a thousand leagues. (fig) Be prudent in speech.

S

380 **Shuōhuǎng bù mán dàng xiāngrén.** 说谎不瞒当乡人。(lit) [When] telling lies, [one can]not deceive the local people. (fig) One can't deceive the local people with lies. [Cf. *JW*, chap. 76; see also *mán tiān, mán dì* above.]

381 **Shuōhuà shí duǎn; jì huà shí cháng.** 说话时短，记话时长。(lit) To speak [takes only a] short time, [but] words are remembered a long time. (fig) Be prudent in speech.

382 **Shuō lái róngyì; zuò shí nán.*** 说来容易，做时难。(lit) Talking is easy, [but] when [it comes to] action [it's more] difficult. (fig) Things are "easier said than done."

383 **Shuōshuō-xiàoxiào, tōngtong qīqiào.** 说说笑笑，通通七窍。(lit) Talking [and] laughing clear out the head. (fig) Talking and laughing are good to health. [Note: *qīqiào*, "the seven apertures of the human head."]

384 **Shuō xiāhuà, zuǐ zhǎng dīng.** 说瞎话，嘴长疔。(If one) speaks nonsense, [one's] mouth [will] grow boils.

385 **Shuō xiào chǎng shàng, wú dàxiǎo.** 说笑场上，无大小。(lit) [In] scenes of talking [and] laughing (i.e., informal situations), there [should be] no distinction between seniors [and] juniors [i.e., elders and youngers, etc.].

386 **Shuō yī shì yī; shuō èr shì èr.** 说一是一，说二是二。Say "one," it's one; say "two," it's two. (fig) One should keep (to) one's word. [Cf. *DRC*, chap. 65; also said *shuō yī, bù èr*; see also *shuō dào nǎli* above.]

387 **Shuōzhe hóngliǎn de, biàn láile Guāngōng.** 说着红脸的，便来了关公。(lit) [When one is] speaking of the red-faced, there comes Guan Gong. (fig) "Speak of the devil (and he will appear)." [Note: Guan Gong or Guan Yu, a famous general of the Kingdom of Shu in the period of the Three Kingdoms, is always portrayed with a red face; see also *shuōdào Cáo Cāo* above.]

388 **Shuōzhě wúyì; tīngzhě/wén zhě yǒuyì/yǒuxīn.** 说者无意，听者／闻者有意／有心。(lit) [Sometimes it happens that a] speaker had no [(particular)] intent, [but the] hearer had [something on his or her] mind [which caused the hearer to interpret what the speaker said in a certain way or to take offense]. [See also *wúxīn rén shuōhuà* above and *yán zhě wúxīn* below.]

389 **Shuōzuǐ lángzhōng wú hǎo yào.** 说嘴郎中无好药。(lit) A glib-tongued quack has no good medicine. (fig) One who boasts of his or her own talents probably is not very good in reality. [Cf. *Hé Diǎn*, chap. 3; also said *màizuǐ . . . etc. (q.v.)*]

390 **Shū qián zhǐ wèi yíng qián qǐ.** 输钱只为赢钱起。(lit) [One] loses money just because [one] began by winning money. (fig) Winning is just a prelude to losing.

391 **Shùqǐ jǐliang zuòshì; fàngkāi yǎnguāng dúshū.** 竖起脊梁做事，放开眼光读书。[One should always hold one's] backbone upright in doing things [and] read with [one's] eyes open wide [i.e., with an open mind.]

392 **Shùqǐ zhāo jūn qí, jiù yǒu chīliáng rén.** 竖起招军旗，就有吃粮人。(lit) [Once the army] enlistment flag is hoisted, there will be enlistees [who will come to join in the army]. (fig) Once an opportunity is made known, (surely) there will be people interested. [Note: *chīliáng*, "be a soldier; serve in the army"; *liángcǎo*, "army provisions."]

393 **Shū sān xiě, yú chéng lǔ, dì chéng hǔ.** 书三写，鱼成鲁，帝成虎。(lit) [If an article is] copied three times, [the character] *yú* ["fish"] will become *lǔ* ["fool-hardy"], [and the character] *dì* ["emperor"] become *hǔ* ["tiger"]. (fig) Mistakes are bound to appear as (ancient) writings are copied and recopied over the ages. [See also *zì (jīng) sān xiě* below.]

394 **Shùshēn shēng de zhèng, bùpà fēng lái yáo.** 树身生的正，不怕风来摇。(lit) A tree grown straight is not afraid of the wind. (fig) An upright and honest person is not to be corrupted by unhealthy tendencies.

395 **Shùshēn zhǎng de zhèng, bùpà yǐngzi xié.** 树身长得正，不怕影子斜。(lit) A tree grown straight is not afraid of a slanting shadow. (fig) An upright and honest person is not afraid of slanderous attacks. [See also *gān shǐ mǒ bù dào* and *gēn shēn bùpà* and *hǎorén shuō bù huài* and *jiǎo zhèng bùpà* and *shēn zhèng, bùpà* above and *xīn zhèng bùpà* below.]

396 **Shū wú bǎi rì gōng.** 书无百日功。[One's] calligraphy cannot be perfected in [only] a hundred days. [Originally from a quotation from a work on calligraphy: *Shūfǎ Yào Lù*, chap. 3; note: *shūfǎ*, "calligraphy"; also said *zì wú bǎi rì gōng*.]

397 **Shǔ wú géyè liáng.** 鼠无隔夜粮。(lit) Rats never keep [their] grain overnight. (fig) Some people seem to be congenitally shortsighted. [See also *láng wú géyè ròu* above.]

398 **Shù xiǎo, fú zhí yì; shù dà, bān zhí nán.** 树小扶直易，树大扳直难。[When a] tree is young, [it is] easier to prop [it] up straight, [but when a] tree is older, straightening [it] is harder. (fig) It's easy to help correct children's shortcomings or bad habits, but (more) difficult to do so with adults. [See also *xiǎo jū kě xùn* below.]

399 **Shù xiǎo, yīnliángr shǎo; zhàoyìng bù dào.** 树小荫凉儿少，照应不到。(lit) [When a] tree is small, [its] shadow is small, [and it can]not produce [a lot of shade]. (fig/pun) A person in a small position cannot take care of too many others. [Usually used self-deprecatingly.]

400 **Shū yào jīngdú; tián yào xì guǎn.** 书要精读，田要细管。Books must [be] read intensively, [just as] fields must [be] cultivated intensively.

401 **Shù yù jìng ér fēng bùzhǐ; (zǐ yù yǎng ér qīn bùdài).*** 树欲静而风不止，(子欲养而亲不待)。(lit) The trees [may] wish [to remain] quiet, but the wind [will] not subside; (the son [may] wish to serve [his parents in their old age,] but they are no more). (fig/originally) Events are not subject to human will. "The wind will not subside." [Originally from the Han dynasty work by Han Yin, *Hán Shī Wàizhuàn*, chap. 9. The first half

was quoted by Mao Zedong in the 1960s to refer to the inevitability of class struggle, meaning that although the proletariat might wish for calm, the bourgeoisie would inevitably try to stage a counter-revolutionary comeback.]

402 **Shù zhí, sǐ; rén zhí, qióng.** 树直死，人直穷。 [Just as a] straight tree [is always the first to] die [i.e., to be cut down, so a] "straight" [i.e., straightforward person is always] poor. [See also the following entry.]

403 **Shù zhí, yòngchù duō; rén zhí, péngyou duō.** 树直，用处多；人直，朋友多。 [Just as a] straight tree [has] many uses, [so a] "straight" [i.e., honest and upright] person has many friends. [See also *rén zhí, yǒu rén hé* above and the preceding entry.]

404 **Shǔ zhōng wú dàjiàng, Liào Huà zuò xiānfēng.** 蜀中无大将，廖化作先锋。 (lit) [Since] in [the Kingdom of] Shu there were no great generals [remaining], Liao Hua, [an assistant to the generals, had to] take the lead. (fig) In the absence of competent leadership, one has to be content with whomever one has available. [Sometimes said modestly of oneself; this refers to an incident in *R3K*; note the colloquial expressions *ǎizi lǐ tiáo chángzi* and *ǎizi lǐ xuǎn jiàngjūn*, (lit) "to choose a tall one/leader from among the dwarves"; meaning "to make do with the best of an inferior lot"; see also *shān zhōng wú lǎohǔ* below.]

405 **Shū zhōng zìyǒu huángjīn wū; shū zhōng zìyǒu yán rú yù.** 书中自有黄金屋，书中自有颜如玉。 (lit) In books there are golden houses and [beauties with] faces like jade. (fig) If you study hard, you'll have fine houses and a beautiful wife someday because you'll become an official and get rich. [A rhyme; originally from the Song dynasty author Zhen Zhong's *Quàn Xuéwen*; traditional advice given before 1949 to encourage young people to study; note: *yánmiàn*, (lit) "face, countenance"; see also *xué ér yōu zé shì* below and the following entry.]

406 **Shū zhōng zìyǒu qiān zhōng sù.** 书中自有千钟粟。 (lit) There are a thousand *zhōng* of grain in books. (fig) If you study hard, you'll become wealthy some day by becoming an official. [Note: a *zhōng* is an ancient measure of grain; originally from the Song dynasty author Zhen Zhong's *Quàn Xuéwen*, followed by the two lines in the preceding entry; traditional advice given before 1949 to encourage young people to study; see also *shí nián chuāng xià* above and the preceding entry.]

407 **Sì bù niù liù.** 四不拗六。 (lit) Four [people can]not overcome six [people]. (fig) A minority cannot defy the will of the majority. [Cf. *Èr Kè Pāi'àn Jīngqí*, chap. 1; see also *sān bù niù liù* and *shuāng quán nán dí* above.]

408 **Sī chǎng yǎn; guānchǎng yòng.** 私场演，官场用。 Practice in private, [and] perform in public.

409 **Sǐ diàn, huórén kāi.** 死店活人开。 (lit) A dead shop [is still] run [by] living people. (fig) Inanimate objects simply exist, but human beings have to be flexible in dealing with life's affairs in order

to be successful; be flexible. [Note: *sǐhuò*, "dead goods," which no one wants to buy.]

410 **Sǐ gǒu fú bù shàng qiáng.** 死狗扶不上墙。 (lit) A dead dog can't be propped up [on top of] a wall. (fig) One cannot help a good-for-nothing person to rise above his station. [Cf. *DRC*, chap. 68; see also the colloquial expression: *fú bù qǐ de Ā Dǒu*, "a worthless person beyond help," referring to Liu Bei in *R3K*, who was supported by Zhuge Liang to no avail.]

411 **Sìhǎi zhīnèi jiē xiōngdì yě.*** 四海之内皆兄弟也。 (lit) Within the four seas all [men] brothers are. (fig) All human beings in the world are as family. [Originally from the Confucian Analects: *Lúnyǔ: Yán Yuān*; also cf. *Xǐngshì Héngyán*, chap. 10.]

412 **Sǐle lóngpáo yě shì sǐ; dǎsǐ tàizǐ yě shì sǐ.** 撕了龙袍也是死，打死太子也是死。 (lit) To tear an emperor's clothes is to die; to beat a prince is also to die. (fig) When one is in desperate straits, one cares little for the consequences. "Hung for sheep, hung for a lamb." [See also *pīnzhe yīshēn guǎ* above.]

413 **Sǐle Zhāng túfū, bù chī hún máozhū.*** 死了张屠夫，不吃浑毛猪。 (lit) [Even if] Zhang the butcher dies, [we] won't eat pork with hairs [on it]. (fig) No one person is indispensable; the work will continue regardless of [one person's] participation. [Note: this is Mao's own negation of *méile Wáng tú, lián máo chī zhū* (q.v.); cf. *JPM*, chap. 73; see also *sǐ zhū bù pà* and *yǒu jī, tiān yě liàng* below.]

414 **Sì liǎng bō qiānjīn.** 四两拨千斤。 (lit) Four ounces can move a thousand catties. (fig) If one is clever, one can accomplish great things with few resources. [Cf. *Dàng Kòu Zhì*, chap. 88; note: literally, one *jīn* or "catty" is equal to one-half kilogram, but *qiānjīn* is figuratively taken to mean "a ton; a great weight."]

415 **Sǐ māo xiào dǎo huó lǎoshǔ.** 死猫笑倒活老鼠。 (lit) A dead cat [can] frighten a live rat [to death]. (fig) An able person can frighten a rival just by taking a stance.

416 **Sī píng wénshū; guān píng yìn.** 私凭文书，官凭印。 Private business relies on contracts, [while] official [business] relies on [official] seals.

417 **Sǐrén chòu yī lǐ; huórén chòu qiān lǐ.** 死人臭一里，活人臭千里。 [The smell of] a dead person stinks for [only] one mile, [but the bad reputation of] a living person will stink far and wide. [Note: one lǐ equals one-half kilometer.]

418 **Sǐrén shēnbiān zìyǒu huó guǐ.** 死人身边自有活鬼。 (lit) Beside the bodies of the dead there are living ghosts. (fig) If someone is murdered, there will be people who will appeal for redress. [Cf. *Shí Diǎn Tóu*, chap. 4.]

419 **Sǐrén tóu shàng wú duìzhèng.** 死人头上无对证。 One cannot make a dead person bear witness. "Dead men tell no tales." [As a *chengyu*: *sǐ wú duìzhèng*; cf. *Chū Kè Pāi'àn Jīngqí*, chap. 14; see also *shārén mièkǒu* above.]

S

420 **Sǐ zé tóng sǐ, shēng zé tóng shēng.** 死则同死，生则同生。[If this is your time to] die, [I will] die with you; [if it is your time to] live, [then I will] live with you. [Said by close friends, sworn brothers, lovers, etc.]

421 **Sǐ zhīfǔ bùrú yī gè huó lǎoshǔ.** 死知府不如一个活老鼠。(lit) A dead district magistrate is not as good as a live rat. (fig) Officials out of power are completely worthless. [Cf. *Rúlín Wàishǐ*, chap. 18; note: from the Tang to the Qing dynasties a *fǔ* ("prefecture") was below the *shěng* ("province") level and above the *xiàn* ("county") level; see also *bále máo de* above.]

422 **Sǐ zhū bù pà kāishuǐ tàng.** 死猪不怕开水烫。(lit) A dead pig is not afraid of being scalded in water [used to soften skin before shaving the hair off]. (fig) When one is in a desperate situation, one will try anything. Desperate people will try anything, as they have nothing to lose.

423 **Sǐ Zhūgé xiàsǐ shēng Zhòng Dá.** 死诸葛吓死生仲达。(lit) The dead Zhuge [Liang] scared off the living Zhong Da [Sima Yi]. (fig) A clever person can outsmart a superior force by trickery. [In the Three Kingdoms period, the master strategist Zhuge Liang, before he died, left instructions that an image of himself be placed in a cart to dismay his enemy Sima Yi, the King of Wei, which ruse in fact succeeded; cf. *Sān Guó Zhì: Zhūge Liàng Zhuàn*; see also Lu Xun's *Qiě Jiè Tíng Záwén: (Mò Biān).*]

424 **Sòng fó, sòng dào Xī(tiān).** 送佛送到西(天)。(lit) [When] seeing off a Buddha, escort him to the West(ern Paradise). (fig) If you're going to help someone, help until help is no longer needed. [Cf. *Érnǔ Yīngxióng Zhuàn*, chap. 9; see also *bāng rén, bāng dàodǐ* above.]

425 **Sòng jūn qiān lǐ, zhōng xū yī bié.*** 送君千里终须一别。(lit) [Although you] escort [your] guest a thousand leagues, [in the] end [there] must [be] a parting. (fig) The time has come for us to part. [Said by the one who is leaving.] [Cf. *Érnǔ Yīngxióng Zhuàn*, chap. 10; see also *liú jūn qiān rì* and *qiān lǐ dǎ cháng péng* and *shèngyàn bì sàn* above and *tiānxià wú bù sàn* below.]

426 **Sòng qīn de lù duǎn; huánxiāng de lù cháng.** 送亲的路短，还乡的路长。[When] seeing close friends and relatives off, [one always feels the] way [is too] short; [when] going back to [one's] home, [one always feels the] way [is too] long. [See also *xīnjí, mǎ xíng chí* below.]

427 **Sòng rén, sòng dàojiā;*** (**wéi rén xū wéi chè**). 送人送到家，(为人须为彻)。(lit) [When you] escort someone, escort [him all the way] home; ([if you] help someone, help [him] thoroughly). (fig) If you help someone, help him or her until help is no longer needed. [The second part is usually omitted; see also *bāng rén, bāng dàodǐ* and *jiù rén, jiù dàodǐ* and *shārén xū jiàn xuè* and *sòng fó, sòng dào Xī* above.]

428 **Sū-Háng bù dào, wǎng wéirén.** 苏杭不到枉为人。[If one has] never been to Su[zhou and] Hang[zhou], one['s life has] not been worthwhile. [Both spots are famous for their scenic beauty; also said *bù dào Sū-Háng, sǐ de yuānwang*; note:

yuānwang, "wasted; unproductive"; see also *shàng yǒu tiāntáng* above.]

429 **Sū-Hú shú, tiānxià zú.** 苏湖熟，天下足。[When the] harvest is good in Suzhou and Huzhou, [people will be] well fed throughout the country. [In ancient China the areas around Suzhou in Jiangsu province and Huzhou in Zhejiang province were the main producers of rice; see also *Hú-Guǎng shú* and *liǎng Guǎng shú* above.]

430 **Suíbǐ dēng zhàng, miǎn hòu sīliang.** 随笔登帐，免后思量。Keep accounts [as] you go along [and you will] avoid [having to] recall [them] later. [Rhyme; note: *sīliang*, "turn over in one's mind"; see also *hǎo jìxing bùrú làn bǐtóu* above.]

431 **Suì má cuō chéng shéng, néng dān qiānjīn zhòng.** 碎麻搓成绳，能担千斤重。(lit) [When] pieces of flax [are] twisted into rope, [they] can bear [the weight of a] thousand catties. (fig) In unity there is strength. [Note: literally, one *jīn* or "catty" is equal to one-half kilogram, but *qiānjīn* is figuratively taken to mean "a ton; a great weight."]

432 **Suī yǒu qīn fù, ān zhī bù wéi hǔ; suī yǒu qīn xiōng, ān zhī bù wéi láng?** 虽有亲父，安知不为虎；虽有亲兄，安知不为狼？(lit) Though [he] is [your] father, how [do you] know [he is] not as [fierce as a] tiger; though [he] is [your] brother, how [do you] know [he is] not as [vicious as a] wolf? (fig) One cannot truly know anyone, even one's closest relatives. [See also *hǎi kū zhōng jiàn* and *huà lóng, huà hǔ* above and *zhī rén, zhī miàn* below.]

433 **Suī yǒu xiōngsuì, bì yǒu fēngnián.** 虽有凶岁，必有丰年。(lit) Although there are bad years, there must [also] be bumper years. (fig) In every life, there are good and bad times. [See also *rén yǒu qī pín* and *shìshì yǒuchéng* above.]

434 **Suī yǒu zhìhuì, bùrú chéngshì; suī yǒu zījī, bùrú dài shí.** 虽有智慧不如乘势，虽有镃基不如待时。(lit) Although [one] has intelligence, [it is] not as good as seizing the right moment; although one has a hoe, [it is] not as good as [plowing] at the right time. (fig) Timing is the most important element in success. [Cf. Mencius, *Mèngzǐ: Gōng Sūn Chǒu, Shàng*; note: *zījī* means "a hoe."]

435 **Sǔn rén zì sǔn.** 损人自损。(lit) [To] injure others [is to] injure oneself. (fig) "What goes around, comes around." [Note the expression (*yǐ*) *sǔn rén kāishǐ*, (*yǐ*) *hài jǐ gào zhōng*, "(to) begin by injuring others and end up ruining oneself."]

436 **Suǒyuè jìn gù, jìng dòu kě yóu.** 锁钥尽固，径窦可由。(lit) [Although] lock and key [are] securely fastened, [a] small hole [will remain] to pass through. (fig) Despite one's precautions, there are always some loopholes to be exploited, (so be careful!)

437 **Súyǔ bù sú.** 俗语不俗。Common sayings are not "common" [i.e., lower class or vulgar]. [Note: *suyu* "proverbial expressions," "common sayings" or "folk adages," as opposed to *chengyu* "fixed phrase literary idioms" and *geyan* "maxims; aphorisms," were traditionally looked upon by the literati as common and vulgar; note: *yōngsú*, "vulgar; philistine"; *súqì*, "vulgar; in poor taste."]

T

1 **Tài gāng zé zhé.** 太刚则折。 (lit) [Anything that is] too rigid will break. (fig) Anyone who is too upright and outspoken will meet with disaster. [Cf. *Dōng Zhōu Lièguó Zhì*, chap. 39.]

2 **Tàigōng diàoyú, yuàn zhě shànggōu.*** 太公钓鱼，愿者上钩。 See *(Jiāng) Tàigōng diàoyú* above.

3 **Tā jìng wǒ yī chǐ; wǒ jìng tā yī zhàng.*** 他敬我一尺，我敬他一丈。 (lit) [If] someone respects me one foot, I'll respect him ten feet. (fig) Help, favors, or respect should be reciprocal. [Also said *nǐ jìng wǒ yī chǐ*, etc.; note: one *zhàng* equals ten Chinese feet or 3.33 meters.]

4 **Tángláng bǔ chán, huángquè zàihòu.*** 螳螂捕蝉，黄雀在后。 (lit) The mantis stalks the cicada, unaware of the oriole behind. (fig) Don't covet gains ahead without being aware of the dangers behind. People who plot evil deeds may suffer the same fate. [Cf. *Xǐngshì Yīnyuán Zhuàn*, chap. 57; see also *què bǔ tángláng* above.]

5 **Táng tián yīkǒu; xīn tián yīshēng.** 糖甜一口，心甜一生。 Sugar [tastes] sweet [only while it's in one's] mouth, [but a clear] conscience [makes one's life] sweet [for] all [one's] life.

6 **Tān jiàn, mǎi lǎo niú.** 贪贱买老牛。 (lit) [If you try to] get things on the cheap, [you'll just get stuck with] buying an old ox. (fig) If one (always) tries to get things on the cheap, one will end up with something useless. [Note: *tānxīn*, "greedy"; *tān piányi*, "anxious to get things on the cheap," see also *guì de bù guì* above.]

7 **Tán kǒu hǎo fēng; rén zuǐ nán wǔ.** 坛口好封，人嘴难捂。 (lit) The mouths of jars are easy to seal, [but] people's mouths are difficult to seal. (fig) People like to gossip. [See also *shuān zhù lú zuǐ* above.]

8 **Tān kuài chū chācuò; màn cháng dé zīwèi.** 贪快出差错，慢尝得滋味。 (lit) A desire for speed produces mistakes, [while] slow tasting [lets one] get the flavor. (fig) "More haste (means) less speed." "Haste makes waste." [See also *jí xíng wú shàn jì* and *jí zhōng yǒu shī* above and *yù sù zé bù dá* below.]

9 **Tānlán de rén bǎo bù liǎo; lìnsè de rén fù bùliǎo.** 贪婪的人饱不了，吝啬的人富不了。 A greedy person never feels full, [while] a penny-pincher never gets rich.

10 **"Tān" zì jìn "pín."** "贪"字近"贫"。 (lit) The Chinese character [for] "greed" [is] close [in shape] to that [for] "poverty." (fig) A greedy person will inevitably end up in poverty.

11 **Tǎofàn pà gǒu yǎo; xiùcái pà suì kǎo.** 讨饭怕狗咬，秀才怕岁考。 (lit) Beggars fear dogs [and] scholars [traditionally] were afraid of the yearly [imperial] examinations. (fig) Everybody has something to fear. [Rhyme.]

12 **Táolǐ bù yán; xià zì chéng xī.** 桃李不言，下自成蹊。 (lit) [Although] peach [trees and] plum [trees do] not speak, [yet] beneath [them] naturally a path [will] form. (fig) Sincere people attract others although they don't speak much. A person of true worth naturally attracts admiration. [Cf. *Hàn Shū: Lǐ Guǎng Zhuàn Zàn*.]

13 **Tàpò tiě xié, wú mì chù; dé lái quán bù fèi gōngfu.** 踏破铁鞋无觅处，得来全不费工夫。 (lit) [One may] wear out [a pair of] iron shoes without finding [a thing, and then] come upon [it] without expending any effort at all. (fig) One may find something by chance after having traveled all over looking for it in vain. [Cf. *WM*, chap. 53; see also *kě yù ér bù kě qiú* and *qiúzhī-bùdé* above.]

14 **Tārén gōng mò wǎn; tārén mǎ xiū qí.** 他人弓莫挽，他人马休骑。 (lit) Don't draw another's bow [and] don't ride another's horse. (fig) Never take anything that doesn't belong to you.

15 **Tiān bùkě wéi.** 天不可违。 (lit) Heaven may not [be] opposed. (fig) Humans can't go against Heaven's will.

16 **Tiān bù néng zǒng qíng; rén bù néng cháng zhuàng.** 天不能总晴，人不能常壮。 (lit) The sky can't always be sunny [and] people can't always be healthy. (fig) Human fortunes are as unpredictable as the weather. [See also *tiān yǒu bùcè* below.]

17 **Tiān bù pà; dì bù pà; jiù pà yǒu rén shuō xiánhuà.** 天不怕地不怕，就怕有人说闲话。 Fear neither Heaven nor Earth; rather fear people gossiping. [Rhyme; note: *tiān bù pà; dì bù pà; jiù pà/zhǐpà . . .* is a standard formula.]

18 **Tiān bù yán, ér zì gāo; dì bù yán, ér zìbēi.** 天不言而自高，地不言而自卑。 (lit) Heaven does not speak, but it's high; earth does not speak, but it's low. (fig) The sky is high and the earth is low, no matter what people say. Good is good and bad is bad, no matter what people may say. [Cf. *JPM*, chap. 62.]

19 **Tiān bù yán zì gāo; dì bù yán zì hòu.** 天不言自高，地不言自厚。 (lit) Heaven [need] not speak of its height, nor earth of its thickness. (fig) If one is good, one is good, and it's not necessary to boast about it. [See the colloquial *suyu* expression *tiān gāo, dì hòu*, (lit) "how high the sky and how deep the earth"; (fig) "the immensity of the universe; the complexity of things; how things are."]

20 **Tiān bù zhuàn, dì zhuàn; (dì bù zhuàn, rén zhuàn.)** 天不转地转，地不转人转。 (lit) If Heaven doesn't turn, the earth will; (if the earth doesn't turn, people will [keep things moving]). (fig) Things keep on happening and changing in life, regardless. [Note: *tiānbuzhuàn dìzhuàn* is a colloquial expression meaning "to happen regardless"; "we are bound to run into each other again some day"; see also *shān bù zhuàn* above.]

T

21 **Tiān cháng dì jiǔ, yǒu shí jìn.** 天长地久，有时尽。(lit) [To the] long existence of Heaven and Earth there [will] come an end. (fig) There is nothing permanent in the universe. [Note the *chengyu: tiāncháng-dìjiǔ,* "enduring as the universe."]

22 **Tián cóng kǔ zhōng lái; fú cóng huò zhōng shēng.** 甜从苦中来，福从祸中生。Sweetness comes from bitterness, [and] fortune from misfortune. [See also *huò xǐ fú suǒ yǐ* and *huò yǔ fú wéi lín* above.]

23 **Tiān dào chóu qín.** 天道酬勤。Heaven rewards the diligent.

24 **Tiāndì wéi dà; qīn shī wéi zūn.** 天地为大亲师为尊。Heaven [and] earth are great; parents [and] teachers are [to be] respected. [In traditional China, students were taught to respect *tiān, dì, jūn, qīn, shī,* "Heaven, Earth, the emperor, parents, teachers."]

25 **Tiān gāo, huángdì yuǎn.*** 天高，皇帝远。(lit) Heaven is high [above and the] emperor is far [away]. (fig) The control of the government is weaker in remote areas. [Cf. *Xǐngshì Yīnyuán Zhuàn,* chap. 12.]

26 **Tiāngōng, rén kě dài; réngōng, tiān bùrú.** 天工人可代，人工天不如。[What] nature creates, man can recreate, [but what] man creates, nature [can]not equal. [Note: *tiāngōng,* "(exquisitely fine) work of nature"; see also *rénshì kěyǐ bǔ* above.]

27 **Tiāngǒu chī bu liǎo rìtou.*** 天狗吃不了日头。(lit) The heavenly dog cannot devour the sun [forever]. (fig) Evil can never prevail over right forever. [Note: it was a popular superstition in traditional China that solar eclipses were caused by a heavenly dog devouring the sun.]

28 **Tiānjī bùkě xièlòu.*** 天机不可泄露。(lit) Heavenly secrets must not be leaked. (fig) Secrets should be kept strictly confidential. [Cf. *WM,* chap. 85; note: *tiānjī,* (lit) "heavenly mysteries," is here being used hyperbolically to refer to ordinary secrets.]

29 **Tiān lěng bù dòng Zhīnǚ shǒu; jīhuang bù è kǔ gēng rén.** 天冷不冻织女手，饥荒不饿苦耕人。(lit) Cold weather won't freeze girl-weavers hands [and] famine won't starve diligent farmers. (fig) Those who work hard will survive cold and hunger. [Note: *kǔgēng,* "hard work"; *kǔgàn,* "work hard."]

30 **Tiān liáng bùrú jiǎn kǒu.** 添粮不如减口。(lit) [Trying to] supply more food is not as [good as] reducing [the number of] mouths [to be fed; e.g., employees, servants, etc.].

31 **Tiān luò mántou, yě yào qǐzǎo qù shí.** 天落馒头，也要起早去拾。(lit) [Even if] steamed bread falls from the sky, [you] have to get up early and pick it up. (fig) Even when good fortune befalls one, one has to exert oneself to accomplish anything. "Heaven helps those who help themselves." [See also *rén hóng dǐpí* above and *tiānshí, rénshì* below.]

32 **Tián pà qiūrì hàn; rén pà lǎolái qióng.** 田怕秋日旱，人怕老来穷。[As] fields dread drought in autumn, [so] people fear poverty in old age. [See also *rén pà lǎolái pín* above.]

33 **Tiān qíng bù kāi gōu, yǔ lái dàochù liú.** 天晴不开沟，雨来到处流。(lit) [If, when] the weather is fine, ditches are not dug, [when it] rains, water [will] run everywhere. (fig) Make preparations well in advance. "Prepare for a rainy day." [Rhyme; see also *qíng gān kāi shuǐdào* above.]

34 **Tiān qíng bùkěn zǒu; zhǐ dài yǔ líntóu.** 天晴不肯走，只待雨淋头。(lit) [If when] the weather's fine [one] won't leave, [then one will] be caught in the rain [later]. (fig) Do things at the right time. [Cf. *Fēngshén Yǎnyì,* chap. 33; see also *qíng gān bùkěn* above.]

35 **Tiānshàng diào bù xià shāo bǐng lái.** 天上掉不下烧饼来。(lit) Sesame seed cakes won't fall from heaven. (fig) Nothing in life is free; one has to work to support oneself.

36 **Tiānshàng méiyǒu duòluò lóng; dìshàng méiyǒu è shā chóng.** 天上没有堕落龙；地上没有饿煞虫。(lit) There will be no dragons falling down from the skies, [and] there will be no worms starving to death. (fig) There will always be some way to make a living or survive. [Rhyme.]

37 **Tiānshàng wú yún, bù xiàyǔ; shì bù chéng.** 天上无云不下雨，地上无人事不成。(lit) [If] there were no clouds in the sky, it wouldn't rain; [if] there were no humans on earth, nothing would get accomplished. (fig) Nothing in life can be accomplished without human effort. [Note the *chengyu: shìzàirénwéi,* "Things are to be done by human beings; it all depends on human effort"; see also *lěngshuǐ yào rén* and the following entry.]

38 **Tiānshàng wú yún, bù xiàyǔ; dìxia wú méi, bù chénghūn.** 天上无云不下雨，地下无媒不成婚。[Just as when] there are no clouds in the sky, it doesn't rain, [so if] there were no go-betweens in the world, [there would] be no marriages. [See also *zhōngjiān méi rén* below and the preceding entry.]

39 **Tiānshàng xiàyǔ, dìxia huá; zìjǐ diēle, zìjǐ pá.** 天上下雨地下滑，自己跌了自己爬。(lit) Everywhere the ground is slippery after it rains; if one slips, one has to get up by oneself. (fig) Life being the way it is, one has to rely on oneself to solve one's own problems. [Rhyme.]

40 **Tiānshàng xiàyǔ, dìxia liú; liǎngkǒur dǎjià bù jìchóu.** 天上下雨，地下流，两口儿打架不记仇。[Just as it's natural that] water flows away on the ground [after it] rains; [so it's equally natural that] "we two" [i.e., husband and wife] bear no grudges [against each other after they/we've] had a fight [Rhyme; note: *liǎngkǒu* is a colloquial expression meaning "we two; both of us"; see also *fūqī wú gé xiū zhī chóu* above.]

41 **Tiān shēng yī gè rén, bì yǒu yī fèn liáng.** 天生一个人，必有一份粮。(lit) [Since] Heaven [permits] one person to be born, there must be one['s] portion of food. (fig) Since one was born,

one is sure to have something to eat. [Cf. Tian Han's modern play *Yú Guāng Qǔ*.]

42　**Tiānshí, rénshì, liǎng xiāng fú.** 天时人事, 两相扶。(lit) Heaven's timing [and] people's [own] efforts are equally important [in accomplishing anything]. (fig) "Heaven helps those who help themselves." [See also *tiān luò mántou* above.]

43　**Tián shì zhǔrén; rén shì kè.** 田是主人, 人是客。(lit) The land is the host [and] people are [merely] guests. (fig) Land owners may change, but the land remains forever. [See also *qiān nián tiándì* above.]

44　**Tiān suàn bù yóu rén suàn.*** 天算不由人算。(lit) Heaven's calculations don't follow man's calculation. (fig) Whatever human minds intend, it's heaven that decides the end; "man proposes, heaven disposes." [See also *móushì zài rén* and *qiān suàn, wàn suàn* and *shì dàotóulái* above.]

45　**Tiān tā bù xiàlái; dì chén bù xiàqù.** 天塌不下来, 地沉不下去。(lit) The sky won't fall down [and] the earth won't sink away. (fig) There's nothing to fear or worry about. [See also the following entry.]

46　**Tiān tā (xiàlai), zìyǒu cháng de chēng zhù.*** 天塌下来, 自有长的撑住。(lit) [Even if] the sky [starts to] fall, there are tall [people who will] prop it up. (fig) Don't worry; (even) if problems come up, there are able people who can deal with them. [Cf. *Xǐngshì Héngyán*, chap. 7; *Wǔ Sōng*, chap. 2; see also *tiān tā, zìyǒu* below.]

47　**Tiān tā, zá zhòngrén.** 天塌砸众人。(lit) [When] the sky falls, everyone [will be] crushed. (fig) No one can escape great disasters (so why should one person worry?). [Also said *tiān tā, dàjiā sǐ*, "If the sky falls, everyone will die."]

48　**Tiān tā, zìyǒu cháng rén dǐng.*** 天踏, 自有长人顶。(lit) [If] the sky falls, there will be taller people [to] hold [it] up. (fig) If anything goes wrong, don't worry about it, there will always be people who are more qualified who will take care of things. [Cf. *Xǐngshì Héngyán*, chap. 7; see also *rù shuǐ jiàn cháng rén* and *tiān tā xiàlái* above.]

49　**Tiānwǎng-huīhuī, shū ér bù lòu.** 天网恢恢, 疏而不漏。(lit) The vast net of Heaven has large meshes, but it lets nothing through. (fig) Heaven's retribution is slow but sure. Crime or injustice will be punished in the end. [Cf. *Érnǚ Yīngxióng Zhuàn*, chap. 18 and *Lǎozǐ: Dào Dé Jīng*, chap. 73; note: the *chengyu*: tiānwǎng-huīhuī, "justice has a long arm"; shū'érbùlòu, "justice is implacable."]

50　**Tiān wúbiān; zhì wúxiàn.** 天无边, 智无限。[Just as] the heavens have no boundaries, [so] wisdom has no limits.

51　**Tiān wú èr rì; mín wú èr wáng.** 天无二日, 民无二王。(lit) There are not two suns in the sky, [and] the people can only have one ruler. (fig) There can only be one ruler in a country. [Cf. *R3K*, chap. 86; note: tiānwú'èrrì is used as a set phrase; see also *yī guó bùróng* below.]

52　**Tiān wú èr rì; rén wú èr lǐ.** 天无二日, 人无二理。(lit) There are not two suns in the sky [and] there are not two truths on earth. (fig) There is only one truth on earth. [Cf. *JW*, chap. 78; see the preceding entry.]

53　**Tiān wú jué rén zhī lù.*** 天无绝人之路。(lit) Heaven has no roads which completely block a person. (fig) Heaven never drives one to desperation. "God never closes one door but he opens another." [Cf. *Xǐngshì Héngyán*, chap. 37: note also the Spanish proverb: *No hieve Dios con dos manos*, "God never wounds with both hands."]

54　**Tiān wú sān rì yǔ; rén méi yīshì qióng.** 天无三日雨, 人没一世穷。[Just as] it doesn't rain for three days in a row, [so] one won't be poor all one's life.

55　**Tiānxià běn wú shì; yōngrén zì rǎo zhī.** 天下本无事, 庸人自扰之。(lit) Originally the world was eventless; [it is only] foolish people [who] create trouble [for] themselves. (fig) Some people imagine trouble out of nothing; people (often) create problems (for) themselves. [Rhyme; cf. *Érnǚ Yīngxióng Zhuàn*, chap. 22; note the *chengyu*: yōngrén-zìrǎo, "worry(ing) about troubles of one's own imagining; bark(ing) at the moon."]

56　**Tiānxià dàolǐ qiān qiānwàn; méi qián bù néng bǎ shì bàn.** 天下道理千千万, 没钱不能把事办。There are thousands upon thousands of principles on earth, [but] without money, nothing can be accomplished. [Rhyme; see also *qián kě tōng shén* above and *tiānxià wú nánshì* below.]

57　**Tiānxià de huàishì zhǐpà bù zuò; bù pà bù pò.** 天下的坏事只怕不做, 不怕不破。(lit) [The] best way [to deal with] all bad acts is not to commit [them], not [just to] worry about being found out. (fig) If you don't want to get caught, then don't do anything wrong in the first place. [See also *ruò yào rén bù zhī* above and *zhǐpà bù zuò* below.]

58　**Tiānxià nánshì bì zuò yú yì.** 天下难事必做于易。[All] difficult things should [be handled by] starting from [the] easy [part]. [Cf. *Lǎozǐ*, chap. 63.]

59　**Tiānxià qiányǎnr dōu yīyàng.** 天下钱眼儿都一样。(lit) All the "eyes" in the world are the same. (fig) Everyone is capable of making judgments about persons or things. [Cf. *JPM*, chap. 15; qiányǎnr refers to the square hole in the center of copper "cash" coins used to string them together in traditional China; here it is a metaphor for the uniformity of people's eyes; see also *gōngpíng chǔyú* and *línjū yǎnjing* above.]

60　**Tiānxià rén guǎn tiānxià shì.** 天下人管天下事。Everyone under heaven has [a right to have] a say about the affairs of the world. [See also *tiānxià wéi gōng* below.]

61　**Tiānxià shì nán jìn rú rényì.** 天下事难尽如人意。(lit) [All the] things in the world [are] hard put to be completely as people wish. (fig) Not everything in life can be completely the way people wish them to be. [Note: jìnrú-rényì is used as a *chengyu* meaning "things develop as wished."]

T

62 **Tiānxià wéi gōng.*** 天下为公。(lit) [Everything] under heaven is public [business]. (fig) The world (and political power) belongs to everyone. Everyone should be concerned with public affairs. [Originally a line from the Confucian *Lǐjì* (Book of Rites): *Lǐ Yùn*; later quoted by Sun Yatsen as a slogan expressing his concept of *mínquán*, "people's rights"; this is sometimes presented as a *chengyu*.]

63 **Tiānxià wú bù sàn de yánxí.** 天下无不散的筵席。(lit) There is no party in the world which does not have an end. (fig) Even the finest feast must break up at last. "All good things must come to an end." [Cf. *Gǔ-Jīn Xiǎoshuō*, chap. 1; see also *liú jūn qiān rì* and *méiyǒu bù sàn* and *qiān lǐ dā cháng péng* and *shèngyàn bì sàn* and *sòng jūn qiān lǐ* above.]

64 **Tiānxià wú bùshi de fùmǔ.** 天下无不是的父母。(lit) There are no incorrect parents in the world. (fig) Parents are always right. Obedience to one's parents should be absolute. [Note: *bùshi*, "fault."]

65 **Tiānxià wú nánshì, zhǐpà yǒuxīnrén.*** 天下无难事，只怕有心人。(lit) There's nothing difficult in the world; it only takes a person with will. (fig) "Where there's a will, there's a way." [Also said *shì shàng wú nán shì*, etc.; see also *shìshàng wú nánshì* above and *yǒuzhìzhě* below.]

66 **Tiānxià wú nánshì, zhǐyào lǎomiànpí.** 天下无难事，只要老面皮。Nothing in the world is difficult for one who is thick-skinned (or brazen-faced) enough. [A sarcastic variant of the preceding entry.]

67 **Tiānxià wú nánshì, zǒng jiào xiàn yínzi.** 天下无难事，总教现银子。Nothing in the world is difficult so long as there is ready cash at hand. [Note: 教 *jiào* is now often replaced by 交 *jiāo*; see also the preceding two entries and *tiānxià dàoli* above and *yǒuqián néng shǐ* below.]

68 **Tiānxià wūyā yībān hēi.*** 天下乌鸦一般黑。(lit) Crows are black the world over. (fig) Bad people are the same everywhere in the world. [Cf. *DRC*, chap. 57; see also *dōng shān lǎohǔ* above.]

69 **Tiānxià yǒu hěnxīn de ér-nǚ; wú hěnxīn de diē-niáng.** 天下有狠心的儿女，无狠心的爹娘。In this world, there are heartless sons [and] daughters, [but] there are no heartless fathers [and] mothers.

70 **Tián yán duó zhì; táng shí huài chǐ.** 甜言夺志，糖食坏齿。Sweet words weaken a person's will [just as] sweet food rots the teeth. [See also *shuō de hǎotīng* above.]

71 **Tián yán měi yǔ, sān dōng nuǎn; èyǔ shāngrén Liùyuè hán.*** 甜言美语三冬暖，恶语伤人六月寒。Sweet, nice words warm [one even in the] coldest days of winter; ill-intended, injurious words [will] chill [one even in the] heat of August. [Cf. *Xīxiāng Jì*, Scene 2, Act 3; *JPM*, chap. 76; note: *sānjiǔ hándōng* refers to the coldest days of winter, and the sixth lunar month generally occurs in late July or August.]

72 **Tián yào dōnggēng; zǎi yào qīnshēng.** 田要冬耕，崽要亲生。(lit) [Just as it is best that] fields be plowed in winter, [so it's best that] sons should be one's own. (fig) It is best to have one's own natural sons, not adopted ones. [Rhyme.]

73 **Tiān yào xiàyǔ, niáng yào jiàrén.*** 天要下雨，娘要嫁人。See *niǎo yào fēi* … above.

74 **Tiān yǒu bùcè fēngyún; rén yǒu dàn-xī huò fú.*** 天有不测风云，人有旦夕祸福。(lit) [Just as in] nature there are unexpected storms, [so in] human [life] there are unpredictable vicissitudes. (fig) Just as storms gather without warning in nature, people's luck can change in a short time. Human fortunes are as unpredictable as the weather. [Cf. *DRC*, chap. 11; note: *bùcè*, "unpredictable"; the first half is usually used alone as a set phrase; see also *tiān bù néng zǒng* above.]

75 **Tiān yǒu shíkè yīn qíng; rén yǒu sān huí, liù zhuàn.** 天有时刻阴晴，人有三回六转。[Just as] the weather is constantly [changing from] dark [to] clear, [so] people['s minds] are [also constantly] changing.

76 **Tiān yǔ bù qǔ, fǎn shòu qí jiù.** 天与不取，反受其咎。(lit) [If] heaven offers [and you] refuse, then [prepare to] receive its punishment. (fig) If "opportunity knocks," and you don't take advantage of it, then be it on your own head. [Rhyme; cf. *Shǐ Jì: Huái Yīn Hóu Lièzhuàn*.]

77 **Tiānzǐ shàngqiě bì zuìhàn.*** 天子尚且避醉汉。(lit) Even the emperor [tries to] avoid meeting drunkards. (fig) Never argue with a drunkard. [Cf. *WM*, chap. 4; *Wǔ Sōng*, chap. 5; see also *ruò yào duàn jiǔ fǎ* above.]

78 **Tiān zuòniè, yóu kě wéi; zì zuòniè, bù kě huàn/huó.** 天作孽犹可违，自作孽不可逭/活。[If] nature causes disasters, there is [still something that] can be done to avoid [them], [but if] humans bring disaster [upon them]selves, nothing can be done to avoid [them]. [More commonly, … *bù kě huó*, "… one cannot live; one is done for"; cf. *JW*, chap. 43 and *Érnǚ Yīngxióng Zhuàn*, chap. 3; note: *zuò'è*; *zuìniè*: "to do evil"; said, e.g., of the *rénhuò*, "man-made disasters" of the Great Leap Forward, which followed the "Three Bad Years" of bad harvests in 1959–1961.]

79 **Tiān zuò, yǒu yǔ; rén zuò, yǒu huò.** 天作有雨，人作有祸。[When] Heaven takes action, it rains; [when] people take action, there are disasters. [See also the preceding entry.]

80 **Tiāoshí de rén bù pàng.** 挑食的人不胖。One [who is too] fussy about food won't get fat [i.e., won't be healthy].

81 **Tiě bù mó, shēngxiù; shuǐ bù liú, fāchòu.** 铁不磨生锈，水不流发臭。(lit) Iron not whetted [will] grow rusty; water [which does] not flow [will] become stale. (fig) One must remain active or become stale. [Rhyme; see also *liúshuǐ bù fǔ* above.]

82 **Tiědǎ de yámen; liúshuǐ de guān.** 铁打的衙门，流水的官。(lit) Government offices [are] made of iron [which remains for ages, but the] officials [working in them are like] running water [changing from time to time]. (fig) Government officials

come and go; that's the way it is. [Note: *tiědǎ (de)*, (lit) "iron-hammered"; (fig) "unshakable."]

83　**Tiědǎ fángliáng mó xiù zhēn; gōng dào zìrán chéng.** 铁打房梁磨绣针, 功到自然成。(lit) An iron roof beam [can be] ground down into an embroidery needle; [when] effort is applied, naturally [things will be] accomplished. (fig) Persistence can grind an iron roof beam (down) into a needle. Persistence can accomplish anything. [Cf. *Érnǚ Yīngxióng Zhuàn*, chap. 5 and 23; *JW*, chap. 36; note: *gōngdào zìránchéng* is used alone (q.v.) as an idiom meaning "constant effort yields sure success"; see also *zhǐyào gōngfu shēn* below.]

84　**Tiě guàn mò shuō guō zhān huī; jìyú mò shuō lǐ tuóbèi.** 铁罐莫说锅粘灰, 鲫鱼莫说鲤驼背。(lit) An iron pot [must] not call a kettle black, nor [should] a crucian carp call a carp hunchbacked. (fig) One should not criticize faults in others which one has oneself. "The pot calling the kettle black." [See also *wūguī mò xiào biē* and *zhū mà wūyā hēi* below.]

85　**Tiě pà luò lú; rén pà luò tào.** 铁怕落炉, 人怕落套。[Just as] iron is afraid to be put into a furnace, [so] people are afraid to be taken in [i.e., cheated or tricked into doing things]. [Cf. *Xǐngshì Héngyán*, chap. 25; *WM*, chap. 61.]

86　**Tiē rén bù fù, zìjiā qióng.** 贴人不富, 自家穷。(lit) [If you] help [other] people, [they will] not [become] rich, [but you your]self [will become] poor. (fig) People do not get rich by relying on others; they must do it for themselves.

87　**Tiě shēngxiù zé huài; rén shēng dù zé bài.** 铁生锈则坏, 人生炉则败。[When] iron gets rusty it's useless; [when] people get jealous [they] will fail.

88　**Tīng bù tīng, zhěntou fēng.** 听不听, 枕头风。(lit) [Whether one wants to] listen or not, [there's bound to be] "pillow talk." (fig) A man has to listen to what his wife says in bed at night whether he wants to or not. A man is sure to be influenced by his spouse's private opinions. [See also *zhěn biān gàozhuàng* below.]

89　**Tīng chuányán, shīluò jiāngshān.** 听传言, 失落江山。(lit) [If a ruler] listens to [and believes] rumors, the country will be ruined. (fig) Anyone who listens to rumors will suffer great losses. [Note: *zuò jiāngshān*, "to rule the country."]

90　**Tīng huà tīngyīn; luó-gǔ tīng shēng.** 听话听音, 锣鼓听声。(lit) [When you] listen to [someone] talk, [you must] listen [to his or her] tone, [just as when you listen to] gongs and drums, [you must listen to the rhythm of the] music. (fig) "The words are the mirror of the mind." [The two halves of this *yanyu* may be in either order; note: *tīngyīn* is a colloquial expression meaning to "take a hint"; note the colloquial *suyu* expression *xiánwàizhīyīn*, (lit) "the sound beyond the strings"; (fig) "overtones; implication"; see also *luó-gǔ tīng yīn* above and *wén qí yán* and *yào zhī xīnfùshì* below.]

91　**Tīng qiān biàn bùrú kàn yī biàn; kàn qiān biàn bùrú zuò yī biàn.** 听千遍不如看一遍, 看千遍不如做一遍。To see [something] once is better than to hear [about it a] thousand times; to do [something] once is better than to look [at it a] thousand times. [See also *bǎiwén bùrú yījiàn* above and *yǎn jiàn qiān biàn* below.]

92　**Tīng rén quàn; chībǎo fàn.** 听人劝, 吃饱饭。(lit) Listen to others' advice [and you] won't go hungry. (fig) One can always benefit from listening to the advice of others. [Technically a rhyme.]

93　**Tóng chuáng dǎ shuì; gèzì zuòmèng.** 同床打睡, 各自做梦。[Even] people who sleep in the same bed each dream their own [separate] dreams. [As a *chengyu*: *tóngchuáng-yìmèng*.]

94　**Tóngháng shì yuānjia.*** 同行是冤家。[Two in the] same trade are [always] rivals. [As a *chengyu*: *tóngháng-xiāngjì*, "People in the same trade always quarrel"; see also *dāng háng yàn* and *géháng rú géshān* above.]

95　**Tónghú bù lòu, shuǐ bù dī.** 铜壶不漏, 水不滴。(lit) [If a] copper kettle doesn't leak, not a drop of water [will] come out. (fig) If there's a problem, there must be a cause.

96　**Tóng jí xiāng lián; tóng yōu xiāng jiù.*** 同疾相怜, 同忧相就。Similarly afflicted people pity each other; fellow sufferers help each other. [Cf. *Dōng Zhōu Lièguó Zhì*, chap. 74; *Jǐngshì Tōngyán*, chap. 12; the first part is now more commonly *tóngbìng-xiānglián*, often used alone as a *chengyu*; see also *zìjǐ tānbēi* below.]

97　**Tónglèi bù xiāng cán.** 同类不相残。One doesn't harm one's own kind.

98　**Tóng míng, xiāng zhào; tónglèi xiāng cóng.** 同明相照, 同类相从。[Just as] similar bright [objects] illuminate each other, [so the] same sort [of people] get together. "Birds of a feather flock together." [Cf. *Shǐ Jì: Bó Yí Lièzhuàn*.]

99　**Tóng pén lànle, jīnliǎng zài; dà chuán lànle, dīngzi duō.** 铜盆烂了斤两在, 大船烂了钉子多。(lit) [When a] copper basin gets rusty, its weight [as scrap metal] remains; [when a] big ship gets rotten, there are many nails [left over]. (fig) Even if a rich family falls into decline, they still have a lot of property left. [See also *dà chuán lànle* and *shòu sǐ de luòtuo* above.]

100　**Tóng pén zhuàngle tiě sàozhou; èrén zì yǒu èrén mó.** 铜盆撞了铁扫帚, 恶人自有恶人磨。(lit) [Like a] copper pan running into [an] iron broom, [so] evil doers always come up against even worse evil doers [in the end]. [Rhyme; cf. *Xǐngshì Héngyán*, chap. 34; see also *cǎo pà yánshuāng* and *èrén zì yǒu* above.]

101　**Tóng sǎn bùtóng bǐng; tóng rén bùtóng mìng.** 同伞不同柄, 同人不同命。[Just as] umbrellas [may be] similar [but have] different handles, [so] people [may be] similar [but] have different fates. [Rhyme.]

102　**Tóngshēng xiāngyìng; tóng qì xiāng qiú.*** 同声相应, 同气相求。(lit) Similar sounds echo one another, [and people of] similar temperament seek each other out. (fig) "Birds of a feather flock together"; "like attracts like." [Cf. *Xǐngshì*

T

Héngyán, chap. 5; note: tóngshēng-xiāngyìng is used as an idiom meaning "act(ing) in unison"; note also the chengyu: qìwèi-xiāngtóu, "to be two of a kind."]

103 **Tóng shì tiānyá lúnluò rén; xiāngféng hébì céng xiāngshí?** 同是天涯沦落人，相逢何必曾相识？ [See xiāngféng hébì below.]

104 **Tóngxíng bù shū bàn.** 同行不疏伴。 (lit) [Those who] travel together don't distance [themselves from their] fellow [travelers]. (fig) Fellow travelers become close companions. [Cf. Rúlín Wàishǐ, chap. 47; see also tóngxíng wú shū bàn below.]

105 **Tóngxìng shì yìjiā.** 同姓是一家。 [People who have the] same surname are [as of] one family. [See also wǔbǎi nián qián and yī bān shù shàng below.]

106 **Tóngxíng wú shū bàn.** 同行无疏伴。 (lit) [Among] fellow travelers there are no distant companions. (fig) Traveling companions stick together and form close friend'ships. [Cf. Suí Táng Yǎnyì, chap. 10; note: shūyuǎn, "separated; estranged"; see also tóngxíng bù shū bàn; vs. lù yù bù shì bàn above.]

107 **Tóng zhōu gòng jì.** 同舟共济。 (lit) [People in the] same boat [should] help one another. (fig) Those who share the same fate should help each other. [Cf. Hòu Hàn Shū and Sūnzǐ's Bīngfǎ: Jiǔ Dì Piān; as a chengyu: tóngzhōu-gòngjì; see also the following entry.]

108 **Tóng zhōu héyī mìng.** 同舟合一命。 (lit) People in the same boat share the same fate. (fig) People in similar circumstances share the same fate. "We're all in the same boat." [See also the preceding entry.]

109 **Tōuchī bù féi; zuò zéi bù fù.** 偷吃不肥，做贼不富。 No one [can] grow fat [or] become rich by stealing.

110 **Tóu cù bù suān; èr cù bù là.** 头醋不酸，二醋不辣。 (lit) [If the] first [batch of] vinegar isn't sour (enough), the second is [sure to be even] blander [because you can't rebrew it]. (fig) The initial step is most important in doing everything (so get it right the first time). [Cf. Jīngshì Tōngyán, chap. 25; WM, chap. 51.]

111 **Tóu dào shēng; èr dào shú; sān dào, sì dào, chéng shīfu.** 头道生二道熟，三道四道成师傅。 (lit) [In doing everything] the first time [one is] not well-skilled, the second time [one] is, [and by] the third and fourth times [one] becomes a master. (fig) "Practice makes perfect."

112 **Tōu de yé qián, méi shǐ chù.** 偷的爷钱，没使处。 (lit) Money stolen from [one's] father [one can]not find a place to spend. (fig) One dare not openly spend money which was obtained by stealing or cheating. [Cf. Èr Kè Pāi'àn Jīngqí, chap. 20; see also tōu lái de luó-gǔ below.]

113 **Tóu duì fēng, nuǎnhōnghong; jiǎo duì fēng, qǐng lángzhōng.** 头对风暖烘烘，脚对风请郎中。 [If you sleep with your] head in a draft, [you'll be] comfortably warm; [if you sleep with your] feet in a draft, call for a doctor. [Rhyme.]

114 **Tóufa suī xì, gè yǒu yǐngzi.** 头发虽细，各有影子。 (lit) Even a tiny hair has a shadow. (fig) Even very insignificant things have some influence.

115 **Tōu fēng, bù tōu yuè; tōu yǔ, bù tōu xuě.** 偷风不偷月，偷雨不偷雪。 (lit) [Thieves] steal [on] wind[y nights, but do] not steal [on] moon[lit nights]; [thieves] steal [on] rain[y nights, but do] not steal [on] snow[y nights, because they might be seen in the moonlight or leave tracks in the snow]. (fig) People generally do evil deeds "in the dark of night" when they are less likely to get caught. [Rhyme.]

116 **Tóu huí shàngdàng; èr huí xīn liàng.** * 头回上当，二回心亮。 (lit) The first time [one is] deceived, [but] the second time [one is] clear-headed (i.e., one can see through the trick). (fig) One won't get taken the second time. [Rhyme; see also chī yī qiàn and shàng huí dàng above.]

117 **Tōu lái de luó-gǔ, dǎbude.** 偷来的锣鼓，打不得。 (lit) Gongs [and] drums [one has] stolen one dare not beat. (fig) Things done or obtained wrongly cannot be revealed. [Cf. DRC, chap. 65; see also tōu de yé qián above.]

118 **Tóumǎ bù huāng, mǎ qún bù luàn.** 头马不慌，马群不乱。 (lit) [If the] lead horse is not spooked, the herd won't run off in different directions. (fig) If the leader is steady, his followers will be well organized. [Note: huāngluàn, "alarmed and bewildered"; see also bǎduò de bù huāng above.]

119 **Tóu nán, tóu nán; wànshì kāitóu nán.** * 头难头难，万事开头难。 Nothing is easy in the beginning; in everything the first step is [the most] difficult. [Rhyme; see also tóu sān jiǎo and wànshì qǐtóu below.]

120 **Tóuqīn bùrú luò diàn.** 投亲不如落店。 (lit) Staying at a relative's (or friend's) [house] is not as good as staying at an inn. (fig) One is not comfortable imposing on one's relatives' or friends' hospitality. [Cf. Suí Táng Yǎnyì, chap. 12; note: qīn here refers to qīnyǒu "relatives and friends"; see also xiāngjiàn hǎo below.]

121 **Tōuqu de quántou, dǎ bù sǐ běnrén.** 偷去的拳头，打不死本人。 (lit) [Martial arts] techniques stolen [from someone secretly] cannot be used to overcome the original person [from whom they were copied]. (fig) One can never defeat one's teacher using techniques one has stolen from him. [Cf. Lu Xun's short story: Bēn Yuè in the collection Gùshì Xīn Biān ("Old Tales Retold").]

122 **Tóu sān jiǎo, nán tī; kāiluó xì, nán chàng.** 头三脚难踢，开锣戏难唱。 (lit) The most difficult [is] to kick the first three kicks [and to] start singing at the very beginning of an opera. (fig) Beginning is the hardest part of doing something. [Note: kāiluó is a theatrical term meaning "to begin the performance"; see also tóu nán, tóu nán above and wànshì qǐtóu nán below.]

123 **Tōu shí (de) māor, xìng bù gǎi.** * 偷食（的）猫儿，性不改。 (lit) A cat that steals food won't change its nature. (fig) "A leopard won't change its spots." [Cf. Xǐngshì Héngyán, chap. 17; Jīngshì Tōngyán, chap. 38; see also gǒu chī shǐ

and *jiǎngshān yì gǎi* and *shé rù zhú dòng* and *shé zuān de kūdòng* above and *yǐ rén, yǐ xiàng* below.]

124 **Tōuzuǐ māor, pà lòuxiàng.** 偷嘴猫儿，怕露相。 (lit) The cat that steals food is afraid of being exposed. (fig) One who does evil deeds is afraid of being found out.

125 **Tǔ bāng tǔ chéng qiáng; qióng bāng qióng chéng wáng.** 土帮土成墙，穷帮穷成王。 (lit) [Just as] earth sticks to earth [and] makes a wall, [so] poor people stick to poor people [and together] create a king. (fig) In unity there is strength. [Rhyme.]

126 **Tǔ bì zé cǎomù bù zhǎng.** 土弊则草木不长。 (lit) [If the] soil is poor, the grass [and] trees won't grow. (fig) Talented people cannot be produced under poor conditions. [Cf. *Lǚ Shì Chūnqiū: Yīn Chū*; see also *jǐngshuǐ wú dà yú* above.]

127 **Tùháo wú yōu-liè; guǎn shǒu yǒu qiǎo zhuō.** 兔毫无优劣，管手有巧拙。 (lit) [It's] not [whether the writing brush made of] rabbit hair is good [or] bad; [it's whether the] hand which controls [the brush is] skillful [or] clumsy. (fig) Good calligraphy depends on the skill of the calligrapher.

128 **Tuǐ cháng zhān lùshuǐ; zuǐ cháng rě shìfēi.** 腿长沾露水，嘴长惹是非。 [Just as] long legs get wet [with] dew-drops, [so] "long tongues" invite trouble.

129 **Tuìhòu yī bù, tiān kuān dì kuò.** 退后一步，天宽地阔。 (lit) [If you] take a step backwards [you will have a] broad expanse of sky and earth. (fig) In doing everything allow for unforeseen circumstances, and in dealing with people, make concessions. [See also *ràng rén yī zhāo* above.]

130 **Tuǐkuài bùpà lù yuǎn.** 腿快不怕路远。 (lit) Fast legs are not afraid of long distances. (fig) Able people are not afraid of difficult tasks.

131 **Tuì yī bù, jìn liǎng bù.*** 退一步，进两步。 (lit) Retreat one step; advance two steps. (fig) One step backwards now can mean two steps forward in the future. "One step back; two steps forward." [This is the Chinese translation of the title of an article by Lenin on making concessions to the Russian bourgeoisie.]

132 **Tǔ jū sānshí zǎi, wú yǒu bù qīnrén.** 土居三十载，无有不亲人。 After living in a locality for thirty years, [one is] bound to have friends and acquaintances. [Cf. *Jǐngshì Tōngyán*, chap. 1; note that traditionally Chinese consider one's home place to be where one's ancestors came from.]

133 **Tuōrén rú tuō shān.** 托人如托山。 Entrusting [things to other] people [entails a risk (to the requester) as] heavy [as holding up a] mountain [so consider carefully before you do so]! [Cf. *Hé Diǎn*, chap. 5; this is a pun on two senses of the verb

134 **Tuó tuó qiānjīn, yǐ fù lì mǐ.** 驮驼千斤，蚁负粒米。 (lit) A camel [can] carry a thousand catties, [and an] ant [can] carry a grain of rice. (fig) People should exert themselves to the utmost (regardless) of their abilities. [Note: literally, one *jīn* or "catty" is equal to one-half kilogram, but *qiānjīn* is figuratively taken to mean "a ton; a great weight."]

135 **Tù sǐ, hú bēi; wù shāng qí lèi.** 兔死狐悲，物伤其类。 (lit) [When] the rabbit dies, the fox mourns; [all] creatures grieve for their [own (bad)] ilk. [Rhyme; cf. *JW*, chap. 62; *R3K*, chap. 89; the two halves are used independently as chengyu with derogatory senses; see also *wù shāng qí lèi* below.]

136 **Tú xiǎolì, dàshì bù chéng.** 图小利，大事不成。 [One who likes to] exploit petty advantages won't accomplish anything great.

137 **Tùzi bù chī wō biān cǎo.*** 兔子不吃窝边草。 (lit) A rabbit never eats the grass beside its burrow [so that it will be protected]. (fig) A criminal does not commit crimes near home. (Even) a scoundrel won't harm his own immediate neighbors or surroundings, (as it is not in his interest to do so). [Also said *tùzi fú chī kē biān cǎo*; cf. *Hé Diǎn*, chap. 8; see also *lùsī bù dǎ* and *měnghǔ bù chī* above.]

138 **Tùzi huítóu, xiōng sì hǔ.** 兔子回头，凶似虎。 (lit) A rabbit [which] turns [in desperation is as] fierce as a tiger. (fig) When overly oppressed, even the meek will turn and fight. "Even a worm will turn." [See also *tùzi jíle* and *zhí xiàng gǎn gǒu* below.]

139 **Tùzi jià bùliǎo yuán.** 兔子驾不了辕。 (lit) A rabbit cannot be harnessed to a carriage. (fig) Don't ask someone weak or incapable to shoulder heavy responsibilities.

140 **Tùzi jíle, hái yǎo rén.*** 兔子急了，还咬人。 (lit) Even a rabbit will bite people [when it's] desperate. (fig) Even a meek person will revolt when pushed too far. "Even a worm will turn." [See also *tùzi huítóu* above.]

141 **Tùzi kào tuǐ, láng kào yá; gè yǒu gè de móushēng fǎ.** 兔子靠腿，狼靠牙，各有各的谋生法。 Rabbits depend on [their fast] legs [and] wolves on [their sharp] teeth; every [creature] has [his or her] own way of making a living. [Rhyme; note: *gèyǒu-gède*, "each had his own involvements."]

142 **Tùzi mǎn shān pǎo, hái děi huí lǎo wō.** 兔子满山跑，还得回老窝。 (lit) A rabbit [may] run all over the hills, [but sooner or later it will] return to [its] hole. (fig) Everybody returns home sooner or later. [See also *shù gāo qiān zhàng* above and *shuǐ liú qiān zāo* below.]

T

W

1 **Wǎguàn bù lí jǐng shàng pò; jiāngjūn nánmiǎn zhèn zhōng wáng.** 瓦罐不离井上破, 将军难免阵中亡。 (lit) [Just as] clay [water-carrying] jugs will [always] break not far from the well, [so] generals will die on the battlefield [sooner or later]. (fig) People who engage in dangerous occupations or activities eventually will be hurt or killed.

2 **Wài cái bù fú rén.** 外财不扶人。 Property [gained by] improper [means] won't make one rich. [See also *xiǎng shí hèngcái* below; vs. *rén wú hèngcái* above.]

3 **Wāi mùtou; zhí mùjiang.** 歪木头, 直木匠。 (lit) A crooked board [but a] straight carpenter. (fig) A board may be crooked, but a good carpenter can make use of it for various purposes. Human effort is the decisive factor.

4 **Wàirén nán guǎn jiāwù shì.*** 外人难管家务事。 Outsiders are hard put to manage the domestic problems of others. [See also *hútuzhàng hǎo suàn* and *qīngguān nán duàn* above.]

5 **Wàisheng duō sì jiù.*** 外甥多似舅。 Nephews are often like [i.e., imitate] [their] maternal uncles. [Note: *jiù* refers to both mother's older and younger brothers; see also *zhínǚ xiàng gūmā* below.]

6 **Wài(tou) yǒu (gè) zhèngqián shǒu; jiā (lǐ) yǒu (gè) jù qián dǒu.** 外(头)有(个)挣钱手, 家(里)有(个)聚钱斗。 (lit) Out(side) there's (a) hand earning money [while] (at) home there's (a) rice container saving it. (fig) The husband earns money outside and the wife saves money at home. [Rhyme; said of a frugal couple; cf. *Wǔ Sòng*, chap. 2.]

7 **Wànbān jiē shì mìng, bàndiǎn bù yóu rén.** 万般皆是命, 半点不由人。 Everything is foreordained by fate, not in the least under human control.

8 **Wànbān jiē xiàpǐn, wéiyǒu dúshū gāo.*** 万般皆下品, 惟有读书高。 All occupations are lowly; only book-learning is exalted. [Said of scholar-officials in traditional China; cf. Guan Hanqing's Yuan dynasty play, *Wàng Jiāng Tíng*, Act 1.]

9 **Wān chǐ huà bù chū zhíxiàn.** 弯尺划不出直线。 (lit) A crooked rule cannot draw a straight line. (fig) If one's basic nature is bad, one cannot do anything good.

10 **Wàn'è, yín wéishǒu; (bǎi shàn, xiào wéi xiān).** 万恶淫为首, (百善孝为先)。 (lit) [Of] all the evils, lewdness is the first; ([of the] hundred goodness, filial piety is the first). (fig) Lewdness is the worst of all sins (and filial piety is the best of all virtues). [Cf. *Jìnghuā Yuán*, chap. 10; the second part is usually omitted; see also *yǒu qí yín zhě* below.]

11 **Wáng shū jiǔ sì shī liáng péng.** 亡书久似失良朋。 To neglect [a certain] book [for a] long [time] is like losing a good friend.

12 **Wáng yáng bǔ láo, (yóu wèi wéi wǎn).** 亡羊补牢, (犹未为晚)。 (lit) [After] losing sheep, mending the fold (is still not too late). (fig) It is not too late to mend the fold, even after (some of) the sheep have been lost. "Better late than never." [The first half is often used alone as a *chengyu*: *wángyáng-bǔláo*; note: this is *not* "locking the barn after the horse has bolted"; see also *jiàn tù gù quǎn* above.]

13 **Wángzǐ fànfǎ, yǔ shùmín tóng zuì.*** 王子犯法与庶民同罪。 (lit) [If a] prince violates the law, [he must be] punished like an ordinary person. (fig) No matter who he is, anyone who violates the law must be dealt with according to the law. All men are equal under the law. [See also *rén suí wángfǎ* above.]

14 **Wàn liǎng huángjīn róngyì dé; zhīxīn yī gè yě nán qiú.** 万两黄金容易得, 知心一个也难求。 Ten thousand taels of gold are easier to come by [than] one true friend. [Cf. *DRC*, chap. 57.]

15 **Wànshì jiē cóng jí zhōng cuò.** 万事皆从急中错。 [In (doing)] all things, all mistakes come from being in a hurry. [See also *jí zhōng yǒu shī* above.]

16 **Wànshì qǐtóu nán.*** 万事起头难。 (lit) [In doing] anything the first step is the most difficult. [See also *tóu nán*, *tóu nán* and *tóu sān jiǎo* above.]

17 **Wànwù wú quán yòng.** 万物无全用。 (lit) [In] all things, there are none [which are] completely useful. (fig) Everything has limits to its uses. [Cf. *Lièzǐ: Tiān Ruì*; note: *wànwù*, "all living things; universe."]

18 **Wàn yán, wàn zhòng bùrú yī mò.** 万言万中不如一默。 (lit) Even better than ten thousand [accurate] words [which] hit [the nail on the head] every time [is] silence. (fig) "Speech is silver; silence is gold."

19 **Wànzhàng gāolóu píngdì qǐ.*** 万丈高楼平地起。 (lit) [Even] a ten-thousand *zhang* high building [has to] start from level ground [and be built up step by step]. (fig) Everything has to start from the very beginning and be built up step by step. [Note: technically one *zhàng* equals 3.33 meters, but *wànzhàng* is used as a metaphor for "lofty."]

20 **Wánzhèng hái xū měng yào yī.** 顽症还需猛药医。 (lit) Stubborn [i.e., chronic] diseases require strong medicine to cure [them]. (fig) Strong measures have to be taken to correct those who persist in wrong-doing.

21 **Wǎpiàn shàng yǒu fānshēn rì.** 瓦片尚有翻身日。 Even [roof] tiles have their day to turn over. (fig) Everybody will have a time of happiness sooner or later. "Every dog has his day."

22 **Wázi bù kū, năi bù zhàng.** 娃子不哭，奶不涨。(lit) [If the] baby does not cry, [the mother's] breasts [will] not engorge. (fig) Don't seek trouble, and you won't have any. [Cf. *Rúlín Wàishĭ*, chap. 45; when mothers hear their babies cry, lactation often automatically starts.]

23 **Wèicéng chūbīng, xiān chóu bài lù.** 未曾出兵，先筹败路。Before dispatching troops into battle, plan the route for retreat. [See also *xiān lù bài* below.]

24 **Wèicéng shuĭ lái, xiān lēi bà.** 未曾水来先垒坝。(lit) Before the floods come, build dikes first. (fig) In good times provisions should be made for bad times. "Save against a rainy day." [Cf. *Shí Gōng Àn*, chap. 147; see also *qíng gān kāi shuĭdào* above.]

25 **Wèi dào bāshíbā, bùkě xiào rén jiǎo zhì, yǎn xiā.** 未到八十八，不可笑人脚踬眼瞎。(lit) Before [you] reach the age of eighty-eight, don't laugh at those [who are] lame or blind. (fig) One should never laugh at old or disabled people or others' defects; it could happen to you. [Rhyme.]

26 **Wèi kàn lǎopo, xiān kàn Ā-jiù.** 未看老婆，先看阿舅。(lit) Before seeing [your] wife [to be], first look at [her] brother. (fig) One can judge (the character of) one's fianceé by first looking at her brother. [Cf. *Èr Kè Pāi'àn Jīngqí*, chap. 17; note: here *jiù* refers to one's future brother-in-law.]

27 **Wéi lǎo bù zūn, jiāohuài zĭsūn.** 为老不尊，教坏子孙。(lit) [If the] elders behave without respect, [it will] set a bad example for [their] descendants. (fig) If the older generation behaves badly, the younger ones will follow their bad example. [See also *shàngliáng bù zhèng* above.]

28 **Wèi liáng tārén, xiān liáng zìjĭ.** 未量他人，先量自己。Before [you begin to] judge others, first judge yourself. [See also *zhèng rén xiān zhèng jĭ* below.]

29 **Wèi lì pĭn, xiān lìzhì.** 未立品，先立志。(lit) Before [one has] established character, [one should] first establish determination. (fig) Have determination first and then you will have a good character.

30 **Wèi niú děi lí; wèi mǎ děi qí.** 喂牛得犁，喂马得骑。(lit) [If you] feed [an] ox, [it should] plow [the fields for you]; [if you] feed [a] horse, [you should be able to] ride [on it]. (fig) One should get some return on one's investment. [Rhyme.]

31 **Wèi qù cháo tiānzĭ, xiān lái yè xiànggōng.** 未去朝天子，先来谒相公。Before one can hope to see the emperor, one must first pay one's respects to the prime minister. [Said before going through one intermediary to see someone else; cf. *Jīngshì Tōngyán*, chap. 3; *Xĭngshì Yīnyuán Zhuàn*, chap. 33.]

32 **Wèi wǎn xiān tóusù; jī míng zǎo kàn tiān.** 未晚先投宿，鸡鸣早看天。Before evening, find somewhere to stay for the night, [and when the] cock crows, [get an] early start on your way [and you will have a safe journey].

33 **Wéiyŏu gǎn'ēn bìng jī hèn; wànnián qiānzǎi bù shēng chén.** 惟有感恩并积恨，万年千载不生尘。(lit) Only gratitude [and] hatred [even after] thousands of years [do] not gather dust. (fig) Gratitude and hatred do not diminish with time. [Rhyme; cf. *Lù Tiān Chĭ Xīxiāng Jì*, Act 16.]

34 **Wèn bǎi rén, tōng bǎi shì.** 问百人，通百事。(lit) Ask a hundred people, learn a hundred things. (fig) The more you ask others, the more you will learn. [See also the following entry.]

35 **Wènbiàn wàn jiā, chéng hángjiā.** 问遍万家成行家。(lit) [If you] ask ten thousand people everywhere, [you'll] become an expert. (fig) You can become an expert by asking others.

36 **Wénchóng zāo shàn dǎ, zhĭ wèi zuĭ shāngrén.** 蚊虫遭扇打，只为嘴伤人。(lit) [The reason] mosquitoes get struck [by] fans [is] just because [they] bite people with [their] mouths. (fig) Talk invites trouble. [Cf. *Xĭyáng Jì*, chap. 63.]

37 **Wén dào bǎi, yĭwèi mò jĭ ruò.** 闻道百，以为莫己若。[One who has] learned many [things] thinks [that] there is [no one] as [good as him]self. [Actually a famous quotation (*míngjù*) from *Zhuāngzĭ: Qiū Shuĭ*.]

38 **Wén de hǎokàn; jiàn de píngcháng.** 闻得好看，见得平常。(lit) [To] hear of [it, it's] beautiful, [but when you] see [it, it's] ordinary. (fig) What one hears is always far better than what the reality actually is.

39 **Wèn kè shā jī, jiǎqíng, jiǎyì.** 问客杀鸡，假情假意。Asking a guest [whether one should] kill a chicken [for dinner is] false hospitality. [Rhyme; this is also used as a *xiēhòuyǔ*.]

40 **Wénmíng bùrú jiànmiàn; jiànmiàn shèngsì wénmíng.** 闻名不如见面，见面胜似闻名。Knowing [people by] reputation is not as good as meeting [them] face to [face]; meeting [them] face [to face] is better than [just] hearing [of their] reputation. [Cf. *WM*, chap. 3; *DRC*, chap. 63.]

41 **Wén qí yán ér zhī qí rén.** 闻其言而知其人。Listen to [someone's] speech and [you shall] know that person. [See also *tīng huà tīngyīn* above.]

42 **Wén yīn, zhī niǎo; wén yán, zhī rén.** 闻音知鸟，闻言知人。[By] hearing [its] song, [you may] know [what kind of] bird [it is]; [so by] hearing [someone's] words, [you can] know [what kind of] person [(s)he] is.

43 **Wénzhāng zìgŭ wú píngjù.** 文章自古无凭据。(lit) Essays since antiquity have never had fixed standards [by which to be judged]. (fig) Critical judgments are always subjective. Just because one's writings are not recognized or praised does not necessarily mean that they're bad. [Said as (self) consolation about not having one's talent recognized, something like "you were born before your time."]

44 **Wènzhe yīshēng, biàn yŏu yào; wènzhe shī-niáng, biàn yŏu guĭ.** 问着医生便有药，问着师娘便有鬼。(lit) [If you] ask a [medical] doctor, then [you'll] get medicine; [if you] ask a shamaness, then [you'll] get ghosts. (fig) One

must ask of the right person to get the right thing. [Cf. *Hòu Xīyóu Jì*, chap. 35; note: *yǒuguǐ* is also a colloquial expression meaning "there's something fishy going on."]

45 **Wòtà zhī cè, qǐ róng tārén hānshuì?** 卧榻之侧，岂容他人鼾睡? (lit) [By the] side of [my] bed, how [can I] let other people snore? (fig) One must not let others interfere with one's self interest.

46 **Wǔbǎi nián qián shì yījiā.** 五百年前是一家。 [People of the same surname came from] the same family five hundred years ago. [This is a polite formula often said by people sharing the same surname upon first meeting; sometimes preceded by *yī bān shù shàng* below (q.v.); see also *tóngxìng shì yījiā* above.]

47 **Wú bìng, yīshēn qīng.** 无病一身轻。 [When one is] in good health, [he feels] completely carefree. [Cf. *Chū Kè Pāi'àn Jīngqí*, chap. 20.]

48 **Wù bì xiān fǔ érhòu chóng shēng.** 物必先腐而后虫生。 (lit) Things first get rotten and [only] later [do] worms appear. (fig) Disaster befalls only after (and because) something has first gone wrong inside, (so beware of small problems within). [From *Xúnzǐ: Quàn Xué*; also said as *wù fǔ shēng chóng*.]

49 **Wū bù lòu, qiáng bù dǎo.** 屋不漏，墙不倒。 (lit) [If a] house does not leak, the walls won't collapse. (fig) Failure results from negligence or mistakes. One should take preventative measures early.

50 **Wú cái, dòu lì; yǒu cái, dòuzhì.** 无才斗力，有才斗智。 [Those who] have no talent vie [with each other in physical] strength, [while those who] have talent compete in intellect. [See also *jūnzǐ dòng kǒu* above.]

51 **Wú chǒu, bù xiǎn jùn; wú jiān, bù xiǎn zhōng.** 无丑不显俊，无奸不显忠。 Without ugliness, beauty won't be seen; without treachery, loyalty won't be shown.

52 **Wú chù táo de lǎoshǔ yǎo límāo.** 无处逃的老鼠咬狸猫。 A rat with no way out [will] bite a leopard cat. [See also *tùzi huítóu* above and *zhí xiàng gǎn gǒu* below.]

53 **Wú dú, bù zhàngfu.** 无毒不丈夫。 (lit) One who is not ruthless [can]not be a great man. (fig) One cannot be a great man without being ruthless. [Cf. *Xīxiāng Jì*, Act 5, Scene 4 and *JPM*, chap. 92; *wúdúbùzhàngfu* has become a set phrase.]

54 **Wú ěr, bù diàoyú; wú mǐ, bù jiào jī.** 无饵不钓鱼，无米不叫鸡。 (lit) Without bait, [one can]not fish; without rice, [one can]not call chickens. (fig) People will not cooperate or work for you without enticements or rewards.

55 **Wú fēng bù qǐ làng; (wú gēn bù zhǎng cǎo).** 无风不起浪，(无根不长草)。 (lit) There are no waves without wind; (there is no grass without roots). (fig) There is always a reason or cause behind things. "Where there's smoke, there's fire." [See also *mù yǒu běn* and *shuǐ lái hé zhǎng* above and *yǒu fēng fāng qǐ làng* below.]

56 **Wú fēng, hán yěhǎo; wú zhài, qióng yěhǎo.** 无风，寒也好；无债，穷也好。 [Just as] without wind, cold can be endured, [so] without debt, poverty can be tolerated. [See also *lěng pà fēng* above and *wú zhài, yīshēn qīng* below.]

57 **Wú fū, bù chéngjiā.** 无妇不成家。 (lit) Without a wife, [a man] is not established. (fig) A man should be married and have a family in order to be considered truly mature and trustworthy. [Cf. *Xǐngshì Héngyán*, chap. 10; note: *chéngjiā*, (lit) "to form a family"; (colloq) "to be married."]

58 **Wù fǔ shēng chóng.** 物腐生虫。 See *wù bì xiān fǔ érhòu chóng shēng* above.

59 **Wǔgēng qǐchuáng, bǎi shì xīngwàng.** 五更起床，百事兴旺。 (S)he who would thrive, must rise at five [i.e., before dawn]. [Note *wǔgēng* refers to the last of the five two-hour time periods into which the night was traditionally divided; see also *yī yè wǔgēng* below.]

60 **Wú gōng, bù shòu lù.*** 无功不受禄。 (lit) [If one has] not [exerted any] effort, [one should] not receive a reward. (fig) [Traditionally said modestly when accepting a gift or honor, or as an excuse to decline:] "I have done nothing worthy of this honor." [See also *jūnzǐ bù chī* above and the following two entries.]

61 **Wú gōng shòu lù, fǎn shòu qí yāng.** 无功受禄，反受其殃。 [One who] receives rewards without merit will get into trouble. [Cf. *Gǔ-Jīn Xiǎoshuō*, chap. 2; note: as a chengyu: *wúgōngshòulù*, "to get an undeserved reward"; see also the preceding entry and the following entry.]

62 **Wú gōng shòu lù, qǐnshí bù ān.*** 无功受禄，寝食不安。 To receive [such a] reward without deserving [it would make one feel] guilty night [and] day. [Cf. *WM*, chap. 28; note: *qǐnshí bù'ān* is a chengyu meaning "to lose sleep and sleep from worry"; see also the preceding two entries.]

63 **Wǔguān huì shā; wénguān huì guā.** 武官会杀，文官会刮。 Military officers can kill [people and] civil officials can exploit [people, in traditional China]. [Rhyme.]

64 **Wú guān, yīshēn qīng.*** 无官一身轻。 (lit) [When one is] relieved of official duties [one feels] completely carefree. (fig) Out of office, out of danger. [See also *wú shì, yīshēn qīng* below.]

65 **Wūguī mò xiào biē; dàjiā ní lǐ xiē.** 乌龟莫笑鳖，大家泥里歇。 (lit) Turtles should not laugh at tortoises, [as] we/they both live in the mud. (fig) People of the same (bad) ilk should not criticize each other. "The pot calling the kettle black." [See also *tiě guàn mò shuō* above and *zhū mà wūyā hēi* below.]

66 **Wú huǎng, bù chéng méi.** 无谎不成媒。 (lit) Without lies, [one] cannot make a marriage match. (fig) There are no matchmakers who don't tell lies. [Cf. *Xǐngshì Héngyán*, chap. 7.]

67 **Wú huǎng, bù chéng zhuàng.** 无谎不成状。 (lit) Without lies, [one] cannot make a lawsuit. (fig) One cannot bring a lawsuit without including some falsehoods. [Cf. *Hé Diǎn*, chap. 2; note: *gàozhuàng*, "to bring a lawsuit."]

W

68 **Wú jī, bù chéng yàn.** 无鸡，不成宴。(lit) Without chicken [on the table], [a dinner can]not [be counted as a] feast. (fig) If a certain crucial element is missing, nothing can be done. [See also *wú jiǔ, bù chéng xí* below.]

69 **Wú jìn wú jì, huángjīn pū dì.** 无禁无忌，黄金铺地。(lit) [If you observe] no taboos, [you will see] gold covering the ground. (fig) Be bold and resolute and don't hesitate to grasp an opportunity whenever it comes. [Rhyme; note: *jìnjì*, "taboo."]

70 **Wú jiǔ, bù chéng xí.** 无酒不成席。(lit) Without wine, [it can]not be [reckoned a] feast. (fig) If a certain crucial element is missing, nothing can be done. [See also *wú jī, bù chéng yàn* above.]

71 **Wú liáng, bù dòngbīng.** 无粮不动兵。(lit) Never dispatch soldiers without provisions. (fig) Do not start anything until all the necessary preparations have been completed. [See also *bīngmǎ wèi dòng* and the following entry.]

72 **Wú liáng bù jù bīng.** 无粮不聚兵。(lit) Without provisions, don't enlist soldiers. (fig) Until all necessary preparations have been made, don't start. [See also the preceding entry.]

73 **Wūlǐ bù shāohuǒ, wū wài bù màoyān.** 屋里不烧火，屋外不冒烟。(lit) [If] inside the house [there is] no fire, outside the house [there will] not be smoke. (fig) There are no results without causes. "Where there's smoke there's fire."

74 **Wū lòu gèng zāo liányè yǔ;** (chuán chí yòu yù dǎtóufēng). 屋漏更遭连夜雨，(船迟又遇打头风)。(lit) A leaky house gets hit by all-night rain; a late boat meets with a head wind. (fig) "Misfortunes never come singly." [Cf. *Xǐngshì Héngyán*, chap. 1; see *fú wú shuāng zhì* and *làn chuán piān yù* and *pò chuán piān yù* above.]

75 **Wū lòu zài shàng, zhī zhī zài xià.** 屋漏在上，知之在下。(lit) [When the] house leaks above, [the ones who] know it [are those who] are underneath. (fig) If mistakes are committed by the superior, it will be known to his subordinates. [Note: *zàixià* is also a traditional term of humility used by an inferior; vs. *shàngmíng bù zhī* above.]

76 **Wú míng bù zhī; yǒumíng biàn xiǎo.** 无名不知，有名便晓。(lit) [When one is] not famous, no [one] knows [him]; [when one becomes] famous, [he] is known to all.

77 **Wù mò néng liǎng dà.** 物莫能两大。Two equally large [opposing] forces cannot coexist; (i.e., one will conquer the other). [Cf. *Zuǒ Zhuàn: Zhuāng Gōng 22 Nián*; also *Qián Hàn Yǎnyì*, chap. 44; see also *yī shān bù néng* and *yī gè shāntóu* and *yī guó bùróng*, etc. below.]

78 **Wúnéng zhě wú suǒ qiú.** 无能者无所求。(lit) Those [who] have little ability do not seek [anything]. (fig) Those who seek nothing are people of no ability or talent.

79 **Wú píng, bù bēi; wú wǎng, bù fù.** 无平不陂，无往不复。(lit) [Just as] there are no [flat] plains without slopes [i.e., ups and downs], [so] there is no "to" without a "fro." (fig) One is bound to suffer revenge if one does evil. "What goes around, comes around." [See also *yī rén yī zāo* below.]

80 **Wú qián chī jiǔ, dù rén miàn chì.** 无钱吃酒，妒人面赤。(lit) With no money to drink wine, [one is] envious of another's red face. (fig) One envies others when one can't get what one wishes for.

81 **Wú qiǎo, bù chéng shū.*** 无巧不成书。(lit) Without coincidence(s) [there would be] no story. (fig) By a happy coincidence. [This expression is commonly found in the traditional popular novels, e.g., *Xǐngshì Héngyán*, chap. 29; cf. *WM*, chap. 24; in speech, also sometimes said *méi qiǎo bù chéng huà*; see also *shì yǒu dòuqiǎo* above.]

82 **Wǔrén bùxī sǐ.** 武人不惜死。Warriors do not hesitate to die. [Cf. *Sòng Shǐ: Yuè Fēi Zhuàn*.]

83 **Wù shāng qí lèi.** 物伤其类。(lit) Creatures mourn their own ilk. (fig) Fellow creatures care about their own kind. [Cf. *DRC*, chap. 73; as a *chengyu*: *wùshāng-qílèi*; see also *tù sǐ, hú bēi* above.]

84 **Wú shì, bù dēng Sānbǎodiàn.*** 无事不登三宝殿。(lit) [If one did] not have any business, [one] would not enter the [Buddhist] temple hall. (fig) One never goes to visit someone unless one is in need of help, e.g., I wouldn't be here bothering you, except I have to ask a favor; (s)he only comes here when (s)he needs a favor, etc. [Cf. *JPM*, chap. 91; see also *lái zài huà shù* above.]

85 **Wǔshí bù zhòng shù; liùshí bù gài fáng.** 五十不种树，六十不盖房。(lit) [At age] fifty don't plant trees [and at age] sixty don't build a house. (fig) Don't wait until late in life to get started, or you will have no time to enjoy the benefits of your labors; start early in life.

86 **Wú shì, yīshēn qīng.** 无事一身轻。(lit) Without [official] tasks, [one's] life [will be] completely carefree. (fig) One can lead a carefree life if one has no official responsibilities. [See also *wú guān, yīshēn qīng* above.]

87 **Wú suǒ qiú zé wú suǒ huò.*** 无所求则无所获。(lit) Without seeking, nothing is obtained. (fig) One must exert some effort in order to get some result. [Note: *not* "nothing ventured, nothing gained," as there is no element of risk.]

88 **Wúxīn rén shuōhuà, zhǐpà yǒuxīnrén lái tīng.** 无心人说话，只怕有心人来听。The only thing a person who talks guilelessly has to worry about is being (over)heard by a listener who is sensitive on a certain topic. [Cf. *Érnǚ Yīngxióng Zhuàn*, chap. 17; see also *shuōzhě wúyì* above and *yán zhě wúxīn* below.]

89 **Wūyā bù rù fènghuáng qún.** 乌鸦不入凤凰群。(lit) Crows [can]not join a flock of phoenixes. (fig) Evil people cannot get along with good people.

90 **Wū, yào rén zhī; rén, yào liáng chēng.** 屋要人支，人要粮撑。[Just as] houses need people to erect [them], so people need food to support [their lives]. [Note: *zhīchēng*, "support; sustain."]

91 **Wūyā qǐ ǒu cǎi fèng.** 乌鸦岂偶彩凤。(lit) How can a black crow be mated to a colorful phoenix? (fig) People from different social backgrounds will not be well-matched in marriage.

92 **Wūyā zhī fēng; chóngyǐ zhī yǔ.** 乌鸦知风，虫蚁知雨。(lit) Crows [are the first to] know [the coming of the] wind, [and] ants, the rain. (fig) Those who are familiar with the environment can foresee changes in the offing. [See also *mǎyǐ lěi wō* above.]

93 **Wù yǐ lèi jù; (rén yǐ qún fēn).** 物以类聚，(人以群分)。(lit) ([Just as]) things come together according to category, ([so] people divide [into similar] groups). (fig) "Like attracts like"; "birds of a feather flock together." [The first half is used alone as a *chengyu*: *wùyǐlèijù*, meaning "like attracts like"; cf. *Xǐngshì Héngyán*, chap. 17.]

94 **Wǔyì wú jiǎ; bǎxì wú zhēn.** 武艺无假，把戏无真。(lit) [True] martial arts skills [can]not be fake[d], [just as conjuring] tricks cannot be real. (fig) If one is going to something, it must be studied well or it will be of no use.

95 **Wù yǒu qiān biàn, rén yǒu wàn biàn; ruò yào bùbiàn, huángtǔ gài miàn.** 物有千变，人有万变；若要不变，黄土盖面。(lit) Things change a thousand times [and] people ten thousand times, if [you] want no change, [wait until the] yellow earth covers [your] face. (fig) Change is inevitable in life. [Rhyme; cf. *Jǐngshì Tōngyán*, chap. 31; note: *huángtǔ*, (lit) "yellow earth," means "loess."]

96 **Wù yǒu suǒ guī; gè jìn qí yòng.** 物有所归，各尽其用。(lit) [All] things have their [proper] placement; each [should be] put to its best use. (fig) Things have their proper places, and best uses. "A place for everything and everything in its place." Let all things serve their best or proper purpose. [As set phrase: *wùjìnqíyòng*; see also *yī wù zìyǒu* below.]

97 **Wú yù, zhì zé gāng.** 无欲志则刚。(lit) [If one] has no [selfish] desires [or self-interest], [one] will be resolute. (fig) One can be free to do what is right if one is not hampered by worldly ambitions.

98 **Wú zhài, yīshēn qīng.*** 无债一身轻。(lit) [When one has] no debts, [one feels] completely carefree. (fig) One who owes nothing, bows to no one. [See also *wú fēng, hán yěhǎo* above.]

99 **Wú zhēn bù yǐn xiàn.** 无针不引线。(lit) [If] there's no needle, [one can]not draw the thread [through]. (fig) Nothing can be accomplished without someone's introduction or recommendation. [Cf. *Wǔ Sōng*, chap. 2; note: as a noun, *yǐnxiàn*, (lit) "thread drawer," refers to a "go-between."]

100 **Wú zhì zhī rén cháng lìzhì.** 无志之人常立志。(lit) A person without resolution always makes resolutions. (fig) One who is always making resolutions never carries them out.

X

1 **Xià bù shuì shí.** 夏不睡石。[In] summer, don't sleep [on] stones. [Note: It's easy to catch cold sleeping on cool stones in summer, because stone absorbs body heat very fast.]

2 **Xià chóng bù kě yǔ bīng; (jǐngwā bù kěyǐ tán tiān).** 夏虫不可语冰，(井蛙不可以谈天)。(lit) [To a] summer insect, [one] cannot speak of ice; ([to] a frog-in-a-well, [one] cannot speak of the sky). (fig) Shallow people are always narrow-minded, (so don't waste your time talking with them). [Cf. *Zhuāngzǐ: Qiū Shuǐ; Èr Kè Pāi'àn Jīngqí*, chap. 37; note: *jǐngwā* or *jǐngdǐzhīwā* refers to a person with a very limited outlook on life, and *tántiān*, (lit) "to talk [about the] sky," as an idiom means "to chat with; to engage in casual conversation"; see also *huìgǔ bù zhī* and *jǐngwā bù kěyǐ* above.]

3 **Xiàděng zhī rén, shuōle bù zuò; zhōngděng zhī rén, biān shuō biān zuò; shàngděng zhī rén, zuòle cái shuō.** 下等之人，说了不做；中等之人，边说边做；上等之人，做了才说。Lower class people talk without doing, middle class people talk while doing, [and] upper class people talk only after doing.

4 **Xià de sān dǒu cù, zuò de gū shuāngfù.** 呷得三斗醋，做得孤孀妇。[As] bitter as sipping three measures of vinegar [it is to] be a lonely widow. [Cf. *Jǐngshì Tōngyán*, chap. 35; here *dǒu* refers to a container used for measuring grain, equal to one deciliter.]

5 **Xiàhǎi fāng zhī hǎishuǐ shēn; shàng shān fāng xiǎo shān nán xíng.** 下海方知海水深，上山方晓山难行。(lit) Until [you] go into the sea, [you] won't know the sea's depth; until [you] go up a mountain, [you] won't know the hardship of climbing. (fig) One cannot truly understand something until one has experienced it oneself.

6 **Xiā māo zhuō bu zhù huó lǎoshǔ.** 瞎猫捉不住活老鼠。(lit) A blind cat won't catch a live mouse. (fig) One who does everything blindly can accomplish nothing.

7 **Xiā mǎ zì jīng.** 瞎马自惊。(lit) A blind horse [always] frightens itself. (fig) If one doesn't know how things stand, one will always have doubts and fears in taking any action.

8 **Xiàn cháng, hǎo fàng yuǎn fēngzheng.** 线长好放远风筝。(lit) [The] longer [the] string, [the] easier [it is to] fly one's] kite higher. (fig) If one takes a long-term point of view, one will obtain benefits in the long run. [See also *yào diào dà yú* below.]

9 **Xiāndān nán zhì méi liángxīn.** 仙丹难治没良心。(lit) [Even] the gods' medicine cannot cure [people] without consciences. (fig) There is no way to convert those without consciences into kind-hearted people. [Note: *xiāndān*, (lit) "immortals' pills," usually refers to a magical "elixir of life."]

10 **Xiān dào mòfáng, xiān shǐ mò.** 先到磨房，先使磨。(lit) The first to come to the mill [is] the first

to do [his] grinding. (fig) "The early bird gets the worm"; "first come, first served." [See also *xiān guò hé, xiān shī jiǎo* below.]

11 **Xiān dào wéi jūn; hòu dào wéi chén.*** 先到为君, 后到为臣。(lit) The first to arrive is the king, [and] the later to arrive are ministers. (fig) Seniority takes precedence. [See also *xiān jìnmén* below.]

12 **Xiān duàn, hòu bùduàn.** 先断后不断。[If one] first [makes a hasty] decision, later [one will have] unceasing [trouble]. [Note: this is a play on words between *pànduàn*, "to decide," and *jìxù bùduàn*, "continuing endlessly."]

13 **Xiāngchūn shù shàng yě yǒu dǎpìchóng.** 香椿树上也有打屁虫。(lit) Even in a fragrant Chinese toon tree, there are stinkbugs. (fig) Even a wonderful person has some shortcomings. [The leaves of the Chinese toon tree are an edible delicacy.]

14 **Xiāng ěr zhīxià, bì yǒu sǐ yú.** 香饵之下必有死鱼。(lit) Under tasty bait, there are bound to be dead fish. (fig) If the enticement is tempting enough, there will always be someone willing to "take the bait."

15 **Xiāngféng hébì céng xiāngshí.** 相逢何必曾相识。(lit) To meet why must [people] already know each other? (fig) One need not necessarily already have been introduced in order to meet (with) someone. Sometimes people are predestined to meet. [Used when two strangers meet; a line referring to two wandering travelers from the poem "Pípa Xíng" from the Tang dynasty poet Bai Juyi; the preceding line is *tóng shì tiānyá lúnluò rén*, so both lines together mean: "Both [of us] are wanderers at the ends of the earth; to meet each other here, why should we already have met before?" (i.e., we were predestined to meet by fate); see also *jì zài fó huì xià* above.]

16 **Xiāngféng zhījǐ huà piān cháng.** 相逢知己话偏长。When congenial friends meet, there'll be endless talk. [See also *jiǔ féng zhījǐ* above.]

17 **Xiāngféng zǒngshì Tiāngōng qiǎo.** 相逢总是天工巧。Chance meetings are always arranged by Providence. [Cf. *Jīngshì Tōngyán*, chap. 12.]

18 **Xiǎng gǔ bùyòng zhòng chuí qiāo.** 响鼓不用重锤敲。(lit) A resonant drum need not be struck with a heavy drum stick. (fig) A wise person requires no detailed explanation. "A word to the wise is sufficient." [See also *míngrén bùyòng* above.]

19 **Xiāngjiàn hǎo; tóng zhù nán.** 相见好, 同住难。(lit) [Occasionally] seeing one another is good, [but] living together is difficult. (fig) It is easier to visit people than to live with them. [See also *tóuqīn bùrú* above.]

20 **Xiāngjiàn yì dé hǎo; gòng zhù nán wéirén.** 相见易得好, 共住难为人。[People who only] meet [occasionally can] easily get along, [but when they have] to live together [under the same roof] it's hard to get along. [Note: *wéirén* "conduct oneself appropriately"; see also *qìngjia péngyou* above.]

21 **Xiāngjiāo mǎn tiānxià, zhīxīn néng jǐ rén.*** 相交满天下, 知心能几人。(lit) [Those whom one] knows casually [may] fill the world, [but] those [who truly understand one] can [only] be few [in number]. (fig) One may have acquaintances all over the world, but very few true friends. [Cf. *Rúlín Wàishǐ*, chap. 23; also said *xiāng shí mǎn*, etc.]

22 **Xiàng mǎ shī zhī shòu; xiàng shì shī zhī pín.** 相马失之瘦, 相士失之贫。(lit) In judging a horse's [ability], [one may] misjudge it [because of its] thinness; in judging a scholar['s ability], [one may] misjudge it [because he is] poor. (fig) A horse may be misjudged because it is thin, and a man because he is poor.

23 **Xiāng mà, wàng rén quàn; xiàng dǎ, wàng rén tuō.** 相骂望人劝, 相打望人拖。[When] quarreling, both [sides] hope [there'll be] someone [who will come to] exhort [them to make peace]; [when] fighting, each [side] hopes [there'll be] someone [who will come and try to] separate [them].

24 **Xiāng mà wú hǎo yán; xiāng dǎ wú hǎo quán.** 相骂无好言, 相打无好拳。In swearing at one another, there are no fine words, [and in] fighting, no light blows will be struck. [Cf. *Xǐngshì Yīnyuán Zhuàn*, chap. 87.]

25 **Xiàng mǎ yǐ yú; xiàng shì yǐ jū.** 相马以舆, 相士以居。[Just as one] judges a horse by the cart [it pulls, so some people] judge a gentleman according to [the place he] lives in. [Rhyme; compare the preceding entry.]

26 **Xiān gōng (ér) hòu sī.*** 先公(而)后私。(lit) First public [business] and [only] later private [business]. (fig) Public business first; private later. [See also *gōng ér wàng sī* above.]

27 **Xiǎng qiǎo bì cuò.** 想巧必错。[One who] resorts to trickery is bound to make mistakes.

28 **Xiàng qíng, xiàng bùliǎo lǐ.** 向情向不了理。(lit) [If one] favors friendship, [one] cannot favor reason/justice. (fig) If one practices favoritism, then one won't be able to adhere to justice. [Note: *jiāoqíng; qíngyì*, "friendship."]

29 **Xiàngshàng pāo shítou; liúxīn zìjǐ tóu.** 向上抛石头, 留心自己头。(lit) [When you] throw a stone upwards [into the sky], mind [your] own head. (fig) Those who intend to harm others will themselves be harmed.

30 **Xiǎng shí héngcái, yīshì qióng.** 想拾横财, 一世穷。[Those who] try to get rich by evil means [will] remain poor all [their] lives. [See also *wài cái bù fú rén* above; vs. *rén wú hèngcái* above.]

31 **Xiànguān bùrú xiàn guǎn.*** 县官不如现管。(lit) A county magistrate['s control over someone] is not as effective as [that of one's] immediate superior. (fig) A higher official may not have as much power as the immediate manager on the spot. [Used in both good and bad senses; see also *guān chà, lì chà* above.]

32 **Xiānguān mànmàn; yuānsǐ zhě bàn.** 其官漫漫, 冤死者半。 (lit) [If a] county magistrate is undisciplined [i.e., not supervised by his superiors], those who die unjustly [by his sentence may be as many as] half [of the cases he hears]. (fig) The great power of a local magistrate in traditional China had to be carefully monitored and exercised with a great sense of responsibility or there could be disastrous results for those who came for judgment. [Rhyme; see also *pò jiā xiànlíng* above.]

33 **Xiánguān qīng; chǒu fù zhēn; qióng chīsù; lǎo kàn jīng.** 闲官清丑妇贞, 穷吃素老看经。 (lit) Idle officials are pure, ugly women are chaste, poor [people] eat vegetarian [meals, and] old [people] read the [Buddhist] scriptures. (fig) Some people's morals and conduct are determined by their circumstances.

34 **Xiān guò hé, xiān shī jiǎo.** 先过河, 先湿脚。 (lit) [The one who is the] first to cross the river [is also the] first [to get his] feet wet. (fig) There are advantages as well as disadvantages in being ahead of others.

35 **Xiāngxià méiyǒu ní tuǐ, chénglǐ èsǐ yóuzuǐ.** 乡下没有泥腿, 城里饿死油嘴。 (lit) [If] there were no muddy legs in the countryside, the "oily-mouths" in the city [would] starve to death. (fig) Without the efforts of the peasant farmers in the rural areas, those in the cities would have no food to eat. [Rhyme; *yóuzuǐ*, (lit) "oily mouths," refers to "slick-tongued glib talkers."]

36 **Xiāngxià shīzi, xiāngxià wǔ.** 乡下狮子, 乡下舞。 (lit) Country lion dancers [will only be welcomed] in the countryside. (fig) The customs of the country won't be welcomed in the city.

37 **Xiàng yǐ chǐ fén shēn; bàng yǐ zhū pò tǐ.** 象以齿焚身; 蚌以珠破体。 (lit) Elephants [are] killed because [they have ivory] tusks; clams [have their] bodies split because [they have] pearls. (fig) One who has treasures invites robberies or attacks.

38 **Xiǎng zhì chuāng, bù néng pà wā ròu.** 想治疮不能怕挖肉。 (lit) [If one] wants to cure a boil, [one] cannot be afraid of cutting out flesh. (fig) Solving problems requires some sacrifice.

39 **Xiánhuà duōbàn jù shì huǎnghuà.** 闲话多半句是谎话。 (lit) [In] idle talk the greater part [of the] sentences are lies. (fig) Too much idle talk becomes lies, (so don't talk too much!)

40 **Xián huò zhèngshì mǎi huò rén.** 嫌货正是买货人。 [The customer who] complains [about the defects of] goods is [a serious] buyer [who wants to buy] the goods [rather than just a casual "window shopper"]. [See also *bāobiǎn shì mǎizhǔ* above.]

41 **Xiān jìnmén yī rì, yě shì dà.** 先进门一日, 也是大。 (lit) The first to enter the gate [even if only by] one day still has seniority. (fig) Seniority must be observed. [Cf. *Píng Yāo Zhuàn*, chap. 8; see *xiān dào wéi jūn* above.]

42 **Xiān lái de chī ròu; hòulái de hē tāng.** 先来的吃肉; 后来的喝汤。 (lit) [Those who] come first [will] eat meat, [while those who] come last [will only] get soup. (fig) Those who go ahead of others usually get some advantage(s). "The early bird gets the worm." [See also *xiān dào mòfáng* above.]

43 **Xiànlìng, xiànlìng; tīng qián diàoyòng.** 县令县令, 听钱调用。 (lit) County magistrates [are] controlled [by] money [in their decision-making]. (fig) Money makes the magistrate go. [Note: *diàoyòng* here means to be controlled by money or financial interest; see also *qián kě tōng shén* above.]

44 **Xiān lǜ bài; hòu lǜ shèng.** 先虑败, 后虑胜。 (lit) Consider first [what to do if you] fail, [and only] later consider [what to do if you] win. (fig) Always prepare for the worst (case). [See also *wèicéng chūbīng* above.]

45 **Xiànqián mǎi de shǒuzhǐ ròu.** 现钱买得手指肉。 (lit) [If one has] cash money, [one] can buy [any] meat [that one can] point to. (fig) "Money talks."

46 **Xiánrén duō cái, zé sǔn qí zhì; chángrén duō cái, zé yì qí guò.** 闲人多财则损其智, 常人多财则益其过。 [If a] worthy person gets rich, [it] will weaken [his] wisdom; [if an] ordinary person gets rich, [it] will increase [his] transgressions.

47 **Xiānrén nán duàn yè jià.** 仙人难断叶价。 (lit) Even gods are hard put to [fore]tell the prices of [mulberry] leaves [used to feed silkworms]. (fig) It is very difficult to predict market prices.

48 **Xiánrén (yě) yǒu máng shí.** 闲人(也)有忙时。 (Even) idle people can [sometimes] be busy. [Often said ironically.]

49 **Xián rén yì chǒu; děng rén yì jiǔ.** 嫌人易丑, 等人易久。 [Just as if one] dislikes a person, [it's] easy [to feel that (s)he is] ugly, [so, if one has to] wait for someone, [it is easy to feel that the waiting time is] long. [Rhyme; cf. *Suí Táng Yǎnyì*, chap. 7.]

50 **Xiān sǎ wōzi, hòu diàoyú.** 先撒窝子, 后钓鱼。 (lit) First scatter the bait [and] then fish. (fig) Make correct preparations before you take action.

51 **Xiánshí zhìxià, máng shí yòng.*** 闲时置下忙时用。 (lit) [When there's] leisure time, buy [things] to use when [you're] busy. [Cf. *Érnǚ Yīngxióng Zhuàn*, chap. 40; see also *yǎngbīng qiān rì* below.]

52 **Xiān shuō duàn, hòu bù luàn.** 先说断, 后不乱。 (lit) First talk about the specifics [and] later [there will be] no confusion. (fig) (It is best to) explain or discuss the plan clearly at first so as to avoid any confusion later. [Rhyme; cf. *JPM*, chap. 7; see also *xiān xiǎorén* below.]

53 **Xiān tiānxià zhī yōu ér yōu; hòu tiānxià zhī lè ér lè.*** 先天下之忧而忧, 后天下之乐而乐。 (lit) [One should] first worry about the worries of (the world) at large; [only] later [after] everyone else is happy should one [seek one's own] happiness. [Said of the scholar-gentry in traditional China; from an essay by the Song dynasty writer Fan Zhongyan entitled "Yuè Yáng Lóu Jì."]

54 **Xiān xià mǐ, xiān chī fàn.** 先下米，先吃饭。(lit) The first to put the rice on [to cook will be] the first to eat. (fig) The one who takes action first will get results first; "first in, first out." [Cf. *JPM*, chap. 84; *Érmǔ Yīngxióng Zhuàn*, chap. 34; note: there is no element of competition implied, unlike "the early bird gets the worm"; see also the following entry.]

55 **Xiān xiǎorén, hòu jūnzǐ.*** 先小人，后君子。(lit) [Be] petty at first, [and a] gentleman later. (fig) In one's dealings, one should be very clear about the terms of negotiation (or business) at first, and then more flexible later on. [Cf. *JW*, chap. 84; see also *xiān shuō duàn* above.]

56 **Xiān xiàshǒu wéi qiáng; hòu xiàshǒu zāoyāng.*** 先下手为强，后下手遭殃。The first to strike will gain [the upper hand, while the one who] delays will meet disaster. [Rhyme; cf. *JW*, chap. 81; see also *zhǐyào xiān shàng chuán* below and the preceding entry.]

57 **Xián xīn shēng qiǎo xīn.** 闲心生巧心。[A clear] calm mind produces clever ideas.

58 **Xiān xué sān nián, tiānxià qù dé; zài xué sān nián, cùn bù nán xíng.** 先学三年，天下去得；再学三年，寸步难行。(lit) [When you] first study [for] three years, [you think you've learned everything and can] go anywhere in the world; [after you've studied for] another three years, [you feel you haven't learned enough and can] hardly budge an inch. (fig) The more one learns, the more modest one will become. [Note: the *chengyu*: *cùnbù-nánxíng*, "unable to do anything"; see also *xuédào zhī xiū chù* and *xué ránhòu zhī bùzú* below.]

59 **Xiān yǒu gēngyún; hòu yǒu shōuhuò.*** 先有耕耘，后有收获。(lit) First there is plowing, [and] later there is harvesting. (fig) One must work before one can enjoy the fruits of one's labor.

60 **Xiān zhǎng de méimao, bǐ bu shàng hòu zhǎng de húzi.** 先长的眉毛，比不上后长的胡子。The eyebrows, [which started] growing first, can't compare with the beard, [which started] growing later. (fig) Youth is stronger than age. The older can't compete with the younger. [Vs. *xiān dào wéi jūn* above.]

61 **Xiān zhě nánwei zhī.** 先者难为知。(lit) Those [who go] first are hard pressed to understand. (fig) The pioneer experiences the most difficulties. [Usually used of pioneering scholars.]

62 **Xiān zuò xuésheng; hòu zuò xiānsheng.*** 先做学生，后做先生。(lit) First be a pupil [and] then be a teacher. (fig) One must learn before one can teach. [Mao Zedong paraphrased this to refer to cadres learning from the masses; see also *yào zuò xiānsheng* below.]

63 **Xiǎo bìng bù zhì, chéng dà bìng; lòu yǎn bù sāi, dà dī bēng.** 小病不治，成大病；漏眼不塞，大堤崩。A slight illness [that is] not cured [can] become a serious illness; a small hole [that is] not blocked [can] collapse a dam. [See also *xiǎo dòng bù bǔ* below.]

64 **Xiǎo bù rěn zé luàn dà móu.** 小不忍则乱大谋。(lit) [If one does] not forbear little [matters, one will create] havoc in greater plans. (fig) (Sometimes) it is wiser to put up with small insults, inconveniences, etc. for a greater good or to achieve greater benefits later on. [Cf. the Confucian Analects: *Lúnyǔ: Wèi Líng Gōng* 26; *R3K*, chap. 13.]

65 **Xiǎo chù bùkě dà suàn.** 小处不可大算。(lit) Small details may not be taken lightly. (fig) Never neglect the details (or they will pile up and cause trouble later). [Cf. *Guānchǎng Xiànxíng Jì*, chap. 47; see also the following entry.]

66 **Xiǎo dòng bù bǔ, dà dòng chīkǔ.*** 小洞不补，大洞吃苦。(lit) [If] small holes are not mended, big ones will cause suffering [later]. (fig) A little neglect may breed great mischief; "a stitch in time saves nine." [Rhyme; see also *xiēxiǎo bù bǔ* and *zhēnjiān dà de* below and the preceding entry.]

67 **Xiǎo'ér fànzuì, zuì zuò jiāzhǎng.** 小儿犯罪，罪坐家长。[When] children commit crimes, the punishment [should] rest on their parents. [Note: *liánzuò*: "to be punished for being related to or friendly with someone who has committed an offense"; vs. *jiā wú quán fàn* above and *yī rén zuò zuì* below.]

68 **Xiǎoguǐ diē Jīngāng.** 小鬼跌金刚。(lit) A minor devil [can] topple a guardian warrior [in a Buddhist temple]. (fig) The weak (can) defeat the strong; David may vanquish Goliath. [Vs. *xiǎoguǐ dòu bu guò* below.]

69 **Xiǎoguǐ dǐng bùliǎo Yánwang zhài.** 小鬼顶不了阎王债。(lit) A minor devil cannot be reckoned as a payment for the debts the King of Hell owes. (fig) The crimes of small criminals are not equal to those of their leader(s); one should punish the major criminal(s), not just the minor one(s). [Note: elsewhere, *yánwangzhài* as one word is a colloquial expresssion for a usurious loan.]

70 **Xiǎoguǐ dòu bu guò Yánwang.*** 小鬼斗不过阎王。(lit) A minor devil in Hell is no match for the King of Hell. (fig) The weak cannot overcome the strong. [See also *mín bù yù guān dòu* above and *xiǎotuǐ niú bu guò* below; vs. *xiǎoguǐ diē Jīngāng* above.]

71 **Xiǎo guò dé chéng, dà cuò bù shēng.** 小过得惩，大错不生。[If] small transgressions are punished, serious mistakes won't occur. [Rhyme.]

72 **Xiǎoháirjia kǒu méi zhēlán.*** 小孩儿家口没遮拦。(lit) Children have no covers on their mouths. (fig) Children often speak of taboo subjects without being aware of it (so don't get upset). [Cf. *Xīxiāng Jì*, Act 3, Scene 2; *DRC*, chap. 49; note: here -*jia* is a coloquial plural suffix: *xiǎoháizijia*, "children."]

73 **Xiǎo háizi de liǎn (xiàng māo liǎn), yī tiān biàn sān biàn.*** 小孩子的脸（象猫脸），一天变三变。(lit) A child's face (is like a cat's face), changing three times every day. (fig) A child's (or woman's) face or attitude is constantly changing. [Rhyme.]

X

74 **Xiǎohái zuǐ lǐ tǎo shíhuà.** 小孩嘴里讨实话。 (lit) In a child's mouth [one may] ask the truth. (fig) If you want the truth, ask a child. "Out of the mouths of babes."

75 **Xiǎo hé zhǎngshuǐ, dà hé mǎn; xiǎo hé méi shuǐ, dà hé gān.*** 小河涨水大河满，小河没水大河干。 (lit) If the water rises in small rivers, the big rivers will be full; if there's no water in small rivers, the big rivers will go dry. (fig) If the individuals are rich, the community will become rich, too; if individuals are poor, the community won't get rich. [Rhyme; see also *dà hé lǐ yǒu shuǐ* above.]

76 **Xiǎo huàn bù mǐ, chéng dà zāi.** 小患不弭，成大灾。 Small troubles [that are] not done away with [will] become great disasters. [Cf. *Hán Fèizi: Yù Lǎo.*]

77 **Xiǎo hú lǐ de shuǐ kāi de kuài.** 小壶里的水开得快。 (lit) The water in small kettles boils quickly. (fig) Small-minded people get impatient and angry easily.

78 **Xiǎo jū kě xùn; lǎo mǎ nán yù.** 小驹可驯，老马难驭。 (lit) Young colts can be trained [but] old horses can hardly be driven. (fig) It's easier to educate the young than the old. If you do not educate the young, when they are older, they will be hard to handle. [See also *shù xiǎo, fú zhí yì* above.]

79 **Xiào kǒu cháng kāi; qīngchūn cháng zài.** 笑口常开，青春常在。 [If one has one's] mouth always open in a smile, [one will] always [feel] youthful. [Rhyme; see also *xīnkuān chū shàonián* below.]

80 **Xiǎo lái, chuān xiàn; dà lái, chuān juàn.** 小来穿线，大来穿绢。 (lit) [When] young, wear cotton; [when] an adult, wear silk. (fig) If one lives a frugal life when young, (s)he will have a comfortable life when old. [Cf. *Gǔ-Jīn Xiǎoshuō*, chap. 10.]

81 **Xiǎo luàn, zhù chéng; dà luàn, zhù xiāng.** 小乱住城，大乱住乡。 [When there are] small disturbances [in society], move to the city; [when there are] great disturbances, move to the countryside.

82 **Xiǎo mǎ zhà xíng, xián lù zhǎi.** 小马乍行，嫌路窄。 (lit) A pony [when] learning to run complains that the road is too narrow. (fig) Callow youth arrogantly complain that they cannot fully bring their talents into play. [Cf. *Érnǚ Yīngxióng Zhuàn*, chap. 33.]

83 **Xiǎoqián bù qù; dàqián bù lái.** 小钱不去，大钱不来。 (lit) [If you are] unwilling to spend a few coppers, big money won't come [to you]. (fig) If you don't make small sacrifices, you won't get great benefits; "spend a penny to gain a pound." [Also said *xiǎo cái bù chū, dà cái bù lái*; note: *xiǎoqián* originally referred to a small coin from the Qing Dynasty, but is also used for a small amount of money; similarly, *dàqián*, "a big sum of money," previously referred to a larger old Chinese coin; see also *zhàn xiǎopiányi* below.]

84 **Xiǎoqì yì yíng.** 小器易盈。 (lit) Small containers are easily filled. (fig) Small-minded people easily become self-satisfied. [Cf. *Jìnghuā Yuán*, chap. 12; note: *xiǎoqì* is also used to refer to small household utensils.]

85 **Xiǎo qū bì yǒu dà shēn.** 小曲必有大伸。 [One who is willing to make] small concessions surely has great ambitions. [Cf. *Sān Guó Zhì: Shú Shū Xì Zhèng Zhuàn.*]

86 **Xiǎorén dézhì, bù kě yī shì.*** 小人得志，不可一世。 (lit) [When a] petty person gets into [a position of] power, [he considers himself] unexcelled in the world. (fig) When a petty person gets into a position of power, (s)he becomes insufferably arrogant. [Rhyme; note: both halves are used as chengyu: *xiǎorén-dézhì*, "villains hold sway"; *bùkě-yīshì*, "(to be) insufferably arrogant"; see also *yīzhāo quán zài shǒu* and the following entry.]

87 **Xiǎorén dézhì, wéi guǐ wéi yù.** 小人得志，为鬼为蜮。 [When] petty people get into [positions of] power, [they] become like devils and beasts [Note: a *yù* is a mythical undersea monster which shoots sand at people; note: *guǐyù*, "devils and monsters"; see also the preceding entry.]

88 **Xiǎorén lè wén jūnzi guò; jūnzi chǐ wèn xiǎo rén è.** 小人乐闻君子过，君子耻问小人恶。 Lowly people [are] happy to learn about great persons' faults, [but] great persons are above inquiring about lowly people's evils.

89 **Xiǎorén zhī jiāo, tián rú mì.** 小人之交甜如蜜。 (lit) Friendship between petty people is [thick and] sweet as honey. (fig) Friendship between petty people is based on material interest. [Usually preceded by *jūnzǐ zhī jiāo, dàn rú shuǐ* (q.v.); originally in *Zhuāngzǐ: Shān Mù*: ... *gān rú lǐ*, "... sweet as wine"; see also *yì dòng jūnzǐ* below.]

90 **Xiǎoshí bù jīn yā, dào lǎo méi jié shā.** 小时不禁压，到老没结煞。 (lit) [One who] when young is not subjected to discipline, when old will accomplish nothing. (fig) "Spare the rod and spoil the child." [Rhyme; cf. *Dàng Kòu Zhì*, chap. 105; note: *jīn*, "to bear; endure"; *yā*, "control."]

91 **Xiǎo shuǐ bùróng dà yú.** 小水不容大鱼。 (lit) A small river can't hold a big fish. (fig) A person of great ability in a small place has no scope for his talents. [See also *shuǐ qiǎn, yǎng bu zhù* above.]

92 **Xiǎo shù suī lǜ, bù chéng yīn.** 小树虽绿不成荫。 (lit) Young trees, although green, give no shade. (fig) Clever children cannot accomplish anything great without education.

93 **Xiǎotuǐ niǔ bu guò dàtuǐ.*** 小腿扭不过大腿。 (lit) The calf cannot twist the upper leg. (fig) The weak cannot overcome the strong. [See also *xiǎoguǐ dòu bu guò* above.]

94 **Xiǎoxīn méi dà chà.** 小心没大差。 (lit) With prudence there are no big mistakes. (fig) One can't be too careful.

95 **Xiǎoxīn tiānxià qù dé; dàdǎn cùn bù nán xíng.** 小心天下去得，大胆寸步难行。 Prudence [allows one to] go everywhere [while] boldness [makes it] difficult to take a small step forward.

[Note: *cùnbù-nánxíng* is used as a *chengyu* meaning "unable to do anything"; vs. *dàdǎn tiānxià* above.]

96 **Xiǎo yào zhì dà bìng.** 小药治大病。 Common medicines [can] cure major illnesses. [See also *piānfāng zhì dà bìng* above.]

97 **Xiào yī xiào, shí nián shào; (chóu yī chóu, báile tóu).*** 笑一笑十年少, (愁一愁白了头)。 (lit) Smile [and feel] ten years younger; (worry, [and you'll] become white haired). (fig) Smiling makes one younger; (worrying makes one age). [Rhyme; see also *nǎo yī nǎo* and *xiào kǒu cháng kāi* above.]

98 **Xiào zāng xiào zhuō, bù xiào bǔ; xiào chán xiào lǎn, bù xiào kǔ.** 笑脏笑拙不笑补, 笑馋笑懒不笑苦。 [You may] laugh at [someone's] dirtiness [and] stupidity, [but] not at his mended [clothes]; [you may] ridicule [someone's] greediness [and] laziness, [but] not his poverty. [Rhyme]

99 **Xià qiǎn shuǐ zhǐnéng zhuā yú-xiā; rù shēn tán fāng néng qín jiāolóng.** 下浅水只能抓鱼虾, 入深潭方能擒蛟龙。 (lit) Go into the shallow waters [and you] can only catch shrimp [and] fish; only if [you] go into the deep waters can [you] catch flood-dragons. (fig) The greater the efforts, the greater the rewards or achievements. [Note: *jiāolóng* refers to a mythical creature capable of invoking storms and floods.]

100 **Xiàqí bù yǔ; luò zǐ bù huǐ.** 下棋不语, 落子不悔。 (lit) [While] playing chess, [do] not talk, [and once you have] made a move, never go back on it. (fig) Think before you act; once you act, have no regrets.

101 **Xiàshān róngyì, shàng shān nán; shàng de shān lái, jǐng gèng kuān.** 下山容易, 上山难; 上得山来, 景更宽。 (lit) It's easier to go down a hill than to go up; once [you] get to the top, [you will have a] broader view. (fig) One has to exert effort to progress, but once you have succeeded, one knows more and has a broader perspective on life. [Rhyme; vs. *shàngshān róngyì* above.]

102 **Xiāyǎn jī chī hǎo mǐ.** 瞎眼鸡吃好米。 (lit) Blind chickens [can] eat fine rice. (fig) One can sometimes get more benefits because of one's misfortune.

103 **Xiāzi shàn tīng; lóngzi shàn shì.** 瞎子善听, 聋子善视。 (lit) The blind [have a] sharp [sense of] hearing, [while] the deaf [have] good vision. (fig) One's defect(s) may be compensated for by bringing into full play ones' strong points.

104 **Xié bù néng shèng zhèng.** 邪不能胜正。 (lit) Evil can never prevail over righteousness. (fig) The upright need not fear the crooked. [Cf. *Xīyáng Jì*, chap. 75; *Jǐngshì Tōngyán*, chap. 19; as a *chengyu*: *xié bù yā zhèng*.]

105 **Xié bù ràng fēn; yī bù ràng cùn.** 鞋不让分, 衣不让寸。 (lit) Shoes do not yield [a] tenth [of an] inch, [and] clothes do not yield [an] inch. (fig) One won't feel comfortable if one's shoes are just a little too small, nor will one feel comfortable if one's clothes are just a few inches too small. [Note: one Chinese *chǐ* contains ten *cùn* or "inches," each of which may be divided into ten *fēn*.]

106 **Xiē chéng de lǎnzi; lèi chéng de hànzi.** 歇成的懒子, 累成的汉子。 Resting makes [one] lazy, [while] working makes [one a] man. [Rhyme.]

107 **Xiélì shān chéng yù; tóngxīn tǔ biàn jīn.** 协力山成玉, 同心土变金。 (lit) [Many people working with] concerted effort can turn mountains into jade, [and many hearts working with] one purpose can turn earth into gold. (fig) "In unity there is strength." [See also *bùpà fēnglàng dà* and *sān rén yītiáoxīn* above and *zhòngrén yìxīn* below.]

108 **Xiě shū bùrú jiě shū rén.** 写书不如解书人。 (lit) The writer of a book is not as good as the annotator of the book. (fig) A reader (or listener) often (claims to) understand more than an author (or speaker) originally intended to mean.

109 **Xiěxiǎo bù bǔ, zhízhì chǐ wǔ.** 些小不补, 直至尺五。 (lit) [If] minute holes are not mended [in time, they will go] right on [to become as big as] five feet [in diameter]. (fig) "A stitch in time saves nine." [Rhyme; more commonly said *xiǎo dòng bù bǔ* above.]

110 **Xìfǎ rénrén huì biàn; gè yǒu qiǎomiào bùtóng.** 戏法人人会变, 各有巧妙不同。 (lit) Everyone can perform [conjuring] tricks, [but] each [one] has [his or her own] special way [which is] different. (fig) Everyone has his or her own way of doing things, (no one of which is necessarily better than any other). "There's more than one way to skin a cat." [Cf. Lu Xun's *Wěi Zìyóu Shū: Xiàndài Shī*, note: *biàn xìfǎ*, "to do conjuring tricks"; see also *gè shīfu, gè chuánshòu* above.]

111 **Xìfú, jīfú.** 惜福积福。 Treasure [your] happinesses [and you'll] accumulate happinesses. [Cf. *Gǔ-Jīn Xiǎoshuō*, chap. 10.]

112 **Xíguàn chéng zìrán.*** 习惯成自然。 What's habitually done becomes natural. [Cf. *Jìnghuá Yuán*, chap. 32; see also *shào chéng ruò tiānxìng* above.]

113 **Xíguàn zhī shǐ rú zhūsī; xíguàn zhīhòu rú shéngsuǒ.** 习惯之始如蛛丝, 习惯之后如绳索。 (lit) The beginning of a habit [is as weak] as a cobweb, [but] after [it has become a] habit, [it is as] strong] as a rope. (fig) Habits once cultivated are hard to break.

114 **Xīn ān máowū wěn.** 心安茅屋稳。 (lit) [He who has] peace of mind feels secure [even living in] a thatched cottage. (fig) One who is contented in poverty and devoted to things spiritual will always feel leisurely and carefree. [Describing scholars who did not wish to be officials; cited in the Ming dynasty author Yang Shen's *Shēng Ān Jīng Shuō*, chap. 4 and his *Yì Lín Fá Shān*, chap. 13.]

115 **Xīnbìng cónglái wú yào yī.** 心病从来无药医。 (lit) A broken heart has never been cured by medicine. (fig) "Where love's the case, the doctor's an ass." [See also the following entry.]

116 **Xīnbìng hái yòng xīn yào yī.** 心病还用心药医。 (lit) A heart's sickness [must] be treated in the heart. (fig) A wounded heart can only be healed in the mind. [Also said *xīn bìng zhòng shì xīn yào yī*, and *xīn bìng hái xū xīn yào yī*; cf. *DRC*, chap. 90; *Chū Kè Pāi'àn Jīngqí*, chap. 6; note also the *chengyu*: *xīn bìng nán yī*, "'heart sickness (is) hard to treat.'"]

117 **Xīn bìng hǎo yī; jiù bìng nán zhì.** 新病好医, 旧病难治。 (lit) A new[ly contracted] illness is easier to cure than an old [i.e., chronic] one. (fig) It is easier to solve problems as soon as they crop up.

118 **Xīn chí wú dà yú; xīn lín wú cháng mù.** 新池无大鱼, 新林无长木。 (lit) [In a] new[ly dug] pond, there are no big fish; [in a] new[ly planted] forest, there are no big trees. (fig) It takes time for things to grow and mature. [Rhyme.]

119 **Xīn chū yěmāo qiángsì hǔ.** 新出野猫强似虎。 (lit) A wild kitten is stronger than a tiger. (fig) Young people, not bound by tradition, will dare to do anything. [See also *chūshēngzhīdú* above.]

120 **Xíng bǎi lǐ zhě, bàn yú jiǔshí.** 行百里者半于九十。 (lit) [For] one who [has to] travel one hundred leagues, [having traveled] ninety [of them] is equal to [no more than] half[way, because the last part is always the most difficult]. (fig) Finishing something is always the most difficult part of any job; a thing is not done until it is completely done. [Cf. *Zhànguó Cè: Qín Cè*, Part 5; note: one *lǐ* equals one-half kilometer.]

121 **Xíngchuán, zǒumǎ, sānfēn mìng.** 行船走马, 三分命。 (lit) [In] traveling, on a boat or on horseback, [there is always at least] thirty percent danger. (fig) There is always a certain element of risk involved when traveling. [Cf. *Hé Diǎn*, chap. 3.]

122 **Xíng de chūnfēng, zhǐwàng xià yǔ.** 行得春风, 指望夏雨。 (lit) [Once the] spring breeze has come, [one can] look forward to the summer rains [coming soon]. (fig) When one has sown, one can expect to reap; when one has done something good, one can look forward to reaping some benefit. [Cf. *Jīngshì Tōngyán*, chap. 25.]

123 **Xíngdòng yǒu sānfēn cái qì.** 行动有三分财气。 [Don't just sit idle;] do *something* and you'll have [at least] a thirty percent [chance of getting] some benefit. [Cf. *JW*, chap. 68; see also *shēnshǒu sānfēn lì* above.]

124 **Xīng duō, tiānkōng liàng; rén duō, zhìhuì guǎng.** 星多天空亮, 人多智慧广。 (lit) The more stars, the brighter the sky; the more people, the greater the wisdom. (fig) "Many heads are better than one." [Rhyme; see also *sān gè chòu píjiàng* above and *yī rén jì duǎn* below.]

125 **Xìngjí diàobude yú; xīnjí chéng bu liǎo shì.** 性急钓不得鱼, 心急成不了事。 (lit) An impatient person won't catch any fish, [and] one who is hasty can accomplish nothing. (fig) Nothing can be accomplished in haste. "Haste makes waste." [See also *jí xíng wú hǎo bù* above.]

126 **Xíng kè bài zuò kè.** 行客拜坐客。 Travelers [from other places should] pay their respects to local hosts. [Cf. *Érnǚ Yīngxióng Zhuàn*, chap. 12; see also *shénxiān xiàfán* above.]

127 **Xíngshàn, dé shàn; xíng è, dé è.** 行善得善, 行恶得恶。 (lit) Do good, receive good; do evil, receive evil. (fig) Charity will have a good recompense and vice an evil recompense. [Cf. *Gǔ-Jīn Xiǎoshuō*, chap. 26; see also *hǎo yǒu hǎo bào* and *shàn yǒu shànbào* above and the following entry.]

128 **Xíngshàn, huò fú; xíng è, dé yāng.** 行善获福, 行恶得殃。 Do good, reap good; do evil, reap evil. [See also the preceding entry.]

129 **Xīnguān shàngrèn, sān bǎ huǒ.** 新官上任三把火。 (lit) A new official assuming office [sets] three fires [i.e., does something to impress his subordinates or the populace]. (fig) Someone assuming a new position deliberately makes some changes just to impress people. [This is *not* equivalent to "A new broom sweeps clean."]

130 **Xīn gū (de) mǎtǒng, sān rì xiāng.*** 新箍(的)马桶三日香。 (lit) A newly-banded nightsoil bucket [only] smells good [for] three days. (fig) New people, new jobs, or new things are usually only favored at the beginning. [Cf. *Hé Diǎn*, chap. 5; also said *xīn gài de cèsuǒ*, etc., "A newly built toilet . . ."]

131 **Xīngxing xī xīngxing; hǎohàn xī hǎohàn.*** 惺惺惜惺惺, 好汉惜好汉。 (lit) The clever cherish the clever, [and the] gallant cherish the gallant. (fig) Kindred spirits respect each other. [Cf. *WM*, chap. 2; *DRC*, chap. 87; see also *hǎohàn shí hǎohàn* above and *yīngxióng shí yīngxióng* below.]

132 **Xīngxing zhī huǒ kěyǐ liáoyuán.*** 星星之火可以燎原。 (lit) A single spark may start a prairie fire. (fig) A small incident or action can have great consequences. [This is an updated paraphrase of a sentence originally in *Shàng Shū: Pán Gēng*; it was used as the title of a famous essay by Mao Zedong, and was widely used as a political slogan during the Cultural Revolution; as a *chengyu*: *xīnghuǒ-liáoyuán*.]

133 **Xíng yào hǎo bàn; zhù yào hǎo lín.** 行要好伴, 住要好邻。 [When] traveling, find good company, [when choosing a place to] live, find good neighbors. [See also *bǎiwàn mǎi zhái* and *qiānjīn mǎi chǎn* above and *xuǎnzé fángwū* below.]

134 **Xīng yī lì, bì yǒu yī hài.*** 兴一利必有一害。 (lit) Promoting a benefit [to someone will] inevitably produce some harm [to someone else]. (fig) Everything in life is a trade-off. Everything has its costs.

135 **Xīnhuāng chuān bùliǎo zhēn.** 心慌穿不了针。 (lit) [One] can't get the thread through [the eye of a] needle in haste. (fig) One cannot do any work that requires meticulous care in haste.

136 **Xīnhūn bùrú yuǎn bié/jiù bié.*** 新婚不如远别/久别。 (lit) [Being] newly married is not as [good as reunion after a] long separation. (fig) Reunion after long separation is better than a wedding night. [Cf. *DRC*, chap. 21.]

X

137 **Xīn jiān, shí yě chuān.** 心坚石也穿。(lit) A determined heart can drill through stone. (fig) One who is determined can accomplish anything. [See also *yǒuzhìzhě* below.]

138 **Xīn jì bùrú mò jì.** 心记不如墨记。A written record is better than [trusting to] memory. [Also said *xīn jì bùrú bǐ jì*; see also *hǎo jìxing bùrú* above.]

139 **Xīn jí chībude rè zhōu.*** 心急吃不得热粥。(lit) [One who is] burning with impatience cannot eat hot rice porridge. (fig) One must have patience to accomplish anything. [See also *jǐn xíng wú hǎo bù* above.]

140 **Xīn jí, děngbude rén; xìngjí, diàobude yú.** 心急等不得人，性急钓不得鱼。[When one is] impatient, it's hard to wait for people, [just as one who is] impatient can't catch fish.

141 **Xīnjí, guō bù gǔn.*** 心急锅不滚。(lit) [When one is] impatient, the pot never [comes to a] rolling boil. (fig) "A watched pot never boils." [Also said *xīnjí, shuǐ bù kāi.*]

142 **Xīnjí, mǎ xíng chí.** 心急马行迟。[When one is] impatient, [one feels that one's] horse travels [too] slowly. [See also *mǎ chí xián biān qīng* and *sòng qīn de lù duǎn* above.]

143 **Xīnjìng, zìrán liáng.** 心静自然凉。(lit) [If one's] heart/mind is calm, [one is] naturally cool. (fig) Those who are calm will be cool (even under the most stressful conditions). It is best to remain calm. "Stay cool."

144 **Xīnkuān bù zài wū kuān.** 心宽不在屋宽。[Whether one's] mind is at ease doesn't [depend] on [whether one's] house is large [or not]. [Note the colloquial expression *xīnkuān tǐ pàng*, "[when the] mind [is] relaxed, [one's] body [gets] fat"; see also *xīn ān máowū wěn* above.]

145 **Xīnkuān chū shàonián.** 心宽出少年。(lit) An easy mind produces youth. (fig) Laugh and grow young. [See also *xiào kǒu cháng kāi* above.]

146 **Xīn lái héshang hào zhuàng zhōng.** 新来和尚好撞钟。(lit) [A] newly arrived monk loves to ring [the] bell. (fig) A newcomer likes to do more work (out of initial enthusiasm or to make a good impression).

147 **Xīn lái, wǎn dào, bù zhī máokēng jǐng zào.** 新来晚到，不知茅坑井灶。(lit) [The] latest newcomer doesn't know [where the] latrine, [the] well, [and the kitchen] stove [are]. (fig) The most recently arrived newcomer doesn't know his or her new environment or situation. [See also *zhà rù lúwéi* below.]

148 **Xīn lái xífù sān rì qín.** 新来媳妇三日勤。(lit) [A] newly married daughter-in-law [is often] diligent [in her duties for the first] three days. (fig) A new employee is often diligent at the beginning. [Cf. *Xǐngshì Yīnyuán Zhuàn*, chap. 84; see also *xīnguān shàngrèn* above and the preceding entry.]

149 **Xìnle dù, màile wū.** 信了肚，卖了屋。(lit) [If all you] believe [is your] stomach, [you'll end up having] sold [your] house. (fig) If you live an extravagant life, you'll have to sell off all your property sooner or later. [Rhyme; see also *rén kùn mài wū* above.]

150 **Xīn lǐ yǒu bìng, shétou duǎn.** 心里有病，舌头短。(lit) [If one] has a guilty conscience, [one will feel oneself to be] short-tongued. (fig) If one has a guilty conscience, it is difficult to speak out boldly. [Vs. *lǐ bù duǎn, zuǐ ruǎn* above.]

151 **Xīn píng, guò de hǎi.** 心平过得海。(lit) [If one's] heart is "level," [one] can cross the sea. (fig) One who has no ambition for wealth or power can weather all sorts of difficult times.

152 **Xīn qù, yì nán liú; liúxia, jié yuānchóu.** 心去意难留，留下结冤仇。(lit) [When one's] heart/mind is gone [elsewhere], it is difficult to hold [his] will, [and if he is forcibly] detained, [he] will bear a grudge. (fig) If someone is determined to leave, you can hardly keep him or her. [Cf. *Fēngshén Yǎnyì*, chap. 18; said, e.g., of one who wants a transfer; also said *xīn qù, rén nán liú*; see also *rén qù, bùzhōng liú* above.]

153 **Xīnrén shàngle chuáng; méirén diū guò qiáng.*** 新人上了床，媒人丢过墙。(lit) [After the] bridal couple has gone to bed, [the] matchmaker [is] thrown over the wall [i.e., ignored]. (fig) When the deal is done, the go-between who made it possible is (often) dropped. [Rhyme.]

154 **Xīn sān nián; jiù sān nián; féngféng-bǔbǔ yòu sān nián.** 新三年旧三年，缝缝补补又三年。(lit) [A suit looks] new [for] three years, old [for another] three years [and if mended it can last] three more years. (fig) Live a thrifty life. [A rhyme popular during the "Three Bad Years" in China, 1959–1962.]

155 **Xīn yǒu língxī yī diǎn tōng.*** 心有灵犀一点通。(lit) [The] hearts [of a lover and his beloved are] linked [like the] white line [which runs through the horn of the divine rhino] *língxī*. (fig) (For those whose hearts or minds are closely linked,) at just a hint, the hearer understands immediately. [This is a celebrated line from the Tang dynasty poet Li Shangyin's poem, "Wú Tí" ("Untitled").]

156 **Xīn yǒuyú, ér lì bùzú.*** 心有余而力不足。The spirit is strong but the flesh is weak. [A rhyme usually said of oneself to reluctantly deny a request for a favor; cf. *DRC*, chap. 25.]

157 **Xīn yù zhuān, záo shí chuān.** 心欲专，凿石穿。(lit) [If one's] heart's desire is concentrated, [one can] chisel through stone. (fig) A determined will can accomplish anything. [Rhyme; note: *zhuānxīn*, "to concentrate one's attention."]

158 **Xīn zhèng bùpà yǐng'r xié; jiǎo zhèng bùpà dǎo dǎo xié.*** 心正不怕影儿邪，脚正不怕倒蹈鞋。(lit) [One whose] heart is upright, is not afraid that his shadow slants; [one whose] feet are straight doesn't care about [having his] shoes reversed [i.e., on the wrong foot]. (fig) One who is correct in behavior is not afraid of gossip.

[Cf. *Érnǚ Yīngxióng Zhuàn*, chap. 26; see also *jiǎo zhèng bùpà* and *shēn zhèng, bùpà* above.]

159 **Xīn zhèng hé chóu zháo guǐ mí.** 心正何愁着鬼迷。 [If one's] heart is righteous why worry [that one will be] led astray by devils? (fig) One who has a righteous heart won't yield to temptation. [Note: *zháomí*, "led astray."]

160 **Xīn zhī guǎn zé sī.** 心之管则思。 (lit) The function of the mind is to think. [Cf. Mencius, *Mèngzǐ: Gào Zǐ Shàng*, also quoted by Mao Zedong in *Xuéxí Hé Shíjú*.]

161 **Xīn zhí, kǒu kuài, zhāo rén zéguài.** 心直口快, 招人责怪。 [A] straightforward [and] outspoken [person will be] blamed by others [i.e., not welcomed]. [Rhyme; cf. *DRC*, chap. 34; note the *chengyu: xīnzhí-kǒukuài*, "frank; outspoken."]

162 **Xiōngdì chán xì, wǔ rén bǎi lǐ.** 兄弟谗阋, 侮人百里。 (lit) Brothers [even if] quarreling [at home will join to] drive off attackers [from without one] hundred leagues away. (fig) Internal disunity dissolves at the threat of external invasion. [Rhyme; cf. *Guó Yǔ: Zhōu Yǔ, Zhōng*.]

163 **Xiōngdì rútóng shǒuzú.*** 兄弟如同手足。 Brothers [are] like hands [and] feet. [Note the *chengyu: qíngtóng-shǒuzú*, "as close as brothers," and *xiōngdì shǒuzú*, "as close as brothers."]

164 **Xiōngdì suī hé, qín suàn shù.** 兄弟虽和勤算数。 (lit) Although brothers live in harmony, accounts [between them] should be settled promptly. (fig) Even (people as close as) brothers should keep clear and careful accounts between them (to avoid trouble later on). [See also *qīnxiōngdì míng suànzhàng* above.]

165 **Xióngpí yǎn zhí; èrén mù héng.** 熊罴眼直, 恶人目横。 The brave [have] straightforward eyes; evil people [have] shifty eyes. [Note: *xióngpí*, (lit) "brown bears," here refers to the brave.]

166 **Xiōngshì bùyàn chí; jí shì bùyàn jìn.** 凶事不厌迟, 吉事不厌近。 Bad things can't happen [too] late, [and] good things can't happen [too] soon.

167 **Xí shàn, zé shàn; xí è, zé è.** 习善则善, 习恶则恶。 [If one always] imitates the good, [one will] become good; [if one always] imitates the bad, [one will] become evil.

168 **Xǐ shí duō shīyán; nù shí duō shīlǐ.** 喜时多失言, 怒时多失礼。 When happy, [it is easy to make] more indiscreet remarks, [and] when angry, to be unreasonable.

169 **Xì shuǐ cháng liú; chī-chuān bù chóu.** 细水长流, 吃穿不愁。 [A] fine [trickle of] water [will] run [for a] long [time]; [if one manages one's finances in a similar manner, one will] never worry [about] food [and] clothing. [Rhyme; *xìshuǐ-chángliú* is used as a *chengyu* meaning "to economize to avoid shortage."]

170 **Xiùcai bùchūmén, néng [/fāng] zhī tiānxià shì.*** 秀才不出门能[/方]知天下事。 [A] scholar, (even) without going outside [of his study] knows [all] the affairs of the world. [A traditional saying, praising the traditional literati; note: *xiùcai* technically refers to one who passed the imperial examination at the lowest (county) level in the

Ming and Qing dynasties; vs. *yīshēng bùchūmén* below.]

171 **Xiùcai bùpà yīshan pò, jiù pà dù lǐ méiyǒu huò.** 秀才不怕衣衫破, 就怕肚里没有货。 A scholar doesn't mind shabby clothes; all [he should] worry about is not "having the goods inside" [i.e., not being sufficiently learned]. [Rhyme.]

172 **Xiùcai èsǐ, bù mài shū.** 秀才饿死, 不卖书。 [Even if a] scholar is starving to death, [he] won't sell [his] books.

173 **Xiùcai rénqíng, zhǐ bàn zhāng.** 秀才人情纸半张。 (lit) A scholar's [expressions of] feeling [are as light as] half a sheet of paper. (fig) Scholars are not rich and can only paint pictures or do calligraphy to present as gifts. [Cf. *Xīxiāng Jì*, Act 1, Scene 2; *xiùcáirénqíng*, (lit) "scholars' feelings," is used metaphorically as a set phrase meaning gifts from scholars (scrolls, paintings, etc.) and more generally, small gifts (usually books).]

174 **Xiùcai tán shū; túhù tán zhū.** 秀才谈书, 屠户谈猪。 Scholars talk of [nothing but] books, [just as] butchers talk of [nothing but] pigs. [Rhyme.]

175 **Xiùcai yùjiàn bīng; yǒulǐ, jiǎng bù qīng.*** 秀才遇见兵, 有理讲不清。 (lit) [When] a scholar encounters a soldier, he [may] have reason [or right on his side, but] is not able to express [it]. (fig) Reason is helpless before force. [Rhyme; also said *shūsheng yùjiàn . . .*, etc.]

176 **Xiùcai zàofǎn, sān nián bùchéng.*** 秀才造反, 三年不成。 Scholars rising in rebellion [will or could] never succeed [even in] three years. [See also *bǎi wú yī yòng* above.]

177 **Xiù dà, hǎo zuò zéi.** 袖大好做贼。 (lit) [With] bigger (and longer) sleeves it's easier to commit theft. (fig) It's easier for the powerful to do evil things. [Wealthy persons and officials in traditional China had long, wide sleeves on their garments.]

178 **Xiùhuāzhēn duì dà tiě liáng; dàxiǎo gèzì yǒu yòngchǎng.** 绣花针对大铁梁, 大小各自有用场。 (lit) [Like] embroidery needles and iron beams, each is useful in its own way. (fig) Big or small, everything is useful in its own way. [Rhyme.]

179 **Xiū jiàng wǒ yǔ tóng tā yǔ; wèibì tā xīn sì wǒ xīn.** 休将我语同他语, 未必他心似我心。 (lit) [Let me] not take my words [and] pass [them] on to others whose minds [may] not necessarily be like mine. (fig) One should be careful who one talks to or confides in.

180 **Xǐ xīn, děi zhēnqíng; xǐ ěr, tú mǎi míng.** 洗心得真情, 洗耳图买名。 [In] doing away with [one's] evil desires, [one] should be sincere; [merely to pretend to] listen respectfully [to others] is a pointless [exercise in] acquiring [a (false)] reputation [for modesty]. [A rhymed line from a Tang dynasty poem by Li Bai; note the colloquial expression *xǐ'ér-gōngtīng*, "to listen respectfully."]

181 **Xuǎnzé fángwū bùrú xuǎnzhé línjū.** 选择房屋 不如选择邻居。Choosing [one's] house is not as important as choosing [one's] neighbors. [Rhyme; cf. *Zuǒ Zhuàn: Zāo Gōng 3 Nián*; see also *bǎiwàn mǎi zhái* and *qiānjīn mǎi chǎn* and *qiān qián mǎi lín* and *xíng yào hǎo bàn* above.]

182 **Xuè bǐ shuǐ nóng; (shū bù jiàn qīn).** 血比水浓, (疏不见亲)。(lit) Blood is thicker than water; (distant [relations should] not interfere [between] close relatives). (fig) Closer relatives are more important than more distant ones, (who should not come between them). [This is a combination of two separate proverbs: the second part (q.v.) may be omitted or used separately (q.v.); see also *rén qīn, gǔròu xiāng* and *shì qīn, sānfēn xiàng* above.]

183 **Xué dào lǎo, bù huì dào lǎo.** 学到老, 不会 到老。[Even if one] studies until [one is] aged, [there will still be things that one does] not know how [to do even when one is] old. [Rhyme; cf. *JPM*, chap. 10; see also *huó dào lǎo* above.]

184 **Xuédào zhī xiū chù, fāng zhī yì bù jīng.** 学到知 羞处, 方知艺不精。Only when [you have] studied to the point [where you feel] ashamed [of how little you know will you] realize [that you have] not learned enough. [See also *xiān xué sān nián* above and *xué ránhòu zhī bùzú* below.]

185 **Xué ér bù sī yóurú shí ér bù huà.** 学而不思 犹如食而不化。Learning without reflecting is like eating without digesting. [See also the following entry.]

186 **Xué ér bù sī zé wǎng; sī ér bù xué zé dài.** 学 而不思则罔, 思而不学则殆。Learning without reflecting gains nothing; thought without learning is dangerous. [From the *Wéi Zhèng* in the Confucian Analects (*Lúnyǔ*); see also the preceding entry.]

187 **Xué ér yōu zé shì.** 学而优则仕。(lit) [Those who] study and do well become officials. (fig) An official career is the natural outlet for good students [under the traditional imperial examination system]. [See also *shū zhōng zìyǒu* above.]

188 **Xuéhǎo sān nián; xué huài sān tiān.** 学好三年; 学坏三天。[It takes] three years [to] learn [to do] good, [but only] three days [to learn [to do] evil. [Rhyme.]

189 **Xuéhǎo shù-lǐ-huà, zǒubiàn tiānxià dōu bù pà.** 学好数理化, 走遍天下都不怕。[If one] studies math, physics, [or] chemistry, [one can] go anywhere without fear [of being unemployed]. [A student saying from the mid-1950s, the modern equivalent of *yī zhāo xiān, zǒubiàn tiān* (q.v.); see also *xuéhuì shù-lǐ-huà* below.]

190 **Xué huài róngyì; xuéhǎo nán.** 学坏容易; 学 好难。To learn badness is easy, [but] to learn goodness is difficult.

191 **Xuéhuì shù-lǐ-huà bùrú yǒu ge hǎo bàba.** 学会 数理化不如有个好爸爸。(lit) Having mastered mathematics, physics, and chemistry is not [worth as] much as having a good father. (fig) Even better than a good education is to have parents with useful social connections (in order to

get a good job placement). [See also *xuéhǎo shù-lǐ-huà* above.]

192 **Xuě lǐ mái bu zhù sǐrén.** 雪里埋不住死人。(lit) Snow cannot cover the dead forever. (fig) Secrets will come out sooner or later. [See also *zhǐ bāo bu zhù huǒ* above.]

193 **Xuě qián sòng tàn hǎo; yǔ hòu sòng sǎn chí.** 雪 前送炭好, 雨后送伞迟。(lit) Sending charcoal *before* it snows is good, [whereas] sending an umbrella after it rains is too late. (fig) One should help those in their time of need; it's no use giving help after the problem is over. [Note: *yǔhòusòngsǎn* is used as a colloquial expression meaning "to give belated help"; see also *jǐnshàng-tiānhuā* above and *zhǐyǒu jǐnshàng-tiānhuā* below.]

194 **Xué ránhòu zhī bùzú.** 学然后知不足。(lit) After [one has] studied [one] knows [one's learning is] not sufficient. (fig) The more one learns, the more one realizes one's own limitations. [Cf. the Confucian Lǐjì: *Xué Jì*; see also *xiān xué sān nián* and *xuédào zhī xiū chù* above.]

195 **Xué rú nìshuǐ-xíngzhōu, bù jìn zé tuì.** 学如逆 水行舟, 不进则退。Learning is like "sailing a boat against the current; not to advance is to drop back." [Note: *nìshuǐ-xíngzhōu* (q.v.) is a *chengyu* meaning "to go against the current."]

196 **Xué rú niúmáo; chéng rú lín jiǎo.** 学如牛毛, 成如麟角。[Those who] study are as [many as the number of] hairs [on an ox], [but those who] succeed are as [rare as Chinese] unicorns' horns. [Rhyme; note the *chengyu: duōrú-niúmáo*, "as numerous as the hairs on an ox" and the *chengyu: fèngmáo-línjiǎo*, "precious and rare as phoenix feathers and unicorn horns."]

197 **Xuéshí hé rú, guān diǎn shū.** 学识何如观点 书。How learned [one is can be judged by] seeing [how one] annotates [one's] books.

198 **Xuéwen qín nǎi yǒu; bù qín fù kōngxū.** 学问 勤乃有, 不勤腹空虚。Learning only comes from diligence; [if one is] not diligent, [one ends up] empty-headed [(lit) "with an empty belly"]. [Note: *mǎnfù jīnglún*, "to have one's mind filled with the Classics; be well-read," and the colloquial expression *tā dùzi lǐ yǒu xuéwen*, "(s)he has a lot of learning."]

199 **Xuéwèn, xuéwèn; yào xué, yào wèn.** 学问学 问, 要学要问。(lit) "Learn-in(g) learn-in(g)"; [if you] want to "learn," [you've] got to "in(g)"-quire. (fig) To gain knowledge, one has to study and ask questions. [A play on the word *xuéwèn*, "learning."]

200 **Xué yī bùmíng, àn dāo shārén.** 学医不明, 暗 刀杀人。(lit) [One who has] studied medicine not well, [can] kill people [just like an] assassin's knife. (fig) A quack can kill people without the victims' realizing it.

201 **Xuèzhài yào yòng xuě lái huán.** 血债要用血 来还。Blood debts must be repaid in blood. "An eye for an eye." [Often used as a political slogan.]

202 **Xuězhōng-sòngtàn, zhēn jūnzǐ; jǐnshàng-tiānhuā shì xiǎorén.** 雪中送炭，真君子；锦上添花是小人。(lit) [One who] "sends charcoal in snow[y weather" is a] true gentleman; [one who only] "adds flowers to the brocade" is a lowly person. (fig) One who provides timely help is a true gentleman, while one who only "jumps on the bandwagon" is not. [Note: *xuězhōng-sòngtàn* and *jǐnshàng-tiānhuā* are used independently as *chengyu*; see also *jǐnshàng-tiānhuā* and *xuě qián sòng tàn* above.]

203 **Xǔ rén yī wù, qiānjīn bù yí.** 许人一物，千斤不移。(lit) [Once] something is promised, a thousand catties [should] not move [it back]. (fig) Once something is promised, it should never be taken back. [Rhyme; note: literally, one *jīn* or "catty" is equal to one-half kilogram, but *qiānjīn* is figuratively taken to mean "a ton, a great weight"; note also the *chengyu: yīnuòqiānjīn*, "a solemn promise"; see also *hǎi yuè shàng kě qīng* above and *yī yǔ wéizhòng* below.]

204 **Xūxīn, xūxīn; dé yín, dé jīn.** 虚心虚心，得银得金。(lit) [Be] modest again and again [and you'll be rewarded] with silver and gold. (fig) Be modest above all else. [Rhyme.]

Y

1 **Yā chī tiánluó, jī chī gǔ; gèrén zì yǒu gèrén fú.** 鸭吃田螺，鸡吃谷；各人自有各人福。Ducks eat river snails and chickens eat grain; every individual has his own blessings. [Rhyme; see also *niú chī qīngcǎo* above.]

2 **Yámen bā zì kāi; yǒulǐ, wú qián, mò jìnlái.*** 衙门八字开，有理无钱莫进来。(lit) The *yamen* [gates] open wide [(lit) like the Chinese character for "eight"], [but if one only] has right [on one's side, but] no money, [one had best] not enter [them]. (fig) Although the gates of the county magistrate's office are theoretically open to all, without money for bribes, one had best avoid them. [Rhyme; also said: *yámen cháo nán kāi*, etc. "Magistrates' offices open [their gates] toward the south, etc."; see also *"bā" zì yámen* above.]

3 **Yámen de qián; xiàshuǐ de chuán.** 衙门的钱，下水的船。(lit) [In a traditional] magistrate's office, the money [to bribe officials flows as fast as a] boat running with the current. [Cf. *Sān Xiá Wǔ Yì*, chap. 37; see also *guān qīng, yámen shòu* above.]

4 **Yámen qián, yī péng yān; shēngyì qián, liùshí nián; zhòngtián qián, wànwàn nián.** 衙门钱一蓬烟，生意钱六十年，种田钱万万年。(lit) [Ill-gotten] money [gained in the] magistrate's court [is spent as fast as a puff of] smoke [disperses]; money [earned by doing] business [lasts] sixty years [i.e., a lifetime]; money made by farming will last a hundred million years. (fig) Easy come, easy go, but hard won lasts forever. People who work hard for their money don't waste it. [Rhyme.]

5 **Yán bì xìn; xíng bì guǒ.** 言必信，行必果。(lit) [One's] words must be credible [and one's] actions must [produce] results. (fig) One's promises must be kept and one's actions must be resolute. [Cf. the Confucian Analects: *Lúnyǔ: Zǐ Lù.*]

6 **Yǎn bùjiàn wéi jìng.*** 眼不见为净。(lit) [What the] eye does not see is clean. (fig) All is clean that you have not seen. What you don't see doesn't upset you. [Most commonly said of unclean food or conditions; see also *bùgān-bùjìng* above and the following entry.]

7 **Yǎn bùjiàn, xīn bù fán.*** 眼不见心不烦。(lit) [What one's] eye does not see, [one's] heart is not bothered [by]. (fig) What you don't see doesn't upset you. "What the eye does not see, the heart does not grieve over." [See also *ěr bù tīng* above and the preceding entry.]

8 **Yán duō le, bù xián; huà duō le, bù tián.** 盐多了不咸，话多了不甜。[Just as] too much salt won't [taste] salty, [so] too many words won't be sweet. [Rhyme.]

9 **Yán duō, shī yǔ; shí duō, shāng shēn.** 言多失语，食多伤身。Too much talk causes slips, [just as] too much food harms the health.

10 **Yàn fēi qiān lǐ, diànjìzhe lúwěi dàng.** 雁飞千里，惦记着芦苇荡。(lit) [Although they have] flown a thousand leagues [away], wild geese [are always] thinking of the reed marshes [where they came from]. (fig) Travelers always miss their home places. [Note: one *lǐ* equals one-half kilometer.]

11 **Yàn fēi qiān lǐ, kào tóuyàn.** 雁飞千里，靠头雁。(lit) Wild geese [may fly a] thousand leagues, [but they always] follow the lead(ing) goose. (fig) People must have a leader. [See also *qún yàn wú shǒu* and *shé wú tóu* above and *yáng qún zǒulù* below.]

12 **Yǎn gāo jiǎo dī rén cháng diē jiāo.** 眼高脚低人常跌跤。(lit) One [who walks with his] eyes upward [and] steps low [will] always stumble. (fig) One who is self-conceited but of little ability will always meet with setbacks, (so be modest).

13 **Yǎngbīng qiān rì; yòngbīng yīshí.*** 养兵千日，用兵一时。(lit) [One] maintains an army [for] a thousand days [in order to] use it once. (fig) One makes one's preparations well in advance against a single emergency. [Cf. *JW*, chap. 36; see also *qiān rì kǎnchái* and *xiánshí zhìxià* above.]

14 **Yǎngbīng rú yǎng hǔ.** 养病如养虎。(lit) Letting [one's] illness go [is as risky] as keeping [a] tiger. (fig) Illness not timely treated is as dangerous as raising a tiger. [Cf. *Sān Xiá Wǔ Yì*, chap. 8; note: *yǎngbīng* here means leaving one's illness untreated.]

15 **Yǎng bù jiào, fù zhī guò; jiào bù yán, shī zhī duò.** 养不教父之过，教不严师之惰。(lit) [If one] raises [children but does] not discipline [them properly, it is the] father's fault; [if the] training is not strict, [it is the] teacher's laziness. (fig) It is the responsibility of parents and teachers to educate children properly. "Spare the rod, and spoil the child." [These are the original lines are from *Sān Zì Jīng* (The Three Character Classic); note: *jiàoyǎng*, "raise, train, educate"; see also *fùxiōng shījiào* above and *yǎng zǐ bù jiào* below.]

16 **Yáng dǐng jiǎo, láng dé shí.** 羊顶角，狼得食。(lit) [When the] rams lock horns, the wolf gets fed. (fig) When people in a group fight among themselves, outsiders profit. [See also *yù bàng xiāng zhēng* below.]

17 **Yǎng ér fáng lǎo; jī gǔ fáng jī.*** 养儿防老，积谷防饥。(lit) [One] raises sons to provide against old [age], [just as one] stores up grain to provide against famine. [Cf. *Jīngshì Tōngyán*, chap. 22.]

18 **Yǎng ér fāng zhī fùmǔ ēn /fù cí.** 养儿方知父母恩/父慈。Not until [one] raises [one's own] children [does one] appreciate [one's] parents'/father's kindness. [See also *bù dāngjiā, bù zhī* above.]

19 **Yǎng ér, yǎng nǚ wàng shàng zhǎng.** 养儿养女望上长。(lit) [Parents] raise [their] sons and daughters [hoping] to rise upwards [in social position]. (fig) Parents hope their children will do even better in life than they did. [Cf. *JPM*, chap. 26; *Érnǚ Yīngxióng Zhuàn*, chap. 39.]

20 **Yánggēng suī měi, zhòng kǒu nán tiáo.** 羊羹虽美，众口难调。(lit) Although mutton broth [maybe] tasty, [it is] difficult to satisfy everybody's taste. (fig) It's hard to please everyone. [Note: *zhòngkǒu-nántiáo* is used as a set phrase meaning: "It's hard to please everyone."]

21 **Yāng hǎo, yībàn gǔ.** 秧好一半谷。(lit) Fine seedlings [are] one-half [of the] harvest. (fig) A good beginning is half the battle. "Well begun is half done."

22 **Yǎng hǔ zì yīhuàn.** 养虎自遗患。(lit) To raise a tiger [is to] bring trouble [upon] oneself [eventually]. (fig) One should consider the future consequences of one's present actions. Appeasement can bring disaster. [Cf. *Shǐ Jì: Xiàng Yǔ Běn Jì*; as a chengyu: *yǎnghǔ-yíhuàn*.]

23 **Yángmáo chū zài yáng shēn shàng.*** 羊毛出在羊身上。(lit) Sheep's wool comes from off a sheep's body. (fig) Just as sheep's wool comes out from a sheep's own body, so any benefits actually cost oneself (although they may seem to come from elsewhere). "There's no such thing as a free lunch." [Cf. *Xǐngshì Yīnyuán Zhuàn*, chap. 1.]

24 **Yáng qún chū luòtuo.** 羊群出骆驼。(lit) A camel [may] run out of a flock of sheep. (fig) Talented person(s) [may] appear out of the common crowd; one may find "a giant among dwarves." [Cf. *DRC*, chap. 88; see also *shēnshān chū jùn niǎo* above.]

25 **Yáng qún lǐ diū le, yáng qún lǐ zhǎo.** 羊群里丢了，羊群里找。(lit) [If you] lose [something] in a flock of sheep, look for it among the sheep. (fig) Look for things you've lost where you last saw them.

26 **Yáng qún zǒulù, kàn tóuyáng.** 羊群走路，看头羊。(lit) [When a] flock of sheep move, [they] watch the lead sheep. (fig) People need a leader to tell them which way to go. [See also *yàn fēi qiān lǐ* above; note: *tóuyáng*, (lit) "lead sheep"; (fig) "bellwether."]

27 **Yáng tāng zhǐ fèi bùrú fǔ dǐ chōu xīn.** 扬汤止沸不如釜底抽薪。(lit) "Scooping up the soup [and pouring it back] to stop the boiling" is not as effective as "removing the firewood from under the cauldron." (fig) A temporary solution is not as effective as removing the root cause. [Note: *yángtāng-zhǐfèi*, referring to an ineffective remedy, and *fǔdǐ-chōuxīn* "take drastic measures to deal with a situation," are both chengyu; cf. *yáng tāng zhǐ fèi mò rú qù xīn* in *Hòu Hàn Shū: Dǒng Zuò Zhuàn*, and *R3K*, chap. 3.]

28 **Yán gù xíng; xíng gù yán.** 言顾行，行顾言。[One's] words must match [one's] actions, and vice-versa.

29 **Yàn gū yī shí; yàn gū yīshì.** 燕孤一时，雁孤一世。[When a] swallow is alone [it's only for] a [short] time [because it can find another mate, but when a] wild goose is alone [it is lost for] a lifetime, [because wild geese are said to mate for life]. [This refers to the pain one suffers when one has lost one's spouse.]

30 **Yàngyàng jīngtōng, yàngyàng xīsōng.** 样样精通，样样稀松。[To] know something [of] everything [is to be] good at nothing. [Rhyme; vs. *yī shì quán zhī* below; see also *shí shì bàn tōng* above.]

31 **Yǎng zǐ bù jiào, fù zhī guò; xùn dào bù yán, shī zhī duò.*** 养子不教父之过，训道不严师之惰。[This is a variation of *yǎng bù jiào, fù zhī guò* above.]

32 **Yānhóu shēn sì hǎi.** 咽喉深似海。(lit) [One's] throat [is as] deep as the sea. (fig) If one just sits idle and eats, without working, one's entire fortune will be exhausted. If one does not work, one will soon "eat oneself out of house and home." [Cf. *Xǐngshì Héngyán*, chap. 33; see also *zuò chī shān kōng* below.]

33 **Yǎn jiàn fāng wéi shì; chuányán wèibì zhēn.** 眼见方为是，传言未必真。(lit) Only [what one's] eyes see is fact; hearsay is not necessarily true. (fig) Seeing is believing, but hearing is not reliable. [Cf. *Xǐngshì Héngyán*, chap. 7; *yǎnjiànshìshí*, "[What one's] eyes see is fact," is used as a set phrase; vs. *yǎn jiàn wèi wéi zhēn* below; see also *bǎiwén bùrú* above.]

34 **Yǎn jiàn qiān biàn bùrú shǒu guò yī biàn.** 眼见千遍不如手过一遍。(lit) [For one's] eyes to see a thousand times is not as [good as one's] hand experiencing [something] once. (fig) It is far better to do something once oneself than to see it done a thousand times. [See also *tīng qiān biàn* above.]

Y

35 **Yǎn jiàn wèi wéi zhēn.** 眼见未为真。(lit) [What one's] eyes see is not [always] true. (fig) Seeing is not always believing. [Vs. *yǎn jiàn fāng wéi shì* above.]

36 **Yán jǐn, hǎo mài; zéi jǐn, hǎo tōu.** 盐紧好卖, 贼紧好偷。[When the trading of] salt is strict[ly controlled, it's] easier to sell [because it's scarce]; [when] burglar[y is] strict[ly suppressed, it's] easier to steal [because people slacken their vigilance].

37 **Yánluówáng miànqián xū méi fànghuí de guǐ.** 阎罗王面前须没放回的鬼。(lit) No ghosts who come before the King of the Underworld can be released. (fig) Officials (in traditional China) would never return any bribes. [Cf. *WM*, chap. 21.]

38 **Yàn pà lí qún; rén pà diàoduì.** 雁怕离群, 人怕掉队。[What] worries wild geese [most is to be] separated [from the] group; [what] worries people [most is] to lag behind. [See also the following entry.]

39 **Yàn pà lí qún; rén pà gūdān.** 雁怕离群, 人怕孤单。(lit) [What] worries wild geese [most is to be] separated [from the] group, [and what] worries people [most is to be socially] alone. (fig) People fear being without friends and relatives.

40 **Yǎn qiǎo hé xū yàngzi bǐ?** 眼巧何须样子比? (lit) [A] skilled eye [has] what need [of a] model [for] comparison? (fig) A skilled person can size things up at a glance without having to investigate every detail. [See also *hángjiā shēnshen shǒu* above.]

41 **Yán qīng, xiū quàn rén; lì xiǎo, xiū lājià.** 言轻休劝人, 力小休拉架。[A person whose] words [carry] no weight [should] not [try to] exhort parties [in a quarrel, just as a] physically weak [person should] not [try to] pull fighting [parties apart].

42 **Yànquè ān zhī hónghúzhīzhì.?** 燕雀安知鸿鹄之志? (lit) How [can] swallows and sparrows understand the ambitions of wild swans? (fig) How can a common, ordinary person understand the mind of a great one? [Originally from *Hàn Shū* (31): *Chén Shèng Zhuàn*; cf. *R3K*, chap. 4; note: *hónghúzhīzhì* is a fused noun phrase metaphor for high aspirations.]

43 **Yánshī chū gāotú.** 严师出高徒。A strict teacher produces talented students. [See also *míngshī chū gāotú* above.]

44 **Yánshuāng piān dǎ kū gēn cǎo.** 严霜偏打枯根草。(lit) Severe frost is inclined to strike grass with withered roots. (fig) Disaster usually befalls the unlucky. "Misfortunes never come singly." One disaster follows another. [Cf. *Chū Kè Pāi'àn Jīngqí*, chap. 11; see also *nóng shuāng piān dǎ* above.]

45 **Yánwáng bù zài, xiǎoguǐ fāntiān.** 阎王不在, 小鬼翻天。(lit) [When the] King of the Underworld is absent, ghosts [can] overturn the heavens. (fig) "When the cat's away, the mice will play." [See also *shān zhōng wú lǎohǔ* above.]

46 **Yánwang hǎo jiàn; xiǎoguǐ nándāng.*** 阎王好见, 小鬼难当。(lit) The King of the Underworld is easy to deal with, [but] minor devils are hard to deal with. (fig) "Better to deal with the master than his servant." It's easier to go straight to the top than to deal with subordinates. [Also said . . . *xiǎoguǐ nánchán*.]

47 **Yánwangyé bù xián guǐ shòu.** 阎王爷不嫌鬼瘦。(lit) The King of the Underworld does not mind [that] ghosts are thin. (fig) Cruel rulers do not care about the poverty of the people they exploit.

48 **Yánwang yě pà pīnmìng guǐ.*** 阎王也怕拼命鬼。(lit) Even the King of the Underworld is afraid of a desperate ghost. (fig) Even the fiercest person is afraid of someone who is desperate.

49 **Yánwang zhùdìng sāngēng sǐ; duàn bù liú rén dào wǔgēng.** 阎王注定三更死, 断不留人到五更。(lit) [If the] King of the Underworld determines that [someone will] die at midnight, [one] absolutely [can]not hold off until dawn. (fig) When the Grim Reaper of Death calls, that's it. [Cf. *JW*, chap. 76; *JPM*, chap. 62; *DRC*, chap. 16; note: *zhùdìng*, "be doomed / destined"; *sāngēng* refers to one of the five two-hour periods into which the night was divided in traditional China; *sāngēng bànyè*, "in the middle of the night"; see also *sān gè wǔgēng* above.]

50 **Yányán zhě miè; lónglóng zhě jué.** 炎炎者灭, 隆隆者绝。(lit) Those who blaze [will be] extinguished, [and] those who are prosperous [will be] finished. (fig) The renowned and powerful will sooner or later come to ruin. [Rhyme; cf. *Hàn Shū: Yáng Xióng Zhuàn*; note: *mièjué*, "to extinguish."]

51 **Yǎn yì néng yǔ.** 眼亦能语。(lit) Eyes also can speak. (fig) One can often read things in other people's eyes.

52 **Yányǔ chuánqíng bùrú shǒu.** 言语传情不如手。Language, [for] conveying feelings, is not as good as hands. [Said, e.g., of music, art, and embroidery.]

53 **Yán zhě wúxīn; tīngzhě yǒuyì.** 言者无心, 听者有意。(lit) [Although] the speaker [had] no definite purpose, the listener [listened] with a definite purpose [in mind]. (fig) One should be careful about loose talk. [See also *shuōzhě wúyì* and *wúxīn rén shuōhuà* above.]

54 **Yán zhě wúzuì; wén zhě zú jiè.** 言者无罪, 闻者足戒。(lit) The speaker is guiltless, [but] the hearer should take heed. (fig) Don't blame the speaker, but rather heed what you hear. [Cf. *Shījīng (Poetry Classic): Dà Xù*; often used by Mao Zedong when speaking of accepting criticism; see also *chéngqián-bìhòu* above.]

55 **Yán zhī tài gān, qí xīn bì kǔ.** 言之太甘, 其心必苦。(lit) [One who] speaks too sweetly [in] his heart must [harbor] evil [intentions]. [Cf. *Guó Yǔ: Jìn Yǔ*.]

56 **Yànzi xián ní, kōngfèi lì; zhǎngdà máo yī, gèzì fēi.** 燕子衔泥空费力，长大毛衣各自飞。 (lit) The swallow carrying [bits of] mud in [her] beak [to build a nest is] wasting [her] effort, [for when the little swallows] grow a coat of feathers, each [will] fly [off on its] own. (fig) When raising children, remember that the day will inevitably come when they will "leave the nest" and go off to lead their own lives. [The second half is also said . . . *zhǎngdà máo gān, gèzì fēi*; see also the following entry.]

57 **Yànzi xián ní, lěi dà wō.** 燕子衔泥垒大窝。 (lit) Swallows, [by] carrying [little bits of] mud in their bills, build big nests. (fig) "Many a little makes a mickle." [See also the preceding entry.]

58 **Yào bǔ bùrú shí bǔ.*** 药补不如食补。 (lit) Medicinal supplements are not as good as good food. (fig) A healthy diet is better than any medicine.

59 **Yào bù (néng) zhì jiǎ bìng; jiǔ bù (néng) jiě zhēn chóu.** 药不(能)治假病；酒不(能)解真愁。 (lit) [Just as] medicine (can)not cure a feigned illness, [so] liquor (can)not resolve real worries. (fig) Liquor can't solve one's problems. [See also *chóu dǎo duàn shuǐ* and *jiǔ bù jiě zhēn chóu* above; vs. *yī zuì jiě qiān chóu* below.]

60 **Yào bù qīng mài; bìng bù tǎo yī.*** 药不轻卖，病不讨医。 (lit) Medicine [should] not be sold casually, nor medical advice offered without its being sought. (fig) Don't offer advice casually or lightly, or you may be sorry later. [Cf. *JW*, chap. 68.]

61 **Yào chī làn ròu, bié nǎozhe huǒtóu.** 要吃烂肉，别恼着火头。 (lit) [If you] want to eat well-done meat, don't anger the cook. (fig) Never offend anyone from whom you might someday need a favor. [Cf. *Xǐngshì Yīnyuán Zhuàn*, chap. 81; note: *huǒtóu* is a colloquial term for a cook.]

62 **Yào dǎ dāngmiàn gǔ; mò qiāo bèihòu luó.** 要打当面鼓，莫敲背后锣。 (lit) Beat the drum in front of [people's] faces; never beat the gong behind [people's] backs. (fig) Say what you think to others' faces; never speak about others behind their backs. [Note: *dǎ dāngmiàn gǔ* may be used alone as a colloquial expression meaning "to say something to someone's face."]

63 **Yào dǎ, kàn niáng miàn.** 要打，看娘面。 [Never] hit [a child until you first] think about [its] mother's reactions. [Cf. *JPM*, chap. 78; note: *qíngmiàn*, "feelings"; see also *dǎ gǒu zhīqián* above.]

64 **Yào dé fù, xiǎn shàng zuò.** 要得富，险上做。 [If you] want to get riches, [you have to] take some risk. [Cf. *JPM*, chap. 14; see also *kǎn bù dǎo dà shù* above.]

65 **Yào dé shì hélǐ, ná rén bǐ zìjǐ.** 要得事合理，拿人比自己。 [If one] wants to be fair [in doing] things, [one should] place oneself in the other person['s position]. [Rhyme.]

66 **Yào diào dà yú, xū fàng cháng xiàn.*** 要钓大鱼，须放长线。 (lit) [If you] want to catch big fish, [you] must let out a long line. (fig) If one wishes to make a big profit, one must invest more capital, effort or risk. [See also *xiàn cháng, hǎo fàng* above and note the colloquial *suyu* expression: *fàng cháng xiàn, diào dà yǔ*, (lit) "letting out a long line to catch a big fish"; (fig) "investing more in the hopes of a greater gain."]

67 **Yào guò ǎi mén, jiù děi wānyāo.** 要过矮门，就得弯腰。 (lit) [If one] wants to get through a low door, [one] has to bend [at the] waist. (fig) One has to make compromises in order to get along in life. [See also *(jì) zài ǎi yán xià* above.]

68 **Yāo jiān yǒu huò, bù chóu qióng.** 腰间有货，不愁穷。 (lit) [If one] has goods about [one's] person, [one is] not afraid of being poor. (fig) If one has some property at hand, one need have no financial worries.

69 **Yào kǔ zhìbìng; tián yán wù rén.** 药苦治病，甜言误人。 (lit) Bitter medicine cures illnesses, [but] sweet words mislead people. (fig) Frank advice may be a "bitter pill" to swallow, but it is often more valuable than what one wants to hear. [See also *liángyào kǔkǒu* above.]

70 **Yào lóng, yào hǔ, bùrú yào tǔ.** 要龙要虎，不如要土。 (lit) Wanting dragons or tigers is not as good as wanting land. (fig) Owning land is most important [in traditional China]. [Rhyme.]

71 **Yào nuǎn, cūbù yī; yào hǎo, zìxiǎo qī.** 要暖粗布衣，要好自小妻。 [If you] seek warmth, clothes [made of] coarse cloth [are best]; [if you] want [a] good [one], take a wife [you've known] since childhood. [Note the *chengyu*: *qīngméi-zhúmǎ*, "male and female childhood playmates."]

72 **Yào pò Dōng Wú bīng, hái děi Dōng Wú rén.** 要破东吴兵，还得东吴人。 (lit) [If you] want to smash the army of [the kingdom of] Eastern Wu, [you] have to [use] people from that kingdom. (fig) If you want to get things done, seek an insider's help. "Set a thief to catch a thief." [The kingdom of Eastern Wu was one of the three contending states in the Six Dynasties period, portrayed in *R3K*; see also *yuán yàoshi kāi yuán suǒ* below.]

73 **Yàoqiú shēnghuó jì, nán xī liǎnpí xiū.** 要求生活计，难惜脸皮羞。 [If one] wants to make a living, [one can] hardly be concerned about the shame of losing face. [Cf. *Xǐngshì Héngyán*, chap. 37.]

74 **Yǎo rén gǒu bù lòu chǐ.** 咬人狗不露齿。 (lit) A biting dog does not show its teeth. (fig) A vicious person doesn't reveal his true nature. [See also *chī rén de* and *ègǒu yǎo rén* above.]

75 **Yào rén zhī, zhòng qínxué; pà rén zhī, shì mò zuò.** 要人知重勤学，怕人知事莫做。 [If you] want to be [well] known, be diligent in studying; [if you] don't want to be known, never do anything bad. [Cf. *Jǐngshì Tōngyán*, chap. 33; *JPM*, chap. 12; *Wǔ Sōng*, chap. 2; see also *ruò yào rén bù zhī* above.]

76 **Yào xiǎng chī mì, bùpà fēng dīng.** 要想吃蜜，不怕蜂叮。 (lit) [If one] wants to eat honey, [one can]not be afraid of bee stings. (fig) "No pain, no gain." [See also *yào xiǎng zhāi méigui* below and the following entry.]

77 **Yào xiǎng chī yú, jiù bù néng pà xīng.*** 要想吃鱼，就不能怕腥。 (lit) [If one] wants to eat fish, then [one] cannot be put off by [its] stink. (fig) If one wishes to attain some benefit, one must put up with some inconvenience or risk.

78 **Yào xiǎng guò hé, xiān dāqiáo.** 要想过河，先搭桥。 (lit) [If you] want to cross the river, first build a bridge. (fig) If you want to succeed, you must first make adequate preparations or connections. [Note: *dāqiáo*, (lit) "to build a bridge," can also mean "to act as a go-between."]

79 **Yào xiǎng zhāi méigui, jiù děi bùpà cì.** 要想摘玫瑰，就得不怕刺。 [If one] wants to pick roses, [one] should not be afraid of thorns. [See also *yào xiǎng chī mì* above.]

80 **Yào xué tiānxià qí nánzi; xū lì rénjiān wèi yǒugōng.** 要学天下奇男子，须立人间未有功。 (lit) [If one] wants to learn to be a distinguished man, [one] must accomplish [something which has] never [been done] before in the world. (fig) If you want to be famous, "build a better mouse trap, and the world will beat a path to your door."

81 **Yáoyán tuǐ duǎn; lǐkuī zuǐ duǎn.** 谣言腿短，理亏嘴短。 (lit) Rumors [have] short legs; unreasonableness [has a] short mouth. (fig) Rumors won't spread far and unreasonable behavior can't be justified.

82 **Yáoyáo zhě yì zhé; jiǎojiǎo zhě yì wū.** 嶢嶢者易折，皎皎者易污。 (lit) Things tall [and] pointed [are] easily broken; things glistening white [are] easily soiled. (fig) Upright and honest people are easily slandered and attacked. [See also *jié guǒ de shù* and *rén pà chūmíng* and *shù dà zhāofēng* above.]

83 **Yào yī bù sǐ bìng; sǐ bìng wú yào yī.** 药医不死病，死病无药医。 Medicine [can] cure [one who is] not mortally ill, [but for one who is] mortally ill, there is no medicine [to cure]. [See also *yīshēng yī bìng* below.]

84 **Yào zhī cháo zhōng shì, cūnyě wèn xiǎo mín.** 要知朝中事，村野问小民。 (lit) [If you] want to know [how] things [are going] at the emperor's court, [go and] ask the common people [in the] rural villages. (fig) Public opinion is a good gauge of the political situation in a country.

85 **Yào zhī hé shēnqiǎn, xū wèn guò hé rén.** 要知河深浅，须问过河人。 (lit) [If you] want to know the depth of the river, best ask someone who has crossed through it. (fig) He knows the water best who has waded through it. Seek the advice of experienced people. [See also *bù zhī shuǐ shēnqiǎn* above and *yào zhī shān xià lù* below.]

86 **Yào zhī shān xià lù, xū wèn guòláirén.** 要知山下路，须问过来人。 (lit) [If you] want to know [about the] road at the foot of the mountain, [you] should ask one who has traveled it. (fig) If you want to learn about something, ask someone who has experienced it. [Cf. *JW*, chap. 21; *Wǔ Sōng*, chap. 25; see also *yào zhī hé shēnqiǎn* above; note: *guòláirén*, "someone who has had a particular experience."]

87 **Yào zhī xīnfùshì, dàn tīng kǒu zhōng yán.*** 要知心腹事，但听口中言。 (lit) [If you] want to know what [is in someone's] heart, just listen to the words in [his] mouth. (fig) "Words are the mirror of the mind." [Cf. *Xīngshì Héngyán*, chap. 13; note: *xīnfùshì*, "secret(s) deep in someone's heart"; vs. *kàn rén, kàn xīn* and *luó-gǔ tīng yīn* above.]

88 **Yào zuò hǎorén, xū xún hǎo yǒu.** 要做好人，须寻好友。 [If you] want to be a good person, [you] must seek good [people as] friends. [See also *bù zhī qí rén* above.]

89 **Yào zuò xiānsheng, bìxū xiān zuò xuésheng.** 要做先生，必须先做学生。 [If you] want to be a teacher, [you] must first be a student. [See also *xiān zuò xuésheng* above.]

90 **Yè bù guān mén, qióng zhuàngdǎn.** 夜不关门，穷壮胆。 (lit) [At] night not shutting the door [is] poor [(people's)] courage. (fig) Poor people do not shut their doors at night because they have nothing to lose.

91 **Yè cháng, mèng duō.*** 夜长梦多。 (lit) The longer the night, the more dreams [one has]. (fig) Long delays cause many hitches. The longer one delays, the more problems one will have. [Cf. *Érnǚ Yīngxióng Zhuàn*, chap. 23; this is also used as a *chéngyǔ*; see also *luó-gǔ chánglè* and *rì cháng, shì duō* above.]

92 **Yèfàn shǎo jìn kǒu, huó dào jiǔshíjiǔ.** 夜饭少进口，活到九十九。 (lit) Put less in [your] mouth for supper [and you will] live to [age] ninety-nine. (fig) Don't eat too much food in the evening and you'll live longer. [See also *zǎofàn chī de bǎo* below.]

93 **Yěhuǒ shāo bùjìn; chūnfēng chuī yòu shēng.*** 野火烧不尽，春风吹又生。 [Even] a prairie fire [can]not completely destroy the grass; [when the] spring breeze blows, [it] grows again. [A line from a Tang dynasty poem by Bai Juyi, entitled "Fù Dé Gǔ Yuán Cǎo Sòng Bié," also used to describe the indomitable revolutionary spirit of communism.]

94 **Yèmāozi bù hēitiān, bù jìn zhái; huángshǔláng bù shēnyè, bù diāo jī.** 夜猫子不黑天不进宅，黄鼠狼不深夜不叼鸡。 (lit) An owl, unless it's night, never enters a house, [and] a weasel, until the dark of night, never steals chickens. (fig) Evil doers wait for an opportune time to commit their evil deeds.

95 **Yěróng huì yín; màn cáng huìdào.** 冶容诲淫，漫藏诲盗。 (lit) A seductive appearance invites lust, [just as] carelessly stored [treasure] invites theft. [Said of women; compare *Proverbs* 11:32, "As a jewel of gold in a swine's snout, so is a fair woman which is without discretion."]

96　**Yèxíng, mò tà bái.** 夜行莫踏白。[When] walking at night, never step onto [anything] white [or you might either fall into the water or bump into a stone]. [A piece of literal advice.]

97　**Yèxíng qiān lǐ, nánmiǎn shījiǎo.** 夜行千里，难免失脚。(lit) [If one] walks a thousand leagues at night, [it's] hard to avoid stumbling. (fig) If one engages in a certain activity for a long time, sooner or later one will inevitably make some mistakes.

98　**Yé yǒu, niáng yǒu, yě yào kāikǒu.** 爷有，娘有，也要开口。(lit) [Even if your own] father and mother have [what you want], [you] still have to open [your] mouth [to ask for it]. (fig) If you need something, it's better to own it yourself. "(Mama may have, Papa may have, but) God bless the child that's got his own." [Rhyme.]

99　**Yībàn rénqíng, yībàn lǐwù.** 一半人情，一半礼物。(lit) [To get things done in life], half [depends on one's] relationships [with other people, and] half [on giving] gifts. (fig) Both gifts and connections are necessary to get things done. [Cf. *Rúlín Wàishǐ*, chap. 50.]

100　**(Yī bān shù shàng liǎng bān huā,) wǔbǎi nián qián shì yījiā.** (一般树上两般花，)五百年前是一家。([Like] two flowers grown from one tree,) [people of the same surname came from] the same family five hundred years ago. [This rhymed couplet is a polite formula often said by people sharing the same surname upon first meeting; the first half is usually omitted; see also *tóngxìng shì yījiā* above.]

101　**Yī bào huán yī bào.*** 一报还一报。(lit) Every deed will be repaid in kind. (fig) Good is returned for good, and evil for evil. No one can escape retribution. [Cf. *DRC*, chap. 19; see also *shàn yǒu shànbào* above.]

102　**Yī bǎ yàoshi kāi yī bǎ suǒ.*** 一把钥匙开一把锁。(lit) Different locks [must be] opened with different keys. (fig) Each problem or person should be dealt with by using a different method.

103　**Yī bēi zài shǒu, wànshì quán diū.** 一杯在手，万事全丢。[With] a cup of wine in hand, all one's troubles vanish. [Rhyme; see also *jiǔ xiāo bǎi chóu* above and *yī zhǎn néng xiāo* and *yī zuì jiě qiān chóu* below.]

104　**(Yī bīng bù néng chéng jiàng;) dú mù bù néng chéng lín.** (一兵不能成将，)独木不能成林。(lit) (A single soldier does not make a general, [just as]) a single tree does not make a forest. (fig) One person alone cannot accomplish anything of any great significance. [The second part is commonly used alone; see also *yī gēn zhúzi* below.]

105　**Yī, bu dǔ lì; er, bù dǔ shí.** 一不赌力，二不赌食。(lit) Never bet on [your physical] strength, nor on [how much you can] eat. (fig) Never overexert yourself or harm your health.

106　**Yī bù gǎn bu shàng; bù bù gǎn bu shàng.** 一步赶不上，步步赶不上。Miss one step, [you will] always be one step behind.

107　**Yī bù gǎn bu shàng, bù bù dǎ jí huāng.** 一步赶不上，步步打急慌。Once [one] lags (even) one step behind, every step taken [will be] hurried.

108　**Yī, bù jī cái; èr, bù jīyuàn; shuì yě ānrán; zǒu yě fāngbiàn.** 一不积财，二不积怨；睡也安然，走也方便。[If one] accumulates neither wealth nor rancor, [one can] sleep soundly [and go] anywhere one likes without difficulty. [Cf. the Ming dynasty work by Lü Kun, *Xù Xiǎo Ér Yǔ*.]

109　**Yī bù niù zhòng.** 一不拗众。One cannot change the minds of the many. One has to conform with the group. [Cf. *Érnǚ Yīngxióng Zhuàn*, chap. 23; see *sān bù niù liù* and *sì bù niù liù* above.]

110　**Yī bù sān shì; bù fú qí yào.** 医不三世，不服其药。(lit) Doctors can't [hand down their skill for] three [successive] generations; [so] don't take their [(i.e., third generation doctors')] prescriptions for] medicine. (fig) Be careful in choosing a doctor. [Note: *fúyào*, "to take medicine."]

111　**Yī bù wèi wěn, xiū kuà èr bù.** 一步未稳，休跨二步。Don't take your second step until you're sure of the first.

112　**Yī bù yà shēn.** 艺不压身。A skill is never a burden. (fig) The more skills one has, the better. [See also *rén duō yì jì* above and *yī zhāo xiān* below.]

113　**Yī bù zǒu cuò; bùbù zǒu cuò.*** 一步走错，步步走错。[Take] one wrong step [and you will] walk in the wrong direction [forever]. [Cf. Cao Yu's modern play *Léi Yǔ* (Thunderstorm), act 3; see also *yī shì chà* below.]

114　**Yī, bù zuò; èr, bù xiū.** 一不做，二不休。(lit) Do not do [it in the] first [place], [and] second, do not stop. (fig) Once some [bad] thing has been started, carry it through to the end; "in for a penny, in for a pound." [Said by desperate doers; see also *yī chútou yě shì* below.]

115　**Yī cài nán hé bǎi rén wèi.** 一菜难合百人味。(lit) A single dish cannot satisfy the tastes of a hundred people. (fig) One person cannot satisfy everyone. [See also *yī rén nán chèn* above.]

116　**Yī chǎng guānsi, yī chǎng huǒ; rèn nǐ hǎohàn méi chù duǒ.** 一场官司一场火，任你好汉没处躲。(lit) A lawsuit [is like a] fire; even a hero can't withstand either. (fig) No matter how good one is, one will be as bankrupted by a lawsuit as by a natural disaster. [Rhyme.]

117　**Yī cháo tiānzǐ, yī cháo chén.*** 一朝天子一朝臣。(lit) Every new sovereign [brings in] his own ministers. (fig) A new leader brings in new aides. [Cf. Tang Xiansu's *Mǔdān Tíng*.]

118　**Yī chén bù shì èr zhǔ.** 一臣不事二主。(lit) A minister cannot serve two masters. (fig) "A man cannot serve two masters." [See also *zhōngchén bù shì* below.]

119　**Yī chútou yě shì dòngtǔ; liǎng chútou yě shì dòngtǔ.** 一锄头也是动土，两锄头也是动土。(lit) [Whether] hoeing one [row] or two, it still disturbs the earth. (fig) Once you start, go all out. "Hanged for a sheep, hanged for a lamb." [Usually said of some bad undertaking; see also *yī, bù zuò; èr, bù xiū,* above.]

120 **Yī cùn guāngyīn, yī cùn jīn; (cùn jīn nán mǎi cùn guāngyīn).*** 一寸光阴一寸金,（寸金难买寸光阴）。An inch of time [is an] inch of gold; (an inch of gold cannot buy an inch of time). [Rhyme; cf. *Xīyáng Jì*, chap. 11; see also *bù guì chǐ zhī bì* above.]

121 **Yīdài bùrú yīdài.** 一代不如一代。Each generation is worse than the last.

122 **Yī dǎ sānfēn dī.** 一打三分低。(lit) One blow lowers [the striker] three grades. (fig) Raising one's fist automatically puts one in the wrong. [Cf. *JW*, chap. 3; see also *jūnzǐ dòng kǒu* above.]

123 **Yī dēng lóngmén, shēnjià shíbèi.** 一登龙门, 身价十倍。(lit) Once a fish climbs over the Dragon Gate, its value increases ten fold. (fig) Once one has become an official, one's prestige increases ten fold. [Note: *dēng lóngmén*, (lit) "jumping over the dragon gate," referred to passing the imperial examinations and becoming an official in traditional China.] ·

124 **Yī dòng bùrú yī jìng.** 一动不如一静。(lit) Moving isn't as good as standing pat. (fig) Better be safe than stir. [Said when questioning the necessity of a move; cf. *DRC*, chap. 57.]

125 **Yì dòng jūnzǐ; lì dòng xiǎorén.** 义动君子, 利动小人。A gentleman is moved by humanity and justice, [while] a petty person is motivated only by self-interest. [See also *jūnzǐ yù yú yì* and *jūnzǐ huái xíng* above.]

126 **Yī dǒu mǐ yǎng gè ēnrén; yī dàn mǐ yǎng gè chóurén.** 一斗米养个恩人, 一石米养个仇人。(lit) A peck of grain wins [one] a friend; a bushel of grain makes [one] a foe. (fig) Carrying one's kindness too far invites trouble. [Cf. *Rǔ Lín Wài Shǐ*, chap. 22; both *dǒu* and *dàn* are Chinese units of dry measure for grain; one *dàn* (= one hectoliter) is equal to ten *dǒu* (= one deciliter).]

127 **Yī fēn gēngyún, yī fēn shōu huò.** 一分耕耘, 一分收获。(lit) [For every] one [per]cent [of] plowing/weeding, [one will get] one [per]cent of harvest. (fig) How much one reaps depends on how much one cultivates. The more effort you make, the better results you'll obtain.

128 **Yī fēn hángqíng, yī fēn huò.** 一分行情一分货。(lit) [For every] one cent of market price, [one gets] one cent['s worth of] goods. (fig) The higher the market price, the better the goods. [Cf. the Qing dynasty novel, *Èrshí Nián Mùdǔ Zhī Guài Xiànzhuàng*, chap. 75; also said *yī fēn qián, yī fēn huò*.]

129 **Yī fēn jiàqian, yī fēn huò.** 一分价钱, 一分货。(lit) [For every] one penny [of] price, [you get] one cent['s worth of] goods. (fig) "You get what you pay for." [See also *guì de bù guì* and *hǎo wù bù jiàn* above.]

130 **Yī fēn qián mǎi yī fēn qíng.*** 一分钱买一分情。(lit) One penny [more] buys one [more] penny['s worth of] friendship. (fig) The better the gift you offer, the better the response you get. [Usually referring to bribery.]

131 **Yīfēn zuìjiǔ; shífēn zuì dé.** 一分醉酒, 十分醉德。Drinking a little is tipsiness; drinking ten times [more] inebriates [one's] virtue. [Cf. *Gǔ-Jīn Xiǎoshuō*, chap. 17.]

132 **Yī fū dāngguān, wàn fū mò kāi.*** 一夫当关, 万夫莫开。(lit) [With] one man guarding [a mountain] pass, ten thousand men cannot break through. (fig) If one occupies a strategically superior position, it will be difficult for others to attack. [A line from the Tang dynasty poet Li Bai's poem, "Shǔ Dào Nán."]

133 **Yī fù dúyào, yī fù jiě yào.** 一付毒药, 一付解药。(lit) [Where there is] a dose of poison, [there is] an antidote. (fig) Different problems must be dealt with by different means.

134 **Yīfu shì xīn de hǎo; péngyou shì jiù de hǎo.** 衣服是新的好; 朋友是旧的好。(lit) [As for] clothes, new ones are better; [(but) as for] friends, old ones are better. (fig) Old friends are better. [See also *rén wéi qiú jiù*; *wù wéi qiú xīn* above.]

135 **Yī fú yà bǎi huò.** 一福压百祸。One instance of good luck will drive away a hundred of ill luck. [Cf. *JPM*, chap. 72.]

136 **Yī gāo, rén dǎndà.*** 艺高人胆大。[When one's] skill is high, one is bold [i.e., not afraid to show it].

137 **Yī gè bāzhang pāibuxiǎng.*** 一个巴掌拍不响。(lit) One hand alone cannot clap. (fig) It takes two to make a quarrel. [Cf. *DRC*, chap. 58; see also *yī zhī wǎn* below.]

138 **Yī gè cáo shàng shuān bù xià liǎng jiàolǘ.** 一个槽上拴不下俩叫驴。(lit) Two [braying] donkeys cannot be tied to the same trough. (fig) Two powerful people cannot coexist in the same place. "When Greek meets Greek, then comes the tug of war." [See also *wù mò néng* above and *yī gè shāntóu* below.]

139 **Yī gè fùnǚ, yī miàn luó; sān gè fùnǚ, bàn tái xì.*** 一个妇女一面锣, 三个妇女半台戏。(lit) One woman [sounds like] a gong, [while] three women [can stage] half [a Chinese] opera. (fig) Women chatter loudly when they get together. [Traditional Chinese operas are accompanied by gongs and cymbals.]

140 **Yī gè gèzao dǐngbuqǐ bèiwō.** 一个虼蚤顶不起被窝。(lit) A flea is incapable of propping up a bed quilt. (fig) One person [acting] alone is incapable of great things. [See also *yī gēn mùtou* and *yī gēn zhúzi* below.]

141 **Yī gè háma, sì liǎng lì.** 一个蛤蟆四两力。(lit) [Even] a toad [has] four ounces of strength. (fig) One may be insignificant, but (s)he can accomplish something. [See also *kùn lóng yì yǒu* above.]

142 **Yī gè jiāngjūn, yī gè lìng; yī gè héshang, yī běn jīng.** 一个将军一个令, 一个和尚一本经。(lit) A new general [issues] new orders [and] a new monk [chants] new scriptures. (fig) Each person has his or her own way of doing things. [Rhyme; see *yī gè shīfu* below.]

143 **Yī gè líba (yào dǎ) sān gè zhuāng; yī gè hǎohàn (yào yǒu) sān gè bāng.*** 一个篱笆(要打)三个桩，一个好汉(要有)三个帮。 (lit) [Just as] a fence needs the support of three stakes, [so] one able fellow needs the help of three others. [A rhyme often used by Mao Zedong, e.g., in his *Lectures to the All China Congress of the Chinese Communist party;* usually abbreviated as *yī gè hǎo hàn, sānge bāng,* etc.; see also *mǔdan suī hǎo* above.]

144 **Yī gēn kuàizi juē de duàn; yī bǎ kuàizi juē bù duàn.** 一根筷子撅得断，一把筷子撅不断。 (lit) One chopstick can [easily] be broken, [but] a bundle of chopsticks cannot. (fig) In unity there is strength. [Based on a popular folk tale about a dying man's instructions to his sons; see also the following entry.]

145 **Yī gēn mùtou zhī bùliǎo tiān.** 一根木头支不了天。 (lit) One single log cannot prop up the sky. (fig) One person alone cannot accomplish anything important. [See also *yī gè gèzao* above and the following entry.]

146 **Yī gēn zhúzi bù chéng pái.** 一根竹子不成排。 (lit) One bamboo does not make a raft. (fig) One person alone cannot accomplish anything. [See also *yī bīng bù néng* above and the preceding entry.]

147 **Yī gè péngyǒu, yī tiáo lù; yī gè yuānjia, yī dǔ qiáng.** 一个朋友一条路，一个冤家一堵墙。 (lit) [Making] a friend [opens up] one [more] avenue [for you, while making] an enemy [builds] a wall [blocking your way]. (fig) One should make friends, not enemies.

148 **Yī gè rén shì sǐ de; liǎng gè rén shì huó de.** 一个人是死的，两个人是活的。 (lit) One person alone is [like a] dead [person, while] two [together] are alive. (fig) Two persons united are more powerful than two people separated. [Cf. *Yuè Fēi Zhuàn,* chap. 74.]

149 **Yī gè shāntóu, yī zhī hǔ.** 一个山头，一只虎。 (lit) One mountain [allows only] one tiger. (fig) Only one powerful leader can exist in each place. [Cf. *Suí Táng Yǎnyì,* chap. 12; see also *yī shān bù néng* below.]

150 **Yī gè shīfu, yī gè chuánshòu.** 一个师傅，一个传授。 (lit) Each master has his [unique] way of teaching. (fig) Everyone has his or her own way of doing things. [See also *yī gè jiāngjūn* above.]

151 **Yī gè xiānglú, yī gè qìng; yī gè rén, yī gè xìng.** 一个香炉一个磬，一个人一个性。 [Just as] an incense burner [differs from] an inverted bell [in shape, so] each person [has] his own personality. [Rhyme; an inverted bell is a Buddhist percussion instrument.]

152 **Yī gè xiǎo jī bù hǎo, dài huài yī lóng.** 一个小鸡不好，带坏一笼。 (lit) One bad chicken spoils the whole coop. (fig) "One rotten apple spoils the whole barrel." [See also *yī kuài chòu ròu* below.]

153 **Yī gè zhuāng bù néng kòu liǎng gè niú.** 一个桩不能扣两个牛。 (lit) [You] can't tie two oxen [onto] one stake. (fig) Rivals can't co-exist in one place. [See also *yī guó bùróng* below.]

154 **Yī guì, yī jiàn, jiāoqing nǎi jiàn.** 一贵一贱，交情乃见。 [When] one [person becomes] rich [and the other] one [becomes] poor, then [their] friendship [will be] tested. [Cf. *Jīngshì Tōngyán,* chap. 17.]

155 **Yī guó bùróng èr zhǔ.** 一国不容二主。 One kingdom does not permit two rulers. [Cf. *R3K,* chap. 60; see also *tiān wú èr rì* above and *yī shān bù néng* below.]

156 **Yī hào téngzi jiē yī hào guā.** 一号藤子结一号瓜。 (lit) [As] the vine, [so] the melon. (fig) Each plant yields its own kind of fruit. Like begets like. "Like father, like son."

157 **Yī huā dú fàng, bù shì chūn.** 一花独放，不是春。 (lit) A single flower blooming does not make a spring. (fig) One instance doesn't make a rule. "One sparrow does not make a spring."

158 **Yī jiā bǎonuǎn, qiān jiā yuàn.** 一家饱暖，千家怨。 One better-off family [is] envied [by a] thousand others. [Cf. *Èr Kè Pāi'àn Jīngqí,* chap. 15; note: *bǎonuǎn,* "amply fed and clothed."]

159 **Yī jiā bù zhī yī jiā; (héshang bù zhī Dàojiā).** 一家不知一家，(和尚不知道家)。 (lit) One family knows nothing of [the troubles of] another, ([just as Buddhist] monks know nothing about Taoists). [Rhyme; see also the following entry.]

160 **Yī jiā bù zhī yī jiā kǔ.** 一家不知一家苦。 One family doesn't know the difficulties an[other] family [has]. [See also *jiājiā dōu yǒu* above and the preceding entry.]

161 **Yī jiā fù nán gù sān jiā qióng.** 一家富难顾三家穷。 (lit) One rich family [would be] hard put to support three poor families. (fig) There are limits to one's resources or to what one (family) can do.

162 **Yī jiàng gōng chéng wàn gǔ kū.** 一将功成万骨枯。 (lit) A general builds his success on ten thousand bleaching bones. (fig) It's the blood of the rank and file that wins a general's promotion. "What millions died that Caesar might be great."

163 **Yí jiāng shèng yǒng zhuī qióngkòu.** 宜将剩勇追穷寇。 (lit) [One] should [use one's] remaining strength to pursue a hard-pressed enemy. (fig) Once the tide has turned and the enemy has started to retreat, one should rally one's forces and continue to pursue them to destruction. [This is a line from Mao Zedong's *qīlǜ* style poem "Rénmín Jiěfàngjūn Zhànlǐng Nánjīng" ("The Peoples Liberation Army Occupies Nanjing"), which contradicts the traditional strategy of *not* pursuing a defeated enemy (*qióngkòu mò zhuī*) expressed in Sūnzǐ's *Bīngfǎ (The Art of War);* see also *guī shī wù yǎn* above.]

164 **Yī jiàng wú móu, lèisǐ qiān jūn.** 一将无谋，累死千军。 If a general is unresourceful, a thousand soldiers will suffer and die. [Said of any leader; see also *bīng hútu yī gè* above.]

165 **Yī jiā qì qiáng, liǎng jiā yòng.** 一家砌墙，两家用。 (lit) [If] one family builds a wall, both families use [it]. (fig) One party's action can benefit two parties. [See also *yīmiàn dǎ qiáng* above.]

Y

166 Yī jiā rén bù shuō liǎng jiā huà. 一家人不说两家话。 (lit) People of one family [or group should] not speak [as though they were] from different families [or groups]. (fig) People in the same family or group should stand united as one. [Cf. the colloquial *suyu* expression: yī jiā wú èr, "one family should have no divisions"; see also yī zhāng chuáng shàng above.]

167 Yī jiā tóngxīn, fèntǔ chéng jīn. 一家同心，粪土成金。 (lit) [When] a family is of the same mind, dung may be turned into gold. (fig) When all members of a family are of one mind, all things are possible. [This rhyme is an exhortation to family unity; see also sān rén yītiáoxīn above.]

168 Yī jiā yǒu nǚ, bǎijiā qiú. 一家有女百家求。 A family with a [marriageable] daughter [will be] sought out by a hundred others.

169 Yī jiā yǒushì, bǎijiā máng. 一家有事，百家忙。 [When] something [good or bad] happens [in] one household, a hundred families [i.e., their neighbors] [will] be busy helping [them; e.g., a marriage celebration].

170 Yī jiā yǒu yī zhǔ. 一家有一主。 Each family has a head, [to whom you must talk if you hope to solve any problem]. [Cf. the *píngshū* story Wǔ Sōng, chap. 5.]

171 Yǐ jǐ zhī xīn, dù rén zhī xīn. 以己之心，度人之心。 (lit) Take [your] own heart [as the] measure of [other] people['s] hearts. (fig) Do unto others only what you would have them do unto you.

172 Yī jùn zhē bǎi chǒu.* 一俊遮百丑。 (lit) One good (or beautiful) point overshadows many defects and deficiencies. (fig) For one merit, a hundred shortcomings may be overlooked.

173 Yī jù yànyǔ, qiān céng yì. 一句谚语，千层意。 One proverb [has a] thousand levels of meaning.

174 Yī kè bù fán èr zhǔ. 一客不烦二主。 (lit) A guest should not trouble two hosts. (fig) One should not impose on two patrons at the same time. [Cf. JW, chap. 3.]

175 Yīkǒu bù néng chā liǎng chí. 一口不能插两匙。 (lit) One mouth cannot hold two spoons. (fig) One cannot do many things at the same time. [See also yīshēn zuòbude below.]

176 Yīkǒu chī bù chéng gè pàngzi.* 一口吃不成个胖子。 (lit) One cannot become fat on one mouthful. (fig) Nothing can be accomplished in one single effort; a person doesn't get to be a certain way overnight; it takes time. [Also said bù néng yīkǒu chī gè pàngzi: see also pàngzi bù shì above.]

177 Yī kuài chòu ròu huàile yī guō tāng.* 一块臭肉坏了一锅汤。 (lit) One piece of stinking pork spoils the whole pot of broth. (fig) One bad person can spoil the whole affair. "One rotten apple can spoil a whole barrel." [See also yī gè xiǎo jī above and yī tiáo yú mǎn below.]

178 Yī láng mùyáng, hé néng chángjiǔ? 以狼牧羊，何能长久？ (lit) If you let a wolf look after the sheep, how can [they] last long? (fig) One should not trust an evil person in doing anything; don't "set a fox to guard a hen house."

179 Yī liǎng jīnzi; sì liǎng fú. 一两金子，四两福。 (lit) One ounce [of] gold [requires] four ounces [of] blessings [so that it can be kept and enjoyed]. (fig) One who has wealth must also have blessings in order to be able to enjoy it. Without good fate, all the money in the world is useless. "Money can't buy happiness."

180 Yī liǎng sī néng dé jǐ shí luò [/lè]. 一两丝能得几时络/乐。 (lit) One ounce [of] silk cannot be spun out [into a long thread]. (fig) Pleasure cannot last forever. [Cf. Guó Shǐ Yí Zuǎn, quoted in Tài Píng Guǎng Jì, vol. 188; in literary Chinese, luò, "thread," is a loose pun on lè, "happiness"; liǎng is a Chinese unit of weight now equal to 50 grams.]

181 Yī liǎo, bǎi dàng. 一了百当。 [One who is capable of] completing one [thing is capable of] handling many [things]. [Cf. Xǐngshì Héngyán, chap. 16; note: tuǒdàng, "properly done."]

182 Yī liǎo, bǎi liǎo.* 一了百了。 (lit) [When the] one [thing] ends, [then] everything ends. (fig) Death ends all one's troubles. All one's worries end when one dies. [Cf. Érnǚ Yīngxióng Zhuàn, chap. 19; as a chengyu: yīliǎo-bǎiliǎo.]

183 Yī lǐ tōng [/jīng], bǎi lǐ tōng. 一理通[/精]，百理通。 [By knowing] one theory completely, [you will] know all others [by analogy]. [Note the chengyu: chùlèi-pángtōng, "to comprehend by analogy."]

184 Yǐ lì xiāngjiāo, lì jìn ér shū. 以利相交，利尽而疏。 A friendship [which is] based [only] on benefits [will become more] distant [when the] benefits run out. [Cf. Jǐngshì Tōngyán, chap. 32.]

185 Yìlǐ zhī yǒng bùkě wú; xuèqì zhī yǒng bùkě yǒu. 义理之勇不可无；血气之勇不可有。 One should have the boldness to argue for justice, not [simply] the vigor to show off [one's] strength.

186 Yī lóng, jiǔ zhǒng; zhǒngzhǒng gèbié. 一龙九种，种种各别。 (lit) One dragon [may have] nine offspring, each one different. (fig) One family may produce both good and bad children. [Cf. DRC, chap. 9.]

187 Yī lóng, sānfēn chī. 一聋，三分痴。 Once [one becomes (partially)] deaf, [one becomes] thirty percent [mentally] slower.

188 Yī mǎ bù kuà shuāng ān. 一马不跨双鞍。 (lit) A horse wears no more than one saddle. (fig) A woman should be betrothed or married twice. [Cf. Xīxiāng Jì, vol. 5. sec. 3; also Yuán Shǐ: Liè Nǚ Zhuàn; see also yī nǚ bù chī below.]

189 Yī mǎ bù xíng, bǎi mǎ yōu. 一马不行，百马忧。 (lit) [When] a horse halts, [a] hundred [will] worry. (fig) One person's action can influence an entire group or situation. [See also yī mǎ yǒu bìng below.]

190 Yī mài bùhé, zhōushēn bùshì. 一脉不和，周身不适。 (lit) [If] one artery (or vein) is in disharmony, [one's] entire body [feels] unwell. (fig) When one part goes wrong, the whole situation will be affected.

191 **Yī máng yǐn zhòng máng, xiāng jiāng rù shuǐ-kēng.** 一盲引众盲，相将入水坑。(lit) [If] one blind [person] leads a crowd [of] blind [people], all will [fall] into [a] pit. (fig) "If the blind lead the blind, both shall fall into the ditch."

192 **Yī mǎ yǒu bìng, bǎi mǎ yōu.** 一马有病，百马忧。(lit) [If] one horse falls ill, [a] hundred [will] be worried. (fig) One person's actions can influence a whole group or situation. [See also *yī mǎ bù xíng* above.]

193 **Yī mén bù dào, yī mén hēi.** 一门不到一门黑。(lit) [If one has] not entered a trade, [one is completely in the] dark [about] that trade. (fig) A person in one trade is completely in the dark about the tricks of others. [See also *géháng rú géshān* above.]

194 **Yīmiàn dǎ qiáng, liǎngmiàn guāng.** 一面打墙，两面光。(lit) A wall built by one side benefits both sides. (fig) One party's act can benefit both parties. [Cf. the Qing dynasty writer Wang Zhuang's *Wú Yàn Shī Chāo*; note: *liǎngmiànguāng* as an idiom also refers to a person who always pleases both sides/parties; see also *yī jiǎ qì qiáng* below.]

195 **Yī míng héshang tiāo shuǐ chī; liǎng míng héshang tái shuǐ chī; sān míng héshang méi shuǐ chī.*** 一名和尚挑水吃，两名和尚抬水吃，三名和尚没水吃。(lit) A single monk brings his own bucket of water to consume, two monks carry their bucket of water jointly, [but when there are] three monks, there is no water to consume at all. (fig) "Everybody's business is nobody's business." [Cf. Lu Xun's essay in *Lǔ Xùn Shū Xìn Jí*: "Zhì Cǎo Jù Rén"; now more commonly said *yī gè héshang*, etc.]

196 **Yī mòrú xīn; rén mò rúgù.** 衣莫如新，人莫如故。[With] clothes, [there is] nothing better than new [ones]; [with] people, there is nothing [better] than old [friends]. [Cf. *Yànzǐ Chūnqiū: Nèi Piān Zá Shàng*; see also *yī shì xīn de hǎo* below.]

197 **Yīn dì hǎo bùrú xīndì hǎo.** 阴地好不如心地好。(lit) Having a good gravesite is not as good as a good character. (fig) It is better to have a good moral nature while one is alive than to have an auspicious location for one's grave after one is dead. [Note: In traditional China, choosing an auspicious gravesite according to the principles of *fēngshuǐ* or geomancy was believed to bring blessings to the living descendants of the deceased.]

198 **Yǐ néng cè shuǐ; mǎ kě shí tú.** 蚁能测水，马可识途。(lit) Ants can foretell rainfall, [and] horses know the way [(back)]. (fig) Only experienced people can solve problems. [See also *lǎo mǎ shí tú* above.]

199 **Yīn fēng chuī huǒ; yòng lì bù duō.** 因风吹火，用力不多。(lit) [If you] blow [on a] fire *with* the wind, [you] won't [have to] exert much effort. (fig) Do things in accordance with (their) nature. It is best to go with the current. [A rhymed suggestion; cf. *Jǐngshì Tōngyán*, chap. 28.]

200 **Yīng lì rú shuì; hǔ xíng shì bìng.** 鹰立如睡，虎行似病。(lit) [An] eagle standing [looks] like [it's] sleeping, [and a] tiger walking looks like [it's] sick. (fig) Sometimes the strong appear weak. Do not be deceived by appearances.

201 **Yīngxióng chū shàonián.** 英雄出少年。Heroes come from the young.

202 **Yīngxióng suǒ jiàn lüètóng.*** 英雄所见略同。(lit) All great men's views are alike. (fig) "(All) great minds think alike." [Usually said humorously to one who holds views similar to one's own; cf. *Hé Diǎn*, chap. 2; *Érnǚ Yīngxióng Zhuàn*, chap. 16.]

203 **Yīngxióng xī yīngxióng.*** 英雄惜英雄。(lit) Heroes cherish heroes. (fig) Great people can sympathize with and respect the feelings of others of their kind. [See also *xīngxing xī xīngxing* above.]

204 **Yīngxióng zào shíshì.*** 英雄造时势。(lit) Heroes create situations. (fig) Great men decide the course of history. [Cf. Liang Qichao's *Zìyóu Shū*; vs. *shíshì zào yīngxióng* above.]

205 **Yīngxióng shí yīngxióng.*** 英雄识英雄。(lit) Heroes recognize heroes. (fig) "Like knows like." [See also *hǎohàn shí hǎohàn* and *xīngxing xī xīngxing* above.]

206 **Yī niáng shēng jiǔ zǐ, jiǔ zǐ lián niáng shí tiáo xīn.*** 一娘生九子，九子连娘十条心。(lit) [If] a woman bears nine sons, the children plus their mother [altogether are] of ten minds. (fig) No matter how closely they are related, every individual in a group has his or her own way of thinking.

207 **Yī nián shù gǔ; shí nián shù mù.** 一年树谷，十年树木。(lit) [It takes] one year to plant [and harvest] grain, [and] ten years to plant [and grow a] tree. (fig) (1) It takes time, effort, and patience to reap benefits. (2) Different life situations require different long and short term planning. [Rhyme; cf. *Guǎnzi: Quán Xiū*; see also *shí nián shù mù* above.]

208 **Yī niàn zhī chā, zhōngshēn zhī lèi.** 一念之差，终身之累。One wrong decision [can] trouble [one's] entire life. [See *niàntóu*, "idea"; note: *yīniànzhīchā* is used as an idiom meaning "a momentary slip with serious consequences."]

209 **Yī nián zhī jì zàiyú chūn.*** 一年之计在于春。(lit) The [whole] year's work depends on [a good start in] spring. (fig) Success depends on a good beginning. "Well begun is half-done." [See also the following entry.]

210 **Yī nián zhī jì zàiyú chūn; yī rì zhī jì zàiyú chén.** 一年之计在于春，一日之计在于晨。(lit) Make your whole year's plan in spring, [and] your day's plans early in the morning. (fig) Spring is the best season to do the year's work, and morning is the best time to do the day's work. [See also *zǎoqǐ sān zhāo* below and the preceding entry.]

211 **Yǐn jí nán yī.** 隐疾难医。(lit) [If you] hide [the true symptoms of your] illness [from the doctor, he will be] hard [put to] cure [you]. (fig) It's hard to correct one's mistakes if one tries to cover them up.

Y

212 **Yǐnshuǐ bù wàng jué jǐng rén.*** 饮水不忘掘井
人。 (lit) [When you] drink water, don't forget
the people who dug the well. (fig) One should not
forget one's past benefactors or supporters, nor
those who produce the food one eats. [Quoted by
Zhou Enlai in reference to those who made possible the resumption of diplomatic relations with
Japan; see also the following entry.]

213 **Yǐnshuǐ sī yuán;*** (yuán mù sī běn). 饮水思
源, (缘木思本)。 (lit) [When] drinking water,
think of [its] source; ([when] climbing a tree, think
of [its] root). (fig) One should not forget one's
origins or past benefactors. [Cf. *Érnǚ Yīngxióng
Zhuàn*, chap. 13; the first half originally a line
from a poem by Sou Xin of the Northern Zhou dynasty, is used as an idiom *yǐnshuǐ-sīyuán*, meaning
"never forget one's origins"; see also the preceding entry.]

214 **Yī nǚ bù chī liǎng jiā chá.** 一女不吃两家茶。
(lit) A girl cannot drink the tea of two families.
(fig) A girl cannot accept betrothal presents from
two families. A woman cannot be betrothed to
two men. [Cf. *Xǐng Shì Héng Yán*, chap. 5; note:
chá lǐ, "betrothal presents"; also *yī mǎ bú kuà*
above.]

215 **Yī nǚ huò chǒng, quánjiā fùguì.** 一女获宠, 全
家富贵。 [When] one girl becomes a favorite
[imperial concubine], [then her] whole family
[naturally becomes] wealthy [and] rises in status.
[Said, e.g., of the daughter Yuan Chun in *DRC*;
see also *yī rén dé dào* and *yī zǐ guìyī* below.]

216 **Yīngxióng nánguò měirén guān.*** 英雄难过美
人关。 (lit) [A] hero is hard put to get through a
pass [controlled by a female] beauty. (fig) (Even)
strong men have difficulty dealing with beautiful
women. "Beauty tames the beast"; "Samson and
Delilah."

217 **Yīnyáng bù kěxìn, xìn le yī dù mēn.** 阴阳不可
信, 信了一肚闷。 Fortunetelling is not to be
believed; if [you] do, [you'll always have] a belly-
ful of worries. [Note: here *yīnyáng*, (lit) "yin [and]
yang," refers to the predictions of fortunetellers;
note also the colloquial expression *xìn yīnyáng*,
"to believe in fortunetellers"; see also *ruò xìn bù*
above.]

218 **Yīnyuán běn shì qiánshēng dìng; bù xǔ jīn ɪén
zuò zhǔzhāng.** 姻缘本是前生定, 不许今
人作主张。 The happy fate that brings lovers
together was originally decided in a previous life
[i.e., predestined, [and is] not decided by people now on earth. [Cf. *Xǐngshì Héngyán*, chap. 27;
note: *yīnyuán* and *yuánfèn*, are Buddhist terms
meaning the lot or luck by which people are
brought together; *qiánshēng* is a Buddhist term
for a previous existence; see also *gèrén yǒu gèrén*
above and *yǒuyuán qiān lǐ* below and the following entry.]

219 **Yīnyuán, wǔbǎi nián qián dìng.** 姻缘五百年前
定。 (lit) The fate which brings marriage partners
together [was] predestined five hundred years
ago. (fig) "A marriage made in Heaven." [Note:
yīnyuán; "the destiny that brings lovers together";
see also the following entry.]

220 **Yīnyuán, yīnyuán; shì fēi ǒurán.** 姻缘姻缘, 事
非偶然。 The fate which brings marriage partners together is not [a matter of] chance. [See
also *qiān lǐ yīnyuán* below and the preceding entry.]

221 **Yī píngzi bù xiǎng; bàn píngzi huàngdang.** 一
瓶子不响, 半瓶子晃荡。 (lit) A [full] bottle
makes no sound [and a] half [full] bottle makes
the most sound. (fig) The dabbler chatters away,
while the wise remain silent. One who knows
least boasts most. "Empty vessels make the greatest sound." [Rhyme; a line from a Tang dynasty
poem by Cao Song entitled "Jǐ Hài Suì."]

222 **Yī qián bù luò xūkōng dì.** 一钱不落虚空地。
(lit) Not one coin falls into an empty place. (fig)
Gifts or bribes are never wasted in the long run.

223 **Yī qián zhē bǎi chǒu.** 一钱遮百丑。 Money
hides a thousand defects.

224 **Yī qiǎo shèng bǎi lì.** 一巧胜百力。 One clever
[technique] is superior to a hundred labor[er]s.

225 **Yī qiào tōng, bǎi qiào tōng.** 一窍通, 百窍通。
[In] knowing one skill, [you] know them all. [Said
of a clever person or a "quick study," e.g., the
Monkey King Sun Wukong in *JW*, chap. 2; as a
chengyu: *yītōng-bǎitōng*.]

226 **Yī qīng, yī huáng shì yī nián; yī hēi, yī bái shì yī
tiān.** 一青一黄是一年, 一黑一白是一天。
(lit) One green [spring and] one yellow [autumn
make up] a year; one black [night and] one white
[day make up] a day. (fig) Time flies and things
change.

227 **Yī quǎn fèi xíng, bǎi quǎn fèi shēng.** 一犬吠
形, 百犬吠声。 (lit) [When] one dog barks
at a shadow, a hundred bark at the sound. (fig)
One person can start everyone talking or guess-
ing, slavishly echoing others. Many people mind-
lessly repeat whatever they hear. [Cf. the Han dynasty author Wang Fu's *Quǎn Fū Lùn: Xián Nán*.]

228 **Yī rén bùdí èr rén zhì.** 一人不敌二人智。
(lit) One person is no match for two in wisdom.
(fig) "Two heads are better than one." [Cf. *Xǐngshì
Yīnyuán Zhuàn*, chap. 84; see also *yī rén jì duǎn*
below.]

229 **Yī rén cáng, shí rén zhǎo.** 一人藏, 十人找。
(lit) [What] one person has put away [for safe-
keeping], it takes ten people to find. (fig) Often
when you put something away for safekeeping, it
takes a long time to find later.

230 **Yī rén chīzhāi, shí rén niànfó.** 一人吃斋, 十
人念佛。 (lit) When one becomes a vegetarian
[as a Buddhist practice], many begin to pray to
Buddha. (fig) Where one leads, many will follow.
[Cf. *Píng Yāo Zhuàn*, chap. 7.]

231 **Yī rén chuán xū, wàn rén chuán shí.** 一人传
虚, 万人传实。 [When] one person tells an
idle story, ten thousand repeat [it as] true. [Cf. *Wǔ
Dèng Huì Yuán*, chap. 11.]

232 **Yī rén dé dào, jī quǎn shēng tiān.*** 一人得道，鸡犬升天。(lit) When a person attains the Tao [i.e., enlightenment and immortality], even his pets ascend to heaven. (fig) When one man is promoted, all those connected with him benefit. [Cf. the Han dynasty materialist philosopher Wáng Chōng's *Lùn Héng: Dào Xū*; *jīquǎnshēngtiān*, has become an idiom for "unabashed nepotism"; see also *yī rén yǒu fú* and *yī rén zàicháo* below.]

233 **Yī rén fànzuì, zhū lián jiǔzú.** 一人犯罪，诛连九族。[If] one person commits a crime, [all] nine generations [of his family will be] killed. [Also said *yī rén zāo fàn, jiǔ zú qián zū*; cf. *WM*, chap. 62; note: *jiǔzú* refers to the nine degrees of kinship in the Chinese extended family system; see also *xiǎo'ér fànzuì* above; vs. *jiā wú quán fàn* above and *yī rén zuò zuì* below.]

234 **Yī rén jì duǎn; èr rén jì cháng; sān rén jì tuǒdang.** 一人计短，二人计长，三人计妥当。(lit) One person['s head] is poor, two people['s heads] are better, [and] three people['s heads] are best. (fig) "Three heads are better than one." [See also *xīng duō, tiānkōng liàng* and *yī rén bùdí* above.]

235 **Yī rén jì duǎn; liǎng rén jì cháng.** 一人计短，两人计长。(lit) One man's plan is limited; the plan of two is better. (fig) Two heads are better than one. [See also *yī rén bùdí* above.]

236 **Yī rén lìzhì, wàn fū mò duó.** 一人立志，万夫莫夺。One person's determined will cannot be shaken by ten thousand others. [Cf. *Xǐngshì Héngyán*, vol. 5.]

237 **Yí rén, mò yòng; yòng rén, mò yí.** 疑人莫用，用人莫疑。[If you] suspect someone, don't employ him; [if you] employ someone, don't suspect [him]. [Cf. *Érnǚ Yīngxióng Zhuàn*, chap. 3.]

238 **Yī rén nán chèn bǎi rén xīn.** 一人难称百人心。(lit) One person can hardly satisfy the wishes of a hundred. (fig) It is difficult to please everyone.

239 **Yī rén pīnmìng, wàn fū mò dàng.** 一人拼命，万夫莫当。When one person fights in desperation, ten thousand cannot defeat [him.] [Cf. *Yīng Lièzhuàn*, chap. 28; *DRC*, chap. 103; note: *wànfūmòdàng* is used as an idiom meaning "mightier than a thousand."]

240 **Yī rén qīng zhèng fǔ; shíwàn xuěhuā yín.** 一任清正府，十万雪花银。[In] one term [of office], [even a] clean and honest official [will get one] hundred thousand [ounces of] snow white silver. [See also *guān jiǔ, zì fù* above.]

241 **Yī rén wéi sī, liù yǎn wéi gōng.** 一人为私，六眼为公。[What] one person [says] is [taken as his] own [opinion, but what] six eyes [(i.e., three people) see] is [taken as] true.

242 **Yī rén xiàngyú, mǎn zuò bù lè.** 一人向隅，满坐[/座]不乐。(lit) [When] one person faces the corner [of the room], everyone [else] sitting [at the table] is unhappy. (fig) One unhappy person makes everyone (else) feel unhappy. [Cf. *Érnǚ Yīngxióng Zhuàn*, chap. 2; note: *xiàngyú*, (lit) "facing the corner," is a literary expression meaning "disappointed; feel(ing) left out."]

243 **Yī rén xiūlù, wàn rén ān bù.** 一人修路，万人安步。(lit) One person fixes the road, [and] ten thousand walk [on it] safely. (fig) When one person does some good, everyone benefits. [Rhyme.]

244 **Yī rén, yī xiàng.** 一人一相。(lit) Everyone has a look of his own [which cannot be changed]. (fig) "A leopard cannot change his spots." [Cf. *Píng Yáo Zhuàn*, chap. 13; see also *gǒu chī shǐ* and *jiāngshān yì gǎi* and *shé zuān de kǔdòng* and *tōu shí (de) māo* above.]

245 **Yī rén yī zāo, tiāngōng-dìdào.** 一人一遭，天公地道。(lit) Each person has a turn, [because] Heaven acts fairly. (fig) Everyone has both good and bad luck. "What goes around, comes around." [Also sometimes used to mean:] "Turn about is fair play." [Rhyme; note: the *chengyu: tiāngōng-dìdào*, "absolutely fair"; see also *wú píng, bù bēi* above.]

246 **Yī rén yǒu fú, dàiqiè yī wū.** 一人有福，带挈一屋。[If] one person has good luck, [it will] lead [his or her] whole family [to riches]. [See also *yī rén dé dào* above and the following entry.]

247 **Yī rén zàicháo; bǎi rén huǎn dài.** 一人在朝，百人缓带。(lit) [If] one person [in a family gets] into the [imperial] court, [then one] hundred [of his relatives will] loosen [their] belts. (fig) One family member in the (imperial) civil service can support and assist all his relatives to get rich. [See also *yī rén dé dào* above and the preceding entry.]

248 **Yī rén zhī jiǎn, yījiā fù.** 一人知俭，一家富。[If] one person [(i.e., the head of the family) plans their living] thriftily, the whole family will prosper. [Note: *qīngjiǎn*, "budget."]

249 **Yī rén zuòshì, yī rén dāng.** 一人做事，一人当。A person must be responsible for his (or her) actions. [Cf. *Fēngshén Yǎnyì*, chap. 12; see also *ér zuò de ér dāng* above and *yī rén zuò zuì* below.]

250 **Yī rén zuò zuì, yī rén dāng.*** 一人作罪，一人当。If a person does wrong, (s)he alone must take the blame. [Cf. *DRC*, chap. 55; vs. *xiǎo'ér fànzuì* above and *yī rén zhùshì* above.]

251 **Yī rì bùjiàn rú gé sānqiū.*** 一日不见如隔三秋。(lit) One day not seeing [a dear one seems] like three autumns. (fig) A day's separation seems as long as three years. "Absence makes the heart grow fonder."

252 **Yī rì bù shíxiū, sān rì bù rěn è.** 一日不识羞，三日不忍饿。Don't feel ashamed [to labor for] one day, [and you] won't know hunger for three days. [Cf. *Gǔ-Jīn Xiǎoshuō*, chap. 22.]

253 **Yī rì bù shū, bǎi shì huāngwú.** 一日不书，百事荒芜。One day without keeping records will undermine many a feat. [Rhyme; cf. *Wèi Shū: Lǐ Biāo Zhuàn*.]

254 **Yī rì bù zuò, yī rì bù shí.** 一日不作，一日不食。(lit) A day of no work; a day of no food. (fig) One should earn one's bread every day of one's life. [Cf. the Song dynasty monk (Shi) Puji's *Wǔ Dèng Huì Yuán*, chap. 8; also the Qing dynasty author Cui Jin's *Tōng Sú Biàn: Xíng Shì*.]

255 **Yī rì [/ yè] fūqī, bǎi rì [/ yè] ēn.*** 一日 [/夜] 夫妻，百日 [/夜] 恩。One day [/night] [together] as husband and wife [means] affection for a hundred [more].

256 **Yī rì gāngē dòng, shí nián bù tàipíng.** 一日干戈动，十年不太平。 (lit) One day of war [means] no peace for ten years. (fig) Once the spears start flying, there will be no peace for ten years. [An injunction against war; note *dòng gāngē*, "take up arms; to go to war."]

257 **Yī rì guānshì, shí rì dǎ.** 一日官事，十日打。 (lit) A lawsuit [which could have been settled in] one day [usually] takes ten days. (fig) Lawsuits take time. [Cf. *JW*, chap. 83; in comtemporary colloquial Mandarin this would be *guānsi*, "lawsuit."]

258 **Yī rì jiào niáng, zhōngshēn shì mǔ.** 一日叫娘，终身是母。 (lit) Call her Mom for one day [and she] is [your] mother for life. (fig) Once she has become your mother, you should remain filial to her all your life. [Cf. *DRC*, chap. 58.]

259 **Yī rì liàn, yī rì gōng; yī rì bù liàn, shí rì kōng.** 一日练，一日功；一日不练，十日空。 [If you] practice [your skill for] one day, [you will] perfect it [a little]; [if you] stop practicing one day, [it will] cancel out ten day['s practice]. [Rhyme; see also *bùpà liàn bù chéng* above.]

260 **Yī rì mài de sān dàn jiǎ; sān rì màibude yī dàn zhēn.** 一日卖得三担假，三日卖不得一担真。 (lit) [One] can sell three hundred weight of false goods in one day, [but] not one hundred weight of genuine goods in three days. (fig) Resorting to deceit is effective, while telling the truth will get you nowhere. [Cf. *Xīhú Èr Jí*, vol. 20; a *dàn* is a Chinese unit of weight equal to fifty kilograms.]

261 **Yī rì nán zài chén.** 一日难再晨。 (lit) One day [can] hardly [have] another morning. (fig) Time is most valuable. [A line from a poem "Zá Shī" by the Jin dynasty poet Tao Qian.]

262 **Yī rì wéi guān, qiángsì qiānzǎi wéi mín.** 一日为官，强似千载为民。One day as an official is better than a thousand years as a commoner.

263 **Yī rì wéi shī, zhōngshēn wéi fù.*** 一日为师，终身为父。 (lit) A teacher for a day [is] a father for a lifetime. (fig) He who teaches me for one day deserves my respect and obedience for life. [Originally a line from a *Yuán qǔ* play by Guan Hanqing entitled *Yù Jìng Tái*, Act 2; *JW*, chaps. 72, 81; *Xǐngshì Yīnyuán Zhuàn*, chap. 35.]

264 **Yī rì zòng dí, shù shì zhī huàn.** 一日纵敌，数世之患。 (lit) [If] one day [you let your] enemy escape, [you will suffer] several generations of trouble. [Cf. *Zuǒ Zhuàn: Xī Gōng 33 Nián*; also *R3K*, chap. 21; see also *fánghǔ-guīshān* above.]

265 **Yī shān bù néng cún èr hǔ.** 一山不能存二虎。 (lit) Two tigers cannot live on one mountain. (fig) Two strong personalities cannot share the same place. "When Greek meets Greek, then comes the tug of war." [See also *wù mò néng* and *yī gè cáo shàng* and *yī gè shāntóu* above.]

266 **Yī shàn guī rén rú zèng gǎnlán.** 以善规人如赠橄榄。Advising others to [do] good [is] like giving [them] olives [to eat; (i.e., although they seem bitter at first, in the end they are good)]. [Cf. *Liáo Zhāi Zhì Yì*, chap. 6.]

267 **Yī shàn zúyǐ xiāo bǎi è.** 一善足以消百恶。One good deed is sufficient to compensate for a hundred ill deeds. [Cf. *Xī Hú Èr Jí*, chap. 10; see *yī zhèng dí qiān xié* and *yī zhèng yà bǎi xié* below.]

268 **Yīshēng bùchūmén, zhōngjiū shì xiǎorén.** 一生不出门，终究是小人。 [One who] never travels all [his/her] life remains a narrow person [i.e., unambitious and narrow-minded]. [Cf. the Mongolian novel *Yī Céng Lóu*, chap. 10; vs. *xiùcai bùchūmén* above.]

269 **Yīsheng yī bìng, bù néng yī mìng.*** 医生医病，不能医命。A doctor [can] cure an illness [but he] cannot cure fate. [A rhyme said when the patient is sure to die; see also *yào yī bù sǐ bìng* above.]

270 **Yīshēn zuòbude liǎng jiàn shì; yī shí diūbude liǎng tiáo xīn.** 一身做不得两件事，一时丢不得两条心。One cannot perform two tasks at once, nor can one set one's mind to two tasks at once. [See also *yīxīn bù néng* below.]

271 **Yīshí bǐbude yīshí.*** 一时比不得一时。 (lit) One time cannot be compared with another time. (fig) Times change; one cannot always keep following the same old ways or rules. [Cf. *DRC*, chap. 72.]

272 **Yī shì chà, bǎi shì cuò.** 一事差，百事错。Do one thing wrong [and] everything will go wrong. (fig) Make one mistake and many more will follow. [See also *yī bù zǒu cuò* above.]

273 **Yī shì chéng, shìshì chéng.** 一事成，事事成。 [If] one thing succeeds, everything will succeed. "Nothing succeeds like success." [See also *yī shì tōng* below.]

274 **Yī shì dào guān, shí shì qiān chán; yī rén rùyù, yī jiā jìn kū.** 一事到官十室牵缠，一人入狱一家尽哭。 [Once] a lawsuit is started, [it will] involve ten households; [when] one person is sent too prison, [it will] set the whole family crying. [Rhyme.]

275 **Yī shì jīng, bǎi shì jīng; yī wúchéng, bǎi wúchéng.** 一事精百事精，一无成百无成。Skillful at one thing, skillful at many; if you cannot succeed at [even] one thing, you cannot accomplish anything. [Cf. *Xīxiāng Jì*, Act 2, Scene 2.]

276 **Yī shì quán zhī shèngyú wànshì zhī.** 一事全知胜于万事知。To know one thing thoroughly is better than to know [something of] ten thousand. [Vs. *yàngyàng jīngtōng* above.]

277 **Yī shì rén zhī wēi; qián shì rén zhī dǎn.*** 衣是人之威，钱是人之胆。Clothes make people important; money makes people bold.

278 **Yī shì tōng, bǎi shì sōng.** 一事通，百事松。Success in one thing makes (success in) other things easier. [See also *yī shì chéng* above.]

279 **Yī shì wù, èr shì gù.** 一是误，二是故。The first [mistake] is accidental; the second is intentional [negligence]. [Rhyme.]

280 **Yī shì xīn de hǎo; rén shì jiù de hǎo.** 衣是新的好，人是旧的好。 [With] clothes new is best; [with] people old [friends] are best. [See also *yī mòrú xīn* above.]

281 **Yī shì zhēn, bǎi shì zhēn.** 一事真，百事真。 [If] one thing is [shown to be] true, all of it must be true. [Rhyme; cf. *Xǐngshì Héngyán*, chap. 16; vs. *yī yán bù shí* below.]

282 **Yī shí zhī shèng zàiyú lì; qiāngǔ zhī shèng zàiyú lǐ.** 一时之胜在于力，千古之胜在于理。 Power wins [one only] a temporary victory, [while] reason wins an everlasting one. [Rhyme.]

283 **Yī shīzú chéng qiāngǔ hèn;* (zài huítóu shì bǎinián shēn).** 一失足成千古恨，（再回头是百年身）。 (lit) One single slip may cause everlasting sorrow; (to go back [and correct it, one would have to be a] hundred year [old] body). (fig) One false step can bring everlasting grief. A moment's error can bring a lifetime of regret. [Rhyme; cf. *Suí Táng Yǎnyì*, chap. 65; see also *yīzhāo shīzú* below; note: *bǎinián zhī hòu*, "after someone's death."]

284 **Yīshí zú érhòu zhī lǐ yì.** 衣食足而后知礼义。 (lit) [Only] after [being well] dressed [and well] fed [does one] know courtesy. (fig) Material well-being enables people to be courteous. Only when a certain basic level of material sufficiency has been attained can one expect people to observe the rules of politeness. "Well fed, well bred." [Compare *bǎonuǎn shēng xiánshì* above; see also the following entry.]

285 **Yīshí zú fāng zhī róngrǔ.** 衣食足方知荣辱。 (lit) Only if [one is well] dressed [and well] fed [does one] know [the meaning of] honor or disgrace. [Rhyme; see also the preceding entry.]

286 **Yī shǒu bù néng yǎn [/zhē] tiānxià mù.*** 一手不能掩[/遮]天下目。 (lit) One hand cannot cover everyone's eyes. (fig) It's impossible for one to hoodwink the public. [Cf. *Qīng Shǐ Yǎnyì*, chap. 87; see the colloquial *súyǔ* expression: *yīshǒu-zhētiān*, "to (try to) hoodwink everyone"; note: *yīshǒu*, (lit) "one hand," in addition to meaning "single-handed(ly)," can also mean "proficiency; skill" or "one trick; one move"; see also *nán jiāng yī rén shǒu* above and *zhī shǒu nán zhē* below.]

287 **Yī shù zhī guǒ, yǒu suān, yǒu tián; yī mǔ zhī zǐ, yǒu yú, yǒu xián.** 一树之果有酸有甜，一母之子有愚有贤。 [Just as] a tree may bear both sour and sweet fruit, [so] a mother may have both stupid and able sons. [Cf. *Fēngshén Yǎnyì*, chap. 4.]

288 **Yī sī wéi dìng, qiānjīn bù yì.** 一丝为定，千金不易。 (lit) An agreement [bound] by a thread cannot be changed for a thousand ounces of gold. (fig) A betrothal sealed with even an insignificant gift cannot be broken off. Once betrothed is forever betrothed. [Note: *qiānjīn*, (lit) "[a] thousand [ounces of] gold," is a metaphor for "a lot of money."]

289 **Yī sǐ yī shēng, nǎi zhī jiāoqíng; yī guì yī jiàn, jiāoqíng nǎi jiàn.** 一死一生乃知交情，一贵一贱，交情乃见。 (lit) True friendship is never known until [critical moments of] life and death or wealth and poverty. (fig) "A friend in need is a friend in deed." [Cf. *Shǐ Jì: Jí Zhèng Lièzhuàn*.]

290 **Yī suì zhǔ, bǎisuì nú.** 一岁主，百岁奴。 [A master is] a master [though only] one year old, [and a servant is] a servant [though a] hundred years old. [Cf. *Érnǚ Yīngxióng Zhuàn*, chap. 22.]

291 **Yī sǔn, jù sǔn; yī róng, jù róng.*** 一损俱损，一荣俱荣。 (lit) Injure one [and] all are injured; honor one [and] all are honored. (fig) When one loses, all lose; when one gains, all gain. When people are bound together for good or evil, their fortunes are intertwined. [Used to describe the families in *DRC*, chap. 4.]

292 **Yī tiáo yú mǎn guō xīng.*** 一条鱼满锅腥。 (lit) One fish makes the whole pot fishy. (fig) "One rotten apple can spoil the whole barrel." [See also *yī gè xiǎo jǐ* and *yī kuài chòu ròu* above.]

293 **Yī tóu rénqíng, liǎng miàn guāng.** 一头人情两面光。 Performing [one] act of kindness [is] satisfying to both parties. [Cf. Chen Canyun's novel *Xiāng Piāo Sìjì*, chap. 20.]

294 **Yī wǎn shuǐ duān píng.*** 一碗水端平。 (lit) A cup of water [must be] carried level. (fig) (One should) treat everyone equally. [Cf. *Érnǚ Yīngxióng Zhuàn*, chap. 26; see also *shuǐ píng bù liú* above.]

295 **Yī wén qián nán dǎo yīngxióng hàn.** 一文钱难倒英雄汉。 (lit) [The lack of] one penny [can] defeat a hero. (fig) Even a hero can be defeated by the lack of money. [Cf. *Érnǚ Yīngxióng Zhuàn*, chap. 19.]

296 **Yī wèn sān bù zhī, shénxian méifǎ zhì.*** 一问三不知，神仙没法治。 (lit) [If to] every question [you reply:] "I don't know," [even] the gods can do nothing [against you]. (fig) If you claim complete ignorance, no one can do anything to you. [Rhyme; see also *bù gān jǐ shì* and *sān gè bù kāikǒu* above.]

297 **Yī wō húli bù xián sāo.** 一窝狐狸不嫌臊。 (lit) Foxes from the same den aren't disgusted by [each other's] foul smell. (fig) People of the same (bad) ilk get along with each other.

298 **Yī wù bù chéng, liǎng wù xiàn zài.** 一物不成，两物现在。 (lit) [If two people] cannot conclude a deal, both things [i.e., your money and my goods] are still there. (fig) No one loses anything. No harm done. [Cf. *WM*, chap. 12.]

299 **Yī wú dé, bù lì.** 艺无德不立。 (lit) [If one's] skills have no morality, [one will] not [be able to] establish [one's self]. (fig) Even though one might have superb skills, if one has no morals, one won't establish oneself in society.

300 **Yī wù xiáng yī wù.** 一物降一物。 (lit) One thing vanquishes one [other] thing. (fig) There is always one thing to conquer another. [See also *mùjiang pà qījiang* and *néngrén zhīwài* and *qiáng zhōng háiyǒu* and *rén wài yǒu rén* and *shān wài*

Y

yǒu shān and *shé tūn shǔ* below; see also the following entry.]

301 **Yī wù xiáng yī wù;*** (**lǔshuǐ diǎn dòufù**). 一物降一物，(卤水点豆腐)。 (lit) One thing always succumbs to another, ([just as] brine curds soybean juice). (fig) There is always one thing to overcome another. Everything has its vanquisher. [Cf. *Érnǚ Yīngxióng Zhuàn*, chap. 31; the first part is commonly used alone (q.v.); the second part is merely added as a rhyme; see the preceding entry.]

302 **Yī wú zhǐ jìng.** 艺无止境。 (lit) Skills [or knowledge] have no limits. (fig) One should never cease perfecting one's skill or knowledge. [Note: *yìwúzhǐjìng* is also used as a set phrase to mean "(possessing) skill that knows no limits."]

303 **Yī wù zìyǒu yī zhǔ.** 一物自有一主。 (lit) Each thing will (come to) have its own master. (fig) Everything will eventually find its proper place, owner, or best use. [Cf. *Fēngshén Yǎnyì*, chap. 47 and JPM, chap. 45; see also *wù yǒu suǒ guī* above.]

304 **Yī xiào jiě bǎi chóu.*** 一笑解百愁。 One laugh scatters a hundred sorrows.

305 **Yǐ xiǎorén zhī xīn dù jūnzǐ zhī fù.** 以小人之心度君子之腹。 (lit) [One should not] use a petty person's heart to [attempt to] gauge a gentleman's feelings. (fig) Small minds can't comprehend the thoughts or noble motives of gentlefolk or their *noblesse oblige.*

306 **Yī xiě dàng shí dú.** 一写当十读。 [A piece of writing is] better learned [by] copying [it] once than [by] reading [it] ten [times].

307 **Yī xí huán yī xí.** 一席还一席。 (lit) [Attending] one feast demands [giving] another [in return]. (fig) Courtesy demands reciprocity.

308 **Yìxīn bù néng èr yòng.*** 一心不能二用。 (lit) One mind cannot [be put to] two uses. (fig) One cannot do two things at once. [See also *yīkǒu bù néng* and *yīshēn zuòbude* above.]

309 **Yí xíng wúchéng; yí shì wú gōng.** 疑行无成，疑事无功。 (lit) [If one] hesitates [in taking] actions [or in] doing things there [can] be no success. (fig) "He who hesitates is lost."

310 **Yíxīn shēng àn guǐ.*** 疑心生暗鬼。 (lit) A doubting heart/mind gives rise to dark devils. (fig) Suspicion creates imaginary fears. [Cf. JW, chap. 32; note: *yíxīn*, "doubt; suspicion."]

311 **Yī yán bù shí, bǎi shì jiē xū.** 一言不实，百事皆虚。 Utter one falsehood [and] everything [you say] will be [taken as] lies. [Vs. *yī shì zhēn* above.]

312 **Yī yàng mǐ yǎng bǎi yàng rén.** 一样米养百样人。 (lit) One type of rice nourishes a hundred types of people. (fig) There are all sorts of people in the world. [See also *bǎi yàng mǐ* above.]

313 **Yī yán jì chū, sìmǎ nán zhuī.*** 一言既出，驷马难追。 (lit) Once a word [has been] said, [even] a team of four horses cannot overtake it. (fig) What has been said cannot be unsaid. [Cf. the Song dynasty author Ouyang Xiu's *Bǐ Shuō*; JW, chap. 83; see also *jūnzǐ yī yán* above; note: *sìmǎ-nánzhuī* is used alone as a set phrase meaning "What has been said cannot be unsaid."]

314 **Yǐ yán jǔ rén ruò yǐ máo xiàng mǎ.** 以言举人若以毛相马。 Choosing a person based on [his] words is like judging a horse by [its] hair [i.e., it's not a good idea]. [Cf. The Confucian Analects: *Lúnyǔ: Wèi Líng Gōng* 15.]

315 **Yī yán qǐ zhìzhě.** 一言启智者。 (lit) One word alerts a clever person. (fig) "A word to the wise is sufficient." [See also *kuàimǎ yī biān* and *míngrén bùyòng* above.]

316 **Yī yán wéi dìng.*** 一言为定。 (lit) One word settles the matter. (fig) One's word is one's bond. [Cf. *Fēng Shén Yǎnyì*, chap. 56; note: *yīyánwéidìng* is also used as an idiom meaning "the matter is settled."]

317 **Yī yè luò zhī tiānxià qiū.** 一叶落知天下秋。 (lit) [From] the falling of one leaf [one may] know the coming of autumn. (fig) A small signifier can indicate a great trend. [Cf. the Tang dynasty author Tang Yan's *Wén Lù*; note also the *chengyu*: *yī yè zhī qiū*, "one leaf heralds autumn"; see also *cǎo yǎn zhī fēngxiàng* above.]

318 **Yī yè wǔgēng, dāngbude yī gè zǎochén.** 一夜五更，当不得一个早晨。 A whole night's sleep [of ten hours] is not the equal of one [good] morning's [sleep]. [Said by those who like to sleep in late in the morning; *wǔgēng* here refers to five of the two-hour time periods into which the night was traditionally divided; see also *wǔgēng qǐchuáng* above.]

319 **Yī yì dǐng sān gōng.** 一艺顶三工。 One skilled [worker] is worth [i.e., earns as much as] three [common] workers.

320 **Yī yī, ē ē; zuò de guān duō.** 依依阿阿，做得官多。 [Always] follow [orders and] flatter [your] superiors [i.e., be a "yes-man," and you will] get more [appointments] as [a government] official. [Note: *yīcóng*, "to follow obediently."]

321 **Yī yǐn, yī zhuó; mòfēi qián dìng.** 一饮一啄，莫非前定。 (lit) Every drink [and] every bite, there is none [which is] not foreordained. (fig) One cannot get what is denied him by destiny, no matter how hard he tries. [Cf. *Xǐng Shì Héng Yán*, chap. 29; see also *mìng lǐ yǒu shí* above.]

322 **Yī yǔ bù chéng, qiān yán wúyì.** 一语不成，千言无益。 If one word does not succeed, ten thousand are of no avail.

323 **Yī yǔ shì fēngxiàng; yī cǎo shì shuǐliú.** 一羽示风向，一草示水流。 (lit) One feather is [enough to] indicate the direction of [the] wind, [and] one [piece of] straw [to] show the direction [the] water [flows]. (fig) Signs of seemingly little significance can indicate general trends to come. [See also *cǎo yǎn zhī fēngxiàng* above.]

324 **Yī yǔ wéizhòng, bǎi jīn qīng.** 一语为重，百金轻。 (lit) One word is heavy [in comparison to which a] hundred catties of gold is light. (fig) One must keep one's promises at all costs. [Cf. *Shǐ Jì: Shāng Jūn Lièzhuàn*; note: *wéizhòng*, "to attach (most) importance to"; one *jīn* or "catty" equals one-half kilogram; see also *hǎi yuè shàng kě qīng* and *xǔ rén yī wù* above.]

Y

325 **Yī zāo guàn; èr zāo fàn.** 一遭惯，二遭犯。[If one is] forgiven [for a mistake] one time, [(s)he will make the same] mistake [a] second time. [Note: *guàn*, "to spoil"; see also *ǒurán fǎncuò* above.]

326 **Yī zāo qíng; liǎng zāo lì.** 一遭情，两遭例。The first gift is [regarded with] affection; the second is taken for granted. [Implying that it is not a good idea to give gifts too frequently.]

327 **Yī zhāng chuáng shàng shuō bù chū liǎngyàng huà.** 一张床上说不出两样话。(lit) [A couple] sharing one bed won't speak two different languages. (fig) Husband and wife (should) always present a "united front" to those outside the family. [See also *yī jiā rén bù shuō* below.]

328 **Yī zhǎng yì tuì, shān kēng shuǐ; yì fǎn yì fù, xiǎorén xīn.** 易涨易退山坑水，易反易复小人心。[Just as] streams in the hills rise and fall irregularly, [so] petty persons are capricious [in not keeping their promises]. [Note: the *chengyu: fǎnfù-wúcháng*, "changeable; fickle; capricious"; the second part of the first half is also said . . . *shān kēngshuǐ*, etc.]

329 **Yī zhǎn néng xiāo wàngǔ chóu.** 一盏能消万古愁。One cup of wine can dispel a thousand years of sorrow. [See also *jiǔ xiāo bǎi chóu* and *yī bēi zài shǒu* above and *yī zuì jiě qiān chóu* below.]

330 **Yī zhàn, zǒu sān lǐ; yì xiē, zǒu sān cūn.** 一站，走三里；一歇，走三村。[When traveling on foot,] one [rest while] standing [up will set you back the time you could] walk three [more] *li*, [and] one rest [will set you back the time you could have] walked [past] three [more] villages. [Note: one *lǐ* now equals one-half kilometer.]

331 **Yīzhāo bèi shé yǎo, sān nián pà jǐng shéng.** 一朝被蛇咬，三年怕井绳。(lit) Once bitten by a snake, [one] fears [coiled] well rope [for the next] three years. (fig) "Once bitten, twice shy." "A burnt child fears the fire." [Cf. *Chū Kè Pāi'àn Jīngqí*, chap. 1; also said . . . *sān nián pà cǎo suǒ*, ". . . one fears hemp rope for three years."]

332 **Yī zhāo bùshèn, mǎnpán jiē shū.** 一着不慎，满盘皆输。(lit) One incautious move spoils the whole [chess] game. (fig) One careless move and you lose the whole game. [Used, e.g., by Mao Zedong in his *Problems of Strategy in China's Revolutionary War*; see also *bùpà qiān zhāo* and *qí cuò yī zhāo* above.]

333 **Yīzhāo qíngyì dàn, yàngyàng bù shùnyǎn.** 一朝情意淡，样样不顺眼。(lit) Once affection thins, everything displeases the eyes. (fig) "Faults are thick where love is thin."

334 **Yīzhāo quán zài shǒu, biàn bǎ lìng lái xíng.** 一朝权在手，便把令来行。(lit) [One who has only had] power in [his] hands [for] one morning [will] begin to issue orders right and left [to promote his or her own power]. [Cf. *Xī Hú Èr Jì*, chap. 5; see also *xiǎorén dézhì* above.]

335 **Yīzhāo rén luòbó, àiqíng shēng yì fēi.** 一朝人落泊，爱情生翼飞。(lit) Once a person is in dire [economic] straits, love sprouts wings [and] flies away. (fig) "When poverty comes in at the door, love flies out the window." "Nobody loves you when you're down and out."

336 **Yīzhāo shīzú, bǎishì mò shú.** 一朝失足，百世莫赎。Once [you make] a blunder, a hundred lifetimes cannot redeem [it]. [See also *yī shīzú chéng* above.]

337 **Yī zhāo xiān, chī biàn tiān.** 一招鲜，吃遍天。[If one has] a specialized skill, [one can] eat [i.e., earn one's living] anywhere. [Said, e.g., of carpenters; see also *rén duō yī jì* above and *yì bù yà shēn* below and the following entry.]

338 **Yī zhāo xiān, zǒubiàn tiān.** 一招鲜，走遍天。[If one develops] a specialized skill, [one can] go anywhere. [See also the preceding entry.]

339 **Yī zhèng dí qiān xié.** 一正敌千邪。One [bit of] uprightness [can] defeat a thousand evils. [See also *yī shàn zúyǐ* above and *yī zhèng yà bǎi xié* below.]

340 **Yī zhèng, liǎng chǒu; yī ràng, liǎng yǒu.** 一争两丑，一让两有。By scrambling for something, both parties look bad; by giving up something, both parties win. [Rhyme; cf. the Ming dynasty writer Xu Desheng's *Xiǎo Èr Yǔ*.]

341 **Yī zhèng, wúbù zhèng; yī xié, wúbù xié.** 一正无不正，一邪无不邪。(lit) Once upright, [one is] invariably upright; once crooked, [one is] invariably crooked. (fig) [If] honest and upright in one matter, [one is] a decent person in all matters; [if] dishonest in one matter, [one is] an evil person in all matters. [Cf. the *píngshū* story *Wǔ Sōng*, chap. 2.]

342 **Yī zhèng yà bǎi xié.** 一正压百邪。One good can overcome a hundred evils. [See also *yī shàn zúyǐ* and *yī zhèng dí qiān xié*.]

343 **Yī zhī wǎn bù xiǎng; liǎng zhī wǎn dīngdāng.** 一只碗不响，两只碗叮当。(lit) One bowl is quiet, two bowls make a racket. (fig) It takes two to make a quarrel. [Cf. *Guānchǎng Xiànxíng Jì*, chap. 30; see also *yī gè bāzhang* above.]

344 **Yī zhōu, yī fàn; dāng sī láizhī-bùyì.** 一粥一饭，当思来之不易。(lit) [In taking a mouthful of] congee or rice, bear in mind that its production is not easy. (fig) Be economical with food. [After the Qing dynasty writer Zhu Bolu's *Zhì Jiā Géyán* (Family Maxims); note: *láizhī-bùyì* is a set literary phrase meaning "hard-earned."]

345 **Yī zhōu yī fàn, lái chù bùyì.** 一粥一饭，来处不易。(lit) One [bowl of] porridge [or] rice is not easy to come by. (fig) Don't waste food. [Advice to children; see the Song dynasty author Zhu Xi's book on educating children: *Zhū Zǐ Jiā Xùn*.]

346 **Yī zǐ guīyī, jiǔ zǔ shēngtiān.** 一子皈依，九祖升天。[Having] one son [who has become a true Buddhist] believer [will allow] nine [sinful] ancestors to ascend to Heaven [on his coat tails]. [See also *yī nǚ huò chǒng*, and *yī rén dé dào* and *yī rén zàicháo* above.]

347 **Yí zǐ huángjīn mǎn yíng, bùrú yī jīng.** 遗子黄金满籯不如一经。(lit) Leaving [one's] son a basket full of gold is not as [good as having him read]

one [of the Confucian] classics. (fig) It is more important to give one's children a good (moral) education than to leave them wealth. [Cf. *Hàn Shū: Wèi Xián Zhuàn*.]

348 **Yī zì rù gōngmén, jiǔ niú bá bù chū.** 一字入公门，九牛拔不出。 (lit) [Once] one word [has been] recorded in a lawsuit, nine oxen cannot pull it out. (fig) Once you instigate a lawsuit, there is no going back. [Cf. *Xíngshì Yīnyuán Zhuàn*, chap. 46.]

349 **Yī zuì bùkě liǎng zhì.** 一罪不可两治。 (lit) One crime [should] not be punished twice. [Compare: "double jeopardy."]

350 **Yī zuì jiě qiān chóu.** 一醉解千愁。 Once drunk, one forgets all one's worries. [Cf. Lao She's modern play *Cháguǎn* [Tea House], Act 2; see also *yī bēi zài shǒu* and *yī zhǎn néng xiāo* above.]

351 **Yòng rén cháo qián; bù yòng rén cháo hòu.** 用人朝前；不用人朝后。 [People who want to] ask [for your] help face [you]; [people who] don't want [your] help, turn [their] backs.

352 **Yòng rén róngyì; shí rén nán.** 用人容易，识人难。 It's easy to direct people, [but] difficult to know them [as people]. [Said by those in authority; see also *shàngmíng bù zhī xià àn* above.]

353 **Yōngyī shārén, bùyòng dāo.** 庸医杀人不用刀。 (lit) [When a] charlatan kills [he] doesn't use a knife. (fig) Quack doctors are dangerous (even if not intentionally so). [See also *yǒu bìng bù zhì* below.]

354 **Yǒu bèi, cái néng wú huàn; wú bèi, bìdìng chīkuī.** 有备才能无患，无备必定吃亏。 (lit) Only [if one] is prepared can [one] be safe; [if one is] not prepared, [one] surely [will] suffer. (fig) Preparedness ensures safety; unpreparedness invites disaster. [This is an expansion of the *chéngyǔ: yǒu bèi, wú huàn*; see the following entry.]

355 **Yǒu bèi, wú huàn.*** 有备无患。 (lit) [If] there are preparations, there [will] be no perils. (fig) Preparedness prevents peril. Always be prepared, just in case. [This is also treated as a *chéngyǔ: yǒubèi-wúhuàn*; see also the preceding entry.]

356 **Yǒu bìng bù zhì, cháng dé zhōngyī.** 有病不治，常得中医。 When [one is] ill, not getting treatment [and just letting the illness run its course] is often [just as good as] getting [treated by] a doctor of mediocre skill. [Cf. *Hàn Shū: Yì Wén Zhì*; see also *yōngyī shārén* above.]

357 **Yǒu chē jiù yǒu zhé; yǒu shù jiù yǒu yǐng.** 有车就有辙，有树就有影。 (lit) [If] there is a cart, then there are tracks [and if] there is a tree, then there is a shadow. (fig) Whatever one does leaves a trace behind. [Usually said of bad activities; see also *máquè fēiguò* and *měngchóng fēiguò* above.]

358 **Yǒu chǐ shuǐ, xíng chǐ chuán.** 有尺水，行尺船。 (lit) [If] there's a foot of water, sail a one-foot boat. (fig) Steer your ship according to the depth of water. It is best to act in accordance with the current conditions. Make the best of what's available. [Cf. *Xíngshì Yīnyuán Zhuàn*, chap. 65;

see also *kàn cài chīfàn* above and *yǒu duōdà de jiǎo* below.]

359 **Yǒu chóu bù bào, fēi jūnzǐ; yǒu yuān bù shēn, wǎng wéirén.** 有仇不报非君子，有冤不伸枉为人。 [One who does] not avenge an injustice is not a gentleman, [and one who does] not seek redress [of a wrong] is not a man.

360 **Yǒu chóu jiē kǔhǎi; wú bìng jí shénxiān.** 有愁皆苦海，无病即神仙。 A troubled [mind] makes a sea of bitterness [and] a healthy body makes [one] a god. [Note: *kǔhǎi* is a Buddhist term referring to the bitterness of earthly life; see *kǔhǎi wúbiān* above.]

361 **Yǒu cuò, gǎicuò, bù suàn cuò.** 有错改错，不算错。 [If, as soon as one] makes an error, [one] corrects the error, [it] is not an error. [See also *zhī cuò, gǎicuò* below.]

362 **Yǒu de bù zhī wú de kǔ.** 有的不知无的苦。 (lit) The "haves" don't know the sufferings of the "have-nots." (fig) The rich do not understand the sufferings of the poor. [Cf. *Hé Diǎn*, chap. 10; see also *bǎo hàn bù zhī* above.]

363 **Yǒu duōdà běnqian, zuò duōdà shēngyi.** 有多大本钱，做多大生意。 (lit) The size of the business one does [depends on] the amount of capital one has. (fig) One should not take on tasks beyond one's abilities.

364 **Yǒu duōdà de jiǎo, zuò duōdà de xié.** 有多大的脚，做多大的鞋。 (lit) Have your shoes made according to the size of your feet. (fig) Act according to the actual circumstances. [See also *kàn cài chīfàn* and *yǒu chǐ shuǐ* above.]

365 **Yǒu ēn, bào'ēn; yǒu chóu, bàochóu.*** 有恩报恩，有仇报仇。 A debt of gratitude must be repaid, [and] an injustice must be avenged. [Cf. *JPM*, chap. 51; see also *yī bào huán yī bào* above.]

366 **Yǒu ēn bù bào, fēi jūnzǐ*** 有恩不报，非君子。 [One who does] not repay a debt of gratitude is no gentleman.

367 **Yǒu fēng bùkě shǐ jìn.** 有风不可驶尽。 (lit) [When you sail] with the wind, don't go full sail. (fig) When you're in a position of power, take it easy and don't ride roughshod over others.

368 **Yǒu fēng fāng qǐ làng; wú cháoshuǐ zì píng.** 有风方起浪，无潮水自平。 (lit) Only when there's a wind are there waves; [only when] there is no current [will] the water be calm. (fig) Everything has a cause. "Where there's smoke, there's fire." [See also *mù yǒu běn* and *shuǐ lái hé zhǎng* and *wú fēng bù qǐ* above.]

369 **Yǒu fú bùyòng máng; méi fú pǎo duàn cháng.** 有福不用忙，没福跑断肠。 The fortunate do not have to busy [themselves, while] the less fortunate [have to] run their guts out [(lit) "until their guts break"] [in order to make a living]. [Rhyme.]

370 **Yǒu fù, kǎndedǎo shù; yǒu lǐ, shuōdefú rén.** 有斧砍得倒树，有理说得服人。 [Just as] with an axe you can cut down a tree, [so] with reason you can persuade people.

Y

371 **Yǒu fú zhī rén bù luò wú fú zhī dì.** 有福之人
不落无福之地。Fortunate people don't land
in unfortunate places. [In present day mainland
China this is commonly used of job assignments.]

372 **Yǒu fú zhī rén, rén fúshì; wú fú zhī rén, fúshì rén.**
有福之人人伏侍；无福之人伏侍人。Fortunate people, others serve, [while] the unfortunate serve others.

373 **Yǒu gāng shǐ zài dāo rèn shàng.** 有钢使在刀
刃上。(lit) Use the [best] steel on the [cutting]
edge of the knife. (fig) Concentrate your efforts
on the key problem. [See also qián (yào) yòng zài
dāokǒu shàng above.]

374 **Yǒugōng bì shǎng; yǒuzuì bì fá.** 有功必赏，有
罪必罚。For [one's] outstanding service, [one]
should be rewarded, [and] for [one's] crimes,
[one] should be punished.

375 **Yǒu guān, bù chóu zàolì.** 有官，不愁皂隶。
(lit) [If one] has [accepted an] official [position,
one need] not worry about [there being] helpers.
(fig) When you assume a position of power, there
will be no shortage of people flocking to help and
seek favors from you. [Note: zàolì refers to "runners" or "go-fers" working for the yámen or local
magistrate's office in traditional China; see also
guān qīng, yámen shòu and dāngchāi de above.]

376 **Yǒu huà shuō gěi zhījǐ rén.** 有话说给知己人。
(lit) [If you] have anything [confidential] to say,
tell it [only] to people who understand you. (fig)
Limit your confidences to intimate friends only.

377 **Yóu jiǎn rù shē yì; yóu shē rù jiǎn nán.** 由俭入
奢易，由奢入俭难。It's easy to change from
a frugal life to a luxurious one, [but] it's difficult
to change the other way round. [See also nìngkě
pín hòu and nìngkě wúle yǒu above.]

378 **Yǒu jiè, yǒu huán, zài jiè bù nán.*** 有借有还，再
借不难。One who borrows and then returns,
when borrowing again will not be spurned. [A
popular rhyme.]

379 **Yǒu jī, tiān yě liàng; méi jī tiān yě míng.** 有鸡天
也亮，没鸡天也明。(lit) Day breaks whether
there are cocks crowing or not. (fig) No one is indispensable; One individual doesn't matter a bit.
[See also sǐle Zhāng túfū above.]

380 **Yǒu le lǎopó, bù chóu hái; yǒu le mùjiàng, bù
chóu chái.** 有了老婆不愁孩，有了木匠不
愁柴。(lit) [If you've] got a wife, don't worry
about [not having] children; [if you've] got a
carpenter [working for you], don't worry about
[not having enough] firewood. (fig) If you have
made the proper preparations, things will work
out properly. [Rhyme.]

381 **Yǒule mǎnfù cái, bùpà yùn bù lái.** 有了满腹
才，不怕运不来。[If you] are full of learning, [you need] not fear that fortune will not visit
[you]. [Rhyme; note: mǎnfù jīnglun, "widely read
in the (Confucian) classics."]

382 **Yǒule qián, wànshì yuán.** 有了钱，万事圆。
[If one] has money, everything [can be] accomplished. [Rhyme; see also the following entry.]

383 **Yǒule yuán lǐ fāng, bǎi shì hǎo shāngliang.** 有了
圆里方，百事好商量。[If one] has money,
everything [can be] easily negotiated. [Rhyme;
note: "yuán lǐ fāng," (lit) "a square (hole) in a
round," is a colloquial name for old fashioned
round copper "cash" coins with a square hole
in the middle for stringing purposes, also known
as "kǒng fāng xiōng," "Brother Square Hole"; see
also the preceding entry.]

384 **Yǒu lì bù xīng; wú lì bù miè.** 有例不兴，无例
不灭。(lit) [As] there exist conventions [to be
observed], [there is] no [need to] propose [new
ones]; [if] conventions did not exist, [there would
be] no [need to] abolish them. (fig) Given that
certain conventions of behavior exist, it is best
to observe them, and not worry about abolishing them or proposing new ones. [Cf. Guānchǎng
Xiànxíng Jì, chap. 41; the second half is an empty
rhetorical flourish.]

385 **Yǒu lǐ bù zài shēng gāo.** 有理不在声高。Being
right does not reside in [having] a loud voice. [Cf.
Xīyáng Jì, chap. 10; vs. rén yuàn, yǔ shēng gāo
above.]

386 **Yǒu lǐ jiǎng de jūnwáng dǎo; bùpà jūnwáng zuò
de gāo.** 有理讲得君王倒，不怕君王坐
得高。(lit) With right [on one's side] one can
talk a monarch down [off his throne], no matter
how high he sits. (fig) Before the truth, everyone
is equal. [Rhyme.]

387 **Yǒu lǐ, sān biǎndan; wú lǐ, biǎndan sān.** 有理
三扁担，无理扁担三。(lit) [If one] is in
the right, [one gets hit] three [times with a] pole;
[and if one is] not in the right, [one gets the] pole
three [strokes]. (fig) One is punished all the same
whether one is right or wrong. [A rhyme originally referring to law cases in traditional China in
which the poor could never win a lawsuit; now
referring to the settlement of any case in this manner.]

388 **Yǒu lǐ, yán zì zhuàng; fùqū, shēng bì gāo.** 有理
言自壮，负屈声必高。With right on one's
side, one naturally speaks boldly and straightforwardly; [when one is] wronged, [one] naturally
[speaks in] a loud voice. [Cf. Jǐngshì Tōngyán,
chap. 15; see also rén yuàn, yǔ shēng gāo above.]

389 **Yǒu lǐ, zǒubiàn tiānxià; wú lǐ, cùn bù nán xíng.***
有理走遍天下，无理寸步难行。With
right [on one's side, one can] go anywhere; without right, [one] can hardly step one inch. [Note:
cùnbù-nánxíng is used as a chengyu meaning:
"unable to do anything."]

390 **Yǒu māo, bù zhī māo gōngláo; wú māo, cái zhī
lǎoshǔ duō.** 有猫不知猫功劳，无猫才知老
鼠多。(lit) [While one] cat is there, [one does]
not notice its meritorious service; only when the
cat is gone, [does one] realize [that the number
of] mice has increased. (fig) One never truly appreciates (the services rendered by) others until
they are gone. [See also chuān wà bù zhī above
and jǐng gān cái zhī below.]

391 **Yòunián xué de, hǎobǐ shí shàng kè de.** 幼年
学的，好比石上刻的。[Things] learned in

childhood are like things inscribed in stone. [See also *yǒuqián, nán mǎi* above.]

392 **Yǒuqián, bù mǎi bànnián xián.** 有钱不买半年闲。(lit) [Even if you] have money, don't buy [anything which will lie around] idle for half a year. (fig) Do not buy anything for which you have no immediate use. [Traditional advice, especially to the poor.]

393 **Yǒuqián cháng jì wú qián rì; mò dài wú qián sī yǒu shí.** 有钱常记无钱日，莫待无钱思有时。[When you] are rich, always remember the days [when you were] poor, so that there won't be poor times when you have to recall the days when you were rich.

394 **Yǒuqián, dé shēng; wú qián, dé sǐ.** 有钱得生，无钱得死。With money [one can] obtain [one's] life, [and] without money [one will] obtain one's death. [Referring to the necessity of bribing judicial officials in traditional China; cf. *Wǔ Sōng*, chap. 3; see also *yǒuqián jiùshì tiāntáng lù* below.]

395 **Yǒuqián de wángba dà sān bèi.** 有钱的王八大三辈。With money [even] a bastard gains seniority. [Note: *bèifèn*, "seniority in the family hierarchy"; see also *yǒuqián gāo sān bèi* below.]

396 **Yǒuqián de yào dǎng; méi qián de mìng kàng.** 有钱的药挡，没钱的命抗。[When ill] the rich have medicine to [help them] resist; the poor [have to] rely on fate. [Rhyme.]

397 **Yǒuqián gāo sān bèi; wú qián gōng biàn sūn.** 有钱高三辈，无钱公变孙。(lit) [If one] has money, [one can be] promoted three generations [in the family hierarchy], [but if one] has no money, a grandfather becomes a grandson. (fig) The rich gain in seniority [and] the poor are demeaned. [See also *yǒuqián de wángba* above.]

398 **Yǒuqián jiùshì tiāntáng lù; wú qián jiùshì dìyù mén.** 有钱就是天堂路，无钱就是地狱门。With money it's the road to Heaven; [but] without money it's the gates of Hell. [Referring to the necessity of having money in traditional China; see also *yǒuqián, dé shēng* above.]

399 **Yǒuqián, nán mǎi bù mài huò.** 有钱难买不卖货。[Even] with money [it's] hard to buy what [others] won't sell.

400 **Yǒuqián, nán mǎi hòuhuǐ yào.** 有钱难买后悔药。(lit) Money cannot buy medicine for repentance [i.e., to cure one's mistakes]. (fig) Be careful; being sorry later won't help.

401 **Yǒuqián, nán mǎi shàonián shí.** 有钱难买少年时。(lit) No money can buy [back] childhood [once it's past]. (fig) Childhood is the best time for learning, so study hard. [Traditional advice to children; see also *yòunián xué de* above.]

402 **Yǒuqián, nán mǎi zì zhǔzhāng.** 有钱难买自主张。[Even if one] has money, one can hardly buy one's independence [i.e., the freedom to hold one's own opinions or make one's own decisions].

403 **Yǒuqián, nánzǐhàn; wú qián, hànzǐ nán.** 有钱男子汉，无钱汉子难。[He who] has money [is] a "real man," [and he who] has no money [is] hard [put to be] a man. [Pun: a play on word order and the homophony of *nán*, "male" and *nán* "difficult"; note: *nánzǐhàn*, "a real man (in the he-mannish sense)."]

404 **Yǒuqián néng shǐ guǐ tuīmò.*** 有钱能使鬼推磨。(lit) [If one] has money [one can even] make the devil turn [one's] millstone. (fig) "Money makes the mare go." [Cf. *Gǔ-Jīn Xiǎoshuō*, chap. 21; *Èr Kè Pāi'àn Jīngqí*, chap. 14; see also *qián kě tōng shén* above.]

405 **Yǒu qiān nián chǎn; méi qiān nián zhǔ.** 有千年产，没千年主。Property may last for a thousand years, [but] not its owners. [Cf. *Xǐngshì Héngyán*, chap. 37; see also *tián shì zhǔrén* above.]

406 **Yǒuqián, shén yě pà; wú qián, guǐ yì qī.** 有钱神也怕，无钱鬼亦欺。Gods fear you if [you're] rich, [and even] devils will bully [you if you're] poor. [Cf. *Chū Kè Pāi'àn Jīngqí*, chap. 15.]

407 **Yǒuqián shǐde guǐ dòng; wú qián huànbude rén lái.** 有钱使得鬼动，无钱唤不得人来。With money devils can be mobilized to serve [one, but] without money no one will come to help. [See also *qián jù rúxiōng* and *yǒuqián néng shǐ* above.]

408 **Yǒuqián, sìshí chēng niánlǎo; wú qián, liùshí chěng yīngxióng.** 有钱四十称年老，无钱六十逞英雄。(lit) A rich person calls [himself] old at forty [and retires from working, while] a poor man poses [himself] a hero at sixty [for still working at that age]. (fig) A rich person can retire from working and enjoy life in middle age, while a poor person has to continue to work for a living until (s)he's really old.

409 **Yǒuqián yǒu jiǔ, duō xiōngdì; jínán, hécéng jiàn yī rén?** 有钱有酒多兄弟，急难何曾见一人？(lit) [When one] has money and wine, [one has] many friends, [but when one is in need of help] in misfortune, have you ever seen [even] one [of them]? (fig) Fair-weather friends flock around one in good times, but nobody wants to know you when you're down and out. [Note: *jiǔròu-péngyou*, "fair-weather friends"; see also *qián jù rúxiōng* above.]

410 **Yǒuqián, zhū shì bàn.** 有钱诸事办。With money everything can be done.

411 **Yǒu qí fù, bì yǒu qí zǐ.*** 有其父必有其子。(lit) [As] is the father, [so] must be the son. (fig) "Like father, like son."

412 **Yǒuqíng, hé pà gé nián qī?** 有情何怕隔年期？(lit) [If one is truly] in love, why fear [waiting] another year's time? (fig) True love can wait (forever). [Cf. *Xī Hú Èr Jí*, chap. 14; said by Zhang Dan in the classical novel *Zhāng Yú Zhǔ Hǎi*.]

413 **Yǒu qīnniáng, yǒu hòu yé; wú qīnniáng, wú téng rè.** 有亲娘有后爷，无亲娘无疼热。[If you] have [your] own mother, [you'll] have a step-father [to take care of you, but if your] mother isn't [around anymore, you'll] get no affection [from either your step-mother, nor from your father, who will focus on his new wife and his children

by her]. [A common occurrence in traditional China; see also *gé chóng dùpí* above.]

414 **Yǒu qí yín zhě, bì yǒu qí huò.** 有奇淫者，必有奇祸。 One who is extremely lewd is destined to invite the greatest disaster. [Cf. *Dōng Zhōu Lièguó Zhì*, chap. 15; see also *wàn'è, yín wéishǒu* above.]

415 **Yǒu qí zhǔ, bì yǒu qí pú.** 有其主必有其仆。 (lit) [As] is the master, [so] is the servant. (fig) The servant imitates or resembles his or her master. "Like master, like man" (or "like servant"). [Cf. *DRC*, chap. 74; *Wǔ Sōng*, chap. 6; note: *púrén*, "servant."]

416 **Yǒuquán bù yòng, guòqī zuòfèi.** 有权不用，过期作废。 (lit) [If you] have power [and do] not use [it for personal benefit], later [when you are out of office] it will be useless [i.e., you won't be able to get anything, so use it while you can]. (fig) "Make hay while the sun shines." [A new saying since the 1980s, supposedly used by (corrupt) officials; see also *dāngmiàn bù qǔ* above.]

417 **Yǒu shè zìrán xiāng, hébì dāng fēng lì?** 有麝自然香，何必当风立？ (lit) [As long as] there's musk, it will naturally be fragrant, [so there's] no need to stand in the wind [to show it off]. (fig) A talented person will be known by others even if (s)he doesn't try to show him or herself off.

418 **Yǒushì, nán mán sìlín.** 有事，难瞒四邻。 [If] anything happens [in one's family, it is] hard to hide [it] from [one's] neighbors. [See also *dàshì, mán bu liǎo* above.]

419 **Yǒushuō-yǒuxiào, bù fēn lǎoshào.** 有说有笑，不分老少。 [When there's] chatting and laughing, young and old are all equal. [Rhyme.]

420 **Yǒuxīn bùpà chí.** 有心不怕迟。 [If you are] determined to do something, don't worry [about starting] late (i.e., there's no need for haste). [Cf. *Zàishēng Yuán*, chap. 69; see also *yǒuxīn bù zài máng* and *yǒu xīn shāoxiāng* below.]

421 **Yǒuxīn bù zài máng.** 有心不在忙。 (lit) Determination does not lie in haste. (fig) If one is determined to accomplish something, there is no need for haste. [Cf. *Sān Kè Pāi'àn Jīngqí*, chap. 23; see also *yǒuxīn bùpà chí* above and *yǒu xīn shāoxiāng* below.]

422 **Yǒuxīn dǎ shí, shí chéng zhuān; wúxīn dǎ shí, shí yuán yuán.** 有心打石，石成砖；无心打石，石原原。 (lit) [Only if you] strike the stone wholeheartedly will it become building blocks; if not, it will remain [just stone] as before. (fig) If one wants to succeed, one must put all of one's efforts into a task. [Rhyme.]

423 **Yǒu xīng jiē gǒng běi; wú shuǐ bù cháo dōng.** 有星皆拱北，无水不朝东。 (lit) All stars surround the North [Star, just as] there are no rivers [in north central China which do] not flow eastward. (fig) The people will naturally turn their hearts toward their rulers.

424 **Yǒu xīn shāoxiāng, bùlùn zǎo-wǎn.** 有心烧香，不论早晚。 (lit) [If one is] sincere in burning incense [to the Buddha, it] doesn't matter [whether one is] early [or] late. (fig) As long as one is sincere, it doesn't matter if it's early or late; it is acceptable to be late (with respects, presents, etc.).

425 **Yòu yào mǎ hǎo, yòu yào mǎ bù chī cǎo.*** 又要马好，又要马不吃草。 (lit) [One cannot] both want his horse to run fast, [and] yet [be] unwilling to let it graze. (fig) It is impossible to get anything without paying the price. [Rhyme.]

426 **Yǒu yī lì, bì yǒu yī bì.*** 有一利，必有一弊。 Advantages are inevitably accompanied by disadvantages. [Cf. Lu Xun's essay: "Guānyu Zhōngguó de Liǎng-Sān Jiàn Shì."]

427 **Yǒu yín, yòng yín; wú yín, yònglì.** 有银用银，无银用力。 [Those] with money can [contribute] money [and those] without money can [contribute] labor. [Cf. *Xīngshì Héngyán*, chap. 10.]

428 **Yǒuyì zhònghuā, huā bù fā; wúxīn chā liǔ, liǔ chéng yīn.*** 有意种花花不发；无心插柳柳成荫。 (lit) [If you] deliberately plant a flower it may not blossom, [but] a willow slip casually stuck in [the ground] may grow to [give] shade. (fig) While the best laid plans of mankind often go awry, sometimes unplanned items can unexpectedly turn out successfully. "Follow love, and it will flee; flee love, and it will pursue you." [Cf. *Xīngshì Héngyán*, chap. 20; see also *kě yù ér bù kě qiú* above.]

429 **Yǒuyuán, qiān lǐ lái xiānghuì; wúyuán, duìmiàn bù xiāngféng.*** 有缘千里来相会，无缘对面不相逢。 If fated, [to do so,] people will come together [though a] thousand leagues apart; if not so fated, they will miss each other [though they come] face to face. [Cf. *WM*, chap. 35; *JW*, chap. 81; note: *yuánfèn*, "lot or luck by which people are brought together"; one *lǐ* equals one-half kilometer; see also *gèrén yǒu gèrén de yuánfǎ* and *jì zài fó huì xià* above.]

430 **Yǒu zhì bù zài nián gāo; (wú móu kōng yán bǎisuì).** 有智不在年高，(无谋空言百岁)。 Having wisdom lies not in advanced years; ([with one who] has no resourcefulness, it's pointless to talk [even if (s)he lives to be one] hundred years old). [Note: *kōng yán*, "to speak in vain"; cf. *Fēngshén Yǎnyì*, chap. 23; *Èr Kè Pāi'àn Jīngqí*, chap. 2; compare the following entry.]

431 **Yǒu zhì bù zài nián gāo; (wú zhì kōng huó bǎisuì).** 有志不在年高，无志空活百岁。 [As long as one] has ambition, [it doesn't] matter [whether one is] old or young, ([but a person] without any determination lives an empty life though (s)he's a hundred years old). [Cf. *Sān Xiá Wǔ Yì*, chap. 85; *Guānchǎng Xiànxíng Jì*, chap. 38; note: *zhìqì*, "ambition"; the first half is often used alone with the meaning: "Success goes to the determined regardless of age"; compare the preceding entry.]

432 **Yǒu zhì dēng shāndǐng, wú zhì zhàn shānjiǎo.** 有志登山顶，无志站山脚。 (lit) [One who] has the will [can] climb to the top of the mountain, [while one who] has no will [will] remain at the foot. (fig) Those who have the will to succeed can accomplish great things, and those who do not will never accomplish anything of any significance.

433 **Yǒu zhì fūrén, shèngrú nánzǐ.** 有志妇人, 胜如男子。 A woman with determination is superior to a man. [Cf. *Jīngshì Tōngyán*, chap. 31.]

434 **Yǒu zhì yíng; wú zhì shū.** 有智赢, 无智输。 With wisdom [one will] win [and] without wisdom [one will] fail.

435 **Yǒuzhìzhě, shì jìng chéng.*** 有志者事竟成。 (lit) [If] one has ambition, things will be accomplished. (fig) Nothing is impossible to a willing mind. "Where there is a will, there is a way." [Cf. *Hòu Hàn Shū: Gěng Yǎn Zhuàn*; note: zhìqì, "ambition"; see also *tiānxià wú nánshì* above.]

436 **Yuàn fèi qīn, nù fèi lǐ.** 怨废亲, 怒废礼。 [When one is] discontented, [(s)he will] ignore [his] relatives; [when one is] angry, [(s)he will] ignore [the] proper courtesies. [Cf. *Jīngshì Tōngyán*, chap. 2.]

437 **Yuǎn guān bùrú jìn dǔ.** 远观不如近睹。 It is better to see things close at hand than at a distance.

438 **Yuānjiā lù zhǎi.** 冤家路窄。 (lit) [For] enemies, the way is narrow. (fig) Enemies or rivals often meet whether they want to or not. [See also *bù shì yuānjia* and *gěng lǐ bù zháo* above.]

439 **Yuānjiā yí jiě, bùyí jié.*** 冤家宜解不宜结。 (lit) [The knot of] enmity [should be] untied, not tightened. (fig) It is always better to resolve one's differences with someone than to make an enemy. [Cf. *Xǐngshì Héngyán*, chap. 20; *WM*, chap. 33; *Gǔ-Jīn Xiǎoshuō*, chap. 38; Mao Dun's "*Zǐyè*" (Midnight).]

440 **Yuānjiā zhài, huán bù chè.** 冤家债还不彻。 (lit) Love accounts can never be settled in full. (fig) Love sickness can't be cured. One cannot stop yearning for one's lover. [Note: here *yuānjia* is a colloquial term for "beloved; darling."]

441 **Yuǎn jìng yīshang, jìn jìng rén.** 远敬衣裳, 近敬人。 [When you are] far [from home] [i.e., if people don't know you, you are] respected [for your] clothes; [if you are] close [to home] [i.e., if people know you, you are] respected [as a] person [i.e., for who you are].

442 **Yuǎn lái de héshang huì niànjīng.*** 远来的和尚会念经。 (lit) Monks who come from afar [are considered to be] better at reading scriptures. (fig) People who come from afar are more valued than local talent. "A prophet is not without honor save in his own country." [Cf. *JW*, chap. 72; see also *běndì jiāng bù là* above.]

443 **Yuǎnlù méi qīng dàn.*** 远路没轻担。 (lit) [On a] long road there are no light burdens. (fig) Light burdens, when carried for a long time, grow heavy. [Cf. *JW*, chap. 80; also said *bǎi bù wú qīng dàn* in *Hě Diǎn*, chap. 5; see also *lù yuǎn méi qīng zài* above.]

444 **Yuǎnqīn bùrú jìnlín.*** 远亲不如近邻。 A nearby neighbor is better than a far-off relative. [Cf. *WM*, chap. 24; see also *jìn xiānglín* and *línjū hǎo* above and *yuǎnqīn, jìnlín* below.]

445 **Yuàn qīn, bù yuàn shū.** 怨亲, 不怨疏。 (lit) Blame oneself; do not blame outsiders. (fig) When anything happens, it is oneself that is to blame, not anyone else.

446 **Yuǎnqīn, jìnlín bùrú duìmén.** 远亲近邻不如对门。 [Neither] a far-off relative [nor] a nearby neighbor are as good as [one's] next door neighbor. [Cf. *Wǔ Sōng*, chap. 2; see also *yuǎnqīn bùrú* above.]

447 **Yuǎn shuǐ bù jiě jìn kě.*** 远水不解近渴。 (lit) Far off water cannot satisfy a present thirst. (fig) Distant, slow, or long-term measures cannot solve an immediate problem. [Cf. *DRC*, chap. 15; see also the following entry.]

448 **Yuǎn shuǐ bù jiù jìn huǒ.*** 远水不救近火。 (lit) Distant water cannot extinguish a nearby fire. (fig) Distant, slow or long-term measures will not solve a present emergency. [Cf. *Hán Fēizǐ: Shuō Lín Shàng*; *Èr Kè Pāi'àn Jīngqí*, chap. 3; see also *è dùzi děngbude* above and the preceding entry.]

449 **Yuǎnxíng wú jí bù.** 远行无急步。 [When] traveling [a] long distance, there is no [need to] make haste [and become tired to no purpose]. [Cf. *Hòu Xīyóu Jì*, chap. 10.]

450 **Yuán yàoshi kāi yuán suǒ.** 原钥匙开原锁。 (lit) [Only the] original key [can] open the original lock. (fig) Only one who knows the (inside) details of a problem can solve it. [Cf. *Wǔ Sōng*, chap. 10; see also *yào pò Dōng Wú bīng* above.]

451 **Yuān yǒu tóu; zhài yǒuzhǔ.*** 冤有头, 债有主。 (lit) [Every] wrong has [its] source, [and every] debt has [its] incurrer. (fig) The culprit must pay for his wrong, and the debtor for his debt. One should complain to or take one's revenge on the person who caused the trouble in the first place. [Cf. *WM*, chap. 26; *JPM*, chap. 87.]

452 **Yuǎn zài érsūn, jìn zài shēn.** 远在儿孙近在身。 (lit) [Wickedness will be punished] sooner upon oneself [or] later upon one's descendants. (fig) One's wrongdoing will catch up with one sooner or later. [See also *shàn yǒu shànbào* above.]

453 **Yuǎn zéi bì yǒu jìn jiǎo.** 远贼必有近脚。 A thief from afar must have "someone on the inside" [in order to succeed]. [See also *jiā zéi nán fáng* above and *zéi wú lì dǐ* below.]

454 **Yú bāng shuǐ; shuǐ bāng yú.** 鱼帮水, 水帮鱼。 (lit) Fish help water [and] water helps fish. (fig) People are mutually interdependent; people (must) help each other. [Often used to mean that the (Chinese) Communist party and the (Chinese) people are mutually interdependent; see also *yú líbukāi shuǐ* below.]

455 **Yù bàng xiāng zhēng, yú rén dé lì.** 鹬蚌相争, 鱼人得利。 (lit) [When a] snipe [and a] clam quarrel, [it is the] fisherman [who] benefits. (fig) When two parties quarrel over something, a third may profit or run off with it. [Based on *Zhànguó Cè: Yàn Cè Èr*; cf. *Èr Kè Pāi'àn Jīngqí*, chap. 10.]

456 **Yù bù zhuó, bù chéng qì.*** 玉不琢不成器。 (lit) If jade is not cut and polished, it cannot be made into anything. (fig) One cannot become useful without being trained/educated/disciplined. "Spare the rod and spoil the child." [Cf. *Lǐjì: Xué Jì*; *Shuō Yuè Quán Zhuàn*, chap. 4; note: *bùchéngqì* is also an idiom for "good-for-nothing; worthless."]

Y

457 (Yuè guò shíwǔ, guāngmíng shǎo;) rén dào zhōngnián, wànshì xiū. (月过十五光明少;) 人到中年万事休。(lit) (After the fifteenth [of the lunar month, when the moon is full] the moon [becomes less and] less bright;) [when] people get to middle age, everything comes to a halt. (fig) After middle age, nothing great can be accomplished. [Cf. *Gǔ-Jīn Xiǎoshuō*, chap. 33; the second part is more commonly used alone (q.v.).]

458 Yuè lǐ Cháng'é ài shàonián. 月里嫦娥爱少年。(lit) [The goddess] Cháng'é in the moon loves youths. (fig) Young girls love *young* men; young girls won't fall in love with old men. [Cf. *DRC*, chap. 46; note: *Cháng'é* refers to the legendary fairy princess on the moon in a popular folk story; also said *zǐgǔ Cháng'é ài shàonián*, (q.v.).]

459 Yuè yǒu, yuè yǒu; yuè méiyǒu, yuè méiyǒu. 越有越有，越没有越没有。(lit) Those who have get even more, and those who have not, have even less. (fig) "The rich get richer and the poor get poorer."

460 Yù guìrén, chībǎo fàn. 遇贵人吃饱饭。(lit) [Whoever] meets a noble person [will] have his fill to eat. (fig) One will benefit from meeting a generous person.

461 Yú guò qiān céng wǎng; wǎngwǎng háiyǒu yú. 鱼过千层网，网网还有鱼。(lit) [Even though] fish pass through a thousand nets, there are still fish in every net; [i.e., some fish are always caught]. (fig) There must be some slips even in the most well organized plan; some are always bound to slip through.

462 Yù jiā zhī zuì, hé huàn wú cí? 欲加之罪，何患无辞？(lit) [If one] desires to frame [someone]'s guilt, why worry [about] not having a case? (fig) If one is out to falsely accuse somebody, it is easy to trump up a charge. [This is a paraphrase of *Zǒu Zhuàn: Xí Gōng 10 Nián*, originally ". . ., qí wú cí hū"; see also *gǒu yǎo rén* and *ruǎndāozi shārén* above.]

463 Yǔ jūn yī xí huà, shèng dú shí nián shū.* 与君一夕话，胜读十年书。One evening's conversation with a gentleman is worth more than ten years of study. [Cf. *Lǎo Cán Yóujì*, chap. 9; note: here *jūn* is an honorific term, often used flatteringly to others.]

464 Yù kě suì ér bùkě gǎi qí bái; zhú kě fén ér bùkě huǐ qí jié. 玉可碎而不可改其白，竹可焚而不可毁其节。(lit) Jade may be shattered, but its whiteness remains unchanged; bamboo may be burned, but its joints remain indestructible. (fig) One must maintain one's integrity even under difficult circumstances. [Cf. *R3K*, chap. 76.]

465 Yú líbukāi shuǐ; guā líbukāi yāng.* 鱼离不开水，瓜离不开秧。(lit) Fish cannot leave the water, nor can melons leave the vine. (fig) The [Chinese] people cannot be separated from the Communist party. [A line in a Communist song popular during the Cultural Revolution: *Dà Hǎi Hángxíng Kào Duòshǒu* (Sailing the Seas Depends on the Helmsman).]

466 Yùn dào shí lái, tiěshù huā kāi. 运到时来，铁树花开。(lit) When luck befalls [one], [even] the iron tree will blossom. (fig) When luck is going one's way, all kinds of rare events can come to pass. [Rhyme; note: the "iron tree" (sago cycas or *Cycas revoluta*) blooms only once every several years; see also *shí dào, huā jiù kāi* above.]

467 Yún lǐ, qiān tiáo lù; yún wài, lù qiān tiáo. 云里千条路，云外路千条。(lit) [There are] thousands of roads in the clouds [and] roads by the thousands beyond the clouds. (fig) There are many ways to do the job. "There's more than one way to skin a cat."

468 Yùn qù, huángjīn shīsè; shí lái, tiě yě shēng guāng. 运去黄金失色，时来铁也生光。(lit) [When one's] luck [has] gone, gold loses [its] splendor; [when one's lucky] time comes, even iron shines bright. (fig) When one's luck runs out, everything seems to go wrong; when luck is running one's way, everything seems wonderful. [Cf. *Jīngshì Tōngyán*, chap. 31; *Chū Kè Pāi'àn Jīngqí*, chap. 1; see also *rén dǎoméi* and *shí lái, wàn tiě* above.]

469 Yùnyòng zhī miào, zàihu yī xīn. 运用之妙在乎一心。(lit) Ingenuity in applying [tactics] lies in the mind. (fig) Ingenuity in application of tactics depends on utilizing one's cleverness of mind, and not just in a rote application of the rules. Tactics depend on how ingeniously they are applied in any one situation. [Originally ". . . cún yú yī xīn" in *Sòng Shǐ 365: Yuè Fēi Zhuàn*; now more commonly ". . . zàihu yī xīn", e.g., in *Rúlín Wàishǐ*, chap. 43.]

470 Yù qióng qiān lǐ mù, gèng shàng yī céng lóu. 欲穷千里目，更上一层楼。(lit) [If one] desires [to see] as far as [one's] eye [can for a] thousand leagues, [one must] ascend even one story [higher]. (fig) If one wants to know more, one must exert even more effort. [A line from a poem entitled "Dèng Guàn Què Lóu" by the Tang dynasty poet Wang Zhihuan.]

471 Yǔqí shòu rén liánmǐn, bùrú bèi rén dùjì.* 与其受人怜悯，不如被人妒忌。It is better to be envied by others than to be pitied by others. [See also *bèi rén jìdu* above.]

472 Yǔ rén fāngbiàn; zìjǐ fāngbiàn.* 与人方便，自己方便。A good turn to someone else is a good turn to oneself. [Cf. *JW*, chap. 30; also said *yǔ rén fāngbiàn; yǔ jǐ fāngbiàn; yǔrén-fāngbiàn* is used as an idiom meaning "to make things easy for others"; note the *chengyu*: *zhùrén-wéilè*, "to find pleasure in helping others"; see also *qīng rén hái zì qīng* above.]

473 Yúrén guān shuǐshì, lièrén wàng niǎo fēi. 渔人观水势，猎人望鸟飞。(lit) Fishermen observe the movement of the water, [and] hunters watch the flight of birds. (fig) Professionals are interested in studying their own trade.

474 Yù rén wù wén, mòruò wù yán. 欲人勿闻，莫若勿言。[If you do] not want others to hear [what you say], better not to say it. [Rhyme; cf. *Shuō Wǎn: Cóng Tán* by Liu Xiang in the Han dynasty.]

Y

475 **Yù shí qí rén, xiān shí qí yǒu.** 欲识其人，先识 其友。 (lit) [If you] want to know this person, first [get to] know his friends. (fig) "A man is known by the company he keeps." [See also *bù zhī qí rén* above.]

476 **Yùshì xiángqíng, fāng suàn míngrén.** 遇事详 情，方算明人。 Only [one who, when (s)he] encounters a situation, [inquires] in detail [may be] reckoned a discerning person.

477 **Yù sù zé bù dá.** 欲速则不达。 (lit) Desiring [more] speed but not attaining [one's goal]. (fig) "The more haste, the less speed." "Haste makes waste." [See also *jí xíng wú shàn jì* and *jí zhōng yǒu shī* and *jǐn xíng wú hǎo bù* and *tān kuài chū chācuò* above.]

478 **Yú zhǎo yú; xiā zhǎo xiā; wángbā jié le gè biē qīnjiā.** 鱼找鱼，虾找虾，王八结了个鳖亲 家。 (lit) Fish seek fish [and] shrimp seek shrimp; a tortoise takes a soft-shelled turtle in marriage.

(fig) "Like attracts like." "Birds of a feather flock together." [Rhyme.]

479 **Yú zhě àn yú chéngshì; zhìzhě jiàn yú wèi méng.** 愚者闇于成事，智者见于未萌。 (lit) [A] foolish person [remains in the] dark about what [has already] happened, [while an] intelligent person [can] predict what will happen before something happens. (fig) A fool is always in the dark, while a clever person can see things coming. [Note: *wèi méng,* (lit) "not yet budded out," (fig) "things to come."]

480 **Yú zhě qiān lǜ, bì yǒu yī dé.** 愚者千虑，必有 一得。 (lit) [If a] fool [makes] a thousand calculations, there must be one [accidentally] correct. (fig) Even a fool occasionally hits on a good idea. [Cf. *Shǐ Jì: Huái Yīn Hóu Lièzhuàn;* often used self-deprecatingly; this often occurs together with *zhìzhě qiān lǜ* (q.v.) below; note the *chengyu: qiānlǜ-yīdé,* "one good idea out of a thousand"; see also *cōngming yīshì* above.]

Z

1 **Zàijiā bù huì yíng bīnkè; chūmén fāng zhī shǎo gùrén.** 在家不会迎宾客，出门方知少故 人。 [If one] doesn't invite guests [when one is] at home, [one will] find out how few friends [one has when one] goes out.

2 **Zàijiā bù shì pín; lù pín, pín shā rén.** 在家不是 贫，路贫贫杀人。 See *jiā pín, bù shì pín* above.

3 **Zàijiā jìng fùmǔ; hé yòng yuǎn shāoxiāng?** 在家 敬父母，何用远烧香? (lit) [If one] respects [one's] parents at home, what need [is there to go] afar to burn incense [in temples]? (fig) One's first and highest duty is toward one's parents. [Cf. *Érnǚ Yīngxióng Zhuàn,* chap. 24; note the traditional Chinese belief that the greater the distance one goes on one's pilgrimage, the more efficacious it will be.]

4 **Zàijiā kào fùmǔ; chūwài kào péngyou.*** 在家 靠父母，出外靠朋友。 At home one relies on one's parents [but] outside one [has to] rely on one's friends. [See also *zàijiā, tóu yéniáng* above.]

5 **Zàijiā qiān rì hǎo; chūmén yīshí nán.*** 在家千 日好，出门一时难。 (lit) It's good to stay at home for a thousand days, [and] it's hard to leave home for a short time. (fig) "There's no place like home"; the world is a dangerous place. [Cf. *Suí Táng Yǎnyì,* chap. 10; see also *chū de mén duō* and *chūwài yī lǐ* above.]

6 **Zàijiā, tóu yéniáng; chūjiā, tóu zhǔrén.** 在家 投爷娘，出家投主人。 At home one relies on one's parents, [but when one] leaves home one [has to] rely on one's superior(s) [for support]. [Often said when looking for a job; also said *zàijiā tóu diēniáng; chūmén tóu zhǔrén;* cf. *Xǐngshì Yīnyuán Zhuàn,* chap. 27; see also *zàijiā kào fùmǔ* above.]

7 **Zài rén ǎi yán xià, zěn gǎn bù dītóu?** 在人矮檐 下，怎敢不低头? See *(jì) zài ǎi yán xià* above.

8 **Zài shēng yī rì, shèng sǐ qiān nián.** 在生一日， 胜死千年。 One day of life is worth more than a thousand years of death. [Usually said by cowards; see also *hǎo sǐ bùrú* above.]

9 **Zǎixiàng jiā rén qī pǐn guān.** 宰相家人七品 官。 A servant in a prime minister's family [is as powerful as a] county magistrate. [Note: *qī pǐn guān* referred to the lowest level magistrate in the county government in the traditional imperial bureaucracy, often colloquially referred to as *qī pǐn zhímǎ guān,* "a county magistrate as small as a sesame seed."]

10 **Zài yī fāng, chī yī fāng.** 在一方，吃一方。 (lit) [If you're] in a place, eat [off] that place. (fig) Wherever you find yourself, make your living there. [See also *fēngzhe hǎochù* above.]

11 **Zāngguān bù dǎ sònglǐ rén.** 赃官不打送礼人。 A corrupt official won't punish one who sends gifts, [so one can safely offer him a bribe]. [More commonly said *guānfǔ bù dǎ sònglǐ de* (q.v.).]

12 **Zǎnqián hǎobǐ zhēn tiāo tǔ; bài jiā yóurú shuǐ tuī shā.** 攒钱好比针挑土，败家犹如水推 沙。 (lit) Accumulation of money is [as slow] as picking up soil with a needle, [while the] ruination of a family is just as [fast as] water washing away the sands. (fig) It takes years of painstaking effort to build up a family's fortune, but it can all be lost overnight. [Note: the first word can be pronounced either *zǎnqián* "to save money," or *cuánqián,* "to piece together small sums of money"; see also *chénglǐ zhī nán* above.]

13 **Zāo bízi bù hējiǔ, wǎng dān xūmíng.** 糟鼻子 不喝酒，枉担虚名。 (lit) [A] red-nosed [man may] not drink liquor, [but he will always] carry the false name [of drunkard]. (fig) People commonly judge others by appearances only.

14 **Zǎochén zāi xià shù, dào wǎn yào chéngliáng.** 早晨栽下树，到晚要乘凉。(lit) [If you] plant a tree in the morning, [it is unrealistic to expect to] sit in the cool [of it's shade] by the evening. (fig) One should be realistic in one's expectations.

15 **Zǎofàn chī de bǎo; zhōngfàn chī de hǎo; wǎnfàn chī de shǎo.** 早饭吃得饱, 中饭吃得好, 晚饭吃得少。Eat a full breakfast, [and] eat a good lunch, [but only] eat a small supper. [Advice for good health; see also *yèfàn shǎo jìn kǒu* above.]

16 **Zào fǎ róngyì; zhífǎ nán.** 造法容易, 执法难。To make a law is easy; to carry it out is difficult.

17 **Zǎoqǐ sān zhāo dāng yī gōng.** 早起三朝当一工。Getting up early for three mornings is equal to one [day of] work. [See also *sān gè wǔgēng* and *yī nián zhī jì* above.]

18 **Zào zhú qiú míng; dúshū qiú lǐ.** 造烛求明, 读书求理。[Just as one] makes candles [in order to] get light, [so one] reads books [in order to] seek truth.

19 **Zéi bèi gǒu yǎo, àn mèn kǔ.** 贼被狗咬, 暗闷苦。(lit) A thief bitten by a dog cannot tell his grief to others. (fig) Wrong doers must suffer in silence. [Cf. *Hé Diǎn*, chap. 6.]

20 **Zéi hàn, ruǎn rú mián.** 贼汉软如绵。A thief [when caught will pretend to be as] soft as silk.

21 **Zéi kǒu chū shèngzhǐ.** 贼口出圣旨。(lit) [What] comes out of a thief's mouth [is always believed as if it were an] imperial edict. (fig) People will generally believe a thief when he accuses someone of being his accomplice; the accused can't avoid the blame. [See also *zéi yǎo yīkǒu* below.]

22 **Zéi méi zhǒng, zhǐpà hǒng.** 贼没种, 只怕哄。(lit) Thieves are not bred, [but are] just misled. (fig) Criminals are not born, but are led into a life of crime. [Rhyme.]

23 **Zéi nán yuān; shǐ nánchī.** 贼难冤, 屎难吃。(lit) Thievery [is as] hard to falsely accuse [someone of as] excrement is hard to eat. (fig) It is difficult to falsely charge someone with theft. [Cf. *Hé Diǎn*, chap. 8; vs. *zéi yǎo yīkǒu* below.]

24 **Zéirén ān de zéi xīncháng; lǎoshǔ zhǎo de mǐ liángcāng.*** 贼人安的贼心肠, 老鼠找的米粮仓。(lit) Thieves [always] harbor evil designs [just as] mice [are always] looking for a grain storehouse. (fig) Evildoers always harbor evil intentions and are not likely to change their characters. [Rhyme; see also *húli zuòmèng* above.]

25 **Zéi shì mùshū; bīng shì zhú bǐ.** 贼是木梳, 兵是竹篦。(lit) Thieves are [like a] wooden comb, [but] soldiers are [like a] sieve. (fig) Thieves just steal a little, but [in traditional China] soldiers take everything. [Cf. Qi Jiguang's *Liàn Bīng Shí Jì*, chap. 9.]

26 **Zéi shì xiǎorén; zhì guò jūnzǐ.** 贼是小人, 智过君子。A thief is a mean person, [but he is] smarter than a gentleman, [so beware!]

27 **Zéi wú jiǎo, tōu bù zháo.** 贼无脚, 偷不着。Without a planted agent [i.e., someone "on the inside"], a thief cannot steal anything. [See also *yuǎn zéi bì yǒu jìn jiǎo* above and *zéi wú lì dǐ* below; see also the following two entries.]

28 **Zéi wú lì dǐ, zhōng dào huí.** 贼无历底, 中道回。(lit) A thief who has no agent inside [to help him will] turn back half way. (fig) A thief will give up his evil intention if he cannot find an inside agent. [See also *jiā zéi nán fáng* and *méi(yǒu) jiā zéi* and *yuǎn zéi bì yǒu* above.]

29 **Zéi wú shú jiǎo, cùnbù nán yí.** 贼无熟脚, 寸步难移。Without a planted agent, a thief can hardly move a tiny step. [See also the preceding two entries.]

30 **Zéi wú zāng, yìng sì gāng.** 贼无赃, 硬似钢。(lit) A thief without loot [will be as] hard as steel. (fig) Unless caught red-handed with the stolen goods, a thief will deny everything resolutely. [Rhyme.]

31 **Zéi yǎo yīkǒu, rù gǔ sānfēn.** 贼咬一口, 入骨三分。(lit) One bite by a thief [is as deep as] three inches into the bone. (fig) One is hard put to prove oneself innocent if falsely charged by a thief. [See also *zéi kǒu chū shèngzhǐ* above; vs. *zéi nán yuān* above.]

32 **Zhǎn cǎo bù chúgēn, chūnfēng chuī yòu shēng.*** 斩草不除根, 春风吹又生。(lit) [When] cutting weeds, [if one does] not dig up the roots, [when] spring comes, [the weeds will] sprout again. (fig) Stamp out the source of trouble completely or you will be sorry later. [Also said *zhǎn cǎo bù chúgēn, fēng chūn fāqīng yòu shēng*; see also the following entry.]

33 **Zhǎn cǎo chú gēn, méngyá bù fā.*** 斩草除根, 萌芽不发。(lit) [When] cutting weeds, remove the roots [so that they will] not germinate sprouts [again]. (fig) Stamp out the source of trouble completely or you will be sorry later. [Cf. *WM*, chap. 49; *Lǎo Cán Yóují*, chap. 5; *zhǎncǎo-chúgēn* is used as an idiom meaning "to destroy root and branch"; see also the preceding entry.]

34 **Zhàn de gāo, kàn de yuǎn.*** 站的高, 看的远。[One who] stands higher can see farther. (fig) One who is educated or in a position of authority has a broader perspective. [Said of one who has a wider perspective or greater vision than others.]

35 **Zhǎng de qiào, cái shì qiào, dǎbàn qiào, rě rén xiào.** 长得俏才是俏, 打扮俏惹人笑。Only [she who is] born a beauty is [a true] beauty; [she who] makes [herself] up as a beauty is a laughing stock. [Rhyme.]

36 **Zhǎngduò de (xīn) bù huāng, chéngchuán de (cái) wěndang.** 掌舵的(心)不慌, 乘船的(才)稳当。(lit) (Only) if [the] helmsman [is] not nervous, [will the] passengers feel secure. (fig) If a leader appears confident, his followers will feel secure. [Also said *bǎduò de bù huāng, chéngchuán de wěndang* (q.v.).]

37 **Zhàngfu yǒu lèi bù qīng tán; zhǐ yīn wèi dào shāngxīn chù.** 丈夫有泪不轻弹, 只因未到伤心处。(lit) [Real] men only weep when deeply hurt. (fig) Real men should not shed tears easily. One should save one's tears for serious hurts. [See also *hǎohàn liúxuè* above.]

Z

38 **Zhāng Sān yǒuqián, bù huì shǐ; Lǐ Sì huì shǐ què wú qián.** 张三有钱不会使，李四会使却无钱。 (lit) "Third Brother Zhang" is wealthy, [but] doesn't know how to [make the best] use [of it], while "Fourth Brother Li" [who does] know, has no money. (fig) That's how life is: those who have the money don't know how to use it, and those who know how don't have any. [Note: *Zhāng Sān Lǐ Sì*, (lit) "Third Brother Zhang and Fourth Brother Li," is an idiom equivalent to "Tom and Jack," meaning "this one and that one."]

39 **Zhǎng shàn ér jiù qí shī.** 长善而救其失。 [To bring into full play one's] strong points [can] make up for [one's] shortcomings. [Cf. *Lǐjì: Xué Jì.*]

40 **Zhǎngxiōng wéi fù; (zhǎng sǎo wéi niáng).*** 长兄为父，(长嫂为娘)。 [In the family] the eldest brother (and his wife) are [regarded] as father (and mother) [in the absence of the parents]. [A traditional Chinese view; cf. *WM*, chap. 24.]

41 **Zhàn xiǎopiányi, chī dà kuī.** 占小便宜，吃大亏。 (lit) [If one seeks] petty benefits, [one may] suffer great losses. (fig) "Gain a penny (only to) lose a pound." [Note: during the Cultural Revolution Liu Shaoqi was criticized for recommending *chī xiǎo kuī, zhàn dà piányi* ("suffer a little to gain a lot") as a strategy for joining the Chinese Communist party; see also *chī xiǎo kuī* and *xiǎoqián bù qù* above.]

42 **Zhāoxiá zhǔ yǔ; wǎnxiá zhǔ qíng.** 朝霞主雨，晚霞主晴。 (lit) Rosy morning clouds indicate rain; sunset clouds mean clear weather. (fig) "Red sky at night, sailor's delight; red sky in the morning, sailor, take warning." [Sometimes said: *zǎoxiá . . .*; "early morning rosy clouds"; this is an example of a *qìxiàng yànyǔ* or "weather proverb."]

43 **Zhà rù lúwéi, bù zhī shēnqiǎn.** 乍入芦圩，不知深浅。 [When one] first enters reed marshes, [one does] not know [where are] the deeps and shallows. (fig) When one first comes into a new situation, one doesn't know how things stand (and therefore may behave tactlessly). [Cf. *JW*, chap. 32; note: *bùzhī-shēnqiǎn* is a colloquial expression meaning "not know(ing) how things stand; behave tactlessly"; see also *xīn lái, wǎn dào* below.]

44 **Zhěn biān gàozhuàng; yīshuō biàn zhǔn.*** 枕边告状，一说便准。 (lit) A complaint lodged by the pillow [by a wife to her husband in bed] is taken as gospel as soon as [it is] uttered. (fig) Husbands tend to believe their wives. [Cf. *Chū Kè Pāi'àn Jīngqí*, chap. 20; see also *nǚrén shì* above and *tīng bù tīng* below.]

45 **Zhēn bù zhēn, kàn biàn zhī.** 真不真，看便知。 [Whether it's] true or false, [one can] tell just by looking [oneself].

46 **Zhēn dāo gè yòng.** 砧刀各用。 (lit) Chopping block [and] knife, each [has its own] use. (fig) Each (person or thing) has its own use. [Cf. *Érnǚ Yīngxióng Zhuàn*, chap. 37.]

47 **Zhēn de, jiǎ bùliǎo; jiǎ de, zhēn bùliǎo.*** 真的假不了，假的真不了。 Truth won't turn into falsehood, nor vice-versa. [See also *shì zhēn, nán jiǎ* and *shì zhēn, nán miè* and *zhēn shì zhēn* above.]

48 **Zhèng bùróng xié.** 正不容邪。 The upright cannot tolerate evil. [Cf. *DRC*, chap. 2.]

49 **Zhèng guō pèi hǎo zào; wāi guō pèi bié zào.** 正锅配好灶，歪锅配鳖灶。 (lit) A good pot for a good stove [and] a bad pot for a bad stove. (fig) People usually find appropriate partners [especially in social status for marriage]. "There's no pot so ugly it can't find a lid." [See also *huā duì huā* and *làn guō zìyǒu* above.]

50 **Zhěng píng bù yáo, bàn píng yáo.** 整瓶不摇半瓶摇。 (lit) Full bottles don't shake, [while] half full ones do. (fig) The learned are modest, while those of little learning brag and boast. [Cf. *Jìnghuā Yuán*, chap. 23; see also *kōng guànzi* and *shuǐ shēn bù xiǎng* above.]

51 **Zhèng rén xiān zhèng jǐ. / Zhèng rén xiān lǜjǐ.** 正人先正己。/正人先律己。 (lit) The upright person first disciplines himself. (fig) One who cannot discipline himself is not fit to discipline others. [Cf. Mencius, *Mèngzǐ: Wàn Zhāng Shàng*; see also *wèi liáng tārén* above.]

52 **Zhèng rú bīngshuāng, jiānguǐ xiāowáng; wēi rú léitíng, kòuzéi bù shēng.** 政如冰霜奸宄消亡，威如雷霆寇贼不生。 [If the] government [is as severe as] ice [and] frost, evildoers [will] disappear; [if] authority [is as powerful as a] thunder bolt, bandits and rebels [will] not appear.

53 **Zhēnhuà hǎoshuō; huǎnghuà nán biān.** 真话好说，谎话难编。 It's easier to tell truth [than to] fabricate lies.

54 **Zhēnjiān dà de kūlong; dǒu dà de fēng.** 针尖大的窟窿，斗大的风。 (lit) A wind as big as a bushel [can get through a] hole as small as the point of a needle. (fig) Small oversights can result in pecks of trouble. [See also *xiǎo dòng bù bǔ* above.]

55 **Zhēn jīn bì fàngguāng; cuìyù bì yào cǎi.** 真金必放光，翠玉必耀彩。 (lit) True gold always glitters [and] jade always sparkles. (fig) Persons of ability will show their remarkable character and wisdom wherever they may be.

56 **Zhēn jīn bù néng zhōng xiàn.** 真金不能终陷。 (lit) True gold cannot be buried [forever]. (fig) A talented person will not remain unemployed (or in obscurity) forever.

57 **Zhēn jīn bùpà huǒ (liàn).*** 真金不怕火(炼)。 (lit) True gold fears no fire. (fig) A person's true worth is revealed under difficult conditions. An honest person can withstand the severest testing. [See also *lièhuǒ jiàn zhēnjīn* above.]

58 **Zhēn púsa shāo ge shénme jiǎ xiāng?** 真菩萨烧个什么假香？ (lit) Why is false incense being burned before a real Buddha? (fig) Never burn false incense before true Buddhas. Don't tell lies indiscriminately before a discriminating person. [See also *zhēnrén miànqián* above.]

59 **Zhēnrén bù lòuxiàng; lòuxiàng bù zhēnrén.*** 真人不露相，露相不真人。(lit) One who has attained the Way doesn't show [it]; [one who] makes a show [of it has] not attained the Way. (fig) One who is really capable doesn't show off, and those who show off aren't really capable. [Cf. *DRC*, chap. 117; *Érnǔ Yīngxióng Zhuàn*, chap. 15; note: *zhēnrén* is a Taoist term referring to one who has attained enlightenment.]

60 **Zhēnrén miànqián shuōbude jiǎhuà.*** 真人面前说不得假话。Before one who [knows] the truth [one] cannot tell lies. [Cf. *Jǐngshì Tōngyán*, chap. 14; *Érnǔ Yīngxióng Zhuàn*, chap. 8; see also *zhēn púsa shāo ge shénme* below.]

61 **Zhēn shì zhēn; jiǎ shì jiǎ.** 真是真，假是假。(lit) Truth is truth; falsehood is falsehood. (fig) Truth cannot be confused with falsehood. [Cf. *DRC*, chap. 104; see also *zhēn de, jiǎ bùliǎo* above.]

62 **Zhēn wǎng nǎlǐ zuān; xiàn wǎng nǎlǐ chuān.** 针往哪里钻，线往哪里穿。(lit) Wherever the needle goes through, the thread follows along. (fig) People follow their leaders.

63 **Zhēnxiū bǎi wèi, yī bǎo biàn xiū.** 珍馐百味，一饱便休。[Even though there are many] dainty meats [and] fine dishes, once [one is really] full [one has to] stop [eating]. [Cf. *JW*, chap. 96.]

64 **Zhēn yínzi bù xiǎng; zhēn cáizhu bù yáng.** 真银子不响，真财主不扬。(lit) [Just as] silver [should] not [be] jingle[d], [so] a truly wealthy person [should] not show off [his wealth to others]. (fig) It is not wise for the wealthy to show off their wealth to others. [Rhyme; see also *jīn-yín bù lòubái* and *qiáncái bù lòu* above.]

65 **Zhè shān wàngjiàn nà shān gāo.** 这山望见那山高。(lit) [Standing on] this hill, [one] finds another hill higher. (fig) One's desire is never satisfied. "The grass is always greener on the other side of the fence." [See also *rénxīn bùzú* above.]

66 **Zhǐ bàng mòrú zìxiū.** 止谤莫如自修。[To] stop slander there is no [better way] than self-cultivation. [Cf. *Sān Guó Zhì: Wèi Shū: Wáng Chǎng Zhuàn*; note: *fěibàng*, "slander."]

67 **Zhǐ bāo bu zhù huǒ.** 纸包不住火。(lit) Paper cannot wrap fire. (fig) The truth cannot be hidden. The truth will come out in the end. [Cf. *Wǔ Sōng*, chap. 2; see also *bèitóu lǐ zuòshì* and *chái duī lǐ cáng* and *xuě lǐ mái bu zhù* above.]

68 **Zhìbìng bùrú fángbìng.** 治病不如防病。(lit) Curing an illness is not as good as preventing an illness. (fig) "An ounce of prevention is worth a pound of cure."

69 **Zhī bùzú zhě hàoxué; chǐ xiàwèn zhě zìmǎn.** 知不足者好学；耻下问者自满。One [who is] not satisfied is good at learning; one [who is] ashamed to ask subordinates is conceited. [Cf. *Shěng Xīn Luò* by the Northern Song dynasty poet Lin Bu; note: *bù chǐ xiàwèn*, "not above asking one's juniors" (if one doesn't know).]

70 **Zhìchéng shí shàng shēng qīngcǎo.** 至诚石上生青草。(lit) Sincerity [makes] grass grow on a stone. (fig) Sincerity makes anything possible.

71 **Zhìchéng (suǒ zhì), jīn shí wéi kāi.*** 至诚(所至)，金石为开。(lit) (Whenever [there is]) sincerity, [even] metals [and] stones [can] be opened up. (fig) No difficulty is insurmountable if one is sincere. [Note: *jīnshí*, (lit) "metal and stone," is a literary expression symbolizing hardness; *jīnshí-wéikāi*, "sincerity can make metal and stone crack," is used alone as a set phrase; see also *jīngchéng suǒ zhì* above.]

72 **Zhǐ chóu bù yǎng; bù chóu bù zhǎng.** 只愁不养，不愁不长。(lit) [People] only worry about not [having a child born to them to] raise, not about [whether it will] grow up. (fig) Just be glad you've got a child born at all, and don't worry about its growing up, which will just happen naturally. [Rhyme; cf. *Xǐngshì Héngyán*, chap. 27.]

73 **Zhī cuò, gǎicuò, bù suàn cuò.** 知错改错不算错。A mistake recognized and corrected is not a mistake. [See also *yǒu cuò, gǎicuò* above.]

74 **Zhīdǐ mò guò dāng xiāngrén.** 知底莫过当乡人。No one knows a person better than his fellow natives. [See also *línjū yǎnjing* above and *zuòfàn mán bu liǎo* below.]

75 **Zhì dí qiān jūn; lì dí yī rén.** 智敌千军，力敌一人。[With] knowledge [one can] fight [any] army [of a] thousand, [but with] physical force [one can only] fight one person. [See also *kào lìliang néng jǔ* and the following entry.]

76 **Zhī ēn bù bào fēi jūnzi.** 知恩不报非君子。(lit) [To] know kindness [and] not repay [it] is not to be a gentleman. (fig) It is ungentlemanly to forget a generous act. [Cf. *JW*, chap. 27.]

77 **Zhǐ ér, bù yǎnglǎo; zhǐ dì, bù dǎliáng.** 指儿不养老，指地不打粮。(lit) Don't count on your sons to support you when you're old, [just as you] don't count on the land for harvests. (fig) Don't count on others to help you. If you pin too much hope on others, you will be disappointed. [See also *zhǐ qīn bù fù* below.]

78 **Zhí gōu diào bùliǎo yú.** 直钩钓不了鱼。(lit) [A] straight fishhook can catch no fish. (fig) A straightforward person often offends people with his frankness. [See also *shénguǐ pà léng rén* above.]

79 **Zhī guò bì gǎi, biànshì shèngxián.** 知过必改便是圣贤。To change [after] realizing [one's own] faults is [to be a] sage.

80 **Zhījǐ dàolái, yán bùjìn.** 知己到来言不尽。[When a] good friend comes there'll be endless talks. [Cf. *Fēngshén Yǎnyì*, chap. 11; see also *jiǔ féng zhījǐ* above.]

81 **Zhíjǐ, zhī bǐ; bǎi zhàn, bǎi shèng.*** 知己知彼，百战百胜。(lit) [If you] know [your]self [and] know them, [in one] hundred battles [you'll have one] hundred victories. (fig) If you know your enemy and know yourself, you'll always be victorious. [This is a colloquial phrasing of the following entry; note: *zhījǐ-zhībǐ*, is used as an idiom meaning "to know one's self and know the enemy," and *bǎizhàn-bǎishèng* is used as an idiom meaning "(be) ever victorious"; see also the following entry.]

82 **Zhījǐ, zhī bǐ; bǎi zhàn bù dài.** 知己知彼，百战不殆。(lit) [If you] know [your]self [and] know them, [in one] hundred battles [you'll] not [be in] danger. (fig) If you know your opposition and know yourself, you'll never be defeated. [This is the original in *Sūnzǐ Bīngfǎ: Móu Gōng* and in *R3K*, chap. 5 of the preceding entry; note: *bǎizhàn-búdài* is used as an idiom meaning "to win battle after battle"; see also the preceding entry.]

83 **Zhì le bìng, zhì bùliǎo mìng.*** 治了病，治不了命。[One's] illness can be cured, [but one's] fate cannot. [Rhyme; cf. *DRC*, chap. 11; see also *yīshēng yī bìng* above.]

84 **Zhī lǐ bù guài rén; guài rén bù zhī lǐ.** 知理不怪人，怪人不知理。[Those who] understand reason(s) won't blame others [and those who] blame others don't understand reason(s). [Cf. *Wǔ Sōng*, chap. 4; note: *zhī lǐ* means "to understand reason or (the reasons) why things are the way they are." The two halves are also used in the reverse order (q.v.).]

85 **Zhínǚ xiàng gūmā.** 侄女象姑妈。Nieces often [behave] like [i.e., take after] [their paternal] aunts. [See also *wàishēng duō sì jiù* above.]

86 **Zhǐpà bù zuò, bù pà bù pò.** 只怕不做，不怕不破。(lit) Just worry about not doing [wrong things in the first place]; don't [just] worry about being exposed. (fig) Whatever one does will become known sooner or later, so don't engage in anything you don't want known. [See also *ruò yào rén bù zhī* and *tiānxià de huàishì* above.]

87 **Zhǐpà qiú ér méiyǒu; nǎpà yǒu ér nán qiú.** 只怕求而没有，哪怕有而难求。(lit) Just worry about seeking [for things that do] not exist; why worry about having difficulties getting [things] which do exist? (fig) If something actually exists, one can get it if one persists. [Cf. *Xǐngshì Héngyán*, chap. 32.]

88 **Zhǐ qīn bù fù; kàn zuǐ bù bǎo.** 指亲不富，看嘴不饱。(lit) [You] won't get rich by counting on [your] relatives [for help, just as you will] never get full by looking at [others] eating. (fig) Don't count on others for help. [See also *zhǐ ér, bù yǎnglǎo* above.]

89 **Zhīqíng bù jǔ, zuì jiā yī děng.*** 知情不举，罪加一等。[If one] knows [the details of a criminal] activity [but does] not report [it to the authorities, one's] punishment [should be even] one degree more [severe than the culprit's]. [Cf. the Qing dynasty novel *Sān Xiá Wǔ Yì*, chap. 81; see also *jiǎnjǔ*, "report an offense to the authorities."]

90 **Zhìqīn wú wén.** 至亲无文。Among close [relatives and friends], there is no [need to stand on] ceremony. [Cf. the Confucian *Lǐjì: Lǐ Qì*; note: *xūwén*, "empty forms of courtesy."]

91 **Zhǐ rènde zhēngyǎn Jīngāng; rènbude bì yǎnjing fó.** 只认得睁眼金刚，认不得闭眼睛佛。(lit) [One can] only recognize the guardian warriors [of the Buddha] with their eyes [glaring] wide open, [but] one does not recognize the Buddha with his eyes closed. (fig) One is usually on guard against frightening-looking people, but one

should be even more wary of the wickedness of quiet people. [Cf. *Wǔ Sōng*, chap. 9; see also *bùpà hóngliǎn Guān Yé* and *míng qiāng yì duǒ* above.]

92 **Zhī rén zhě zhì; zìzhī zhě míng.** 知人者智，自知者明。[One who] knows others [is] intelligent; [one who] knows himself is wise. [Cf. *Lǎozǐ (Dào Dé Jīng)*, chap. 33; also said *zhī rén zhě zhì; zhījǐ zhě míng*.]

93 **Zhī rén, zhī miàn; bù zhī xīn.*** 知人知面不知心。(lit) [To] know people [is to] know [their] faces, [but] not [to] know [their] hearts. (fig) It is easy to know people's faces, but not to know what is in their minds. [Cf. *JPM*, chap. 51; *DRC*, chap. 94; also said *zhī rén, zhī miàn; zén zhī qí xīn*; see also *hǎi kǔ zhōng jiàn* and *huà lóng, huà hǔ* and *suī yǒu qīn fù* above.]

94 **Zhī shǒu nán zhē tiānxià mù.** 只手难遮天下目。(lit) [A] single hand cannot cover the eyes of all the people under heaven. (fig) "You can't fool all the people all the time." [Note: *zhēyǎn, zhēgài*, "to hide; to cover up"; see also *nán jiāng yī rén shǒu* and *yī shǒu bù néng* above.]

95 **Zhì sǐ, wú dàshì.** 至死无大事。[To one who is] near to death, nothing is dreadful.

96 **Zhì wù bù qióng; mài wù bù fù.** 置物不穷，卖物不富。(lit) Buying [ordinary household] things [will] not [make one] poor, nor [will] selling them make [one] rich. (fig) Whether one is rich or poor does not depend on one's occasional expenditures or incidental income, but rather on one's regular source of income, so live within your budget.

97 **Zhī wú bù yán, yán wú bù jìn; (yán zhě wúzuì, wén zhě zú jiè).*** 知无不言，言无不尽；(言者无罪，闻者足戒)。(lit) [Of what you] know there [should] be nothing [which] is not said, [and in what is] said there [should] be no holding back; (the speaker [will] be guiltless [and the] hearer [will] learn a lesson). (fig) Say all you know and say it without reserve; (you will not be blamed, and your hearers will learn from it). [The first part is from *Jìn Shū: Liú Cōng Zài Jì*; the second part is from *Shījīng* (Poetry Classic): *Dà Xù*; often quoted together by Mao Zedong; see also *chéngqián-bìhòu* above.]

98 **Zhí xiàng gǎn gǒu, huítóu yīkǒu.** 直巷赶狗，回头一口。(lit) [A] dog [being] driven [in a] straight lane (i.e., with no outlets] [will] turn around [and] bite. (fig) Don't press people too hard. "Even a worm will turn." [Rhyme; see also *gǒu jí tiào qiáng* and *hàozi jíle* and *tùzi jíle* above.]

99 **Zhǐ xǔ zhōu guān fànghuǒ; bùxǔ bǎixìng diǎndēng.** 只许州官放火，不许百姓点灯。(lit) Only the officials are permitted to set fires, [but] the common people are not [even] permitted to light lanterns. (fig) Great folks may set the town on fire, but the common people can't even light lanterns. "One may steal a horse while another may not look over a hedge." [This *yanyu* refers to a prefectural governor named Tian Deng who is said to have tabooed the use of any words homophonous with any part

of his name. Thus he declared that the traditional displaying of lanterns at the Lantern Festival could not be referred to as *fàng dēng*, "displaying lanterns," but only as *fànghuǒ*, "setting fires," and the common people were forbidden to refer to *diǎn dēng*, "lighting lanterns." See *Gǔ-Jīn Tán Gài* (chap. 1) by Féng Mèng Lóng. Note: *(lǎo)bǎixìng*, (lit) "(old) hundred surnames," is a traditional term for the common people.]

100 **Zhì yǎng qiān kǒu; lì yǎng yī rén.** 智养千口，力养一人。 Knowledge [can] support [a] thousand people, [but physical] strength [can only] support one person. [See also the preceding entry.]

101 **(Zhǐyào gōngfu shēn,) tiěchǔ móchéng zhēn.*** (只要工夫深，)铁杵磨成针。 (lit) (With enough hard work,) an iron rod can be ground [down] into a needle. (fig) Persistence and hard work can accomplish great feats; "many strokes fell great oaks." [Rhyme; cf. Sun Jinbiao's *Tōng Sú Cháng Yán Sū Zhèng*, vol. 3; *Píng Yáo Zhuàn*, chap. 10. This saying is also the basis of a popular story about the famous Tang dynasty poet Li Bo as a child. The second half is often used alone as an idiomatic phrase. See also *gōng dào, zìrán chéng* and *tiědǎ fángliáng* above.]

102 **Zhǐyào jiǎng huā qí, bùpà lànghuā jí.** 只要桨花齐，不怕浪花急。 (lit) As long as [everyone] rows in unison, [there is] no [need to] fear rough waves. (fig) As long as everyone "pulls together," difficult situations can always be surmounted. [Rhyme; see also *bùpà fēnglàng dà* above.]

103 **Zhǐyào rénshǒu duō, páilóu tái guò hé.** 只要人手多，牌楼抬过河。 (lit) As long as there are enough people's hands, a memorial arch can be carried across the river. (fig) Any difficulty can be overcome so long as there is enough manpower. [Cf. *Dàng Kòu Zhì*, chap. 77; note: *rénshǒu*, (lit) "human hands," means "manpower"; see also *zhòng qíng yì jǔ* below.]

104 **Zhǐyào xiān shàng chuán, zìrán xiān dào àn.** 只要先上船，自然先到岸。 (lit) Just be the first on board [the ship, and you'll] naturally be the first on shore. (fig) Act sooner and you'll achieve your goal sooner. [Rhyme; cf. *Érnǚ Yīngxióng Zhuàn*, chap. 30; see also *xiān xià mǐ* and *xiān xiàshǒu* above and *zhōngyuán zhú lù* below.]

105 **Zhǐyǒu bù kuài de fǔ; méiyǒu pībùkāi de chái.** 只有不快得斧，没有劈不开的柴。 (lit) There are only blunt axes, [but] no firewood that cannot be split. (fig) There are incapable people, but no difficulties that cannot be surmounted.

106 **Zhǐyǒu cuò zhuō; méiyǒu cuò fàng.** 只有错捉，没有错放。 (lit) There may be [cases of] wrongful arrest, [but] there [should] never be [cases of criminals] wrongly set free. [Cf. *JW*, chap. 97.]

107 **Zhǐyǒu dòngsǐ de cāngying; méiyǒu lèisǐ de mìfēng.** 只有冻死的苍蝇，没有累死的蜜蜂。 (lit) There are flies that freeze to death, but no bees that die of fatigue. (fig) There are lazy people who die of cold, but there are no hard-working people who die of diligence.

108 **Zhǐyǒu jǐnshàng-tiānhuā; nǎ dé xuězhōng-sòngtàn?** 只有锦上添花，哪得雪中送炭？ (lit) There are [people who] add flowers onto brocade," [but] when did [anyone ever] "send charcoal in snowy weather." (fig) There will always be people who come to flatter you when you are successful, but no one will come to help you when you are in need; the world is full of "fair weather friends," but "nobody knows you when you're down and out." [Cf. *Chū Kè Pāi'àn Jīngqí*, chap. 20; also said *jǐnshàng-tiānhuā* . . . (q.v.). Note: *jǐnshàng-tiānhuā* and *xuězhōng-sòngtàn* are both *chengyu*; see also *jǐnshàng-tiānhuā* and *xuězhōng-sòngtàn* above.]

109 **Zhǐyǒu qiān rì zuò zéi; nǎ yǒu qiān rì fáng zéi?** 只有千日做贼，哪有千日防贼？ (lit) One may be a thief for a thousand days, but one cannot be on guard against thieves for an equally long time. (fig) It's easy to be a thief, but difficult to be on guard against thieves; one's vigilance is always bound to slacken. [Cf. *Suí Táng Yǎnyì*, chap. 33.]

110 **Zhǐyǒu shèng zhōu, shèngfàn; méiyǒu shèng ér, shèng nǚ.** 只有剩粥剩饭，没有剩儿剩女。 There may be porridge or rice left over, [but] there are no leftover sons or daughters [who cannot find a match in marriage]. [Cf. *Wǔ Sōng*, chap. 4.]

111 **Zhìzhě guì yú chéng shí.** 智者贵于乘时。 (lit) A wise person values an opportune time. (fig) A wise person seizes the chance when he can; "*carpe diem*." [Cf. *R3K*.]

112 **Zhìzhě kàn huǒ; yú zhě kàn guō.** 智者看火，愚者看锅。 (lit) An intelligent person watches the fire [while] a foolish person watches the pot. (fig) A clever person pays attention to the crucial points of a problem, while a foolish person only observes superficial phenomena. [See also *cǎo bù mí yíng yǎn* above.]

113 **Zhìzhě lè shuǐ; rén zhě lè shān.** 智者乐水，仁者乐山。 (lit) Wise people are fond of water [and] kindhearted ones like mountains. (fig) People of different characters have different interests. "Different strokes for different folks." [Cf. the Confucian Analects: *Lúnyǔ: Yōng Yě*.]

114 **Zhìzhě qiān lǜ, bì yǒu yī shī; (yú zhě qiān lǜ, bì yǒu dé).** 智者千虑必有一失，(愚者千虑必有一得)。 (lit) [Even though a] wise person [may] consider [issues a] thousand [times, nevertheless] there must be [at least] one error; (a fool [may] consider [issues a] thousand [times, and] there must be one [time (s)he] gets [it right]). (fig) Even the wise are not always free from error, (and sometimes even a fool can get lucky). "Even Homer sometimes nods." [Cf. *Shǐ Jì: Huái Yīn Hóu Lièzhuàn*, the two halves are often used independently or in reversed order. The second part may be omitted. Note the *chengyu: qiānlǜ-yīshī*, "one miss in a thousand"; see also *cōngming yìshì* and *shèngrén yě yǒu* above.]

115 **Zhī zhǐ cháng zhǐ, zhōngshēn bù chǐ.** 知止常止，终身不耻。 [One who] knows [when] to stop [and] always does [is] never humiliated. [Rhyme; see *chǐrǔ*, "humiliation."]

116 **Zhǐ zhī wǒ wàimiàn xíngzhuàng; nǎ zhī wǒ dù nèi wénzhāng?** 只知我外面形状，哪知我肚内文章？ (lit) One may know [someone's] appearance, [but] how can one know what's in [someone's] mind? (fig) One can never truly know what is in others' hearts or minds. [Rhyme; see also *rén dào nánchù* and *sān nián shí mǎ xìng* above.]

117 **Zhīzú bù rǔ; zhī zhǐ bù dài.** 知足不辱，知止不殆。 [One who] knows how [to be] content [will] not be disgraced; [one who] knows [when to] stop [will] not be in danger. [Cf. *Lǎozi (Dào Dé Jīng)*, chap. 44.]

118 **Zhīzú, shēn cháng lè; néng rěn, xīn zì ān.** 知足身常乐，能忍心自安。 Being content with what one has brings happiness; [one who] can exercise forbearance [will be] peaceful at heart. [Also said *zhīzúzhě cháng lè . . .* and *zhīzú, xīn cháng lè . . .*; as a chengyu: *zhīzú-chánglè*; see also *rú bù zhīzú* above.]

119 **Zhōng bù dǎ, bù xiǎng; huà bù shuō, bùmíng.*** 钟不打不响，话不说不明。 (lit) [Just as a] bell not struck won't make sounds, [so if] explanations are not made, [matters will] not be understood. [Cf. *Érnǚ Yīngxióng Zhuàn*, chap. 5; see also *huà bù shuō, bùmíng* above.]

120 **Zhòng guā, dé guā; zhòng dòu, dé dòu.** 种瓜得瓜，种豆得豆。 (lit) [If one] plants melons, [one will] get melons; [if one] plants beans, [one will] get beans. (fig) "As one sows, so shall one reap." [See also *ná fù dé dé* above.]

121 **Zhònghuā yī nián; kàn huā shí rì.*** 种花一年，看花十日。 (lit) [Those who] look at flowers [for] ten days [can't appreciate the labors of those who] tended the flowers [for] one year. (fig) Those who enjoy the fruits of other people's labors don't know, or ought to consider, the hard work of those who produced them. [See also *kàn rén tiāodàn* above.]

122 **Zhōngjiān méi rén, shì nán chéng.** 中间没人事难成。 Nothing can be accomplished without go-betweens. [See also *tiānshàng wú yún* above.]

123 **Zhòng kǒu nán tiáo.** 众口难调。 (lit) [All] people's tastes [are] difficult to cater to. (fig) It's hard to please everyone. [Note: *zhòngkǒu-nántiáo* is used as a set phrase.]

124 **Zhòng kǒu shuò jīn.** 众口铄金。 (lit) The masses' mouths [can] melt metals. (fig) Popular opinion can confound right and wrong. If enough mud is thrown, some of it will stick. [Note: *zhòngkǒu-shuòjīn* is sometimes treated as a set phrase.]

125 **Zhòng nù nán fàn.** 众怒难犯。 It is dangerous to incur public wrath. [Note: *zhòngnù-nánfàn* is sometimes treated as a set phrase; see also the following entry.]

126 **Zhòngnù rú shuǐhuǒ.** 众怒如水火。 The people's indignation is as [fierce as] flood [and] fire. [Cf. *Zuǒ Zhuàn: Zhāo Gōng 13 Nián* and *Shǐ Jì: Chǔ Shì Jiā*; see also the preceding entry.]

127 **Zhòng qíng yì jǔ.** 众擎易举。 (lit) [When there are a] multitude lifting, [it's] easy to lift [a load]. (fig) "Many hands make light work." [Note: *zhòngqíng-yìjǔ* is sometimes treated as a set phrase.]

128 **Zhòngrén de zhìhuì; yī rén de cáihuá.** 众人的智慧，一人的才华。 [A proverb is the] wisdom of many people, [and the] talent of one person.

129 **Zhòngrén shíchái, huǒyàn gāo.*** 众人拾柴火焰高。 (lit) [When there are] many people [to] gather firewood, the fire burns high. (fig) "Many hands make light work." [Quoted by Mao Zedong in opposition to a policy for population control proposed by Ma Yanchu in the 1950s; see also *rén duō, lìliàng dà* above.]

130 **Zhòngrén shì shèngrén.** 众人是圣人。 (lit) A group of people is [equal to one] sage. (fig) "Many heads are better than one." [See also *sān gè chòu píjiàng* above.]

131 **Zhòngrén (yǎnjing) shì gǎnchèng; jīnliǎng chēng fēnmíng.** 众人(眼睛)是杆秤，斤两称分明。 (lit) (The eyes of) the masses are [like a] steelyard [scales on which] catties [and] ounces are weighed accurately. (fig) Public opinion is objective. [Note the Communist slogan: *zhòng mù zhāozhāng*, "the masses are sharp-eyed"; note: *jīnliǎng*, (lit) "catties [and] ounces," means "weight"; see also *lùshang xíngrén* and *rén yǎn shì* and *tiānxià qiányǎnr* and *zhīdǐ mò guò* above.]

132 **Zhòngrén yīxīn, fèntǔ biàn jīn.** 众人一心，粪土变金。 [If] many people [are of] one mind, dung [and] dirt [can be] turned into gold. [Rhyme: see also *sān rén yītiáoxīn* and *xiělì shān chéng yù* and *yī jiā tóngxīn* above.]

133 **Zhòngshǎng zhīxià, bì yǒu yǒng fū.*** 重赏之下必有勇夫。 Under [the influence of a] weighty reward, there must be someone brave [enough to take on any difficult task]. [Cf. *Fēngshén Yǎnyì*, chap. 87; see also *gǔlái fāng ěr* above.]

134 **Zhōngshēn rànglù, bù wǎng bǎi bù.** 终身让路，不枉百步。 (lit) [If] all [one's] life [one] yields [the right of] way to others, [it will] not cost [you a] hundred steps. (fig) It costs one nothing to be modest and polite. [Rhyme; see *yuǎnwang*, "in vain."]

135 **Zhòngtián bù shú bùrú huāng; yǎng ér bùxiào bùrú wú.** 种田不熟不如荒，养儿不孝不如无。 [Just as] tilling the land [and] not [getting a] harvest is not as good as [just leaving it lie] fallow, [so] raising a son [who is] not filial is not as good as having no [son at all]. [Cf. *Xǐngshì Héngyán*, chap. 17.]

136 **Zhòngtián fú (/bù) lí tiántóu; dúshū fú (/bù) lí àntóu.** 种田弗(/不)离田头，读书弗(/不)离案头。 (lit) A farmer never leaves [his] fields, nor a scholar his desk. (fig) One has to be diligent and persistent in one's work. [From the Qing dynasty proverb collection *Yuè Yàn*, vol. 1 by Fan Yan.]

137 **Zhōngyán nì'ěr (lìyú xíng).** 忠言逆耳(利于行)。 Honest advice [although it] is unpleasant to the ear (induces good conduct). [Cf. *Shǐ Jì: Liú Hòu Shì Jiā*; the first part, often used alone as a chengyu: *zhōngyán-nì'ěr* meaning: "the truth

hurts," or like the first part of a *xiehouyu*, paraphrases *Hán Fēizǐ: Wài Chǔ Shuō Zuǒ Shàng*; see also *liángyào kǔkǒu* above.]

138 **Zhōngyuán zhú lù, jié zú xiān dé.** 中原逐鹿, 捷足先得。(lit) [When] chasing deer [on the] plains, [the one who] runs faster [will] achieve [his goal] first. (fig) When there are many rivals competing, the one who strikes first will win. [Note the *chengyu*: *zhúlù-zhōngyuán*, "to fight among rivals for the throne"; see also *xiān xià mǐ* and *xiān xiàshǒu* and *zhǐyào xiān shàng chuán* above.]

139 **Zhōng zài sì lǐ, shēng zài wàibiān.** 钟在寺里, 声在外边。(lit) [Although the] bell is housed in the temple, [its] sound [spreads] outside. (fig) No secret can be hidden forever. [Cf. *Niè Hǎi Huā*, chap. 16.]

140 **Zhōng zài sìyuàn, yīn zàiwài.** 钟在寺院, 音在外。(lit) [The] bell is [in the] temple, [but its] sound is outside. (fig) What happens inside will become known outside. It's impossible to keep secrets for long. [See also *gǔ zhōng yú gōng* above.]

141 **Zhòng zhì chéng chéng.** 众志成城。(lit) [The united] will of the masses becomes [like a] fortress. (fig) In unity there is strength. [Cf. *Guó Yǔ: Zhōu Yǔ, Xià*; note: *zhòngzhì-chéngchéng* is treated as a set phrase.]

142 **Zhǒngzǐ gé nián liú; zǎi nǚ qián shì xiū.** 种子隔年留, 崽女前世修。[Just as] good seeds are kept [and passed on] from one year to the next, [so good] sons [and] daughters [are born because in a] previous life [their parents were] virtuous. [Rhyme: a popular superstition in traditional China.]

143 **Zhōu fù nǎi jiàn shàn yóu.** 舟覆乃见善游。[When the] boat turns over, then [it will be] seen [who is the] best swimmer. [Cf. *Huái Nán Zǐ: Shuō Lín Xùn*.]

144 **Zhóulǐ duōle, shìfēi duō; xiǎogū duōle, máfan duō.** 妯娌多了是非多, 小姑多了麻烦多。(lit) The more brothers' wives [there are], the more disputes [there will be]; the more [unmarried] husbands' sisters [there are], the more trouble [there will be]. (fig) The more women, either married in or not yet married off, that there are in a family, the more quarrels and disputes there will be. [Said of large extended families in traditional China.]

145 **Zhuāngjiārén kàn tiān, dǎyú rén kàn cháo.** 庄稼人看天, 打鱼人看潮。(lit) Farmers [always] watch the sky [and] fishermen watch the tides. (fig) People in different specialties must be concerned with different things. [See also the following entry.]

146 **Zhuāngjiārén shí bù wán gǔ; dǎyú rén shí bù wán yú.** 庄稼人识不完谷, 打鱼人识不完鱼。(lit) [A] farmer doesn't know all [kinds of] grain; nor [does a] fisherman know all [kinds of] fish. (fig) Even a specialist doesn't (necessarily) know everything. [See also the preceding entry.]

147 **Zhǔ bù chī, kè bù yǐn.** 主不吃, 客不饮。[At a dinner if] the host hasn't [invited the guests to] eat, the guests [should] not [even take a] drink. (fig) Guests should wait for their host(ess) to invite them to begin eating. [Cf. *Jīnghuā Yuán*, chap. 37.]

148 **Zhǔ bù qī bīn.** 主不欺宾。A host should not bully his guests. [Cf. *Érnǚ Yīngxióng Zhuàn*, chap. 15.]

149 **Zhū duō, ròu jiàn.** * 猪多肉贱。(lit) The more pigs [there are], the cheaper the [price of] pork. (fig) The more common things are, the less they are valued.

150 **Zhǔ gùn, yào zhǔ cháng de; jiēbàn yào jiē qiáng de.** 拄棍要拄长的, 结伴要结强的。[When] leaning on a walking stick, lean on a long one; [when] making friends, choose powerful ones. [Rhyme.]

151 **Zhū kùn, zhǎng ròu; rén kùn, mài wū.** 猪睏长肉, 人困卖屋。(lit) [Just as a] lazy pig gains weight, [so a] lazy person sells [his] house. (fig) Laziness can ruin a family.

152 **Zhū mà wūyā hēi.** 猪骂乌鸦黑。The pig scolds the crow [for being] black. (fig) One should not criticize faults in others which one has oneself. "The pot calling the kettle black." [See also *wūguī mò xiào biē* and *tiě guàn mò shuō* above.]

153 **Zhūmén jiǔròu chòu, lù yǒu dòngsǐ gǔ.** 朱门酒肉臭, 路有冻死骨。The vermilion gates [of the rich] reek of [leftover] wine [and] meat, [while by the] roadside lie the bones [of those who have] frozen to death. [A line from a poem paraphrasing Mencius by the Tang dynasty poet Du Fu entitled: "Zì Jīng Fù Féngxiān Yǒnghuái Wǔ Bǎi Zì"; note: *zhūmén* refers to the red-lacquered doors of wealthy homes.]

154 **Zhūmén shēng èpiǎo, bái wū chū gōngqīng.** 朱门生饿殍, 白屋出公卿。Descendants from the vermilion gates [of the rich may] starve to death, [and] the thatched houses of the poor [may] produce high officials. [Cf. *Liàn Bīng Shí Jì*: chap. 9, by the Ming dynasty patriot Qi Jiguang; *Xǐngshì Héngyán*, chap. 2; note: *zhūmén* refers to the red-lacquered doors of wealthy homes.]

155 **Zhuōjiān jiàn shuāng; zhuō zéi jiàn zāng; shārén jiàn shāng.** 捉奸见双, 捉贼见脏, 杀人见伤。(lit) To catch adulterers, find [the adulterous] pair; to catch a thief, find the loot; [to prove] murder, show the injuries. (fig) In order to prove that a crime has been committed, evidence must be presented. [Cf. *WM*, chap. 26; *Gǔ Jīn Xiǎoshuō*, chap. 38; *Lǎo Cán Yóujì*, chap. 19.]

156 **Zhuōzhù Púsa, bùpà Jīngāng bùfú.** 捉住菩萨, 不怕金刚不服。(lit) [When one] catches a Buddha, never fear [that his] guardians [will] not submit. (fig) When a leader is caught, his subordinates will also (have to) surrender.

157 **Zhǔ yǎ, kè lái qín.** 主雅客来勤。[When] the host is refined, guests [will] come frequently. [Cf. *DRC*, chap. 32.]

Z

158 **Zhù zài yī xiāng, dǎ zài yī bāng.** 住在一乡，打在一帮。 (lit) [When you] settle down in a locality, [it's best to] hit [it off] with the [local] gang. (fig) When you move somewhere, it's best to integrate yourself with the local people. [Rhyme.]

159 **Zhū zhuǎ zhǔ qiān gǔn, zǒngshì cháo lǐ wān.** 猪爪煮千滚，总是朝里弯。 (lit) Pigs' feet [even if] boiled a thousand times [will] always bend inwards. (fig) One is always inclined to be partial to members of one's own group. [See also *gēbo zǒngshì* above.]

160 **Zìgǔ Cháng'é ài shàonián.*** 自古嫦娥爱少年。 See *yuè lǐ Cháng'é ài shàonián* above.

161 **Zìgǔ hóngyán duō bómìng.*** 自古红颜多薄命。 Since ancient [times] beauties [have] mostly [had] ill luck. [Cf. *JW*, chap. 70; also said *hóngyán bómìng* in Chū Kè Pāi'àn Jīngqí, chap. 23; note: *hóngyán*, (lit) "red color(ed)," is a literary expression for beautiful women.]

162 **(Zìjiā) yǒu bìng, zìjiā zhī.** (自家)有病，自家知。 (lit) One knows one's (own) illness best. (fig) Only oneself really knows the true nature of one's problem. [Often said of *xiàngsī bìng*, "lovesickness"; *zìjiā* is colloquial for *zìjǐ*, "oneself."]

163 **Zìjǐ de mèng, zìjǐ yuán.*** 自己的梦自己圆。 (lit) [From one's] own dreams [one has to] predict [good or ill luck] oneself. (fig) One has to realize and correct one's own shortcomings or mistakes. [Note: *yuánmèng*, "to interpret dreams."]

164 **Zì jīng sān xiě, "wū" yān chéng "mǎ."** 字经三写，"乌"焉成"马"。 (lit) [When a] character has been copied thrice, "bird" becomes "horse." (fig) There are bound to be copying mistakes. [See also *shū sān xiě* above, now more commonly used.]

165 **Zìjǐ tānbēi, xǐ zuì rén.** 自己贪杯惜醉人。 (lit) [One who] himself is fond of drinking sympathizes with one who is drunk. (fig) One is sympathetic to those with problems similar to one's own. [Note the *chengyu*: *tóngbìng-xiānglián*, "those who have the same illnesses sympathize with each other"; see also *tóng jí xiāng lián* above.]

166 **Zì shuō zìhǎo, làn dàocǎo.** 自说自好，烂稻草。 (lit) Talking [about how] good one is [is like] rotten rice stalks. (fig) Boasting of oneself is useless.

167 **Zì tuī, zì diē, zì shāng jiē.** 自推，自跌，自伤嗟。 (lit) [If one] pushes oneself [and] stumbles, [one has to] lament alone. (fig) If you suffer setbacks which you have brought upon yourself, you have no one else to blame. [A rhyme; note: *bēishāng*, "sad; sorrowful"; *jiē* or *juē* is an exclamation in ancient Chinese.]

168 **Zǐ yòng fù qián, xīn bù tòng** 子用父钱，心不痛。 Sons spend their fathers' money [with] carefree hearts.

169 **Zhōngchén bù shì èr jūn; zhēnnǚ bù jià èr fū.** 忠臣不事二君，贞女不嫁二夫。 (lit) [Just as a] loyal minister does not serve two rulers, [so a] faithful woman won't marry two husbands. (fig) A widowed woman will not re-marry. [Cf. *Shǐ Jì: Tián Dān Lièzhuàn*; note: *zhēnnǚ*, "faithful widow"; see also *yī chén bù shì* and *yī mǎ bù kuà* above.]

170 **Zòng yǒu dàshà qiān jiān, bùguò shēn mián qī chǐ.** 纵有大厦千间，不过身眠七尺。 (lit) Even if [one] has houses by the thousands, [all one needs] to sleep in [is] only seven feet [long]. (fig) It is not necessary to have a spacious and luxurious building to live in. [Cf. *Sān Xiá Wǔ Yì*, chap. 42.]

171 **Zǒu píng lù, fáng shuāijiāo; shùnshuǐ chuán, fáng ànjiāo.** 走平路防摔跤，顺水船防暗礁。 (lit) [Even when] walking [on a] level road, [one should be careful and] guard against tripping [and] falling; [even when] sailing [with the current], [one should] guard against submerged reefs. (fig) One should always be careful. [See also *qiǎn shuǐ yānsǐ* and *quàn jūn mò dǎ* above.]

172 **Zǒu sān jiā bùrú zuò yìjiā.** 走三家不如坐一家。 (lit) [When seeking help it's] better to sit at one family than to go to three families. (fig) When seeking help it's better to go to one person persistently than to run here and there to a number of different people. [Cf. *JW*, chap. 50; see also *qiú, biàn qiú Zhāng Liáng* above.]

173 **Zú hán shāng xīn; mín hán shāng guó.** 足寒伤心，民寒伤国。 [Just as if one's] feet are [exposed to the] cold, [it will] harm [one's] heart, [so if] the [common] people [suffer from] cold, [it will] harm the country. [Cf. *Shí Guó Chūnqiū: Chù Tuō Bǎ Héng Zhuàn*; see also *tóu duì fēng* above.]

174 **Zuǐ bù ráorén, pí chīkǔ.*** 嘴不饶人，皮吃苦。 (lit) [If one's] mouth [does] not pardon others, [one's] skin will suffer. (fig) One will suffer physically if one is too severe in one's speech. [Note: *pírou zhī tòng*, "pain from a beating."]

175 **Zuǐ dǐxià jiùshì lù.** 嘴底下就是路。 (lit) Just under one's mouth lies the way. (fig) All you have to do is keep asking for directions and you'll find your way. [See also *dàlù shēng* and *lù zài zuǐ biān* above.]

176 **Zuǐ qiáng de zhēng yī bù.** 嘴强的争一步。 Those [who have a] glib tongue [can] gain petty advantages. [Cf. *JPM*, chap. 43.]

177 **Zuǐ shàng wú máo, bànshì bù láo.*** 嘴上无毛，办事不牢。 (lit) [If] there is no hair on [one's] face, [one can] not handle affairs securely. (fig) Young people cannot be entrusted with important tasks because they lack experience. "Downy lips make thoughtless slips." [Rhyme; cf. *Guānchǎng Xiànxíng Jì*, chap. 15.]

178 **Zuì shì xǐng shí yán.** 醉是醒时言。 (lit) [In] drunkenness [there] are the words of sobriety. (fig) One speaks one's true mind when drunk; *in vino veritas*. [Cf. *WM*, chap. 45; see also *jiǔ dào zhēnxìng* above.]

179 **Zuìwēng zhī yì bù zài jiǔ.*** 醉翁之意不在酒。 (lit) The drunken old man's [true] motivation lies not in liquor. (fig) One's true motivation is (often) not the ostensible one. [Cf. the Song dynasty essayist Ouyang Xiu's popular essay entitled: "Zuìwēng Tíng Jì" ("Notes on the Drunken Old Man Pavilion").]

180 **Zuò chī shān kōng,* (lì chī dì xiàn).** 坐吃山空，(立吃地陷)。 (lit) [If one] sits [idle, one will] eat away a mountain [of wealth], ([and if one] stands [idle, one will] eat [a hole] into the ground). (fig) If one does not work, one will eat up one's capital. [The first half is used alone as a *chengyu: zuòchī-shānkōng*, meaning "to fritter away a great fortune"; see also *yānhóu shēn sì hǎi* above.]

181 **Zuò dào lǎo, xué dào lǎo.*** 做到老，学到老。 (lit) [If one] works to an old age, [one should continue] studying to an old age. (fig) One is never too old to learn. It's never too late to learn. [Rhyme; see also *huó dào lǎo* above.]

182 **Zuò de chuántóu wěn, bùpà làng lái diān.** 坐得船头稳，不怕浪来颠。 (lit) Sit steady at the head of a boat, [and you] need not fear the rocking of the waves. (fig) If one's conduct is respectable, one need not fear being defamed.

183 **Zuò de zhèng, xíng de zhèng; nǎpà tóng héshang hé bǎndèng?** 坐得正，行得正，哪怕同和尚合板凳？ (lit) [If a woman] sits straight and walks upright, there's no need [for her] to fear sharing a bench with a [Buddhist] monk. (fig) If a woman bears herself respectably, she need not fear any gossip or slander. [Rhyme; cf. *Wǔ Sōng*, chap. 2; see also the preceding entry.]

184 **Zuò dòu zhě shāng.** 佐斗者伤。 Those who help [others] fight [will be] injured, [so mind your own business]! [Also said as *zhù dòu dé shāng*.]

185 **Zuòfàn mán bu liǎo guōtái; tiāo shuǐ mán bu liǎo jīngtái.** 做饭瞒不了锅台，挑水瞒不了井台。 (lit) Cooking can't be hidden from the stove top, [and] water carrying can't be concealed from the well. (fig) Whatever one does can't be concealed from one's neighbors. [Rhyme; see also *zhǐdǐ mò guò* and *zhòngrén yǎnjing* above.]

186 **Zhuó fù mòrú qīngpín.** 浊富莫如清贫。 Filthy riches are not as good as honest poverty.

187 **Zuò hǎo, qiān rì bùzú; zuò huài, yīzhāo yǒu yú.** 作好千日不足，作坏一朝有余。 To do good [deeds for] a thousand days is not enough; to do evil [even for] one day is too much.

188 **Zuò jīng, bài dào; gè yǒu yī hào.** 坐经拜道，各有一好。 (lit) Sit [and chant Buddhist] sutras [or] worship the Tao; each [person] has [his or her] preferences. (fig) Everyone has his or her own preferences (in anything). [Rhyme.]

189 **Zuǒjiǔ, dé cháng.** 佐酒得尝。 (lit) [One who] accompanies [others in] drinking [will] be rewarded. (fig) One who helps others will be rewarded in the end. [Note: formerly *zuǒjiǔ* referred to those who kept others company while drinking.]

190 **Zuò shě dào biān, sān nián bù chéng.** 作舍道边，三年不成。 (lit) [If one is to] build a house by the side of the road, [it will] not be completed in three years [because each passerby will have a different opinion as to how things should be done]. (fig) Too many opinions will come to nothing. "Too many cooks spoil the broth." [See also *rén duō, shǒu zá* above.]

191 **Zuòshì guò chí, bùrú bù wéi.** 做事过迟，不如不为。 (lit) Doing things too late is not as [good as] not doing [them at all]. (fig) Either do things at the right time or not at all. Better never than late. [Vs. *dān chí, bù dān cuò* above.]

192 **Zuò shì yào wěn; gǎicuò yào hěn.** 做事要稳，改错要狠。 (lit) [In] doing things [one] should be prudent, [and in] correcting [one's] mistakes [one] should be resolute. [Rhyme; note: *wěnzhòng*, "steady; circumspect; prudent."]

193 **Zuò yǐn jiāxiāng shuǐ yě tián.** 坐饮家乡水也甜。 [Even when just] sitting [and] drinking the water [in one's] native place, [the water] tastes sweeter. (fig) "There's no place like home." [See also *měi bù měi, xiāng zhōng shuǐ* above.]

194 **Zuò zéi sān nián, bù dǎ zì zhāo.** 做贼三年，不打自招。 (lit) [If one] has been a thief for three years, [even if] not caught [by others], [he will] expose himself [sooner or later]. (fig) If one has been doing something evil for a long time, one will expose oneself sooner or later, even if not caught and punished first. [Note: *bùdǎ-zìzhāo* is an idiom meaning "to make an unforced confession."]

195 **Zuò zhě bù bì; bì zhě bù zuò.** 做者不避，避者不做。 [If you] do [something], don't hide [it from others]; [if it is something that ought to be] hidden, don't do [it]. [See also *ruò yào rén bù zhī* above.]

196 **Zuò zhě bù jū; jū zhě bù zuò.** 作者不居，居者不作。 (lit) Those who build [houses] don't live [in them, and] those who live [in them] don't build [them]. (fig) The laboring classes don't get to enjoy the fruits of their labor, and the rich don't have to work for what they have. [Cf. *Liǎng Jiù Yǎnyì*, chap. 92.]

Z

Bibliography

In this bibliography of works of and about *yànyǔ* and related topics, the authors are listed alphabetically by their surnames as written in *Hànyǔ Pīnyīn* unless the author and/or work in question uses another system of romanization. Similarly all authors' names and titles are printed either in simplified characters or in "old style" complex characters (*fántǐzì*) as they appear in the work listed.

Anonymous. "Cíhuìxué 词汇学." *Cí Hǎi (Xiūdìng Běn)* 辞海(修订本) pp. 15–16. Shànghǎi: Shànghǎi Císhū Chūbǎnshè 上海: 上海辞书出版社, 1978.

——. *Gǔyǔ Jīnghuá* 古语精华. Nánchāng: Jiāngxī Rénmín Chūbǎnshè 南昌: 江西人民出版社, 1983.

——. *Hànyǔ Yànyǔ Xiēhòuyǔ Súyǔ Fēnlèi Dà Cídiǎn* 汉语谚语歇后语俗语分类大词典. Hūhéhàotè: Nèiměnggǔ Rénmín Chūbǎnshè 呼和浩特: 内蒙古人民出版社, 1987.

——. *Jīn Píng Méi Líyǔ Súyǔ* 金瓶梅俚语俗语. Běijīng: Bǎo Wén Táng Shūdiàn 北京: 宝文堂书店, 1988.

——. *Mín Yàn Shí Cuì* 民谚拾粹. Xī'ān: Shaǎnxī Rénmín Chūbǎnshè 西安: 陕西人民出版社, 1983.

——. *Pín-Xiàzhōngnóng Pīpàn Fǎndòng Yànyǔ Wǔshí Lì* 贫下中农批判反动谚语五十例. Běijīng: Nóngyè Chūbǎnshè 北京: 农业出版社, 1975.

——. *Táiwān Lǐ Yàn Jí Lǎn* 臺灣俚諺集覽. Táiběi: Táiwān Zǒngdū Fǔ 臺北: 臺灣總督府, 1942.

——. *Xīnbiān Xuéshēng Yànyǔ Zàojù Shǒucè* 新編學生諺語造句手冊. Hong Kong: Míng Huá Chūbǎn Gōngsī 香港: 明華出版公司, 1990.

——. *Yǔlín Jíjǐn* 语林集锦. Xiàmén: Xiàmén Yīzhōng Yǔwén Jiāoyánzǔ 厦门: 厦门一中语文教研组, 1979.

——. *Zhōngguó Nóngyàn* 中国农谚. Běijīng: Nóngyè Chūbǎnshè 北京: 农业出版社, 1980.

——. *Zhōngguó Yànyǔ Zǒnghuì: Hànyǔ Juàn: Súyǔ* 中国谚语总汇: 汉语卷: 俗语. Běijīng: Zhōngguó Mínjiān Wényì Chūbǎnshè 北京: 中国民间文艺出版社, 1983.

Arkush, R. David. "Orthodoxy and Heterodoxy in Twentieth-Century Chinese Peasant Proverbs." *Orthodoxy in Late Imperial China*, ed. by Kuang-Ching Liu, pp. 311–331. Berkeley, CA: University of California Press, 1990.

Běijīng Wàiyǔ Xuéyuàn 北京外语学院. *Hàn-Yīng Chéngyǔ Cídiǎn* 汉英成语词典. Běijīng: Shāngwù Yìnshūguǎn 北京: 商务印书馆, 1982.

——. *Hàn-Yīng Cídiǎn: A Chinese-English Dictionary* 汉英词典. Běijīng: Shāngwù Yìnshūguǎn 北京: 商务印书馆, 1978.

Brown, Brian, ed. *Wisdom of the Chinese: Their philosophy in sayings and proverbs.* New York: Brentano's, 1920.

Bueller, William M. *Chinese Sayings.* Rutland, Vermont: Charles E. Tuttle, 1972.

Cáo Cōngsūn 曹聪孙. *Zhōngguó Súyǔdiǎn* 中国俗语典. Chéngdū: Sìchuān Jiàoyù Chūbǎnshè 成都: 四川教育出版社, 1991.

———. *Zhōngguó Súyǔ Xuǎn Shì* 中国俗语选释. Chéngdū: Sìchuān Jiàoyù Chūbǎnshè 成都: 四川教育出版社, 1985.

Char Tin-yuke, trans. 谢廷玉. *Chinese Proverbs*. San Francisco: Jade Mountain Press, 1970.

Cheah Toon-hoon 謝敦倫. *Chien Ju Hun and Sam Ju Keng* 昔時賢文. Rangoon: American Baptist Mission Press, 1890.

Chén, John T. S. 陳佐舜. *Zhōngguó Yànyǔ Xuǎnjí—1001 Chinese Sayings* 中國諺語選集. Hong Kong: Xiānggǎng Zhōngwén Dàxué Cóngjī Xuéyuàn 香港: 香港中文大學崇基學院, 1973.

Chén Wàngdào 陈望道. *Xiūcíxué Fāfán* 修词学发凡. Shànghǎi: Shànghǎi Wényì Chūbǎnshè 上海: 上海文艺出版社, 1962.

Chén Xīnwàng 陈欣望. *A Collection of Chinese Idioms, Proverbs and Phrases with English Translation* 汉语成语, 谚语, 常用词语汇编. Běijīng: Zhīshi Chūbǎnshè 北京: 知识出版社, 1984.

Chéng Fúpíng and Chéng Shànqīng 成扶平, 成善卿. *Gǔ Jīn Xiēhòuyǔ Shíyí Jiān Zhù* 古今歇后语拾遗兼注. Běijīng: Nóngcūn Dúwù Chūbǎnshè 北京: 农村读物出版社, 1984.

Ch'eng Yu K'ao. *Manual of Chinese Quotations*. Shanghai: Kelly & Walsh, Ltd., 1893.

Chéngdū Shì Qúnzhòng Yìshùguǎn 成都市群众艺术馆. *Sìchuān Chéngyǔ, Yànyǔ, Xiēhòuyǔ Yùnběn* 四川成语, 谚语, 歇后语韵本. Chéngdū: Sìchuān Rénmín Chūbǎnshè 成都: 四川人民出版社, 1980.

Chiang Ker Chiu 蔣克秋. *Chinese Proverbs* 中國格言. Táiběi: Jīn Shān Túshū Chūbǎn Yǒuxiàn Gōngsī 臺北: 金山圖書出版有限公司, n.d.

Chinnery, John D. and Cuī Míngqiū 秦乃瑞, 崔鳴秋. *Yīng Hàn Lǐyàn Hébì* 英汉俚谚合璧. Běijīng: New World Press 北京: 新世界出版社, 1984.

Chu Chieh-fan 朱介凡. *Pìyù Yànyǔ Jí* 譬喻諺語集. Táiběi: Tiānyī Chūbǎnshè 臺北: 天一出版社, 1974.

———. *Shāndōng Yànyǔ Jí* 山東諺語集. Táiběi: Tiānyī Chūbǎnshè 臺北: 天一出版社, 1974.

———. *Tīng Rén Quàn* 聽人勸. Táiběi: Tiānyī Chūbǎnshè 臺北: 天一出版社, 1974.

———. *Yànyǔ de Yuánliú, Gōngnéng* 諺語的源流, 功能 (亞洲民俗, 社會生活專刊, 第五集). Táiběi: Orient Cultural Service (Asian Folklore and Social Life Monographs, vol. 5.) 臺北: 東方文化供應社, 1970.

———. *Yànyǔ Jiǎ Biān* 諺語甲編. Táiběi: Tiānyī Chūbǎnshè 臺北: 天一出版社, 1974.

———. *Zhōngguó Fēngtǔ Yànyǔ Shì Shuō* 中國風土諺語釋說. Táiběi: Xīnxīng Shūjú 臺北: 新興書局, 1962.

———. *Zhōngguó Nóng Yàn* 中國農諺. Táiběi: Tiānyī Chūbǎnshè 臺北: 天一出版社, 1974.

———. *Zhōngguó Yànyǔ Lùn* 中國諺語論. Táiběi: Xīnxīng Shūjú 臺北: 新興書局, 1965.

———. *Zhōngguó Yànyǔ Zhì (vols. 1-11)* 中國諺語志 (全十一冊). Táiběi: Táiwān Shāngwù Yìnshūguǎn 臺北: 台湾商务印馆, 1989.

Dawson-Grone, Herman. *Ming Hsien Chi, being a collection of proverbs and maxims in the Chinese language.* Shanghai: Kelly and Walsh, 1911.

Diàoyú Wēng (pseud.), ed. 釣魚翁. *Miào Yǔ Rú Zhū* 妙語如珠. Táiběi: Nánjīng Chūbǎn Gōngsī 臺北: 南京出版公司, 1977.

Eberhard, Wolfgang. "Some Notes on the Use of Proverbs in Chinese Novels." *Proverbium (15)* pp. 201–209, 1967.

——. "Proverbs in Selected Chinese Novels." *Proverbium (2)* pp. 21–57, 1985.

Edmonson, Monro E. *Love: An Introduction to the Science of Folklore and Literature.* New York: Holt, Rinehart & Winston, 1971.

Fán Rén 樊仁. *Zhōngguó Gè Zú Yànyǔ huìcuì* 中国各族谚语荟萃. Fúzhōu: Fújiàn Rénmín Chūbǎnshè 福州: 福建人民出版社, 1986.

Fèi Jiéxīn 費潔心. *Zhōngguó Nóngyàn* 中國農諺. Zhōnghuá Shūjú 中華書局, 1937.

Féng Péngnián 馮鵬年. *Měi Rì Yī Yàn* 每日一諺. Táiběi: Lián Jīng Chūbǎnshè 臺北: 聯經出版社, 1983.

Gài Rǎng 盖壤. *Zhōngguó Súyǔ Gùshi Jí* 中国俗语故事集. Shěnyáng: Liáoníng Dàxué Chūbǎnshè 沈阳: 辽宁大学出版社, 1990.

Gěng Wénhuī 耿文辉. *Zhōnghuá Yànyǔ Dà Cídiǎn* 中国谚语大辞典. Shěnyáng: Liáoníng Rénmín Chūbǎnshè 沈阳: 辽宁人民出版社, 1991.

Giles, Herbert A. *A History of Chinese Literature.* New York: Appleton Century, 1901, 1935.

Giles, Lionel. "Introduction to the Proverbs of China." *Racial Proverbs: A Selection of the World's Proverbs arranged Linguistically* pp. xl–xlii, 349–384. George Routledge & Sons, Ltd., 1938.

Goody, Jack. *The Interface of the Written and the Oral.* Cambridge: Cambridge University Press, 1987.

Guāng Wén; Dé Gēn; and Kuí Yuán 光文, 德根, 魁元. *Zhìhuì de Huāduǒ* 智慧的花朵. Xīníng: Guǎngxī Rénmín Chūbǎnshè 西宁: 广西人民出版社, 1978.

Guǎng Lù 广路. "Gòngchǎnzhǔyì de 'Yōulíng' Shì Zěnme Yóudàng Dào Zhōngguó Lái de 共产主意的《幽灵》是怎么游荡到中国来的." *Shū Lín (1)* 书林 (1) pp. 40–41, 1979.

Guitorman, Arthur. *Chips of Jade.* New York: E.P. Dutton & Co., 1920.

Gunn, Edward. *Rewriting Chinese: Style and Innovation in Twentieth-Century Chinese Prose.* Stanford, CA: Stanford University Press, 1991.

Hā Jīngxióng 哈經雄. *Zhōngguó Yànyǔ Jíchéng* 中國諺語集成. Hong Kong: Zhōngyāng Mínzú Dàxué Chūbǎnshè 香港: 中央民族大學出版社, n.d.

Hànyǔ Pīnyīn Cíhuì Biānxiězǔ 汉语拼音词汇编写组. *Hànyǔ Pīnyīn Cíhuì* 汉语拼音词汇. Běijīng: Yǔwén Chūbǎnshè 北京: 语文出版社, 1991.

Hart, Henry H. *Seven Hundred Chinese Proverbs.* Stanford University Press, 1937.

Hé Xuéwēi 何学威. *Zhōngguó Fēngtǔ Yáo Yàn Shì* 中国风土谣谚释. Chángshā: Húnán Měishù Chūbǎnshè 长沙: 湖南美术出版社, 1986.

——. *Zhōngguó Gǔdài Yànyǔ Cídiǎn* 中国古代谚语词典. Chángshā: Húnán Chūbǎnshè 长沙: 湖南出版社, 1991.

Heng Xiaojun and Zheng Xuezhi. *A Chinese-English Dictionary of Idioms and Proverbs (Lexicographia: Series maior: 24).* Tubengin: Niemeyer, 1988.

Hóng Jiāhuì 洪嘉惠. *Wǒ Bú Zài Yòngcuò Yànyǔ* 我不再用錯諺語. Hong Kong: Xīn Fēng Chūbǎnshè 香港: 新風出版社, n.d.

Huang, Huanyou. *Chinese Proverbs, Quotations, and Fables*. Felinfach/Wales: Llanerch, 1998.

Jí Tiánlóng 吉田隆. *Zhōngguó Yànyǔ Jí Xiēhòuyǔ* 中國諺語及歇後語. Táinán: Hàn Fēng Chūbǎnshè 臺南: 漢風出版社, 1990.

——. *Zhōngguó Yànyǔ Xuǎn. 2 vols.* 中国谚语选. Lánzhōu: Gānsù Rénmín Chūbǎnshè 兰州: 甘肃人民出版社, 1981.

Jì Chéngjiā, et al. 季成家, 等. *Zhōngguó Yànyǔ Xuǎn* 中国谚语选 (上/下). Lánzhōu: Gānsù Rénmín Chūbǎnshè 兰州: 甘肃人民出版社, 1981.

Jiāng Fēng and Wáng Cí 江枫, 王慈. *Zhōngguó Hànzú Yànyǔ Xuǎn* 中国汉族谚语选. Chángshā: Húnán Wényì Chūbǎnshè 长沙: 湖南文艺出版社, 1987.

Jīn Lù and Xú Yùmíng 金路, 徐玉明. *Zhōngguó Yànyǔ* 中国谚语. Shànghǎi: Shànghǎi Wényì Chūbǎnshè 上海: 上海文艺出版社, 1989.

Jǐng Lóng 景龙. *Shǎoshùmínzú Yànyǔ Huìcuì* 少数民族谚语荟萃. Héféi: Ānhuī Rénmín Chūbǎnshè 合肥: 安徽人民出版社, 1984.

Kordas, Bronislawa. *Le Proverbe en Chinois Moderne*. Taibei: Editions Ouyu, 1987.

——. "The Poetic Function and the Oral Transmission of Chinese Proverbs." *Chinoperl Papers* (15) pp. 85–94, 1990.

Kui, Lilian Lin 桂林. *A Comparative Study of Proverbialism* 中西諺語之比較研究. Táiběi: National Táiwān University 臺北: 臺灣國立大學, 1965.

Lai T'ian-ch'ang. *More Chinese Sayings*. Hong Kong: Swindon Book Co., 1972.

——. *Selected Chinese Sayings*. Hong Kong: Swindon Book Co., 1972.

Lai T'ian-ch'ang and Y. T. Kuong. *Chinese Proverbs*. Hong Kong: Swindon Book Co., 1978.

Lau, Theodora. *Best-Loved Chinese Proverbs*. New York: Harper Collins, 1995.

Lee, Davis L. C. *Chinese Proverbs: A Pragmatic and Sociolingustic Approach*, Ph.D. thesis. Washington, D.C.: Georgetown University, 1978.

Lǐ Dàoyī 李道一. "Shìlùn Pǐ Jiě Yǔ Jí Qí Yǔ Xiēhòuyǔ, Chéngyǔ, Yànyǔ de Qūbié 试论譬解语及其与歇后语, 成语, 谚语的区别." *Zhèjiāng Shīfàn Xuéyuàn Xuébào (1)* 浙江师范学院学报 (1) pp. 67–76. Hángzhōu: Zhèjiāng Shīfàn Xuéyuàn 杭州: 浙江师范学院, 1981.

Lǐ Gēngxīn 李更新. *Gǔyàn Diǎn Yīngyì* 古諺典英譯. Táizhōng: Guāng Qǐ Chūbǎnshè 臺中:光啟出版社, 1979.

——. *Tái Yàn Jíjǐn* 臺諺集錦. Táizhōng, Táiwān 台湾, 臺中, 1979.

——. *Zhōnghuá Mínsú Yànyǔ* 中華民俗諺語. Táizhōng: Hóngdá Měishù Yìnshuāchǎng 臺中: 弘達美術印刷廠, 1982.

Lǐ Jìxián 李繼賢. *Lù Gǎng Yànyǔ Shì Shuō* 鹿港諺語釋說. Lù Gǎng Zhèn: Lù Gǎng Wénjiào Jījīnhuì 鹿港鎮: 鹿港文教基金會, 1986.

Lǐ Mèngběi 李孟北. *Yànyǔ Xiēhòuyǔ Qiǎn Zhù* 谚语歇后语浅注. Yúnnán: Rénmín Chūbǎnshè 云南人民出版社, 1980.

Lǐ Yùchuān 李玉川. *Shúyǔ Qù Huà* 熟语趣话. Běijīng: Shìjiè Zhīshi Chūbǎnshè 北京: 世界知识出版社, 1990.

Lin, Marjorie and Leonard Schalk. *Dictionary of 1000 Chinese Proverbs (Hippocrene Bilingual Proverbs).* New York: Hippocrene Books, 1998.

Lister, Alfred. "Chinese Proverbs and their Lessons." *The China Review (3)* pp. 129–138, 1874–1875. Reprinted in Meider, W. & A. Dundes, eds. pp. 242–256, 1981.

Liú Dàiwén, Hú Zhìwěi and Wú Jùnhé 刘代文, 胡志伟, 吴俊和. *Qúnzhòng Yǔhuì Xuǎnbiān* 群众语汇选编. Tàiyuán: Shānxī Rénmín Chūbǎnshè 太原: 山西人民出版社, 1983.

Liú Yùnyǔ 劉運宇. *Zhōngguó Súyǔ Dà Diǎn* 中國俗語大典 (上/下). Táiběi: Xīngguāng Chūbǎnshè 臺北: 星光出版社, 1986.

Mǎ Juéwēng and Tián Huónóng 馬矍翁, 田活农. *Huáběi Nóngyàn* 华北农谚. Běijīng: Cáizhèng Jīngjì Chūbǎnshè 北京: 財政經济出版社, 1957.

Mateo, Fernando. "Linguistic and Literary Structure of the Chinese Proverbs." *Tamkang Review (2–3)* pp. 453–466, 1971–1972.

McCunn, Ruthanne Lum. *Chinese Proverbs.* San Francisco: Chronicle Books, 1991.

Mèng Shǒujiè, et al. 孟守介, 等. *Hànyǔ Yànyǔ Cídiǎn* 汉语谚语词典. Běijīng: Běijīng Dàxué Chūbǎnshè 北京: 北京大学出版社, 1990.

Mieder, Wolfgang. *International Proverb Scholarship: An Annotated Bibliography.* New York: Garland Publishing Co., 1982.

Mieder, Wolfgang and Alan Dundes, eds. *The Wisdom of Many: Essays on the Proverb.* New York: Garland Publishing Co., 1981.

Moule, A. E. "Chinese Proverbial Philosophy." *Chinese Recorder (5)* pp. 72–77, 1874.

Nánhǎi Xiàn Dà Xī Gōngshè Xī Zhōng Dàduì Lǐlùn Fǔdǎo Zǔ, Guǎngdōng Shěng Zhéxué Shèhuì Kēxué Yánjiū Suǒ Dà Pīpàn Zǔ 南海县大西公社西中大队理论辅导组, 广东省哲学社会科学研究所大批判组. *Pīpàn Fǎndòng Yànyǔ* 批判反动谚语. Guǎngzhōu: Guǎngdōng Rénmín Chūbǎnshè 广州: 广东人民出版社, 1975.

Níng Jǔ 宁榘. *Yànyǔ, Géyán, Xiēhòuyǔ* 谚语, 格言, 歇后语. Wǔhàn: Húběi Rénmín Chūbǎnshè 武汉: 湖北人民出版社, 1980.

Norrick, Neal R. *How Proverbs Mean.* New York: Mouton, 1985.

Obelkevich, James. "Proverbs and Social History." *The Social History of Language* pp. 43–72. Cambridge: Cambridge University Press, 1987.

Ong, Walter J. *Orality and Literacy: The Technologizing of the Word.* London: Meuthen and Co. Ltd., 1982.

Pān Lǐwén 潘禮文. *Súyǔ Diǎn* 俗語典. Táiběi: Wǔzhōu Chūbǎnshè 臺北: 五洲出版社, 1976.

———. *Zhōngwài Súyǔ Diǎn* 中外俗語典. Hong Kong: Chángxīng Shūjú 香港: 長興書局, 1975.

Park, Nancy. "Power in Imperial Chinese Proverbs." *Proverbium (15)* pp. 243–263, 1998.

Pinerro, Jaime. *Los Mejores Proverbios Chinos.* Barcelona: Editorial Bruguera, S.A., 1975.

Plath, Heinr. Johan. *Ming Hsien Chi—Proverben chinesischer wersheit, nach dem chin. des Ming Sin Paokien.* Munchen: G. Franz, 1863.

Plopper, Clifford H. *Chinese Religion Seen Through the Proverb.* Shanghai: The China Press, 1926. Reprint: New York: Paragon, 1969.

Qián Yì 錢毅. *Zhuāngjia Huà* 莊稼話. Táiwān: Huánghé Chūbǎnshè 臺灣: 黃河出版社, 1947.

Qiū Chóngbǐng 邱崇丙, ed. *Súyǔ Wǔ Qiān Tiáo* 俗语五千条. Xī'ān: Shǎnxī Rénmín Chūbǎnshè 西安: 陕西人民出版社, 1983.

———. *Súyǔ Chángyán Cídiǎn* 俗语常言词典. Xī'ān: Shǎnxī Rénmín Jiàoyù Chūbǎnshè 西安: 陕西人民教育出版社, 1991.

Qū Pǔ 屈朴. *Súyǔ Gǔjīn* 俗语古今. Shíjiāzhuāng: Héběi Rénmín Chūbǎnshè 石家庄: 河北人民出版社, 1992.

Redfield, Robert. *Peasant Society and Culture: An Anthropological Approach to Civilization.* Chicago: The University of Chicago Press, 1956.

Rohsenow, John S. *A Chinese-English Dictionary of Enigmatic Folk Similes (Yanyu).* Tuscon: The University of Arizona Press, 1991.

———, trans. "Appendix I: Basic Rules for Hanyu Pinyin." *ABC Chinese-English Dictionary* pp. 835–845. Honolulu: The University of Hawai'i Press, 1996.

———. "Proverbs." *The Columbia History of Chinese Literature* pp. 149–159. New York: Columbia University Press, 2001.

Scarborough, Wm. *A Collection of Chinese Proverbs.* Changsha, China: Union Theological School, 1926. Reprinted New York: Paragon, 1964.

Scarborough, Wm. and E. W. Allen. *Chinese Proverbs.* Shanghai: Presbyterian Mission Press, 1926.

Shàng Yīngshí 尚英時. *Huāyán-qiǎoyǔ* 花言巧语. Táiběi: Chángchūnshù Shūfāng 臺北: 常春树书坊, 1977.

———. *Zhōngguórén de Súhuà* 中國人的俗話. Táiběi: Chángchūnshù Shūfāng 臺北: 常春树书坊, 1979.

Shào Zhìzhōng and Mèng Chánglín 邵知中, 孟长麟. *Yànyǔ Xuǎn Chāo* 谚语选抄. Běijīng: Zhōngguó Shàonián Értóng Chūbǎnshè 北京: 中国少年儿童出版社, 1980.

Shēn Jùn, ed. 申俊主编. *Zhōngguó Shúyǔ Dà Diǎn* 中国熟语大典. Shànghǎi: Shànghǎi Wényì Chūbǎnshè 上海: 上海文艺出版社, 1990.

Shěn Àilián 沈爱莲. *Yànhǎi Míngzhū* 谚海明珠. Tàiyuán: Shānxī Rénmín Chūbǎnshè 太原: 山西人民出版社, 1983.

Shěn Huìyún, et al. 沈慧云, 等. *Gǔjīn Súyǔ Jíchéng, Vol. 5* 古今俗语集成, 第五卷. Tàiyuán: Shānxī Rénmín Chūbǎnshè 太原: 山西人民出版社, 1989.

Shī Yíngfù and Zhèng Huáishèng 施盈富, 郑怀盛. *Jīngshén Wénmíng Jīn Yán Jí* 精神文明锦言集. China: Zhōngguó Rénmín Jiěfàngjūn Zhànshì Chūbǎnshè 中国人民解放军战士出版社, 1983.

Shǐ Xiāngzhāi 史襄哉. *Zhōnghuá Yàn Hǎi* 中華諺海. Zhōnghuá Shūjú 中華書局, 1927. Reprint: Shànghǎi Wényì Chūbǎnshè 上海文艺出版社, 重印, n.d.

———. *Zēngbǔ Zhōnghuá Yàn Hǎi* 增補中華諺海. Táiběi: Tiānyī Chūbǎnshè 臺北:天一出版社, 1975.

———. *Zhōnghuá Yàn Hǎi* 中华谚海. Shànghǎi, China: Shànghǎi Wényì Chūbǎnshè 上海: 上海文艺出版社, 1986.

Shih, Vincent Yu-chung. *The Literary Mind and the Carving of Dragons*. Hong Kong: The Chinese University Press, 1983.

Smith, Arthur H. *Proverbs and Common Sayings from the Chinese*. Peking: American Presbyterian Mission Press, 1914. Reprint: New York: Paragon Book Reprint Corp. and Dover Publications, 1965.

Sŏu Tóng 叟童. *Kàn Tú Zhī Súyǔ* 看圖知俗語. Hong Kong: Nán Huá Chūbǎnshè 香港: 南華出版社, n.d.

Street, Brian V. *Literacy in Theory and Practice*. Cambridge: Cambridge University Press, 1984.

Su Tzǔ-ch'ang and Liang Ta-shan 徐子常, 梁达善. *Chinese Proverbs Explained*. Shànghǎi: Commercial Press 上海: 商务印书馆, 1926.

Sun, C. C. *As the Saying Goes*. St. Lucia: University of Queensland Press, 1981.

Sūn Wéizhāng 孙维张. *Hànyǔ Shúyǔxué* 汉语熟语学. Chángchūn: Jílín Jiàoyù Chūbǎnshè 长春: 吉林教育出版社, 1989.

Sūn Xīlù 孫錫祿. *Zhōngguó Míngyán Jīngxuǎn* 中國名言精選. Táiběi: Guójiā Chūbǎnshè 臺北: 國家出版社, 1970.

Sūn Zhìpíng and Wáng Fǎng 孙治平, 王仿. *Súyǔ Liǎng Qiān Tiáo* 俗语两千条. Shànghǎi: Shànghǎi Wényì Chūbǎnshè 上海: 上海文艺出版社, 1985.

Sūn Zhìpíng, Zhōu Zhèngrén, Yáo Jīnxiáng, Wáng Shìjūn, and Yán Liánghuá, eds. 孙治平, 周正仁, 姚金祥, 王士均, 严良华, 编. *Yànyǔ Liǎng Qiān Tiáo* 谚语两千条. Shànghǎi: Wényì Chūbǎnshè 上海: 文艺出版社, 1984.

Tán Dáxiān 譚達先. *Zhōngguó Mínjiān Míyǔ Yánjiū* 中國民間謎語研究. Hong Kong: Shāngwù Yìnshūguǎn 香港: 商務印書館, 1982.

Táng Qǐyùn 唐启运. *Chéngyǔ Yànyǔ Xiēhòuyǔ Diǎngù Gàishuō* 成语谚语歇后语典故概说. Guǎngzhōu: Guǎngdōng Rénmín Chūbǎnshè 广州: 广东人民出版社, 1981.

Tannan, Deborah, ed. *Spoken and Written Language*. Norwood, NJ: Abelex Publishing Corporation, 1982.

Taylor, Archer. *The Proverb and an Index to "The Proverb"*. Cambridge, MA: Harvard University Press Associates, 1931. Reprint: Hatboro, PN: Folklore Associates, 1962.

Wang, Juan. "Fatalism Seen Through Chinese Proverbial Expressions and Folk Beliefs." *Folk Narrative and World View*, ed. by Leander Petzoldt, pp. 823–834. Frankfurt am Main: Peter Lang, 1996.

Wāng Zhì 汪治. *Yànyǔ Xīn Biān* 谚语新编. Guǎngzhōu: Guǎngdōng Rénmín Chūbǎnshè 广州市: 广东人民出版社, 1982.

Wáng Chángzài 王常在. *Yànyǔ Shǒucè* 谚语手册. Běijīng: Zhōngguó Qīngnián Chūbǎnshè 北京: 中国青年出版社, 1985.

Wáng Chūn, ed. 王春. *Zhōngguó Yànyǔ Cídiǎn* 中国谚语辞典. Xī'ān: Sān Qín Chūbǎnshè 西安: 三秦出版社, 1991.

Wáng Fǎng 王仿. *Zhōngguó Míyǔ, Yànyǔ, Xiēhòuyǔ* 中国谜语, 谚语, 歇后语. Hángzhōu: Zhèjiāng Jiàoyù Chūbǎnshè 杭州: 浙江教育出版社, 1989.

Wáng Guózhōng, et al. 王国忠等. *Chángyòng Yànyǔ 600 Tiáo* 常用谚语600条. Běijīng: Shāngwù Yìnshūguǎn 北京: 商务印书馆, 1981.

Wáng Qín 王勤. *Yànyǔ Xiēhòuyǔ Gàilùn* 谚语, 歇后语概论. Chángshā: Húnán Rénmín Chūbǎnshè 长沙: 湖南人民出版社, 1980.

Wáng Shùshān, Shàng Héngyuán and Shēn Wényuán 王树山, 尚恒元, 申文元. *Gǔjīn Súyǔ Jíchéng (v. 1)* 古今俗语集成 (第一卷). Tàiyuán: Shānxī Rénmín Chūbǎnshè 太原: 山西人民出版社, 1989.

Wáng Táoyǔ 王陶宇. *Yànyǔ Zhé Lǐ Shī* 谚语哲理诗. Hūhéhàotè: Nèi Měnggǔ Jiàoyù Chūbǎnshè 呼和浩特: 内蒙古教育出版社, 1984.

Wáng Yì 王毅. "Lüèlùn Zhōngguó Yànyǔ 词汇学." *Mínjiān Wénxué (10)* 民间文学 (10) pp. 44–58, 1961.

Wáng Zōngjié and Hóng Huìzhēn 王宗傑, 洪慧貞. *Zhōngguó Géyán Yànyǔ Sì Yòng Dà Cídiǎng* 中国格言谚语四用大辞典. Jīn Wén Túshū Yǒuxiàn Gōngsī 金文图书有限公司, 1979.

Wēn Duānzhèng 温端政. *Hànyǔ Yànyǔ Xiǎo Cídiǎn* 汉语谚语小词典. Běijīng: Shāngwù Yìnshūguǎn 北京: 商务印书馆, 1989.

———. *Yànyǔ* 谚语. Běijīng: Shāngwù Yìnshūguǎn 北京: 商务印书馆, 1985.

Wēn Duānzhèng, et al. 温端政, 等. *Zhōngguó Súyǔ Dà Cídiǎn* 中国俗语大辞典. Shànghǎi: Shànghǎi Císhū Chūbǎnshè 上海: 上海辞书出版社, 1989.

Wu, C. K. and K. S. Wu. 吳志鋼, 吳黃縈琇. *Chinese-English 2000 Selected Chinese Common Sayings* 漢語兩千中國俗語選. Monterey, CA: Chinese Language Research Association 中国语文研究学会, 1968.

Wú Yíngtāo 吳瀛濤. *Táiwān Lǐyǔ Jí* 臺灣俚語集. Táiwan: Yīngwén Chūbǎnshè 臺灣: 英文出版社, n.d.

———. *Táiwān Yànyǔ* 臺灣諺語. Táiwān: Yīngwén Chūbǎnshè 臺灣: 英文出版社, 1975.

Wǔ Guānhuá, et al. 伍关华. *Zhōngguó Gǔdài Géyán Xiǎo Cídiǎn* 中国古代格言小词典. Xī'ān: Shǎnxī Rénmín Chūbǎnshè 西安: 陕西人民出版社, 1988.

Wǔ Zhànkūn and Mǎ Guófán 武占坤, 马国凡. *Yànyǔ* 谚语. Hūhéhàotè: Nèi Měnggǔ Rénmín Chūbǎnshè 呼和浩特: 内蒙古人民出版社, 1980.

Wúxī Shīfàn Xuéxiào 无锡师范学校. *Hànyǔ Yànyǔ Cídiǎn* 汉语谚语词典. Jiāngsū: Rénmín Chūbǎnshè 江苏人民出版社, 1981.

Wyss-Vogtlin, M. *Siebenhundert Chinesesche Sprichworter*. Zurich, 1945.

Xià Tiān, ed. 夏天编. *Xì Yàn Yìqiān Tiáo* 戏谚一千条. Shànghǎi: Shànghǎi Wényì Chūbǎnshè 上海: 上海文艺出版社, 1985.

Xú Hànhuá 徐汉华. *Zhōngwài Yànyǔ Fēnlèi Cídiǎn* 中外谚语分类词典. Xī'ān: Shǎnxī Rénmín Jiàoyù Chūbǎnshè 西安: 陕西人民教育出版社, 1987.

Xú Zǐcháng and Liáng Dáshàn, eds. 徐子長, 梁達善. *Mín Yàn* 民諺. Shànghǎi: Shāngwù Yìnshūguǎn 上海: 商務印書館, 1926.

Xú Zōngcái and Yīng Jùnlíng, eds. 徐宗才, 应俊玲编. *Chángyòng Súyǔ Shǒucè* 常用俗语手册. Běijīng: Běijīng Yǔyán Xuéyuàn Chūbǎnshè 北京: 北京语言学院出版社, 1985.

Xǔ Huáishí 许怀石. *Qiàopi Huà* 俏皮话. Zhuāngjiā Chūbǎnshè 庄家出版社, 1979.

Yáng Guāngzhōng 楊光中. *Qí Yán Miào Yù* 奇言妙喻. Táiběi: Lín Bái Chūbǎnshè 臺北: 林白出版社, 1978.

Yáng Guìshēng, et al. 杨贵生, 等. *Súyǔ Xiǎo Diǎn* 俗语小典. Hénán Jiàoyù Chūbǎnshè 河南教育出版社, 1991.

Yáng Shèn (Míng Dynasty), ed. 楊慎 [明]. *Fēngyǎ Yǐ Piān, Gǔjīn Fēng Yáo, Gǔjīn Yàn* 風雅 逸篇, 古今風謠, 古今諺. Shànghǎi: Gǔdiǎn Wénxué Chūbǎnshè 上海: 古典文 学出版社, 1958.

Yáng Tíngyáng, et al. 杨廷洋, 等. *Gǔ-jīn Súyǔ Jíchéng, Vol. 3* 古今俗语集成, 第三卷. Tàiyuán: Shānxī Rénmín Chūbǎnshè 太原: 山西人民出版社, 1989.

Yáng Wéizhēn, et al. 杨为珍, 等. *Gǔ Jù Xīn Yòng* 古句新用. Jílín: Jílín Rénmín Chūbǎnshè 吉林: 吉林人民出版社, 1980.

Yáng Yuán and Jì Yuè 杨沅, 季岳. *Méi Yàn Huì Jiān Fù Érgē Quán Yī Cè* 梅諺彙箋附兒 歌全一冊. Yóutóu Wàimǎ Lù Xiǎohúa Yīyuàn 油頭外馬路小華醫院, 1932.

Yáo Fāngmiǎn, et al. 姚方勉, 等. *Yànyǔ Cídiǎn* 谚语词典. Jiāngsū: Gǔjí Chūbǎnshè 江 苏古籍出版社, 1990.

Yīn Bǐnyōng and Hán Huī 殷斌庸, 韩晖. *100 Pearls of Chinese Wisdom (Gems of the Chinese Language Through the Ages)* 博古通今学汉语丛书: 谚语 100. Běijīng: Sinolingua 北京: 华语教学出版社, 1999.

Yīn Bāngyàn, ed. 尹邦彦. *A Chinese-English Dictionary of Commonly Used Idiomatic Expressions* 汉语常用熟语词典. Jiāngsū: Jiāngsū Jiàoyù Chūbǎnshè 江苏教育出版 社, 1989.

Yoo, Young H. *Wisdom of the Far East: A Dictionary of Proverbs, Maxims, and Famous Classical Phrases of the Chinese, Japanese, and Korean.* Washington, D.C.: Far Eastern Research and Publications Center, 1972.

Yuǎndōng Túshū Gōngsī Biānshěn Wěiyuánhuì 遠東圖書公司編審委員會. *Zhōngguó Géyán Dà Cídiǎn* 中國格言大辭典. Táiběi: Yuǎndōng Túshū Gōngsī 臺北: 遠東 圖書公司, 1972.

Zhang, Hong. "Images of Women in Chinese Proverbs." *Locating Power*, ed. by Kira Hall, et al., v. 2, pp. 601–609. Berkeley, CA: Berkeley Women and Language Group, University of California, 1992.

Zhāng Fó 張佛. *Nóngyàn Yī Cè* 農諺一冊. Shànghǎi: Shāngwù Yìnshūguǎn 上海: 商務 印書館, 1935.

Zhāng Lǔyuán and Hú Shuāngbǎo 张鲁原, 胡双宝. *Gǔ Yànyǔ Cídiǎn* 古谚语辞典. Běijīng: Běijīng Chūbǎnshè 北京: 北京出版社, 1990.

Zhāng Xùnqí 张迅齐. *Zhōngguó Míngyán Jí* 中国名言集. Chángchūn: Chángchūn Shūfāng 常春: 常春书坊, 1975.

Zhāng Yě 张野. *Hànyǔ Súyǔ Yīngyì Dàquán* 汉语俗语英译大全. Húběi, Hónghú: Hǎitiān Chūbǎnshè 湖北, 洪湖: 海天出版社, 1993.

Zhāng Yì 张毅. *Chángyòng Yànyǔ Cídiǎn* 常用谚语词典. Shànghǎi: Shànghǎi Císhū Chūbǎnshè 上海: 上海辞书出版社, 1987.

Zhào Zhòngyì 赵仲邑. *Wén Xīn Diāo Lóng Jízhù* 文心调龙集注. Guǎngxī Líjiāng Chūbǎnshè 广西漓江出版社, 1982.

Zhèng Xùnliè 郑勋烈. *Yànyǔ Shǒucè* 谚语手册. Shànghǎi: Zhīshi Chūbǎnshè 上海: 知 识出版社, 1985.

Zhèng Xùnliè and Zhèng Qíng 郑勋烈, 郑晴. *Zhōngguó Yànyǔ* 中国谚语. Shànghǎi: Dōngfāng Chūbǎn Zhōngxīn 上海: 东方出版中心, 1997.

Zhōng Mǐnwén, ed. 钟敏文. *Súyǔ Dàquán* 俗语大全. Běijīng: Dàzhòng Wényì Chūbǎnshè 北京: 大众文艺出版社, 1997.

Zhōngguó Mínjiān Wénxué Jíchéng Quánguó Biānjī Wěiyuánhuì 中国民间文学集成全国编辑委员会. *Zhōngguó Mínjiān Wénxué Jíchéng—Níngxià Juàn* 中国民间文学集成—宁夏卷. Běijīng: Zhōngguó Mínjiān Wényì Chūbǎnshè 北京: 中国民间文艺出版社, 1990.

Zhōu Pánlíng 周盤林. *Zhōng Xī Yànyǔ Bǐjiào Yánjiū* 中西諺語比較研究. Táiběi: Wén Shǐ Zhé Chūbǎnshè 臺北: 文史哲出版社, 1975.

Zhōu Róngjié 周榮杰. *Táiwān Yànyǔ Quán Biān* 臺灣諺語詮編. Gāoxióng: Dà Wǔtái Shū Yuàn Chūbǎnshè 高雄: 大舞臺書苑出版社, 1978.

Zhōu Shàohuái, Zhōu Yuán and Lí Shìchéng 周绍淮, 周元, 黎世诚. *Zhìhuì de Huāduǒ: Yànyǔ Xuǎn Xùjí* 智慧的花朵: 谚语选续集. Nánníng: Guǎngxī Rénmín Chūbǎnshè 南宁: 广西人民出版社, 1982.

Zhōu Wénbīn, et al. 周文彬, 等. *Zhōnghuá Chéngyǔ Dà Cídiǎn* 中华成语大词典. Chángchūn: Jílín Wénshǐ Chūbǎnshè 长春: 吉林文史出版社, 1986.

Zhū Bǐnghǎi 朱炳海. *Tiānqì Yànyǔ* 天气谚语. Běijīng: Nóngyè Chūbǎnshè 北京: 农业出版社, 1987.

Zhū Xiānlì, Chén Jìshēng and Rén Huìrú, eds. 朱先立, 陈济生, 任惠儒. *Nóng Yàn Zhùjiě* 农谚注解. Běijīng: Tōngsú Dúwù Chūbǎnshè 北京: 通俗读物出版社, 1957.

Zuǒ Xiùlíng 左秀靈. *Yànyǔ Cídiǎn* 諺語辭典. Táiběi: Jiàn Hóng Chūbǎnshè 臺北: 建宏出版社, 1991.

Index

Indexed terms are the names, places, topics, and so forth contained *within* the entries themselves and do not refer to the first Chinese words of each entry. This fact should be kept in mind when checking cross-references. English terms shown in ALL CAPITAL LETTERS in the index refer to the topic(s) addressed by each proverb.

A

ABILITY   B195, C2, D162, F65, F68, G6, G7, G19, G32, G33, H6, H54, H60, H108, H184, H231, K47, K48, L40, L46, L75, L100, L174, M68, M75, M76, N21, N32, N33, N35, N91, N106, N107, P30, P35, Q9, Q19, Q29, Q45, Q80, Q103, Q181, R36, R91, R249, S91, S92, S95, S101, S126, S144, S150, S183, S199, S223, S353, S362, S415, T46, T48, T130, W78, X22, X91, Y140, Y143, Y175, Y181, Y270, Y301, Y363, Z39, Z55, Z59, Z105

ABSENCE   S101, Y45, Y251

ABSTINENCE   Q196

ACCENT   G56

ACCEPTANCE   J129

ACCOMMODATION   C49, D132, G5, R6, R268, S62, Y340

ACCOMPLISHMENT   B176, C65, C67, C75, C164, C167, C194, D93, D107, D113, D168, H24, H27, H76, H77, H123, J58, J113, J130, J131, L71, M30, M52, M58, M64, M65, M71, M123, N88, P2, Q76, R151, S37, S308, S414, T31, T37, T42, T44, T56, T83, W99, X90, X125, X137, X139, Y72, Y104, Y141, Y145, Y146, Y176, Y275, Y382, Y421, Y432, Y457, Z101, Z122

ACCOUNTING   G68, H65, Q154, R169, X164, Y253

ACCOUNTS   Q150, R217, S430

ACCUMULATION   J185, J237, Y57

ACCUSATIONS   G17, G101, J75, R265, S176, X158, Y462, Z21, Z23, Z31

ACHIEVEMENT   D109, H27, J30, J196, J244, L13, L115, M59, S123

ACQUAINTANCES   B23, T132, X21

ACTION   B120, B121, D154, D222, F42, G193, J54, J121, J160, K1, L48, L64, L167, M16, M32, M124, M128, Q105, R161, R255, S155, S169, S185, S201, S237, S275, S328, S376, S382, T81, T91, T110, W79, X3, X54, X100,

X123, X132, Y34, Y119, Y124, Y308, Y309, Z104

ACTIONS   D166, H175, L62, L124, M39, M131, P6, Q66, Q79, Q197, R94, S152, S273, S285, T57, T76, T79, W15, W19, W100, Y5, Y22, Y28, Y75, Y94, Y165, Y189, Y192, Y194, Y249, Y250, Y272, Z185, Z192, Z195

ACTIVITY   L131, T81

ADAPTING   K6, K18, S78, Y358, Y364

ADEQUACY   L150

ADMIRATION   S163, T12

ADOPTION   T72

A Dou   S410

ADULTERY   L164, M130, Z155

ADULTS   R285, X90

ADVANTAGE   B90, D26, D137, F17, H33, H169, H180, R74, S74, S220, S295, X34, X191, Y1, Y132, Y426, Z176

ADVERSITY   D204, M54, S192

ADVICE   B22, B130, B173, B200, B203, B212, D5, D46, D104, J101, J134, L92, L135, N38, Q62, Q193, Q194, Q196, Q198, R277, S4, S20, S21, S143, T92, Y60, Y69, Y85, Y86, Y266, Y345, Z137

AFFECTATION   C148

AFFECTION   C36, E18, H152, N66, Q138, R129, R130, R131, R233, Y255, Y333

AGE   B21, B168, B170, B172, C54, C109, C111, C200, F3, G13, G60, G188, H102, J38, J47, J101, J197, L35, L36, L37, L38, L39, L40, L47, L50, L52, L53, L56, L59, L60, L104, M18, M90, N23, N24, N37, Q34, Q107, Q121, R23, R30, R36, R39, R70, R89, R90, R91, R93, R105, R109, R110, R111, R113, R148, R149, R151, R152, R154, R158, R183, R191, R277, S47, S100, S104, S111, S112, S115, S149, S203, S292, S359, S360, S361, S362, S363, S364, T32, W25, W85, X33, X60, X78, X80, X97, X183, Y17, Y92, Y290, Y408, Y419, Y430, Y431, Y457, Y458, Z181

AGING   R39, R91, R92, R93

AGREEMENT   H136, J214

AGRICULTURE   C202, J178, Q178, R49, S13

àiwū-jíwū   A4

Ài Yīng   H247

Albania   H3

ALERTNESS   L42

ALLIANCES   H204

ALLOTMENT   B46, B47

ALOOFNESS   R248

ALTERNATIVES   C185, C186, C187

AMBIGUITY   S378

AMBITION   B161, B169, C80, D146, E27, F29, H246, L104, M80, Q208, R121, R149, W97, X85, X85, X151, Y431, Y433, Y435

AMIABILITY   H48, H113

Amida Buddha   R270

Āmítuófó   J164, R270

AMNESTY   Q183, R275

Analects   R30

ANALOGY   Y183

ANCESTORS   Q64, Q67, Q68

ANGER   B152, B172, H196, J133, J187, J200, L78, N108, P20, Q132, R236, S22, S153, X77, X168, Y436, Z125

Anhui province   D116

ANNOTATIONS   X197

ANTS   M53

aphorisms   S437

APOLOGIES   J285

APPEARANCES   A2, B1, B52, B70, B82, C14, C80, C121, C180, C181, D35, F56, G167, H103, H128, H153, H185, H208, J118, L152, M20, M93, P42, Q63, R21, R84, R98, R120, R164, R194, R199, R210, R231, R269, S12, S145, S151, S168, Y74, Y95, Y200, Y244, Y340, Y441, Z13, Z35, Z36, Z116

APPETITE   H165, S207

APPLICATION   Y469

APPRECIATION   H40, H230, J137, Q21, S175, Y205, Y390

APPRENTICES   S218

APPROPRIATENESS   A19, B87, D43, D199, G135, G145, G207, H196, H206, J128, J242, K30, M65, M100, N99, Q12, Q127, Q139, S58, S79, S81, S147, S340, W44,

About the Author

John S. Rohsenow, who has taught and conducted research in Beijing, Nanjing, Hangzhou, and Taiwan, is author of *A Chinese-English Dictionary of Enigmatic Folk Similes (Xiehouyu)* (1991) and co-editor, with Yin Bingyong, of *Modern Chinese Characters* (1994). He is currently associate professor of linguistics at the University of Illinois at Chicago.